Hammond's

Nature Encyclopedia of America

COMPRISING

Hammond's Nature Atlas of America

AND

Hammond's Guide to Nature Hobbies

By

E. L. JORDAN, Ph.D.

Rutgers University

WITH THE ASSISTANCE OF A GROUP OF SPECIALISTS
IN THE VARIOUS BRANCHES OF THE NATURAL SCIENCES

CLASSICS EDITION

1954

C. S. Hammond and Company

MAPLEWOOD, N. J. NEW YORK, N. Y.

PRINTED IN THE UNITED STATES OF AMERICA

PRINTING HISTORY

The following are the dates of the numerous printings of these beautiful Nature subjects:

FIRST PRINTING .... August, 1952
SECOND PRINTING .... October, 1952
THIRD PRINTING .... November, 1952
FOURTH PRINTING .... April, 1953
FIFTH PRINTING .... July, 1953
SIXTH PRINTING .... November, 1953

The total of these printings is over one-half million

Introduction

PART I

Hammond's Nature Atlas of America

One of the most fascinating and thrilling experiences you can have is exploring Nature. Here brought together in one volume is a reference library of Nature in America, showing you wild animals, birds, wildflowers, fish, amphibians and reptiles, insects, rocks and trees. It tells where each is likely to be found and answers many Nature questions you or your youngsters are likely to have. Pages 1 to 256.

PART II

Hammond's Guide to Nature Hobbies

Discover for yourself the pleasure and thrill of a Nature Hobby. Many are described, with detailed instructions — from shell collecting to bird banding, wildlife photography, and numerous others. Pages N1 to N64.

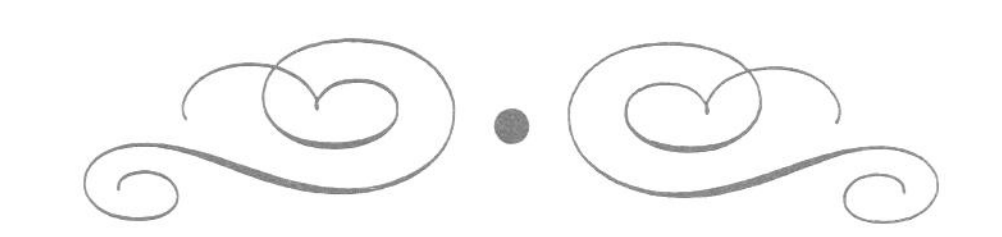

Hammond's

Nature Atlas of America

By

E. L. JORDAN, PH.D.

Rutgers University

WITH THE ASSISTANCE OF A GROUP OF SPECIALISTS
IN THE VARIOUS BRANCHES OF THE NATURAL SCIENCES

320 Original Paintings

282 By

WALTER FERGUSON

and 38 By

JOHN CODY

C. S. Hammond and Company

MAPLEWOOD, N. J. NEW YORK, N. Y.

Foreword

THIS ATLAS has been written and compiled for nature lovers who are not scientists. It is a general, first introduction to our natural environment and restricts itself to those aspects of nature with which we come into contact in our daily lives: the rocks, trees and wildflowers; the birds and animals; the amphibians, reptiles, fishes and insects.

All technical data are held to a minimum. Any readers who are stimulated by the maps, paintings and text to probe more deeply into any of the fields covered, will find good guidebooks and scientific works available which supplement and extend this Nature Atlas on every desired level and for every type of study.

By virtue of its topic, this Atlas touches also upon an issue which is close to the heart of America: the problem of conservation. Our great nature heritage was so abundant that little or no thought was given to preservation for future generations — possibility of scarcity or extinction was inconceivable. This resulted in the "great slaughter" of the 19th Century. Not even the oldest lumberjacks in Maine can recall the giant, virgin white pines. When young Lincoln split his fence rails, much of his timber, we can assume, was black walnut, — so abundant was this valuable tree; trailing arbutus covered thousands of sunny slopes a hundred years ago, and red cardinal flowers fringed the brooks; blue passenger pigeons darkened the sky and trumpeter swans sailed over mountains and forests in their V formations; pronghorn antelopes grazed among the buffaloes by the tens of thousands; clumsy sea cows floated in flocks of 12 or 15 in Biscayne Bay; schools of sturgeon abounded in the lower Delaware. Although the word conservation is seldom used herein, the facts that made America conservation-conscious crop up in every section.

The Atlas also presents the counter-action. In maps, tables and text it shows the national parks, national monuments and state parks which keep alive the giant sequoias and the redwoods, the bald cypresses and white cedars. It outlines the huge wooded territories we have assembled over the years and organized as National Forests, not to "preserve" our nature assets but to manage them scientifically. It describes the hundreds of wildlife refuges in the U.S. and Canada which, in spite of the draining of swamps and the clearing of woods, have kept the Atlantic, central and Pacific fly-ways open for our migratory birds; which maintain herds of elk and pronghorn and other big game; and which, in northern Canada, have restored the buffalo to a semi-wild status.

In this continental conservation program, the practical aspect — the continuous use of our natural resources — is only of secondary importance. Its other values are infinitely greater: Our nature heritage is primarily there to be enjoyed, understood, and loved; for it is a unifying, all-embracing bond, an heirloom of strength and beauty, a common possession in which American life is growing its deepest roots.

A few technical remarks may be in order. All measurements given in the nature sections of this atlas are approximate: in the case of trees and wildflowers, they refer to fully-grown, mature plants; in the case of animals, to average adult males. The range maps also are only approximate, for obvious reasons. In spelling and capitalization, various systems are in use in different fields. For the sake of uniformity, the Atlas has adopted the following method: The names of orders, families and genera are capitalized; the names of species are not capitalized except in titles.

As far as we know, this is the first volume to present all national public outdoor facilities for the observation and study of nature which are at everybody's disposal in the United States and southern Canada, from National Parks and National Monuments to National Forests (with numerous Wilderness Areas), and National Wildlife Refuges.

Acknowledgments

THE CREATION OF THIS ATLAS has truly been a cooperative enterprise. First and above all, my sincere thanks go to those authorities in the various branches of the natural sciences who assisted in this venture. They carefully reviewed the portions of the text which concerned their own special fields, and their constructive advice was followed in every section of the atlas. They are:

in the field of minerals and rocks, Dr. A. K. Lobeck, Chairman of the Department of Geology, Columbia University, New York;

in the fields of trees and wildflowers, Dr. Edwin B. Matzke, Professor of Botany, Columbia University, New York, who examined the botanical sections of the text and checked many of the detailed facts dealing with plants;

in the fields of birds and mammals, Dr. L. A. Hausman, Professor of Zoology, Rutgers University, and Consulting Ornithologist, the Agricultural Experiment Station of the State of New Jersey, New Brunswick, N. J.;

in the fields of fishes, amphibians and reptiles, Dr. Max K. Hecht of the Department of Biological Sciences, Hunter College of the City of New York, and of the Department of Amphibians and Reptiles, The American Museum of Natural History, New York;

in the field of insects, Dr. B. B. Pepper, Chairman of the Department of Entomology, College of Agriculture, Rutgers University, New Brunswick, N. J.;

as to the chapters "Climate and Nature in America" and "Landforms and Nature in America", Dr. G. G. Weigend, Acting Chairman of the Department of Geography, Rutgers University, New Brunswick, N. J.

A number of federal authorities supported this project by furnishing a great amount of informative material on both general and specific questions. I gratefully acknowledge the assistance of the following agencies:

in the field of minerals and rocks, the Geological Survey and Bureau of Mines of the U.S. Department of the Interior, Washington, D.C.;

in the field of climate and weather, the Weather Bureau, the Bureau of Agricultural Economics, and the Soil Conservation Service of the U.S. Department of Agriculture, Washington, D.C.;

in reference to national parks and national monuments, the National Park Service of the U.S. Department of the Interior, Washington, D.C.;

in reference to national forests and wilderness areas, the Forest Service of the U.S. Department of Agriculture in Washington, D.C.; and its regional offices in: Missoula, Montana; Denver, Colorado; Albuquerque, New Mexico; Ogden, Utah; San Francisco, California; Portland, Oregon; Philadelphia, Pennsylvania; Atlanta, Georgia; and Milwaukee, Wisconsin;

in reference to national wildlife refuges, the Fish and Wildlife Service of the U.S. Department of the Interior in Washington, D.C.; and its regional offices in: Portland, Oregon; Albuquerque, New Mexico; Minneapolis, Minnesota; Atlanta, Georgia; and Boston, Massachusetts;

additionally, a large number of superintendents of national monuments, national forests, and wildlife refuges answered specific questions and gave valuable information about the areas under their supervision.

I had the same friendly and effective cooperation from the Canadian authorities, and wish to express my appreciation, particularly, to the following agencies:

in reference to Canadian minerals and rocks, the Mines and Geology Branch of the Bureau of Geology and Topography, Ottawa;

in reference to Canadian national parks, the National Parks Branch of the Department of Resources and Development, Ottawa; and the Canadian Government Travel Bureau, Ottawa.

I enjoyed greatly the collaboration of the two artists whose original paintings illustrate this atlas; Walter Ferguson, fresh from his studies at Yale and Pratt, brought to his task an unusual combination of artistic talent and biological knowledge, and John Cody switched from painting exotic tropical insects in the jungles of Trinidad (as staff artist of one of Dr. Beebe's scientific expeditions) to the portraying of honey bees and butterflies of temperate North America.

My step-by-step cooperation with the publisher was cordial and close, and I am grateful to Mr. C. D. Hammond, Jr., and Mr. George W. Lapham for their effective help in the organization of the material. My wife, Ethel Jordan, acted as general adviser, consultant, editor and secretary of the project; to her practical assistance and sound judgment this book owes more than I can express here.

The idea of the Nature Atlas of America was conceived in the northwoods where mountain and airplane views of countless lakes and endless forests suggested a giant nature map. The idea matured during various long and pleasant stays in northern Maine at my brother-in-law's Shin Pond House, where the loons cry at night and bears raid the blueberry patches.

E. L. J.

Contents

Your own backyard and flower garden may be the most rewarding place to observe nature, or the nearest brook, lake, or forest will serve the purpose, depending on the circumstances. A friend of mine, a widely known ornithologist, maintains that an old orchard is a necessity for every nature lover's farm. He does not mean the scientific kind of orchard with well-pruned, properly trimmed and frequently sprayed trees, but the neglected kind — the gnarled old trees with trunks that are partly decayed, and with many limbs that are dead. Such an orchard provides dozens of ideal nesting sites: holes and cavities for nuthatches and woodpeckers, chickadees and bluebirds, wrens and other birds of the hole-dwelling varieties. During spring the old crowns look lovely at blossom time, humming with nest-building activities; during the summer the orchard is a happy and lively bird community which is a joy to observe; and if, in the fall, the fruit crop is negligible, only a materialist will complain.

The vantage points available for the first-hand study of nature are almost as numerous and varied as the forms of nature itself. But speaking in a general way, it can be assumed that the most satisfying areas of contact are the huge tracts of land and water set aside to keep our natural environment as untouched and unspoiled as it can be kept. They are our well-known national parks; our numerous national monuments which, on a smaller scale, have the same purpose; and our almost 300 national wildlife refuges scattered throughout the U.S., serving our migratory birds along their principal routes, creating a favorable environment for dwindling big game, and carrying out other projects of conservation. The national forests, which cover 179 million acres of land and are organized principally for timber production and watershed protection, are also enormous wildlife reservoirs open to hunters, fishermen, and nature lovers. In addition to national agencies, numerous state parks in every section of the country follow a similar program. In Canada a network of national and provincial parks is maintained along the same lines. Finally, there are the Indian reservations in the U.S. and Canada which comprise a large area; the Navajo Reservation alone is three times the size of the Commonwealth of Massachusetts. The reservations are not nature preserves proper, but usually they are located in the unspoiled sections of the country, and the Indian way of life insures protection to wildlife found in their domain.

Within the national forests great tracts are set aside which are called "wild areas" if they comprise 5,000 to 100,000 acres, and "wilderness areas" if their size is greater than 100,000 acres. These lands, comprising approximately 8% of our national forests, remain in the same state of primitive grandeur which was admired by the first settlers. They are kept roadless and include many of the mountain ranges and peaks that are the landmarks of the West. While these areas are without roads, they are not without trails, and as they are open to the public, pack trips into the wilderness are becoming increasingly popular. The only restrictions in these areas refer to fire prevention, or to the preservation of any wildlife of national interest which is in danger of extinction; for instance, the nesting grounds of the rare California condor in Los Padres National Forest in California are closed to unauthorized visitors. In the Superior Roadless Areas of Minnesota, long wilderness journeys can be made by canoe. Special "Natural Areas" are set aside as experiment stations for scientific research. In the following chapter these untouched areas are listed under "national forests."

Almost all of the facilities mentioned above are indicated on the maps on pages 17 to 29; visitors are welcome everywhere, and if certain national parks, monuments, forests, reservations or refuges seem of special interest to a reader and he plans to visit them, it is suggested that he write a note to the superintendent of the area concerned. A circular will be returned giving all necessary information on exact road connections, accommodations, flora and fauna, and other items of interest.

The following pages present a survey of the facilities for nature observation and enjoyment in the six major sections of the U.S. and Canada. National monuments and parks of purely historical significance are not included. Wild life refuges are listed in the tables on pages 245 to 249.

The North Eastern Sector. Maps on pages 18 and 19.

NATIONAL PARKS: *Acadia National Park* is located above Bar Harbor, Maine; its Cadillac Mountain rises 1,530 feet out of the ocean, the highest peak on the Atlantic shore north of Rio de Janeiro. Its sea caves, particularly Thunder Hole Chasm, are famous. Rare wildflowers like the pale purple orchid, the blue iris and the red cardinal flower may be observed. Sea birds of all descriptions abound, among them the osprey and bald eagle.

Shenandoah National Park in Virginia, famous for its Skyline Drive, is perhaps the most accessible of our native preserves; the distance to Washington, D.C. is only 75 miles, to Philadelphia, 200 miles. While climbing Old Rag Mountain or hiking to White Oak Canyon, red and grey foxes may be encountered, also deer, bobcats and bear.

NATIONAL FORESTS: Those national forests which are indicated on the map but are not mentioned in this chapter are "Purchase Units," i.e. their land is in process of being acquired and developed. NEW HAMPSHIRE: The *White Mountain N.F.*, parts of which are in Maine, is located near the Presidential Range; mountain stream fishing, deer and bear hunting. VERMONT: The *Green Mountain N.F.* is traversed by the "Long Trail;" it offers lake and stream fishing, bird shooting, deer and bear hunting. PENNSYLVANIA: The *Allegheny N.F.* boasts of some fine virgin timber stands and 300 miles of trout streams in the Heart's Content and Tionesta Natural Areas; trout and bass fishing; deer and bear hunting. VIRGINIA: A part of the *George Washington N.F.* was originally surveyed by George Washington himself; it includes limestone caverns, the Crabtree Falls, and Ranney's Draft Natural Area; trout and bass fishing; turkey, grouse, deer and bear hunting. *Jefferson N.F.* is an interesting transition zone of northern and southern flora; white-tailed deer hunting. WEST VIRGINIA: *Monongahela N.F.* contains a number of unexplored limestone caves and the spectacular Seneca Rocks on the historic Seneca Indian Trail; the Cranberry Glades are botanically interesting.

Canadian National Parks: *St. Lawrence Islands N.P.* in Ontario comprises a mainland area and 13 of the famous Thousand Islands which in reality number 1,700. Rising out of the dark green waters of the great river, their granite and limestone cliffs are topped by groves of dark pines and white birches, big oaks and stands of maple, Canada's national tree.

Fundy N.P. in New Brunswick, on the Bay of Fundy, is an ideal sanctuary for small fur-bearing animals, among them mink, otter and weasel; reports of the presence of mountain lions are investigated. Great blue herons and peregrine falcons dwell in the park.

Prince Edward Island N.P. is the territory that in 1534 was described by Jacques Cartier as "low and flat and the fairest that may possibly be seen, and full of beautiful trees and meadows." The description still holds true after 420 years.

Cape Breton Highlands N.P. in Nova Scotia is a rugged mountain preserve on whose wild summits bald and golden eagles build their nests. The park counts the snowshoe rabbit among its inhabitants, besides black bears and smaller beasts of prey. A flotilla of sword-fishing boats works out of South Ingonish Harbour.

Canadian Provincial Parks and Preserves: Ontario, Algonquin Park; Quebec, La Vérendrye Park, Mt. Tremblant Park, Laurentides Park, Gaspesian Park; New Brunswick, Plaster Rock-Renous Game Refuge.

The South Eastern Sector. Map on pages 20 and 21.

National Parks: *Great Smoky Mountains National Park,* between Tennessee and North Carolina, includes the highest mountains east of the Rockies, with 17 peaks over 6,000 feet. Its fauna resembles that of Shenandoah N.P.; its flora is famous for the catawba rhododendron which sometimes grows to a height of from fifteen to twenty feet. Laurel shrubs of 14 feet have stems up to 17 inches thick. Both rhododendron and laurel form so-called "slicks" or "hells," which are inpenetrable, giant thickets.

Hot Springs National Park in Arkansas is a reservation of 47 mineral hot springs. Its significance is largely of a medical nature.

Everglades National Park on the southern tip of Florida is a unique subtropical wilderness of grass, water and wood islands. It contains the largest mangrove forest in the Americas, with trees more than 80 feet tall; there is saw grass as high as a man; ferns grow fronds 15 feet long; 80 kinds of wild orchids thrive among the pines, palms and cypresses some of which are at least 1,000 years old. In freshwater pools, alligators sun themselves, in saltwater inlets crocodiles survive. Sea cows, the mermaids of the ancient mariners, graze on river bottoms, unmindful of the numerous fish which surround them; the largest of the latter is the Florida tarpon which attains a weight up to 200 pounds. Giant loggerhead turtles with 300-pound bodies frequent the seashore near Cape Sable, and serpents abound, from cottonmouth moccasins and indigo snakes to king snakes and diamond-back rattlers. Black bears, bobcats, otters, white-tailed deer and marsh rabbits inhabit the wet wilderness, and the panther makes his last stand east of the Mississippi. Some of the world's greatest rookeries are located in this park.

Fort Jefferson National Monument is a sanctuary of bird and marine life on an island of the Dry Tortugas. The fort was built in 1846 to control the Florida Straits.

National Forests: National forests indicated on the map but not mentioned in this chapter are "Purchase Units," i.e. their land is in process of being acquired and developed. North Carolina: *Croatan N.F.* has interesting stands of swamp hardwoods, only three miles from the Atlantic Ocean; there is hunting of bear, deer, quail, turkey and migratory birds. *Nantahala N.F.* is famous for its azaleas and rhododendrons; lake and stream fishing for bass and trout; hunting for wild boar, deer, bear, turkey and birds. *Pisgah N.F.* is at its best when the purple rhododendron is in bloom in the Craggy Gardens and on Roan Mountain; fishing for trout, bass and perch; hunting for deer, bear and small game; annual big game hunts are held in the cooperative game management areas of the forest. Tennessee: In the *Cherokee N.F.* the Ducktown Copper Basin is an outstanding example of land deformation and erosion; lake and stream fishing for rainbow and brook trout; hunting for small and large game, including the wild boar. Arkansas: *Ouachita N.F.* encompasses the Ouachita, Kiamichi and Winding Stair Mountains, with Crystal Cave, Little Missouri Falls and several medicinal springs; here De Soto fought the Indians, and La Salle and de Tonti explored the wilderness, which accounts for the many French names in this region; fishing for bass; hunting for deer, quail and squirrel. *Ozark N.F.* is largely composed of beautiful oak forests; stream and lake fishing; small game and deer hunting.

South Carolina: *Francis Marion N.F.* offers fine old moss-draped oaks and flowering yucca, dogwood and holly trees; fishing for bass and other varieties; hunting for deer, turkey, quail and alligator. *Sumter N.F.* in the Piedmont and the Blue Ridge Mountains, is another area of big old stands of rhododendron and flowering shrubs; fishing for trout and bass; quail hunting. Georgia: In *Chattahoochee N.F.* in the Blue Ridge Mountains deer hunting with bow and arrow is popular; fishing for trout and bass. Alabama: *William B. Bankhead N.F.* includes several limestone gorges and two natural bridges; fishing for bass and bream; hunting for deer, squirrel and turkey. *Conecuh N.F.* offers bass and bream fishing in large, clear ponds; hunting for turkey, deer and small game. *Talladega N.F.* is known for bass bream and perch fishing; hunting for deer, squirrel, duck and turkey. Mississippi: *Bienville N.F.* contains 80 acres of outstanding virgin loblolly pine; fishing and quail hunting. *Delta N.F.* has extensive stands of virgin bottomland hardwoods; fishing and deer hunting. *De Soto N.F.* provides fishing and quail hunting. In *Holly Springs N.F.* some of the largest known erosion gullies as well as several erosion control projects can be examined; quail and small game hunting. *Homochitto N.F.* is one of the finest natural timber-growing areas in the U.S.; near Natchez spectacular eroded loess country can be observed.

FLORIDA: *Apalachicola N.F.* contains some unusual tree varieties like the rare Florida yew and the stinking cedar; fishing for bass, bream and perch; hunting for quail, deer, and bear. In *Ocala N.F.* both hardwoods and various subtropical palms are thriving; its Juniper Springs have a daily flow of 8 million gallons of fresh water; fishing and deer hunting. *Osceola N.F.* is located in flat country dotted with ponds and cypress swamps; fishing for bass, perch and bream; hunting for quail, dove, turkey and deer. LOUISIANA: *Kisatchie N.F.* still has a touch of the original deep South, with its stands of virgin pine and its bayous and lakes screened with Spanish moss; fishing, and hunting for deer, quail and migratory birds.

The North Central Sector. Map on pages 22 and 23.

NATIONAL PARKS: *Mammoth Cave National Park,* one hundred miles south of Louisville, Kentucky, shows fascinating rock formations in many miles of underground halls, like the Methodist Church (near the old, abandoned saltpeter works), the Star Chamber, and others. Interesting cave flowers which look like roses, camellias, chrysanthemums and similar blossoms are formed of gypsum. The Echo River contains unusual adaptations to the cave environment: white, eyeless fish, blind crawfish, and blind crickets.

Isle Royale National Park lies in a group of approximately 150 islands in Lake Superior, about 20 miles from Minnesota and Canada and 50 miles from Michigan. The island contains more than 30 lakes, and its Lake Siskewit with Ryan Island is "a lake within a lake, with an island within an island." There are, on Isle Royale, more than a thousand ancient copper pits which were worked by prehistoric Indians, and one of America's largest moose herds thrives in its forests.

Wind Cave National Park, ten miles north of Hot Springs, S. D., is noted for the fine boxwork and frostwork in its underground halls; the calcite crystal formations are most beautiful in the Garden of Eden.

NATIONAL MONUMENTS: *Pipestone National Monument* near the town of Pipestone, Minnesota, preserves the quarry of soft, red stone from which the American Plains Indians carved their ceremonial pipes for many centuries.

South Dakota contains several national monuments of interest. *Badlands National Monument* is a weird region of eroded mountains where prehistoric animal fossils are found. *Fossil Cycad N.M.* has also many fossil beds, but the area is undeveloped. *Jewel Cave N.M.* is decorated with lovely calcite crystals (see also Wind Cave N.P.). In North Dakota, the *Theodore Roosevelt National Memorial Park* shows, on a section of the old Roosevelt ranch, a portion of the badlands.

NATIONAL FORESTS: National forests indicated on the map but not mentioned in this chapter are "Purchase Units," i.e. their land is in process of being acquired and developed. OHIO: *Wayne N.F.* consists of stands of fine hardwoods; old iron and charcoal furnaces and the Amesville "coonskin library" are reminders of pioneer days; stream and lake fishing; small game hunting. KENTUCKY: *Cumberland N.F.* is known for its rock formations such as the Red River gorge, sandstone cliffs, natural rock arches, limestone caves and mineral springs; bass and pike fishing. INDIANA: *Hoosier N.F.* has excellent stands of black walnut; an old trail of migratory buffalo, between Western Plains and French Lick, is a relic from Indian days; here the final outlet of the Lost River is located, and the Ten O'Clock Indian Boundary Line crosses the area; the forest is at its best when dogwood and redbud are in bloom in spring; fishing for catfish, bass, bluegill; hunting for fox, squirrel, quail. MICHIGAN: *Huron N.F.* offers fishing for trout and hunting for small game and birds. *Manistee N.F.* has good lake and stream fishing, deer and small game hunting. *Ottawa N.F.* is known for its waterfalls (Bond, Sturgeon, Rainbow, and others); lake and stream fishing; deep sea trolling in Lake Superior; deer and bear hunting. *Hiawatha and Marquette N.F.* in upper Michigan are known for the Pictured Rocks on Lake Superior; the forests offer lake and stream fishing.

ILLINOIS: *Shawnee N.F.* contains prehistoric Indian mounds and stone forts, near the confluence of the Ohio and Mississippi Rivers; hunting for quail, water fowl, squirrel, rabbit, raccoon; stream fishing. WISCONSIN: *Chequamegon N.F.* consists of good stands of various pines and spruces, balsam and jack pine; lake and stream fishing, particularly for muskellunge; deer and small game hunting. *Nicolet N.F.* contains both pine-spruce-balsam and hardwood forests; its cedar-spruce swamp is interesting; lake and stream fishing for muskellunge, pike, bass, trout; hunting for deer, bear, grouse and duck. MISSOURI: *Rolla-Clark N.F.* with its stands of oaks and pines, its big springs and clear, fast-flowing streams, is located in the Ozark Mountains; here the spring bloom of dogwood and redbud is especially beautiful; small-mouth bass and other fishing; squirrel and fox hunting. *Mark Twain N.F.,* also in the Ozark Mountains, is studded with many coves, rock cairns, and springs; fishing for bass, pike and panfish.

MINNESOTA: In *Chippewa N.F.* stands of virgin red pine surround the headwaters of the Mississippi River; it is the home of the Chippewa Indians; lake fishing for wall-eyed pike, northern pike, pan fish; hunting for water fowl, upland game, birds, deer, bear. *Superior N.F.* contains millions of acres of virgin forests and 5,000 lakes; the Superior and Little Indian Sioux Roadless Areas are located here, and the historic water route to the Northwest skirts the forest's shores; lake and stream fishing; deer hunting. NEBRASKA: *Nebraska N.F.* includes a game preserve with a large herd of mule deer; it is a nesting ground for the great blue heron, grouse, and prairie chicken; outside of the preserve there is hunting in season for pheasant, other birds and small game; fishing. SOUTH DAKOTA: *Black Hills N.F.* offers spectacular canyons, waterfalls and crystal caves; fishing, and hunting for deer and migratory birds; this is the historic gold rush area of the fabulous Homestake Mine and of such colorful, early characters as Calamity Jane, Wild Bill Hickok, Deadwood Dick and Preacher Smith. *Custer-Harney N.F.* is the site of the famous Rushmore National Memorial which depicts, in gigantic outlines, the faces of Washington, Jefferson, Lincoln and Theodore Roosevelt carved in granite; gold, silver and feldspar mining can be observed there; trout fishing; deer and elk hunting.

The *Quetico-Superior* area, a huge wilderness northwest of Lake Superior, has been established jointly by the U.S. and Canada as an International Peace Memorial Forest. It combines Superior National Forest in Minnesota with Quetico Provincial Park in Ontario as one wildlife management unit.

CANADIAN NATIONAL PARKS: *Georgian Bay Islands National Park* is located in Georgian Bay, Ontario. It includes the unusual Flowerpot Island at the mouth of Georgian Bay; here two rock columns stand on the shore like two huge flowerpots; they have been separated by erosion from the limestone cliffs which rise 300 feet above the water.

Point Pelee National Park is the southernmost spot of the Canadian mainland, in the southwest corner of Ontario on Lake Erie; and the residents of the region like to point out that here Canada, in the minds of most people a country of the far north, almost touches the latitude of the northern state line of California.

Riding Mountain National Park in Manitoba, northwest of Winnipeg, is a large plateau rising to a height of 2,200 feet and offering a sweeping view of the endless plains below. It is a big-game sanctuary of mule deer and white-tailed deer, moose and bear. One of America's largest elk herds is grazing on its meadows, and near Lake Audy a herd of buffaloes leads a semi-wild existence.

The South Central Sector. Map on pages 24 and 25.

NATIONAL PARKS: *Platt National Park* in Oklahoma, outside of the town of Sulphur, contains 32 large and several small cold mineral springs; 18 of them are sulphur springs, 6 are freshwater, 5, iron, and 3, bromide springs.

Big Bend National Park in Texas, on the Big Bend of the Rio Grande 110 miles from the town of Alpine, is a desert wilderness with high mountain ranges and great forests. It encompasses Boot Canyon, Santa Elena and two other canyons of the Rio Grande, with a fine desert flora of creosote bushes, cactus plants in a wide variety, yucca and ocotillo, mesquite and century plants. Also a varied fauna flourishes, undisturbed by civilization: The mountain lion, here called puma, is in evidence, as is the peccary, the wild pig. Other animals encountered in the park are the Mexican black bear, the kit fox, the mule deer, the white-tailed deer, the pronghorn antelope, and the zebra-tailed lizard. Also fossil remains of prehistoric animals can be seen, among them shells of oysters and clams three feet wide and four feet long.

Carlsbad Caverns National Park lies 28 miles south of Carlsbad, New Mexico. Its seven-mile-long underground halls and rooms have huge dimensions: One cave is 3/4 of a mile in length, 600 feet wide, 350 feet high. The Queen's Chamber is decorated with gleaming stone curtains and draperies, and there are impressive stalagmites like the Totem Poles and the Twin Domes. One of the most fascinating aspects of this park is its population of bats. At dusk every day, three million of them leave the cave, soaring into the evening on their nightly insect hunt.

NATIONAL MONUMENTS: *Capulin Mountain National Monument* lies in the northwestern corner of New Mexico. It is an extinct volcano more than 8,000 feet above sea level, with a symmetrical crater in its crest.

White Sands National Monument, in south central New Mexico, preserves a rare and spectacular phenomenon: a gleaming white desert of gypsum. The gypsum sand is blown by the wind into huge dunes which are forever shifting, causing the few surviving plants to perform miracles of adaptation. In order to keep their crowns above the crest they grow a longer and longer stalk, and plants with 40 foot stems have been discovered. Receding dunes leave other plants, whose roots have bound the gypsum around the stem, on top of tall and lonely pillars. The animals, too, have adapted themselves to their environment, and have developed a pale coloration that is not too conspicuous on the white backdrop. The prize probably goes to the pocket mice: in the black lava beds a few miles to the north, they are black; in the red hills nearby, they have a reddish fur; and in the gypsum sands they are white.

NATIONAL FORESTS: National forests indicated on the map but not mentioned in this chapter are "Purchase Units," i.e. their land is in process of being acquired and developed. TEXAS: *Angelina N.F.* surrounds the Angelina River with forests of longleaf pine and hardwoods along the river bottom; river and lake fishing of bass and catfish; hunting of dove and quail. *Davy Crockett N.F.* is a mixture of hardwoods and shortleaf-loblolly pines; river and lake fishing for bass and catfish; deer hunting. *Sabine N.F.* consists of hardwoods and southern pines; fishing for bass and catfish in Sabine River and overflow lakes; fox hunting. *Sam Houston N.F.* is part of the "Big Thicket" area, with shortleaf-loblolly pine woods and hardwoods in bottoms; lake and river fishing for bass and catfish. NEW MEXICO: *Carson N.F.* in the Sangre de Cristo Mountains, includes the Taos Indian pueblo and several hot springs; lake and stream fishing for trout; hunting for wild turkey and brown bear. *Cibola N.F.* is known for its prehistoric ruins and the ancient "sky city" of Acoma; considerable antelope herds are found here; limited fishing; hunting for deer and antelope. *Gila N.F.* includes the Mogollan, Black, Pinos, Altos and Diablo Mountain Ranges, also the Gila and

Black Range Wilderness Areas; prehistoric ruins and cliff dwellings are found in the Gila National Monument; stream fishing; hunting for black bear, mule deer, white-tailed deer, antelope, mountain lion and turkey. *Lincoln N.F.* adjoins the Carlsbad Caverns National Park and the White Sands National Monument; it contains the White Mountain Wild Area with extensive stands of fir and ponderosa pine; fishing and big game hunting; the highest golf course in the world is located at Ruidoso and Cloudcroft, within the forest's territory. *Santa Fe N.F.*, in the Sangre de Cristo Range, includes Indian villages and ruins of ancient pueblos and Spanish missions, also the San Pedro Peak Wild Area and the Pecos Wilderness Area; trout fishing in clear lakes and streams; hunting for turkey, elk, deer and bear.

The North Western Sector. Map on pages 26 and 27.

NATIONAL PARKS: *Yellowstone National Park* in the northwest corner of Wyoming is known the world over for its geysers; the most famous among them is Old Faithful which erupts every 65 minutes; the tallest is the Giant with a water jet 200 feet high; the Beehive is considered the most beautiful; Grand Geyser spouts its jet in the form of a giant fan. Firehole Lake seems to produce underwater flames at its bottom; the Mud Volcano and mud springs, like the Fountain Paint Pots, are interesting phenomena as are the Mammoth Hot Springs with their huge terraces. There are remarkable rocks, like Roaring Mountain, with a steam vent near the top; Sulphur Mountain; Obsidian Cliff, a mountain of glass; Amethyst Mountain; and the petrified trees of forests buried for millions of years. Yellowstone Lake with the Fishing Cone used to provide old-timers with a chance to catch a cutthroat trout in the lake and boil it in the hot spring without taking it from the pole. Two-Ocean Pass offers a vivid illustration of the Continental Divide: A stream branches; one arm flows toward the Pacific, the other toward the Atlantic. Countless water and land birds enliven the scene, among them sea gulls and white pelicans. The park is a veritable natural zoo.

Grand Teton National Park lies eleven miles south of the border line of Yellowstone Park. Its great attraction is the Teton Range which has been compared with a giant saw whose teeth reach into the sky. The Grand Teton, with a height of almost 14,000 feet, is the tallest. Elk and big-horn sheep, mule deer and moose are among the park's residents.

Glacier National Park in northwestern Montana offers a symphony of colors: Its red and green, purple and yellow mountains form the picturesque background to more than 60 glaciers — the largest is Sperry Glacier of about 330 acres — and approximately 200 glacial lakes. Triple Divide Peak is a living demonstration in American geography: From the same mountain, water drains northeastward to Hudson Bay, westward to the Pacific Ocean, and southward to the Gulf of Mexico. The wildflowers of the park are lovely in season. The Mackinaw trout is renowned among its fish population, and among its birds, a white species of the ptarmigan is unusual; it is hardly noticeable in the snow. Besides, there are black and grizzly bears, otter, moose and elk, mule deer and white-tailed deer.

Mount Rainier National Park, 56 miles from Tacoma and 90 miles from Seattle, Washington, presents the fourth highest peak in the U.S., rising to a height of 14,408 feet. Rainier is considered America's most beautiful mountain; it towers two miles above the surrounding valleys, standing alone and aloft; above the timberline a two-mile wide belt of the loveliest wildflowers surrounds its peak like a brightly colored, fragrant wreath. The finest flower specimens can be found at an altitude of about 5,500 feet; a famous flower meadow is Indian Henry's Hunting Ground. The park contains 28 glaciers, most of which are live glaciers, i.e. they move. Emmons and Nisqually Glaciers are the largest. Strangely, even these glaciers have their fauna and flora. In the "rose-colored snow" the rose hue is caused by a tiny plant, and in the ice of the Rainier glaciers a species of slender, dark-brown worm and a type of "ice flea" are regular residents.

Olympic National Park lies 6 miles south of Port Angeles on the Olympic Peninsula of Washington. Here the "rain forests" are preserved — virgin stands of woods climb from sea level to a height of 5,000 feet; 200-foot Douglas firs can be seen, 20-foot garlands of moss, and huge ferns. On the meadows of the Olympic Mountains the exquisite white avalanche lily is the first to blossom in spring, among myriads of wildflowers. Bear and mountain goat, black-tailed deer and Roosevelt elk are part of the park's fauna.

Crater Lake National Park, 62 miles from Klamath, and 80 miles from Medford, Oregon, surrounds Crater Lake which is geologically fascinating and naturally beautiful. The lake is the crater of an extinct volcano, "a giant cup half full of water," 6 miles in diameter and almost 2,000 feet deep. It is surrounded by 20 miles of cliffs of picturesque colors; these walls rise to 2,000 feet above the lake's emerald surface. The mirror of the water is pierced by the Phantom Ship, a lava island, and Wizard Island whose 300-foot wide crater once was a volcano within a volcano.

NATIONAL MONUMENTS: *Devils Tower National Monument* in northeastern Wyoming is a spectacular landmark of the West, a tower of rock that rises 1,280 feet above the Belle Fourche River. It stands alone in a countryside of pine forests and rolling grasslands. Its top plateau, an area of about an acre and a half, is a favorite nesting site for falcons and hawks.

Shoshone Cavern N.M., also in Wyoming, is a cave decorated with fine crystals. It is not open to the public.

Craters of the Moon National Monument is located in southern central Idaho. Its 75 square miles contain a wide variety of stone formations resulting from volcanic activity, such as cinder cones and craters, lava bombs and lava tubes, lava flows and tree molds. On the whole, this desolate area reminds the visitor of the landscapes of the moon as they are observed through a telescope.

Where to See American Nature Best

Oregon Caves National Monument lies southeast of Crater Lake National Park, near the California line.

NATIONAL FORESTS: National forests indicated on the map but not mentioned in this chapter are "Purchase Units," i.e. their land is in process of being acquired and developed. WYOMING: *Bighorn N.F.* is located in the Bighorn Mountains, an area of more than 300 lakes; a prehistoric Indian medicine wheel may be examined on Medicine Mountain; the forest includes the Cloud Peak Wild Area; trout fishing; hunting for elk, deer, bear and duck. *Bridger N.F.* contains several live glaciers and the Bridger Wilderness Area; lake and stream fishing; hunting for bear, moose, elk, mountain sheep, deer. *Medicine Bow N.F.* includes the Snowy Range Natural Area with numerous beaver colonies; fishing and deer hunting. *Shoshone N.F.* can boast of the largest glaciers in the Rocky Mountains; its Beartooth Plateau is covered with perpetual snow; fishing; hunting for mountain sheep, elk, deer, moose, bear and game birds. *Teton N.F.* includes the Teton Wilderness Area with its big game herds, a section of the Continental Divide, and the famous Jackson Hole country; stream and lake fishing.

MONTANA: *Beaverhead N.F.* contains the Anaconda-Pintler Wilderness Area with alpine lakes and hot springs; fishing; hunting for deer, elk, moose, antelope, bear. *Bitterroot N.F.* is known for the Selway-Bitterroot Wilderness Area, the largest in the U.S., with mountain lakes and hot springs; rocks with Indian hieroglyphics are found here; lake and stream fishing; hunting for elk, deer, bear and mountain goats. *Cabinet N.F.* extends over rugged mountain ranges; 100 miles of the Clark Fork River Valley offer a varied landscape of farms, forests and picturesque mountains; lake and stream fishing; hunting for bear, elk, black and white-tailed deer. *Custer N.F.* has glaciers and ice caverns, rich fossil beds and Indian hieroglyphics; the Beartooth Wilderness Area is in its territory; trout fishing, big game hunting. *Deerlodge N.F.* offers fishing in alpine lakes and streams; hunting for bear, deer and elk; special seasons for moose hunting. *Flathead N.F.* is known for its interesting geological formations such as the so-called Chinese Wall, hanging valleys, glaciers and glacial lakes; the Mission Mountains and Pentagon Wild Areas and the Bob Marshall Wilderness Area are included in the forest's territory; fishing; hunting for elk, deer, moose, mountain sheep and goats. *Gallatin N.F.* is located in the Crazy Mountains with their canyons, snow-clad peaks, and thousands of miles of trout streams; the Spanish Peaks and Absaroka Wilderness Areas are included in this territory; lake and stream fishing; hunting for bear, moose, elk, deer. *Helena N.F.* straddles the Continental Divide at the Big Belt and Elkhorn Mountain Ranges; a boat trip to Gates of the Mountains on the Missouri River, the original blockhouse of Fort Logan, and the ghost towns of Diamond City, Marysville, and Crow Creek Falls are special attractions; the Gates of the Mountains Wilderness Area lies within its territory; lake and stream fishing; hunting for elk and deer. *Kootenai N.F.* includes the Cabinet Mountains Wilderness Area, with Whitefish Range, Yaak River, Kootenai Canyon and Fisher River; lake and stream fishing; hunting for black bear and deer. *Lewis and Clark N.F.* boasts of scenic limestone canyons and rolling mountains with an open, park-like landscape; within the range of the forest are the Little Belt Mountains and parts of the Bob Marshall Wilderness Area, the Chinese Wall, and the Continental Divide; stream and lake fishing; hunting for deer, elk, grizzly and black bear, and antelope. *Lolo N.F.* straddles the Mission, Bitterroot and Swan Ranges and is crossed by the Lewis and Clark Trail; stream and lake fishing; hunting for grouse, pheasant, elk, deer and bear.

IDAHO: In *Boise N.F.* the ancient gold rush areas with their ghost towns and abandoned pits are revitalized today with active placer, hydraulic and shaft mining and dredging; this is rugged back country with magnificent stands of virgin ponderosa pine and sites of early Indian camps; lake and stream fishing for trout and salmon; hunting for bear, elk and deer. *Caribou N.F.* is crossed by beautiful valleys which are separated by narrow mountain ranges with towering peaks; it is a country of lovely streams and waterfalls, historic trails and natural soda springs; here the world's largest known reserve of phosphate is located, large enough to fill almost one-third of the world's needs; stream fishing; hunting for game birds, deer and bear. *Challis N.F.* comprises such spectacular scenery as the Lost River Range, the majestic Sawtooth Primitive Area and the Stanley Basin; the Middle Fork of the Salmon River in the Idaho Wilderness Area, the White Knob mountain ranges, and the headwaters of the Salmon River; stream and lake fishing for trout and salmon; hunting for deer, elk, mountain goat, mountain sheep, antelope and bear. *Clearwater N.F.*, on the Lewis and Clark route, contains large stands of virgin white pine; fishing for trout and salmon; hunting for elk and bear, and for deer in part of the forest. *Coeur d'Alene N.F.* adjacent to the beautiful Coeur d'Alene Lake with 104 miles of shore line, is a rich mining district and important producer of zinc, lead and silver; stream fishing; deer hunting. *Kaniksu N.F.* is rugged back country with the Selkirk Mountain Range, several big lakes, Chimney Rock and Roosevelt Ancient Grove of Cedars; lake and stream fishing; hunting for big game, grouse and duck. In *Minidoka N.F.* an area of fantastic wind-and-water-worn rocks is called "silent city of rocks;" the Snake River Valley offers wide scenic views and lovely alpine lakes; small stream fishing; deer hunting. *Nezperce N.F.* includes the Seven Devils Range, Hell's Canyon of the Snake River, Red River Hot Springs, historic Elk City, and part of the Selway-Bitterroot Wilderness Area; lake and stream fishing; hunting for elk, deer and bear. *Payette N.F.* comprises part of the Idaho Wilderness Area, the Grand Canyon of the Snake River, Payette Lakes and Seven Devils Mountains; fishing for trout and salmon in 154 lakes and 1,530 miles of streams; hunting for deer, elk, goats, sheep and bear. *St. Joe N.F.* has timber stands of virgin white pine and rugged scenery in the Bitterroot Range of the Idaho-

Montana divide, St. Marie's River Valley, and the canyon areas of Little North Fork of Clearwater River; lake and stream fishing; hunting for elk, deer, bear and mountain goat. *Salmon N.F.*, with the Big Horn Crags, Lewis and Clark Trail, and Salmon River Canyon, offers hunting for deer, elk, sheep, goats, bear, cougar and antelope. *Sawtooth N.F.* comprises the Sawtooth, Pioneer and Smoky Ranges and the Sawtooth Wilderness Area with hot springs and numerous glacial lakes ranging in size from 1 to 1,500 acres; some Pacific salmon ascend the Columbia River for a thousand miles to spawn and die in this area; lake and stream fishing; hunting for deer, elk, bear. *Targhee N.F.* is the "Island Park" country with the Grand Teton Peaks, Big Falls and Cave Falls; lake and stream fishing.

WASHINGTON: *Chelan N.F.* includes Lake Chelan, a 55-mile long body of water surrounded by precipitous ranges, alpine meadows, snow peaks and glaciers; the North Cascade Wilderness Area is located here; lake and stream fishing. *Colville N.F.* is the site of Roosevelt Lake, the 151-mile long artificial lake impounded by Grand Coulee Dam; this is both historic territory, with the old mission at Kettle Falls constructed without the use of nails in 1845, and a rich mineral-producing area; huckleberries and mushrooms abound in season; lake and stream fishing; hunting, notably for mule deer which is exceptionally large in the forest (a top weight of 440 pounds has been recorded). *Gifford Pinchot N.F.* is crossed by the scenic Evergreen Highway; it contains the Goat Rocks and Mount Adams Wild Areas with many lakes, mineral springs, and snow-capped peaks, also the Wind River forest nursery; lake and stream fishing for trout; deer and bear hunting. *Mt. Baker N.F.* presents a superlative mountain scenery with snow-capped peaks, glaciers, alpine lakes, and heavy stands of giant Douglas fir; the North Cascade Wilderness Area is included here; trout fishing; deer and bear hunting. *Olympic N.F.* is a wilderness of dense "rain forests" with huge trees, scores of lakes and streams, and snowy peaks; lake and stream fishing; hunting for deer, bear, cougar and elk. In *Snoqualmie N.F.* the world's largest known Douglas fir can be seen; here the 250-foot high Snoqualmie Falls, the Naches Pass with its "pillars of the Dalles," and the Goat Rocks Wild Area are located; stream and lake fishing, particularly for steelhead trout; hunting for black-tailed and mule deer. *Wenatchee N.F.* is known for its alpine meadows with lovely, rare wildflowers, along clear lakes in which snow-capped peaks are mirrored; stream and lake fishing.

OREGON: *Deschutes N.F.* is studded with beautiful mountain lakes and waterfalls, snowy peaks, ice caves and lava caves; the Deschutes River, Newberry Crater, Mount Jefferson Wild Area and Three Sisters Wilderness Area are located in the forest's territory; fishing for rainbow trout, hunting for deer. *Fremont N.F.* contains the geologically interesting Abert fault east of Lake Abert, the second largest vertical fault in the world; Indian paintings and writings are found here; protected herds of antelopes live in the Gearhart Mountain Wild Area; also the Oregon Desert is within the boundaries of the forest; hunting for deer. *Malheur N.F.* is known for its fossil beds of prehistoric plants and animals and its extensive stands of ponderosa pine; the Strawberry Mountain Wild Area is located here; miles of streams offer trout fishing; elk and deer hunting, with bow and arrow in an archers' hunting reserve. *Mount Hood N.F.* on the Oregon Trail presents world-famous views, glaciers, lakes and alpine meadows with colorful wildflowers; the widely-known Timberline Lodge, the Multnomah Falls, the Mount Hood and Mount Jefferson Wild Areas are in the forest's territory; stream and lake fishing. *Ochoco N.F.* is a park-like landscape with ponderosa pine groves and forests in which numerous beaver colonies are thriving; this was the scene of fierce range wars in pioneer days; trout fishing and deer hunting. *Rogue River N.F.* contains extensive forests of sugar pine and Douglas fir; this is the site of a bloody Indian war, and of the Mountain Lakes Wild Area; fishing for rainbow and steelhead trout, hunting for deer and migratory birds. *Siskiyou N.F.* is of great botanical interest as the original home of the Port Orford cedar and the Oregon myrtle; there are profuse growths of wild lilac and rhododendron, azaleas and pitcher plants, Brewer weeping spruce and Saddler oak; ghost camps of gold-rush days are encountered here; the Kalmiopsis Wild Area is also located in the forest's territory; the fishing grounds in the lower Rogue River gorge are famous for salmon, cut-throat and steelhead trout; hunting for deer, bear and cougar. *Siuslaw N.F.* is bordered by the Pacific Ocean; it includes the sand dunes of Cape Perpetua and heavy stands of Sitka spruce and western hemlock, cedar and Douglas fir, pitcher plants, azaleas and rhododendrons; Cascade Head Experimental Forest is located in this territory; ocean, lake and stream fishing; hunting for deer, bear, cougar and migratory birds. *Umatilla N.F.* on the old Oregon Trail contains the Blue Mountains and the Starkey Experimental Forest and Range; there are a number of hot sulphur springs; hunting for elk, deer and pheasant. *Umpqua N.F.* is known for the spectacular North Umpqua Cataracts, the Toketee and Lemolo Falls, Umpqua River and Diamond Lake; fishing for steelhead and rainbow trout; hunting for deer, bear and cougar. *Wallowa N.F.* offers a grand panorama of the Snake River and the Imnaha Canyons from Grizzly Ridge Road, with snowy peaks and glaciers, lakes and alpine meadows which in season abound with rare and colorful wildflowers; the Eagle Cap Wilderness Area is included here; trout fishing in lakes and streams, especially in the famous Minam River; hunting for elk, deer and bear. *Whitman N.F.* straddles the Blue and Wallowa Mountains; stream and lake fishing; hunting for deer, bear and elk. *Willamette N.F.* is the most heavily timbered national forest in the U.S., with snow-capped peaks and cool, clear lakes, waterfalls and hot springs; the Mount Jefferson Wild Area and the Three Sisters Wilderness Area are located in the forest's territory, the latter showing extraordinary volcanic formations.

CANADIAN NATIONAL PARKS: *Prince Albert National*

Park is located in the center of Saskatchewan, just inside of the map on pages 26-27. A gateway to the north country, the park includes lovely, cool lakes surrounded by forests of jack pine, spruce, white birch, trembling aspen and poplar. Besides the regular big game, woodland caribou and a herd of buffalo are protected there.

Waterton Lakes National Park in Alberta merges, on the Canadian side, with Glacier National Park on the American side; they form the Waterton-Glacier International Peace Park.

Elk Island National Park in Alberta possesses a large herd of buffalo, besides other big game. *Wood Buffalo National Park,* outside of the map on the northern borderline of Alberta, consists of 17,300 square miles of immense forests and open plains; there, amidst all sorts of other animals, numerous wood buffaloes live in an approximation of their original status; they are larger and darker than the plains buffaloes.

Banff National Park is known the world over for its majestic beauty. The nature lover will find there, besides the breath-taking scenery, some 500 varieties of lovely wild flowers; framing the lakes and rocks and thriving on the lower slopes are heavy stands of lodgepole pine and Engelmann spruce, of Douglas fir and alpine larch, of aspen and black poplar. The park's list of animal residents is most impressive: It includes mountain sheep and mountain goat, mule deer and elk, black bear and grizzly bear, coyote and mountain lion; among the smaller animals such unusual species as marten and marmot ("the whistler") are encountered.

Jasper National Park is a continuation of the Banff region, with the same grandiose scenery and fascinating fauna and flora. Several additional parks are in process of development in Alberta.

In British Columbia four smaller parks offer superb, alpine mountain scenery: *Mt. Revelstoke, Glacier, Yoho,* and *Kootenay National Parks.*

The South Western Sector. Map on pages 28 and 29.

National Parks: *Rocky Mountain National Park,* about 50 miles northwest of Denver, Colorado, presents "the shining mountains," 16 towering peaks more than 13,000 feet high and 65 peaks over 10,000 feet. Its bright and varied wildflowers include the blue columbine and the snow buttercup which, in early spring, pushes its blossoms through the snowfields.

Mesa Verde National Park, 56 miles from Durango, Colorado, preserves the prehistoric Indian cliff dwellings built into the canyon walls of the Mancos River.

Bryce Canyon National Park, 90 miles east of Cedar City, Utah, contains thousands of fantastic rock formations in a spectacular array of colors, ranging from white and yellow to pink, orange, red, brown and purple. Hundreds of these rocks seem to be "stone people."

Zion National Park, 60 miles south of Cedar City, Utah, is a unique canyon: Its walls of bright red sandstone are topped by white cliffs. Among its various mountains the Great White Throne, a huge stone block in red, buff and white, is the most famous.

Grand Canyon National Park, 60 miles north of the town of Williams, Arizona, is so well-known, as one of the world's most spectacular sights, that no attempt to describe it is necessary. The fauna of the park is interesting; besides mule deer, antelope, mountain sheep and bobcat, it includes mountain lions. One small animal is the park's own: The Kaibab squirrel with the white tail.

Lassen Volcanic National Park is located 50 miles east of Red Bluff and 150 miles north of Sacramento, California. Its area contains the only recently active volcano in the U.S. It erupted sporadically between 1914 and 1921, and at times spouted clouds of black smoke six miles high. To this day, steam rises from 35 vents on top of the mountain—which also offers a superb view.

Yosemite National Park, 200 miles east of San Francisco on the west slope of the Sierra Nevada, is famous for its waterfalls which are among the world's highest and most beautiful. The waters of Upper Yosemite Fall tumble down 1,430 feet, a height which equals 9 Niagara Falls. Other magnificent falls, at their best in May and June, are Lower Yosemite, Ribbon, Bridalveil, Nevada, Illouette and Vernal. The "fire fall" on Glacier Point, 3,000 feet above the valley, is admired nightly. The park also includes three groves of giant sequoias; the Mariposa grove contains 200 big trees.

Sequoia National Park, 220 miles from Los Angeles and 253 miles from San Francisco, preserves approximately 1,000,000 big trees, almost half of them in the Giant Forest. The most famous sequoia is the General Sherman which has been called the biggest and oldest living organism on earth; it is 36 feet wide at the bottom, and is as tall as a 27-story skyscraper measuring 272 feet. Its age is estimated at 3,000 years or more. Other great trees are the Roosevelt, the Abraham Lincoln, and Chief Sequoyah. The Chimney Trees have been hollowed by lightning and fire. In this region the country's highest peak, Mt. Whitney (14,495 feet), looks down on the country's lowest point, Death Valley. Black bear and mule deer occur in the park. Golden Trout Creek is the original home of this species of trout.

Kings Canyon National Park is in the same region as Sequoia N.P., 60 miles east of Fresno, California. It contains hundreds of big trees in the General Grant Grove and the Redwood Mountain Area. Hollow Log Tree is a big tunnel; Converse Basin is a grove ruined by logging operations. Some rare wolverines live in the park.

National Monuments: *Great Sand Dunes National Monument* is located in the San Luis Valley of south central Colorado.

Wheeler National Monument, nine miles from Wagon Wheel Gap, Colorado, is an extinct volcanic area studded with fantastic pinnacles and cut by deep gorges and canyons. *Black Canyon of the Gunnison N.M.,* also in Colorado, is mainly of geological interest. *Colorado N.M.* is known for its weird rock formations; towering monoliths stand by sheer-walled canyons. *Holy Cross N.M.* in Eagle County in central Colorado honors a peak almost 14,000 feet high which presents every year, until late July, a giant cross of snow on its northeast side.

Dinosaur National Monument, in the canyon plateau country of northeastern Utah and northwestern Colorado, is one of the richest fossil deposits in America. This was a tropical lowland with an abundant vegetation in the days of the dinosaurs and their relatives, reptiles ranging in size from a few inches to 80 feet. The largest animals became so bulky and unwieldy that they were often trapped in quicksand and drowned by floods. Their corpses rotted away and their bones piled up in shallow waters, were covered with silt, impregnated with silica, and thus preserved to our day. The last dinosaurs perished about 60 million years ago. Conservation is so perfect that the bone structure may be studied with a microscope.

Arches N.M. in southeastern Utah contains a large number of giant arches, windows, spires and pinnacles carved, by erosion, out of red sandstone rocks. *Natural Bridges N.M.,* also in the southeast of Utah, shows similar phenomena, including three huge, natural bridges, while *Rainbow Bridge N.M.* in southern Utah boasts of an immense stone arch of the same name; it has a span of 278 feet and is 309 feet high; with its salmon-pink sandstone set off against a canyon of darker stone walls, it is strikingly beautiful. *Capitol Reef N.M.* in Wayne County, Utah, is an area of highly colored cliffs and spectacular erosional forms visible from the highway. *Cedar Breaks N.M.,* also in Utah, presents the work of erosion in another fashion: It is a big, natural ampitheater with walls of pink rock. *Timpanogos Cave N.M.* in Utah is a limestone cavern, and *Zion N.M.* is an extension of Utah's Zion National Park.

The Petrified Forest National Monument is a part of the Painted Desert in northern Arizona. It is the greatest deposit of petrified wood known in the world and, in its beds of shale, also contains perfectly preserved fossil leaves of a remote era. In six separate "forests" huge logs of agate lie on the ground; in their day, the living trees had crashed into a stream and had been buried under sand; gradually silica had penetrated the cell tissues and the trees had become petrified.

Sunset Crater N. M., about 20 miles north of Flagstaff, Arizona, is dedicated to a huge volcanic cone with a brightly colored rim.

Saguaro N.M., 17 miles east of Tucson, Arizona, is a bizarre forest of giant Saguaro cactus plants, of fluted columns 20 or 30 feet high which, in May, are crowned with caps of gleaming, magnificent white blossoms. The latter turns into edible, scarlet fruit later in the year. The cactus trees in this area are as old as 200 years. *Organ Pipe Cactus N.M.* in the Sonoran Desert, east of Tucson, Arizona, is a native Mexican desert garden in which the long-armed Organ Pipe Cacti are the most spectacular plants. Several clusters contain as many as 30 unbranched columns, some of them 20 feet tall, and give, indeed, the impression of a pipe organ. In May their white blossoms, with a tinge of lavender, open after sunset and close after sunrise. *Chiricahua N.M.* in southeastern Arizona is a wilderness of weird and beautiful pinnacles and turrets eroded in volcanic rocks. *Lehman Caves N.M.,* a group of caverns in grey and white limestone, is located five miles west of Baker, Nevada.

Death Valley N.M. lies in southwestern Nevada, east of California's High Sierra. Closed in by two forbidding mountain ranges, it is a country of superlatives and one of America's most widely known spots. Here is the lowest land of the western hemisphere, at Badwater, 280 feet below sea level; altogether 550 square miles of the valley floor are lower than the ocean surface. It is also the driest spot, and the hottest in summertime, with 134°F. recorded in the shade.

Joshua Tree N.M. in southern California is a huge and beautiful desert of more than 800,000 acres. Its vegetation includes large stands of the spectacular Joshua Tree which elsewhere is becoming rare. This plant, a member of the Lily Family, reaches a maximum height of 38 feet. Creamy white blossoms grow in magnificent clusters at the ends of its angular branches. The name has probably been coined by the Mormons on their westward trek.

Pinnacles N.M. in California is an area of rock formations whose spires rise 500 to 1,200 feet. *Devil Postpile N.M.,* also in California, preserves the remaining column of a huge basaltic lava flow. *Muir Woods N.M.,* just north of San Francisco, contains a virgin stand of superb coastal redwoods; it is so-called in honor of the famous western naturalist. *Channel Islands N.M.,* off the coast of southern California, is an outpost of fascinating wildlife, but undeveloped and not open to the public.

NATIONAL FORESTS: National forests indicated on the map but not listed in this chapter are "Purchase Units," i.e. their land is in process of being acquired and developed. COLORADO: In *Arapaho N.F.* gold and silver mining operations may be watched, also old ghost towns which are falling into ruin; the Gore Range — Eagles Nest Wild Area is in this territory; lake and stream fishing; hunting for elk, deer, bear and small game. *Grand Mesa N.F.* is a plateau 10,500 feet high, with 250 lakes and reservoirs, cliffs and canyons, water falls and wildflowers; lake and stream fishing; hunting for deer, bear and duck. *Gunnison N.F.* is a spectacular mountain wilderness with 27 peaks more than 12,000 feet high; it includes the Ruby Range and the West Elk and Maroon Bells-Snowmass Wilderness Areas, with high lakes and the Taylor Park reservoir; fishing in 1,000 miles of streams; hunting for elk, deer, mountain sheep and bear. *Pike N.F.* offers a whole array of famous sights and places: Pikes Peak, historic Cripple Creek, and the Alma gold camps; the Rampart Range Road with its splendid panoramas, Devil's Head Forest Fire Lookout, and Monument Forest Nursery; the Manitou Forest Experiment Station and the watersheds of the Platte and Arkansas Rivers; fishing and hunting. In *Rio Grande N.F.* active mining camps may be observed; within its boundaries the rugged mountains of Wolf Creek Pass, the Wheeler National Monument, and the Upper Rio Grande and La Garita — Sheep Mountain Wilderness Areas are included; trout fishing; hunting for deer, elk and duck. In *Roosevelt N.F.* the Continental Divide is particularly rugged, with many alpine lakes and the Arapaho, Isabelle and South St. Vrain Glaciers; trout fishing and hunting for deer, bear, mountain lion, grouse and duck. *Routt N.F.* includes a stretch of the Continental Divide where ice and snow are perpetual; the Mount Zirkel-Dome Peak Wild Area and the Big Creek Lakes Recreation Area are in the forest's confines; trout fishing; hunting for deer, elk, grouse and duck. *San Isabel N.F.* has the highest average elevation of all national forests in the U.S.; within the boundaries of the forest are the Sangre de Cristo Range with 12 peaks taller than 14,000 feet, including Mount Elbert, second highest in the U.S., and the Lake Isabel Recreation Area; there are more than 40 timberline lakes, molybdenum mines, and the Snow Angel on Mount Shavano; fishing for trout; hunting for small game, birds, deer, elk, bear and mountain lion. *San Juan N.F.* offers alpine lakes and cataracts, canyons and peculiar geological formations, archaeological ruins and historic mines. *Uncompahgre N.F.* contains numerous peaks higher than 13,000 feet; on the Uncompahgre Plateau gold mines are points of interest; the Uncompahgre Wild Area and the Ouray Scenic Area are located here; trout fishing; hunting for grouse, elk, bear and mountain lion. *White River N.F.* is a famous producer of zinc, silver and marble.

UTAH: *Ashley N.F.* includes the eastern half of the Uinta Mountain Range, the tallest American range extending east and west; there are numerous natural erosion formations and scenic gorges, among them the Red Gorge of the Green River, 1,500 feet deep, and exposed geological formations estimated to be a billion years old; the High Uintas Wilderness Area has an elevation mostly above 10,000 feet; lake and stream fishing; hunting. *Cache N.F.* contains the rugged peaks of the Bear River and Wasatch Ranges, Minnetonka Cave and Logan and Ogden Canyons; fishing for trout; hunting for deer and elk. *Dixie N.F.* is a majestic mountain wilderness; from its Table Cliff Point peaks in four states (Arizona, Colorado, Nevada and Utah) can be seen in clear weather; its Pine Valley Mountains and its Boulder Top Plateau have many lakes which are not accessible by road; stream and lake fishing; hunting for deer, elk and cougar. *Fishlake N.F.* includes the Tushar Mountains, the Thousand Lake Mountain Scenic Area, and the Petrified Wood Scenic Area; lake and stream fishing; hunting for deer and elk. *Manti-La Sal N.F.* on the Wasatch Plateau stands on huge deposits of coal in its eastern part; its Skyline Drive winds through alpine meadows and sylvan glades, colorful canyons and rocks with Indian writings; the Great Basin Forest Research Center is located here; fishing and hunting. *Uinta N.F.* is of special interest to geologists because of the Wasatch upthrust limestone strata which are bisected by deep canyons and waterfalls near Provo; the forest is a beautiful open range with stands of oak, maple, aspen, spruce and fir; hunting for mule deer and a limited number of elk. *Wasatch N.F.* is rugged back country with the Wasatch, Uinta, Stansbury and Onaqui Ranges and the High Uintas Wilderness Area; the Alpine Scenic Highway leads to Timpanogos Cave; lake and stream fishing and hunting.

ARIZONA: *Apache N.F.* is a country of spruce woods and mountain meadows, traversed by the Scenic Coronado Trail; the prehistoric Blue River Cliff Dwellings are located here; lake and stream fishing for trout; hunting for turkey, deer, elk and bear. *Coconino N.F.* is in the neighborhood of Grand Canyon National Park and the National Monuments of Sunset Crater, Walnut Canyon with its cliff dwellings, Wupatki with its ancient ruins, and Montezuma Castle; Lowell Astronomical Observatory is within the boundaries of the forest; hunting for deer, elk and mountain lion. In *Coronado N.F.* rugged mountains rise abruptly from the desert so that the transition from cactus thickets to pine forests, and from swimming to skiing can be negotiated in an hour's drive; interesting plants are found here, like the Chihuahua pine, the chilicote and the madrona, with its red-brown trunk and limbs and its shiny evergreen foliage; the forest's bird life is varied and includes the pine-loving, picturesque trogon, a southerner of brilliant plumage of bronze-green and black, white and rosy-pink hues; among the forest's unusual animals are the Chiricahua squirrel, the coatimundi (a southern cousin of the raccoon), and the javelina or peccary; there is hunting for deer and javelina. *Crook N.F.* is a semidesert ascending to alpine country, from 3,500 to 10,700 feet; it encompasses the Mogollon Rim and Pinaleno Ranges, parts of the Gila and Superstition Wilderness Areas, and the Galiuro Wild Area; hunting for quail, turkey, peccary, deer, elk, bear and mountain lion. *Kaibab N.F.* includes the Grand Canyon National Game Preserve with the famous Kaibab deer and buffalo herds; this forest is the only habitat of the Kaibab squirrel; both the north and the south rims of the Grand Canyon are accessible from here; hunting for turkey, deer, elk, antelope, bear and mountain lion. *Prescott N.F.* is typical back country in the high mountains; rugged Granite Mountain is mirrored in Granite Basin Lake; the Jerome "billion dollar copper camp" is located here; some fishing, and deer hunting. *Sitgreaves N.F.* is known for its large elk herd, its Pueblo ruins and the Mogollon Rim drive which offers vast panoramic views. *Tonto N.F.* has a varied and colorful topography, ranging from semidesert to large ponderosa pine forests in the mountains; it includes the famous Tonto Basin, the Tonto National Monument with its prehistoric ruins, and the Pueblo Canyon ruins; a band of Mexican bighorn sheep lives in the Superstition Mountains; fishing and hunting.

NEVADA: *Humboldt N.F.* includes the Wildhorse Reservoir and the Owyhee River Canyon; stream fishing and deer hunting. *Nevada N.F.* is best known for its Charleston Division, a beautiful forest of large pine trees and cool climate surrounded by hot desert country; Nevada's only elk herd lives here; the forest adjoins the Lehman Caves National

Monument; deer hunting. *Toiyabe N.F.* is located in the Sierra Nevada, Toiyabe, and Santa Rosa Ranges; the Hoover Wilderness Area is included here; fishing in streams and alpine lakes for golden and Piute trout; hunting for black-tailed deer, mule deer and antelope.

CALIFORNIA: *Angeles N.F.* is unique insofar as its steep, wild mountains adjoin the metropolitan area of Los Angeles; it is predominantly a chaparral forest which serves as watershed for the Los Angeles area and offers delightful panoramic views, especially of the illuminated city at night; the forest contains Devil's Canyon and the Bear Canyon Wilderness Area; fishing and hunting. *Cleveland N.F.* is a watershed forest between the desert and the sea; it has an unusually mild climate; the Agua Tibia Wilderness Area and the Palomar Observatory with the world's largest telescope are within the boundaries of the forest; warm water fishing; pigeon, quail and deer hunting. *Eldorado N.F.* is an interesting backwoods territory in the Sierra Nevada mountains; it is studded with hundreds of mountain lakes, including the south end of famous Lake Tahoe; early mining camps were located here, among them Coloma, the site of Sutter's mill where the discovery of gold nuggets started the gold rush of 1849; the Carson Pass Highway follows the route of the Fremont expedition of 1844 which was guided by Kit Carson; lake and stream fishing; deer and bear hunting. *Inyo N.F.* covers some glorious mountain country, with the highest point in the continental U.S., Mount Whitney, and the southernmost glacier in the U.S., Palisade Glacier, which is also the largest in the Sierra Nevada; there are, in this back country, many more spectacular peaks with elevations of over 14,000 feet; also the High Sierra Wilderness Area and the Minarets Wild Area are located here; lake and stream fishing; deer hunting. *Klamath N.F.* includes the Marble Mountain and Salmon-Trinity Alps Wilderness Areas; its high mountain lakes and streams, particularly the Klamath River and its tributaries, are famous for salmon and steelhead trout fishing; deer hunting. *Lassen N.F.* is a fascinating volcanic area, the southern end of the so-called Cascade Wonderland; it abounds with volcanic lava flows and tubes, craters, hot springs and mud pots; Indian pictographs and hieroglyphics can be seen not far from the old immigrant trails; Caribou Peak and Thousand Lakes Wilderness Areas are within the forest's boundaries; lake and stream fishing for rainbow, steelhead and Lochleven trout; deer and bear hunting. *Los Padres N.F.* is a primitive mountain and forest territory with fine stands of redwood near the coast ascending to a semidesert surrounded by snow-capped peaks; this is the home of the rare California condor, one of the largest and most majestic birds; the Ventana and San Rafael Wild Areas are included here; fishing for trout; hunting for quail, pigeon, and some deer and wild boar. *Mendocino N.F.* contains the Middle Eel-Yolla Bolly Wilderness Area; some fishing, and hunting for black-tailed deer. *Modoc N.F.* is the winter range of a large interstate deer herd and a migratory bird refuge at Clear Lake Reservoir; the Glass Mountain lava flows and the South Warner Wilderness Area are within the forest's boundaries; lake and stream fishing; hunting for mule deer and water fowl. *Plumas N.F.* lies in the Feather River Country whose Feather Falls are among America's highest and most picturesque; the historic gold mining areas of La Porte and Johnsville are now a famous winter sports region; in the lovely mountain valleys extensive hydro-electric developments are carried out; lake and stream fishing; hunting for dove, quail, geese, duck, black-tailed deer, mule deer and bear. *San Bernardino N.F.* encompasses the highest mountains of southern California, including the San Jacinto, San Gorgonio, and Cucamonga Wild Areas; fishing in streams and in Big Bear, Arrowhead, and other lakes; deer hunting. *Sequoia N.F.* is a wilderness area with 200 peaks more than 11,000 feet high; within the territory of the forest are located the Mineral King Recreation Area, a stretch of the John Muir Trail, Kings River Canyon, Hume Lake, Kern River Canyon, Boyden's Cave, and the Sequoia National Game Refuge; mountain lake and stream fishing; hunting for mule deer and bear. *Shasta N.F.* includes Mount Shasta, Shasta Lake with 365 miles of mountainous shore line, and five living glaciers; also the Trinity Alps Wilderness Area and such geologically interesting formations as Glass Mountain, Lava Beds, and Castle Crags; lake and stream fishing, particularly for Dolly Varden trout which has its home here; hunting for small game, upland birds, deer and bear. *Sierra N.F.* is the watershed of the San Joaquin and Kings Rivers; it contains the Nelder and McKinley groves of big trees and the central sierra section of the John Muir Trail, also several wilderness areas and the Devil Postpile National Monument; lake and stream fishing; hunting for quail, deer and bear. *Six Rivers N.F.* consists of giant redwoods and old firs; it is primitive back country around the Klamath, Smith, Eel and Mad Rivers, with an unusually steady climate, cool in summer and mild in winter; fishing for steelhead trout and salmon, hunting for deer and bear. *Stanislaus N.F.* is a portion of the San Joaquin Valley, the mountain country nearest to San Francisco Bay, rising from an elevation of 1,100 feet to a height of 11,575 feet; it is covered with fine stands of timber and traversed by deep canyons that have been cut by the Merced, Tuolumne, Stanislaus, and Mokelumne Rivers; the Emigrant Basin Wild Area and the Sonora and Ebbets Pass abound with memories of the routes and wanderings of pioneers and early settlers; fishing in 715 miles of streams and numerous lakes; hunting for deer and bear. *Tahoe N.F.* with its lovely streams and lakes, among them the beautiful Lake Tahoe, is the scene of much of the gold rush history of California; this is the country of the mother lode and the Trail of the Forty-niners; today it is famous as a winter sports center with ideal snow conditions; lake and stream fishing; hunting for deer and bear. *Trinity N.F.* contains extensive stands of virgin timber in the Salmon-Trinity Alps and Yolla Bolly Middle Eel Wilderness Areas; lake and stream fishing, particularly for salmon and steelhead in the Trinity River.

Where to See American Nature Best

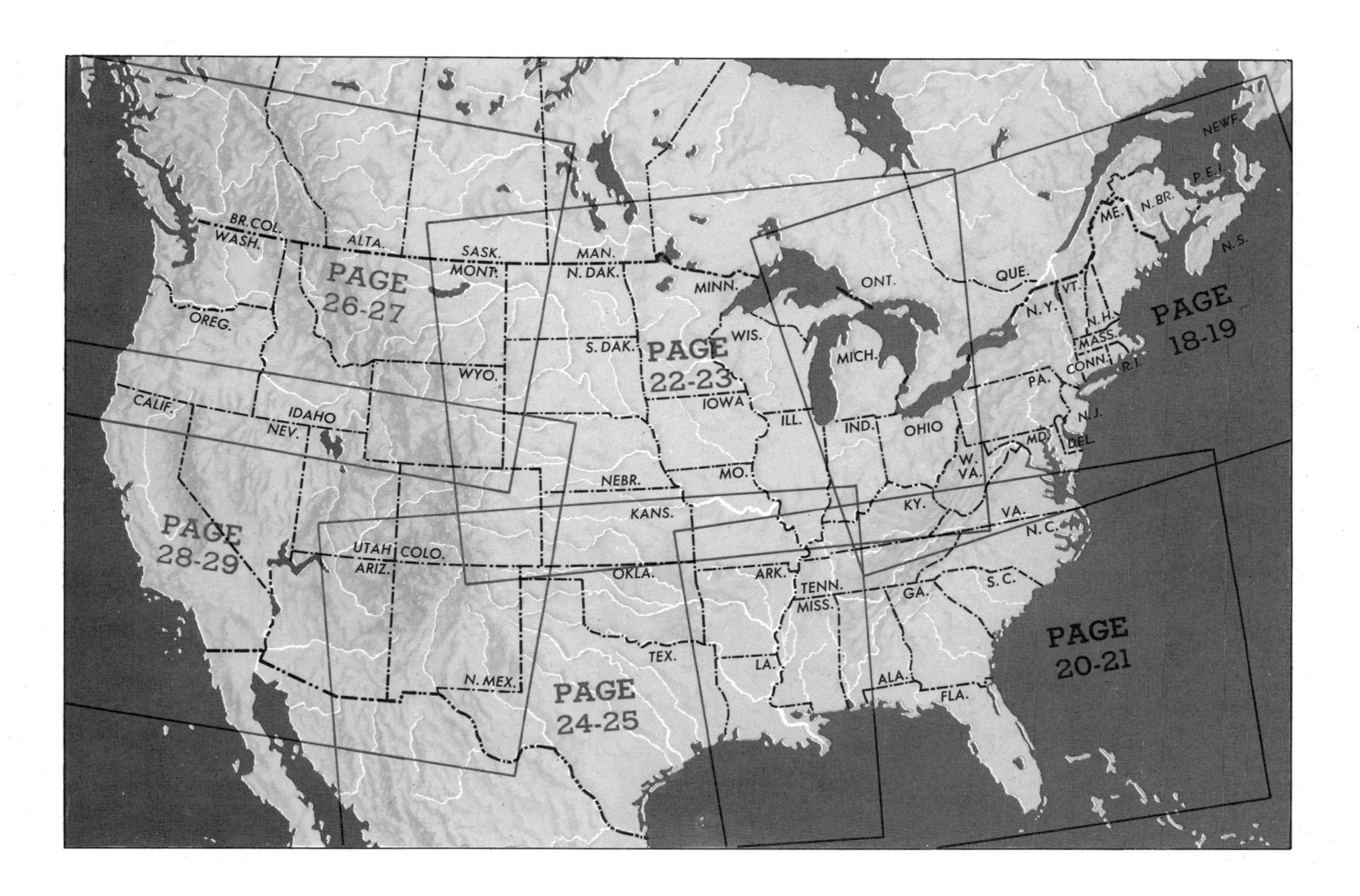

LEGEND

- National Parks and Monuments
- National Parkways
  - Completed sections
  - Projected or under construction
- National Recreational Areas
- Indian Reservations and Reserves
- National Wildlife Refuges
- National Forests and Forest Reserves
- State and Provincial Parks
- State and Provincial Forests
- Highways to National Park Service Areas
- Highways to State and Provincial Recreational Areas
- U.S. Highway Numbers (24)
- State and Provincial Highway Numbers (9)
- Trails
- National Boundaries
- State and Provincial Boundaries
- Cities and Towns
- National Capitals
- State and Provincial Capitals
- Deserts
- Mountain Peaks

LIST OF ABBREVIATIONS

C.H.=Court House
CHAN.=Channel
CO.=County
CR.=Creek
EXPER. STA.=Experimental Station
FED.=Federation
I., IS.=Island, Islands
IND. RES., I.R.=Indian Reservation or Reserve
MEM'L FOR.=Memorial Forest
MT., MTN., MTS.=Mount, Mountain, Mountains
NAT'L MEM'L=National Memorial
NAT'L MON.=National Monument
N.F.=National Forest
N.W.=Northwest
N.W.R.=National Wildlife Refuge
PKWY.=Parkway
PROV.=Provincial
P.S.=Plant Sanctuary
R.A.=Recreational Area
R.D.A.=Recreational Demonstration Area
S.F., S.F.P.=State Forest, State Forest Park
S.P.=State Park

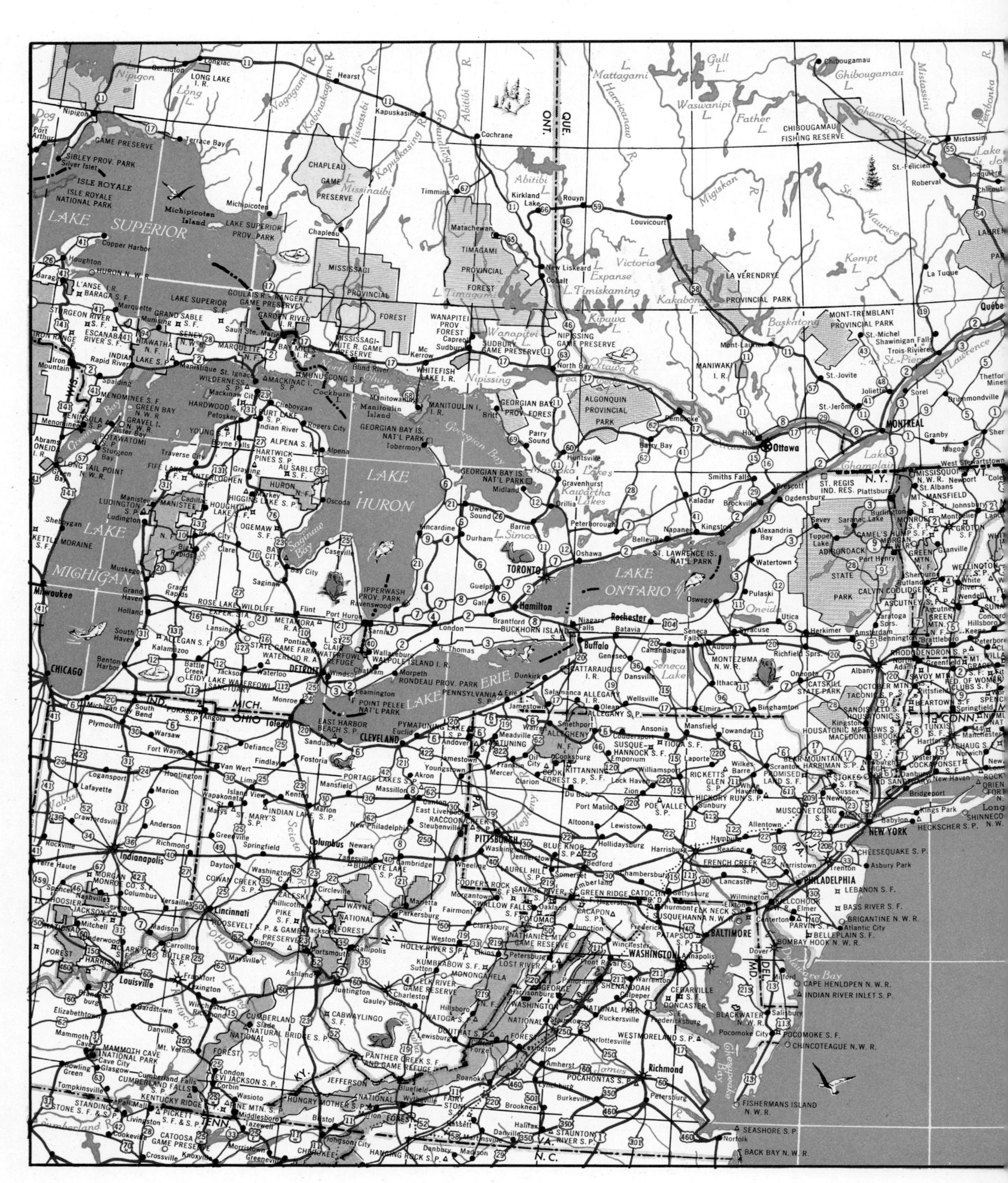
LAKE SUPERIOR
LAKE MICHIGAN
LAKE HURON
LAKE ERIE
LAKE ONTARIO
Georgian Bay
ISLE ROYALE NATIONAL PARK
CHAPLEAU GAME PRESERVE
MISSISSAGI PROVINCIAL FOREST
TIMAGAMI PROVINCIAL FOREST
ALGONQUIN PROVINCIAL PARK
LA VÉRENDRYE PROVINCIAL PARK
MONT-TREMBLANT PROVINCIAL PARK
CHIBOUGAMAU FISHING RESERVE
ONT.
QUE.
N.Y.
VT.
CONN.
PA.
OHIO
MICH.
IND.
KY.
TENN.
VA.
W. VA.
MD.
DEL.
N.C.
Cochrane
Kapuskasing
Hearst
Timmins
Rouyn
Louvicourt
North Bay
Sudbury
Ottawa
MONTREAL
Quebec
Toronto
Hamilton
Rochester
Buffalo
Syracuse
Albany
NEW YORK
PHILADELPHIA
BALTIMORE
WASHINGTON
Richmond
PITTSBURGH
CLEVELAND
Toledo
DETROIT
CHICAGO
Milwaukee
Indianapolis
Columbus
Cincinnati
Louisville
ADIRONDACK STATE PARK
MAMMOTH CAVE NATIONAL PARK
SHENANDOAH NATIONAL PARK
CHINCOTEAGUE N. W. R.
FISHERMANS ISLAND N. W. R.
BACK BAY N. W. R.

Where to See American Nature Best

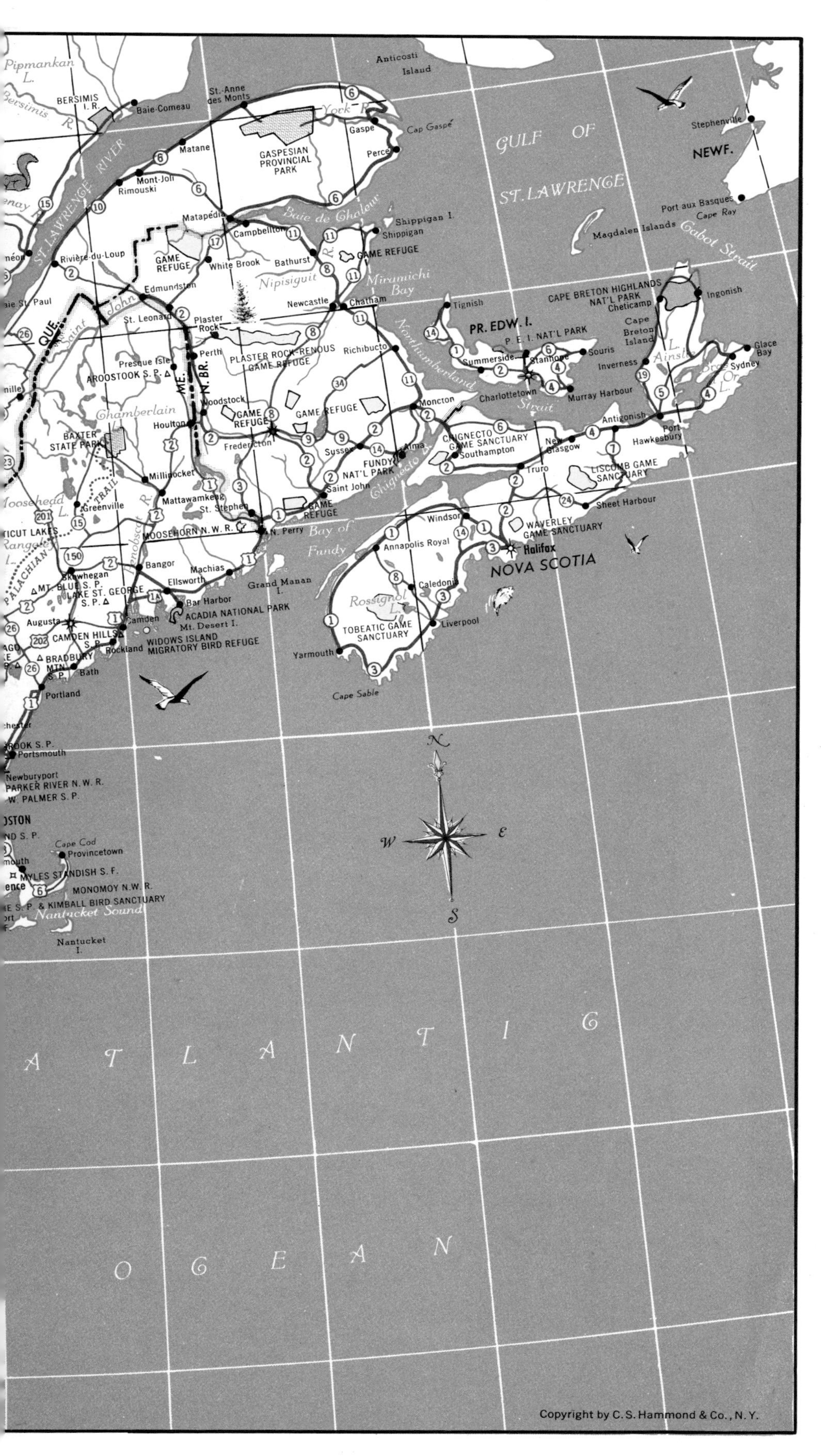

THE NORTH EASTERN SECTION

This map, showing the vantage points for the observation of nature and wildlife in the north-eastern corner of the continent, is explained in the chapter "Where to See American Nature Best." In the physical picture of this region the following mountain ranges (peaks only, not ranges, are shown on map) are outstanding: The *Laurentian Hills* are a 3,000-mile crescent of ridges 1,500 to 3,000 feet high, in eastern Canada. *The Adirondacks* of New York are geologically so ancient that many summits have been rounded by erosion; only in the north picturesque peaks of naked stone remain; the highest is Mt. Marcy (5,344 ft.). This is one of America's great hunting regions for deer, grouse and waterfowl. All other ranges of the East are parts of the Appalachian system. The *White Mountains* of New Hampshire include the Presidential Range with Mt. Washington (6,288 ft.), New England's highest peak. Numerous summits are naked rocks, huge cones of gneiss or granite. The *Green Mountains* of Vermont are as lovely as they are useful: Granite, marble and slate are quarried there. Their highest peak is Mt. Mansfield (4,393 ft.). They are covered with mixed forests; among their hardwoods the maples make Vermont the classical maple sugar country. To the south the *Berkshire Hills* of western Massachusetts have a similar character. The *Blue Ridge Mountains* of Virginia are heavily wooded; their tallest peaks, attaining a height of about 4,000 feet, are found in the Black Mountain group, so called because of the dark foliage of the hemlocks and balsam firs.

Among the numerous rivers of the region the *St. Lawrence* is the most impressive, with a grandiose estuary in a setting of unspoiled nature, while the *Hudson* is the most picturesque; its crystal-clear mountain waters rush down from the Adirondacks, mix with the salty tides of the ocean, and form one of the world's greatest harbors.

Among the birds, flowers and trees of the North-East the following favorites have been chosen by the various states as symbols of their wildlife: Maine—chickadee, white pine cone and tassel; New Hampshire—purple finch, purple lilac, white birch; Vermont—hermit thrush, red clover, sugar maple; Massachusetts—chickadee, mayflower (trailing arbutus), elm; Rhode Island—bob-white, violet, maple; Connecticut—robin, mountain laurel, white oak; New York—rose; New Jersey—eastern goldfinch, purple violet, red oak; Pennsylvania—ruffed grouse, mountain laurel, hemlock; Delaware—"blue hen's chicken" (game cock), peach blossom, holly tree; Maryland—Baltimore oriole, black-eyed Susan; Virginia—American dogwood, cardinal; West Virginia—cardinal, great laurel, sugar maple; Kentucky—cardinal, goldenrod.

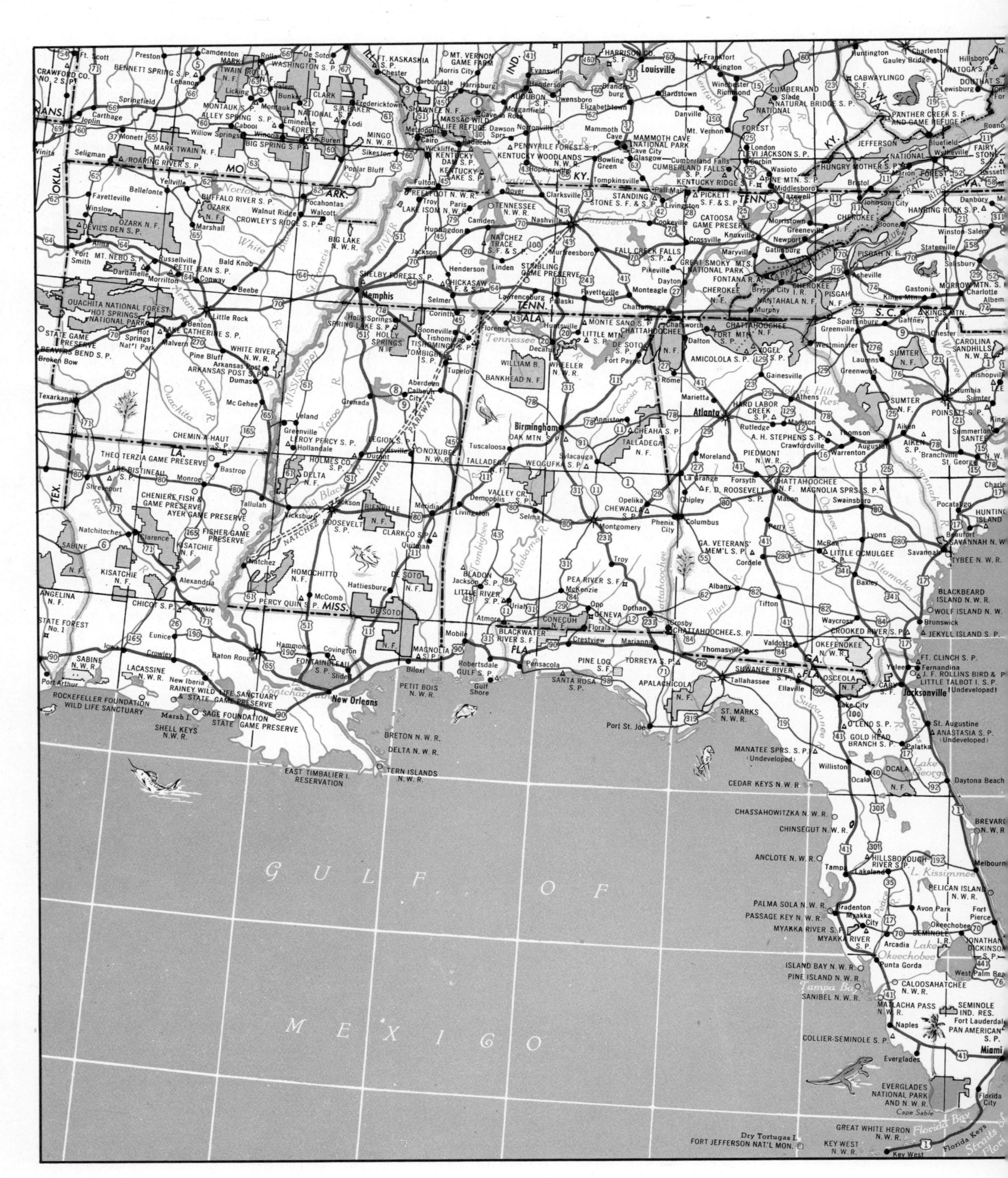
GULF OF MEXICO
Louisville
Memphis
Nashville
Birmingham
Atlanta
New Orleans
Jacksonville
Little Rock
Chattanooga
Montgomery
Mobile
Pensacola
Tallahassee
Tampa
Miami
Key West
Savannah
Charlotte
Asheville
Knoxville
Vicksburg
Jackson
Baton Rouge
Shreveport
Alexandria
Texarkana
Hot Springs
Springfield
Evansville
Frankfort
Lexington
Columbia
Augusta
Macon
Columbus
Tuscaloosa
Meridian
Hattiesburg
Biloxi
Gulfport
Lake City
Ocala
St. Augustine
Daytona Beach
Naples
Fort Lauderdale
OUACHITA NATIONAL FOREST
HOT SPRINGS NATIONAL PARK
MAMMOTH CAVE NATIONAL PARK
GREAT SMOKY MTS. NATIONAL PARK
EVERGLADES NATIONAL PARK AND N.W.R.
OKEFENOKEE N.W.R.
FORT JEFFERSON NAT'L MON.
Dry Tortugas I.
ROCKEFELLER FOUNDATION WILD LIFE SANCTUARY
SAGE FOUNDATION STATE GAME PRESERVE
SHELL KEYS N.W.R.
BRETON N.W.R.
DELTA N.W.R.
TERN ISLANDS N.W.R.
EAST TIMBALIER I. RESERVATION
CEDAR KEYS N.W.R.
CHASSAHOWITZKA N.W.R.
CHINSEGUT N.W.R.
ANCLOTE N.W.R.
PALMA SOLA N.W.R.
PASSAGE KEY N.W.R.
ISLAND BAY N.W.R.
PINE ISLAND N.W.R.
SANIBEL N.W.R.
GREAT WHITE HERON N.W.R.
KEY WEST N.W.R.
Lake Okeechobee
Florida Bay
Cape Sable
Straits of Florida
Florida Keys
MO.
ARK.
TENN.
KY.
ALA.
MISS.
LA.
GA.
FLA.
S.C.
TEX.
OKLA.
KANS.
ILL.
IND.
VA.
W. VA.

Where to See American Nature Best

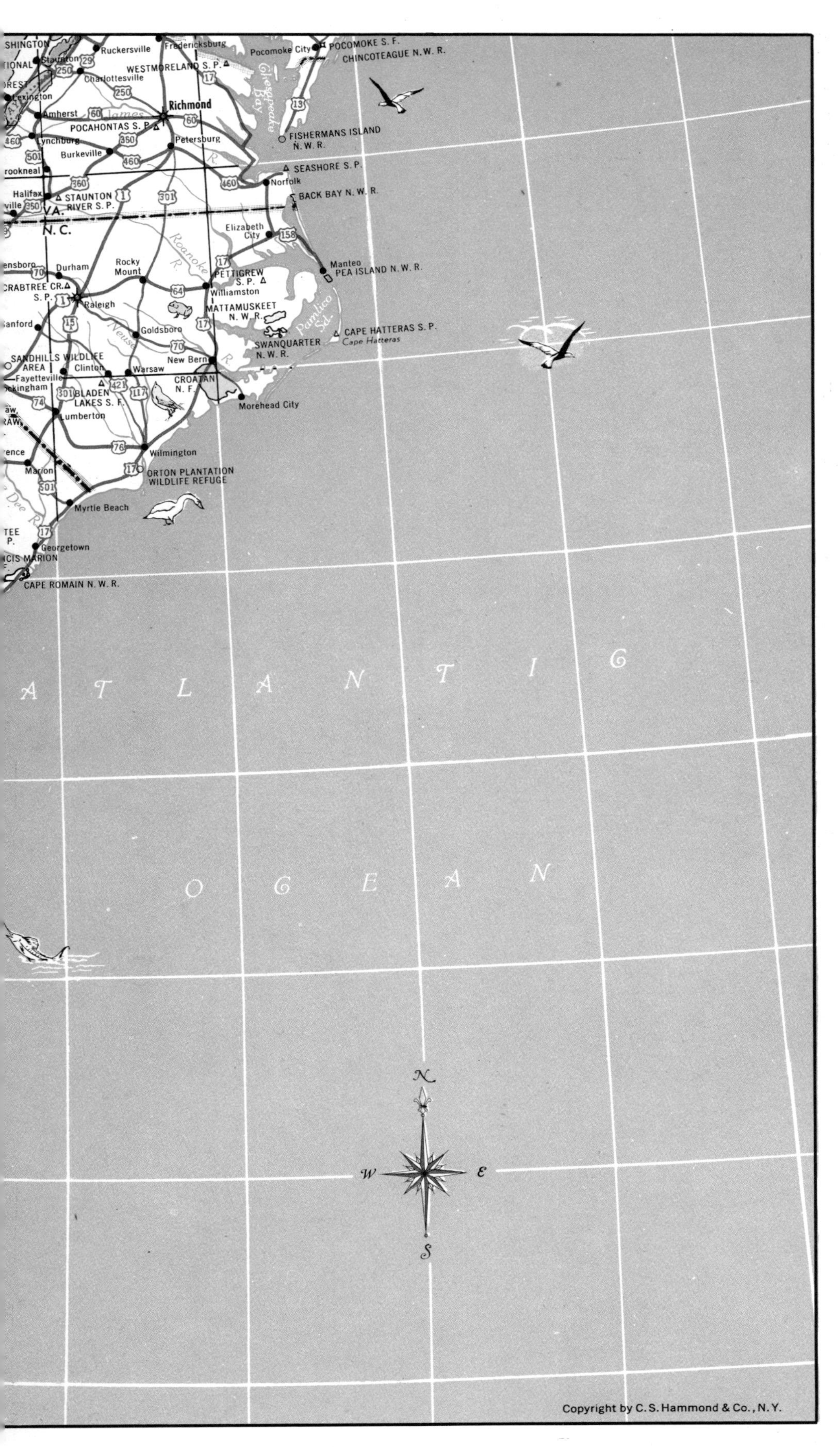

THE SOUTH EASTERN SECTION

This map, which shows the vantage points for nature and wildlife observation in the south-eastern part of the United States, is explained in the chapter "Where to See American Nature Best." In the physical picture of this section the following mountain ranges (peaks only, not ranges, are shown on map) are important: The *Great Smoky Mountains,* on the borderline between North Carolina and Tennessee, are so called because of the frequent haze rising from the valleys. They reach their highest point in Clingman's Peak (6,642 ft.). The *Ozark Plateau* lies largely in Missouri but slopes down into Illinois, Arkansas, Oklahoma and Kansas. Geologically very ancient, it consists of many separate "knobs" 1,200 to 1,800 feet high. Great forests prevail in the southern parts.

Among the many rivers of the South-East the *St. Johns* is fascinating. It rises in the Florida wilderness of Saw Grass Lake, and for its final 150 miles forms a 6 to 7 mile-wide basin of wild marshes and ponds studded with a luxuriant plant growth and clusters of huge old trees. Toward the west the *Mississippi* dominates the scene. For its last 1,100 miles it flows through an immense fertile garden of its own making; here an ancient ocean was gradually changed into land by the silt deposits of the current. The surface of the stream is higher than the surrounding land, for the heavy silt settles both on the bottom and on the sides of the banks and raises the river's "groove" above the countryside. Unique is the network of bayous sent out through southern Louisiana to the Gulf. Its southernmost tributary is the *Red River,* so called because on its upper course its waters receive a reddish tint from the red soil of the prairies; farther downstream it forms "the raft," a 70-mile-long swampland obstructed by logs, trunks, and rotting vegetation. The *Arkansas River* cuts through the state of Arkansas before entering the Mississippi. On its upper course in Colorado it rushes through the Royal Gorge, a very deep canyon. The *Tennessee River,* made famous through the TVA, rises in the southern Appalachians and empties into the Ohio.

Some nature favorites of the region are indicated by the birds, flowers and trees adopted by the various states: North Carolina—cardinal, dogwood; South Carolina—mockingbird, yellow jessamine, palmetto tree; Georgia—brown thrasher, Cherokee rose, live oak; Florida—mockingbird, orange blossom; Tennessee—mockingbird, iris, tulip poplar; Alabama—yellowhammer (woodpecker), goldenrod; Mississippi—mockingbird, magnolia blossom, magnolia tree; Louisiana—brown pelican, magnolia blossom; Arkansas—mockingbird, apple blossom, pine tree.

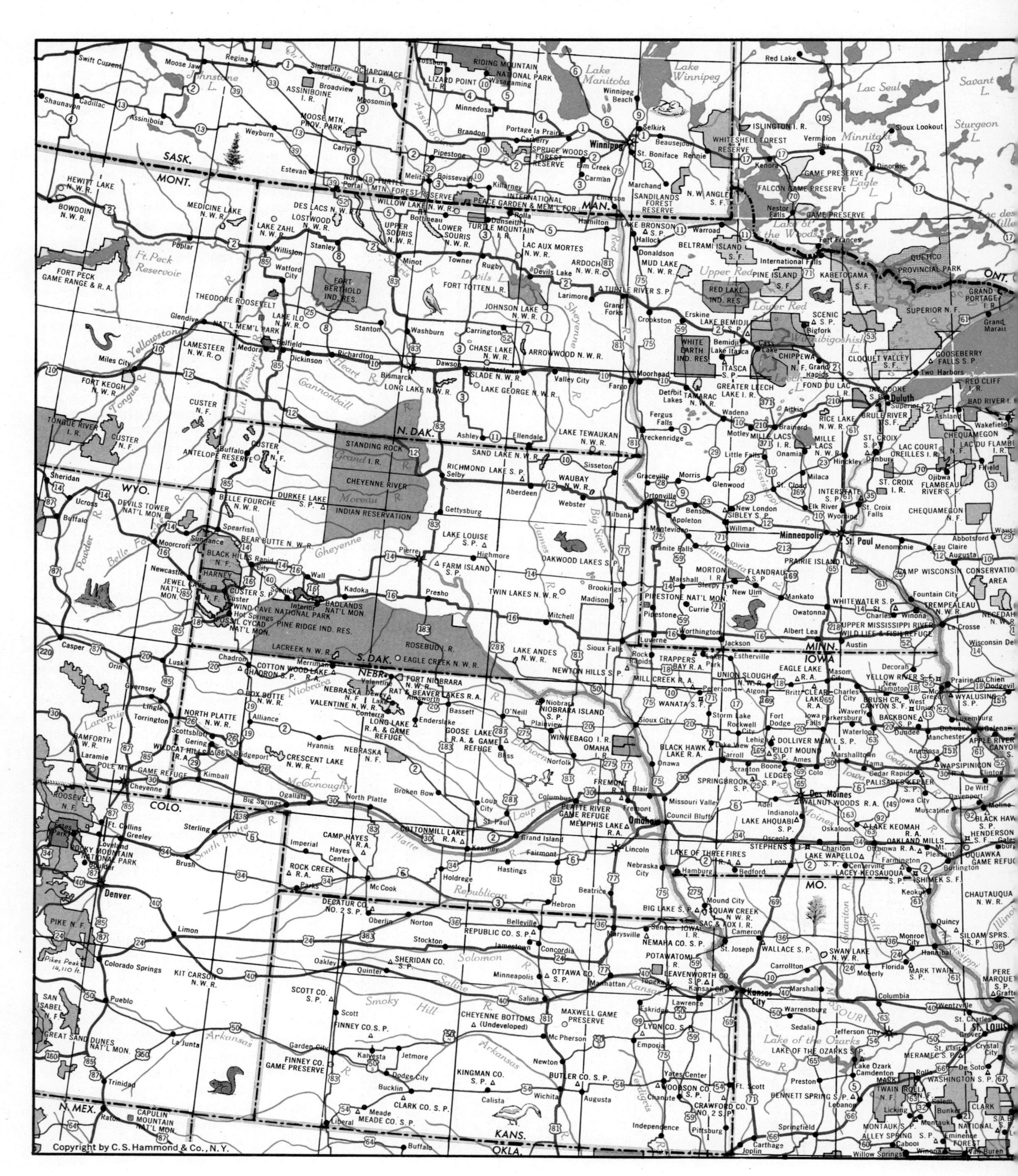
SASK.
MONT.
MAN.
ONT.
N. DAK.
S. DAK.
WYO.
NEBR.
COLO.
KANS.
N. MEX.
OKLA.
MINN.
IOWA
MO.
Regina
Moose Jaw
Swift Current
Winnipeg
Brandon
Lake Manitoba
Lake Winnipeg
RIDING MOUNTAIN NATIONAL PARK
Lake of the Woods
QUETICO PROVINCIAL PARK
SUPERIOR N. F.
Duluth
Minot
Bismarck
Fargo
Grand Forks
Devils Lake
Aberdeen
Pierre
Rapid City
BLACK HILLS N. F.
BADLANDS NAT'L MON.
WIND CAVE NATIONAL PARK
PINE RIDGE IND. RES.
ROSEBUD I. R.
CHEYENNE RIVER INDIAN RESERVATION
STANDING ROCK I. R.
FORT BERTHOLD IND. RES.
THEODORE ROOSEVELT NAT'L MEM'L PARK
DEVILS TOWER NAT'L MON.
Ft. Peck Reservoir
FORT PECK GAME RANGE & R. A.
CUSTER N. F.
Sioux Falls
Minneapolis
St. Paul
Omaha
Lincoln
Des Moines
Kansas City
St. Joseph
Denver
Cheyenne
Colorado Springs
Pueblo
ROCKY MOUNTAIN NATIONAL PARK
PIKE N. F.
Pikes Peak 14,110 ft.
GREAT SAND DUNES NAT'L MON.
CAPULIN MOUNTAIN NAT'L MON.
Wichita
Salina
Dodge City
Topeka
St. Louis
Lake of the Ozarks
MARK TWAIN N. F.
CLARK NATIONAL FOREST
Missouri R.
Platte R.
Arkansas R.
Yellowstone R.
Copyright by C. S. Hammond & Co., N. Y.

Where to See American Nature Best

THE NORTH CENTRAL SECTION

This map is explained in the chapter "Where to See American Nature Best," particularly in reference to the outstanding vantage points for the observation of nature and wildlife. In the physical geography of the eastern part of this section the *Great Lakes* play a dominant role, as the largest body of fresh water on earth. Like a gigantic terrace the levels of the five lakes descend from Superior's elevation of 600 feet to Ontario's 250 feet. *Superior's* northern shore consists of a chain of cliffs up to 1,500 feet tall, while the southern shore is mostly sandy. *Lake Michigan* is famous for its shifting sand dunes, notably to the east and south, and a great area of orchards, vineyards and berry plantings on the eastern shore. Like the other lakes, *Huron* must at one time have extended much farther than it does today: Freshwater shells are occasionally discovered as far as 20 miles inland, and up to 200 feet above the present lake level. *Lake Erie,* with the outlet of the Niagara River, is the shallowest of the group, while *Ontario* has the considerable average depth of 490 feet.

In the western part of this section the *Mississippi-Missouri* system is the outstanding physical feature. The Mississippi rises in Itasca Lake in northern Minnesota while the Missouri originates 8,000 feet high in the Rockies. When they unite and form one river bed their currents do not merge for 100 and more miles but retain their individuality flowing side by side, one clear, calm and white, the other dirty and reddish-muddy. They blend only after they have been tossed into each other by river bends. In the Great Plains the Missouri frequently changes its course, and its floods wash away farm lands and destroy villages. According to a local saying the "Big Muddy" is "too rapid for rowing, too deep for poling, too winding for sails." The *Ohio* is formed by the Allegheny and the Monongahela Rivers. It drains a mountain territory which stores huge masses of snow in wintertime, so that spring floods are often heavy.

The states of this region have chosen the following favorite birds, flowers and trees as symbols of their wildlife: Ohio—cardinal, scarlet carnation; Indiana—cardinal, zinnia, tulip tree; Michigan—robin, apple blossom; Wisconsin—robin, violet; Illinois—cardinal, violet, native oak; Missouri—bluebird, hawthorn; Iowa—eastern goldfinch, wild rose; Minnesota — goldfinch, moccasin flower; North Dakota—wild prairie rose; South Dakota — ring-necked pheasant, pasque flower, Black Hills spruce; Nebraska—western meadowlark, goldenrod, elm; Kansas—western meadowlark, sunflower.

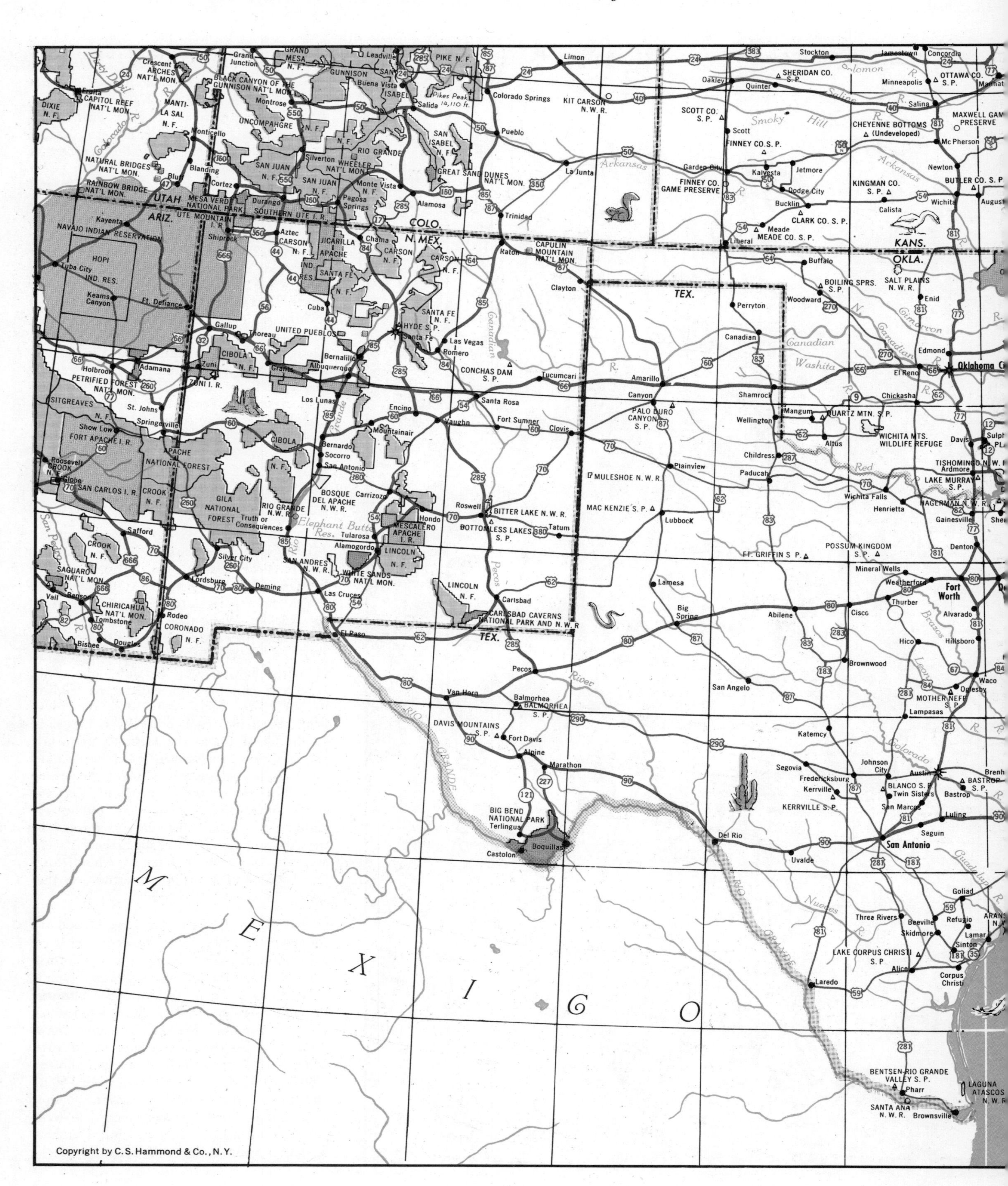
UTAH
ARIZ.
COLO.
N. MEX.
KANS.
OKLA.
TEX.
M E X I C O
Grand Junction
Leadville
PIKE N. F.
Limon
Stockton
Concordia
Crescent
ARCHES NAT'L MON.
GRAND MESA N. F.
BLACK CANYON OF THE GUNNISON NAT'L MON.
GUNNISON
Buena Vista
Pikes Peak 14,110 ft.
Colorado Springs
KIT CARSON N. W. R.
SHERIDAN CO. S. P.
Oakley
Quinter
Minneapolis
OTTAWA CO. S. P.
Fruita
CAPITOL REEF NAT'L MON.
DIXIE N. F.
MANTI-LA SAL N. F.
Montrose
Salida
Pueblo
SCOTT CO. S. P.
Scott
Salina
MAXWELL GAME PRESERVE
UNCOMPAHGRE N. F.
SAN ISABEL N. F.
FINNEY CO. S. P.
CHEYENNE BOTTOMS (Undeveloped)
Mc Pherson
Monticello
NATURAL BRIDGES NAT'L MON.
Blanding
RIO GRANDE
Silverton
SAN JUAN N. F.
WHEELER NAT'L MON.
La Junta
Garden City
Jetmore
Newton
RAINBOW BRIDGE NAT'L MON.
Bluff
Cortez
Monte Vista
GREAT SAND DUNES NAT'L MON.
FINNEY CO. GAME PRESERVE
Kalvesta
KINGMAN CO. S. P.
BUTLER CO. S. P.
MESA VERDE NATIONAL PARK
Durango
Pagosa Springs
Alamosa
Dodge City
Wichita
UTE MOUNTAIN I. R.
SOUTHERN UTE I. R.
Trinidad
Bucklin
CLARK CO. S. P.
Calista
Kayenta
NAVAJO INDIAN RESERVATION
Shiprock
Aztec
CARSON N. F.
JICARILLA APACHE IND. RES.
Chama
Meade
MEADE CO. S. P.
Liberal
Raton
CAPULIN MOUNTAIN NAT'L MON.
Buffalo
HOPI IND. RES.
Tuba City
SANTA FE N. F.
Clayton
BOILING SPRS. S. P.
SALT PLAINS N. W. R.
Keams Canyon
Ft. Defiance
Cuba
Woodward
Enid
Perryton
Gallup
Thoreau
UNITED PUEBLOS
HYDE S. P.
Santa Fe
Las Vegas
Romero
Canadian
Edmond
Holbrook
Adamana
CIBOLA N. F.
Zuni
Grants
Bernalillo
Albuquerque
CONCHAS DAM S. P.
Tucumcari
Amarillo
El Reno
Oklahoma City
PETRIFIED FOREST NAT'L MON.
ZUNI I. R.
Los Lunas
Santa Rosa
Canyon
Shamrock
Chickasha
SITGREAVES N. F.
St. Johns
Springerville
Encino
Vaughn
Fort Sumner
PALO DURO CANYON S. P.
Mangum
QUARTZ MTN. S. P.
Show Low
FORT APACHE I. R.
Mountainair
Clovis
Wellington
Altus
WICHITA MTS. WILDLIFE REFUGE
Roosevelt
Globe
APACHE NATIONAL FOREST
Bernardo
Socorro
San Antonio
Childress
TISHOMINGO N. W. R.
Ardmore
SAN CARLOS I. R.
CROOK N. F.
GILA NATIONAL FOREST
BOSQUE DEL APACHE N. W. R.
Carrizozo
Plainview
Paducah
LAKE MURRAY S. P.
MULESHOE N. W. R.
Wichita Falls
Henrietta
Roswell
BITTER LAKE N. W. R.
HAGERMAN N. W. R.
Gainesville
RIO GRANDE N. W. R.
Truth or Consequences
Elephant Butte Res.
Tularosa
MESCALERO APACHE I. R.
Hondo
BOTTOMLESS LAKES S. P.
Tatum
MAC KENZIE S. P.
Lubbock
Safford
Silver City
Alamogordo
LINCOLN N. F.
POSSUM KINGDOM S. P.
Denton
SAGUARO NAT'L MON.
SAN ANDRES N. W. R.
WHITE SANDS NAT'L MON.
FT. GRIFFIN S. P.
Mineral Wells
Lordsburg
Deming
Las Cruces
Weatherford
Fort Worth
Vail
Benson
CHIRICAHUA NAT'L MON.
Tombstone
Rodeo
LINCOLN N. F.
Carlsbad
Lamesa
Thurber
Alvarado
CORONADO N. F.
CARLSBAD CAVERNS NATIONAL PARK AND N. W. R.
Big Spring
Abilene
Cisco
Hico
Hillsboro
Bisbee
Douglas
El Paso
Pecos
Brownwood
Waco
San Angelo
Oglesby
Van Horn
Balmorhea
BALMORHEA S. P.
MOTHER NEFF S. P.
Lampasas
DAVIS MOUNTAINS S. P.
Fort Davis
Katemcy
Alpine
Marathon
Segovia
Johnson City
Austin
Fredericksburg
Kerrville
BLANCO S. P.
Twin Sisters
BASTROP S. P.
Bastrop
KERRVILLE S. P.
San Marcos
Luling
BIG BEND NATIONAL PARK
Terlingua
Castolon
Boquillas
Del Rio
Uvalde
San Antonio
Seguin
Goliad
Three Rivers
Beeville
Refugio
Skidmore
Lamar
Sinton
LAKE CORPUS CHRISTI S. P.
Alice
Corpus Christi
Laredo
BENTSEN-RIO GRANDE VALLEY S. P.
Pharr
LAGUNA ATASCOSA N. W. R.
SANTA ANA N. W. R.
Brownsville
Colorado R.
Arkansas R.
Smoky Hill
Solomon R.
Canadian R.
Cimarron
Washita
Red
Brazos
Pecos
RIO GRANDE
Nueces R.
Guadalupe R.
Leon R.
San Pedro R.
River

Where to See American Nature Best

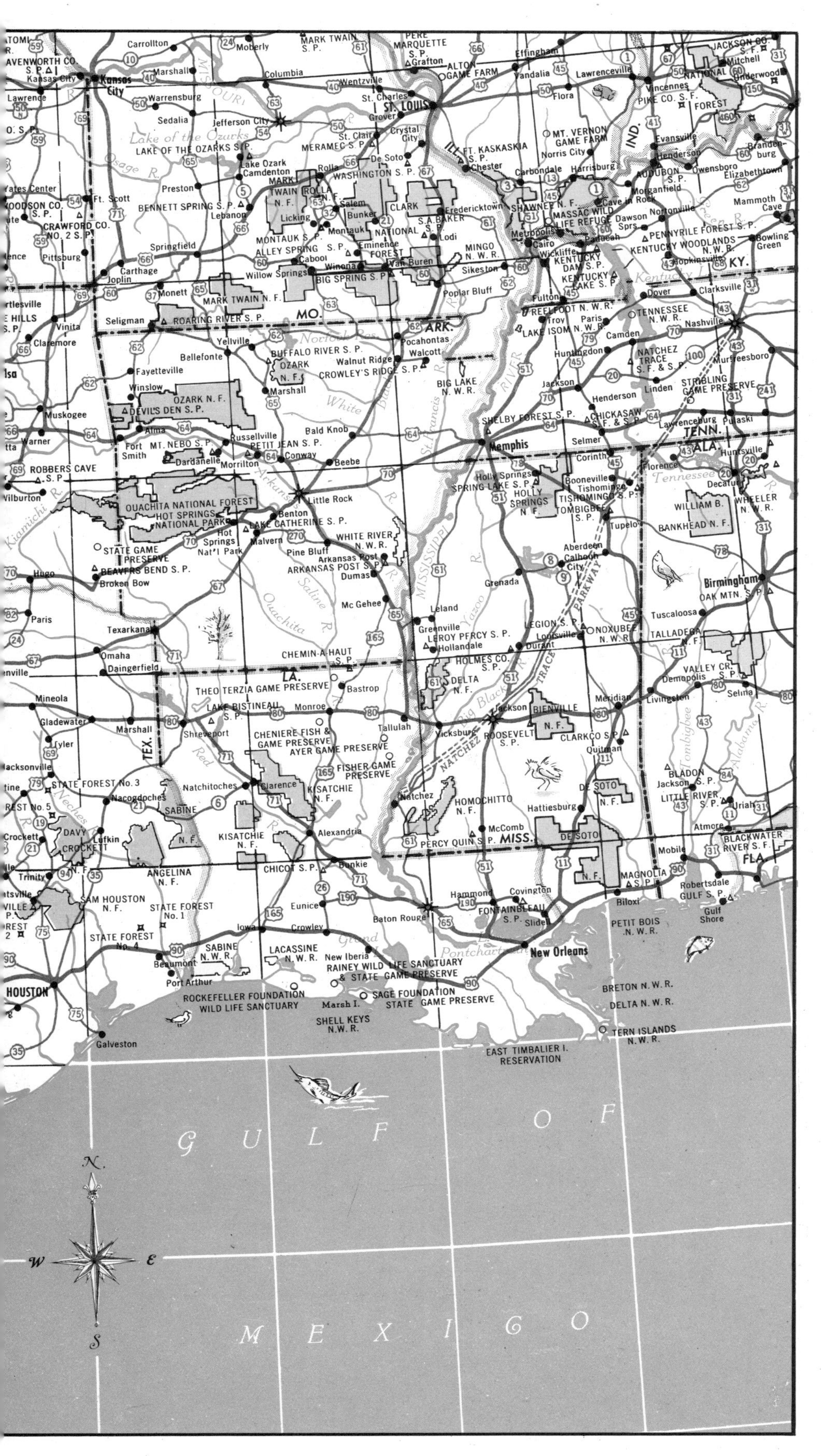

THE SOUTH CENTRAL SECTION

This map, designed to show the vantage points for the observation of nature and wildlife in the south-central part of the United States, is explained in the chapter "Where to See American Nature Best." To a large extent the region is an enormous plateau that slopes downward from the north-west to the south-east; consequently all its rivers flow in that direction. The state of Oklahoma is a good example for the structure of the whole section: Its north-western corner has an altitude of 4,900 feet, its southeastern corner of 400 feet. On sea level, the coast forms a number of sandy islands and peninsulas, shallow bays and broad lagoons. The thirteen deepwater ports are largely man-made, *i.e.* they are dredged. For fifty miles inland the plain is almost flat, a fertile, rich grassland with woods along the rivers and brooks. On the opposite side, the southern Rocky Mountains (peaks only, not ranges, shown on map) reach both into Texas and New Mexico. In Texas, Guadalupe Peak in Culbertson County attains a height of 8,751 feet, while the tallest summits in New Mexico, Wheeler and North Truchas in the Sangre de Cristo range, rise to more than 13,000 feet. The mean altitude of New Mexico is 5,700 feet. Between the coastal grasslands and the western mountain chains various types of plains and prairies occur. In some parts tree growth is very sparse, in others cedar and oak groves thrive and mesquite thickets abound. In the arid districts cactus and yucca plants give a distinct character to the countryside while on the slopes of the mountains oak and pine forests prevail. Deep canyons are found on the plateaus, particularly those of the Panhandle.

Several independent ranges like the *Arbuckle and Ouachita Mountains* (not indicated on the map) cross southern Oklahoma; parts of the Ozarks reach into the northeastern corner of Oklahoma.

Natural lakes are rare, but a considerable number of artificial lakes have been created in connection with flood control and water power projects. Among the rivers the *Rio Grande* is the best-known water course; its upper part is studded with rapids and falls, with waters rushing between high, rocky banks. On its shallow lower course it forms the boundary between Mexico and Texas. The *Pecos River* is its main tributary.

Among the birds, flowers and trees of the south-central United States, the following favorites have been chosen by the various states as symbols of their wildlife: Oklahoma—bobwhite, mistletoe, redbud; Texas—mockingbird, bluebonnet, pecan tree; New Mexico—roadrunner, yucca.

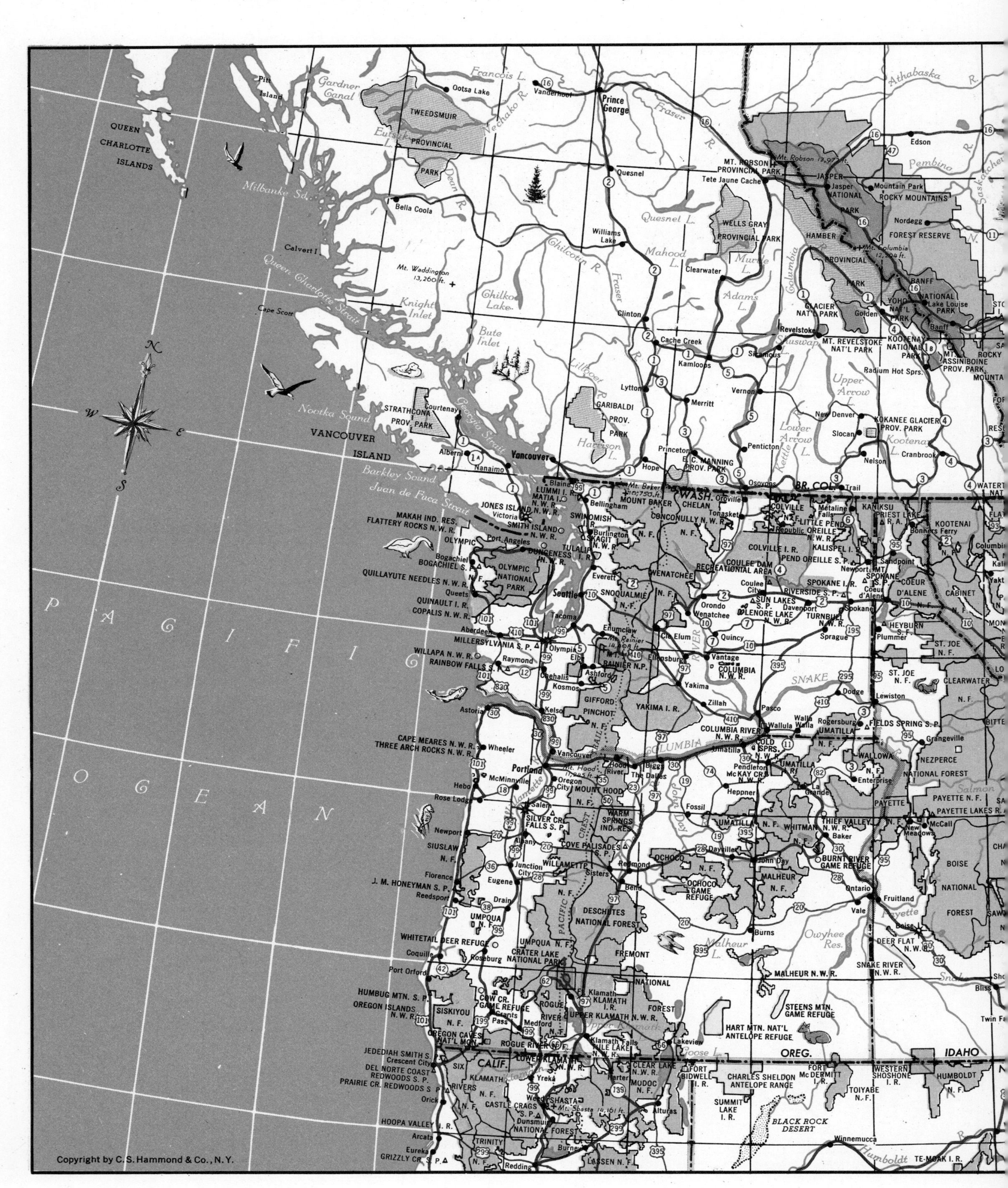
QUEEN CHARLOTTE ISLANDS
Pitt Island
Gardner Canal
Milbanke Sd.
Calvert I.
Queen Charlotte Strait
Cape Scott
Knight Inlet
Bute Inlet
Chilko Lake
Mt. Waddington 13,260 ft.
Bella Coola
Dean R.
Oatsa Lake
TWEEDSMUIR PROVINCIAL PARK
Francois L.
Vanderhoof
Nechako R.
Prince George
Fraser R.
Quesnel
Quesnel L.
Williams Lake
Chilcotin R.
Mahood L.
Clearwater
WELLS GRAY PROVINCIAL PARK
Murtle L.
Adams L.
MT. ROBSON PROVINCIAL PARK
Mt. Robson 12,972 ft.
Tete Jaune Cache
JASPER NATIONAL PARK
Jasper
HAMBER PROVINCIAL PARK
Mt. Columbia 12,294 ft.
Edson
Pembina
Athabaska R.
Mountain Park
ROCKY MOUNTAINS FOREST RESERVE
Nordegg
BANFF NATIONAL PARK
Lake Louise
Banff
YOHO NAT'L PARK
Golden
GLACIER NAT'L PARK
KOOTENAY NATIONAL PARK
MT. ASSINIBOINE PROV. PARK
Radium Hot Sprs.
Revelstoke
MT. REVELSTOKE NAT'L PARK
Shuswap
Sicamous
Upper Arrow L.
Lower Arrow L.
New Denver
Slocan
KOKANEE GLACIER PROV. PARK
Kootenay L.
Nelson
Cranbrook
Trail
Clinton
Cache Creek
Kamloops
Lytton
Lillooet R.
Vernon
Merritt
GARIBALDI PROV. PARK
Harrison L.
Princeton
Penticton
E.C. MANNING PROV. PARK
Hope
Osoyoos
STRATHCONA PROV. PARK
Courtenay
Nootka Sound
Georgia Strait
VANCOUVER ISLAND
Alberni
Nanaimo
Vancouver
Barkley Sound
Juan de Fuca Strait
Victoria
BR. COL.
WASH.
Blaine
LUMMI I. R.
MATIA I. N.W.R.
JONES ISLAND N.W.R.
SMITH ISLAND N.W.R.
Mt. Baker 10,750 ft.
MOUNT BAKER
Bellingham
SWINOMISH
Burlington
SKAGIT N.W.R.
TULALIP I.R.
DUNGENESS N.W.R.
Port Angeles
MAKAH IND. RES.
FLATTERY ROCKS N.W.R.
OLYMPIC
OLYMPIC NATIONAL PARK
Bogachiel
BOGACHIEL S.P.
QUILLAYUTE NEEDLES N.W.R.
Queets
QUINAULT I.R.
COPALIS N.W.R.
Aberdeen
MILLERSYLVANIA S.P.
Olympia
WILLAPA N.W.R.
RAINBOW FALLS S.P.
Raymond
Everett
Seattle
SNOQUALMIE N.F.
Tacoma
Enumclaw
Mt. Rainier 14,408 ft.
MT. RAINIER N.P.
Ashford
Chehalis
Kosmos
GIFFORD PINCHOT N.F.
Kelso
Astoria
CHELAN
CONCONULLY N.W.R.
Oroville
Tonasket
COLVILLE N.F.
COLVILLE I.R.
WENATCHEE
Wenatchee
COULEE DAM RECREATIONAL AREA
Coulee City
SUN LAKES S.P.
LENORE LAKE N.W.R.
Orondo
Davenport
TURNBULL N.W.R.
Quincy
Cle Elum
Ellensburg
Vantage
COLUMBIA N.W.R.
Yakima
YAKIMA I.R.
Zillah
Pasco
SNAKE
Walla Walla
Wallula
COLUMBIA RIVER N.W.R.
COLD SPRS. N.W.R.
METALINE FALLS
LITTLE PEND OREILLE N.W.R.
Republic
KANIKSU
PRIEST LAKE
PEND OREILLE S.P.
KALISPEL I.R.
SPOKANE I.R.
RIVERSIDE S.P.
Spokane
Sprague
Newport
Sandpoint
COEUR D'ALENE
Coeur d'Alene
HEYBURN S.P.
Plummer
ST. JOE N.F.
CLEARWATER
Lewiston
Dodge
FIELDS SPRING S.P.
Rogersburg
UMATILLA
Grangeville
NEZPERCE NATIONAL FOREST
KOOTENAI
Bonners Ferry
CABINET
CAPE MEARES N.W.R.
THREE ARCH ROCKS N.W.R.
Wheeler
Vancouver
Portland
McMinnville
Hebo
Rose Lodge
Salem
Oregon City
MOUNT HOOD N.F.
Mt. Hood 11,245 ft.
Hood River
The Dalles
Biggs
Pendleton
McKAY CR. N.W.R.
UMATILLA I.R.
Heppner
John Day
La Grande
WALLOWA N.F.
Enterprise
Newport
SIUSLAW N.F.
Albany
SILVER CR. FALLS S.P.
WARM SPRINGS IND. RES.
COVE PALISADES S.P.
Florence
J. M. HONEYMAN S.P.
Reedsport
Eugene
Junction City
WILLAMETTE N.F.
Sisters
Redmond
Bend
OCHOCO N.F.
OCHOCO GAME REFUGE
Drain
UMPQUA N.F.
DESCHUTES NATIONAL FOREST
Fossil
UMATILLA N.F.
WHITMAN N.F.
THIEF VALLEY N.W.R.
Baker
BURNT RIVER GAME REFUGE
MALHEUR N.F.
Dayville
Ontario
Vale
Fruitland
Boise
PAYETTE N.F.
PAYETTE LAKES
McCall
New Meadows
BOISE NATIONAL FOREST
DEER FLAT N.W.R.
SNAKE RIVER N.W.R.
WHITETAIL DEER REFUGE
Coquille
Roseburg
UMPQUA N.F.
CRATER LAKE NATIONAL PARK
FREMONT
Burns
Malheur L.
Owyhee Res.
MALHEUR N.W.R.
Port Orford
HUMBUG MTN. S.P.
OREGON ISLANDS N.W.R.
SISKIYOU N.F.
COW CR. GAME REFUGE
Grants Pass
ROGUE RIVER N.F.
Medford
OREGON CAVES NAT'L MON.
Klamath Falls
UPPER KLAMATH N.W.R.
KLAMATH I.R.
Ft. Klamath
NATIONAL FOREST
Lakeview
Goose L.
STEENS MTN. GAME REFUGE
HART MTN. NAT'L ANTELOPE REFUGE
OREG.
IDAHO
CALIF.
JEDEDIAH SMITH S.P.
Crescent City
DEL NORTE COAST REDWOODS S.P.
PRAIRIE CR. REDWOODS S.P.
Orick
SIX RIVERS N.F.
KLAMATH N.F.
LOWER KLAMATH N.W.R.
TULE LAKE
Yreka
CLEAR LAKE N.W.R.
MODOC N.F.
Alturas
FORT BIDWELL I.R.
CHARLES SHELDON ANTELOPE RANGE
FORT McDERMITT I.R.
WESTERN SHOSHONE I.R.
HUMBOLDT N.F.
TOIYABE N.F.
SUMMIT LAKE I.R.
BLACK ROCK DESERT
Winnemucca
Humboldt
TE-MOAK I.R.
Mt. Shasta 14,161 ft.
SHASTA N.F.
CASTLE CRAGS S.P.
Dunsmuir
Weed
HOOPA VALLEY I.R.
Arcata
Eureka
GRIZZLY CR. S.P.
TRINITY N.F.
Redding
Burney
LASSEN N.F.
PACIFIC OCEAN
N
S
E
W
Copyright by C.S. Hammond & Co., N.Y.

Where to See American Nature Best

THE NORTH WESTERN SECTION

This map, which emphasizes the vantage points for the observation of nature and wildlife in the north-western corner of the continent, is explained in the chapter "Where to See American Wildlife Best." In the physical picture of this region the various great mountain ranges (peaks only, not ranges, shown on map) are the dominating factor. The *Rocky Mountain* Range rises suddenly out of the central plain in the form of numerous single huge cones which blend into ranges and ridges farther west, forming an almost unbroken, massive barrier. In the northern Rockies the Selkirk Mountains and the Bitterroot Mountains are outstanding: the latter are the watershed between the Colorado and Missouri river systems. The Rockies are the roof of America; the streams they send out reach the Arctic, the Pacific, and the Atlantic Ocean in all its parts from Hudson Bay to the Gulf of Mexico. In their upper courses these rivers cut through deep canyons whose walls often rise skyward for thousands of feet. The streams receive their water mostly from the western slopes of the mountains where the clouds drifting in from the Pacific discharge heavy rains. The *Black Hills* are separated from the principal ranges, a mountain mass towering 4,000 feet high above the plains of eastern Wyoming and western South Dakota. The *Cascade Mountains,* spectacularly rugged in shape, run through Oregon and Washington into British Columbia. They have been named for the beautiful cascades of the Columbia River which cuts through the range on its way to the Pacific. Their towering peaks include some famous names: Mt. Shasta (14,162 ft.), Mt. Rainier (14,408 ft.), and Mt. Hood (11,245 ft.). Many summits in this group once were volcanoes, but all are extinct now. The northern part of the *Coast Range* is a series of separate groups of low ridges; only the *Olympic Mountains,* which rise between Puget Sound and the Pacific Ocean, attain a considerable height (Mt. Olympus—7,954 ft.). Rainfall is abundant there, and the slopes bear a thick cover of evergreen forests. The *Columbia River,* the largest stream in western America, rises in British Columbia and in a tortuous course flows over numerous falls and rapids into the Pacific. Its salmon fisheries are famous.

Some of the nature favorites of this section are indicated by the birds, flowers and trees adopted by the various states as symbols of their wildlife: Wyoming—meadowlark, Indian paintbrush, cottonwood tree; Montana—meadowlark, bitterroot, ponderosa pine tree; Idaho—mountain bluebird, syringa, white pine tree; Oregon—western meadowlark, Oregon grape, Douglas fir; Washington—willow goldfinch, western rhododendron, western hemlock.

PACIFIC
OCEAN
GULF OF
CALIFORNIA
M
OREG.
IDAHO
NEV.
CALIF.
UTAH
ARIZ
HUMBUG MTN. S. P.
OREGON ISLANDS N. W. R.
SISKIYOU N. F.
ROGUE RIVER N. F.
KLAMATH I. R.
UPPER KLAMATH N. W. R.
LOWER KLAMATH N. W. R.
TULE LAKE N. W. R.
JEDEDIAH SMITH S. P.
Crescent City
DEL NORTE COAST REDWOODS S. P.
PRAIRIE CR. REDWOODS S. P.
Orick
SIX RIVERS N. F.
KLAMATH N. F.
Yreka
SHASTA
Mt. Shasta 14,161 ft.
Dunsmuir
CASTLE CRAGS S. P.
HOOPA VALLEY I. R.
Arcata
Eureka
GRIZZLY CR. S. P.
Cape Mendocino
HUMBOLDT REDWOODS S. P.
Weott
Benbow
E. R. HICKEY S. P.
ROUND VALLEY I. R.
RUSSIAN GULCH S. P.
Mendocino
MENDOCINO WOODLANDS S. F.
Willits
Ukiah
MENDOCINO N. F.
TRINITY N. F.
Redding
Red Bluff
Chico
LASSEN N. F.
LASSEN VOLCANIC NATIONAL PARK
Manzanita Lake
Susanville
PLUMAS N. F.
MODOC N. F.
Alturas
CLEAR LAKE N. W. R.
Lakeview
Goose L.
FORT BIDWELL I. R.
HART MTN. NAT'L ANTELOPE REFUGE
MALHEUR N. W. R.
STEENS MTN. GAME REFUGE
CHARLES SHELDON ANTELOPE RANGE
SUMMIT LAKE I. R.
FORT McDERMITT I. R.
BLACK ROCK DESERT
SMOKE CREEK DESERT
Winnemucca
Humboldt R.
HUMBOLDT N. F.
WESTERN SHOSHONE I. R.
TOIYABE N. F.
Pyramid L.
PYRAMID LAKE I. R.
WINNEMUCCA N. W. R.
ANAHO N. W. R.
CARSON SINK
FALLON N. W. R.
Fernley
Fallon
Reno
Carson City
Truckee
TAHOE N. F.
Lake Tahoe
ELDORADO N. F.
WALKER RIVER I. R.
Walker L.
Hawthorne
Austin
TOIYABE NATIONAL FOREST
Tonopah
Goldfield
Beatty
SACRAMENTO N. W. R.
SUTTER N. W. R.
COLUSA N. W. R.
Williams
Marysville
Roseville
Sacramento
Davis
Santa Rosa
Bodega Bay
MUIR WOODS NAT'L MON.
FARALLON N. W. R.
Sausalito
Berkeley
Oakland
SAN FRANCISCO
San Francisco Bay
Stockton
Bigtrees
CALAVERAS BIG TREES S. P.
STANISLAUS N. F.
YOSEMITE NATIONAL PARK
Yosemite
El Portal
Wawona
DEVILS POSTPILE NAT'L MON.
SIERRA N. F.
INYO N. F.
Bishop
Big Pine
San Joaquin R.
San Jose
Gilroy
BIG BASIN REDWOODS S. P.
Santa Cruz
Monterey Bay
Monterey
Hollister
Salinas
Merced
PINNACLES NAT'L MON.
Pinnacles
MILLERTON LAKE RECREATIONAL AREA
Fresno
KINGS CANYON NATIONAL PARK
Mt. Whitney 14,495 ft.
Visalia
SEQUOIA NATIONAL PARK
Independence
Lone Pine
Olancha
Stovepipe Wells
DEATH VALLEY NAT'L MON.
Furnace Creek
280 ft. below sea level
Death Valley Jc.
Shoshone
Big Sur
PFEIFFER BIG SUR S. P.
LOS PADRES N. F.
San Lucas
Coalinga
Tulare
TULE RIVER I. R.
Tulare L.
Famoso
MORRO BAY S. P.
Morro Bay
Atascadero
San Luis Obispo
Bakersfield
TULE ELK RESERVE S. P.
Buena Vista L.
Mojave
Freeman
Baker
Barstow
ANGELES N. F.
Santa Barbara
Santa Barbara Channel
San Miguel I.
Santa Cruz I.
Santa Rosa I.
Anacapa I.
CHANNEL ISLANDS NAT'L MON.
Santa Barbara I.
Santa Catalina I.
San Nicolas I.
San Clemente I.
Gulf of Santa Catalina
San Pedro Channel
Saugus
LOS ANGELES
SAN BERNARDINO N. F.
San Bernardino
MT. SAN JACINTO S. P.
Palm Springs
JOSHUA TREE NAT'L MON.
Twentynine Palms
Amboy
CLEVELAND N. F.
PALOMAR MTN. S. P.
Oceanside
Rincon
Salton Sea
SALTON SEA N. W. R.
ANZA DESERT S. P.
Borego
Julian
CUYAMACA RANCHO S. P.
El Centro
San Diego
Imperial
FORT YUMA I. R.
Yuma
Needles
CHEMEHUEVI I. R.
FORT MOHAVE I. R.
HAVASU LAKE N. W. R.
COLORADO RIVER I. R.
KOFA GAME RANGE
GILA BEND I. R.
Gila Bend
MARICOPA
CABEZA PRIETA GAME REFUGE
ORGAN PIPE CACTUS NAT'L MON.
PAPAGO I. R.
Las Vegas
BOULDER CANYON N. W. R.
BOULDER DAM VALLEY OF FIRE S. P.
Lake Mead
LAKE MEAD R. A.
DESERT GAME RANGE
HUALPAI I. R.
Kingman
GRAND CANYON NAT'L MON.
GRAND CANYON NATIONAL PARK
Bright Angel
KAIBAB I. R.
KAIBAB N. F.
Williams
Flagstaff
Ash Fork
PRESCOTT N. F.
Prescott
Wickenburg
Phoenix
KERSHAW CANYON-RYAN S. P.
CATHEDRAL GORGE S. P.
BEAVER DAM S. P.
Pioche
Caliente
ZION NAT'L MON.
ZION NATIONAL PARK
St. George
CEDAR BREAKS NAT'L MON.
BRYCE CANYON NAT'L PARK
DIXIE N. F.
FISHLAKE NATIONAL FOREST
Sevier Lake
Fillmore
Beaver
Baker
LEHMAN CAVES NAT'L MON.
RAILROAD VALLEY N. W. R.
NEVADA N. F.
Ely
Wells
RUBY LAKE N. W. R.
RUBY VALLEY IND. RES.
GOSHUTE I. R.
Wendover
GREAT SALT LAKE DESERT
Great Salt Lake
Salt Lake City
SKULL VALLEY IND. RES.
TIMPANOGOS CAVE NAT'L MON.
Utah Lake
BEAR RIVER MIGRATORY BIRD REFUGE
Ogden
Brigham
LOCOMOTIVE SPRS. N. W. R.
CARIBOU N. F.
MINIDOKA N. W. R.
CRATERS OF THE MOON NAT'L MON.
American Falls Res.
Pocatello
FORT HALL IND. RES.
Blackfoot
Twin Falls
Shoshone
Bliss
SNAKE RIVER N. W. R.
Snake R.
Copyright by C. S. Hammond & Co., N.Y.

Where to See American Nature Best

THE SOUTH WESTERN SECTION

This map, which shows the vantage points for nature and wildlife observation in the south-western part of the United States, is explained in the chapter "Where to See American Nature Best." In the physical geography of this region the western mountain ranges (peaks only, not ranges, shown on map) are the outstanding feature. The tallest masses of the *Rocky Mountain Range* are found in Colorado where more than 40 peaks exceed 14,000 feet in height. Pike's Peak (14,110 ft.) is especially well known. The *Great Basin* consisting of the western parts of Utah and Nevada, the south-western parts of New Mexico, and the south-eastern parts of California, is a desert region without visible outlets to any ocean; it includes Death Valley, the lowest point on the continent. The *Sierra Nevada* in eastern California, a range 430 miles long and up to 80 miles wide, has many attractions for the nature lover: Mount Whitney whose peak rises to an altitude of 14,495 feet, Yosemite Valley with its splendid water falls, and the Giant Forest in Sequoia National Park. Evergreen forests cover the slopes of the range. The southern part of the *Coast Range* consists of a number of hills and low mountain ridges which rise with abrupt suddenness from the Pacific Ocean, hardly leaving room for a coastal plain. In the south the Coast Range and the Sierra Nevada merge; the Santa Inez Mountains, an east-west ridge north of the Mexican border, is about 4,000 feet tall. On account of the dry climate much of the southern Coast Range is covered with chaparral, a thicket of thorny undergrowth.

Among the rivers of the region the *Colorado River* with its more than 50 tributaries takes a most unusual course before it empties into the Gulf of California. From the ice-capped peaks of the continental divide, 14,000 feet high, its waters travel through some of the world's most magnificent mountain scenery to the bottom of the Colorado Desert. For about a thousand miles it runs through deep canyons of which the Grand Canyon has become world-famous. The river's basin is one of the most thinly settled regions in our hemisphere, yet the remnants of pre-historic cliff dwellings prove that it is ancient human ground.

The various states of this section have chosen the following favorite birds, flowers and trees as symbols of their wildlife: Colorado—lark bunting, columbine, blue spruce; Utah—sea gull, sego lily, blue spruce; Arizona—cactus wren, Saguaro cactus, blossom and tree; Nevada—mountain bluebird, sagebrush, aspen; California—valley quail, California poppy, California redwood.

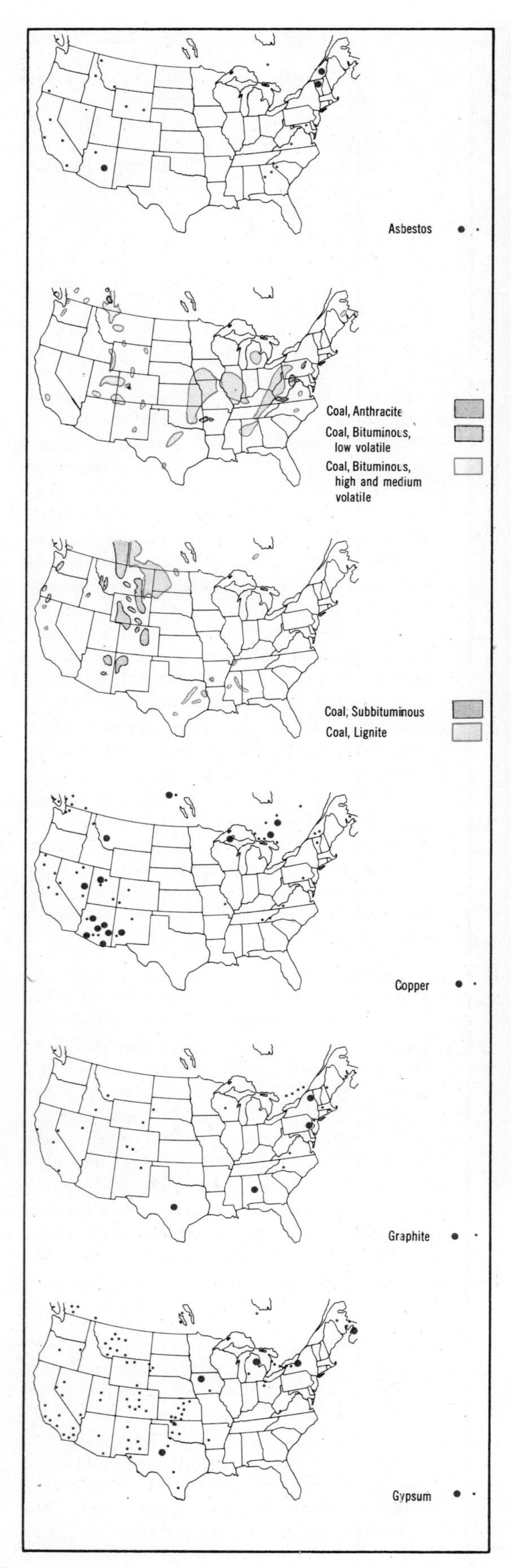

MINERALS AND ROCKS IN THE U.S. AND SOUTHERN CANADA

The following pages describe and illustrate a number of minerals and rocks which are frequently encountered in the U.S. and southern Canada, or are of general interest for other reasons. The first sixteen items are minerals; they are either rock-building like feldspar, quartz, mica and garnet, or otherwise important; the rest of the list refers to rocks proper. As reliable and up-to-date material on their locations and ranges is limited, only a few representative examples are presented on the range maps on this page. The physical map in the center shows important outcroppings of granite and related rocks; the other maps indicate, in alphabetical order, the occurrence of various other minerals and rocks. No

Minerals and Rocks

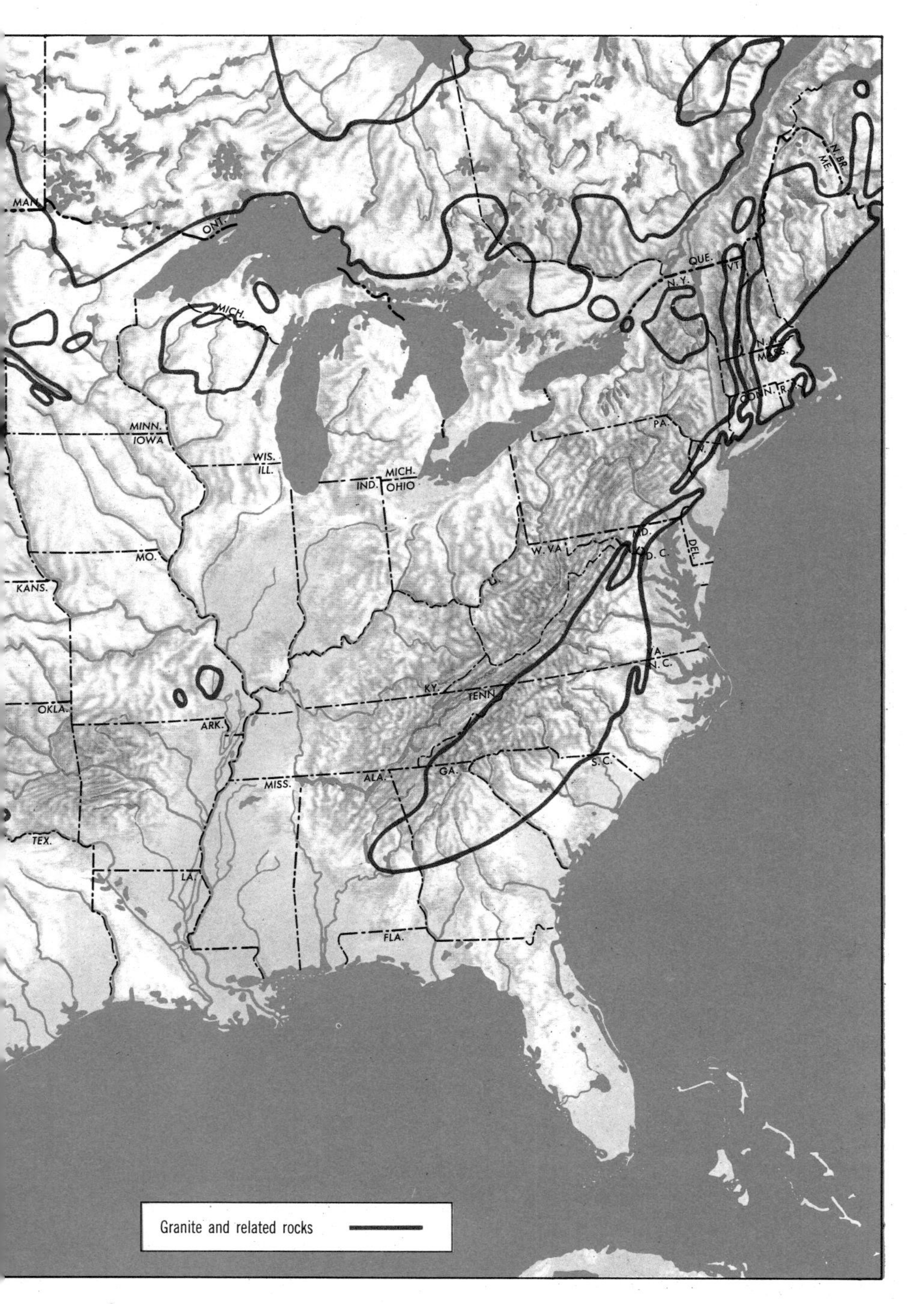

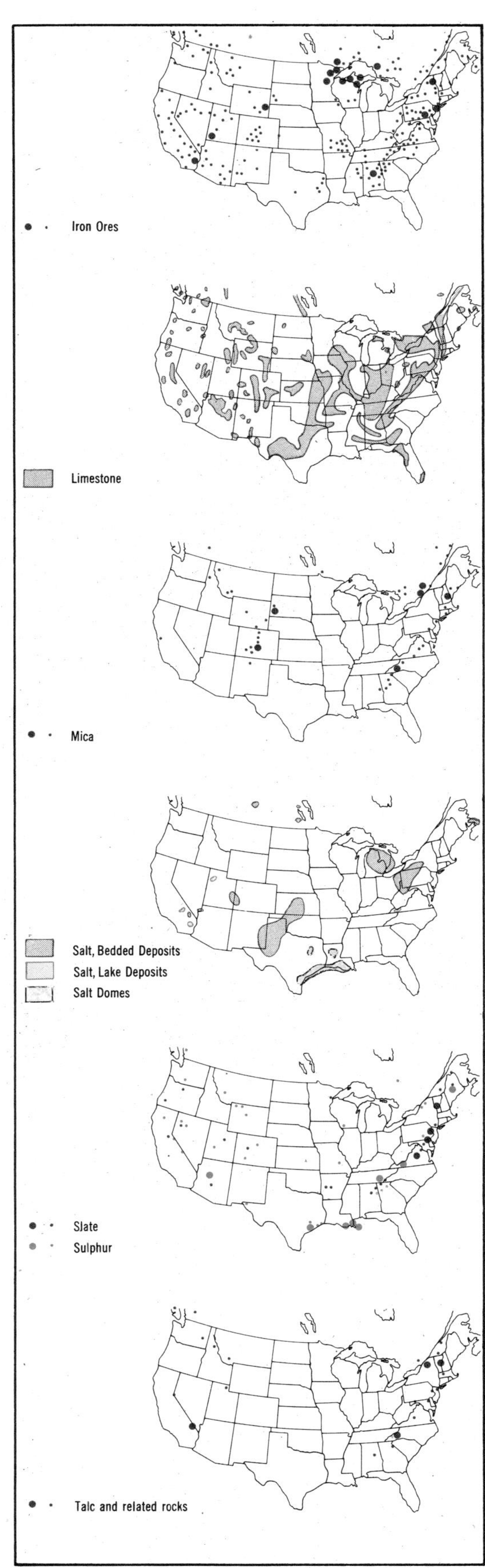

maps are provided for rocks that are common throughout the continent, such as sandstone and shale. A key to the principal groups and varieties of rocks will be found on page 209.

The following notes refer to the maps. *Iron Ores* — the deposits indicated on the map include hematite, brown iron ore, magnetite and siderite. The huge iron ore deposits recently discovered in northern Quebec will give Canada a leading role in iron ore and steel production. *Salt* — salt domes are underground ridges of salt, in the U.S. mostly of circular outline; they occur primarily near the Gulf Coast. *Sulphur* — the deposits indicated on the map include beds of native sulphur, of pyrites, and deposits of metallic ores from which pyrites are obtained as a by-product.

AGATE

Beauty in Bands — While collectors of minerals are particular about keeping their collections free of anything that is artificial, they do not seem to mind a man-made touch on their agates. What happens is this: Agate is a mineral belonging largely to the quartz variety called chalcedony; when essentially dark-colored, mostly black or grey, a type of chalcedony results which is called onyx; when of lighter color, frequently with blue, green and brown tints, it is named agate. Agate is a striated chalcedony — with its color arranged in bands or stripes. It is the porous quality of the bands that has made agates possible. Minerals in solution, deposited in cavities notably in ancient lavas, formed first along the cavity wall; these outer layers surrounding the cavity wall allowed water to seep through them and form additional layers until the cavity was filled. Being more resistant than the surrounding lava, the agates weathered into pebbles and nodules and are found in stream beds and gravel banks. The bands, in many cases approximately concentric, are sometimes so incredibly thin that about 17,000 of them crowd into one inch. They are also very hard, yet many are porous and take certain dyes readily. Soaking the agates first in a sugar solution and then in sulphuric acid will produce black or dark brown bands. Agates are used as mortars, as ornaments, and in similar ways. They are quite common in the lava deposits of the Lake Superior district.

ASBESTOS

The Insulator — The Greek word asbestos means "unquenchable," an appropriate name for a mineral that is not affected by an open fire and does not conduct heat except at high temperatures; it is also pliable, so that its unusual qualities can be put to human use by combing, spinning and weaving it into cloth; as an effective insulating material it is finding ever wider applications. One well-known commercial asbestos is the mineral chrysotile; it is the fibrous variety of the mineral serpentine, a compound of hydrogen, magnesium silicon and oxygen found both in igneous and metamorphic rocks. While the green, mottled, massive type of serpentine is sawed and polished for decorative uses — for instance to fashion tops of soda fountains because it resists corrosion by carbonic acid — the fibrous variety is found in veins which cut through massive serpentine. It has a silky luster and yellowish-green color; however, when separated, the cotton-like fibers are white; the longest are 3 or 4 inches in length, but most are shorter. Serpentine asbestos is mined in Arizona and, in particularly large quantities, in Quebec. Another type of asbestos is amphibole asbestos. The fibers of amphibole asbestos are long, measuring up to 18 inches or more; but they lack the flexibility of serpentine asbestos and break easily into small pieces. This variety occurs in Idaho, Georgia and several adjoining southern states.

BERYL

Gem and Tool — Such words as emerald, golden beryl, morganite and aquamarine are suggestive of expensive jewelry. All are composed of the mineral beryl, a silicate of the metals beryllium and aluminum, and differentiated by their colors. When bright, deep green, because of the presence of chromium oxide, it is an emerald; the yellow types are golden beryl; the pink ones are named morganite in honor of J. P. Morgan; and those of the bluish green tints are called aquamarine, a word meaning sea water. Common beryl is light green, white, or colorless. Beryl usually occurs in granite, particularly in veins of pegmatite, traversing the granite mass. Crystallized in the hexagonal system, it is sometimes found in huge crystals; 2-ton specimens have been discovered in New Hampshire, and an 18-ton crystal, 4 feet across and 14 feet long, was found in Maine. Common beryl is the principal source of beryllium which has important industrial uses: Combined with aluminum it produces various light-weight alloys, and in conjunction with copper it makes tough, long-lived copper alloys, especially for tools and springs. On the whole, beryl is a by-product of feldspar, mica and quartz quarries in the Black Hills of South Dakota, in Connecticut, Maine, New Hampshire, and notably North Carolina. Connecticut has also produced golden beryl and aquamarine, and in North Carolina, the discovery of a few emeralds caused a sensation.

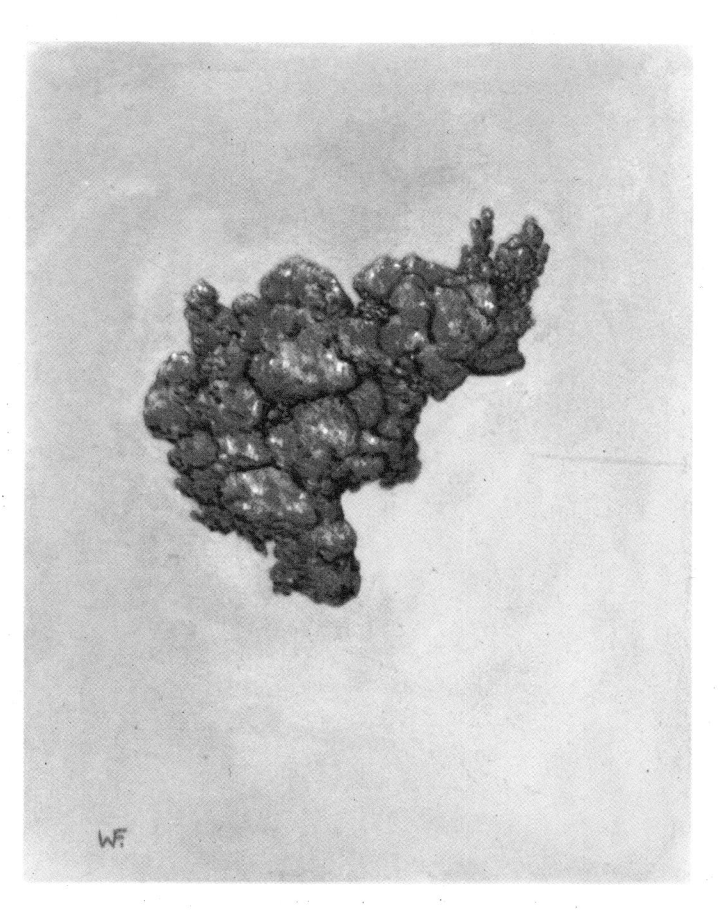

COPPER

Mined Here Before Columbus — The only metal known to the Indians was native copper; it was mined by them on Isle Royale in Lake Superior where more than 1,000 prehistoric copper pits testify to their appreciation of this malleable and ductile metal that was bartered throughout the continent. Native copper still occurs in fair quantities. It fills cracks or pores in rocks, taking on the form of sheets, frond-like plates, grains, or crystals of the cubic system, but usually distorted. One of the largest chunks of copper was found in the Lake Superior region in 1857; it weighed 420 tons. There, in the deep mines of the Michigan peninsula, masses weighing many tons occur more frequently than elsewhere; the rocks, mostly ancient basaltic lavas of a dark color, have been mineralized with copper, apparently by water solutions. Native copper is usually tarnished to a dull, brown color, sometimes with a greenish hue. Only new fractures show the bright luster and the familiar copper color. In the Michigan mines transparent calcite crystals are sometimes encountered which enclose flakes of copper; as these crystals are air-tight envelopes, the copper inside is not oxidized and remains bright and shiny. For industrial purposes the amount of copper metal gained from the native copper mineral is far exceeded by the quantities reduced from the various copper ores. Like lead and zinc minerals, copper frequently occurs in compounds.

◄ CORUNDUM

In Factory and Ballroom — Hardness is the outstanding characteristic of this mineral which is an oxide of aluminum. Only diamonds are harder. Its crystals are shaped like barrels or are prisms, and its colors range from white to grey and brown to black. Often it is found in the form of pebbles in the gravel of rivers. Its granular variety, colored black or grey, is called emery and has long been used as an abrasive in the form of sharpening stones, emery cloth, corundum wheels, or as powder for grinding precious stones. In America corundum deposits occur in Georgia, Massachusetts, Montana, North Carolina and Ontario. Lately, however, corundum has been succeeded, as an abrasive, by carborundum, an artificial silicide of carbon. Sometimes small quantities of inorganic coloring materials of various types are present in the corundum crystals, so that the latter are colored without losing their transparency. Such stones attain the status of "precious corundum"; they are gems. Though all colors of the rainbow are represented, by far the best-known varieties are the red one — the ruby — and the blue type — the sapphire. When cut with a convex surface, the star ruby and the star sapphire result. They present a star of reflected light, with six rays. Principal producers of "precious corundum" are Burma, Ceylon and Siam; in America, sapphires are found in Montana. The synthetic gems manufactured today differ only in source.

FELDSPAR ►

The Heart of Granite — Feldspar is more generally represented on earth than any other single mineral. Sixty per cent of all igneous rocks are made up of the various forms of the feldspar group; they are silicates of aluminum combined with either potassium, sodium, or calcium. They have the luster of glass or silk and a cleavage in two directions at right angles(this is called "orthoclase," the Greek word for "splitting at right angles"), or at almost right angles (this is called "plagioclase," the Greek word for "splitting obliquely"). The breaking down of feldspars by weathering produces clay. Orthoclase, a potassium feldspar, is colorless in its pure state, but usually tinted pink, red, or buff by iron oxides. An opalescent variation is called "moonstone." Microline is closely related to orthoclase — they have the same chemical formula — but it has cleavages at almost right angles, as contrasted with the right angles of orthoclase. A bright bluish-green form of microline is the famous Amazon stone (see illustration), one of the most beautiful minerals; it is found in the Pikes Peak region of Colorado and other localities in the U.S. and Canada. The decomposition of the potassium feldspars yields potash, the plant food, and kaolin, a raw material for porcelain. Among the plagioclase types, the sodium feldspar albite is used by potteries for a smooth glaze; the grey labradorite shows, in a mass, an interesting metallic iridescence.

FLINT

The Mineral that Strikes Sparks — Fire was struck by flint on steel; the flint lock was a part of the pioneer's rifle; and the arrows that wounded or killed him had flint heads. Flint has a great many associations with our early history, although today it has almost outlived its usefulness to man. It is a compact mineral, a variety of quartz, containing silica as its principal component or actually consisting of it. The grain is so fine that it can be discerned only by a powerful microscope and, on account of organic impurities, its color is usually dark: grey, brown, or black. Nevertheless, flakes of flint are translucent on thin edges, and when a chip is heated by a blow pipe, the organic coloring matter disappears. The luster is waxy, and like obsidian, flint breaks with a sharp curving or conchoidal fracture, a quality which was highly valued by primitive peoples who could chip it into tools, spear heads and other weapons. It is encountered in many limestones, forming veins, layers, or irregular nodules which may be as large as a pea or attain considerable bulk. Most silicas in flint are probably inorganic deposits, but in some varieties interesting remains of organic matter are found: one-celled animals of the sponge type called radiolarians, and one-celled plants called diatoms. In the U.S. and Canada flint is widely distributed in rocks of all geological eras, but it is not as abundant as in the chalk deposits of western Europe.

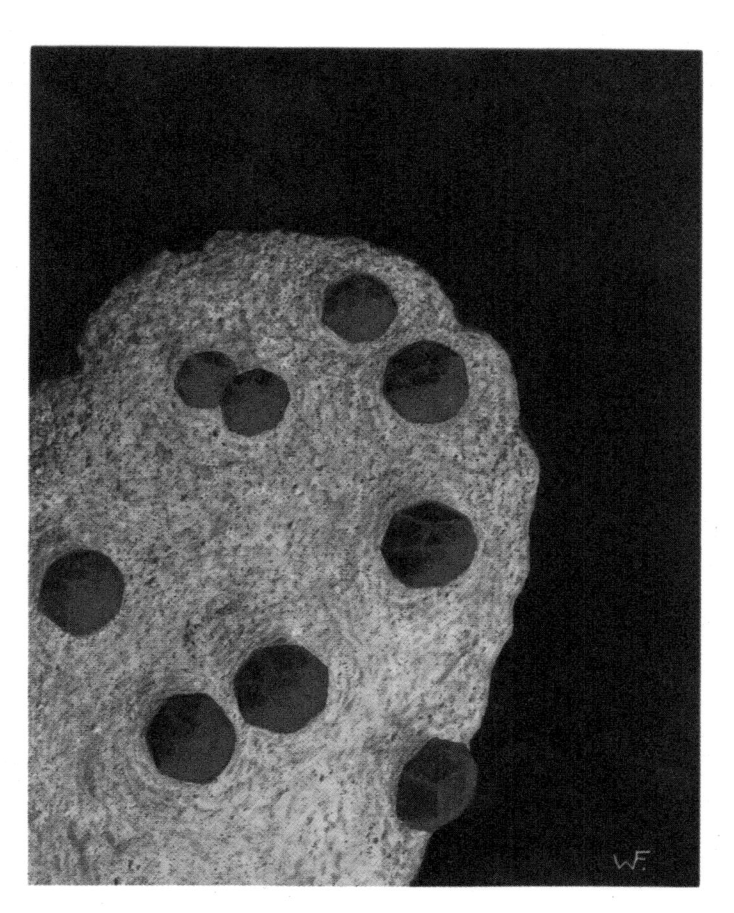

GARNET

Everybody's Ruby—"Garnet red" is a color shade so named after the familiar cut gems. The crystals of this mineral may be of any color ranging from green and yellow to black, but the red variety is most famous and makes indeed a lovely jewel if it is free of the cracks that fill so many garnets. This is a group of silicate compounds which are all alike in their crystalline form; the most usual shapes are of the types known as dodecahedron (a solid with 12 plane faces) and trapezohedron (a form whose faces are irregularly four-sided). Probably the most common variety is almandite, an iron garnet deep red to brownish black which occurs in many localities on earth; Alaska produces fine gems near Fort Wrangel, and in the neighborhood of Salida, Colorado, an almandite crystal of 14 pounds was once discovered. Andradite, a calcium iron silicate, is greenish-yellow, or wine-red and brown; black andradite garnets are called melanite, bright green ones (with chromium as the coloring agent) uvarovite. Pyrope, a magnesium silicate, is the so-called precious garnet that appears in the celebrated Czechoslovakian (or rather Bohemian) garnet jewelry. However, this deep-red mineral occurs also in Arizona, Colorado, Kentucky and New Mexico. Most abundant in metamorphosed rocks, common garnets are mined in New York's Adirondacks, in New Hampshire and North Carolina for manufacture of "red sandpaper."

◄ GOLD

The Standard — Gold is everywhere. As dust it is widely scattered throughout the world; grains and nuggets are found in gravels; in quartz it appears as veins, sheets, or irregular patches; in some localities in Colorado and California the sands are gold-bearing; it is found in stream beds and is in all salt water in solution. But, of course, the quantities are small, and upon its rarity and indescructibility its position as a world medium of exchange is based. In nature, gold never appears pure; it is always alloyed with silver which sometimes makes up more than a third of the compound; on other occasions silver represents only 1 per cent, but it is always there. Gold, one of the softest metals, is too soft to be worked in its pure state; therefore it is alloyed with copper, or more rarely with silver, to increase its qualities of hardness and durability. To indicate the gold contents, the measure "carat" is used, and an expression like "a 14 carat gold object" means that out of 24 metal parts 14 are pure gold. The distinguishing characteristics of gold are its color, lustre and its great weight (it has a specific gravity of 19.3). It is also malleable and ductile to a high degree; gold crystals, usually eight-sided, are rare. In the famous Mother Lode of California the native gold is visibly exposed in the quartz veins. In Alaska it is gained from gravel and quartz.

GRAPHITE ►

The Diamond's Unequal Twin—Graphite and the diamond are of pure carbon and have the same chemical formula. The latter is the hardest of all minerals, the former is one of the softest. There are other interesting differences: The diamond is colorless, transparent, and the very symbol of purity; its shape is almost always that of an eight-sided crystal; it is a very poor conductor of electricity. Graphite, on the other hand, is opaque and grey-black, soils everything it touches, and feels greasy; it is imperfectly crystallized, and while it occurs in the form of deficient six-sided plates, it is usually found in irregular fibrous masses in various crystalline rocks such as marble, schist, granite and gneiss. It is an effective conductor of electricity. The scales possess perfect cleavage parallel to their surface, i.e. they can be separated into thinner leaves. The seemingly undesirable quality of blackening everything with which it comes in contact, makes it the ideal filler for lead pencils: the expression "black lead" being the trade name for a mixture of graphite and clay which is compressed into various grades of hardness. Impure graphites are important ingredients in stove polish, foundry facings and paints; graphite crucibles are highly heat-resistant. Its special contribution to modern industry is its use, in a purified, powdered form, as a dry lubricant. There are considerable deposits in the U.S., also in Canada, but actual production of graphite is small.

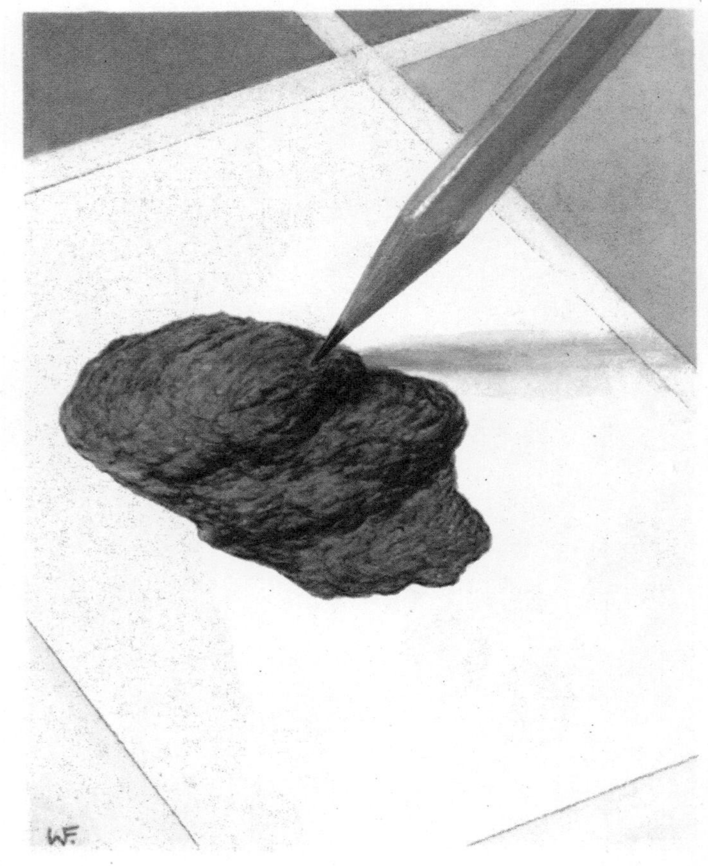

HEMATITE (RED IRON ORE) ►

Machine Age Mineral — This is the most important of all iron ores and is the basis of most of our iron and steel. It occurs in many forms from hard rock to soft earth. When the ore appears in crystalline form it is grey to black in color and has a metallic, mirror-like lustre. Because of this reflective quality it is termed iron-glance or specular iron ore. Hematite may also consist of tiny flakes or scales—so thin that they are almost translucent—which resemble flakes of mica; hence the name micaceous iron-ore. Most commonly, it appears as a dull red earthy mass. It is named hematite (derived from the Greek word meaning "blood-like") because all forms, from the hard black crystals to the soft red earthy mass, show when crushed or scratched a characteristic blood red powder or streak. The rock hematite consists of the mineral hematite (a compound of iron and oxygen) in its pure form or mixed with clay, silica or sand. If the amount of clay is considerable, the hematite is called red ocher. The mineral when powdered is used in pigment, red pencils and rouge. Hematite occurs in vast deposits in Ontario, Michigan and Wisconsin. Most of the ore mined in the famous Mesabi Range in Minnesota is hematite. Here the deposits are so close to the surface that the ore is removed by steam shovels and loaded directly for shipment.

◄ MICA

Glass and Snow — The word "isinglass" awakens pleasant, old-fashioned thought associations: the old iron stove had an isinglass window through which a red glow spread through the room; the isinglass curtains were put up on the surrey on a rainy ride. The scientific name of isinglass is muscovite (they used it in old Muscovy in their windows) or white mica. All the varieties of the mineral mica are silicates which have a perfect cleavage: they split into layers which are thin but tough and bounce back into shape when bent. Their crystals are six-sided plates with shiny, glassy, flat surfaces and rough sides; they occur also as irregular flakes. Muscovite is found in granites and pegmatites, sometimes in sheets 10 feet wide. It is mined in the Black Hills of South Dakota, North Carolina and Virginia; granite quarries in New England also yield considerable quantities. Today it is an even more important product than in the era of the isinglass curtains; it finds a great variety of uses in modern industry, from insulation to lubrication. "Snow" for Christmas trees and movie sets is ground-up muscovite. Biotite is a mica which iron has tainted black, dark green, or brown; it has little economic significance. Phlogopite is almost free of iron and therefore particularly valuable for all electric uses; large brown or amber crystals are encountered in eastern Canada and New Jersey. Lepidolite, a lithium mica, is lavender, pink, or yellow.

QUARTZ

Radar Parts and Crystal Balls — "Krystallos" is the Greek word for clear ice, and the ancient world believed the rock crystals were ice frozen so hard that it would not melt again. Rock crystal is a form of quartz, the very common mineral that is abundant in the rocks and sands around us. It is a compound of silicon (1 atom) and oxygen (2 atoms to 1 molecule), is transparent, and without color in a pure state; it has no cleavage and appears in masses of grains or in crystals which are prisms with pyramids on either or both ends. It is so hard that it cannot be scratched with a knife. Rock crystal is extensively used in the optical and electronics industries; a very specialized product is the crystal ball which, as the crystal gazers pretend to believe, reveals the future. For decorative purposes clear quartz is transformed into "rhinestones." Although rock crystal occurs in Arkansas and California, North Carolina and New York, the principal supply is imported from Brazil. Many forms of quartz are colored by impurities and make well-known gems: If stained purple or violet, probably by manganese, it is an amethyst; citrine is a yellow quartz often known as "Spanish topaz"; rose quartz, frequently cut into gems, may lose its color in bright light, but when kept in the dark, the color returns; chalcedony is a variety of quartz that is described in connection with agate; and many of the gold-bearing veins are of milky quartz.

SILVER

Pounds and Dollars — Fine twisted wire embedded in rock is the most common form in which native silver occurs. It does not look impressive as it is usually tarnished black; untarnished it is white and has the well-known metallic silver luster. Crystals occur occasionally but they are usually distorted. Native silver is often alloyed with gold or copper, and has been found in considerable quantities in Colorado (one chunk weighed over 1,800 pounds) and the Lake Superior region. In silver production, silver ores are also important, and an appreciable amount is extracted from silver-containing lead ores. Utah, Nevada, Montana, Idaho and Colorado are rich in silver-bearing ore, as is the province of Ontario. A certain amount of silver is absorbed by the metal ware, chemical and photographic industries, and silver jewelry is more common today than ever. Silver retains its status as a monetary standard in several Asiatic countries, and the U.S. still clings to a theoretical gold and silver currency. But the impact of silver on our nation's life has rather been historical; the pound sterling we used in colonial days referred originally to a weight, a pound of silver, and the term dollar can be traced to one of the world's richest silver mines, that of Joachimstal in Bohemia. In the middle ages the coins produced there were called Joachimstaler, or taler for short; by a circuitous route the latter word became our "dollar".

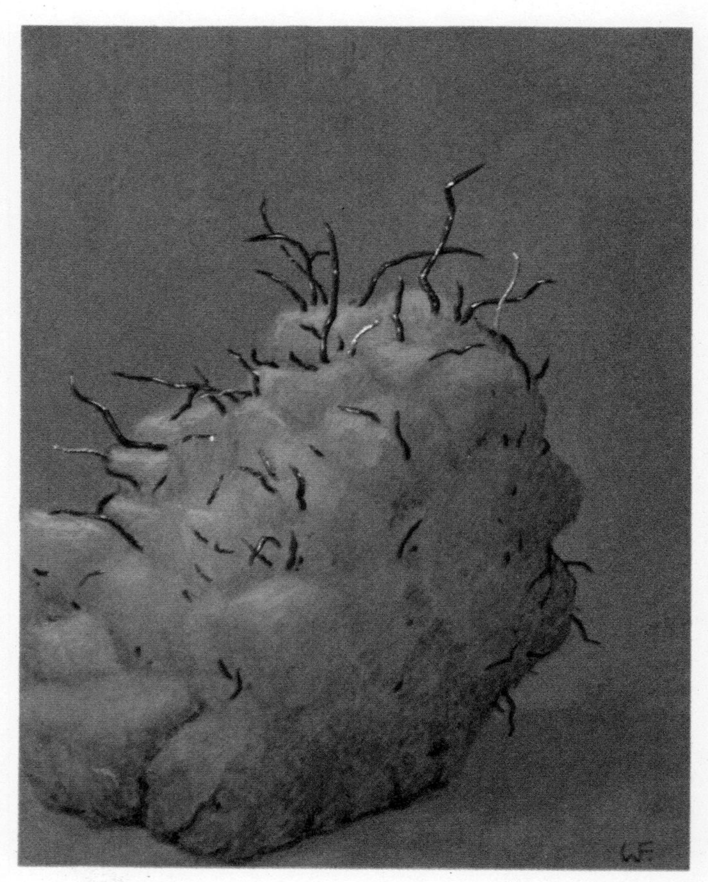

SULPHUR

On the Rim of Craters and Deep in the Earth — According to folklore, sulphur and molasses make an ideal spring tonic, and sulphur and brimstone are two attributes of hell. The mineral supposedly capable of such diverse functions consists of crystals which are as yellow as an evening primrose, transparent or translucent, and normally have the shape of a pyramid; with their bright and smooth faces they are prized items in a mineral collection but have to be handled with care; they are poor conductors of heat, and when held in a warm hand, a crackling noise emanates from them and fissures appear. Sulphur is soft, light and brittle; it burns with a blue flame and creates a suffocating odor. In the crystallized form it is found in deposits which are often associated with limestone, gypsum, or rock salt; in Louisiana and Texas, for instance, sulphur beds and salt domes are encountered in the same neighborhood; some of the sulphur veins of that region are 120 feet thick. Vast quantities are also obtained in compounds found elsewhere. As a powdery substance sulphur is formed in the craters of volcanoes, by the action of sulphurous gases; occasionally it is mined there. The practical applications of sulphur are numerous and important in the manufacture of gun powder, matches, rubber and fireworks; in the chemical and pharmaceutical industries; and as a bleaching agent in the production of wood pulp and paper.

TALC

Soapstone and Sea Froth — Talcum powder is crushed and ground from talc, the softest of all minerals. It is hydrated magnesium silicate which hardly ever crystallizes; it forms masses which often are lamellar or foliated. The cleavage is parallel to the surfaces, and while the thin, wavy flakes are bent easily, they do not snap back into their original position as the flakes of mica; i.e. they are flexible but not elastic. The surface has a silvery and pearly luster and is colored grey, green or yellow; it can be scratched with a fingernail and cut with a knife. Translucent to opaque, it feels greasy to the touch. Generally it occurs in metamorphic rock and, in a mass, talc is the principal ingredient of the rock called soapstone, which will be discussed later. The cosmetic and pharmaceutical industries make use of considerable amounts of talc; in paper manufacturing it serves as a filler; and as a dry lubricant, it has specialized uses. Large deposits are located in New York, North Carolina, California and Vermont. A close relative of talc is the white mineral sepiolite, known to the western world as meerschaum, the raw material out of which fine tobacco pipes are carved. The German name meerschaum means "sea froth" and refers to the fact that, due to its porous nature, the dry mineral floats on water. It is mined in Asia Minor, carved in central Europe, and prized by American pipe collectors.

◄ GRANITE

The Stuff of Our Mountains — Many of the hills of New England are solid granite masses; so also are many peaks of the Appalachians as far south as Georgia. Also many parts of the Rockies and the West Coast chains are formed of granite, and the "Needles" of the Black Hills in South Dakota are spectacular granite erosion forms. This rock of our mountains is also the material of our monumental buildings; for it is the stone par excellence: Hard and durable, it can be highly polished, and appears in a wide range of colors from white to dark grey, from pink to deep red, from yellow to green and brown. It is not easily chiseled, and granite sculpture may be coarse; but it is often bold and impressive. Delicate inscriptions and ornamentations, notably on tombstones, are produced by sand-blasting. Granite is a coarsely crystalline igneous rock composed of quartz and feldspar, sometimes with an addition of mica and other minerals, and forms the basis for a vast number of deposits of gold, tin, tungsten, and bismuth. Some of its several varieties are especially interesting. "Pudding granite" of Vermont is filled with black lumps of mica; and the handsome foliated granite is shot through with twisted bands of different color and composition. Weathering breaks granite down into sand, gravel and soil releasing such valuable substances as lime, magnesia, potash and silica, to be used as building materials for stems and leaves.

BASALT ►

The Columns of Pliny — One thousand nine hundred years ago, Pliny the Elder, for the first time, described some black stone formations in Ethiopia as "basalt". It is an old name for an old rock which occurs both in the Old and New Worlds. In most forms it is true lava that erupted from volcanoes or flowed through cracks, and the steam formed bubble holes and other characteristics of lava flows are still visible. It is a dense igneous rock of dark grey, green purple or black color, containing a great deal of lime, magnesium and iron. Its jointing is platy, or it forms columns with three to six sides; good examples can be seen in Yellowstone Park, near the Snake River in Idaho, and in other places, especially in the Northwest where many thousands of square miles have a base of basaltic lava flow. An interesting weathered form is an oval spheroid with peeling scales or layers. Basalt is crushed for the surfacing of roads both in the West and in large eastern quarries, for instance, in the Palisades of the Hudson. In the basalts of the Lake Superior region copper is found, and occasionally a sapphire or other gem is embedded in the dark rock. A glassy phase of basalt is called tachylite or basaltic glass. This brittle rock is black and has a resinous luster; it is commonly ejected by volcanoes in the form of cinders and bombs, and is found frequently on the Hawaiian Islands.

OBSIDIAN

A Glassy Rock for Man's First Tools — In volcanic regions, nature made glass. We call it obsidian. It is harder than window glass, which it will scratch. Normally it is black, but grey, red and brown varieties are also found. The microscope reveals that obsidian is really colorless, as glass should be, but it is full of minute dust particles which consist probably of magnetite; they represent crystals that had just begun to grow; it is supposed that high viscosity and rapid cooling prevented the formation of real crystals and made obsidian the glassy rock which it is. The tiny particles stain it black; where they have been oxydized to hematite dust, they are responsible for the red or brown color found in some varieties. The composition of obsidian is similar to that of granite, about two-thirds feldspar and one-third quartz. Because obsidian is homogeneous and lacks structure, its fracture is conchoidal (i.e. like one-half of a bivalve shell). This quality was recognized by man in earlist days and highly prized by primitive peoples; for it enabled them to shape obsidian into the form of weapons and tools by simple chipping. In the Old World, the traveler who brought this rock from Ethiopia to Rome was Obsidius, godfather of obsidian, and in the New World the Indians, particularly those of ancient Mexico, made knives of slender flakes that were as sharp as razors. In the U.S., obsidians are encountered throughout the West.

SANDSTONE

The Common Rock Around Us — Sandstone has a simple formula: It is sand held together by a cementing material. Sand grains consist largely of quartz, with a possible admixture of other minerals, and the most common "binders" are silica or lime; occasionally clay or oxide of iron serves the purpose. When a piece of sandstone breaks, the sand stands out on the surface like sugar grains. The color range is wide: white, grey, or green; yellow or buff; red or brown. There are approximately ten important varieties: Grit is the densely cemented, hard and large-grained rock that was much used for millstones. Flagstone breaks easily into slabs and is a popular garden path material; of interest to palaeonthologists, flagstone often contains prehistoric markings and tracks of wind, rain and animals. For building purposes, sandstone is easily quarried in regular blocks; "brownstone houses" were the landmarks of eastern cities in the late 19th century. The very pure St. Peter sandstone of Illinois is removed by pumps and used in optical and plate glass. Other sandstones usable for glassmaking crop out in the Appalachians from Virginia to the Gaspé Peninsula of Canada. Nature, too, uses sandstone for an important function — that of underground storage. Sometimes as much as 30% of the rock's volume consists of pores, and if the sandstone is covered by a lid of impervious shale, it acts as a reservoir for water, petroleum, and natural gas.

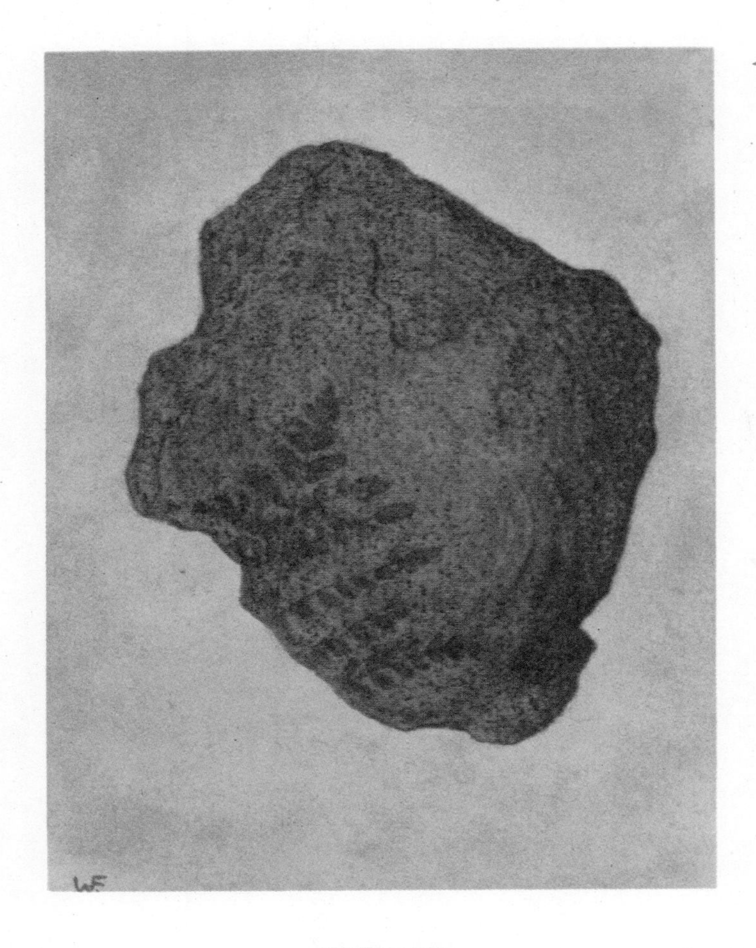

SHALE

A Great Preserver — Tracks of prehistoric worms and of dinosaurs; dots where the rain struck and marks where the water rippled; fossils of ferns and corals, jellyfish and crawling creatures — all such reminiscences of previous geological ages are well preserved in shales. Shale took these imprints readily because it was originally soft mud, and it preserves them because it has not changed greatly after hardening. It consists largely of clay minerals and is so fine-grained that its component particles can be determined only by a strong microscope. In many cases it can be cut with a knife; such shales crumble easily when dry. Other varieties are hardened by silica. All shales split, parallel to beds and layers, into flat fragments that look like shells. Grey is the predominant color, but white, yellow, buff, red, brown, purple, greenish and black shales are also encountered. Some types contain a great deal of organic matter, usually carbon; they are the carbonaceous shales, normally black. A similar type which has attracted considerable public attention lately is oil shale; although it does not contain oil as such, it can be distilled, and its carbonaceous matter yields petroleum and tar. In Europe oil shales are utilized; in America they are considered only as reserves. The biggest reserve is the Green River shale in Colorado, Utah and Wyoming, an Eocene lake deposit. It is estimated to contain 100 billion barrels of oil.

GYPSUM

The Plaster of Paris — Heat this rock, and all water will be driven out of it. Then add water, and the lost molecules will replace themselves. That such a substance makes an ideal plastering material which can be moulded and then hardens, was discovered long ago. Gypsum was first quarried for such a purpose, according to an ancient story, at Montmartre near Paris, which accounts for the name Plaster of Paris. In the U.S., gypsum is found throughout the country, and in Canada, in the Province of New Brunswick and elsewhere. It is mined in huge quantities in New York and Michigan, Iowa, Kansas, Texas and elsewhere. The title of "Gypsum State" goes to Oklahoma because of its enormous deposits. Gypsum is a precipitate from water charged with calcium sulphate, possibly settled in prehistoric salt lakes or lagoons, and commonly appears in a solid mass without distinct layers; its thickness ranges from a few inches to more than a thousand feet. It may be the white mineral in pure form, or it may have an admixture of clay, iron oxides, marl and bitumen, which accounts for its variety of colors: light grey, yellow, brick-red. It is fine-grained and can be scratched with the fingernail. Alabaster, a white or delicately tinted variety, is easily carved into small statues and ornamental vases. Gypsum sand, formed in dry desert lakes, is blown by the winds into the beautiful dunes of White Sands National Monument in New Mexico.

Minerals and Rocks

ROCK SALT ►

Rock from the Sea — Salt, an essential to man and beast, has been utilized by peoples of all ages and in the ancient world was of great economic and religious significance. It is evaporated from sea water, mined like coal and pressure pumped from wells. Rock salt is composed of the grains of the mineral salt whose scientific name is halite or sodium chloride; its grain ranges from fine to coarse, and its natural color is white; minute impurities change it occasionally to yellow, red, grey or black. In the U.S. and Canada rock salt forms several huge basins; the biggest extends over more than 100,000 square miles from upstate New York to Michigan and contains approximately 185 million tons. Another basin underlies parts of Kansas, Oklahoma, Texas and New Mexico; in both regions salt beds of 250, 400 and 600 foot thickness are found. The process by which such enormous layers developed was, in a simplified explanation, this: Salt water evaporated in a lake in an arid region; before it dried up entirely, a new flow of sea water broke through and mingled with the concentrated brine; in time the waves built up the barrier again, closed the lake, and evaporation continued; this alternating process went on for millions of years until the deposits reached their present thickness. In Louisiana and Texas so-called salt domes occur; they are underground ridges of salt, usually circular, capped by layers of other rocks.

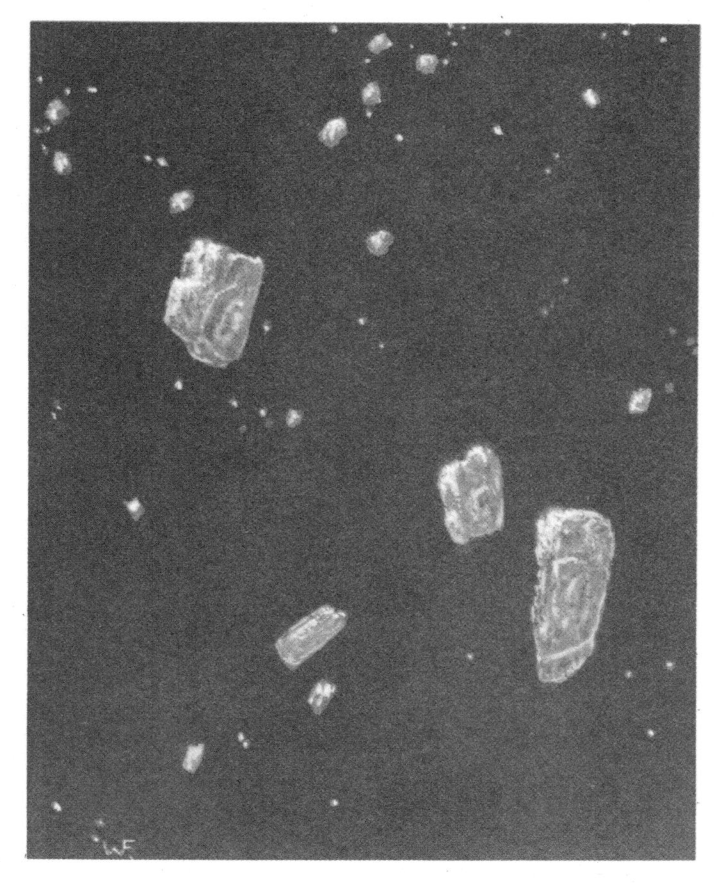

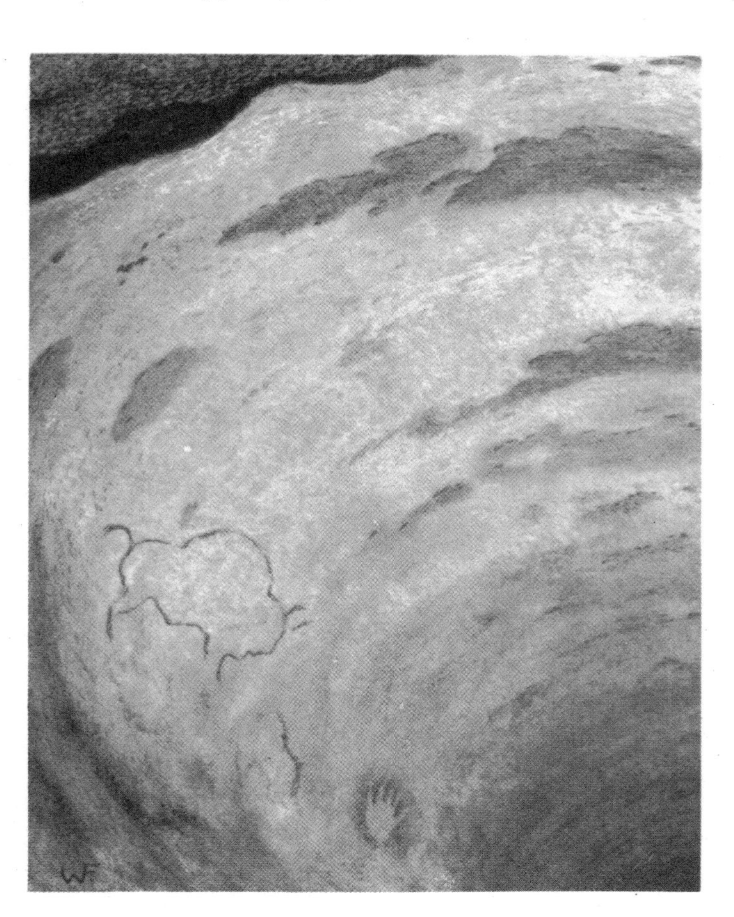

◄ LIMESTONE

"Limestone Country, Rich Country" — Limestone insulates our houses as rock wool; it is the stone of many public buildings; it gives body to the cement of our foundations and to the concrete of our highways; it restores health to acid pastures and fields, and is carved into statues of heroes; the number of industries that require limestone is legion, ranging from sugar and soap manufacturing to paper and aluminum production. It occurs in every state, but the production centers for building stone are in Indiana and Missouri, Wisconsin and Minnesota. Limestone is a rock that consists essentially of calcium carbonate, the remainder consisting of such components as sand or iron oxides. When pure, it is white or cream-colored, but it is commonly stained grey, yellow, red, brown, or black by impurities. There are fine-grained and crystalline, firm and porous, strong and weak varieties. Limestone is slowly dissolved by water but rain water saturated with carbon dioxide and acids from the soil eats it quickly. Thus, erosion attacks limestone beds. Funnel-shaped "sinks" and tunnels appear, and gradually the great limestone caves with stalagmites, stalactites and underground rivers come into being. Crystalline limestone takes a high polish and is sold as marble; shell limestone consists mostly of fossil shells, and coral limestone of coral, algae and shells; lithographic limestone is occasionally employed in printing.

PEAT

Between Plant and Stone — When plants decompose on the ground, they give off their carbon to the atmosphere and leave behind only mineral matter. However, if they decay under water, a much slower process is carried out by bacteria, the oxygen is removed from the dead leaves, roots and stalks and the proportion of carbon in the remains is greatly increased. Gradually the plant material is converted into rocks of the coal series whose earliest stage is peat. Peat develops in swamps, bogs and marshes, largely from plants of a low order — such as certain mosses that grow upward while they die off below — which accounts for the great thickness of many peat deposits. The upper part of a peat bed consists of a matted, spongy layer of fibrous material in which, sometimes, remains of stems and roots can still be recognized; it has a yellowish to brown color. The mass below is dark brown or black and looks like wet clay: it is compact and homogeneous. A great part of it is water, so it shrinks considerably when dried. In Europe it is cut and pressed into blocks and used as fuel, with a heating value between that of wood and soft coal. In the U.S. and Canada it is employed as fertilizer and for mulching, as bedding for livestock and as packing material. It is estimated that the Canadian peat deposits cover about 37,000 square miles, those of the U.S. 11,200 square miles; they are widely distributed.

BITUMINOUS COAL

Coke and Smoke — When examining a piece of bituminous coal, or soft coal as it is commonly called, the structure of layers is conspicuous. Some layers are shiny black; these were at one time flattened tree trunks, and in their woody portions the pores absorbed decaying compounds that turned into lustrous carbon. Other bands are dull; here the minute particles of plant material are mixed with clay and other substances. Still other layers are powdery; we do not know why, but huge fires raging in prehistoric forests while the coal was in process of formation, are suggested as a cause. Soft coal consists of ashes, carbon (60 to 85 per cent), and volatile matter like gas (15 to 40 per cent). Varieties that have a large amount of volatile contents are turned into coal gas and coke (burnable clinker). "Smokeless coal" has a low content of volatile matter (15 to 20 per cent), and possesses, consequently, a high heating value per pound; it is in demand for steam engines and ships. But the bulk of bituminous coal does not perform any specific tasks; it is a satisfactory heating coal, though sometimes a great smoke producer. Soft coal beds may be a few inches or several feet thick. In the U.S. and Canada bituminous coal fields are widely distributed; production centers are in the East, South, Midwest and West. Intermediate stages between peat and soft coal are lignite and subbituminous coal, a black, coaly rock which sometimes crumbles but burns well.

ANTHRACITE ►

Black Gold — In mountainous regions where rocks were folded and squeezed, as for instance in the Appalachians in Pennsylvania, the weight of mountains was sometimes pushed over a soft-coal bed and pressed on it heavily; in this way water and gas were driven out gradually, and an ever higher proportion of carbon was left. By this process anthracite was gradually produced — a hard, dense, compact, brittle rock with a carbon content of 80 to 90 per cent (occasionally even higher) and a small quantity of impurities. It is jet black; some types display, on broken surfaces, an iridescent film that reflects the colors of the spectrum, a quality from which the name peacock coal has been derived. Strong heat is necessary to ignite anthracite; it burns slowly with a pale blue flame and yields heat with hardly any smoke or odor. Therefore it is an ideal fuel for household use, especially in cities which enforce smoke control ordinances. In the U.S. the largest anthracite deposits are those of Pennsylvania which contain 99½ per cent of our domestic reserves. Nature's process of coal-making is still going on in innumerable shallow lakes and bogs. In the Dismal Swamp of southern Virginia, for instance, a layer of soil filled with roots is found under the peat, just as it is frequently encountered under the seams of coal; on the surface, peat can be observed to settle around the giant old cypress stumps, obviously earmarking them as future coal.

◄ GNEISS

Ancient Rock in Changed Form—The miners in Germany's Harz Mountains and in the Erzgebirge, two of the world's oldest mining regions, used the word gneiss to denote crystalline rock with mineral veins. From there, the term spread and is now universally accepted to describe a banded rock with a roughly developed foliation. The bands are straight, wavy or folded. The expression "gneiss" itself refers to texture only, and if we use such terms as granite gneiss or muscovite gneiss, the first word concerns the composition of the rock. Consequently "gneiss" may mean a large number of highly diverse rocks, some weakly metamorphosed, others strongly metamorphosed, some derived from sedimentary rocks, others from igneous rocks. In some cases the metamorphic process has gone so far that the nature of the original rock can no longer be determined with certainty. The color of gneiss also is so varied that it cannot serve for diagnostic purposes; all shades of grey, green, pink, red and brown occur, and in rare instances even white or black. These are, on the whole, the colors of granite, and in its general appearance gneiss resembles granite. Various kinds of feldspar, quartz and mica are important components—the feldspars occurring as elongated, shapeless grains, and the quartz in round grains or lenticles while the micas have no definite crystal form but appear in flakes or patches. Gneiss formations occur throughout the continent.

◄ SOAPSTONE

Pans and Statues — Soapstone played an important part in the history of mankind; it made its appearance in human affairs when primitive man, both in the Old and the New Worlds, added the art of cooking to the technique of roasting his food in an open fire. Even before pottery was invented, there was one material available that could be cut and easily shaped into a pot or pan — soapstone. It did not crack, when placed over the flames; water could now be boiled. One of the greatest advances in housekeeping had been accomplished. Soapstone also had a bearing on the birth of art: from it were sculptured some of man's earliest ornamental figures. The same qualities that made soapstone a rock highly prized by the Indians and other Stone Age peoples, its resistance to heat and acids, make it valuable for modern use in sinks, laundry tubs, table covers in chemical laboratories, switchboards and similar objects. Soapstone is a compact rock without cleavage — so soft, that it can be sawed into slabs of any thickness, and of a grey or greenish color. Talc is an important component, and the scales of talc, chlorite and other minerals are closely interwoven. One variety of soapstone (also called steatite or pot-stone) is the common French chalk used by tailors. In areas where metamorphic rocks abound, soapstone is found in good-sized deposits. In the U.S. it is mined or quarried in New York, Vermont, California and other states.

SLATE ►

The Blackboard Rock — Such expressions as "a clean slate" or "the slate of officers" indicate that at one time slate played an important role in human communications. On a slab of slate the young scholar learned his 3 R's, and on a slate board the innkeeper recorded his charges. Houses were, and still are, roofed with slate, for it is durable, easily prepared for use and impervious to weather. Slate is so homogeneous and fine-grained that the unaided eye cannot distinguish the constituent particles. As a rock, it represents the mildly metamorphosed form of the finest materials produced by erosion, i.e. various clays, silts and shales, with an admixture of volcanic dust and other impurities. Its cleavage, the quality which makes it useful to man, is interesting. While it splits into thin layers, the splitting does not occur parallel to the original bedding, or does so only accidentally. It proceeds at all angles depending on the tilting and squeezing to which the bed was subjected in the upheavals of mountain building. The mineral composition of this dense rock is mainly quartz, sericite (a mica variety), chlorite and carbonaceous material; the latter determines the color of slate which is light grey, dark grey, or black. Abundant chlorite may color it green, and iron oxides will give it yellow, red and brown tints. Slate is common in eastern North America, the chief producing states being Pennsylvania, Vermont and New York.

Minerals and Rocks

MARBLE ►

First in Beauty — Throughout history, marble has served to symbolize man's highest aspirations — in the columns of the Acropolis and the temples of Rome, the marble statues and monuments. Marble is the name given metamorphosed limestone. Its grain ranges from fine to coarse; in blocks reserved for statuary the fracture surface has a silky, shimmering luster; while in coarser varieties, the grains resemble those of cube sugar. In the best marble, the color is pure white; but carbonaceous materials and iron oxides color it grey, black, yellow, pink, or red. The coloration may be uniform, but usually it is not; in fact, the veined or spotted distribution of tints is called "marbled" because it is so characteristic for this rock. The hardness is the same as that of calcite. In its structure, it is devoid of foliation, i.e. it is massive and has no cleavage. In the quarrying and building trades, any limestone that can be cut into good-sized blocks and take a high polish is sold as marble. For instance, much of the famous "Tennessee marble" is a very pure but little metamorphosed limestone. In architecture, compact white marbles that can be carved without difficulty are named "statuary." Those of uniform grain and color, preferably white to pink, are "architectural," and those of bright colors and striking patterns of veins are "ornamental." Vermont, Massachusetts, Georgia, Tennessee and eastern Canada are known for their large deposits of marble.

◄ JADE

The Carver's Stone — Some of the world's finest art objects are Chinese carvings of jade; they reflect the infinite care and excellent taste of their artist-creators. In fashioning them, the first difficult task was to find a large and pure piece of jade; then the tough, fibrous material was carved with painstaking attention to the most minute details; and finally, the polishing gave a rich depth to the luster of the statue, bowl, or vase. Jade has always been highly prized throughout history back to the Bronze and Stone Ages; the Swiss Lake Dwellers, for instance, used jade hammers and jade knives. Technically, jade is one of two metamorphic rocks — either jadeite or nephrite. Some geologists prefer to classify both varieties as minerals. Jadeite is fine-grained, compact and of uncertain origin; sometimes it is snow-white in color but the usual hues are apple-green or dark green; occasionally the green permeates the white in the form of veins or clouds. Nephrite is similar to jadeite in its properties and applications, but somewhat softer and easier to carve. It occurs in a variety of colors, with green and yellow, grey and white predominating. The finest jadeite is quarried in Tammaw in upper Burma, the principal source of supply for the Chinese jade carvers. But jade is also found in Alaska, British Columbia, Wyoming, and Mexico where the ancient Aztecs appreciated jade, had a name for it, and fashioned it into ornaments and tools.

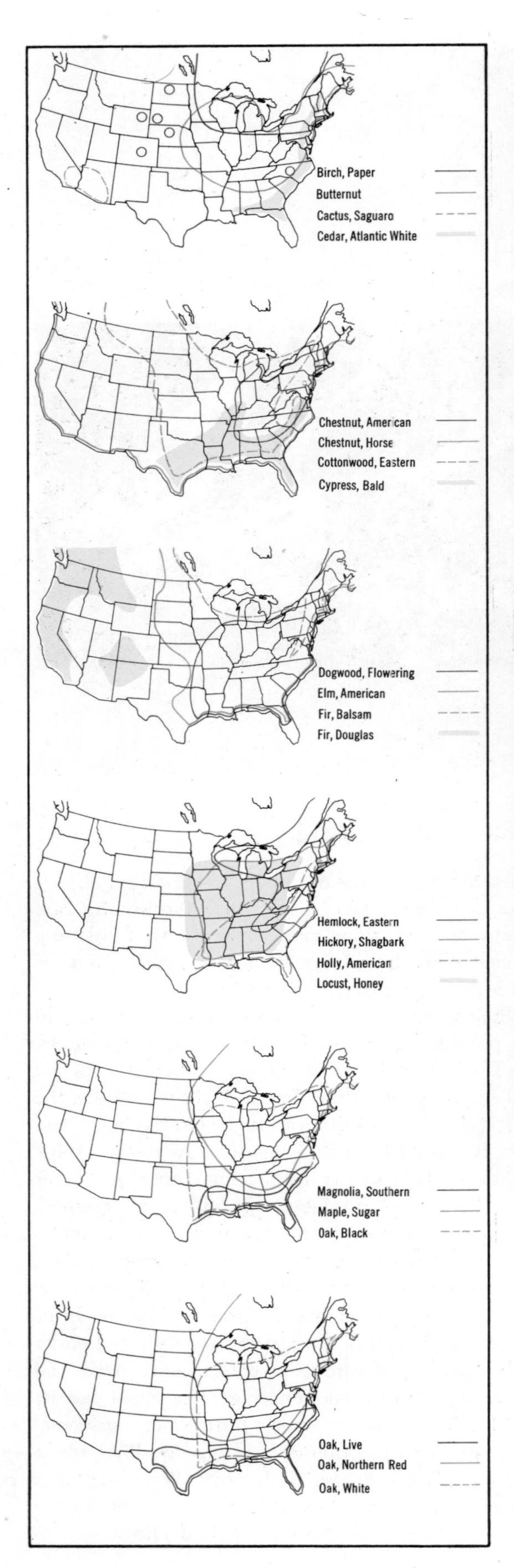

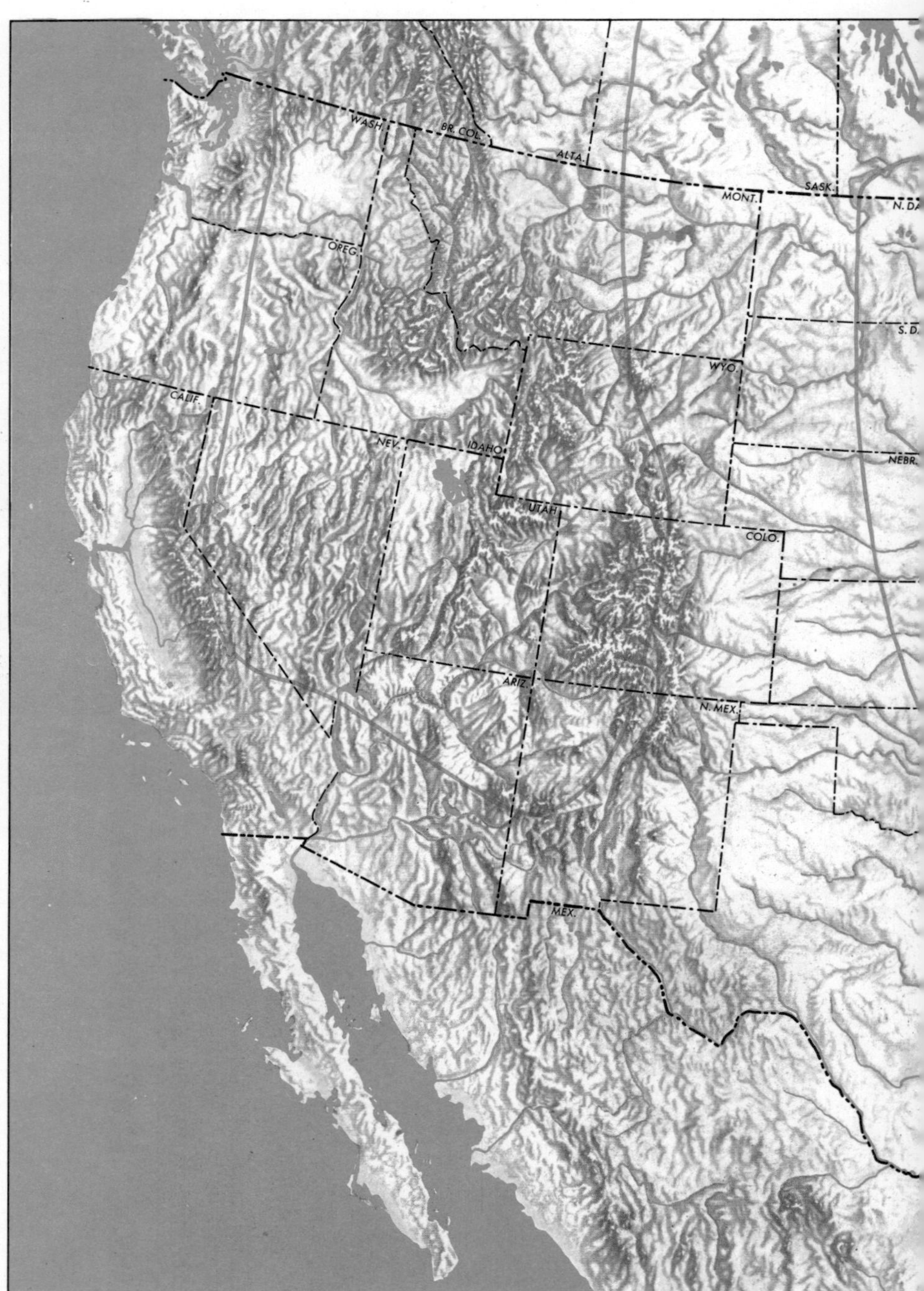

TREES IN THE U.S. AND SOUTHERN CANADA

The following pages describe and illustrate those trees which are most frequently encountered in the U.S. and Canada, or are of general interest for other reasons. The distribution of these trees is outlined in alphabetical order on the range maps on this page. The stands of coniferous, deciduous and mixed forests are indicated on the vegetation map on page 207. A key to the principal orders and families of trees will be found on page 211.

The following notes refer to the maps on this page. *Aspen, Quaking* — the range extends to the arctic tree line, throughout Canada to Alaska. *Birch, Paper* — its northern limit is the tree line from Labrador to Manitoba. *Chestnut, Horse* — introduced from Europe. *Elm, American* — within its range it is absent from the mountain ranges and the immediate seacoast. *Fir, Balsam* — its main stands

Trees

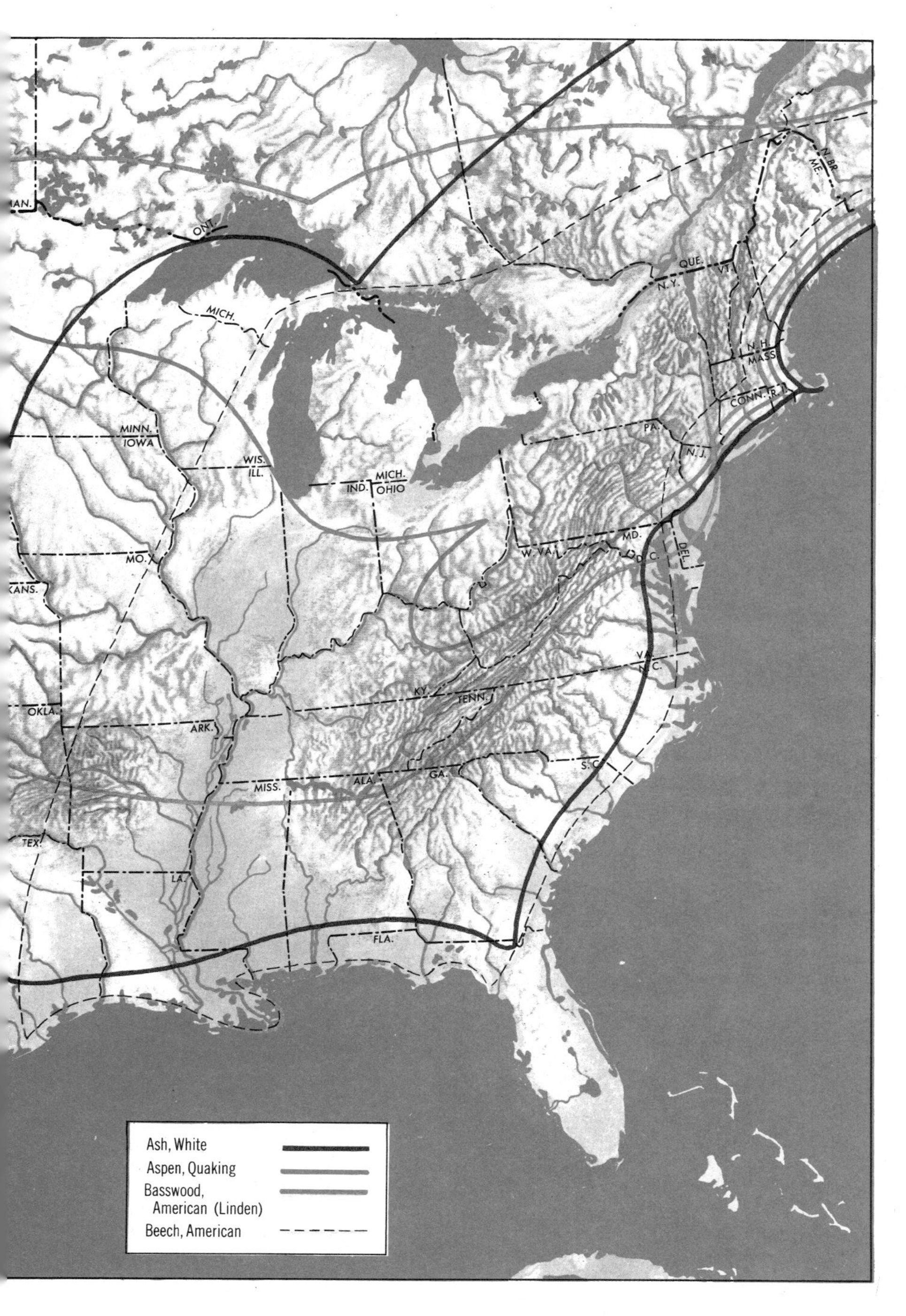

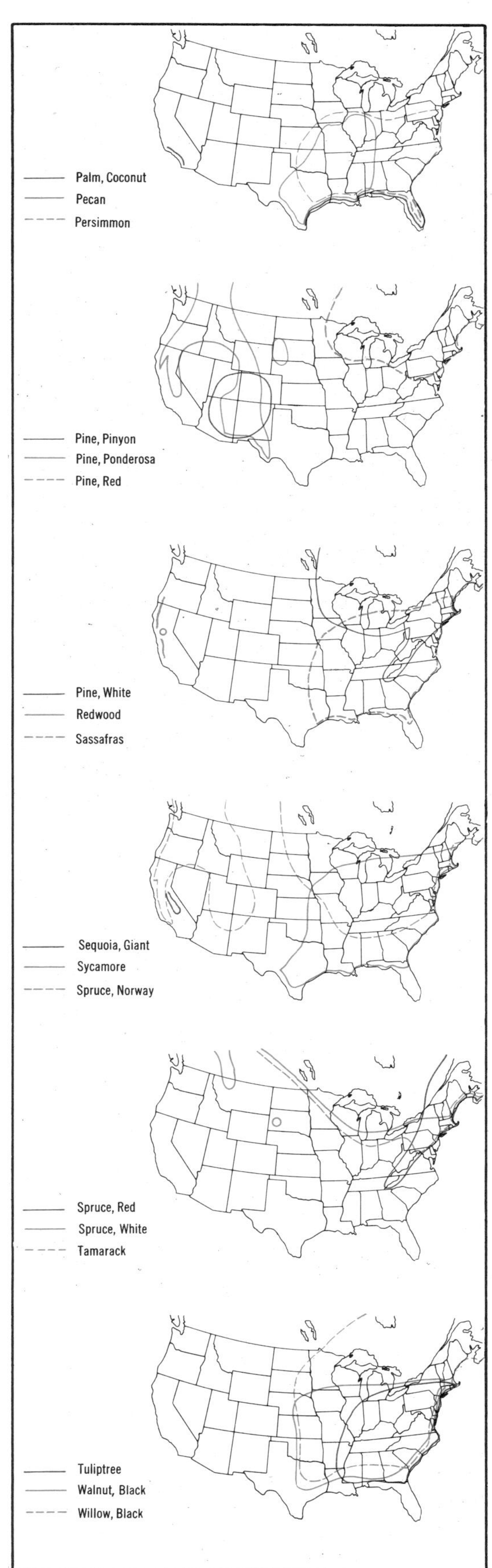

are in Canada, from Labrador to Yukon Territory. *Locust, Honey* — as this tree has been planted extensively, the natural range shown here is only approximate. *Oak, Black* — absent from the immediate seashore on the south Atlantic and Gulf Coasts. *Oak, Northern Red* — in Tennessee and Kentucky it occurs only in the mountainous parts. *Palm, Coco* — introduced from the Tropics. *Pecan* — planted far beyond its natural range. *Persimmon* — absent from higher Appalachians. *Sycamore* — absent from higher Appalachians. *Spruce, Norway* — introduced from Europe. *Spruce, Red* — above 3,500 feet in Pennsylvania, Virginia and West Virginia, and above 4,500 feet in Tennessee and North Carolina. *Spruce, White* — its range extends to the timberline from Labrador to Alaska. *Tamarack* — its main stands are in Canada from Labrador to Yukon Territory.

◄ WHITE PINE

A Part of American History — Early explorers of the eastern wilderness discovered that much of southern Canada, New England, New York and Pennsylvania was covered with white pine, not to speak of the vast stands toward and beyond the Great Lakes. These forests became a most valuable source of masts, as some of the trees reached a height of 240 feet, and when the British crown claimed the tallest specimens for its navy, and the "royal arrows" appeared on the straightest trunks, such an interference was greatly resented. The superior qualities of white pine — it is light and strong, the least resinous of all eastern pine woods, warps less than other timber, and is easily worked — soon were recognized in the world markets, and it was sold in the West Indies and Europe, Africa and Indonesia. At home it built the frame houses which seemed so typically American to the European immigrants who for the most part knew only stone and brick structures. The picturesque figures of the lumberjack and the lumber baron which had originated in the white pineries, combined forces to cut down the virgin woods, and in the early 1900's few accessible stands were left. Since then the third growth has been reaching maturity, and the beautiful tree with its distinct "layers" of branches is regaining a place in timber production. Among its enemies are white pine blister rust and white pine weevil which destroys the "leaders." *Pinus strobus.*

RED PINE ►

Landmark of the Sandy Plains — As the reward of an inconspicuous life is survival, the red pine has done better than its handsomer and more famous sister, the white pine which was tragically decimated. Its name is derived from its reddish-brown bark whose ridge-like plates seem to glow deeply in the rays of the setting sun. Frequently it is called Norway pine, a name based on a misapprehension of the early explorers. Its straight, clean trunk usually reaches a height of 80 feet, with a diameter of two to three feet, although some occasional giants grow to be 135 feet tall. It does not get very old, rarely living to an age of 300 years and usually beginning to grow old after 200 years. Its thick bark, rich in tannin, is fairly fire-resistant, and after a forest blaze the tree is able to reproduce with redoubled vigor. Its heartwood is slightly red and close-grained, its sapwood light yellow; it has greater weight and strength than white pine. Red pine masts were bought extensively by the British Navy, and in the days of the sailing vessels the heartwood of red pine was often ordered as ship's flooring. It is serviceable for all construction purposes. The tree's range covers an area from Newfoundland to Minnesota, to West Virginia and Pennsylvania. Its finest stands are encountered on the gravelly ridges of the eastern states and on the plains around the Great Lakes. *Pinus resinosa.*

PONDEROSA PINE ►

Ridge Runner — Ponderous — that was the first impression David Douglas received of this tree when he saw it on the Spokane River in Washington in 1826; on his suggestion it was christened ponderosa pine. Lewis and Clark had first mentioned its existence in 1804, on their journey along the upper Missouri. Ponderosa pine, strongly represented on all of our western ranges, turned out to be one of our important timber trees. In the southwestern states it thrives on elevations up to 12,000 feet, and in the vast forests of the Colorado plateau, 5,000 to 10,000 feet above sea level, it comprises over ¾ of the trees represented. The tallest specimens reach a height of 225 feet, with a diameter of 8 feet. They attain an age of 400 to 500 years. In the older trees the scaly bark is brown and has an orange-yellow tinge, from which the tree's commercial designation of western yellow pine is derived. In the younger trees the bark is nearly black — which explains the name blackjack pine. Its needles, 5 to 10 inches long, grow in clusters of 2 or 3. The brown cones, about 5 inches long, turn down when they mature; the scales open and the seeds, with wings an inch long are carried away by the wind as far as 500 or 800 feet. The strong, hard and light wood is primarily used as construction material. *Pinus ponderosa.*

◄ PINYON PINE

In the Tradition of the Southwest — While the great forests of the East were still unknown to white man, the pinyon pine, in our Southwest, was described, named, and used by the early Spanish explorers. Cabeza de Vaca, particularly, was attracted by the tree and christened it in 1536. As this small and rather scraggy pine usually grows only to a height of about 18 feet, it was not the size that called his attention, but the tree's reddish brown, mottled nuts which were a staple diet of the Indians; the nuts were a Godsend to explorers and early settlers; they are considered a delicacy to this day. Their development begins with the purplish flowers growing at the ends of the twigs; small cones start to grow, and in the fall of the second year they mature; shaped like eggs, they measure an inch or two; as many as two dozen nuts may be gathered from the scales in the center of the brown cone. As much as 6 to 9 bushels have been harvested from a single pine, and over 250 pounds of seed from a grove of an acre. As the nuts lose their flavor easily and spoil, it is the practice to bake them shortly after the harvest. A typical southwesterner, the pinyon pine is encountered more frequently in poor and stony soils than in rich ground. It can stand elevations of over 8,000 feet, an annual rainfall less than 14 inches, temperature extremes from over 100° to below zero. *Pinus edulis.*

◄ RED SPRUCE

Paddles and Fiddles — If the imaginative southern mountaineers speak of the she-balsam and he-balsam, they mean, according to Peattie, the balsam fir whose swollen blisters of resin supposedly look like milk-filled breasts, and the red spruce, the frequent companion of the fir on the eastern mountain ranges. On certain northern peaks it rises to about 70 feet on the lower slopes, and recedes to shrub height higher up. In the warmer South, however, many a high peak or ridge is covered by the beautiful, symmetrical pyramids of the red spruce which provide the mountain with a dark green cap over the light green wreath of its foliage trees below. In fact it occurs rarely in the southern mountains below about 4,000 feet. The name of the spruce is derived from its red cones. The dark, four-sided, shiny needles, about half an inch in length, grow incurved from all sides of the branches. When crushed, they give off a spicy fragrance. The tree's resinous juice is enjoyed as chewing gum by the children of the mountain folk. The light, strong and soft wood is excellent for canoe paddles and ladder rails; it also makes good paper and is much in demand as pulpwood. This latter use is almost too humble for a timber that is so resonant and uniform, in its finest growth, that it produces our best sounding boards for violins, guitars and mandolins. *Picea rubens.*

WHITE SPRUCE ►

Pulp and Polecat — This is a Canadian tree: It grows from Newfoundland to the Yukon Territory. In the Rockies of western Canada it is an outstanding forest tree, and its beautiful bluish-green conical crowns may reach a height of 150 feet, with a diameter as great as 4 feet. In eastern Canada the trees, growing 50 to 70 feet high, form dense cathedral-like woods, reminiscent of the Black Forest. The splendor of this majestic stand of pine creates a dramatic backdrop for one of America's most beautiful landscapes. Its range reaches south into U.S. territory in Montana, the Great Lakes region, New York and New England; in Alaska its groves almost touch the Arctic Sea. The wood is straight-grained and yellowish; although it is widely used for construction and interior finish, by far its most important role is played in the pulp industry. Enormous tracts in Canada are cut in a system of rotation, and it is hoped that white spruce will serve our newspapers without interruption for decades to come. The four-sided needles are short, measuring ¾ of an inch or less; they grow from all sides of the twigs curving toward the top. The oblong-cylindrical cones, about 2″ long, consist of shiny, light-brown scales. When the needles are crushed they expose the only unpleasant feature of the tree: They smell like a polecat. Skunk spruce is the name resulting from this shortcoming. *Picea glauca.*

NORWAY SPRUCE ►

A Naturalized American — A native of Europe where it is the common spruce, not only in Norway but also all over Sweden, Central Europe and Russia, it was introduced to America at an early time and adapted itself so readily to a variety of conditions that it is now found in all states except those of the southern tier. It is also wide-spread in Canada. Its uses are manifold: As an ornamental tree grown in the open it presents a lovely, symmetrical dark-green cone 50 to 60 feet tall, with a straight trunk surrounded by whorls of usually pendulous branches; exceptional specimens may grow to a height of 150 feet. It is sometimes planted as a Christmas tree, although in a warm room it sheds its needles earlier than a fir. It is giving excellent protection to midwestern farms in the form of windbreaks and shelters. Its soft, straight-grained wood is easily worked and used in the construction industry although the timber's contact with the soil should be avoided. Finally, it is a good raw material for paper pulp, and widely planted for that purpose. Its shiny, four-sided needles, 3/4 of an inch long or less, surround the branch but are directed upward and forward. Like all spruces, it matures its cones in a single year; they are light-brown and 5 to 7 inches long. The winged seeds are freed late in winter or in spring. *Picea excelsa.*

◄ TAMARACK

A Conifer that Sheds its Needles — This northern tree, which is also called American or eastern larch, has a double face: One is graceful and friendly, the other somber and forbidding. It is beautiful in spring when its yellow flowers are succeeded by its delicate, lace-like needles, and in the fall when its leaves turn yellow just before they are shed. The needles are solitary, or 12 to 20 of them form a cluster of soft bristles; averaging an inch in length, the needles are keeled below, rounded above. They are light green but so thin that the northern sun shines right through them to the ground. Those who have seen it in spring in the highest north near the Arctic Sea where the midnight sun shines on the most northerly groves, have found it enchanting. On the other hand, it will often look melancholy in winter: Standing in some dismal swamp, its needles gone, its rusty bark having a scorched appearance, its blackish cones of former years still clinging to the branches, one might imagine he sees a grove of dead trees killed by some catastrophe. The tree ranges from the middle-Atlantic and Great Lakes States northward to Labrador and the Yukon Territory, and appears also in Alaska. It is 50 to 60 feet tall on the average, with a characteristic arrangement of branches: the upper ones are more or less ascending, the middle ones horizontal, and the lower ones point downward. *Larix laricina.*

◄ EASTERN HEMLOCK

Slow and Brittle — This is a tree of the ages. It is of ancient lineage: its needles, cones and timber have been found in America's early geological strata. It grows slowly, enters maturity in about the middle of its life span, most trees living to a ripe old age of more than 500 years. It is not a pathfinder but will take root only in a soil moist with humus where other trees have already formed a roof providing shade. It produces a great many seeds: Its small, reddish-brown cones cover the tree from the nodding top to the lowest branches, and its seeds (with transparent wings) are so tiny that as many as several hundred thousand go into a pound. Yet only the smallest fraction will reach maturity: those which are protected from direct light while young, and those which find the right slope, or moving water, or rocks for the roots to embrace. The ones that survive will slowly but surely outgrow their neighbors and raise their crowns 70, perhaps 100 feet high. Woodsmen in New England and the Appalachians, the Great Lakes region and southern Canada have often used the reddish bark to heal wounds and burns. The tannin in the bark is the curative element, a chemical which also has been and still is in great demand by the leather tanning industry. In fact, hemlock bark has probably been more valuable than hemlock wood which is usable but coarse-grained, brittle and not resistant to the elements. *Tsuga canadensis.*

BALSAM FIR ►

The Christmas Tree — When, not so many generations ago, the western world decided to celebrate the birth of Christ by decorating and lighting Christmas trees, the balsam fir had all the qualifications to perform the new task graciously: It is one of the straightest and most regular of all conifers; its bluish-green needles do not shed for weeks in the warmth of the house, and they spread the balsam fragrance of the northwoods. While some conservationists bemoan the fact that so many thousands of young trees are cut before they reach maturity, others point out that scientific thinning improves the groves. Besides, balsam firs can be grown commercially for the Christmas trade, and for that purpose land is often used on which crops could not be raised. The numerous resin blotches under the thin bark furnish a transparent substance called Canada balsam which is of great importance in mounting biological material on microscopic slides. In a burning forest, however, these concentrations of resin turn the tree into a crackling firebrand. The balsam fir ranges from Newfoundland to the Canadian Northwest and occurs as far south as the Appalachians of Virginia. In our northeast its average height is from 30 to 60 feet, with 90 as a maximum. Its narrow needles are approximately an inch long, with blunt ends, and show a shiny blue-green on the upper side. The soft, coarse-grained wood is used for pulp, excelsior, crating. *Abies balsamea.*

DOUGLAS FIR ►

Tall Timber of the Rockies — When in the 1820's the Scotchman, David Douglas, rediscovered this tree — it had been reported 30 years earlier by Dr. Archibald Menzies — all he had in mind was to send seeds home and introduce to England the tree which bore his name. Since then Douglas fir has been growing satisfactorily in the British Isles, but it can be really appreciated only in its natural range, the western mountain chains of the U.S. and Canada. There it stands out as one of our most majestic trees, its oldest and tallest specimens rivaling the redwoods with heights of 300 feet and trunk diameters up to 17 feet. The age of the largest trees is estimated as ranging from 500 to 1,000 years. When the tree's characteristics were explored to determine its scientific name, the puzzled botanists found a great resemblance to not less than 4 different groups: the hemlocks, yews, spruces and firs. So they gave it a Latin name meaning "a pseudo-hemlock with leaves of yew". The pointed needles, ½ to 1½ inches long, make the branches appear thick and full by growing all around them. The pendulous, oval cones, 2 to 4½ inches long and maturing in the first fall, spread their winged seeds widely and usually are the first ones to occupy forest areas ravaged by fire. The wood is, though comparatively light, one of the strongest in America, and an important building material. *Pseudotsuga taxifolia.*

◄ GIANT SEQUOIA

King of the Conifers — Some of the same sequoias now standing in the Sierras were nodding their lofty boughs in Biblical days. And after seventy more generations of man they will, most probably, still flourish in cool California summers and mountain winters that bring six feet of snow and zero temperatures. The sequoias and the redwoods are, since the glacial period, the only American survivors of an ancient race that spread as far north as the Arctic Zone. The sequoias grow in California in about 70 groves of from 4 or 5 to over 1000 trees. They are native to the western slopes of the Sierra Nevada and spread over an area 260 miles long, at elevations from 4,500 to 8,500 feet. These giants may attain a height of 300 feet, with a diameter of 30 feet above the stump-swell. Many of them are 2,000 years old; on one tree stump 3,400 annual growth rings have been recorded, and John Muir reported counting 4,000 rings on another. For how many centuries or millennia our present sequoias will go on living nobody knows; their chances seem excellent as they are almost indestructible. Their red-brown bark is up to 24 inches thick and has an outer layer of fibrous scales which do not catch fire easily. Fungus and insect enemies cannot destroy them either. There are no pitch tubes in the wood, as in pines, through which the pests can spread. Lightning is their principal foe. *Sequoiadendron giganteum.*

◄ REDWOOD

Pacific Sentinels — The tallest living tree in America grows on Dyerville Flat, California. It measures 364 feet and is a redwood. Much of this continent was covered with redwoods before the ice age descended from the north. Today less than a million and a half acres are left, and the fact that these trees commonly yield 100,000 board feet of saw timber per acre, is a serious temptation to cut down the stands. Fortunately some of the finest redwoods are preserved in the Muir Woods National Monument and in various state parks so that these ancient Americans seem safe from extinction. They are the tallest trees, but they are neither as big nor as old as their cousins the giant sequoias. It is believed that a 300-foot redwood with a 20-foot diameter represents an age of 2,000 years. Most commercially cut specimens are 200 to 275 feet high and 400 to 800 years old. Their range is a narrow strip of land along the coasts of California and southern Oregon where the tree receives its breath of life: the fogs of the Pacific ocean. In the old trees the brown bark with the greyish hue is perhaps a foot thick, and no ordinary fire can penetrate it. Besides, the redwood is resistant to fungus diseases and quite immune to attacks by insects. Its flat, yellow-green needles point to opposite sides on lower limbs and saplings. The purplish-brown cones are only an inch long. *Sequoia sempervirens.*

BALD CYPRESS ►

"The Wood Eternal" — The heartwood of the bald cypress has been so called because of its extreme durability; even when exposed to the elements or in direct contact with the ground it seems to last forever. The timber, varying in color from light to very dark, emits a rancid odor and is easily worked. It is used in ships, water tanks, and general construction. Like the giant sequoia and the redwood the bald cypress is the remnant of an ancient race; it may be 1,000 years old, 170 feet tall and 15 feet across; specimens of 120 feet are fairly common in its last stand in our southeastern and Gulf States and along the Mississippi. Shallow roots creep far from its base which is often reinforced by buttresses; if the roots stand in water part of the time, they grow sharp cones called "knees" which rise above the surface of the mud, sometimes as high as 6 feet. They are hollow and thought to provide the roots with air. The bald cypress is a conifer but not an evergreen; in the autumn it loses its yellow-green, feathery needles which grow on the twigs in spirals. Before the needles fall they turn yellow or brown, and the immature twigs are shed with them. The round, purplish cones, about an inch in diameter, release the winged seeds. It is fairly immune to insect pests, and forest fires do not invade wet swamps. But during droughts great stands are often burned. *Taxodium distichum.*

ATLANTIC WHITE CEDAR ►

A Tree that is Mined — The gloomy darkness of a medieval church descends upon you when you enter the 900-acre cedar swamp in New Jersey's Green Bank State Forest. The spire-like trees, sometimes reaching a height of 70 or 80 feet, huddle together, and the branches are so densely laced that little sunlight invades the melancholy grandeur of this piece of untouched America. The tree is not a member of the genus Cedrus, and for that reason some scientists prefer the usage of "whitecedar" as one word. It occurs from Maine to Mississippi where there are freshwater swamps, streams and frequently flooded lands. Its fan-shaped boughs, covered with tiny, scale-like leaves, are bluish-green when young, turn reddish-brown when winter comes, and dark-brown when dying. The spherical cones, only ¼ of an inch in diameter, stand upright like candles on the leafy branches; in the fall they release the winged seeds which sprout readily in moist soil. The wood is light and of fine texture; like that of most swamp trees it is water-resistant, and has an aromatic fragrance; before new roofing materials came into use, cedar shingles were the most durable house protection available. Today most of the timber goes into boats, crates, siding, and telephone poles. Supplementing the original stands, large deposits of sound cedar trunks were discovered at the bottom of coastal swamps. *Chamaecyparis thyoides.*

◄ COCO PALM

In the Sway of the Trade Winds — Wherever the tropical seas throw up a sand bank and establish a new island, a botanical phenomenon may occur: Coconuts leisurely floating on the waves hit the land, roll into a favorite spot and germinate. They do not often get water-logged because of their leathery skin, and they sprout readily on the beach. In time the barren new land becomes a lovely grove of palms which offer to sailors and settlers their fronds for shelter, cool coconut milk as a drink and coconut meat as food. In that way the first stands of coco palms may have grown in Florida, although the fine specimens that now dot our subtropical coasts are introduced from the tropics for the sole purpose of lending a touch of more leisurely lands to our southernmost shores. So closely in harmony with the ocean are these trees that they will not spread far inland by themselves, although they grow there when planted. On our coasts they may not rise to a height of 100 feet as in the tropics; they may not bear fruit regularly except in southern Florida; they may not yield us "palm cabbage" or great quantities of copra; but with their rosettes of gracefully swaying leaves and white or yellow blossoms they have become a symbol of our semi-tropical resorts. The timber of the cylindrical trunk, called "porcupine wood" is used for construction purposes and in cabinet making. *Cocos nucifera.*

◄ BUTTERNUT

Dyes and Altars — This is the poor relative of the famous black walnut. The tree has usually a short trunk and a low crown; its sweeping branches are broken by wind and ice; its leaves fall early and its nuts litter the ground; the kernels are good eating but turn rancid fast; it is short-lived and usually dies when it reaches an age of 75. Yet, with all these shortcomings the butternut tree is an integral part of the American scene and of American folk life in the Northeast, the southern mountains and the Central States. Its fresh bark and the rind of its nuts contain a yellow-brown dye which for generations has been applied by the mountain folks to their homespun cloth, and from the nuts the Indians obtained a ceremonial oil. The soft, light, coarse-grained wood can be highly polished, and as it neither warps nor cracks, it is a favorite for cabinet work and for the interior finish of fine homes and boats. Peattie made the interesting discovery that many altars in our churches are carved of butternut wood. The tree averages 30 to 50 feet in height and measures 2 or occasionally 3 feet in diameter. Its alternate, compound leaves consist of 11 to 17 leaflets; the yellow-green, drooping catkins bear the pollen while the inconspicuous flowers grow into pear-shaped, greenish, hairy fruits; within the pulp an oblong nut with sharply notched ridges contains the oily kernel. *Juglans cinerea.*

BLACK WALNUT ►

"Jupiter's Acorn" — The gaunt rail splitters — that's how we like to imagine the pioneer youths — found so many gigantic walnut trees in the virgin forest that they put them to lowly use, transforming them, for instance, into fences of the snake-rail type. Those ax-men would marvel at the modern industrial processes which today carve thousands upon thousands of square feet of veneer out of a single big walnut tree, now quite a rare specimen. The grain of the veneer shows delicate and often fascinating patterns whose artistic effect is heightened by skillful matching. Standing singly or in small groves, the trees with their straight trunks and deeply furrowed black-brown bark frequently reach a height of 100 feet, with a breast-high diameter of three feet, while their crowns spread into lofty cupolas. The black walnuts are ripe in September and October; they are highly appreciated as they preserve their spicily delicious flavor in cooking, baking, or in ice-cream. Enjoying a centuries-old fame in Europe, the Latin name of the genus is a tribute to its role in western civilization. "Juglans" is a contraction of "Jovis glans," meaning "Jupiter's Acorn." The range area of the black walnut follows the Atlantic coast from Massachusetts to North Carolina, then continues along a fairly straight line to the northern Gulf States, eastern Texas, and north to Nebraska and southern Ontario. *Juglans nigra.*

PECAN ►

The Candy Tree — The oldest living trees in Mount Vernon are said to be pecans, planted by George Washington in 1786 from nuts sent him as a gift by Thomas Jefferson. They were then called "Illinois nuts", and were a symbol of the magnificent and distant west that lay beyond the mountains. In New Orleans pecan nuts were already a staple confection at that time. This great tree attracted attention with its commanding height of 90 or 100 feet (the greatest recorded height, according to Collingwood and Brush, is 170 feet), and with its massive trunk and its crown of huge spreading limbs. The leaves consist of 9 to 17 toothed leaflets which are dark green above, pale green beneath. The dark brown nuts grow in clusters of 3 to 11 and are freed when the thin husks open into 4 sections. Poineer tales relate how in the days when our forests were considered inexhaustible, old giants were often cut down for a single year's harvest; boys had the job of climbing all over the fallen trees and gathering the nuts. On the other hand, planting started early, and in 1846 a slave-gardener in Louisiana proved that, as with orchard trees, the finest pecans were grown by grafting good varieties on wild stock. Since that time pecan groves have been planted far beyond the tree's original range of Alabama, the Mississippi Valley and Texas; Georgia is the principal pecan producer today. *Carya pecan.*

◄ SHAGBARK HICKORY

The Homely Tree — Why was General Jackson called "Old Hickory"? The word hickory implied toughness and resilience, excellent qualities for an American president. There are a great many other thought associations with hickory, all pleasant: It makes us think of roaring bonfires and the unique flavor of hickory-smoked hams; not so long ago cracking parties, at which the shelling of hickory nuts alternated with kissing games for the young people, took their rightful place besides quilting and husking bees. The very appearance of the tree has, in accordance with its name, a homely, shaggy, backwoods appearance: Thick plates of grey-brown bark, sometimes a foot long, are attached to the trunk in the middle but turn one or both loose ends outward. To this day the tree is a common and welcome sight in most of the eastern half of the U.S. It occurs rarely in pure stands; the finest specimens are encountered mixed with oaks and other deciduous trees in the Mississippi river bottoms and the Cumberland region; there they reach a height of 120 feet. The compound leaves consist of 5 or 7 leaflets, and the fruits ripen with the October frosts; then each husk splits and releases a thin-shelled nut with a kernel of exquisite taste. The wood is not only one of the toughest and strongest available, but also one of the most elastic. It is still irreplaceable for ax handles, and the best for athletic equipment. *Carya ovata.*

◄ QUAKING ASPEN

A Tree with a Task — This is America's liveliest tree. Its small, egg-shaped leaves tremble almost incessantly, touching our ears with a high, soft rustle and our eyes with the flashing of myriads of little reflectors catching the sun. For generations the quaking aspen was despised as worthless: It dies before it reaches an age of 80; it is susceptible to fungus diseases, and heart rot kills many trees before they are 50; it rarely grows beyond a height of 40 or 50 feet; and its wood is soft and undistinguished. Yet it is a tree with a mission: Where valuable forest stands are destroyed, either by the ax or by fire, it usually becomes the conserving element. Easily adapted to all sorts of surroundings, from sea level to an elevation of 10,000 feet, spreading from Labrador to Alaska, and climbing the Appalachians, the Rockies and the Sierras, it moves in on scarred surfaces with millions of saplings; prevents soil erosion; and provides the shade in which more valuable forest trees will grow later on. The old-time lumberjacks had only contempt for popple, as they called it; yet while their conifers are transformed into common newspaper pulp, the despised aspen today produces fine magazine paper. In the fall the tree is a thing of beauty: Its straight, greenish to yellowish brown trunk is topped with a golden-yellow crown that glows in the autumn sun after the leaves of other trees have fallen. *Populus tremuloides.*

EASTERN COTTONWOOD ►

Shelter of the Plains — This member of the poplars grows so fast that it is said to reach a height of 100 feet in 15 years, under especially favorable conditions. As it is anchored by a shallow but widespread system of roots, it withstands gales, blizzards and droughts, and is an ideal shelter tree in the prairies west of the Mississippi. Growing 4 to 5 feet a year under regular circumstances, it ought to be an excellent shade tree for city streets, but what is an admirable trait in the prairies is a nuisance in town: Its tiny rootlets search for water so diligently that they clog the drain pipes; besides, the spreading roots like to heave the sidewalk. In most sections of the East, except on the mountains and in the neighborhood of the ocean, cottonwood trees grow to 80 or 100 feet and rarely more; their glossy, leathery, toothed leaves have somewhat the shape of a triangle and give off a pleasant fragrance of balsam when crushed. Male and female flowers are borne on separate trees, and in May the tiny seeds, attached to fluffy white down, are blown by the wind over great stretches. But in order to take root they must find an exposed spot of mineral soil within a few hours; after that they lose their productive power. The wood is soft, weak, porous, and warps in seasoning. Therefore it is used largely for pulp, excelsior, crating and fuel. *Populus deltoides.*

Trees

BLACK WILLOW ►

Mirrored in Rivers — To see the black willow in all its glory you have to go to our slow-flowing great rivers. There it leans over the water, rising from a bulky root system to a height of 60 or 70 feet. Its trunk is forked a few times and almost black, and its bark covered with narrow cracks. How did it get there? Perhaps a willow twig drifted down the river, was embedded in the mud and began to sprout; for as everybody knows, a willow tree may grow whenever a branch is placed in the ground. The great black willows with their sweeping branches are not only a picturesque ornament above the lazy waters, they are useful dam builders and, in emergencies, may prevent the break-through of a flood and save homes, cattle and human lives. Wherever embankments have to be reinforced for flood control, the strong roots of the willow trees will help, and where the levees are threatened by the rushing waters, "mattresses" woven of willow branches and weighted with stones will hold the crumbling sides. Black willows occur in moist settings in southern Canada and in many regions in the East and South of the U.S. Their thin, light-green leaves are 3 to 6 inches long; the male and female blossoms grow on different trees as catkins with yellowish scales. The wood is light and weak, but usable for wickerwork furniture because of its flexibility. *Salix nigra.*

◄ PAPER BIRCH

A Tree of Clear, Cool Waters — Slender, white-stemmed birches, dark-green spruces and the blue waters of a lake — this blend means New England to us, or Canada. It also means an American tradition, and a grand American invention: The canoe, built of birch bark and sewed with the long, tough roots of the tamarack, shooting over the waters as swiftly as hardly any other boat made by man anywhere, and carrying ten times its own weight. There are other ways in which the birch is intertwined with the life of the forest: Birch bark makes the moose-calling horn for the hunter, and birch twigs are winter food for moose and deer. The beaver loves birch almost as dearly as aspen. Best of all: There are more paper birches in America now than there were at the time of white man's arrival, for each fall its catkins are packed with numerous tiny, single-seeded winged fruits that love the mineral soil of burned-over land. The paper birch, so called because of its chalky-white outer bark that peels in thin, paper-like layers, graces our East from Labrador to Manitoba, and from New Jersey to Iowa. Growing in a variety of soils, it prefers rich, moist, and rocky ground and grows to a height of 60 to 70 feet. The wood is hard and quite tough, and used for specialties like snow shoes, clothespins, tooth picks and spools, also for wood pulp. *Betula papyrifera.*

◄ AMERICAN BEECH

Deep Roots in Soil and Story — Since times immemorial men have carved words and symbols into the smooth, grey bark of the beech tree. It bears not only the hearts and arrows of lovers; when hunters and scouts performed a daring exploit, they too sometimes recorded it on a nearby beech. Many consider it the most beautiful tree; to walk through a beech grove on a summer day is indeed a joy to remember: The ground, free of underbrush, is soft with leaves; the silvery trunks rise like pillars; and the crowns form a continuous, sun-touched roof. A slow-growing hardwood, it may reach the mature age of 300 to 400 years. Beechnuts develop in short-stalked burs which ripen in early fall; two or three triangular nuts, brown, highly polished and fair to eat, are packed in downy lining. The reddish-brown wood, though hard to split, is used in woodenware, handles, and furniture; because of its clean smell it is a favorite material for barrels. Beeches range along the Atlantic all over the eastern half of the continent, the northern line extending from Canada's New Brunswick to central Wisconsin, the southern line from eastern Texas to northern Florida. They thrive in the alluvial soils of the Ohio and Mississippi Valleys and on the western slopes of the Appalachian Mountains where they may attain a diameter of four and a height of 120 feet. Because of their thin bark, forest fires take a heavy toll. *Fagus grandifolia.*

AMERICAN CHESTNUT ►

A Fight for Survival — There are three stages in this drama: Up to the beginning of our century millions of these glorious trees flourished in our eastern, southern and Midwestern forests, parks and gardens, raising their huge crowns 80 or even 100 feet high, growing their trunks to a 10-foot diameter, and spreading their limbs to give deep, cool shade. In spring the great chestnut stands were seas of snowy white blossoms, and in the fall their sweet nuts stuffed our Thanksgiving birds. The second stage began in 1904 in New York zoological garden; there the blight was first discovered, probably introduced on Chinese chestnuts. It spread to Pennsylvania, Illinois, everywhere, and as the spores of the disease were carried by the wind from state to state, the burning of the sick trees did not stop the blight. Ghastly grey tree skeletons dotted the woods. The lumbermen rushed in to cut whatever chestnuts were left because the trees were doomed anyhow. Not even the new saplings developed immunity; they lived for a time and died. The third stage is marked by intensive research; for years it was dishearteningly unsuccessful, but lately definite progress has been made in developing blight-resistant hybrids, and there are encouraging reports of healthy young groves in Wisconsin, and several western states. In the days of our grandchildren the American chestnut may again be as common as it is beautiful. *Castanea dentata.*

NORTHERN RED OAK ►

Fastest-Growing Oak — Lumberjacks divide the oaks into white oaks and red oaks; so do the scientists because the botanical distinguishing marks confirm the judgment of the lumbermen who base their distinction largely on the color of the wood. Nature has allotted about half of the stands to each group, favoring the red oaks a little. Commercially the white oak timber is considered more valuable, and the cutting of red oak began only when the former became less accessible, for the red oak wood is lighter, more difficult to season, and more porous. Nevertheless, it is close-grained, strong lumber used in the building industry for posts, poles, railroad ties and inexpensive furniture. Ranging from Nova Scotia to Minnesota, and south to Arkansas and the Appalachian regions, the northern red oak grows to a height of 70 to 90 feet; in the southern mountains some 150-foot specimens with 6-foot diameters are reported. The leaves, their unequal lobes tipped with bristles, turn red in the fall and help to glorify the American autumn. They hang on to their branches far into the winter months. In May or June, male and female flowers grow on the same tree but on different limbs; inconspicuous pistillate blossoms are fertilized by wind-borne pollen from male catkins and develop into reddish-brown acorns about an inch long, in the fall of the second season. *Quercus borealis.*

◄ BLACK OAK

The Tanner's and Dyer's Tree — To say that the black oak is one of the red oaks sounds strange, but that is the common classification; when cut, it is usually sold as red oak. The name is derived from the tree's bark which is almost black. It is a familiar sight in the forests of the east (extending into southern Maine and Ontario), the Midwest (as far as eastern Nebraska and Kansas), and the South (except Florida), and comprises about 15% of all oak stands. Not so long ago the outer bark was used by leather tanners because of its high tannin content; the orange inner bark made a good dye, called "quercitron", for home-spun clothes, and the wood is considered good fuel; it is also in demand for construction work and furniture making. While there are considerable upland stands of black oak in rich soils, the tree is abundant in the poorer ground of the slopes, or high up on the ridges, and it grows long tap roots which reach the water. It attains a height of 80 to 100 feet, although in the lower Ohio valley 150-foot specimens are recorded. The leaves are bristle-tipped and their indentations are deep. The acorns ripen in the fall of the second season; they are ½ to ¾ of an inch long and sit in deep cups. A serious enemy is the oak blight which has been spreading through the Midwest in the last few years. *Quercus velutina.*

LIVE OAK

Evergreen Aristocrat — There is something awe-inspiring about the huge, old live oaks of our South Atlantic Coast and the Gulf States. Their gnarled, thick limbs spread 60 or 70 feet in all directions until their ends touch the ground, and when you step under the tree, you seem to enter a great, green cathedral. Although the foliage itself is not as beautiful as some trees, the garlands of Spanish moss which generally hang from its boughs give it a fairyland grace and beauty. Avenues of these oaks give to some southern plantation houses a grandeur that is never attained by northern mansions. However, tradition links the live oak not only with the drowsy cotton fields but also with the sea, the pursuit of pirates, the clipper ship. Before the coming of iron ships, wood of the live oak was indispensible to shipbuilding. Natural "knees" — plates connecting girders to the side of the ship — were made from the angle formed by the joint of the heavy routes to the trunk. The live oak is so called because it is evergreen; its egg-shaped leaves are shiny above, downy below, with their margins rolled under, and stay on the tree for about 13 months, until new leaves are formed. The chestnut-brown acorns, about an inch long and held by scaly cups on rather long stalks are sweet and an excellent food for pigs. *Quercus virginiana.*

WHITE OAK

King of the Eastern Forest — When white man arrived in America, the white oak bade him a friendly welcome. The Pilgrims saw it growing on the shores of New England, recognized it as a close relative of the English oak, and had visions of sturdy cabins and oaken ships. The early settlers on the streams and rivers of Chesapeake Bay found many beautiful specimens there, some of which are still standing; these trees have lived through all of American history. When the pioneers crossed the mountains they encountered, on the western slopes of the Alleghenies and in the lower Ohio valley, white oak giants over 100 feet tall, 8 feet in diameter and perhaps 750 years old. Aside from these spectacular patriarchs, the regular specimen of 60 to 70 feet height is an outstanding American tree on almost every count: It is beautiful; when grown in the open, it develops side branches up to 50 feet long, creating an airy, green summer house for its owner. The pale grey bark, which is responsible for the name white oak, is attractive; and the acorns, developed in one season, are sweet and in great demand with squirrels and birds; with the tannin removed, the acorns were eaten by Indians and pioneers. The light-brown wood weighs nearly twice as much as that of white pine; it is strong, adaptable, and serves almost any purpose. *Quercus alba.*

Trees

AMERICAN ELM ►

Designed like a Fountain — This tree plays an intriguing role: It is a symbol of public life in America. Indian tribes used elms as council trees. Under elms white men and red men smoked the peace pipe and concluded their deals. The names of Penn and Daniel Boone were connected with various "treaty elms" and "justice trees". Some of these reminders of the past are still alive. Elms shade court houses, town halls and village greens all over New England. Elms played their part in the lives of Washington and Lincoln. They have the affection of the American people to this day; their fountain-like crowns shelter thousands of farms, they form gothic arches over our city streets, and permeate our eastern forests. Although their natural range is the American East (excepting the mountain ranges) they are now planted in the West also, with equal success. The elm's silhouette is unmistakable: At a height of 10 to 20 feet the main trunk divides into several limbs which rise fairly straight to a height of 50 or 60 feet, then suddenly branch out into a round cupola; elms 100 feet tall are not unusual. The bark is greyish and cracked into scaly ridges. The leaves have double teeth and sharp points, and the flat, single-seeded fruits germinate readily. The wood is hard, tough, and cross-grained, therefore difficult to split. The dreaded Dutch elm disease is making destructive inroads into most stands. *Ulmus americana.*

◄ SOUTHERN MAGNOLIA

Art in Nature — "The most splendid ornamental tree in the American forests", — that is the verdict of Charles Sprague Sargent, a foremost tree scientist. Its beauty is threefold: The velvety white flowers which stud the tree from April to June are a glorious sight; they are large (6 to 8 inches across), and as they sit singly at the ends of small branches, they stand out strikingly on the dark-green, lustrous foliage. The petals look as if they are molded of wax, and the spots of purple that show at their base, create a colorful center. The second asset is the magnolia's highly decorative foliage. The oval leaves with smooth edges have a glossy, leathery sheen above and a rusty-brown coat of down beneath; they are 5 to 8 inches long. Beloved as Christmas decorations, branches are shipped north every year for the holiday season. Finally, the tree itself is impressive: Up to 40 feet from the ground the trunk may be clear of branches; the limbs, sometimes spreading but more often pointing straight upward, give the crown a compact, characteristic silhouette. Trees 60 to 80 feet tall and aged 90 to 120 years are not uncommon; Baton Rouge is the heart of the magnolia country, and Louisiana's sky-scraper capitol looks down on numerous magnificent specimens. Magnolia wood has a straight-grained, uniform texture and is adapted to some specific purposes; for instance, it is used for slats of venetian blinds. *Magnolia grandiflora.*

TULIP TREE

Soft Hardwood — Like the other members of the Magnolia Family, the tulip tree is of very ancient descent; as the examination of fossils shows, it is one of the oldest broad-leafed trees in the world. Commercially it is sold as yellow poplar, although it has no relationship whatever with the poplar family; but as "tulipwood" is a trade term for an imported timber, the lowly commercial name will not be changed. In the Tennessee mountains the expression canoe-wood is heard, and indeed numerous fine canoes have been hollowed out of the broad and straight trunks whose wood is so easy to work. Nominally a hardwood, it is softer than most softwoods in the U.S. and can easily be milled; it is used in huge quantities for crating and boxing. As it is also very light, it is employed effectively as an insulation material, and turned into high-quality paper for books. The inner bark is bitter, and a heart stimulant is derived from it. With this abundant usefulness it is also a majestic tree of the eastern states which, in the sheltered valleys of the Appalachians, attains a height of almost 200 feet with a 10-foot diameter and a 100-foot stretch free of branches. The local expression "saddle-leaves" describes the form of the sharply cut, glossy leaves, and the tulip-like flowers, orange at the base and greenish-yellow on top, are its crowning glory; they stand erect on the branchlets. *Liriodendron tulipifera.*

SASSAFRAS

The Tonic Tree — Sassafras was a magic word during the first 100 years of the New World, for the oil obtained from the roots and bark of this American tree was considered a miraculous cure-all in Europe, a medicine which the Indians supposedly used with incredible effectiveness. Early in the 17th century the price of sassafras bark in London had risen to fantastic heights, and in Bristol a company of "adventurers" was founded to exploit America's sassafras resources. The boom did not last, of course, yet for almost three more centuries sassafras tea was the acknowledged spring tonic in rural America. Poor folks in the deep South were said to build their floors and beds of sassafras wood to keep the bedbugs out. To this day the oil is employed in flavoring medicines and perfuming soaps; the Creole cuisine uses it as a spice. A shrub or small tree in New England, it grows to 40 or even 80 feet in the South. It is easily recognized by its unsymmetrical crown and upward-spreading, gnarled and twisted branches. Its fragrant, yellow-green leaves appear in three forms; some are lance-shaped, others look like a mitten with a "thumb" lobe, and still others are three-lobed. Country children like to chew the leaves or aromatic twigs. The inconspicuous flowers develop into dark-blue fruits that resemble berries. The wood is soft and brittle but durable in contact with water and the soil. *Sassafras albidum.*

SYCAMORE

The Mark of Good Soil — John James Audubon describes how he once came upon a huge old hollow sycamore. Putting his ear to the trunk he heard a rumbling noise, and then saw the cause: Thousands of swallows circled overhead, and in groups of 3 or 4 darted into the hole. The next morning before daybreak he stood again at his listening post; all was quiet, then suddenly the roar started again. It sounded like a big, revolving water wheel, and the very trunk seemed to rock. Then he saw the swallows pour out of the sycamore's crown in a black stream, soaring into the dusk for about 30 minutes. The tree stood near Louisville, Kentucky, in the heart of the sycamore country; in Audubon's days the Ohio River was lined with huge specimens. The old giants are gone now, but among American hardwoods it is still one with most massive proportions, growing in the eastern and southern states to heights of 60 to 120 feet. As the trunk expands patches of grey bark flake off to expose smooth green new bark beneath giving the tree a mottled look; also characteristic is its fruit cluster, a dense ball dangling from a slender stem all winter; it releases its one-seeded fruits in spring. These round buttons have given the sycamore the familiar name "buttonwood". The leaves have three to five pointed lobes, frequently with a few teeth. Sycamore wood cannot be split and makes an ideal butcher's block. *Platanus occidentalis.*

HONEY LOCUST

Tree in Bristling Armor — "Honey and locusts" were the food on which St. John subsisted in the wilderness, according to the Bible. Peattie explains that the term locusts was applied to the rattling pods of the carob plant, also called St. John's bread. So it happened that an American tree which could also boast of large, rattling, sweet pods, received the Biblical name locust. The flat, twisted, brown pods (which indicate the tree's membership of the Pea Family) grow a foot or more long, ripen in the fall and cling on to the branches until winter. Because of the juicy pulp inside, they are a favorite food of cows and deer, rabbits and certain birds; these animals pick them up from the ground, eat them and spread the seeds from pasture to pasture and grove to grove. While generous, the tree does not want to be annoyed, and keeps man and beast away with an armor of thorns; trunk and branches bristle with them and, as they are needle-sharp, up to a foot long, and grown from the innerwood, they fulfil their task well; squirrels never climb a honey locust. It is an eastern inland tree, forming groves in the open country or islands in the hardwood forest. A medium-sized tree, its average height is 75 feet. The leaves consist of gracefully curved stems with 18 to 28 dark-green leaflets. The wood is coarse and decay-resistant in contact with the soil. *Gleditsia triacanthos.*

◄ AMERICAN HOLLY

Christmas Songs and Piano Keys — In the case of the holly the foliage is better-known than the tree, and it is an almost overwhelming Christmas-like experience to come upon a grove of southern holly trees and see the lustrous, dark-green crowns with their clusters of red berries rise to a height of 70 feet. In the middle states holly may become 30 or 40 feet tall, and in Massachusetts, its northernmost limit, it usually remains a shrub. The evergreen leaves are leathery, shiny green above and lighter below; staying on the branches 3 years until replaced by new ones in spring. Male and female blossoms normally appear on separate trees, and the inconspicuous white flowers, scattered among the new growth, ripen into the familiar clusters of red, berry-like fruits. Birds eat them with relish but digest only the pulp; the seeds are thus distributed widely. The wood of the American holly tree is not marketed to any great extent, but it is sought for several special purposes. Because of its whiteness and fine grain it resembles ivory more closely than any other American wood; it also takes on dyes readily and may be highly polished — qualities which make it ideally suited for white and black piano, organ and accordian keys, for unusual patterns of inlaid furniture, and for wood engraving. The ilex tree which yields the famous Paraguay tea of South America, is a relative of the American holly. *Ilex opaca.*

SUGAR MAPLE ►

Spring Sweetness, Fall Glory — Although there are sugar maples in every eastern and Midwestern state, they thrive best and have their closest human relations in New England. And although they are fine trees at any time of the year, they are the shining glory of the eastern forest in the fall when clear yellow and bright orange glisten through the deep crimson. Together with corn husks, pumpkins and apple cider, maple foliage is the symbol of our autumn. In certain sections of the country, notably in Vermont and New York, Ohio and Michigan, the sugar maples come into their own again in February when the sap begins to flow. The picturesque ancient paraphernalia are gone, the ox team and the row of kettles over the roaring open fire, the biggest pan taking the sap and the smallest yielding the syrup. Today some groves are so modern, the sap runs in pipes from the maples into the central receptacle. But "sugaring off" is as popular as ever. Figures on yields vary greatly; 2 to 3 pounds of sugar or ½ to ¾ of a gallon of syrup is the approximate average production per tree. The sugar, hard, or rock maple, as it is called, grows to heights of 70 to 120 feet; its five-lobed leaves and winged fruits are familiar to all, and the excellent wood is lighter and stronger than white oak. Bird's eye maple is valued for furniture because of its grain pattern. *Acer saccharum.*

HORSE CHESTNUT ►

A World Favorite — Southern Asia is the natural habitat of this tree. It was brought to Europe in early times, and introduced in the U.S. and Canada 200 years ago. Its wood is not outstanding in any way, and its chestnuts are too bitter to be eaten. Yet it is welcome and has been planted in every state and province, for it grows rapidly so that it can be enjoyed by the planter, not only by his grandchildren; and it pleases the eye: It rises to imposing heights in a symmetrical form, its branches and twigs curving upward at the ends. Its big leaves consist of a number of leaflets growing fan-fashion from a stout stalk — the scar of the leafstem resembles the imprint of a horses hoof, hence the name horse chestnut. The blossoms open in June when the tree has its green foliage; standing erect, like huge candles, they cover the whole crown with their beautiful white flower clusters, each 6 to 12 inches high. The 5 white petals of every blossom are dotted with yellow and purple; the curved yellow stamens reach out far beyond the petals, and give the clusters an elaborate, embroidered appearance. The fruits are spiny capsules enclosing one to three large brown nuts which are inedible. The brown-black bark used to be a raw material for tannin and a yellow dye. The wood is white and soft and employed in woodenware and artificial limbs. *Aesculus hippocastanum.*

◄ AMERICAN BASSWOOD (LINDEN)

The Fragrance of Summer — Thoreau remarked in his journal that there were only a few basswood trees in Concord, but there was no way of ignoring them at blossom time; far away the humming of bees could be heard — it seemed to envelop the crowns — and far away the strong, sweet fragrance could be smelled. When, in June, the white or cream-colored flowers appear and send out their waves of perfume, the bees seem indeed to ignore the other plants and flock to the basswoods. The honey is whitish and of superior quality, and every 2 or 3 years there is a particularly heavy honey flow. The grey fruits that develop from the blossoms have the shape and size of a pea and hang from a stalk singly or in bunches. The tree occurs in the eastern and Midwestern states, and grows most vigorously in the central lowlands; its height ranges from 70 to 90 feet, with a reported maximum of 140 feet; it reaches maturity at an age of 90 to 140 years. There used to be pure groves of basswoods, but today they are encountered only in association with other hardwoods. The dark-grey outer bark is deeply furrowed and has typical horizontal cracks; the inner bark contains long and tough fibers of which the Indians used to make very usable ropes. The wood is prized for its white color and lightness, and is employed in woodenware and boxes, toys, cooperage and paper pulp. *Tilia americana.*

SAGUARO CACTUS

Survival in the Desert — Trees that look like exclamation marks 40 feet long, or like people wildly gesticulating or sternly folding their arms over their chests, are found in one of America's strangest forests, in southern Arizona east of Tucson. They are the plants of the giant or Saguaro cactus. Growing in a desert wilderness, they seem to have only one aim: conservation of water. As there are no obvious leaves, the evaporation surface is small, and the thick growth of spines shades the outer skin and keeps away animals in search of moisture. The stem consists of a skeleton of vertical ribs numbering 12 to 30; they support a body of spongy tissues. This is, so to say, the storage plant, while the wide-spread roots are ready to receive huge quantities of water. During a torrential rain a mature plant may take in as much as a ton of water. As it uses this moisture during the following weeks, it shrinks and develops wrinkles and pleats. After another rain, it puffs up again proudly. The oldest specimens have an age of approximately 200 years, and the tallest reach a maximum height of 50 feet. In April the fluted columns are crowned with splendid creamy-white blossoms; they mature into edible fruits which split open in midsummer and show their bright red pulp with shiny black seeds. The Saguaro cactus occurs in California, Mexico and southern Arizona whose state flower it is. *Carnegiea gigantea.*

FLOWERING DOGWOOD

White Stars and Shuttles — This small tree with the humble name is famous on two counts: One is the beauty of its white or, rarely, pink blossoms which appear just before the leaves come out. The flowers proper are inconspicuous, and what we usually admire as the four, waxy petals is really a foursome of bracts, i.e. leaves. Lovely in themselves, they grow like an artistic flower exhibit in the best of taste: They present themselves on graceful sprays, in receding layers, low enough to be admired by all. The small scarlet fruits with a single seed are almost as handsome. Dogwood's second claim to fame lies on the practical side: The world's textile industry depends on its hard, smooth, close-textured, shock-resistant wood for the weaving shuttles it needs. There is no other material that fills the qualifications as ideally as dogwood: It does not wear the thread and becomes smoother in usage. Many small shops in the southern states manufacture these dogwood shuttles for the looms of the world, using about nine tenths of the annual cut. The remaining tenth goes into such specialties as golf club heads and mallets, wedges and jewelers' blocks. The dogwood tree grows to a height of about 40 feet; it is encountered in a variety of soils, frequently as the "understory" in an open forest, or at the edge of the woods. It occurs in the East, Midwest and South, the largest stands in Arkansas. *Cornus florida.*

PERSIMMON ►

American Ebony — "Diospyros," the scientific name of this familiar tree, means "food for the gods." Such a flattering term is correct if the fruit is eaten ripe. Otherwise its astringent tannin will pucker mouth and tongue. Green at first, the persimmon gradually takes on a yellow-orange color; at that well-known stage it appears on our fruit stands. When it hangs on the tree long enough, its skin becomes purplish and its pulp mushy; in that condition it is said to be sweetest. The fruit's food value is high, second only to that of the date. Wild persimmons vary in size, and often they load the branches in great numbers. In some southern localities trees bear fruit successively from August through fall and winter to March, and generously supply food to birds, deer, the hogs, and other wild life. Early settlers roasted the seeds for coffee, a practice supposedly renewed in the South during the blockade of the Civil War. The tree grows to a height of 50 feet, reaching 100 or more feet under favorable conditions; often, however, it develops as a large shrub in thickets on abandoned land. As it belongs to the ebony family, the wood of the older specimens is almost black; it is also close-grained and tough and serves in the same way as dogwood. The range extends from southern Connecticut to Iowa and southward to the Gulf States. *Diospyros virginiana.*

◄ WHITE ASH

With a Part in the Story of Mankind — Wotan's spear with which he ruled the world was made of ash. Egypt's ancient chariots were built of ash. Baseball bats are made of white ash. So are hockey sticks and polo mallets. Wherever strength and lightness must be combined with elasticity, white ash is the wood to be used. Found in various soils, the tree prefers fertile ground on north and east exposures; it grows in small groups among other hardwoods, or with pine or spruce, and it is a favorite in the woodlots of farms, for when old ashes are felled the young sprouts rise rapidly out of the existing root system. The tree averages 70 to 80 feet in height, and the very straight trunk is often free of branches for half of its length. The broadly rounded crown seems to have particularly thick foliage on the outside, while you can see right through to the tree top when standing by the trunk: There is no better place to observe bird life. The compound leaves consist of 5 to 9 pointed leaflets. The inconspicuous flowers develop into pendant clusters of brown fruits which are shaped like paddles, 1 to 2 inches long. Old white ashes develop big horizontal limbs, strong and sweeping, like beams holding up the green dome, and such an ash, according to Germanic mythology, is the world; the gods live in the crown, the gnomes among the roots, the people in between. *Fraxinus americana.*

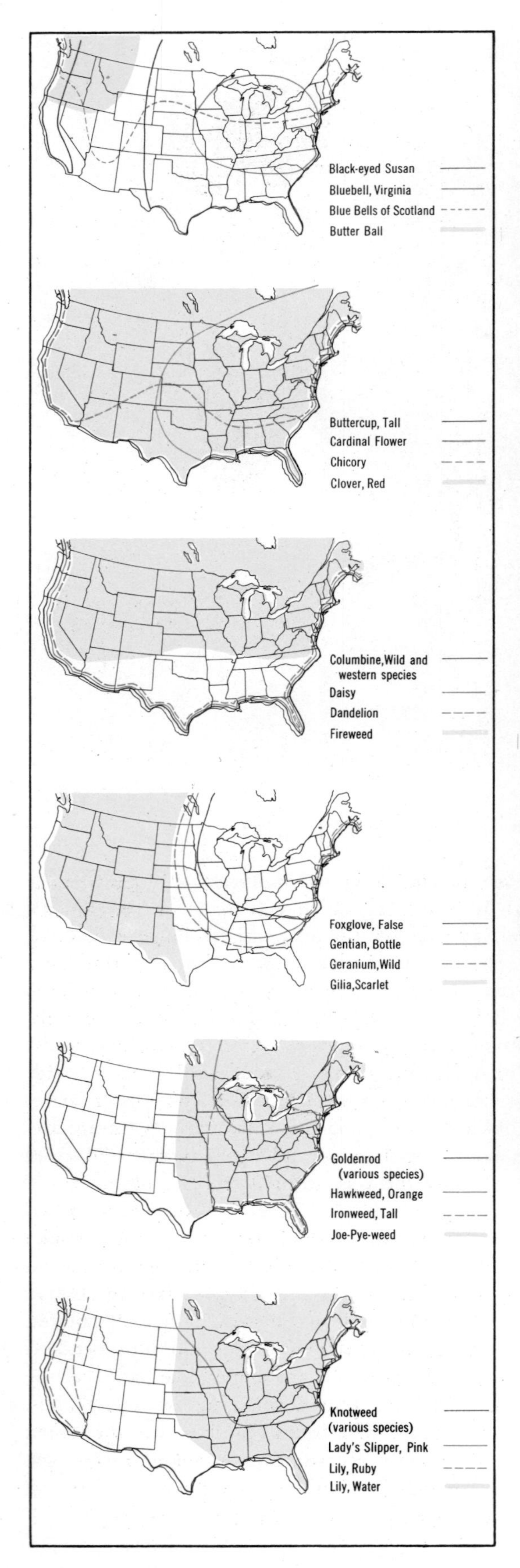

WILDFLOWERS IN THE U.S. AND SOUTHERN CANADA

So many foreign visitors are impressed by our skyscrapers and assembly lines that it is refreshing to find at least one who thinks America remarkable because of her wildflowers. "The flora of America is incredibly rich," writes Sigrid Undset, the Norwegian Nobel Prize winner, and glowingly describes her impressions of our wildflowers; how she loved the yellow jasmine in Florida and Alabama in early spring; the sunflowers along the railroad tracks of Wyoming; the purple wild asters with myriads of small blossoms spreading everywhere; and the black-eyed susans she wanted to transplant to Norway. We salute Miss Undset.

The following pages describe and illustrate those wildflowers which are most frequently encountered in the U.S. and southern Canada, or are of general

Wildflowers

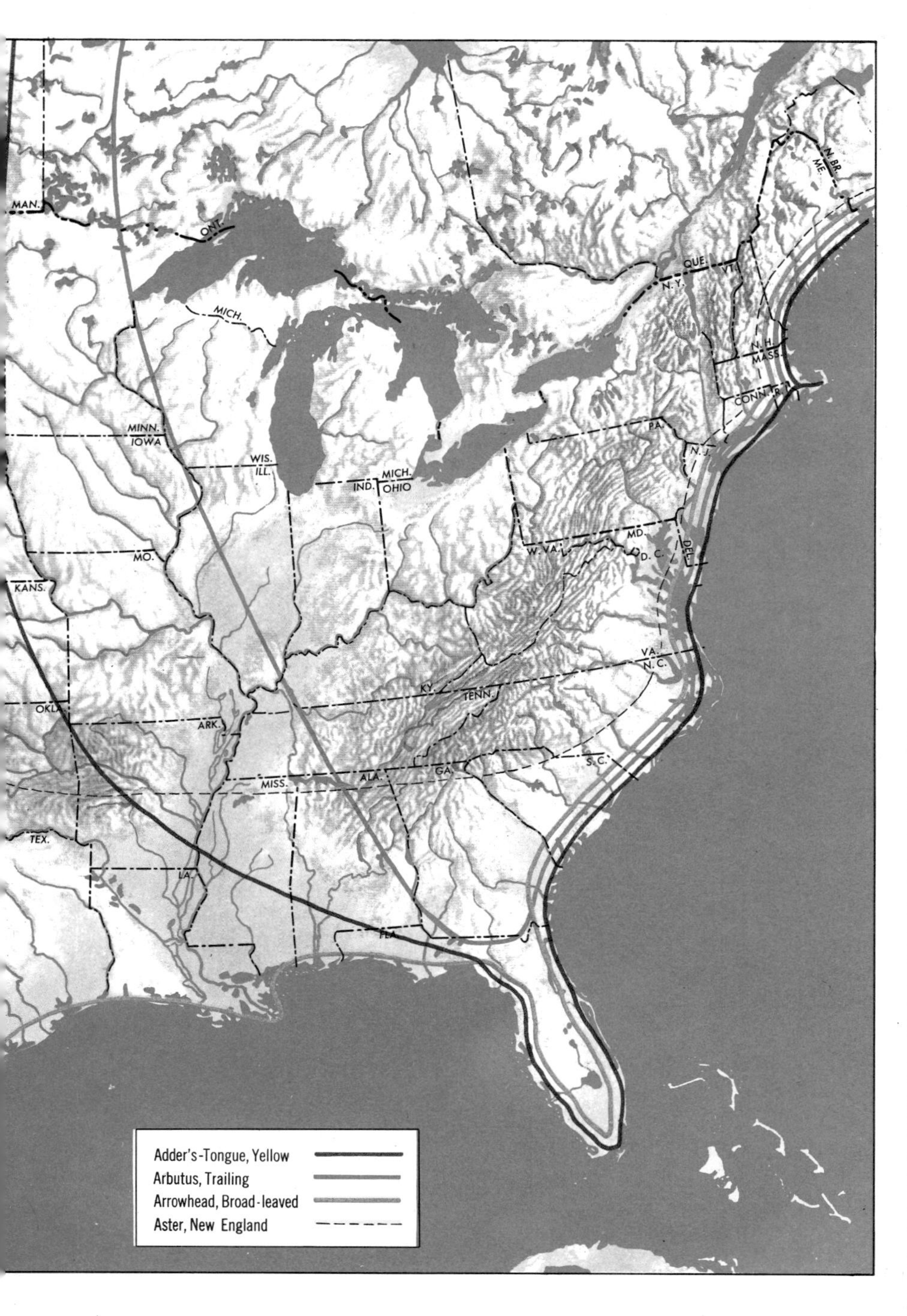

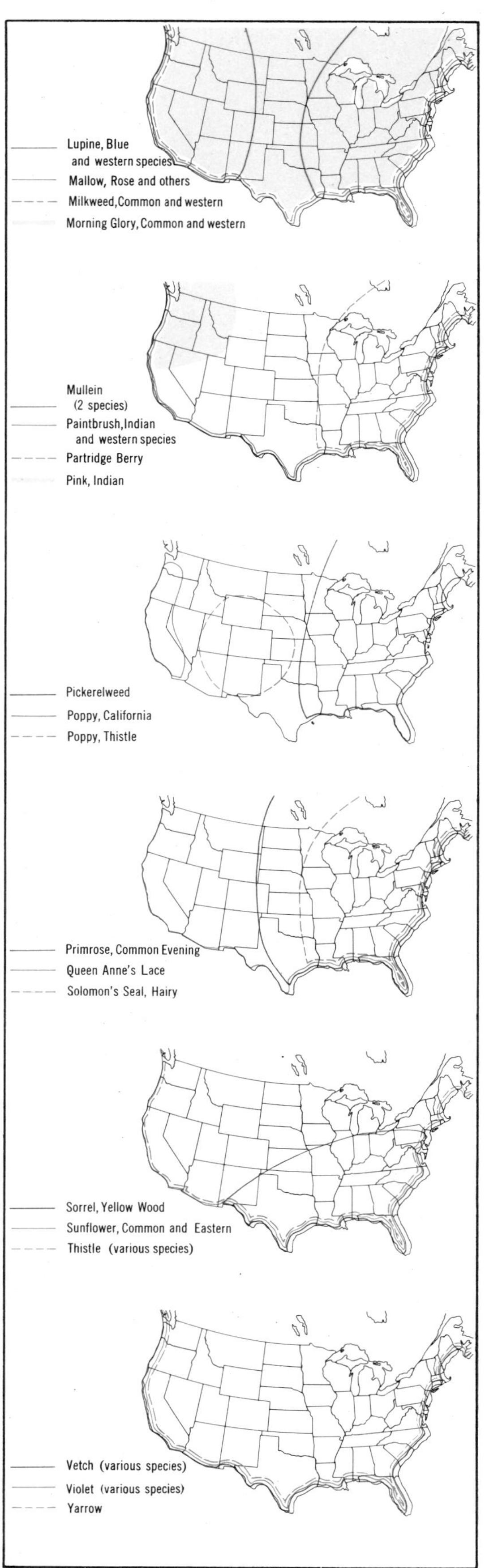

interest for other reasons. The distribution of these wildflowers is outlined in alphabetical order on the range maps on this page. The borderlines must be considered more or less fluid as seeds spread and flowers are transplanted. A key to the principal families will be found on page 215.

The following notes refer to the maps. *Columbine, Wild* — most species occur in the Rocky Mountains. *Foxglove* — the range refers to the fern-leaved false foxglove. *Geranium, Wild* — numerous related species occur in the West. *Hawkweed, Orange* — other species occur in the western states. *Lady's Slipper, Pink* — while in the U.S. its range is limited to the North and Central East, it reaches as far north as the Great Slave Lake in Canada; numerous other members of the Orchid Family occur throughout the continent. *Morning Glories* — they are particularly abundant in the South.

◄ BROAD-LEAVED ARROWHEAD

Handsome and Useful — Indians used to roast and eat the tubers of the arrowhead's fibrous roots which they found in the soft mud. Following the natives' example, the early settlers considered these rootstocks a welcome addition to their diet. They called them swan potatoes and swamp potatoes, duck potatoes and tule potatoes, and wapatoes. The ducks love to eat them to this day. Thus the arrowhead combines utility and beauty. Its graceful spire of three-petaled, white flowers rises one to two feet above the bouquet of leaves which are arrow-shaped, glossy-green and molded with prominent veins. Sometimes the leaf-form of the arrow is absent and a modified stem acts as a leaf blade. The plant juices are milky. It is easily cultivated in garden pools but, as it spreads rapidly by underground stems, it may prove domineering and undesirable. On the edges of ponds and streams and the margins of swamps, the broad-leaved arrowhead is encountered throughout North America with the exception of the far Canadian north. It is more frequent in the East than in the West and blooms from July to September. About 40 species of arrowheads are recorded on the continent, both in the Temperate Zone and in the Tropics. They are also called sagittaria, derived from the Latin word sagitta, meaning arrow, although the leaves of several species are sword-shaped, like those of the iris. They belong to the Water Plantain Family. *Sagittaria latifolia.*

PICKERELWEED ►

Blue Spikes on Blue Ponds — An unsuspecting fish swimming by a bed of pickerelweed may soon breathe its last, for a fierce pickerel may shoot out, from under the ambush of thick leaves, and devour its prey. Both the pickerel and the pickerelweed love swampy ponds and sluggish streams, and the plant forms extensive stands there. It grows 1 to 3, or even 4 feet high, has thick root-stocks which creep along in the mud, and glossy, heart-shaped leaves, with rounded bases, which grow to a length of 10 inches. The rich blue flowers are in a spike, with a green spathe below; sometimes its hues are lighter; it blooms from June to October. The range of the pickerelweed extends from Nova Scotia to Minnesota in the west, and to Texas and Florida in the South. Ducks eat its seeds, and the plant is a handsome and desirable addition to water gardens and lily pools. Dogtongue is another name for it, and the Indians called it wampee. It belongs to the Pickerelweed Family which boasts of another famous member — the water hyacinth. This plant is well-known throughout the South for its massive floats of purple, turquoise and sapphire-blue blossoms which cover numerous acres and are a gorgeous sight. But frequently they clog up lakes, bayous and canals, and are an annoying obstacle to the navigation of our inland waterways, particularly in Florida. Latin name of the pickerelweed: *Pontederia cordata.*

SOLOMON'S SEAL ►

Stamped on the Rootstock — Out of the horizontally creeping roostocks the aerial stem arises; in the fall it withers again and leaves a scar which has some resemblance to a seal pressed in wax; nature lore asserts that King Solomon has given the plant his stamp of approval. There may be quite a few such seals, over the years, on one rootstock. Of the three species, the hairy Solomon's seal has pale-green, bell-shaped flowers which hang beneath the alternate leaves, two by two. Th plant attains a height from 1 to 3 feet, grows in moderately acid soil in forests where it prefers wooded slopes and thickets; it blossoms from April to July. Its plump, globular berries are of blue-black color, and its name is derived from the hairy underside of its leaves. It occurs from New Brunswick to Ontario in the north, as far as Kansas in the west, and as far south as Florida and Texas. Smooth Solomon's seal is a larger plant, growing to a height of 2 to 8 feet and blossoming in clusters which contain 2 to 8 flowers; its range extends from New Hampshire to South Carolina to Oklahoma. There are also several species of false Solomon's seal; their leaves are similar to those of the true Solomon's seal but their flowers are starry and form terminal clusters. All these plants belong to the large Lily Family which comprises more than 2,000 species. The Latin name of the hairy Solomon's seal which is illustrated here, is *Polygonatum pubescens*.

◄ ADDER'S-TONGUE

The Dog-Tooth Violet — There is a movement under way to discredit the ancient names of adder's-tongue and dog-tooth violet as inept, and to supplant them with the terms fawn lily or trout lily. Some of the latest books recognize only this last name. Whether American nature lore is gaining by such a move is doubtful. Trout lily is certainly a prettier word but adder's-tongue, with its naive touch of superstition, has a greater charm and appeal to our imagination. There are three species of these delightful small plants that grow 5 to 10 inches high on flats and slopes in the eastern forest, especially where the stands of trees are thin. One has a nodding, yellow blossom, a single flower of six parts, and occurs from the Nova Scotia-Ontario-Minnesota line in the north, to Kansas in the west, and Florida and Arkansas in the south. The white species grows as far north as Albany, N. Y., and southern Ontario, and streches south to Georgia, Tennessee and Texas. Both the yellow and the white adder's-tongue have decoratively mottled leaves; the pattern is more pronounced in the yellow variety. The third species, called midland adder's-tongue, is pale lavender and inhabits the heart of the continent: Nebraska, Kansas, Iowa and Missouri; its leaves are not mottled. All bloom in spring, from April or May to June; western species are called avalanche lilies. Yellow species: *Erythronium americanum*.

◄ RUBY LILY

"Consider the Lilies of the Field" — For thousands of years the beauty of the lilies has excited man's imagination; ancient legends, fairy tales and religious stories use them as symbols of splendor. They are as widespread in the Old as in the New World, and the most fragrant of them all is an American westerner, the ruby lily of the Pacific Coast Ranges. It is as sweet and spicy to smell as it is magnificent to see. The plant may be 6 or 7 feet tall, and it is topped by clusters of, perhaps, 20 flowers; the highest are pure white buds; with them are the freshly opened blossoms which are dotted with purple; the older flowers that grow on the lower stalks have taken on a pink hue; and at the bottom, a few of the earliest calices fade into ruby and purple. Their leaves, with undulating margins, radiate from the stems and form decorative whorls. The setting which this superb flower-piece chooses is often as striking as the lily itself; the fragrant display may stand under an age-old, sky-high redwood tree, or under a huge live-oak whose thick branches stretch out like the beams of a hall. Ruby lilies also bloom among the chaparral, i.e. a thicket of shrubs or dwarf trees. In accordance with its background preferences, the flower is also called redwood lily or chaparral lily. Its period of bloom extends from June to August. *Lilium rubescens.*

PINK LADY'S SLIPPER ►

Orchid of the Cooler Ranges — A whole list of imaginative names has been invented for this lovely orchid; besides pink lady's slipper, it is called camel's foot, old goose, Noah's ark, whip-poor-will's shoe, moccasin flower. The several allusions to foot, shoe, slipper and moccasin refer to the round, inflated sac of the blossom called the lip; this modified petal is used for nectar secretion and insect pollination, while the two others are long and narrow. In the large, slightly fragrant flower of the pink lady's slipper the sac-like petal is conspicuous, and the lip has a "closed fissure" down the front. The plant has two leaves at the base, rises from fleshy roots, and attains a height of 6 to 15 inches; it grows in woods and bogs, preferably in a soil which is rich in humus and strongly acid; it blooms in May and June. Its range extends from Newfoundland to Manitoba and south along the Appalachians to North Carolina and Tennessee. Other famous American orchids are the showy lady's slipper whose front petal is tinted with crimson-magenta hues, and the widely distributed yellow lady's slipper. Most orchids are hard to cultivate; they do not grow easily from their minute seeds, develop slowly, are difficult to transplant and are attacked by mice, fungi, and other pests and parasites. With nearly 20,000 species, the orchids probably form the largest plant family. *Cypripedium acaule.*

KNOTWEEDS ►

Bonanza for Seed-Eaters — Game and water birds search in wasteplaces and along damp roadsides, in marshes and in moist meadows for one of their food favorites: the large, dark-colored choice seeds of the knotweeds. Numerous species are in this group, all of them spreading weeds which grow to a height of 1 to 4 feet. There is, for instance, the species called heart's ease, a spiraling annual plant with dense spikes of flowers in bright, rosy-pink shades; the leaves are lanceolate and quite shiny. Moist soil is the favorite habitat of this weed that can be seen almost anywhere from the Nova Scotia-Ontario-Minnesota line in the north to the Florida-Texas line in the south. Another common species, whose leaves show a dark triangle across the center, is called heartweed; it ranges throughout the continent except in the far Canadian north. The aquatic version is known as water persicaria or lady's thumb; it spreads over much of North America from Quebec to Kentucky and to Colorado and California in the west; its floating or submerged stems grow to a length of 4 to 20 feet; ducks are fond of its seeds. Most knotweeds bloom throughout the summer, the heart's ease from July to September. A number of climbing plants are close relatives, such as smartweed, climbing buckwheat and tearthumb, which will tear your thumb when you pull it. *Genus Polygonum.*

◄ BUTTER BALLS

Bright Spots on the Western Plains — "Wooly knees" is the meaning of the Greek word Erigonum, the name of the genus of annual or perennial herbs to which this flower belongs; the allusion is to the stems of the plants which are both woolly and jointed like knees. There are more than 200 species in the group and most of them are westerners. The butter balls flourish in the Northwestern States and western Canada, and the bright-yellow sulphur flowers, a close relative, range from New Mexico and Wyoming to California. Butter balls have white or yellow flowers; their spheres, about 1½ inches in diameter, sit on top of thin stems which may be 4 to 12 inches tall. The small leaves surround the base of the plant; the new ones are almost white with down. The butter balls and most other erigonums select dry places as their habitat and prefer the high plateaus of the West. Many are actually desert plants; in one species the stem is enlarged and it is often called desert trumpet. There are also other varieties with blossoms of pink and orange-red shades. All carry their small, perfect flowers in dense clusters or heads. They belong to the Buckwheat Family whose approximately 800 species are widely distributed throughout the U.S. and Canada. Some relatives of the butter balls are important food plants, others have been developed into ornamental garden flowers; many are just weeds, some are shrubs. *Genus erigonum orthocaulon.*

◄ INDIAN PINK

Delicate All-Americans — Yerba del Indio is the Spanish name of this lovely western plant; for the Indians made a medicine of its downy leaves, and to this day the leaves are used for pharmaceutical purposes. Its flowers are red, not pink, but they seem to be "pinked" as by scissors, since their five petals have sharp indentations and deep clefts. The blossom grows to more than an inch in diameter; the lanceolate leaves measure 1½ to 4 inches in length. A two-foot-long tap root sends up the downy stems which are semi-erect and have branches; they grow to a height of approximately 15 inches. It is a flower of the open mountain woods, brightly dotting the sloping hillsides and rocky highlands of the Northwestern States (including parts of California), during June, July and August. The best-known eastern representative of the Pink Family is the wild pink, a delicate, low perennial with pink to crimson, wedge-shaped petals. It rises from 4 to 10 inches above the ground on sandy and often rocky soil. Its Latin name "pennsylvanica" indicates its habitat, although it occurs as far north as Maine and as far south as Georgia. Also well-known is the fire pink or catchfly whose scarlet flowers, with deeply-cleft petals, look like stars; throughout the summer they enliven dry woods and slopes from Ontario to Georgia, and westward to Minnesota, Missouri and Arkansas. Indian pink: *Silene californica.*

WATER-LILY ►

Chalice of Fragrance — The mysteriously dark and blackish surface of a mud-bottom pond is an effective background for the magnificently pure blossoms of the water-lily. Frosty white and sometimes pink, they float majestically between their bright-green leaves. With handsomely clean surfaces and contours the leaves also contrast sharply with the dark and sluggish water out of whose slime they arise. They are thick, often egg-shaped, deeply indented at the base, with a blade of 5 to 12 inches in diameter. The blossoms which measure 3 to 6 inches in diameter, open in the early hours of the morning and are closed again in the late afternoon; various species bloom from June to September in ponds, lakes and slow streams from Newfoundland to Manitoba, as far west as Kansas and as far south as Florida and Louisiana. Another famous member of the Water-Lily Family is the American lotus, also known as great yellow water-lily, water chinkapin, or duck acorn; its thick stems, 3 to 7 feet long, arise from horizontally creeping, starchy tubers which were considered good food by the Indians and early settlers; its acorn-shaped seeds are also edible. The long stalks lift the round leaves — some of them measuring 2 feet across — high out of the water. Though overpicked, it occurs locally from New England to Minnesota in the west and Louisiana in the south. All the members of the relatively small family are aquatic. Water-lily: *Castalia odorata.*

WILD COLUMBINE ►

Enchantment Among the Rocks — The dove and the eagle, symbols of gentleness and of strength, figure in the names of this lovely group of flowers: the Latin "columba," meaning dove, in columbine, and the Latin "aquila," eagle, in their scientific name aquilegia. The latter association is more easily explained. Each of the 5 flower petals tapers off into a long, slender, slightly curving, nectar-containing spur which looks like an eagle's talon. In various parts of the country the columbine is represented in different colors: The eastern species combines the colors of red and yellow, an abundant variety of the Rocky Mountains is blue, and honored as the state flower of Colorado; there is also an all-yellow species, and a white columbine in the Northwest. As it is an easy wildflower to cultivate, it is grown and enjoyed in thousands of gardens. Its general popularity is attested to by a proposal to name it the national flower of the United States, and by the many affectionate local terms in use: meeting house, capon's tail, lady's shoe, cock's foot, jack-in-trousers. The blossoms of the wild or eastern columbine hang at the ends of slender stems which are branching and grow to a height of 1 to 2 feet. An underground rootstock sends up new shoots every year. The olive-green leaves are formed in three clean-cut lobes. It blooms from April to July in stony woodlands from Nova Scotia to Alaska, and south to Texas and Florida. *Aquilegia canadensis.*

◄ TALL BUTTERCUP

A Handsome and Deceptive Weed — In the first century after Christ, Pliny the Elder examined a common plant with yellow blossoms and, as he found it in wet places frequented by frogs, he called it "ranunculus," little frog. That is the plant's scientific name to this day. Of the approximately 40 species, growing in the U.S. and Canada, many still prefer moist meadows and roadsides, and some are even submerged aquatic plants. The tall or meadow buttercup has bright yellow flowers whose 5 overlapping petals look as shiny as if they had just been waxed. Its branched stalks are hairy and hollow and from 2 to 3 feet tall, and their sharply indented leaves have 3 to 7 parts. While several buttercups are native, some of the more conspicuous ones have been introduced from Europe, among them the tall variety which by now has spread over most of the U.S. and southern Canada. But it is not considered a blessing; it is not only an annoying weed, but also produces acrid juices which are quite poisonous. In spring, cattle nibble its young leaves and have their mouths and intestines inflamed. Sometimes even death results. Another generally accepted name for the buttercup is crowfoot, a term which has been adopted for the whole family; it includes about 1,100 species of perennial and annual herbs in the Arctic, Temperate and Tropical Zones; of the buttercups proper, there are about 275 species spread over the globe. *Ranunculus acris.*

◄ CALIFORNIA POPPY

Symbol of the Western Spring — When the Spanish rancheros galloped across their valleys and found their spring meadows carpeted with innumerable acres of "copas de oro," cups of gold, they were enchanted. When the Americans took possession of the coastal lands, they too loved this brilliant blossom, called it California poppy, and made it their state flower. The move was logical, for it is a truly California plant which does not grow anywhere else, except for limited stands in neighboring states. The blossom is open only during the day; it measures 2 to 3 inches in diameter, and sits on top of a blue-green stem which attains a height of 12 to 18 inches. The leaves are greatly dissected. Cultivated varieties are planted in countless gardens, and white, cream, and pink blossoms have been developed. The Poppy Family itself is quite large, and its approximately 115 members are widely distributed in the Northern Temperate Zone. All have cloudy, milky juice which is acrid or, in some cases, narcotic. An eastern and Midwestern representative of the family is the gold or celandine poppy which grows in the rich soil of open woods from Pennsylvania to Tennessee in the South and to Wisconsin in the West. Out of a thick underground stem, noted for its yellow sap, a leafy stalk with four-petaled, bright yellow flowers arises. The widely introduced European celandine is a similar plant. Scientific name of the California poppy: *Eschscholtzia californica.*

THISTLE POPPY ►

A Prickly Desert Dweller — The secondary names, Mexican poppy and milk thistle, well describe the characteristics of this plant. It is a flower of dry places in the arid Southwest, ranging throughout plains and slopes from Kansas westward to New Mexico, Wyoming and Utah. As is the case with much desert growth, its spiny-toothed leaves and its stalks are covered with sharp prickles and rigid hairs. This stout, leafy, thistle-like plant attains a height of 2 to 3 feet and at the top of the stalk bears a large blossom more than 3 inches in diameter; the 6 petals look ruffled, but the flower as a whole is attractive. Its yellow juice is bitter, like that of other poppies. There are about 6 species in this group of bushy desert dwellers; some are white, others are yellow, and at least a few, like Argemone mexicana (whose leaves are often mottled with white), are poisonous. Their pods contain seeds which are round, like miniature bird shot. Another western poppy that is also bushy is encountered in the Matilija Cañon and other valleys and canyons of California. It is called Matilija poppy after its home; a shrub 5 to 8 feet tall, it produces beautiful, fragrant white flowers 5 to 6 inches in diameter, with 6 petals; their filaments are yellow above and purple beneath; the whole is a large, handsome version of the thistle poppy blossoms. *Argemone hispida.*

BLUE LUPINE ►

A Misnamed Benefactor—"Wolf among the plants,"—that is the meaning of Lupine, derived from the Latin "lupus," wolf. According to our ancestors it consumes the nourishing elements in the soil and leaves them impoverished and barren. Of course, there could not have been a worse mistake; for far from being harmful, lupines improve the soil as they fix free nitrogen in the ground, and are cultivated to restore exhausted fields. Game birds love their smooth seeds, but on cattle the plants have a poisonous effect. There are over 100 native species, most of them thriving in the West, although the blue lupine is an eastern representative which ranges from the Maine-Ontario-Minnesota line southward to Florida and Louisiana. But just like most of its western cousins it likes dry soil of sand or gravel which may actually be sterile. The straight stem, firm and hairy, rises 10 to 18 inches out of a wide-spread root system, with a spectacular raceme of handsome flowers; the cluster is 6 to 10 inches long and the blossoms are purplish-blue, and sometimes pink or white. The star-like leaves consist of 7 to 9 leaflets which are slender at the base and broad on top. The blue bonnet, famous state flower of Texas, is a beautiful blue lupine in which the upper broad petal of the corolla is dotted with a yellow or white spot. A field of blossoming blue lupines and golden poppies is a sight to remember. *Lupinus perennis.*

◄ RED CLOVER

Everybody's Friend — When the better-known kinds of clover were introduced from Europe — our native varieties are quite inconspicuous — our bumblebees took a liking to them, pollinated them and helped to spread them all over the United States and southern Canada. Everybody has benefited from the wide distribution of clover: The farmers find it a nitrogen-fixer which improves the soil; it is an excellent pasture plant for cattle; clover honey is among the best on the market; partridges and countless other birds love to eat the hard clover seeds; and to some it foretells the future (for people who find four-leaf clovers are supposed to have good luck). Red clover is a branching perennial which grows to a height of 6 inches to 2 feet; its dense, globular flower-head, consisting of magenta or roseate florets, is known to everybody. The oval leaflets, usually 3 in number, show the design of a light-colored triangle. In meadows and pastures it grows from Newfoundland to British Columbia, and southward from California to Florida. Vermont, with its rich Green Mountain pastures, has adopted it as the state flower. It blooms from late spring to late fall. Of the approximately 75 species of clover growing in North America, only about 20 occur in the East; they are most abundant in the West where a few species grow 6 or 7 leaflets. Colors vary from purple, red and pink to yellow and white. *Trifolium pratense.*

◄ COMMON VETCH

"Wild Sweet Peas" — Throughout Europe, Asia and North America the vetches are plentiful. In the U.S. and Canada approximately 25 species occur, thriving over most of the continent. The best-known varieties are the common vetch, the American vetch and the cow vetch which differ only in minor details. They are trailing herbs with weak stems and climb with the help of tendrils which grow out of the tops of their leaves. The petals of their blossoms are blue, purple, or sometimes white. Their shallow pods enclose a few round seeds which in some cases are edible. The vines climb or trail for 2 to 4 feet; its purple-blue and occasionally white flowers are about an inch long; each leaf is terminated by the tendrils and consists of thin leaflets which are oblong, olive-green and bristle-tipped. It blooms from June to August in pastures and waste places. The cow vetch occurs in the north from Newfoundland to British Columbia and in the south along a line from New Jersey to Kentucky, Iowa and Washington. The American vetch is abundant in central and eastern North America and the common vetch, which usually is the cultivated forage plant, occurs throughout the country. The vetches, like the clovers and lupines, belong to the Pea Family and have attained a certain importance in farming. They should not be confused with the milk vetches which belong to a different genus and include the dreaded loco weeds of the West. *Vicia sativa.*

YELLOW WOOD-SORREL ►

Is This the Original Shamrock?—St. Patrick is said to have explained the doctrine of the trinity with the help of a shamrock, a triple-parted, deep-green leaf which has become a symbol of the Irish. The original plant on which this design is based, is either one of the clovers or the white wood-sorrel. Indeed, wood-sorrel leaves look like clover leaves; they fold at night and have a sour, agreeable taste. Shamrock and sour grass, wood sour and sour trefoil, toad sorrel and sheep poison are various names under which the members of this family are known. The group is mostly tropical, but about 30 species occur throughout the U.S. and southern Canada. Some are violet, others are purple, pink, and white, but a common species is the yellow wood sorrel, a low herb whose branching stem is 3 to 12 inches long and has a slight growth of hair. The blossoms measure about half an inch in diameter. The heart-shaped, dark-green leaves sometimes show purple hues. In waste places and along roadsides, in fields and pastures, it ranges from New Jersey to Oklahoma and Mexico in the West, and to Florida in the South. In warm climates it blooms as early as February; in the North it is later and goes on blooming into November. The violet wood sorrel is a dweller of rocky forest lands. A Brazilian species is popular as a potted plant. *Oxalis corniculata.*

WILD GERANIUM ►

Country Cousin of a City Flower — The geranium is probably the world's best-known potted plant. However, the cultivated species is a member of the sub-tropical genus Pelargonium and not too closely related to the wild geranium, although both belong to the same family. The wild species has not such fleshy stems, and its leaves are more sharply indented. The Latin word "geranium" means crane, and crane's bill is indeed its popular second name; it refers to the long, beak-shaped seed capsule; when the ovary is ripe the "bill" splits open. Of the various species inhabiting our continent a large number prefer the West, although the range of the wild geranium proper extends only from Maine to Manitoba, then south to Kansas, Alabama and Georgia. Its straight, hairy stems grow 1 to 2 feet tall and terminate in five-petaled flowers that are light purple or pink in color. The leaves also are hairy and divided into 3 to 5 finely-cut parts. It blooms from April to July and chooses woodlands as its habitat; however, many western species are encountered in the open country. Herb Robert is another wild geranium, distinguished by the heavy musk scent emanating from its glands; its blossoms have a magenta color. Finally, the pink filarees (a Spanish word for the pin-like "bills") should be mentioned; they have lace-like leaves and abound in the orchards of California and the West and furnish seeds for innumerable birds. *Geranium maculatum.*

◄ ROSE MALLOW

The Hibiscus of the North — Speaking of mallows conjures up many pleasant thoughts: The word marsh mallow brings recollections of bonfires and picnic roasts (the confection is made from the gelatinous root of the plant); musk mallow means heavily scented leaves; Indian mallow, a velvety annual with yellow flowers, has a strong fibre in its inner bark and is used in making twine and paper; and rose mallows fringe, with gay pink flowers, the river banks and swampy shores in the lowlands of the Great Lakes region and in the Eastern States; near the Atlantic ocean they often lend a touch of beauty to drab and somber saltwater marshes. Other species find their proper habitat in the western parts of the U.S. and Canada and brighten the prairies and plains with their scarlet and purple, magenta, pink, white and yellow blossoms. There are more than 30 species in North America; they range in height from 1 to 7 feet and occur throughout the U.S. and Canada, but are rare in our Southwest. Beyond our continent, they thrive throughout the Tropical and Temperate Zones of the world, approximately 900 species strong. The rose mallow grows on a hairy stem to a height of 4 to 7 feet, and its blossom measures 4 to 7 inches in diameter; the five pink petals are marked with a handsome pattern of white stripes. The flower matures into a seed capsule 1 inch long. The plant thrives in mud and can easily be grown by a garden pool. *Hibiscus palustris.*

◄ PRAIRIE VIOLET

Beloved Fragrance — The dainty flowers of the violet are so lovely that not less than four states have adopted it as the official state flower (Illinois, New Jersey, Rhode Island, Wisconsin). Yet, in many cases, these blossoms are sterile and reproduction is complicated. After the pretty, more showy flowers have spent their virginal lives, during spring, other inconspicuous but vigorous green, bud-like blossoms appear on short stems. Normally they do not even have petals, nor do they ever open. But they pollinate themselves from their own anthers and produce abundant seeds. Between 70 and 80 species of wild violets occur throughout the continent in the U.S. and Canada, all low plants not more than 10 inches high. They range in color from purple and blue to yellow and white; in the East the purple varieties prevail, in the West the yellow ones, and the Canadian violet is the best-known white species. Many cultivated violets, and also the pansy, have been developed from European species. Many violets have heart-shaped leaves, but others show a greatly indented pattern, like the prairie or larkspur violet. The later species arises from a massive underground stem, spreads its fan-shaped leaves, and opens its five-petaled, purple blossoms from April to June. The grasslands of the prairies are its natural habitat, particularly where the soil is rich in humus; its range is the Midland States and adjoining area. *Viola pedatifida.*

COMMON EVENING PRIMROSE ►

A Night-Scented Weed — This abundant flower of our fields prefers the night life. When twilight falls, it opens its bright yellow blossoms and closes them in the morning. In dull weather, when the sky is overcast, they may stay open all day. That a lemon scent should emanate from the lemon hue of these nocturnal flowers is an odd coincidence. Though a pure yellow color is the rule, pink and white appear in some other species. Once upon a time, curative medicinal properties were ascribed to the evening primrose, and it was called fever plant and king's cure-all. It is a biennial growing 2 to 4, and sometimes 6 feet tall; its flowers, of 1 inch or more in diameter, develop on stems covered with soft hairs; the rough leaves are basal or alternate, elliptical and hairy; their margins are wavy and toothed, but only to a slight degree. It thrives readily in any barren spot and spreads throughout dry meadows, waste areas and along roadsides; it tends to invade and dominate old, neglected fields. As a typical summer flower, it is in bloom from June to October, and occurs east of the Rocky Mountains. These herbs, or weeds, form their own group, the Evening Primrose Family, whose annual or perennial members flourish throughout America; some are cultivated widely, especially the clarkia and fuchsia. *Oenothera biennis.*

Wildflowers

FIREWEED ►

A Flower With a Mission — Nature has reserved a pleasant task for the fireweed. Wherever forest fires occur and leave ugly black scars on our northern lands, the fireweed frequently does the first repair work, at least in an aesthetic sense: It spreads rapidly over the blighted area and blankets the damage with magenta-pink and purple blossoms. It grows tall and stout enough to be very much in evidence, the smooth, straight stems attaining a height of 2 to 5 and sometimes 6 feet. The four-petaled blossoms, each about one inch in diameter, form large, spike-fashioned racemes at the ends of the stalks. The lance-shaped leaves are up to 6 inches long and on the lower side paler than on the upper side. The seeds are provided with tufts of hairy, white down and, while the plants are handsome during their period of bloom from June to September, they look unkempt when the fuzzy seeds begin to scatter in the fall. Open woods and low ground are their habitat; they range from the Arctic throughout Canada into the U.S., along the Appalachians to North Carolina, on the prairies south to Kansas and eastern Colorado, in the Rocky Mountain area to Arizona, and along the Pacific coast. From the Arctic, by the way, they radiate also in all other directions, southward into Europe and Asia. There are a number of related species but they are of smaller growth and less conspicuous. *Epilobium angustifolium.*

◄ QUEEN ANNE'S LACE

A Royal Cinderella — Although the flower with this regal name is a lovely and delicate creation, and although, on the useful side, our garden carrot was developed from it long ago, farmers consider it a noxious weed that is hard to keep out of pastures and causes an unpleasant flavor in milk. That is the reason why they call it devil's plague, in preference to the aristocratic appellation; those practical minds who consider the vegetable garden, refer to it as wild carrot. A biennial, it has a fleshy conelike root and hairy stems 1 to 2 feet high. The stem is topped by a lacy flower mass up to 4 inches in diameter; the individual blossoms sit on stalks which branch out from the same point of the stem; the result is a kind of flat top, dull white in color, sometimes pink. But in the center of each cluster a purple floret accents the whitish lace. Its leaves are deeply divided. The blossoming period extends from June to September. In meadows and fields, in vacant lots and along roads, Queen Anne's lace flourishes throughout the U.S. and Canada except in the highest north; it is particularly in evidence in the Northeast. A smaller species ranges throughout the West but is not abundant. It is a member of the large and extremely important Parsley or Carrot Family whose approximately 2,000 species of herbs spread around the globe, particularly in the temperate and northern zones. *Daucus carota.*

◄ TRAILING ARBUTUS

The Mayflower of the Pilgrims — That the Pilgrim Fathers should have lovingly commented on this delicate plant, raises it to a certain sentimental status and makes it the logical state flower of Massachusetts. But there are other, more direct reasons why it has become a favorite in the eastern woods. To the wintry forest the evergreen leaves give a color touch before the snow falls; they creep along the ground close to the cold earth, protected by a rough-hairy underside; of a light olive-green shade, the leaves become rusty-spotted and yield to new growth in June. Its white or pink-tinted flowers are not nearly as spectacular as those of its cousins the laurel, the azaleas and rhododendrons, but they are subtle and delicate, have a lovely frosty sheen and are spicily scented. Blooming soon after the snow has melted, they are among the first messengers of spring. At one time the sandy slopes and the wooded ranges of the New England hills and the Appalachian chains were a maze of trailing arbutus blossoms, but because of overpicking the plant has become rare now; this rarity has enhanced its value, as there is only one species in America. March, April and May are the flowering months. The blossom is nectar-bearing and it is often visited by the early queen bumblebees. Its preferred habitat are the sandy soils and the pine woods, from Canada west to the Minnesota-Wisconsin-Kentucky line and south to Florida. *Epigaea repens.*

BOTTLE GENTIAN ►

Pleasant, Hardy, Modest — If on a cold October day, with winter already in the air, you still find a brave wildflower in bloom, its tight blossoms closed to the wind, it will probably be a bottle gentian. It is a well-known and well-liked perennial in the East, 1 to 2 feet tall; its blossoms are club-shaped and of a deep blue, although sometimes white specimens occur. The flower is about 1½ inches long and a late-comer, appearing in August and lasting throughout the fall. The opposite leaves, 2 to 4 inches in length, are lance-shaped and have sharp tips. The seeds develop in a small capsule which cracks open when mature. Moist soil and damp thickets are its preferred locations. Its range extends from Quebec to Manitoba and southward to Kansas and Georgia. There are a number of gentians, both in the East and in the West. Probably the most beloved member of the family is the fringed gentian which, however, has paid dearly for its fame; it is rare now and in danger of extermination due to overpicking. Its violet-blue flowers are delicately fringed and have the shape of a vase; they bloom in the plant's second year. The roots of some gentians have medicinal qualities and are used in preparing tonics; according to Pliny, it was King Gentius of Illyria who detected these curative properties, and in his honor the plant family was named. *Gentiana andrewsii.*

COMMON MILKWEED ►

A Pleasant and Familiar Sight — This fragrant, perennial plant is so abundant that its main characteristics are known to almost everybody: the milky juice that is contained in all its parts; the dull purplish, fragrant flower clusters; and the seeds with their "parachutes," searching for a place to take root with the help of the wind. The common milkweed has strong, straight stems covered with soft hair and grows to a height of 3 to 5 feet. The oval leaves, often more than 6 inches long, are short-stalked and opposite. The flat-topped clusters of its blossoms are usually of a subdued purple, but variations from pink to green and brown occur. The large seed pods, 3 to 5 inches in length, are matted with woolly hair and contain brown, flat seeds which are arranged in shingle-like rows. The seeds are tufted with silky floss which is as warm as fur and as light as a dry sponge; therefore it is gathered for commercial purposes and used in the filling of life preservers. For many centuries milkweeds were also considered outstanding medicinal plants, and their family name, Asclepiadaceae, was chosen in honor of Aesculapius, the Greek-Roman god of medicine. In fields, empty lots and along roads, the common milkweed blossoms in profusion from June to August; its range extends from New Brunswick to Saskatchewan, and south to Kansas, Missouri, and North Carolina. But other species occur all over the U.S. and Canada. *Asclepias syriaca.*

◄ COMMON MORNING GLORY

A Work of Art — The morning glories called heavenly blue, now enjoying a wave of popularity, decorate trellises, porches and barns in wide parts of the country with their gorgeous bright blossoms. But their more modest brother in the country is just as attractive. The morning glories are originally a tropical family, well represented in South America, and in our country they still prefer the warm, deep South. But if they have good soil, they adapt themselves readily to all kinds of conditions. The common morning glory has twining stems that climb or trail 4 to 6 feet, and its leaves, deeply green and heart-shaped, have a wide indentation at the base. Its flower has the form of a bell or funnel or trumpet, 2 or 2½ inches in length, and is pink, purplish or blue. Other species are scarlet or white. Having escaped from gardens, it blooms in waste places from July to October, its range extending from Nova Scotia to Ontario, and southward to Kansas, Texas and Florida. Another interesting member of the family sends its slender, climbing vines from an enormous root which is sometimes 2 feet long and weighs up to 30 pounds. It is the wild potato vine or big-root morning glory, a brother of the cultivated sweet potato. Its flowers, decoratively draped over the bushes it has climbed, are magnificent: Their funnels, 3 inches in diameter, are white or pink while their throats are marked with purple. *Ipomoea purpurea.*

◄ SCARLET GILIA

Bright Spot in Western Sands — The stems are sticky, the leaves are sticky, the seeds are sticky when damp, and the odor of the plant is rather obnoxious. But it looks handsome with its curved stem which is 2 to 4 feet long and takes on purplish hues toward the top; with its bluish-green leaves that are finely dissected and alternate on the stem; and with its pretty red flowers which are stars on tubes 1 to 1½ inches long. They form clusters on top, but appear along the stem also. The scarlet gilia blooms in dry ground from May to September and ranges from Nebraska to British Columbia, our Pacific states, and Mexico. It is a perennial or biennial plant and a member of the Phlox Family, one of the approximately 100 varieties of gilias which brighten the western sections of the U.S. and Canada. In the deserts and on the mountains some dwarfed species lend a gay touch to an otherwise dry and monotonous landscape, and on open mountainsides and hill slopes, other species carpet the country with yellow and white, blue and purple, scarlet and pink blossoms. All are 5-petaled and funnel-shaped, but their variable development often makes it hard to distinguish the different species. Other well-known relatives are wild sweet william with its purple-blotched stems and pink, purple, or sometimes white flowers, the Jacob's ladder with its blossoms in bluish purple, and our ornamental garden phloxes. *Gilia aggregrata.*

VIRGINIA BLUEBELL ►

Ringing in the Spring — The beauty of the Virginia bluebell is manyfold: In itself, its nodding clusters of trumpet or cup-shaped flowers are lovely, graceful and varied; they are pink as buds and mature into bright blue or lavender blossoms. Besides, they grow in rich bottom lands in broad stands forming a soft, deep, colorful, solid carpet that is magnificent. And finally, they do not drag their lives into a drawn-out and withered old age; for as their seeds ripen, about a month after blossom time, their foliage dies. The succulent, straight stems of the Virginia bluebell grow to a height of 1 to 2 feet, and its leaves are oval, alternate and short-stemmed, smooth, strongly veined and broadly pointed. It thrives in well watered meadows, on the shores of streams, in wet ground, also on rocky, moist slopes, and blossoms as early as March; by the end of May it is usually finished. Its range extends far beyond the confines of Virginia, from Ontario to Minnesota in the north, and from Nebraska and Kansas to South Carolina in the south. Other names for this well-loved flower are Roanoke bells, mertensia and, somewhat prosaically, Virginia cowslip and tree lungwort. It can be raised easily in a wildflower garden. It is a member of the Borage Family which includes also the heliotrope and the forget-me-not. Many of its ornamental species are cultivated, and a few possess pharmaceutical properties. *Mertensia virginica.*

MULLEIN ►

Coarse and Stately — Majestically, the mullein rises from the earth like a 5 or 7-foot torch, a green pyramidal structure crowned by a long, erect spike of yellow flowers. The Germans call it Königskerze, royal candle, while such American names as old man's flannel, blanket leaf, and Adam's flannel are less respectful. The more common a plant is the more names it acquires and, as the mullein is an abundant dweller of pastures, fields, and waste lots, it has widely aroused popular imagination; Aaron's rod and Jacob's staff allude to the Bible; in other localities it is known as shepherd's club, hedge taper, candlewick, velvet dock and feltwort. Some of these terms refer to the fact that the mullein is velvety like fine wool, with thick leaves that look like felt. The latter grow around the base of the plant in a decorative, large rosette, some leaves attaining a length of more than a foot; smaller leaves grow on the stem. Mullein blooms from June to September and ranges as far north as Nova Scotia, as far west as South Dakota and Nebraska, and as far south as Florida. The moth mullein, a similar species whose flowers are pale yellow or white, occurs in much of the U.S. Both have been introduced from Europe and thrive conspicuously in their new habitat. They belong to the Figwort or Snapdragon Family, a large group spreading over many parts of the globe. *Verbascum thapsus.*

◄ FALSE FOXGLOVE

An Ornamental Exploiter — This handsome plant is a root parasite. It fastens its own roots to those of a tree, links up with the life of its host, and derives a part of its food energy from that source. An annual, the branching herb grows to a height of 1 to 4 feet; it is sticky and covered with downlike hairs. Its five-petaled, tubular, lemon-yellow flower is shaped like a bell, is 1 to 1½ inches long, and looks lovely on the background of the lacy, deeply serrated leaves. The leaves are 1 to 3 inches long and spread like ferns. It is encountered in open woodlands where the soil is dry, and blooms rather late, in August and September. It is an eastern wildflower which ranges from Maine to Ontario and Minnesota, and southward to Illinois and North Carolina. As to its classification, it belongs to the group of flowers called Gerardia, in honor of the famous botanist John Gerard, and to the Figwort Family. Most members of this family have a bitter juice, and quite a few have narcotic and poisonous properties. The cultivated brother of the false foxglove, the garden plant called foxglove or digitalis, has played an important part as a medicinal plant. The several wild species are confined to the East. Even the western false foxglove, whose bright yellow flowers are a little larger, does not spread as far west as the Great Plains. *Gerardia pedicularia.*

◄ INDIAN PAINTBRUSH

Painted Leaves on Indian Lands — The fan-like bracts (i.e. the leaves directly under the blossom) on this herb look as if they have been dipped in scarlet paint. They are so bright and conspicuous that they obscure the flowers themselves; the latter are indeed unspectacular: tubular, green-yellow, up to an inch in length. The plant's whole appearance is attractive and has inspired such additional names as scarlet painted cup and red Indian; somewhat on the violent side are terms like bloody warrior and nosebleed, and a more compromising local appellation is election posy. The name prairie fire refers to the plant's bright brilliance. An annual or biennial, it raises its erect stem to a foot or two. The basal leaves grow in a rosette, the stem leaves alternate and are slightly toothed. Both stem and leaves are hairy. Like the false foxglove, it is a partial parasite and receives a portion of its nourishment from other plants, particularly from grass roots. It blossoms from spring to early summer in fields, meadows and grassy spots from Maine to Manitoba, southward through the Dakotas to Texas, and through Arkansas to North Carolina. The western species whose "painted" bracts are red, yellow, or red and yellow, often form brilliant patches on mountain meadows and prairies in a setting of towering rocks and snowy peaks. They are rarely higher than 20 inches. One lovely species has been adopted by Wyoming as its state flower. *Castilleja coccinea.*

PARTRIDGE BERRY ►

Trailer in the Northern Woods — Partridges and other birds love to eat these red berries with eight nutlets in pulpy flesh; the berries are edible for human beings also. The "twinberries" are developed from twin flowers, pretty, small stars of creamy-white to light pink color whose four petals merge into a single tube or funnel. They sit on smooth, trailing vines that are 6 to 12 inches long and bear round or oval, opposite, shiny, evergreens leaves; they measure ¼ to ¾ of an inch in length. The plant takes root along its stem as it creeps over the ground. It is a familiar sight in Canada and our northern tier of states, but also occurs everywhere else east of the Minnesota-Texas line. It blossoms in the woods during April, May and June; a favorite habitat is a forest border rich in humus. It also adapts itself readily to a woodland garden. Why, in nature lore, it has been affiliated with the Indian squaw is difficult to see, but its additional names are squaw berry, squaw plum and squaw vine. It is related to the tropical and subtropical coffee plant whose fruit is a two-seeded berry and contains what we call the coffee "bean." Another important relative is the cinchona tree of South America whose bark produces quinine. All three belong to the large cosmopolitan Madder Family which comprises approximately 6,000 species, mostly in the tropics. *Mitchella repens.*

BLUE BELL OF SCOTLAND ►

Wiry Grace — A number of Scotch virtues are united in these universally liked flowers. They may not look very hardy but they are, and they adapt themselves readily to various surroundings, even to what might be called straightened circumstances. Meadows and sandy hillslopes, rocky places, cliffs, shores, — almost any environment will serve, and the blue bell will grow taller or smaller according to conditions. Its five petals are merged into one bell, an arrangement which prevents the waste of pollen. Insects are welcome for pollination, but if they fail to arrive, the stigmas bend down and come into contact with the pollen dropped to the base of the flower. It is also called varied-leaf bell because it produces two types of leaves; the ones at the base are roundish and frequently wither when the flowers begin to open. The leaves on the stem are alternate, slender and smooth, and often quite numerous. The stems are wiry, 6 to 18 inches tall, and the drooping bells, approximately 3/4 of an inch long, are blue-violet; they bloom throughout the summer, from June to September, and flourish best in the northern parts of North America from Labrador to Alaska. Also in the Sierra Nevada, Rockies and hills of New Jersey. Blue bells belong to the Bellflower Family whose characteristics are a milky plant juice and bell-shaped blossoms. The Canterbury bells are a famous member. *Campanula rotundifolia.*

◄ CARDINAL FLOWER

King of the Wildflowers — Descending the cliffs by the side of Saddle Brook Falls in the northwoods of Maine, one comes upon a bed of cardinal flowers in full bloom, stretching for 20 feet along the churning waters, almost under the spray of the falls. It is a perfect setting for one of America's most beautiful, rare flowers. A poll of American naturalists conducted to determine the showiest and most fascinating species, conferred the grand prize upon this cardinal flower, and you would agree: The bright color, the sophisticated irregularity of its blossom, and the attraction it has for humming birds combine to give it an aura all its own. The plant raises its smooth stem to a height of 2 to 4½ feet; it is topped by the brilliant flowers measuring 1 to 1½ inches in length. The leaves are dark green and often have a bronze hue; they are toothed and approximately 5 inches long. A summer flower, it blooms from July to September in the eastern half of the U.S., including parts of Colorado and Texas. It occurs also in New Brunswick and Ontario. Because of overpicking it has become quite rare and is on the protection list. Its habitat is the border of streams and swamps, of ditches and ponds in the moist woodlands of the East. It is one of the few red members of the Lobelia Family. *Lobelia cardinalis.*

◄ TALL IRONWEED

Purple Tufts of Early Fall — This stout plant has an air of strength about it; that is perhaps the reason for the "iron" in its name. The woody, leafy stem attains a height from 4 to 8 feet, and branches loosely at the top to bring all its abundant terminal flower heads to approximately the same level. This arrangement accounts for the weed's additional name of flat top. The dark purple blossoms consist of many tiny tubular florets and look like little thistles, but the plant is not rough and does not possess spines. The leaves are dark green and smooth, quite narrow and finely toothed, and the fruit is provided with purple bristles. Tall Ironweed blooms during the late summer and early fall, mainly in August and September. It thrives in low, damp meadows, thickets and roadsides, preferring the South as a habitat but also ranging over the Eastern States as far north as New York, and the Midwestern States to the prairies. There are a number of other species in the same area, for instance the New York ironweed with dark purple and sometimes white flower-heads; the great ironweed of the Middle States that reaches a height of 12 feet; the Illinois ironweed, also purple, of the Prairie States; and the western ironweed which, in spite of its name, does not grow beyond the Great Plains. All are members of the very large Composite Family which comprises more than 15,000 species. *Vernonia altissima.*

JOE-PYE-WEED ►

Tall Tops of Eastern Thickets — Joe Pye, it seems, was a noted Indian doctor in New England. His fame is perpetuated in the Joe-Pye-weed, a name more original than the terms "king of the meadow" and "queen of the meadow" which are also applied to this common plant. Kidney root and fever weed are additional names testifying to the flower's one-time status as a medicinal herb. It is a stately, stout and straight plant, 4 to 8 or sometimes 10 feet tall, and its huge terminal plume is probably its most outstanding characteristic. That plume is a cluster of numerous tiny heads of dull pink or lavender, tubular florets. The coarsely-toothed leaves, 4 to 12 inches long, grow in whorls of 3 to 6, and are often slightly hairy on the lower surface along the veins. The fruits have tips of small, coarse, grey bristles. Joe-Pye-weed is a common sight in the early fall — August and September — in moist, low ground, in thickets and along roads. Its range extends from New Brunswick southward to Texas and Florida. There are a number of closely related species in the same area; a common species with white flowers is the upland boneset of New England, the Southeast and the Middle States. White snakeroot, a considerably smaller but handsome plant with velvety white heads in flat tops, has a wide range east of the Rocky Mountains. All belong to the Composite Family. *Eupatorium purpureum.*

NEW ENGLAND ASTER ►

A Blaze of Color — Aster is the Greek word for star, and each star-shaped blossom is a multiple compact flowerhead in which the center flowers are bright yellow and the 40 or more outer flowers or rays (deceptively looking like petals) are deep purple or violet. They grow on tall stems which are 2 to 8 feet high; the stalks are rough and hairy, sticky and branching, and often show a reddish tinge. The lance-shaped alternate leaves, 2 to 5 inches long, clasp the stalk. Pinkish bristles tip the fruit. The New England aster flourishes in open fields and meadows, also in thickets, waste lots and swamps; it ranges from Quebec to Saskatchewan, southward to Wyoming and Colorado, and eastward again from Missouri to North Carolina. The one place where it is quite rare is northern New England. More than 250 native species of asters occur in the U.S. and Canada, but they are more properly an eastern flower. Grasslands are carpeted and roads are fringed, from late summer to the late fall, with millions of purple, violet, blue, pink, or white asters. Often they hybridize in their wild state, and horticulturists have produced beautiful garden flowers from hardy asters, for instance the well-known Michaelmas daisies. Widely spread wild species are the blue-violet New York aster, the white woodland aster with the zig-zag stems, and the purple southern swamp aster. They belong to the Composite Family. *Aster novae angliae.*

◄ PLUME GOLDENROD

Stars and Plumes of the Eastern Fall — For many years goldenrod was denounced as a major source of hay fever. However, that is not so as its pollen is normally insect-borne and not carried by the wind. Ragweed rather should be blamed. In fact, the thousands of acres of meadowland that are covered with bright yellow goldenrod blossoms, are a friendly symbol of late summer and early fall. There are about 125 species in this country and Canada, all native. Their blossoms are similar and their flowering period extends approximately from August to October; but otherwise they show considerable differences. The sharp-leaved goldenrod is a common and graceful species with plumelike golden clusters (New Hampshire to Virginia to South Dakota); the late goldenrod does not bloom later than the others; it develops yellow blossoms with a lilac "bloom" on the stem while the silverrod produces creamy white flowers (Maine to Georgia to Missouri); the tall and coarse Canadian goldenrod thrives as far south as New York and Pennsylvania. While most species have a pungent aroma, the sweet goldenrod (Maine to New York to Kentucky to Texas) smells strongly of anise. In size, goldenrod plants differ greatly, measuring eight inches to seven feet in height; their habitat is similarly varied, according to the species; they range from meadow and mountain to swamp and seaside. The plume goldenrod (illustrated) is *Solidago juncea.*

◄ BLACK-EYED SUSAN

Bright American Star — Sigrid Undset, the Norwegian novelist and Nobel Prize winner, liked the black-eyed susan best of all American wildflowers. Stem and leaves, she thought, look robust and healthy, and the flowers exquisite both in color and shape. Many of us will agree with her (for instance, the people of Maryland, who made it their state flower), and we heartily endorse its nation-wide range of growth. A native of the Central States, it has spread far and wide to the Atlantic, to the Pacific, and northward into Canada. It is the same plant as the brown-eyed susan, the yellow daisy and the golden Jerusalem. This biennial herb has a rough, hairy stem 1 to 3 feet tall; the well-known blossom, 2 to 4 inches in diameter, has 10 to 15 orange-yellow rays; its blackish-brown disk florets are arranged in a cone, the "black eye." The thick, hairy upper leaves, 2 to 6 inches long, are alternate and directly fastened to the stem; usually they are sparingly toothed. On the prairies and plains, in grassy spots and thickets it blossoms throughout the summer, sometimes in quite sterile soil. It is one of that group of daisy-like weeds which occur widely in sandy soils in the center and east of the continent. Their cone-like center, which is at first green and later becomes dark brown, distinguishes them from the sunflowers. They are members of the Composite Family. *Rudbeckia hirta.*

COMMON SUNFLOWER ►

A Midland Sunburst — There is more than one reason why these fine, big blossoms are called sunflowers. Obviously, they look like symbols of the sun. Besides, the flowers always gaze toward the sun; in fact the whole stem turns so that as much of the leaf surface as possible is continually exposed to the sun. The plant is useful; its seeds produce a fine oil, and in themselves they are a favorite bird food. Consequently the common sunflower is widely cultivated. In its wild state it will grow 8 to 10 feet tall, in cultivation it will reach 15 feet; the flowerhead will have a diameter of 3 to 6 inches in waste places and along roads, and of 12 and more inches in cultivated stands. The stem of the plant is covered with bristly hairs; the rays of the flowerhead are bright yellow, the disk florets have a brown and sometimes purple color. The leaves are up to 12 inches long, toothed, and coarse on both sides; they grow in opposite pairs on the lower stem, alternate on the upper branches. Blossom time extends from July to September, and the range reaches from Minnesota southward to Oklahoma and Texas and westward to the Pacific. But quite a few are encountered in the East also where they escape from cultivated patches. They are approximately 60 species of native sunflowers in North America; they are most typical of the prairies and particularly of Kansas, the official sunflower state. Composite Family. *Helianthus annuus.*

YARROW ►

Familiar Road Companion — This aromatic weed is one of the few plants that are known to almost everybody not only in the U.S. and Canada but in many parts of the world; it lines the sides of the roads nearly everywhere in the temperate zone. Although it is very common, it has at times been highly regarded as a medicine, supposedly curing minor ills and serving as a tonic. Such additional names as nosebleed, soldier's woundwort and sanguinary refer to its pharmaceutical properties. Such terms as milfoil and thousand-leaf allude to the leaves which are dissected into numerous small, toothed parts. The stiff, slightly hairy stems are occasionally forked; they attain a height of 1 to 2 feet and carry the flat tops of small flowers which measure $\frac{1}{4}$ of an inch or less across and have a dull, greyish-white color, with an occasional pink, purple or rarely crimson floret. The dull green leaves taste bitter and have a spicy fragrance, are alternate and, on the lower levels, up to 10 inches long. Yarrow blooms throughout the summer and fall, from June to November, in fields, on waste lots and along roads, with a continental range. There are several species in different parts of the country; they are members of the Composite Family. One close relative is the sneezewort or sneezewort-yarrow, of the Eastern and Midwestern States. Also related to the yarrow are the various species of chamomile of drugstore fame; they occur on the East and Pacific Coast. *Achillea millefolium.*

◄ DAISY

Friendly and Abundant — This is a welcome immigrant from Europe; while it has impressive and noble relatives— the cultivated chrysanthemum, for instance, — its straightforward, simple beauty has an air of sincerity that speaks to the heart. It is by no means rare either, but brightens fields and roadsides throughout the U.S. and Canada, with particular abundance in the East. The plant is a perennial which raises its slender, delicately-grooved stem to a height of $1\frac{1}{2}$ to $2\frac{1}{2}$ feet. The yellow flower disks are approximately $\frac{1}{2}$ inch in diameter, surrounded by white ray florets 20 to 30 in number. The narrow, alternate leaves are coarsely toothed. The blossoms are in evidence during all of summer and early fall, in fields and meadows, waste areas and along roads. A variety of names are applied to the plant, like white daisy, field daisy, ox-eye daisy, moon-penny, and, to shed light also on the other side of the medal, farmer's curse. A close relative is the feverfew or featherfew, a leafy daisy with branched stems, yellow flower disks measuring $\frac{1}{2}$ to $\frac{3}{4}$ of an inch in diameter, and 10 to 20 toothed, white rays. The common tansy belongs to a related genus, the so-called bitter-buttons whose flat clusters have golden flower heads but no conspicuous rays. This aromatic perennial has escaped from oldfashioned gardens to which it was brought from Europe. All these forms belong to the Composite Family. *Chrysanthemum leucanthemum.*

◄ COMMON THISTLE

Prickly and Pernicious—Is there someone who likes thistles, the pernicious weeds that crowd their way into fields and pastures? Well, the Scotch made a thistle the floral symbol of Scotland, and the Indians appreciated some thistle roots as vegetable. Among the birds, the goldfinches have a preference for thistles; they eat the seeds and line their nests with thistle down; they build their nests later than most other birds because they have to wait for the thistles' down to ripen. Otherwise thistles are considered noxious weeds. Some are of European extraction; the plumed thistles are mostly native Americans. The common thistle, also called spear or bull thistle, is naturalized from Europe. It is a plant of leafy stalks which grow to a height of 3 to 5 feet, and bears fragrant magenta or lavender flowerheads which attract bees and butterflies because of their richness in nectar. The bracts are provided with sharp spines, as are the alternate, hairy leaves which are divided into lobes; the lobes carry the white spines at their tips. The common thistle blooms during the summer and early fall and ranges from Newfoundland to North Dakota and Oregon, and southward to Georgia in the East, and to California in the West. Thistles, as a group, cover all of the U.S. and much of Canada; the various species have blossoms of lilac, purple, yellow or white. They are members of the Composite Family. *Cirsium lanceolatum.*

DANDELION ►

A Nuisance with Benefits — Doonhead clock and witch's gowan, blowball and lion's tooth are only a few of the numerous English names by which this cosmopolitan weed is known. The latter term is a translation of the French dent-de-lion which in turn has been corrupted into the English dandelion. It refers to the jagged edge of its leaf which bears a remote resemblance to a row of teeth in an animal's jaw. This plant should be popular considering the long list of its virtues. Its blossom, with an orange-golden center and light yellow bands on the margin, is lovely and its globe of silky fuzz, when the seeds ripen, is beautiful; children play at telling time by blowing away all the fuzz — the number of blows, the hour of the day. Spring salad of dandelion leaves abounds in vitamins, and dandelion wine distilled from the flowers has a flavor enjoyed by many. From the roots, a drug is extracted for treating diseases of the liver, and the native western dandelions are welcomed by bee keepers as a source of honey. Its seeds, finally, are a favorite bird food. Yet, with all these blessings, the common dandelion is the despair of the lawn owner. For this weed with the deep tap root has domineering vitality and is prolific, several species are found throughout the U.S. and Canada, blossoming from spring to fall. Fields, lawns, and waste places are its habitat. The dwarf dandelion thrives in dry soil or sandy banks; its flower is less than ¾ of an inch. *Taraxacum officinale.*

CHICORY ►

The Coffee Weed — In New Orleans a demitasse has a spicier flavor than in Boston. For in the deep South chicory is added to the coffee, an old French custom. In some parts of the world "coffee" is actually brewed from roasted chicory roots, a cheap substitute for the tropical product. Chicory leaves are widely used as salad greens and the plant is grown as cattle fodder. The plant that furnishes millions of pounds of chicory every year is a common but handsome weed, also called succory or blue sailors. Its light-blue blossoms, at their best from July to October, sit tightly on rigid stems and keep open only in sunshine; they close in rainy or cloudy weather. Occasionally white or pink flower heads supplement the blue blossoms, looking like colorful ribbon medallions. They all welcome bees as visitors, but in the absence of insects the structure of the flowers assists in effecting self-fertilization. Their lance-shaped leaves are grey-green and coarse-toothed, and their stout and stiff stems branch out to a height of four or even five feet. Originally a native of Europe, the plant was brought to America and is thriving here by the thousands along country roads and pastures, empty town lots and waste places, particularly in the neighborhood of the seaboard towns; its long tap roots manage to extract nourishment even from poor soils. It does not occur, however, in the dry climate of the Southwest; it is a common sight everywhere else. *Cichorium intybus.*

◄ ORANGE HAWKWEED

A Brush Dipped in Paint — A New England summer meadow covered with an orange-red carpet that seems suspended a foot or more above the green grass, is a magnificent sight for the nature lover, while the farmer is less enthusiastic about the spreading of the weed; for this plant, introduced from Europe, grows from runners and builds up dense patches. The slender stalk, 1 to 2 feet tall, possesses black hairs and ends in a cluster of orange flowerheads, an inch or less in diameter. The leaves, overlaid with greyish hairs, are arranged in a rosette at the base. Orange hawkweed blooms in summer and early fall in dry fields and pastures, open waste lots and clearings, mainly in the Northeast, from New Brunswick to Ontario in Canada and in the U.S. as far south as New Jersey and Pennsylvania, also in certain localities toward the west. Of its various names, devil's paintbrush is quite common in New England; others are tawny hawkweed, devil's weed, flora's paintbrush. There are a number of species of hawkweeds, some with yellow flowers; they are widely distributed in the East and West, but prefer the northern latitudes; they are members of the Composite Family. The rattle-snake-weed is closely related; in spite of its name it is an attractive plant with clusters of flowerheads in deep yellow. The Canada hawkweed, also yellow, thrives from Newfoundland to British Columbia, and Pennsylvania to Oregon. *Hieracium aurantiacum.*

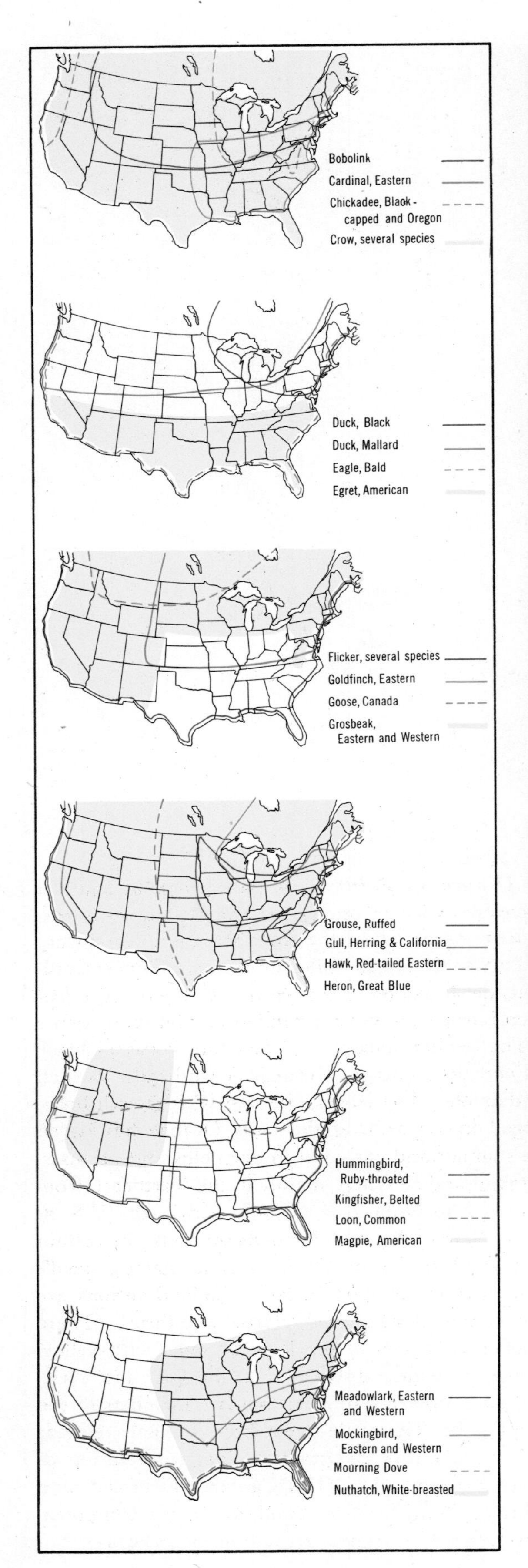

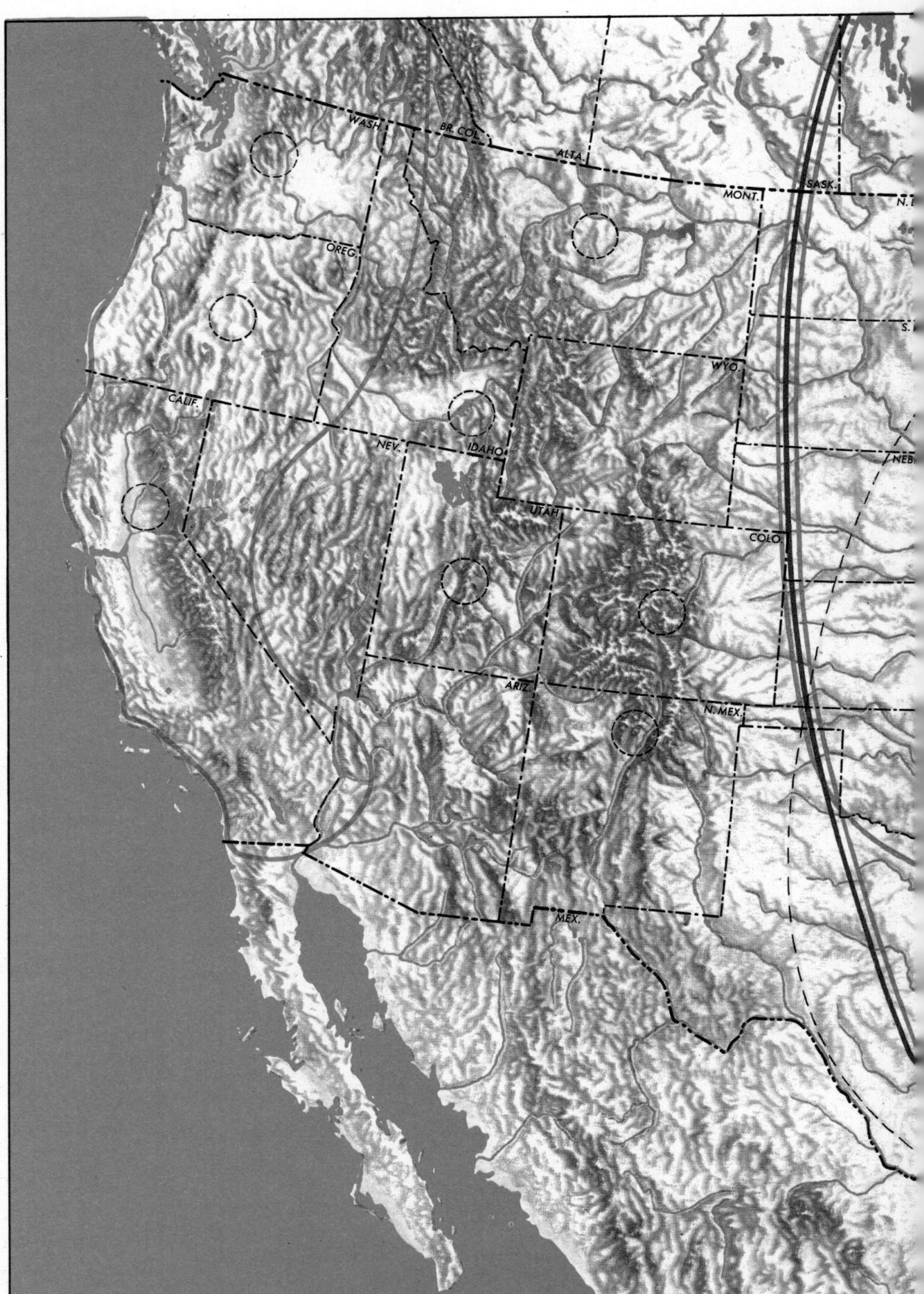

BIRDS IN THE U.S. AND SOUTHERN CANADA

The following pages describe and illustrate those birds which are most frequently encountered in the U.S. and Canada, or are of general interest for other reasons. The distribution of these birds is outlined in alphabetical order on the range maps on this page. The picture presented is that of the summer months. A key to the principal orders and families will be found on page 220.

The following notes refer to the maps. *Bob-White, Eastern* — has been introduced to several western localities. *Blue Jay, Northern* — related species occur in the West. *Crow* — the eastern, western and several other species are all similar in appearance. *Chickadee* — the black-capped species is best-known in the East, the Oregon spécies in the West. *Flicker* — the eastern species is

Birds

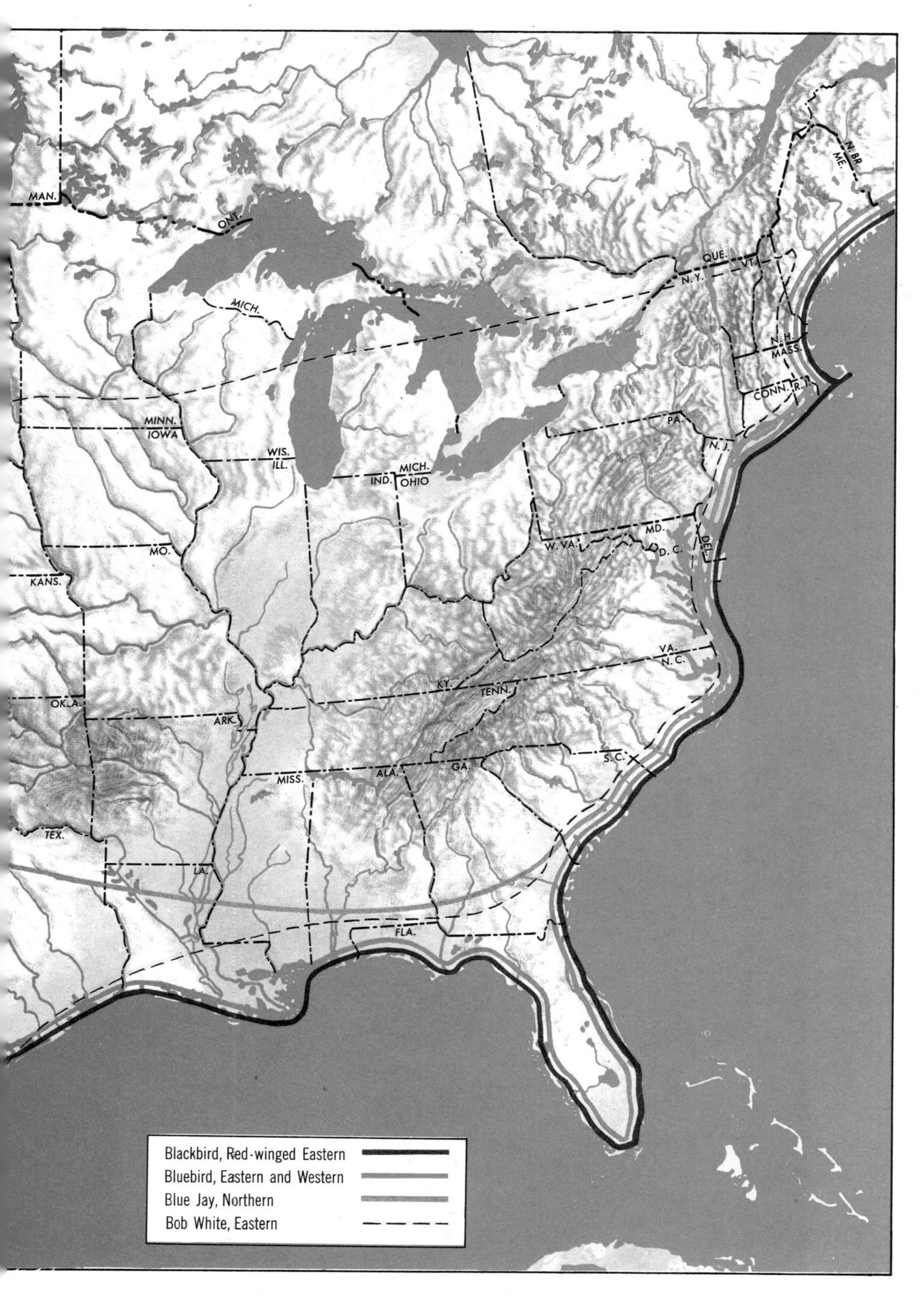

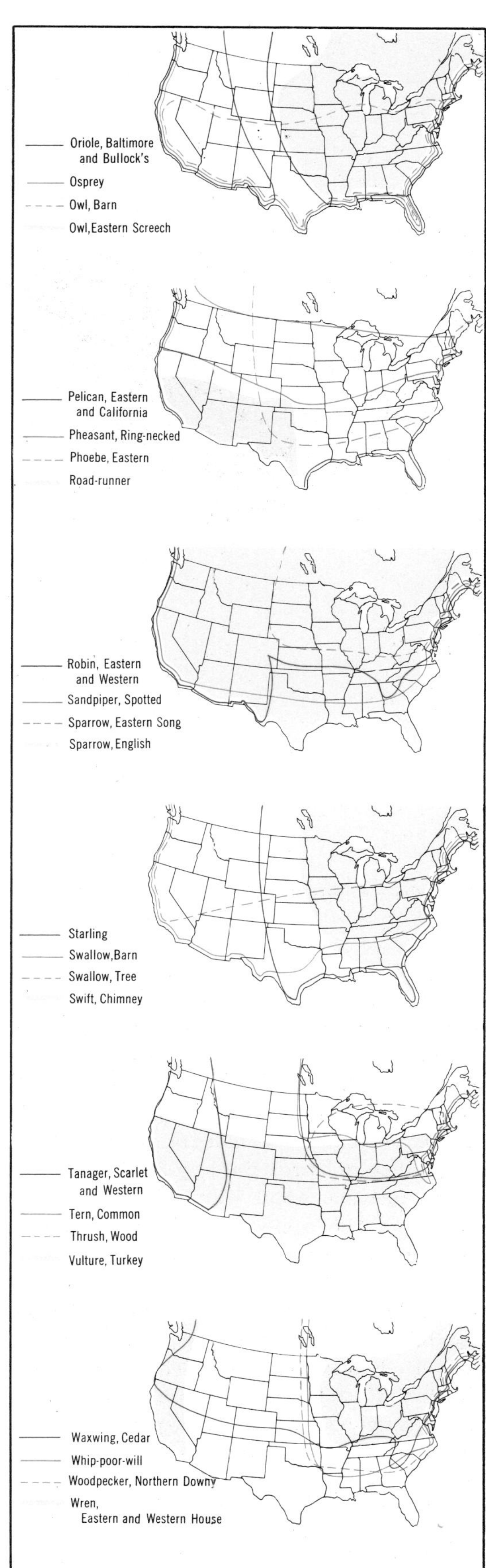

yellow-shafted, the western, red-shafted. *Grosbeak* — the rose-breasted species is outstanding in the East, the black-headed in the West. *Grouse, Ruffed* — similar species occur in the Northeast and Northwest. *Gull, Eastern Herring* — during the winter it is abundant on Atlantic and Gulf coasts. *Hummingbird, Ruby-throated* — several other species of hummingbirds occur in the West. *Mockingbird*—its range is gradually extending farther north. *Oriole*—Bullock's oriole is the western counterpart of the Baltimore oriole. *Pelican* — ranges are shown for eastern brown and California brown pelicans. *Pheasant, Ring-necked* — has also been introduced to Northwest and West. *Phoebe, Eastern* — its western counterpart is Say's phoebe. *Song Sparrow* — in the West the Lincoln sparrow is a similar species. *Terns* — they occur locally in the Gulf States also.

◄ COMMON LOON

Sailor of the Northern Lakes — The weird cry of the loon might sound like the hollow laughter of a hysterical woman, its spooky overtones heightened by the loneliness of the lake and the echo from the silent northwoods. Yet the loon is a sober and realistic bird, and supremely skillful in its daily chores. Its equipment is excellent: The plumage is so compact that the bird "feels hard" if you lift it with your hands; the bill is strong and straight, with a sharp tip and knife-like edges; three toes are webbed, the fourth is free and short. There are few birds as fascinating to watch. Their diving, for instance, is unique: Slowly the body submerges under the surface until only the neck and head swish through the water like a submarine periscope. Suddenly they too disappear; not even a ripple is caused on the water. From then on you will look around for five minutes before you notice the resurrected loon calmly floating far away in a bay. Under water it "flies," i.e. it uses its wings together with its feet; it proceeds so swiftly that it overtakes and catches fish which are its principal food. The nest is a casual depression near the shore with a few sticks on the margin, and the number of olive or brownish eggs is usually two. Its range is northern North America, and it winters from the latitude of Illinois to the Gulf Coast. Length: 2½ feet. *Gavia immer immer.*

EASTERN BROWN PELICAN ►

Fisherman of the Southern Coasts — The pelican town is built on a marshy southern island: Hundreds of coarse, big nests are constructed of branches and sticks on mounds of mud or soil, 6 to 8 inches high, with some on low bushes. Here an enormous colony of pelicans goes about the business of living in a gregarious and sociable way, in many localities protected by law. In these huge rookeries they lay their chalk-white eggs, 2 or 3 in number, and attend to the breeding. From here, little groups take off on foraging trips that may extend for 50 miles or more; their wings skim the waves, then the birds rise to a height of 20 or 30 feet and plunge into the water with a loud, explosive splash; up they come with a fish which is promptly devoured. After the young are born, they have to be provided with food; so the parents bring it home from their fishing excursions in their bellies, then regurgitate it into the pouches of their long bills, and from there the young retrieve it by sticking their heads into the pouch. They relish greatly the half-digested, stinking mass of fish fragments. The eastern, brown variety is, like the other species, at ease in the water, has a curious but graceful way of flapping its huge wings in the air, and looks grotesque on land. Their range extends from South Carolina to Texas on the coast. Length: 4 feet. *Pelecanus occidentalis occidentalis.*

GREAT BLUE HERON ►

Proud American Bird — A beautiful landmark of the American scene from the Arctic to Colombia and Venezuela is the great blue heron, a familiar and decorative sight in ponds and streams, on lakesides and shallows, inlets and estuaries, in saltwater and freshwater. Like a philosopher it stands on its straight long legs, its neck in a graceful S curve, motionless and seemingly in deep thought. But its mind is very much on the fishes that pass by, and if a small one comes near enough, it is struck with a snake-like thrust of neck and bill, tossed into the air, caught in the beak head first, and swallowed. If it is a large one, it is stabbed and killed before it is devoured. Or the bird wades along cautiously, stalking the fish, frogs, tadpoles, salamanders, and snakes that form its main diet. It is said to be a more skillful trout fisher than most sportsmen who naturally dislike this competition. In addition, it is also a great hunter, preying on shrews and mice, young rats and muskrats, salamanders and dragonflies. On the whole it leads a solitary life, only during the mating season do many herons unite in large colonies, building their nests close together on trees or rocks, near the water. Their pale bluish or greenish eggs number 3 to 4, and food is delivered to the young from their parents' stomachs in a regurgitated form. Its call is a low croak. Length: 4 feet. *Ardea herodias herodias.*

◄ AMERICAN EGRET

Southern Belle — The huge, elegant ladies' hats of the Edwardian era almost caused the extermination of this bird, for the long, finely dissected aigrette plumes arising between its shoulders and covering the tail, about 20 inches long and 50 in number, were the height of fashion. In those days thousands upon thousands of these beautiful snow-white birds with black legs and yellow bills populated the lake shores of Florida and the Gulf States, and patroled the beaches when the tide brought in small fishes. Then the wholesale slaughter began; as the American egrets grow their aigrettes only during the nesting season, the parent birds were killed and the young were left to starve. Protective legislation stopped the practice before it was too late, and today their numbers are increasing again. They had the habit of straggling northward after the breeding season and when, after a long interval, they appeared again as visitors in our northern states along the Canadian border, only a few years ago, they were greeted as long-lost friends. Their regular range extends from Virginia to central California and south into the Tropics. Their nests are big platforms constructed in trees over a lagoon or a swampy lake; a famous rookery can be observed in the easily accessible Jungle Gardens of Avery Island in Louisiana. They eat fish, frogs, snakes, grasshoppers, beetles, large moths, spiders, etc. Length: 3½ feet. *Casmerodius albus egretta.*

◄ CANADA GOOSE

"It tells the Sweep and Loveliness of Things . . ." — Flocks of Canada geese flying northward, painting perfect V's on the evening sky and sending their deeply resounding honking notes down to earth, are, to Americans, symbols of longing, of spring, and of wanderlust. More prosaically, they are also good eating, and conspicuous targets for sportsmen. Nevertheless, they are far from extinct, which is due largely to two traits: They are extremely watchful and wary, and they breed in the far North, from the northern Prairie States through Canada to the Yukon. Far from civilization, they are able to raise most of their young with little disturbance. They are also very adaptable in their nesting sites which may be dry ground on an island, a muskrat house, a tree or a cliff. Brooks reports that they sometimes take over old osprey nests early in the season. When the proprietors return, a battle ensues in which the ospreys emerge victorious. They evict the squatters but considerately leave the goose eggs where they are and lay their own alongside. What happens at hatching time nobody knows. The Canada goose is easily recognized not only by its black head and neck and white collar but also by the extremely large size. Its 4 to 10 eggs are cream or greenish white. Seeds, grasses and insects are its food, and its winter quarters are the southern states. Length: 3 to 3½ feet. *Branta canadensis canadensis.*

COMMON MALLARD ►

Of Ancient Lineage — The mallard is said to be one of the first animals to be domesticated by man; it has been bred on Chinese farms since prehistoric days and is the ancestor of almost all domestic species. The wild mallard, however, is somewhat larger than its tame cousin. It is a familiar sight in most parts of the world. It breeds in the North and winters in the South, and although the hordes of mallards feeding and quacking on Louisiana lagoons and Florida marshes seem enormous, they are but a fraction of the veritable clouds of migratory fowl that used to make the annual voyage. What restricts the mallard population, besides over-hunting, is the fact that in its southern breeding grounds from Indiana and Iowa to California, many swamps have been drained, wild lands have been cleared and, where there used to be ponds, there now are farms. But it still finds many suitable nesting sites from Labrador to Alaska. Its diet includes pond weeds, herbs, grasses, insects and other small animal life. The nest is built among the reeds, not far from water, and is lined with soft down. Here, half a dozen or more eggs are laid, buff in color with grey or greenish tints. The young are among the most independent and self-reliant babies in the animal world. The length of the adult male is approximately 2 feet, while the mottled brown female is smaller. *Anas platyrhynchos platyrhynchos.*

BLACK DUCK

A Rugged Northeasterner — The black duck is not black but dark brown; in the interplay of light and shadow, however, it often appears black. It is remarkable in many ways; it is incredibly rugged in its constitution; it does not seem to mind freezing temperatures and is so attached to its home quarters that it stays there in cold and snow until the ice covers the feeding grounds. While it can often be seen at the seashore, riding the waves like a canoe, it takes its meals rather on inland ponds and salt marshes or on the estuaries of small rivers. There it searches for its vegetables — seeds and wild rice, roots and plants, nuts and berries — and hunts for its prey — worms and insects, leeches and tadpoles, toads and frogs, salamanders and small fish. In turn it is shot and eaten by some hunters; they claim that it makes a fair dish when it has been on a vegetable diet. Its quack is like that of the mallard, but in its character it is much wilder, shyer and warier. Its breeding grounds extend along the Atlantic Coast from Maine to Delaware, and westward to the Great Lakes. There it builds its nest on grassy or bushy ground, often quite far away from water bodies, and lines it with feathers. The 6 or more eggs are similar in color to mallard eggs. It spends the winter from New England to Louisiana. Length: 2 feet. *Anas rubripes tristis.*

TURKEY VULTURE

The Clean-up Team — A flock of these big birds tearing to pieces the putrid flesh of a dead horse or devouring a freshly killed fox, stuffing themselves greedily and then relieving the pressure by disgorging a part of their stomach contents — such are not sights for the delicate. But other sights are: These same birds have a wingspread of nearly 6 feet and are among the world's most graceful and skillful soarers, wheeling through the air in wide circles and broad spirals, often above the clouds, and maintaining their flight level with nothing more than an occasional adjustment of the wings. They are so specialized in the art of gliding that on windless days they would rather stay on their roost than exert themselves in the air. Their reputation may be doubtful, and the appellation "vulture" or the alternate term "buzzard" may have no flattering connotations. Yet, their work in cleaning nature of undesirable carrion is so valuable that they are protected by law in many places, particularly in the South. Their labor as scavengers is aided by the fact that they are gregarious, and flocks from 8 to two dozen often cooperate in the disposal of carrion and garbage. They do not trouble themselves with building nests but lay their brown-spotted, white eggs — usually 1 to 3 — on rocky ledges, hollow branches, or on the ground. Their range is the territory of the U.S. except in its northernmost portions. Length: 2½ feet. *Cathartes aura septentrionalis.*

◄ RED-TAILED HAWK

A Maligned Helper — This hawk sails through the air just for the joy of it, soaring so high that it is reduced to a tiny spot and then vanishes. It is not, as may be supposed, on a foraging expedition trying, from above, to locate a meal. When seeking food, it perches on top of a dead tree or some other vantage point with a commanding outlook over brushlands or weedy fields, watches the ground carefully and, with a sudden thrust, pounces on its prey which in most cases will be a mouse or a gopher or wood-rat, a snake or lizard, or even a rabbit. The western species gorges itself with obnoxious grasshoppers and helps the crops and the farmers. Unfortunately a few specimens acquire a taste for poultry, but to call the whole species "chicken hawks" or "hen hawks" is unjustified, and to shoot them at sight, as has been done for a long time in many parts of the country, is against the farmer's interest. The call of the red-tailed hawk is a hissing, high-pitched scream. It builds its nest on tall trees in the forest or in small stands, sometimes as high as 80 feet above ground; there the female lays 2 to 4 brown-spotted, white eggs. The eastern species ranges throughout Canada and the U.S. to the Great Plains; the western species, from the Rockies to the West Coast. Length: 20 inches. Eastern species: *Buteo borealis borealis.*

OSPREY ►

Invitation by Cartwheel — This bird, also called fish hawk, is a solid citizen: It minds its own affairs and does not molest smaller birds; it is intent only on its daily chores which it carries out with supreme skill, and is an affectionate parent; and it chases crows and other pests from its neighborhood. No wonder, then, that farmers in the coastal regions or near the Great Lakes erect long poles with an old wagon wheel on top, an invitation to the osprey to build its nest there. The hint is often taken, and the osprey sets up a huge structure of twigs, sticks, and corn stalks, so big that sometimes, in its lower tiers, grackles arrange their own nests. They are welcome. Fish are practically the only food of the osprey; they are caught by 30 to 100-foot plunges. Emerging from the water, the bird holds its prey with both claws which are as strong as steel hooks; they twist the fish lengthwise in the direction of flight to decrease wind resistance. Usually the meal is eaten on a favorite, frequently visited perch under which the ground is strewn with fish bones. The source of the fish does not make much difference; it may be saltwater or freshwater. The whole of North America is the osprey's range; during the winter it migrates south when its northern feeding grounds freeze over. Its call is a high-pitched whistle. Length: 2 feet. *Pandion haliaëtus carolinensis.*

BALD EAGLE ►

The Bird on the Quarter — On June 20, 1782, the Second Continental Congress adopted the bald eagle as our national emblem. Public opinion was doubtful, though, the dissenters including Benjamin Franklin. They pointed out at least one un-American character-trait of this bird: It steals. It lets the osprey capture a good-sized live fish, then scares the smaller bird into dropping it, swoops below and catches the falling fish. In spite of this robber habit, the majestic beauty of the bald eagle — its 7-foot wingspread and the masterful domination of its environment — won the day and the necessary votes. Of course, the eagle also fishes on its own, and has been observed to drag ashore big catches that were too heavy to be lifted. It also hunts small mammals and waterfowl, but the reports of its attacks on pigs, lambs and babies are fairy tales. Its huge nest of sticks and twigs, placed in tall trees or on cliffs, is used recurrently — Dr. F. H. Herrick reports one was used for 35 years — and, as the volume increases with the annual repairs, it often attains a height of 6 feet and also a diameter of 6 feet. The 1 to 3 eggs are white. The emblem bird is the southern bald eagle which ranges throughout the U. S. and southern Canada, while the larger, northern bald eagle does not occur south of the Great Lakes during the summer. Length: 2½ to 3 feet. *Haliaeetus leucocephalus leucocephalus.*

◄ RUFFED GROUSE

Chicken of the Forest — Thump-thump-thump. The drumming starts like slow, great heartbeats, a booming roll that increases rapidly until it fades into silence with a soft subdued tremor. That is the male grouse's call of love or his challenge, heard most often in spring, but also in the fall and winter. It is done by the wings beating the air, not striking an object. The grouse has another strange habit that hardly ever fails to scare the woodsman. When almost underfoot it will start up with an explosive whir of wings, and the wanderer's heart will skip a beat. The name of America's finest upland game bird (called partridge in New England) is derived from the "ruff" of greenish-black feathers that is draped around the neck and shoulders. Definitely a forest bird, it will not venture into the open country. It resembles in appearance a plump barnyard hen, and its clucking sounds are also reminiscent of the farmyard. 8 to 14 pale buff eggs are laid in a shallow depression in the ground and, as soon as the brood is hatched, they follow their mother around like a hen's chicks. If a walker approaches, the hen will tumble away with whining cries as if her wing were broken, to draw his attention from her young which crouch on the ground, quiet and invisible. The eastern ruffed grouse is a permanent resident from Massachusetts to Minnesota, to Tennessee and Georgia. Length: 17 inches. *Bonasa umbellus umbellus.*

◄ BOB-WHITE

A Character All Its Own — A cluster of pretty little birds arranged in a circle, the tails touching like the spokes of a wheel and the heads pointing outward — that is the bob-white's curious way of sleeping. The purpose is twofold: If an alarm is sounded, all birds take off simultaneously in the direction they are headed, i.e. everywhere, to the confusion of the marauding fox; the second factor is the warmth which the bodies of the circle provide for each other. On a winter night snow may begin to fall, but the birds do not stir; to them it is just a protective, warm blanket. The bob-white, also called quail in the North and partridge in the South, has other little habits that are ingratiating: It is sociable and lives in bands or bevies which wander through the fields or woodlands; when they come to an unprotected clearing, they run across at top speed with heads erect and crests raised. It flies swiftly, and sometimes has a characteristic way of gliding through the air with wings bent downward. Its 2 or 3 whistle notes, the last one sliding upward abruptly, are known universally. As it feeds on insect pests and the seeds of weeds, it should be protected. Epicures praise its meat, but there is very little of it on the plucked body. It ranges over the eastern half of the U.S. and has been introduced in many western states. Length: 10 inches. *Colinus virginianus virginianus.*

RING-NECKED PHEASANT ►

A Resplendent Immigrant — To combine Chinese and English ancestry seems unusual; yet the American ring-necked pheasant descends from a Chinese and an English species that were imported to the U.S. and interbred here. The pheasant family, comprising about 100 species, is most distinguished, and for thousands of years has been the particular pride of Asia where it is native from the eastern shores of the Mediterranean Sea eastward to Malaya. In our country pheasants are raised systematically on game farms and then liberated. Consequently they have spread throughout most of the northern U.S. They are permanent residents throughout this range, displaying a striking appearance with brilliantly lustrous plumage in fascinating color patterns. Because they provide a meat that is a top delicacy, the pheasant has become a favorite game bird. During the hunting season it is easier to shoot the female as the wary male is extremely shy. Its diet consists of wild fruits and insects, but as it also consumes great quantities of wheat, barley and corn, it sometimes becomes a nuisance to the farmer. The nest of dead leaves, grass and straw is constructed on the ground in overgrown meadows and bushy pastures, in moorlands and grainfields; rarely a deserted nest in a tree is taken over. The 6 to 12 eggs are buff to dark olive, or pale bluish-green, or light brown. A large bird, about 35 inches. *Phasianus colchicus torquatus.*

Birds

SPOTTED SANDPIPER

Pan American Shore Runner — This little bird teeters. It is called "teeter-tail." Teeter, according to Webster, is "to seesaw — as children do for sport." The spotted sandpiper does just that when it stands still; it raises its head and lowers its tail, then bends down its head and lifts its tail in a balancing act. But it does not stand still very often. Usually it runs busily along the water line in search of worms and spiders, insects and small crustaceans. It may be the water line of the Atlantic or of a small inland pond, of a water hole in the prairies or of the Pacific. Its coloration is an excellent camouflage and at a distance the picture of the bird merges with its surroundings. Its call is a shrill "sweet-sweet." The conspicuous blackish spots on the breast are not permanent but vanish before the autumn migration. A slight depression, lined with grass, will do for a nest; it may be set up on a sandy shore or an open field quite far inland, or the rocky bank of a stream. Here, four eggs are laid, white or tan, with brown and black marks. The downy grey young take to the shore immediately and run with their parents on wobbly legs. The bird's migratory range is large. During the summer spotted sandpipers enjoy themselves on Hudson Bay, in the winter specimens may be seen on the La Plata River in Argentina. Length: 7½ to 8 inches. *Actitis macularia.*

HERRING GULL

Strong, Tough, and Unafraid — When sailing in Maine waters, where these birds breed in huge colonies on the thousand little islands, bays and capes, herring gulls always accompany your boat. They snatch up every bit of refuse you discard, and in the small ports they are so tame, they will pull pork scraps right out of your hand. When you land on a beach where the outgoing tide leaves rocks and flats exposed, you will see hundreds of gulls searching there for organic matter. Besides, small fish are picked up, and mollusks and crustaceans. One great virtue of these birds is to keep the bays and estuaries free of floating garbage. They have also a peculiar liking for blueberries and fly far inland to secure them. Washington County, Maine, swarms with gulls at blueberry time. Their summer breeding grounds extend from the far North to a line running from British Columbia to the Great Lakes to Massachusetts. In the fall they migrate southward and are found on every American coast, lake, and river to Lower California and Cuba. Their call is loud and raucous. The nest of the herring gull, sometimes protected by heavy vegetation, is built of marsh plants, seaweeds and feathers; for strength and decor, shells are added. The 3 or 4 eggs, quite variable in color and usually blotched with brown, produce young whose plumage is much darker than that of their parents. Length: 2 feet. *Larus argentatus smithsonianus.*

◄ COMMON TERN

Swallow of the Sea — Schools of bluefish or mackerel swimming in deeper water drive schools of minnows to the surface. The minnows attract flocks of common terns which sail above the fish with shrill shrieks and dive for a meal; the antics of the terns bring fishermen to the scene who catch the mackerel or bluefish. This is the tern's practical contribution to ocean fishing. But nature-lovers are fond of the tern for another reason: It is one of the most graceful shore birds; with its deeply-forked tail, its streamlined body and slender wings, it looks like a black-capped white swallow. Sea swallow is indeed a name often applied to it. Terns are smaller and less compact than gulls, and are bolder fishermen: They plunge into the sea head on, in search of small fish which, besides some insects, are their only food. Observers have discovered that their way of living is not too easy: Innumerable dives are made in vain, and a minnow for the young is often carried in the bill over miles of ocean. In early summer, hundreds and sometimes thousands of common terns gather in breeding colonies, selecting an isolated island beach or a rocky shore. They scratch out a depression for a nest and line it prettily with shells, or construct a real mound of seaweed. They lay 2 to 4 spotted eggs. Roughly, the eastern half of the continent is their range. Length: 15 inches. *Sterna hirundo hirundo.*

MOURNING DOVE ►

A Quiet Countryman — There is a certain historic interest about the mourning dove. It looks like a smaller edition of the beautiful passenger pigeon which once was one of our most common birds. Since the great slaughter, the passenger pigeon has been extinct (not even the zoological gardens have been able to preserve the strain), and the mourning dove lives on as an image and reminder. In that sense, the name is well chosen, although the real reason for the term "mourning" is the bird's soft, melancholy cooing. Like all pigeons, it is a ground feeder, its diet consisting almost entirely of seeds. In the late summer, little flocks follow the harvesting crews and, after the crops have been taken, they search among the stubbles for corn, wheat and barley, and inspect what used to be the pea, bean and buckwheat patches. Some wild berries are welcome, too. These quiet, brown birds are friendly dwellers of the countryside, the orchards and groves, the farms and prairies throughout southern Canada and the U.S. They spend the winter south of the parallel of southern Connecticut. In spring they fly about in pairs: they are solitary in their breeding habits and build their nests of straw, stalks and moss in trees, preferably pines. As they lay only 2 white eggs, their protection by law has been rightfully demanded. Length: 12 inches. The western mourning dove is similar but smaller. *Zenaidura macroura carolinensis.*

Birds

ROAD RUNNER ►

Clown of the Desert — X marks the track of this astonishing bird, with two toes pointing forward and two backward. As the casual observer is mystified about the direction in which the bird has been running, the X is quite appropriate. The appearance of the road runner is as strange as its trail, considering the sly look in its light-colored eyes, its fine crest, and its huge tail which, at the end of a run, is raised straight up and used as a wind brake. The mesquite and cactus country of the Southwest is its home, and as there is plenty of room to run, it has developed this capacity to a surprising degree. It flies well, but it would rather run. In stagecoach days it greatly enjoyed running ahead of horses and wagons for miles, and always won the raçe, as it is said to attain a speed of 18 miles per hour. Its call is a series of cooing notes, and when alarmed, it clacks its bill and produces a rattling sound. Its menu consists of the offerings of the arid brush: It picks up insects, lizards and centipedes, mice and snakes. The story, often heard in the Southwest, that it builds a hedge of thorny cactus around a coiled rattlesnake to trap it is, of course, a fairy tale. The nest is built of sticks, in bushes or low trees; it contains 4 to 9 eggs of buff-white color. Length: 22 inches. *Geococcyx californianus.*

◄ BARN OWL

Hunter in the Darkness — A ghastly face; a nocturnal life; a noiseless flight; a call that sounds like a scream yet is subdued, repressed; a nesting place in an abandoned mansion, in the ruins of a church, a deserted tower — these are the reasons why the barn owl has been associated with ghosts and witches, spooks and haunted houses for centuries. By daylight it is seldom seen, and when disturbed by accident, it makes a bewildered and erratic getaway. But it is fully at ease in the night; its ears are large and so sensitive that they detect the slightest stir; its eyes are constructed for acute night vision; its plumage is soft and downy and enables it to glide eerily through the darkness without a sound. Yet it does not mind the neighborhood of man. For years, barn owls used to live in the northwest tower of the Smithsonian Institution in the heart of Washington; perhaps they still do. Like all owls, it regurgitates the indigestible bones and fur of its prey in the form of pellets, and thus offers a check of its diet which consists largely of mice and other rodents harmful to field and garden crops. In the West it also destroys a great many gophers and crickets; everywhere it is one of our most helpful birds of prey. It occurs in the central and southern U.S. and is an occasional straggler in Canada. Length: 17 to 20 inches. *Tyto alba pratincola.*

◄ SCREECH OWL

Poor Prophet, Good Provider — This small owl does not screech. It wails plaintively, it quavers tremulously, it utters a long, melancholy whinny. Some southern folks are greatly disturbed when the "shivering owl" dolefully cries near their cabin. To them it means the sure approach of death or trouble; fortunately they have their counter measures; to cast a handful of salt into the fire is one way to nullify the evil forebodings. Meanwhile the little screech owl goes about its nightly chore of hunting mice and rodents, snails and snakes and an occasional small bird. The latter practice makes many enemies, and when a screech owl is discovered by day in its resting place, perhaps a hollow in an apple tree, a flock of flickers and jays, cardinals and goldfinches will gather there to curse loudly the killer of their young. If the hideout is accessible, an actual attack may follow; annoyed by the daylight, the owl takes to flight. The screech owl is friendly to man and likes the neighborhood of farms. It does not build a nest but lays its 3 to 5 white eggs in a tree hollow or on a ledge of a house. The eastern species has two color phases, one grey and the other reddish brown; sometimes both are represented in the same nestful of young. Screech owls range throughout most of the U.S. and southern Canada. Illustrated is the eastern species. Length: 9 inches. *Otus asio naevius.*

WHIP-POOR-WILL ►

Blending With Nature — This bird makes its presence known by calling its own name loudly and repeatedly, at dusk and before dawn, often preceding it by a low cluck. The vibrant, throbbing caller is, however, a sort of hermit in other ways. Few people ever see it, for its plumage has a mottled camouflage coloration — a mixture of black, grey, buff, brown, yellow and white — which merges perfectly with its background in nature; to make itself even more inconspicuous, the bird always perches lengthwise on the branch. It spends much time on the ground, and even its short insect-hunting flights rarely take it to the tree tops or great heights. Low valleys or brooks and meadows are its haunts, and there it captures with its big mouth the moths and other nocturnal insects which are its only food; most of its prey is caught on the wing in a noiseless flight. During the day it sleeps in thickets. On well drained ground perhaps on the margin of a brushwood, a slight depression is found in some leaves, and on this secluded spot the female deposits her 2 eggs which are white and spotted with brown or lilac. No attempt is made to construct a nest. The range of the whip-poor-will extends from Nova Scotia to the northern Gulf States, and westward to the Great Plains. Stephen's whip-poor-will, of similar color but larger in size, occurs in the Southwest. Length: 10 inches. *Antrostomus vociferus vociferus.*

CHIMNEY SWIFT ►

The Bow and Arrow of the Sky — How did the chimney swift get along before there were chimneys on this continent? It built its nest in hollow trees and caves, or attached it to cliffs; it curiously adapted itself to civilization when white man arrived. The saliva-cement with which it glues the tiny twigs to its nest sticks well to a brick or mortar surface; also the darkness of the chimney is appealing to a bird which is not nocturnal but likes dusk and dawn and cloudy days. The chimney swift is fascinating in other ways: As the name implies, it shoots through the air with swiftest speed, yet zig-zags a great deal with erratic dashes that resemble the flight of a bat. Its crescent wings beat so rapidly, they seem a mechanical gadget rather than part of a living creature. The bird is so much at home on the wing that it hunts in the air — mosquitoes, flies, and other insects — drinks in the air, and takes its bath by dashing from the air into the water for a refreshing shower. It does not perch on branches but clings to vertical surfaces; the young, hatched from 4 to 6 white eggs, do the same as soon as they leave the nest. The chimney swift ranges throughout the eastern half of the continent. Where it spends the winter is not definitely known, but probably in Central or South America. Related species live in the West. Length: 5½ inches. *Chaetura pelagica.*

◄ RUBY-THROATED HUMMINGBIRD

An Incredible Dynamo — This tiny bird weighs only as much as a copper cent, and half a silver dollar will cover its neat little nest that is built of plant down and lichen, spider web and saliva threads. Its flying capacities are astonishing; its wings vibrate so rapidly that all one can see is a dull blur; the beating of wings also produces the humming sound that gives the bird its name. Like a helicopter, it can hover in front of a blossom to drink its nectar, and it flies forward and backward with equal ease. Sometimes it swings back and forth through the air as if it were sitting on a trapeze. As to endurance, it seems to enjoy greatly its annual round trip flight which may take it from Guatemala to Labrador and back. The brilliant ruby-red of the male's throat glistens with a metallic sheen as the bird darts about, but it is not always visible since the refraction of light from the feathers produces the color. Once or twice a year two tiny white eggs, about half an inch long, are laid in the nest saddled on a tree branch, 3-50 feet high. The hummingbird family is truly all-American, its approximately 500 species ranging from the Argentinian Andes to the Canadian northwoods. But east of the Mississippi the ruby-throated hummingbird is the only species, summering from the Hudson Bay region to eastern Mexico, and wintering from Florida to Central America. Length: 3¾ inches. *Archilochus colubris.*

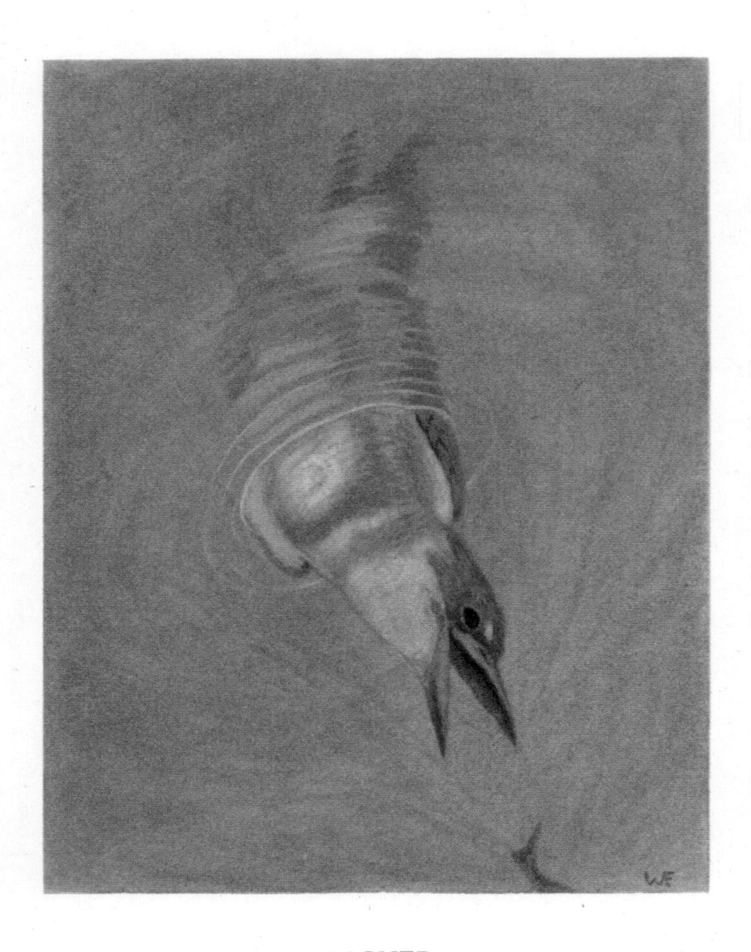

◄ BELTED KINGFISHER

A Top-Heavy Original — Energy and character mark the ways of the kingfisher: Sitting on a branch over the water, its appearance is somewhat grotesque, with a head too big for its body, a crest of "uncombed hair," and small, weak feet. But the bird is not idling away its time. It observes the water alertly, awaiting the least movement; suddenly it plunges head on from its branch, as if it were dropping dead and, after a splash, emerges with a fish in its long, sharp bill; a small one is swallowed without delay, a big one is beaten repeatedly against a stone until it is lifeless and manageable. Occasionally, the menu is varied by frogs, salamanders, tadpoles, lizards, beetles and crickets. Fish bones and other indigestible parts are regurgitated, after digestion, in the form of pellets, but they are not wasted; many are used as bedding in the nest. To construct the latter is an arduous task; in a clay or gravel bank a tunnel is dug, perhaps 3 or 4 or sometimes more than 10 feet long, with a chamber at the end where 5 to 8 white eggs are deposited. Except during the mating season, the kingfisher is solitary and does not tolerate intruders on its fishing grounds. On the whole it is a freshwater fisher, but occurs also on tidal inlets. Its range is the entire continent. Its call is a rattle. Length: 13 inches. *Megaceryle alcyon alcyon.*

FLICKER ►

Man About Town — Knock at a tree with a large hole in its trunk, preferably a dead tree, and a flicker may stick out its head and greet you. This friendly woodpecker is so common, it has acquired more than 20 names, most of them cheerful like high-holer, wickup, yellow-hammer and wood pigeon. It is also a good fellow as far as the bird world is concerned, and seemingly lives on the best of terms with the songbirds, the sparrows, the hawks. Flickers are a hardy race and thrive anywhere in the U.S. and southern Canada. The northern or eastern species is yellow-shafted, the western is red-shafted; in the area between they interbreed, and hybrids are common in the Midwest. They like every type of country where there are trees, except dense thickets. City parks, orchards and bird houses in the suburbs are welcome quarters. The flicker's nest is usually a deep hole in a tree, and is lined with chips. Here its 5 to 9 white eggs are laid. While enjoying some wild berries and seeds, its main food consists of beetles, ants and other insects which are speared with its long and sharp tongue. The latter can be flung out for 2½ inches beyond the bill, and its sticky saliva acts as an adhesive to which small creatures are instantly attached. Its clear "flickering" cries are responsible for its name, and its "wick wick" is sometimes repeated a dozen times. Length: 12 to 13 inches. Illustrated is the northern species. *Colaptes auratus luteus.*

DOWNY WOODPECKER ►

A Friendly Woodsman — Apple borer, coddling moth, pine weevil, birch borer, maple borer, aphids, gall insects and leaf miners — all these insects, badly injurious to orchards, parks and forests, are on the menu of this valuable, small bird. The service it renders in this way has endeared it to man. Another list is equally significant of its popularity: Chickadees, cardinals, nuthatches, creepers and titmice are its friends and associates, particularly in wintertime when they visit feeding stations all together. In the mating season the male performs a vigorous drumming act, rolling a jubilant tremolo on dry wood, a cheerful substitute for the lack of a singing voice. It builds its nest in a cavity of a tree trunk which it usually hollows out with its own bill; this is more easily done on dead timber, but live trees of soft wood are selected also. The nest of this little lumberjack is appropriately 8 or 10 inches deep. Here 4 to 6 white eggs are laid which have the porcelain-like surface of most woodpecker eggs. A close relative is the hairy woodpecker, almost a replica of the downy species but larger by about 2 inches or more and equipped with a heavier bill. The northern downy variety ranges throughout the east as far south as South Carolina, but related woodpeckers cover the whole of the U.S. and southern Canada. Length: 6¾ inches. *Dryobates pubescens medianus.*

◄ EASTERN PHOEBE

Tail-Bobber — When the ice melts in brooks and streams, and during the first warm sunny days when the swarms of gnats rise and fall in dancing spirals, the little phoebe is there to watch the coming of spring, to catch some flies, bob its tail cheerfully (a habit practiced so often that it is a distinguishing mark of the bird), and sing its famous call which is supposed to be a pronouncement of its name. According to some authorities, however, the singing is a rather uncertain, whispered performance, and frequently the bird gets credit for the clearly whistled fee-bee spring call of the chickadee. One of the earliest birds to nest, the phoebe prefers some very definite localities as home sites, for instance ledges under bridges spanning wooded streams, or a culvert, an outhouse, or a beam under a porch, or the root base of a fallen tree. The nest is constructed of mud, moss and leaves, and is lined with soft materials like feathers and rootlets. Its 3 to 6 white eggs are sometimes marked with small dots of brown. Year after year it returns to its old nesting site. Its favorite observation post is a branch overhanging a pond or brook, and from there it darts out after moths, gnats or flies. The eastern phoebe's range extends from Newfoundland to the Rockies in the west, to South Carolina and Texas in the south. Say's phoebe is its western counterpart. Length: 7 inches. *Sayornis phoebe.*

◄ TREE SWALLOW

Convention on the Telephone Wire — A flock of these birds circling in the air, the sun playing on their iridescent greenish-blue backs and their breasts a gleaming pure white, are a delightful sight. They are among the earliest arrivals in spring, and before they leave again in the fall they gather in huge assemblies, feeding in marshes and lining telephone wires in close rows. These big social gatherings start when the breeding season is over and are carried on for many weeks, from July to October. Flying insects are their principal diet, while in the colder months they enjoy wild berries, particularly bayberries of which they are fond. Woodpecker holes, natural cavities in trees, and crevices in rocks and buildings are their nesting sites, but they will also use bird boxes erected for them. Pearson reports of a couple settling in an old open can, which was a mistake, for the sun heated the tin and the young died. The nest is woven of grass and lined with feathers, and holds 4 or 5, or sometimes even 7 white eggs. The call does not rise above a high-pitched twittering chatter, but during the mating season the male utters a sweet little warbling twitter. The tree swallows' range extends from the arctic regions of Alaska and Labrador to a southern line from central California approximately to northern Connecticut. They spend the winter in our South, in Mexico, Cuba, and Central America. Length: 6 inches. *Iridoprocne bicolor.*

BARN SWALLOW ►

"Watch the swallers skootin' past! 'Bout as peert as you could ast." — A rich blue, a glossy chestnut, a delicate salmon — there could be no more intriguing pattern of colors. Also, the body of this bird, with the deeply forked tail and the crescent wings, is lovely, particulraly in flight; it is not only graceful but also skillful as it darts into the air, skims over the fields, or zig-zags over the pasture, and it is admirably enduring. Some barn swallows summer in Alaska, winter in southern Brazil. As the name implies, this bird uses a barn as a nesting site, i.e. beams or walls within the structure. The swallow which attaches its house to the outside walls under the eaves is the cliff swallow. The question arises, where did these birds do their breeding before barns existed in this country? Well, they built their nests in caves or cavities of trees. Their building material is a mixture of mud, straw, and other vegetable material, and they line the cradle with feathers and fine grasses; their 4, 5, or 6 eggs are white, marked with brown spots. Like other members of their family they feed on the wing, catching insects such as flies, beetles and bugs and, to a lesser extent, wasps, flying ants, moths and others. Barn swallows occur in most parts of North America, as far north as Greenland and as far south as Alabama. The winter is spent in South America. Length: 7 inches. *Hirundo erythrogaster.*

NORTHERN BLUE JAY ►

Cop and Robber — The spotlight is on the blue jay. Just as the mourning dove stands for quiet and reserve, the dashing jay is the symbol of sass and noise; minding everybody's business, it scolds and shrieks in various nasal screams or flutelike calls, singly or in chorus. It annoys smaller birds and gives a piece of its mind to owls and hawks, teases cats and scares snakes. It stands in the midst of the struggle for life; on the one hand it robs and eats eggs and young birds; in turn, many a significant mound of blue jay feathers can be found under a hawk's perch. The general diet of this common bird also includes dragonflies and other large insects, nuts and seeds. It is especially fond of acorns and hides so many in various spots, without retrieving them, that it has been called a "planter of oak forests." It builds its nest of twigs and small roots in the fork of a tree, preferably of the evergreen kind, and while the forest is a satisfactory environment, life on a farm, in a village or suburb is more exciting. Consequently few birds are as well known in the eastern and central parts of the continent. It lays 4 to 6 greenish eggs, spotted with brown. During the winter it stays in its range, which extends from Hudson Bay south to the Gulf States and west to the Great Plains. Length: 11¾ inches. *Cyanocitta cristata cristata.*

◄ AMERICAN MAGPIE

Pet and Pest — Who keeps the countryside clean of offensive carcasses, of butchering scraps, offal and refuse? The magpie, an associate of the vulture. It also devours great numbers of injurious grasshoppers, weevils, grubs and caterpillars. Besides, it is an amusing pet in captivity, and some birds learn to imitate the human voice. On the other side of the balance sheet the flocks of magpies that gather around western ranches may become serious pests. They destroy the eggs and young of game birds, plunder the melon and berry patches, and are reported to annoy newly born calves and freshly sheared sheep by pecking them viciously. Traditionally, they have the reputation of being impudent thieves. For these reasons occasional campaigns have been waged locally to destroy the magpies, yet they hold their own; fortunately so, for the conspicuous bird with the enormous tail is a diverting and sociable addition to the western landscape. It seems to be forever chattering, using many expressive sounds; the whole flock appears to carry on an animated conversation. In a bulky nest of mud and sticks, sometimes lined with horsehair, it lays 4 to 8 greyish-brown eggs. Its range is a belt extending from the far north to Arizona and New Mexico; there it stays summer and winter. A close relative, the somewhat smaller yellow-billed magpie, occurs in the countryside of central California. Length: 18 inches. *Pica pica hudsonia.*

◄ EASTERN CROW

Living Well by Its Wits — Approach a crow with a gun and it will fly away. Carry a wooden stick and it will pay no attention to you. If you have a gun, the crow will know its range. You can kill one only by matching wits with it. Collectively they are just as smart. When feeding on the ground, a sentinel relays any sign of danger. When one of their enemies appears, they take immediate action; they hound a fox across an open field and, with noisy scolding, advertise its presence; if they detect an owl on a hidden branch, they swoop at it and drive it from tree to tree. In captivity they are hilarious pets and learn to pronounce certain words; their thievish tendencies, however, are irritating. Their various cawing sounds and additional cackling and stuttering noises seem to imply various meanings. Whether the crow is a useful or a harmful bird is probably to be decided on a local basis; it devours great numbers of slugs, grasshoppers and other injurious insects, but it also plunders corn and grain fields, and the fact that the device to keep away birds is called a scarecrow, expresses the farmer's opinion. Crows build their nests in trees, usually pines, and lay 3 to 6 eggs which are greenish-blue marked with brown. The range of the eastern crow extends from Canada to Texas, but similar species are encountered throughout the country. Length: 19 inches. *Corvus brachyrhynchos brachyrhynchos.*

BLACK-CAPPED CHICKADEE ►

Black Bib, Black Hat — To alight on a branch upside down and nonchalantly eat a meal in that position, is one of the most amusing habits of this little bird. It is intriguing also in other ways: It is not just a fair-weather friend, but stays with us all winter; indeed, we see much more of it during the cold months when a piece of suet or a handful of sunflower seeds will bring a flock of chickadees to the feeding station. They enjoy their meal but are never rough and greedy; in fact, they will leave if other visitors try to bully them, and return later. During the summer, they retire to the woods and, from twigs and crevices in the bark of trees, pick all sorts of noxious insects, weevils, larvae, and moth eggs, among them the eggs of the tent-caterpillar moth. They also consume seeds and fruits. The nest is built in an old woodpecker hole, or a new cavity is excavated in the soft wood of a dead limb or trunk; it is lined with plant down and filled with 5 to 8 eggs, half an inch wide, white, and dotted with reddish-brown spots. The chickadee calls its own name, and the last syllable is often prolonged into a dee-dee-dee-dee; in spring it has an especially clear, whistled double-note. It occurs from Labrador to North Carolina and throughout the Midwest. Length: 5¼ inches. *Penthestes atricapillus atricapillus.*

WHITE-BREASTED NUTHATCH ►

A Forest Acrobat — How to open a nut? The nuthatch does it this way: He wedges it into a crevice in the rough bark of a tree, gives it a few strong hammer blows with the bill, splits it open and gets the kernel. The bird's name is derived from this operation. Sometimes it leaves the nut in the crack, to store it for a rainy day. Another outstanding trait of the nuthatch is its peculiar method of walking: It crawls up as fast as down along the tree trunks and branches, its head always forward, and proceeds on a limb right side up or upside down. It can do so because its feet are very large for its size, and exceptionally strong. It does not even use its tail for a prop, as the woodpeckers do. Besides eating nuts and seeds, it is forever .busy flying, crawling, swinging, and hunting beetles, ants, spiders, bugs and insect eggs. While running, it utters its well-known yank yank or wank wank, and in spring it has some joyous musical notes. In an abandoned woodpecker hole or a cavity in a big tree, sometimes as high as 60 feet above ground, it builds its nest of plant fibres, rabbit's fur, feathers, and twigs. Here 4 to 8 brown-spotted eggs are deposited. There are nuthatches almost everywhere in the U.S. and Canada. In the East, the white-breasted species is most common. Length: 6 inches. *Sitta carolinensis carolinensis.*

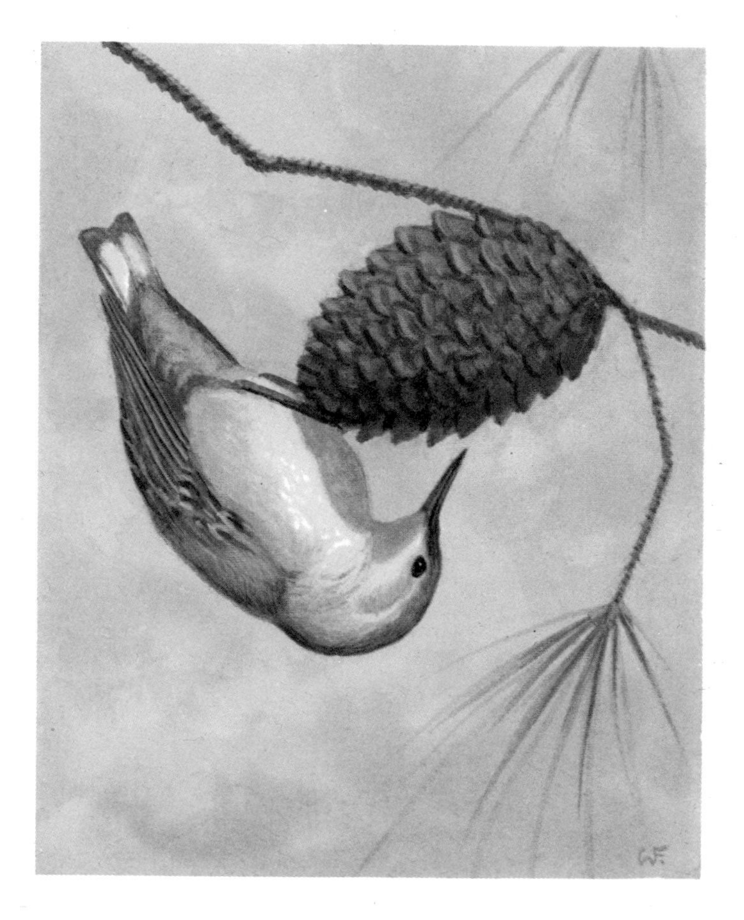

◄ HOUSE WREN

An Exciting World — It scolds in a harsh voice. It chatters monotonously. It sings musically but repeats the same theme over and over again. It cocks its tail up over the back and jumps up and down, up and down, on its tiny legs. Nervous? Worried? Well, life isn't easy. For one thing the male takes the nesting problem very seriously. When arriving in a new territory, it fills every hole and cavity in that neighborhood with twigs, so that there will be a good selection of reserved sites. It may take one birdhouse in a garden and fill up two others to keep out undesirable neighbors. The final choice is often most original: a tin can, an old coat, a dead horse's bleached skull which a farm boy has hurled into a tree. Old apple orchards are popular sites. Then there is the other problem: The male house wren is often a bigamist, and to support two separate households and feed two families is not easy. No wonder there is always an air of bustling, hustling, and rattling activity about the wren world. Their diet consists of caterpillars, spiders, beetles and other insects, a menu commended by gardeners. 4 to 9 white eggs, thickly spotted with brown or lilac dots, are laid in their bulky nests. The familiar eastern house wren occurs in most eastern states, and there are other species in almost every region of the U.S. and southern Canada. Length: 5 inches. *Troglodytes aëdon aëdon.*

◄ MOCKINGBIRD

A Star Performer — It is good news that the mockingbirds are spreading. The eastern species is occasionally heard now as far north as Maine and Quebec, and some of the western species are so numerous they can be observed on city streets. They are welcome, for they have a passion for singing and a beautiful, liquid voice. They sing all day and sometimes half the night, and not only in spring but also in summer and often in winter; rightly they have been called the American counterpart of the European nightingale. They have their own lovely passages, themes, and calls, and they mimic to perfection almost any other song bird. Forbush followed up the imitations of one mockingbird in the Arnold Arboretum in Boston and made a list of 39 bird songs and 50 bird calls he heard from that one source. Besides, the mockingbird has what to human ears appears to be a sense of humor: It produces the chirping of a cricket, the barking of a dog, the croaking of a frog, the meowing of a cat, the creaking of a door with rusty hinges, and the whistling of a city "wolf." Mockingbirds are useful insect eaters, and add some wild fruit in season to their diet. Their nests are built in shrubs near houses, and consist of weed stalks and twigs, shreds and pieces of string; their 4 to 6 bluish-green eggs are marked with brown. They are permanent residents. Length: 10½ inches. Eastern species: *Mimus polyglottos polyglottos.*

ROBIN ►

A Great American — The return of the robin is a regular topic of conversation in the month of March, throughout the central and northern states including our metropolitan cities. It means that spring is in the air, heralded by a dependable friend. Early in the morning there is a concert to greet the day. Sweet warbling notes fill the air. During the day, earthworms are hunted in an efficient manner. Briskly the robin runs over the lawn, then stops dead in its tracks, straight and still, and bears down on its prey with an energetic blow. Insects, seeds and fruits (including cherries and strawberries), supplement the earthworm diet. When mating time arrives, the nest is built in a substantial and solid fashion, of mud reinforced with grass blades and plant stalks, and to give the bowl just the right shape, the female employs her breast, making turn after turn. The 3 to 5 eggs have a delicate blue color which, under the name of "robin-egg blue," has become a fashionable shade. The robin, a thrush by family ties, was named by homesick pioneers after an English songbird of the same name which, however, has a redder breast and is much smaller. Of the various species, the famous eastern robin ranges from Canada and Alaska southward to Virginia, along the Appalachian Mountains to Georgia, and to the Rocky Mountains in the West; a western variety, from the Rockies to the Pacific. Length: 10 inches. *Turdus migratorius migratorius.*

WOOD THRUSH ►

Classical Themes in the Forest — The thrushes are a distinguished family and include such celebrities as the robin, the bluebird and the European nightingale. The wood thrush, too, is an outstanding bird, with its rich brown back and the prominent dark spots on its white breast and abdomen; its liquid song is lovely, and as it repeats its passages often, each time in a slightly changed version, its singing has been compared to the "theme with variations" of the classical composers. There is indeed an air of classical serenity about this calm bird, as it sits motionless on its green, leafy perch and sings on and on. It loves the woods, is seen also in orchards and gardens, and does not like the mountains. On a sapling in the forest or on the crotch of a big tree it builds its nest with great care, weaving it firmly of twigs and rootlets, and reinforcing it with an inner wall of mud; here 3 to 5 greenish-blue eggs are deposited. Its diet is varied and includes the seeds of weeds and some wild fruits as well as caterpillars and ants, beetles and bugs, and other insects. Its range is the East and much of the South; in the North, however, it does not occur beyond Vermont, New Hampshire and southern Quebec. The winter is spent in Central America. Its cousin, the eastern hermit thrush, is a mountain and northwoods dweller and an even more famous singer. Length: 8¼ inches. *Hylocichla mustelina.*

◄ BLUEBIRD

"Soft as an Angel's Wing" — A pair of bluebirds dreamily floating before an old elm in the bright afternoon sun are a glorious summer sight. The vivid blue of the male rivals the northern summer sky; its orange-brown breast reflects the color of a setting sun, and the white belly has the purity of snow. As the blue is a refractionary, not a pigment color, it can be observed only when the light is favorable. With its sweetly warbled song, it is a beautiful, friendly bird — also an affectionate mate — and very gentle. Perhaps it is too gentle, for it used to be common in our city parks and suburban gardens but has been crowded out of many areas by such upstart-immigrants as the English sparrow and the starling. Practically speaking, the bluebird is a very desirable resident, eating pests like cutworms and cankerworms, grasshoppers and weevils. In fall and winter its diet shifts to wild fruits, especially berries of dogwood and holly. Its 5 or 6 pale-blue eggs are deposited in a nest of grass, hair and rootlets in a tree cavity or a bird house. The range of the eastern species extends from Nova Scotia and Manitoba to the Gulf States, while the western variety occurs from British Columbia to California. The birds winter in the warmer parts of the same ranges. The mountain bluebird is found high in the Rockies. Length: 7 inches. Eastern species: *Sialia sialis sialis.*

◄ CEDAR WAXWING

A Crested Aristocrat — If a bunch of berries hangs so far out on a branch that it can be reached only by the bird nearest to them, the latter will pick one after another and, in its bill, hand them down the line to its associates. Which bird is to swallow it? Sometimes they cannot make up their minds and pass the berry back and forth. Such considerate manners go with a tailored and distinguished appearance. Its varicolored coat is sleek, and on the tips of the secondary wing feathers red drops of pigment appear which are shiny and bright as sealing wax; they have given the bird its name. Its voice, however, is not remarkable, consisting of a thin note so high-pitched that it is perceptible only to some ears. The cedar waxwing is a fruit eater and includes mulberries and grapes, hawthorn and dogwood berries in its diet; it is also fond of choke cherries and cedar berries and devours some insects. The nest is built rather late in the season and looks bulky and untidy with bark and moss among the grasses and roots. Its 3 to 5 eggs are greyish-blue and speckled. The young are fed by regurgitation. Cedar waxwings occur throughout southern Canada and the northern half of the U.S. from the Atlantic to the Pacific; they usually spend the winter in the South. In some years, however, surprisingly large numbers stay in the north. Length: 7¼ inches. *Bombycilla cedrorum.*

STARLING ►

The Interloper — When, in 1890 and '91, one hundred starlings were brought over from Europe and released in New York's Central Park, it seemed a good deed at the time. The starling is a handsome bird, with its metallic summer coat on which the sunlight plays in the colors of the rainbow, and its spotted brown winter coat. Its song is pleasant and, like its cousin, the mynah bird of Asia, the starling has the gift of imitating other bird calls; in captivity both may learn to speak. Most important, however, this bird is a great consumer of insect pests, and at present it helps to control the obnoxious Japanese beetle. On the other hand, nobody dreamed in 1890 that in half a century the 100 immigrants would multiply into a horde of descendants numbering millions, and would occupy the country from Canada to Florida, and westward to the Rockies; it seems only a question of time before they will spread to the West Coast. They are tough and adaptable, and build their slovenly nests almost anywhere in a tree or building. They are dirty and noisy; worst of all, they have driven from our gardens and parks thousands of downy woodpeckers and flycatchers, flickers and bluebirds, by annoying them and appropriating their nest holes. They also steal cherries and other cultivated fruits. For the winter they leave their northernmost range, but are permanent residents in the rest. Length: 8½ inches. *Sturnus vulgaris vulgaris.*

ENGLISH SPARROW

Making Himself at Home — This bird comes from northern Europe and Asia, not just from England. It is not a sparrow either, but a member of the weaver finches. It was imported to America to exterminate the cankerworms, but it showed much more interest in horse dung and grains, and the cankerworms are still with us. In 1850 and '52, flocks of these sparrows were released in Brooklyn and nearby, and within 20 years every city on the Atlantic seaboard swarmed with them; then they took to the country, and today are permanent residents throughout the U.S. and most of Canada. Their hordes have declined in the cities since the automobile replaced the horse. There are several reasons for the sparrows' triumphant acclimatization; They are tough, rugged and cheerful; they build their nests on any place 5 or more feet above ground, and of any material; and they breed throughout most of the year. A warm, sunny day in January starts both the male and female on their nest building activities. Their 3 to 7 eggs are greyish-white or dull brown, and speckled. As they eat large quantities of corn and wheat, oats, barley and other grains, besides some insects and weed seeds; as they are dirty and noisy — they have no real song; and as they are pugnacious and aggressive and drive bluebirds, martins, and other desirable birds from their nesting sites, they are considered a pest. Length: 6-1/3 inches. *Passer domesticus domesticus.*

BOBOLINK

Commuter Between the Continents — "A bright black wedding coat" with white trimmings is the bobolink's summer attire. His "quaker wife, pretty and quiet, with plain brown wings" is inconspicuous, and while the male fits perfectly into a bright meadow of daisies, soaring low over the blossoms and singing his exuberant, sparkling melodies, the female belongs to the nest which is almost invisibly tucked into a depression on the ground where the grasses are thick and tall. The 4 to 7 white eggs are camouflaged with blotches of brown and grey, and the yellowish-brown young are also protected by their coloration; besides, the parents never fly directly to their home, in order to conceal its location. As they feed on grasshoppers and other injurious insects, they are highly welcome in their summer quarters which extend throughout southern Canada and the northern tier of the U.S. from the Atlantic to Alberta, Montana, and Utah. In the fall the males change into plain winter coats, the tribe gathers in huge flocks, and they head for the southern states. There they are not at all popular, for they devour great quantities of wild and cultivated rice. Fortunately, they do not linger long and start out on one of the longest voyages in the bird world; they sail to the pampas of southern Brazil and northern Argentina. But in spring they are back in the North, having flown maybe 9 thousand miles. Length: 7½ inches. *Dolichonyx oryzivorus.*

◄ BALTIMORE ORIOLE

"A Scrap of Sunset with a Voice" — That work of art, the nest of the Baltimore oriole, is the achievement of the plain, yellowish female. On a shade tree or orchard tree by a village road or in a city park, a long, sweeping branch is selected, and here she begins to weave the pendant nest which looks like a dangling Christmas stocking; she works, of course, from the top down. Originally, her building materials were plant fibres and hair, and they still are, but now human subsidies of string, cloth and yarn are welcomed and worked into the grey-brown texture; the resulting basket is so strong, it will stick to its branch through winter storms of snow and sleet. While the female weaves, the male flies through the tree tops, flashing his flaming colors in the sun, and whistles his loud, rich love song. Thoreau thought that one song goes: "Eat it, Potter, eat it," while Hausman translates another song into "Oh here here; see me up here." Whatever it may be, the female pleasantly responds with her own sweet song. The oriole's diet consists mostly of caterpillars and boll weevils, grasshoppers and plant lice, other injurious insects and also some fruit. Its 4 or 5 white eggs are irregularly marked with brown and black. The range extends from southern Canada almost to the Gulf, and west to the Rocky Mountains; for the winter it travels to Central and South America. Length: 7½ inches. *Icterus galbula.*

MEADOWLARK ►

Master of the Daisy Fields — Although not related either to our horned lark or to the famed European skylark, it is a fine-looking and useful bird in its own right. The black V on its yellow breast is an unmistakable distinguishing mark; its song is flute-like and cheery, and its diet is of a kind that helps the farmer: It feeds on grasshoppers and cutworms, crickets, hairy caterpillars, and other harmful insects, and eats grain and wild grass seeds only to a small extent. The eastern species occurs throughout the Canadian and American east, approximately to the Nebraska-Texas line; there it meets the similar, though somewhat paler, western meadowlark which ranges to the Pacific Coast. Both are permanent residents in the southern sections of their areas; those that go north often arrive in March when there is still snow on the ground. A male newcomer selects his territory and guards it jealously against intruders; the love songs he pours out from his perch sometimes win him more than one mate, though normally he is content to be monogamous. The nest is constructed in the dry grasses of the past year, and sometimes a tunnel of a foot or more has to be traversed before the arched nest is reached. Here 3 to 6 white eggs, speckled with brown, are laid and, although the male does not share in the egg-sitting, he is a good provider for his young. Length: 10¾ inches. *Sturnella magna magna.*

RED-WINGED BLACKBIRD ►

Soldier of the Marshlands — Soaring through the air like clouds of smoke, huge flocks of blackbirds descend upon our marshes in spring time. The males are first on the scene, proudly displaying their bright scarlet shoulder patches edged with yellow. Swamps fringed with bushes are favorites; they resound with their loud screams — of a musical kind, though — and their deep, throaty call notes that resemble a rattle when many birds merge their voices. Then the plain-looking, unspectacular females arrive, and over the plains and pastures a merry chase begins: The red-winged males are fiery suitors, and the ensuing game has been described as a "head-long-dash courtship." When the excitment dies down to responsible housekeeping, the nest of coarse plants is attached to a bush, quite low and usually in a marsh or bog. The 4 or 5 eggs are bluish-white and irregularly marked. Seeds of swamp plants and weeds are their principal food, supplemented by insects and berries. Various species of redwings are encountered throughout southern Canada and the U.S., the eastern variety ranging to the Great Plains. They are permanent residents in the southern and western states, but migratory in the north and the Appalachian Mountains. The tricolored red-winged blackbird, its deep-red epaulettes set off with white, is a familiar sight in Oregon and California. Length of eastern species: 9½ inches. *Agelaius phoeniceus phoeniceus.*

◄ SCARLET TANAGER

In a Gala Uniform — The wardrobe of this bird is varied indeed. The young have an inconspicuous coat, a mixture of brown, yellow, and olive, and are slightly streaked below. When they grow up the males put on that bright scarlet summer garment that makes them delightful, tropical color flashes in our shade and forest trees. The females get an attire which is dull greenish above and green-yellow below; they appear so different from their mates that laymen may take them for another species. However, in the fall, the males, too, change into an inconspicuous travel suit; at that time they look greenish-yellow blotched with red paint. They resemble the females (although they keep their black wings) when they set out on their long voyage to Colombia and Bolivia. In spring they are back with us, as bright red as ever. Their song is quite loud and pretty but possesses a certain wheezing quality; it has been compared to the voice of a robin with a cold. Their menu includes berries and wild fruits but consists mainly of caterpillars and other insects. The nest is built on a tree branch, sometimes as high as 70 feet above ground, and often toward the end of the limb. 3 or 4 greenish-blue eggs are marked with brown specks. The range of the scarlet tanager extends from Canada to the mid-South and westward almost to the Great Plains. Length: 7¼ inches. *Piranga erythromelas.*

◄ CARDINAL

Prince in Scarlet — To watch the little ways of a cardinal family is fascinating. Father, with his red uniform and black chin, has, of course, the spotlight; he sits on an exposed perch for all to admire and pours out his series of whistles while the female and the young, their coats more brown than red, remain hidden in the foliage, occasionally uttering a sharp call note. The male is an attentive husband; late in April or in May, the female selects a vine or thicket for a site, builds the nest of twigs and rootlets, blades of grass and pieces of bark, and lays 3 or 4 bluish-white eggs with reddish-brown specks, while the male brings her tidbits of berries and insects and feeds her gently. When the young brood leaves the nest he takes complete charge of them, with solicitous seriousness, while his mate starts to build another nest for a second set of eggs. Usually two rounds are considered sufficient for one year, but sometimes the performance is repeated a third time. Cardinals stay with us throughout the winter, although the young birds do a good deal of local wandering and, as their red plumage seems doubly bright in the white snow, they are honored guests at every feeding station. The best-known cardinal is the eastern species which ranges from central New York to the Gulf States and to Oklahoma - Nebraska in the west. Length: 8 inches. *Richmondena cardinalis cardinalis.*

ROSE-BREASTED GROSBEAK ►

A Model Husband — Although the female in her brown and white clothes is not nearly as handsome as her husband, she has a way of endearing herself to her mate. When she builds the nest, he follows her around, shows great interest in her work, and even helps her; however, the result is a rather loose and poorly woven structure. When she sits on the eggs, he brings her food, and nearly half the time he has to take care of the sitting himself. Later in the year when a friendly observer watches the male, the latter will probably fly to the female and the young to show them to the visitor. These gentle and cheerful manners are enhanced by a beautiful, robin-like song of rapid warbles. On the practical side, farmers welcome rose-breasted grosbeaks because of their fondness for potato beetles, caterpillars and other injurious insects; wild fruits in season are also included in their diet. Their nests are found in small trees or elderberry bushes, not lower than 5 feet and not higher than 20 feet above the ground. The eggs, blue spotted with brown, can often be seen from below through the nest's thin bottom. Rose-breasted grosbeaks occur from Canada to New Jersey and Ohio, and as far west as the Great Plains. They also breed in the higher Allegheny Mountains southward to North Carolina. For the winter they fly to Central and South America. Length: 8 inches. *Hedymeles ludovicianus.*

GOLDFINCH ►

Caroler of the Tree Tops — Joy of life seems to be the outstanding characteristic of this lovely, small bird, and "the goldfinch way" must be the ideal standard for song birds; small gay flocks are forever cavorting in a tree top or about a fence rail, playing and chattering, warbling a tuneful canary rhythm or calling each other in sweet, musical notes. On and on they sing, even when flying or gobbling down their favorite seeds. They bound along in the air as if they are riding on imaginary waves or on a roller-coaster. Long after the other birds have settled down to their staid family duties, the goldfinches continue a merry club life. Among the last birds of the season to nest, they protract the raising of their young to July and even well into August. For that they have a practical reason, however. Accustomed to line the cradle of their babies heavily with thistledown, they have to wait until the thistledown ripens. When the brooding on the bluish-white eggs (3 - 6) begins, the male will feed the female faithfully, and both parents provide the young with partially predigested seeds by regurgitation from their bills. Fruit, plant lice and caterpillars are also on their diet. The nest of fine grasses, bark and moss is built in bushes or on trees 5 to 35 feet high. Their range extends from Labrador and Manitoba to Virginia and Missouri, and from the Atlantic to the Rockies. In winter they spread over the South. Length: About 5 inches. *Spinus tristis tristis.*

◄ SONG SPARROW

Our Native Vocalist — Whatever our complaints may be about that noisy immigrant, the English sparrow, we can be proud of our own native sparrows. They are desirable birds, healthy and clean; in addition, our song sparrows have an exuberant, energetic song. In bushy meadows, along village lanes, almost anywhere in the open country these melodious performers may be heard in the morning or evening, in spring or at any other season. Their food consists of seeds and insects, and their nests are built on the ground or in low thickets; their 4 or 5 white eggs show brown spots. Various species inhabit southern Canada and the northern and western parts of the U.S.; they are migratory only in the colder regions. The eastern song sparrow ranges from Quebec to Virginia to the Great Plains. Mrs. M. M. Nice, an outstanding student of our song sparrows, has compiled statistics that show the birds' precarious existence; according to her observation's two-thirds of the first nests were destroyed by rats, snakes, rainstorms and similar causes; the following attempts were more successful, but even in the fourth set of the year not more than 60% of the young were raised. One observation is intriguing: At nesting time the male takes bits of grass to several places which he suggests as nesting sites. The female thinks differently, and the final site is selected only after a great bustle. Length of the eastern species: 6½ inches. *Melospiza melodia melodia.*

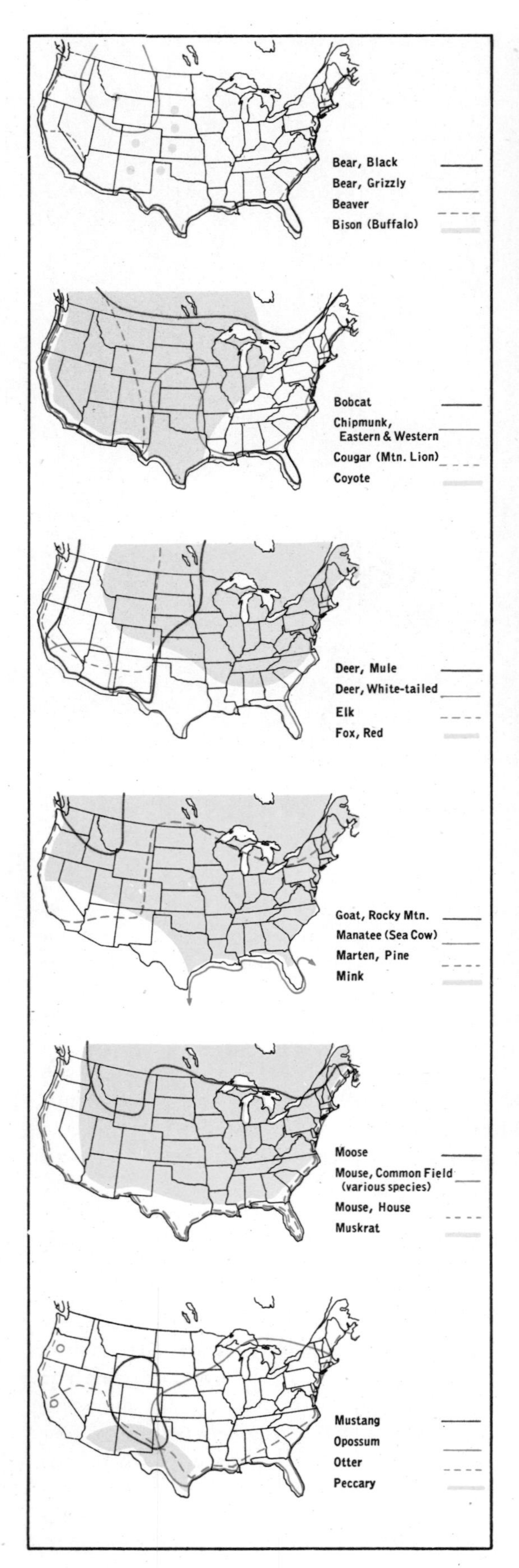

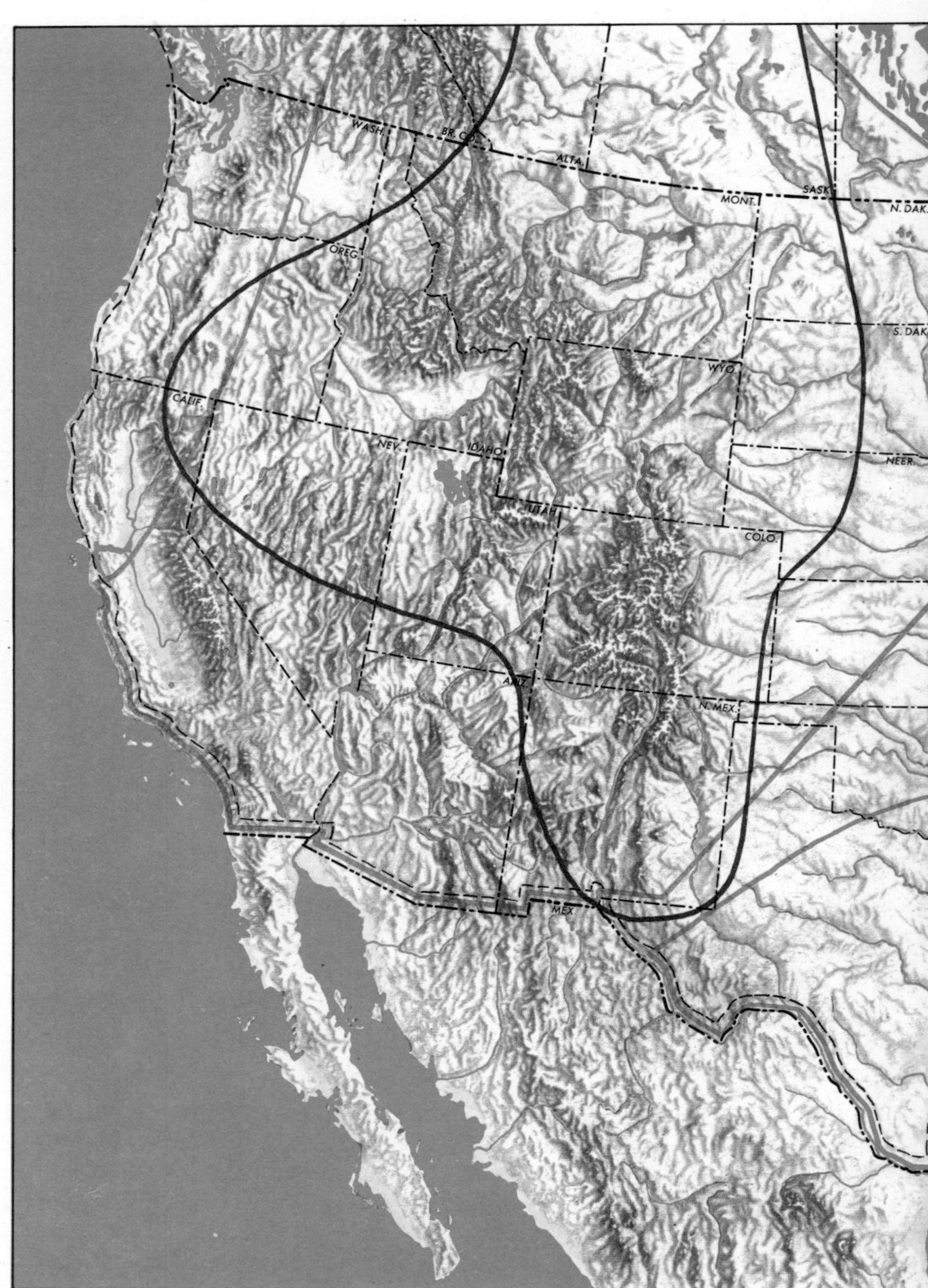

WILD ANIMALS IN THE U.S. AND SOUTHERN CANADA

The following pages describe and illustrate those wild animals which are most frequently encountered in the U.S. and Canada, or are of general interest for other reasons. The distribution of the animals is outlined in alphabetical order on the range maps on this page. A key to the principal orders and families will be found on page 227. The term "animal" is used here in the sense of "mammal".

The following notes refer to the maps. *Bison* — kept in preserves and parks, mainly in Montana, South Dakota, Oklahoma, Nebraska, Texas. *Chipmunk* — the eastern and western species overlap in the Great Lakes region; the eastern is rusty, the western grey. *Coyote* — sporadic in every eastern state; lately it has been reported in the Adirondacks. *Opossum* — it has also

Animals

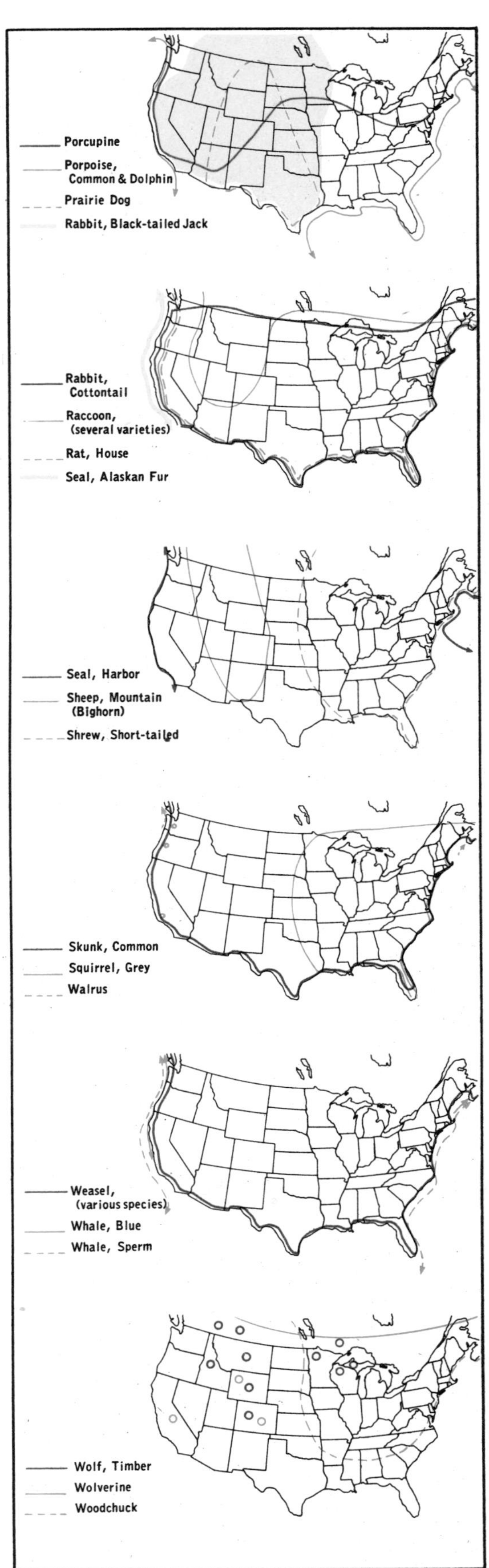

been introduced in the Pacific States. *Shrew* — other species occur in the West. *Squirrel, Grey* — outside of its principal range it is also found in the extreme West. *Walrus* — its range is beyond the map, on the Atlantic coast from Arctic to Newfoundland, on Pacific coast from Bering Sea to Pribiloff Islands. *Whale, Blue* — the arctic waters are its range. *Whale, Sperm* — occurs in all oceans; most frequent, according to old whaling charts, between 35° north and south latitudes. *Wolf, Timber* — uncommon in the U.S., more frequent in uninhabited sections of Canadian north. *Wolverine* — sporadic in U.S., more frequent in northern Canada.

Arctic America, beyond the limits of the maps, has an interesting animal population which includes the musk ox, the caribou, the white wolf and the polar bear.

SHORT-TAILED SHREW

Diminutive Cannibal — The Taming of the Shrew may be accomplished in Shakespeare's comedy, but it could not be done in nature, for the tiny shrews are solitary, morose and ill-tempered to such a degree that when two are placed together they will probably attack each other with tooth and claw. Dr. C. Hart Merriam put a tumbler over three common shrews; soon there were only two, and by nightfall there was only one. Behind a fierce instinct there is a voracious appetite and a rapid digestion which causes this tiny beast to eat its own weight every day. The short-tailed species is the largest of the family, reaching a length of 5 inches from tail end to pointed snout which acts like a drill in burrowing. It feeds on worms, insects and vegetable matter, but also likes meat and will attack and tear to pieces a mouse much bigger than itself. A poisonous secretion that flows into the wound inflicted by the incisors, makes it a sure killer. Its incredible appetite turns it into a restless creature, and it forages in daytime and at night, summer and winter, having no time to hibernate. Although among our most numerous mammals, it is rarely seen because of its shyness. The short-tailed shrew ranges from southern Canada over most of the eastern half of the continent. Of the common or long-tailed shrew different varieties live from the tundras of Labrador and Hudson Bay to North Carolina. *Blarina brevicauda.*

LITTLE BROWN BAT

A Radar-Equipped Night Flyer — Close the eyes of a bat with any kind of glue and it will fly with greater assurance than with its eyes open. Close its ears and it will stumble into obstacles. These experiments seem to prove that the bats use a kind of sixth sense for direction-finding, and that their "radar" is located in their ears. If their technical equipment is an intriguing puzzle, their social habits are also fascinating. As the father bat builds no nest and shows no interest in his offspring, the mother bat has to shelter her young; she lets them cling to her body while she is asleep or when in flight, and when they grow larger, she hangs them up by their hooked claws on a tree or in a cave while she goes on her errands; later she returns to give them a breast-feeding. When a baby falls it cries, and adult bats will swoop down in an attempt to rescue it; but as they are awkward on the ground, they will probably not succeed. In caves that are illuminated for tourists, whole pailfuls of fallen baby bats are gathered. The little brown bat is the most widely distributed representative of this ancient and primitive family of night flyers and insect eaters. They hibernate in caves, most species huddling close together to keep warm. Their little bodies are 4 inches long, or less. Their range extends from Alaska and Labrador throughout the continent. *Myotis lucifugus.*

NINE-BANDED ARMADILLO ►

His Cousins Are Fossils — While it is true that most of the relatives of the Armadillo, for instance the 12-foot monsters called glyptodonts, lived several million years ago; and while it is also true that its armor of 9 shell-rings hinged together looks like a remnant of a prehistoric era, the animal itself is very much alive and indeed invading the U.S. A dweller of Mexico 40 years ago, it is now found in Texas, Louisiana, and Oklahoma; it is still extending its range, possibly to the frost line; however, it cannot stand freezing temperatures. It is quite easy to observe this recent immigrant for it is nearsighted and so concentrated on its business of hunting worms, insects and caterpillars in a clump of bushes, that it will not notice you; when scared it will run for its nest or burrow. Some varieties are said to curl up in a ball protected by its flexible armor plates, and you will probably not be able to uncurl it. This harmless small animal — usually weighing about 13 pounds — has not many natural foes; man is its worst enemy, killing large numbers of armadillos for the sake of their good meat and their armors which the hunters transform into baskets and curios. The female is a very systematic mother, giving birth to four young at a time; they are always of the same sex and they are always identical. Even the number of hairs on their undersides is the same. *Dasypsus novemcinctus texanus.*

◄ GREY SQUIRREL

A Friendly Easterner — Watching a squirrel interring a nut in the ground, we wonder if it will ever again find its buried treasure. Most authorities agree that it will, even when the earth is covered with snow. Provident storing of food for the time of need marks the solid citizen, but there are also other ways in which the grey squirrels have ingratiated themselves to us. Their movements are graceful, their fluffy tails undulating elegantly as they run or leap; wary and clever in the wilds, they are tame and good-natured in our gardens, in contrast to the quarrelsome red quirrels; daintily they sit up to eat their pine cones and beechnuts, seeds, hazelnuts and hickory nuts. But they have not always been as welcome as they are now. In American pioneer days they existed in myriads and undertook gigantic migrations across the country, even swimming lakes and rivers like the Ohio and the Hudson, and destroying every corn and wheat field in their path. In 1749 Pennsylvania settlers killed 640,000 and in 1808 Ohio required each free white man to deliver 100 squirrel scalps a year or pay a $3 fine. The range of the grey squirrel, its black variation, and several subspecies extends throughout the deciduous forests of the U.S. and Canada east of the treeless Great Plains. It is a North American species and not closely related to the squirrels of Europe. *Sciurus carolinensis.*

◄ EASTERN CHIPMUNK

Handsome Hoarder — Is this a case of misdirected foresight? To hoard half a bushel of hickory nuts for winter use surely is hard work for a small chipmunk. And when the time comes to enjoy the fruits of its diligence, the foresighted householder is overcome with drowsiness and falls asleep for three months. At any rate, food storing seems to be uppermost in the mind of this busy and shy gnawer. It stuffs the pouches of its cheeks with acorns and buckwheat, hazelnuts and beechnuts, ragweed seeds and corn, mushrooms and blueberries. It also likes to eat beetles and snails, frogs and snakes, young birds and eggs, and in Minnesota a chipmunk family was reported to have stolen a whole nestful of grouse eggs and hidden them away without breaking a single one. Its burrow is located under a tree root or fence post or rock ledge, and its oval nest chamber, two or three feet underground and a foot or more in diameter, is lined with soft vegetable matter; of the passageways and side chambers one is usually set aside as a "washroom," for sanitary purposes. When not alarmed, this cheerful, alert, sun-loving little animal cavorts over the ground and from a ledge chirps and clucks, but scolds angrily at intruders. It is seen from the Nova Scotia-Great Lakes line as far south as Georgia and as far west as Oklahoma. There are also many western species with similar habits. *Tamias striatus.*

PRAIRIE DOG ►

A Sociable Town Dweller — Human towns were dwarfed by dog towns. One colony of prairie dogs recorded in western Texas stretched continuously for 250 miles, and was 100 miles wide; it had hundreds of millions of inhabitants. There are still enormous settlements throughout the Grêat Plains and the semi-arid plateaus of the Rocky Mountains. Water is not vital to their towns for they don't often drink. Their numerous natural enemies cannot decimate them to any great extent, no matter how many fall prey to coyotes and foxes, badgers and ferrets, owls and snakes, Navajos and Pueblos who prize their meat. But now the white man has declared a relentless war on them, and poison is reducing them in many areas. According to stockmen even a few prairie dogs eat as much grass as one sheep, and as they strip the soil of their towns of vegetation, they are a major cause of soil erosion. It is unforunate that these sociable, pleasant little creatures are pests by human standards, for its is a joy to observe them by the craters of their burrows leisurely stretching out in the sun or excitedly sitting up. During the day the whole town is astir with life, with chattering and high-pitched barking, with neighborly intercourse. Their burrows are almost straight shafts 8 to 16 feet deep, ending in a horizontal side passage and a nest chamber. The more common species have black-tipped tails, others have white tips. *Cynomys ludovicianus.*

WOODCHUCK ►

A Would-Be Weather Prophet — When American folklore set February 2nd as the day on which the ground hog or woodchuck leaves its burrow to watch its shadow and forecast the weather, it acted a little hastily, for obviously a woodchuck in Georgia will test the coming of spring much earlier than a ground hog in Labrador. It is true, however, that in the north the animal often emerges from its winter sleep several weeks before the snow melts. Correspondingly, it begins its hibernation early, often by late September. It does not hoard a stockpile of food for winter like many other rodents, but toward fall stuffs itself with clover and all the vegetables it can steal until it is excessively fat. It is a solitary animal of about 10 pounds weight, most frequently seen in a motionless pose, sitting bolt upright. Its call is a shrill, short, explosive whistle, and when disturbed it also rattles its teeth. A favorite place for its burrow is a pastoral hillside where it digs its passageways and chambers from 20 to 40 feet underground, slanting them upward to prevent the rain from entering. Here its blind young are born, up to 9 in number; a few weeks later they play by the mound of fresh earth at the burrow entrance, where the adults also like to take an occasional sun bath. The woodchuck's range extends from Labrador to North Dakota in the west and Georgia in the south. *Marmota monax.*

◄ AMERICAN BEAVER

An Engineering Genius — When a colony of young beavers tried in vain to build a difficult dam, they engaged, as a consultant, an old experienced neighbor. The veteran took command and the project was promptly completed. Incidents of this kind have been reported by reliable observers. Perhaps they endow the beaver with too high an intelligence, but even its every-day work is remarkable. By building dams of branches, stones and mud it creates the beaver pond. By cutting poplars, willows and other trees along the bank so that their crowns will fall into the water, they provide an easy access to their favorite food, green bark. And if there are desirable trees inland, they dig a canal to float them. The beaver house is a dome 8 to 10 feet wide, built in the pond but with its main chamber above the water line; the entrance, however, is usually below the surface. The beaver weighs 30 to 40 pounds, and sometimes attains a weight of 70 pounds. Its hind feet are fully webbed, its fore feet are used like hands when it carries mud pressed against its breast. The tail is a scaly paddle and under their long outer hairs they wear silky-smooth fur which made American history. Beaver skins spurred the conquest of the West, were used as currency, caused wars and international disputes. Beavers range through most of the woodlands of the U.S. and Canada; although not abundant, they are on a rapid increase. *Castor canadensis.*

PORCUPINE

Unhurried, Unafraid—How porcupines bristling with sharp quills have young without harm to either, is somewhat of a mystery; but young porkies are born, though usually just one baby a year; it comes into this world covered with fur and already armed with spines. After only a week it is independent of its mother and takes up its slow, sluggish, solitary life. The porky's strength lies in its defense; its bristles stand up, loosely attached in its thick skin. A slap with the tail will drive the spines deeply and painfully into a dog's or fox's head, and sometimes will result in the attacker's death. Occasionally a hungry beast will succeed in turning the porcupine on its back and devour the defenseless underpart; the pine marten and fox are said to be skillful at such an operation. On the whole the porcupine's life is quiet, spent in trees or on the ground, with only a tree trunk for shelter; in summer it feeds on leaves, twigs and berries, and in winter on tender under-bark of hemlocks, pines, spruces, oaks and other trees. Its one passion is for salt, and it will invade camps to chew boards or any objects with a salty flavor. Of its two species the smaller and paler yellow-haired porcupine occurs from Alaska to Arizona, the Canadian porcupine from Nova Scotia to the Great Lakes region to Pennsylvania. It reaches a length of 3 feet and a weight of 35 pounds. *Erethizon dorsatum.*

COMMON FIELD MOUSE

A Harassed Native — A strange phenomenon in the life of these tiny animals is the cycle of recessions and scarcity in numbers, and of upsurges when they overrun wide sections of the country by the millions. In 1906-8, for instance, the field mouse colonies of the Humboldt Valley of Nevada merged into one great army and, like a Biblical scourge, swarmed over the alfalfa fields and destroyed tens of thousands of acres. After a few years they decreased again. The nature of these cycles is still uncertain. The numerous species of this shy, peace-loving animal have greyish winter coats and brownish summer coats. Their grass houses are so constructed that they will keep the mouse family dry and warm even in rain and snow storms. They also burrow, living above ground mostly in winter. Fields they live in are a maze of surface runways to feeding grounds for grasses, seeds, roots and barks. They have more than six litters a year, each of about six young. Their enemies are legion, swooping down from the air in the form of hawks and owls; and pursuing them on the ground, beasts of prey, even wolves and bears, catch and eat them. Their only weapon is vigilance, and the numerous inch-wide runways are always kept clear of obstacles for a quick getaway. Various members of the group range from the treeless arctic tundras to Mexico. Eastern field mouse: *Microtus pennsylvanicus.*

MUSKRAT

The World's Leading Fur Bearer — Muskrats lived in the marshes of Staten Island when the Indians sold Manhattan to the Dutch; they still live there, undisturbed by the sky-line across the bay. They don't mind man. They are trapped by the millions, and all beasts of prey hunt them, yet they live in nearly the same territory which they occupied in Indian days. They are prolific; that is their means of survival. Several litters of 3 to 11 young every year keep the race alive. They are fastidious eaters, combining a diet of water lily roots, cattails and other choice vegetables with shellfish, crawfish and turtles. They are trapped systematically because of their soft brown fur which is protected by an overcoat of long coarse hair and is sold throughout the western world under various trade names. For shelter, they dig burrows in high river banks or build beaver-like houses in shallow water, with the chamber above the water line. The winter cold does not affect them; indeed, the warmth of their bodies melts the snow on the roofs of their houses. Not even an ice sheet on the pond disturbs them although the entrances to their lodge are subaquatic; courageously they dive into the water, under the ice, and forage for roots; in an emergency they eat some of the material of which their house is built. In various geographical races, but without conspicuous differences, they occur from the Arctic barrens to Mexico. *Ondatra zibethica.*

HOUSE MOUSE

A Cosmopolitan Parasite — Half hostile and half amused, that seems to be man's attitude toward this small rodent, as reflected in the world's folklore and fables, proverbs and nursery rhymes. A native of Asia, it has migrated to every part of the earth that is settled, and has shown tremendous vitality in adapting itself to any climatic conditions except the frigid Polar regions. When living in a house, it will build its warm nest of fibres or fabrics in any nook or cranny, eating almost anything it can find. When moving to a meadow it will live like a native field mouse and feed largely on grain. With several litters of 4 to 9 blind and naked young each year, it multiplies rapidly, and in spite of a legion of cats and other foes, of traps and poison, it holds its own. To a certain degree house mice are subject to the same life cycle of abundance and scarcity that affect the American field mice and the Norwegian lemming. In 1926, for instance, a mass migration of millions of house mice emerged in the San Joaquin Valley in California and overran the thickly settled oil fields of that region; highways became slippery with dead mice, and in the morning people found their clothes swarming with them. The main difference between this introduced rodent and our native mice is the long, hairless tail, and the nearly uniform color of its upper and lower body parts. *Mus musculus.*

◄ HOUSE RAT

The World's Worst Vermin — Here is the rat's sad record: It is host to the flea that used to spread bubonic plague throughout the world, and it is probably the carrier of half a dozen other dreaded diseases. It devours millions of tons of human food and pollutes and spoils many times that amount as it lives in sewers and garbage dumps; it is tough, growing to a length of 16 inches and occasionally 20 inches and a weight of 2 pounds, and not hesitating to wander over miles of rugged country and to swim broad rivers; it has such a fierce disposition that several rats in a cage will soon be reduced to one, the stronger specimens eating the weaker ones; they are so smart that they will avoid poison after a few companions have died from it, and when the mongoose was introduced to Hawaii to war on rats, the latter became arboreal, safe in the trees from their ground-dwelling pursuer. They have several litters every year, averaging 10 young and sometimes as many as 20. These hordes of young rats begin to breed when they are about 3 months old. Obviously, we are confronted with a major problem, and it is hoped that modern research will find a solution for it. The house rat is a native of Asia; it "jumped ship" in American ports in the 18th century. It is distinguished from our native rats by its long, naked tail and coarser hair. *Rattus norvegicus.*

BLACK-TAILED JACK RABBIT ►

The Champion Racer — Leap, leap, bound — leap, leap, leap, bound — that is the rhythm of the jack rabbits as they are frequently observed by western highway and railroad travelers. The bound is extra high, probably to survey the lay of the land. When pursued, they do not indulge in such capers but run along at top speed, their long ears held back on their shoulders. Coursing jack rabbits with greyhounds used to be a popular pastime in the western states; no other dogs had a chance in such a competition. Even the young know by instinct the ways of the runner; when pursued, they skillfully evade the enemy by a sudden dash or zigzagging. They are born with open eyes and fur in litters of 2, 4, or sometimes 6, and fend for themselves a few weeks later, when they are still round, fluffy balls. Like all members of their family, they run on their toes, and frequently can be seen sitting on the ankles of their hind feet. When living in the desert, on sagebrush and cactus, the jack rabbits are harmless, but in agricultural regions they do great damage to clover, alfalfa, grain and other fields. Since many of their natural enemies, like the wolf and the coyote, have been decimated by man, they have to be controlled by poison. Jack rabbits do not dig a burrow or build a nest but simply hollow out a resting spot called "form" under a shrub or cactus. *Lepus californicus.*

Animals

COTTONTAIL RABBIT ►

Dweller of the Brier Patch — No lover of Uncle Remus' Brer Rabbit can hate a cottontail, the soft-eyed, handsome animal whose trademark is, in nearly all its numerous species, the puff of white hair on the underside of its tail. Only on a few far western members of the family the tails are brown. Living throughout the countryside and the suburbs of cities from Canada to Mexico, they have adapted themselves to all kinds of conditions, thriving at sea level as vigorously as at timberline. In the West they often occupy the abandoned holes of prairie dogs, and are therefore called dog rabbits, while in the East they simply settle in "forms," i.e. shady hiding places in hedges, bushes or under a log. It appears that each form is the personal property of one cottontail, respected by all others. The nest is a hole concealed by plant growth and lined with the mother's own soft, downy hair; several litters of five blind and almost naked young are born. In the northern places they breed in spring and summer; year-round in the South one litter follows another. Accordingly, their number does not decrease although owls and eagles, hawks and coyotes, foxes and weasels feast on them constantly, and millions of pounds are consumed by man every year, in the rural sections of the U.S. and Canada. Indeed, rabbit meat has been an American staple food since colonial days. The eastern species: *Sylvilagus floridanus.*

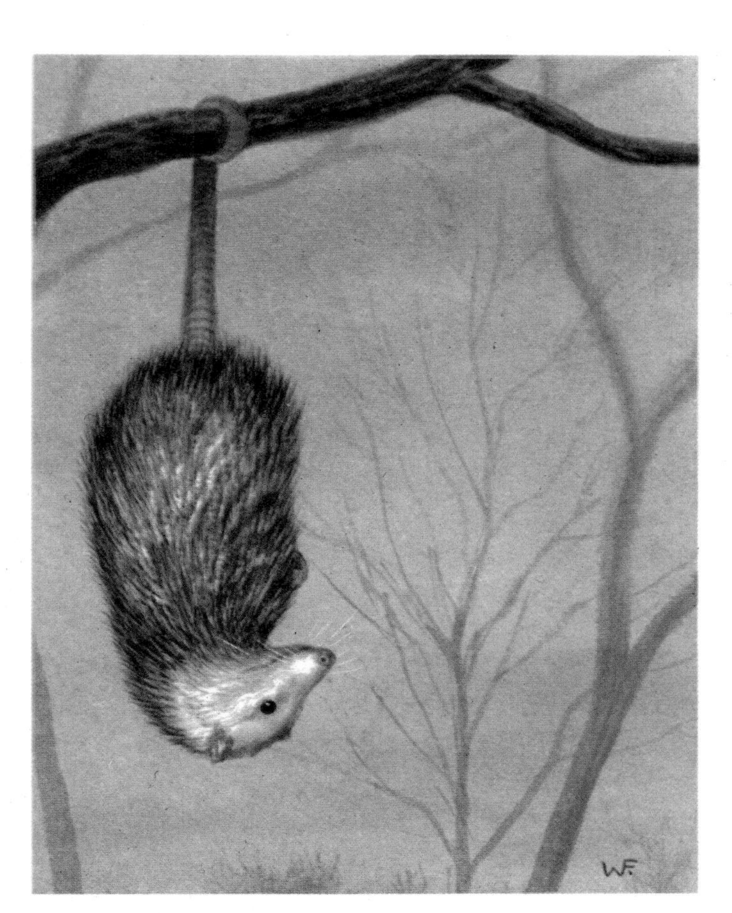

◄ OPOSSUM

Star of Southern Folklore — How has brother 'possum become a leading character in the folk songs and animal tales of the South? Because it is an amusing creature. Its ears are hairless, its monkeylike, prehensile tail is slung around a branch, and its free toes look like miniature hands. If confronted by an enemy, it "plays possum," i.e., it falls to the ground with eyes closed and tongue lolling out, completely limp and apparently dead. After the puzzled attacker has left, the "corpse" revives to great vitality; in fact, it is so tough that it is difficult to kill an opossum. As a survivor of an ancient family of animals which was thriving before the rise of modern mammals, its home life is strange. The mother's 5 to 14 naked babies, smaller than honey bees, attach themselves so firmly to the teats in her pouch that they cannot be shaken off. After they grow a coat of fur they look like miniature replicas of their parents; but for 30 days more they go on riding on their mother, clinging to her hair with their strong little hands while she goes about her nightly routine. An omnivorous prowler, eating everything from birds and mice to box-turtles and snakes, it ranges throughout the eastern woodlands south of the Ontario-Wisconsin-Nebraska line, but is much more frequent in the South; it has also been introduced to California. Of the several species the Virginia opossum is the largest. *Didelphis virginiana.*

◄ AMERICAN BISON

Symbol of the Old West — 60,000,000 buffaloes roamed our continent, according to historical estimates, when white man took possession of America. They ranged from Great Slave Lake in the high North way into Mexico, and from the plateaus of Idaho and Wyoming to the Carolinas, western Pennsylvania and New York. The Spanish explorers compared them to the multitude of fish in the sea. As late as 1871 a herd was reported on the Arkansas River which had millions. Then came transcontinental railroads and the great slaughter, and in 1895 approximately 800 buffaloes were left alive. America's most magnificent animal was practically extinct. Since then several new herds have been built up from these remnants, amounting to about 5,000 bison in the U.S. and to approximately 15,000 in Canada; in the immense reservation of Wood Buffalo, straddling the border between Alberta and the Northwest Territory, they live again in a semi-wild state. Bulls stand 5 to 6 feet high at the shoulder and often weigh over a ton, while the females are somewhat smaller in size. Both grow horns. They shed their bushy coats in the spring, and at that time their matted hides look moth-eaten. But their new fall coats of rich, deep brown color look sleek and handsome. The common term buffalo is really a misnomer as the bison does not belong to the true buffaloes of the Old World. *Bison bison.*

MOUNTAIN SHEEP (BIGHORN) ►

The Champion Climber — Snowy peaks and the cool, crystal-clear air above the clouds; graceful bounds from high cliffs to higher ledges where no other animal would dare to follow; beautiful spiral horns, perhaps the most highly prized trophy of the western hunter — there is a certain glamour associated with America's wild mountain sheep. The glory of the landscape surrounds them by day when they browse over the steep slopes and nibble on mountain plants, and by night when even their beds are made on some rock promontory with a magnificent view, where they can scan the broad valleys for potential attackers. Every sheep has its own bed, scraped out of the rocky surface, to which it returns each night. A dozen or more of these beds lie close together, forming the herds' dormitory. Up here near the clouds they are safe, and even their babies are now less frequently stolen as the golden eagles have become scarce. Only in winter time when they migrate to the valleys in search of food, are many killed by wolves and mountain lions. The mountain sheep, standing over 3 feet high at the shoulders and growing to about 5 feet long, have adapted themselves remarkably well to their surroundings; the Alaskan species thrive in sub-zero temperatures, the southern varieties, in the barren desert mountains where the heat is excessive and water scarce. They raise but one lamb annually, born in March or April. *Ovis canadensis.*

Animals

ROCKY MOUNTAIN GOAT ►

On the Roof of America — Like thick woolen jacket and leggings, so hangs the dense coat of beautiful white hair around its body and legs, down to its ankles. This shaggy garment, the profuse whiskers and the small black horns give the mountain goat a mirth-provoking appearance. Yet the presence of these big and sure-footed climbers lends a touch of life to the forbidding mountain vastness. Their range extends from the Columbia River to Alaska, and on the slopes of the coastal ranges they sometimes descend to sea level; but normally they remain high up among the bleak and barren peaks where they browse on mountain plants and brave even winter blizzards. They do not seek refuge in the valleys where mountain lions might prey on them. Since their meat is inferior and their horns are too inconspicuous to make a valuable trophy, they are not hunted as much as the mountain sheep and survive in greater numbers, especially in Alberta and British Columbia. Several years ago a small herd of Rocky Mountain goats was exhibited in South Dakota; one ram and one ewe escaped into the Black Hills and have been thriving in the new habitat ever since. Their family herd has increased to 25, and they have adapted themselves well to the warmer climate. The average weight of the male is under 300 pounds. They are uniquely North American, and not true goats but closely related to antelopes. *Oreamnos montanus.*

◄ PRONGHORN ANTELOPE

Western Beauty — Flash! Danger! — The two clumps of hair on the antelope's rump suddenly stand up like two flashing white rosettes; then it bounds away. But a friend two miles distant has spotted the signal and is warned. It is one of the most unique communication systems in nature. Another unique feature is their horns which, unlike those of true antelopes, are branched and the horny outer sheath is shed. Unlike the antlers of the deer family which are shed completely each year, or the hollow, permanent horns of cows or goats, the pronghorn has a permanent bony core about which is grown each year a new protective covering. Their hair is coarse and their skin spongy; it is not tough enough to make good buckskin. Once upon a time the pronghorn antelopes were as numerous as the bison; they ranged from Alberta to Mexico, and in herds of thousands shared the Great Plains with the buffaloes. The monumental slaughter came with the transcontinental railroads, and only a pitiful remnant was left. But protective legislation and wild life management have raised their number again to more than 200,000. They are nervous and shy but exceedingly curious, and sometimes they are lured into rifle shot distance by a red rag. They also love to race, even with a horseman, and usually have no difficulty overtaking him. Their fawns, commonly twins, are born in spring, and are fiercely defended by their mother. *Antilocapra americana.*

◄ PECCARY

The Only Native Pig — These little wild pigs, also called javelinas, can be heard and smelled more easily than seen. Running about in bands of up to 25 animals, they grunt and bark back and forth as if discussing various topics. When alarmed, the hair on the head stands on end, and from a large musk gland a secretion is released which fills the air with a penetrating, obnoxious odor. Your nose will smell it hundreds of feet away. However, to see the nervous and active peccaries is not easy; they vanish swiftly under the shrub oaks or in the mesquite. They have probably a common ancestor with the domestic hog, but they do not belong to the same family; peccaries are native Americans; pigs, fattening in the farmyard or running wild in the mountains, are foreigners introduced from Europe. The peccary mother usually bears twins in a burrow or hollow log; after two days the young are strong enough to join the band. With their pig-like snouts they grub for frogs and snakes, lizards and worms, turtle eggs and bird eggs, cactus fruits and acorns. They love prickly pears, and their stomach linings are sometimes full of spines. But they are too busy to get as fat as hogs; 40 to 60 pounds is their average weight. Overhunting nearly exterminated them, but under today's protective laws they have staged a comeback; they are quite numerous again in southern Texas, Arizona and New Mexico. *Pecari angulatus.*

MULE DEER ►

A Broad-Jump Acrobat — To spring from the ground with all four feet at once does not seem an efficient method of locomotion. Yet it is the common gait of the mule deer, and as this "venado burro" lives in the broken terrain of badlands and forest, this horizontal leaping is superior to running. The agility with which it ascends or descends rough, steep slopes in jerky, stiff-legged bounds is amazing. Its name refers to its large ears; otherwise it has no resemblance to a mule, although it is heavier set than the white-tailed deer. The tip of its tail is black, and in action is not raised like a flag, as with its white-tailed cousin. Its antlers possess branching prongs. During the summer months the stags like to browse on high, rocky ridges for a twofold reason: no enemy can approach them from below unseen, and the breezes keep away the flies from their sensitive, velvety, growing antlers. As the mating season draws near, the horns lose their velvet, and the bucks in small bands, now in perfect condition, roam the open fall forest. Their glossy coats reflecting the sun and their beautiful antlers held aloft majestically, they are a magnificent sight. Their wide range extends from the Pacific coast to the Great Plains, from Alberta and Manitoba to the Mexican tableland. There are several species of mule deer, but their variations are slight. *Odocoileus hemionus.*

WHITE-TAILED DEER ►

Symbol of the American Woods—In buckskin breeches and moccasins the early settlers cleared the wilderness, eating venison as a staple diet; the white-tailed or Virginia deer was their reliable stand-by. This dweller of our forests has been hunted incessantly these past 330 years, yet its story is not that of the buffalo or the pronged antelope. It is estimated to be as numerous today as it was when white man conquered America, and ranges from the Atlantic to the Pacific, and from Canada to Mexico. Indeed, it has spread into hundreds of miles of new territory, particularly in northern Ontario and Quebec. And while it is shy, it is not afraid of the neighborhood of man; hundreds of deer live within 30 miles of Times Square. Its white flag raised at every bound, its graceful fleetness, its rusty-red summer coat which seems to glow in the afternoon sun, have made it one of America's best-known and best-loved animals. While quite solitary during the summer, herds band together when their grey winter coats begin to grow; they form a "yard" where they keep a system of trampled snow paths open, to have access to bushes, trees, and pine and spruce needles. Their summer fare is more varied, including leaves of many plants, mosses and berries, beechnuts and acorns, and a little grass. Their fawns, usually two, are spotted with white; they lose this color pattern with their first winter coat. *Odocoileus virginianus.*

◄ ELK

The Indians' Wapiti — The bugle call of the elk bull resounding through the lonely valley wilderness is an awe-inspiring challenge to combat over the cows. Another bull responds, and soon the huge animals struggle fiercely, their four or even five foot antlers pushing and stabbing. Sometimes a tragedy occurs: The antlers interlock, the animals cannot separate, and both are doomed to death. Elks are even more polygamous than the other deer, and during the mating season the bulls surrond themselves with a small harem. Bigger than the white tailed bucks which may weigh 300 pounds, they attain weights of 700 to 1,000 pounds. Originally these handsome deer ranged throughout the U.S. and Canada, but were exterminated in the East; the last elk in Pennsylvania was killed a hundred years ago. But they survive in considerable numbers in the Rocky Mountains, particularly in the Yellowstone Park region, in the west Coastal Ranges, and in British Columbia, Manitoba and Saskatchewan. In spring they ascend the mountain forests to the timberline, browsing on leaves and twigs; in the fall they return to the more hospitable valleys. The fawns are born from May to July, numbering one, two, or rarely, three. The name elk is based on a misconception of the early settlers; the Old World elk is our moose, and the Indian term wapiti seems more appropriate. *Cervus canadensis.*

MOOSE

Aloof Giant — In uncanny silence the bull moose stalks through the forest, an almost incredible feat for a body weighing 900 to 1,400 pounds and carrying a pair of shovel-like antlers that may reach a width of 6 feet. With its huge rump on thin legs, its shaggy beard, its big upper lip hanging over the underlip; with strange shambling gait and constantly nodding head as it runs along; and with its summer habit of standing in lonely lakes and feeding on water plants with its head entirely submerged—the moose seems a relic of other geological epochs. In the main, it is a Canadian animal occuring in the U.S. only in the north woods of Maine and Minnesota, south in the Rockies to Idaho and Wyoming. Thoreau describes it fascinatingly in his book on the Maine Woods. Shy and silent, aloof and dignified during most of the year, the bull moose becomes bold and aggressive during the mating season, crashing through the underbrush and challenging its rivals with its loud call. When a fight ensues, the two bulls use not only their antlers as weapons but also hit each other fiercely with their front hoofs. The birch bark horn, imitating the call of the cow moose, is an effective lure to bring a bull into gunshot range. One calf is born the first year, two and rarely three the next. In contrast to the other fawns of the deer family, they are not spotted. *Alces americanus.*

MUSTANG

The Bucking Bronco—The dawn horse, a midget 12 inches high at the shoulders, lived in North America in the Lower Eocene Age. It was undoubtedly an ancestor of the modern animal. In a later epoch true wild horses galloped over the western plains, as the Pleistocene fossil beds of Texas prove. For reasons unknown, they perished before the Indian emerged on our continent. When white man arrived, the dog was the only beast of burden in the New World. But the Spaniards brought the horse along, usually animals of spirited Arabic strains. Some mares and stallions escaped, multiplied, and for three centuries wild horses again roamed the western plains. Left to themselves, the mustangs became a small, hardy breed of their own, and made history in our western states. They changed whole tribes of Indians from wanderers to horsemen; the Comanches and Apaches, for instance, became such skillful riders that they appeared on their fleet mustangs out of nowhere, plundered and burned white settlements, and vanished in the prairie without traces. Today the mustangs are largely rounded up to prevent their stallions from breeding ranch mares. But some herds still inhabit the remote western mesas, in full freedom. Wild burros also live in the West, in such arid wastelands as the Painted Desert and Death Valley. Just as the mustangs, they descend from animals imported by Mexican explorers and American prospectors. *Genus Equus.*

WEASEL ►

A Handsome Killer — Put a small weasel and a big rat into a cage, and the rat will cringe in terror and give up without a fight. Nothing could furnish stronger proof of the weasel's ferocity. The blood of its prey is its natural food, but it kills beyond its needs just for the love of killing, and has been recorded to murder 40 chickens in a single night. It must be added, however, that it also kills rats and mice by the hundreds. For its bloody calling it is superbly equipped. Its body is sinuous, its long neck and pointed head are snake-like; when attacking an animal perhaps larger than itself, it holds its head high and sways it back and forth, waiting for its chance in tense excitement. Then suddenly it strikes, and with sure instinct it always pierces a deadly spot: the back of the neck, the brain, the jugular vein on the side. All rodents and birds live in terror of it. In various species it inhabits the whole of the U.S. and Canada, but while the southern weasels retain their brown coat with the white belly throughout the year, the northern species change into ermines, donning snow-white coats with a black tip on the tail. Ermine is, and always has been, the symbol of royalty, but today the brown fur is considered just as valuable. The change of color takes about one month; the farther north, the earlier it occurs. *Mustela noveboracensis.*

◄ MINK

Purveyor of Elegance — No matter how many glossy mink coats warm handsome women on Fifth Avenue and Michigan Boulevard, the original range of this sleek savage has remained constant for its various subspecies throughout the years, extending from the arctic barrens to Florida and the Gulf, also throughout the forests of the West; but is not found in the arid and desert sections of the West and Southwest. It is one of the few fur bearers that breed well in captivity, and as carefully selected stock is used, the rich brown pelts of "farmed" mink often command higher prices than the natural product. A restless animal of approximately 2 feet in length and 2 pounds in weight, it has somewhat amphibian feeding habits. On land it is a great wanderer and kills rabbits and muskrats, squirrels and birds; it will also raid an occasional hen house, destroying more fowl than it can devour. In water it is even more at home, and as an excellent swimmer it catches trout and crayfish, frogs and salamanders, snakes and mussels. In the lower Yukon territory where small fishes of just the right size, 4 to 5 inches, abound, the minks are so numerous that the Eskimos living there are called "the mink people." Mink dens are usually located in the banks of streams, and the annual litter of 4 to 10 young is born in April or May; they stay with their mother until fall. *Mustela vison.*

◄ COMMON SKUNK

A Controversial Figure — The Dr. Jekyll-Mr. Hyde of the American animal scene is a gentle and intelligent beast, dignified, fearless and easily tamed. On the other hand it wreaks havoc with its chemical weapon and has only to raise ominously its big bushy tail to turn to flight much larger creatures. If there is a show of resistance, two little tubes of the scent sac on each side of the vent will eject a well aimed double squirt of a malodorous fluid, hitting goals as far as twelve feet away. Touching the eye, the liquid may cause severe pain and momentary blindness. There is another dilemma in the skunk's life: It has a marked fondness for the neighborhood of man, will frequently visit farms and settle under buildings; yet it loves to eat game birds, water fowl, chickens and eggs and is therefore trapped and shot. That is unfortunate, for the skunk exterminates large quantities of farm pests like rodents, grubs, larvae, cutworms, grasshoppers and beetles. The skunk's family life is close; during the summer the young ones trail behind their mother, often in Indian file, and the following winter the family remains united; as many as eight or ten have been counted in one den. The range of the common skunk, which reaches a weight of twelve pounds, is the whole U.S. and much of Canada; with the exception of deep forests and deserts, it occupies mixed woodlands from sea level to timberline. *Mephitis mephitis.*

PINE MARTEN ►

Hermit in the Tree Tops — A hunter on skis in the wintry pine and spruce forests of Colorado may scan the crowns of the trees, but he is not looking for birds, he is hunting the pine marten, a weasel which has taken to the tree tops where it spends much of its life. There it chases and catches red squirrels and occasional birds; it also descends to the ground to devour rats and hares, mice and chipmunks, frogs and fish, nuts and fruit. Occasionally it does not mind eating one of its cousins, a weasel or mink. Very retiring, it lives in the remotest thickets of the forest and is not only solitary but shows violent antagonism when meeting another marten. This character trait has been a great obstacle in attempts to mate these nervous and excitable beasts in captivity. When confined with a female, the male will probably not breed her but bite her through the skull and kill her. However, recent research in their mating habits is reported to have improved the situation and fur farming of martens seems to be a promising possibility now. With a length of 22 to 30 inches, the male reaches a weight of 2 to 3 pounds. Its rich brown fur, called American sable, is valuable and much sought. It occurs throughout the wooded areas of Canada from the Atlantic to the Pacific, and in the U.S. in northern New England, the Adirondacks, and the western mountains. *Martes americana.*

WOLVERINE ►

A Disagreeable Countryman—A despicably mean character is the outstanding trait of this northern savage. It will kill every creature in sight, attacking and felling even deer and caribou. It will bury in the snow the meat it cannot devour, and in doing so will taint it with the acrid smell from its musk glands so that it might not be of any use to other animals. In fact, none will touch it. This robber will steal every imaginable object from camps, even if it is entirely useless to its own needs. It will patrol trap lines, and not only eat or destroy the catch, but sometimes will actually hide the traps. Its strength and courage are unmatched, and for hundreds, perhaps thousands of years the Eskimos of Alaska have trimmed their hoods with wolverine fur, and have used the skin of the head and legs to make their belts and hunting bags, so that the animal's fearless spirit might enter their own bodies. It is also true that the coarse wolverine fur does not collect moisture, and is therefore highly appropriate for arctic clothing. Growing to a length of 3 to 3½ feet, its weight averages from 20 to 30 pounds. Its range is now reduced to a territory bounded by the Arctic Circle in the north and reaching down into the U.S. only in the Yellowstone Park region and northern California. 3 to 5 young are born annually in a burrow. *Gulo luscus.*

◄ AMERICAN BADGER

Prospector of the Western Plains — If on a bright western morning we see on the grassy plain a line of tracks meandering from hole to hole, each one flanked by a little mound of fresh earth, we have before us the nocturnal labor of a badger. If more than one badger has been operating here and we are on horseback, we have to watch out for the pony's legs. The digger's wanderings probably have brought a rich harvest of pocket gophers and ground squirrels, mice and praire dogs, rats and insects, scorpions and lizards, turtle eggs and the eggs of ground-nesting birds. Scenting that a burrow is occupied, the hunter's sharp, inch-long claws dig down with lightening speed and seize the frightened inmate. Man on foot can easily overtake the slow animal whose furry hair drags at its sides; but no badger is easily caught; it will fight with vicious desperation and overcome an attacking dog, a raccoon, a fox and even a deer. Little is known about its family habits; it seems to mate for life. In May or June the young are born, the litter averaging four. In the north, badgers hibernate during the coldest months. Their original range was the U.S. and Canada west of the Saskatchewan-Michigan-Kansas-Texas line, but today they are greatly reduced in numbers and in some areas extinct. For although they are valuable hunters of destructive pests, it is the unfortunate custom to shoot them at sight. *Taxidea taxus.*

OTTER

Exuberant Sportsman — Tobogganing is the favorite sport of these intelligent, good-natured animals. On a chute of wet mud, a group of fullgrown playmates will slide down the steep bank in a whizz, their legs turned backwards. With a splash they land in the water, one after another; then they return to the top by a side path and start the game all over again, in a spirit of friendly rivalry. The sport is even more fun in wintertime when the icy chute is as slippery as glass. They don't mind the cold on their bottoms as a layer of fat beneath the skin keeps them warm. When the rivers freeze, they have to migrate and their tracks usually lead in a straight line over many miles; they end at some rapids or other open water spots which are found with sure instinct. A swift swimmer with webbed feet, the otter feeds on fish, frogs, and crayfish, but sometimes attacks muskrats or ducks, also. Their dens are in the banks of streams and lakes, with entrances above or below the water level. There, 1 to 3, rarely 5, young are born. The males are 3½ to 4½ feet long and weigh up to 25 pounds. Their range is enormous: It extends from the Canadian treeline south throughout the U.S., with the exception of the western and southwestern desert country; while they are not abundant, they hold their own. Their fur is highly valued throughout the world. *Lutra canadensis.*

RACCOON

Black-Masked, But No Bandit — A furry, ringed coontail hangs from the cap of a trapper, a gay symbol of pioneer days; two eyes shine behind a black mask; a small raccoon by the water's edge vigorously washes a frog before eating it; another catches a fish with a front paw that looks like a monkey's hand; a coon mother carries a baby in her mouth, by the nape of its neck; a cornered male fiercely bites and cripples two or three dogs although it may be badly torn itself; another one, chased by a coon dog, leads its pursuer into a lake, jumps on the dog's head, holds it under water and drowns it — the number of our thought associations with this plucky woods-dweller are legion and make it a truly American animal. The Europeans call the raccoons "wash-bears," but they neatly wash their food only when water is near. That, to be sure, is usually the case as they love to patrol the brooks and ponds and feed on crayfish and frogs, turtles and eggs. They are also fond of fruits in season and visit cornfields and watermelon patches; they love honey and will raid beehives. They are expert tree climbers and have their dens in hollow trees where 4 to 6 babies are born. Their range is southern Canada and the whole U.S., except the high Rockies and western deserts. Their total length is 30 to 36 inches. *Procyon lotor.*

TIMBER WOLF ►

Cruel Killer, Kind Parent — The wolf is a brother of the dog. Both belong not only to the same family but to the same genus. Yet in freedom and independence the wolf seems to have preserved a stronger personality than the civilized dog. To survive in a unanimously hostile world, the timber wolf must sharpen his intelligence, and he does. When hunting in packs of not more than 30, consisting of a few friendly families, they apply successfully every rule of strategy, and by ruse and ambush, surprise and terror, bring down their prey which may be a deer or a calf, a colt or even a moose. In silent agreement every member of the pack knows what to do as they roam over the wide, irregular circle that comprises their territory. They also eat rodents. Once they were common throughout the temperate and arctic North America, but retreated when, with the settlements, the game supply dwindled. The last wolf in the Adirondacks was shot in 1893, in Maine in 1936. It still occurs in the Rocky Mountains, and in the woods around the Great Lakes, and hunts freely in large sections of northern Canada. It survives because of its fecundity, bringing forth 8 to 12 whelps. The young are well taken care of by their most devoted and conscientious parents which seem to mate for life; their friendly family circle contrasts sharply with our image of the cruel, yellow-eyed killer. Length: 4 to 7 feet. *Canis lycaon.*

◄ COYOTE

A Clever Schemer — When pursued, a jack rabbit races in a wide circle which it describes again and again; this is a good opportunity for two coyotes to take turns in the chase; one works, the other rests; between them, they run down the rabbit and divide the prey. No wonder, then, that a whole literature has sprung up around the smart little wolf of the western prairies. Besides its cleverness, its eerie howl which sounds like that of a creature in agony, has made the coyote a frequent topic of American folklore. Usually coyotes hunt in pairs, or groups of three, and in many ways are useful destroyers of pests, feasting on prairies dogs and rabbits, mice and other harmful rodents; adapting themselves to their environment, the Arizona coyotes like kangaroo rats, cactus fruits and mesquite beans. The Minnesota coyotes are fond of muskrats and apples. But they all love to eat calves, lambs, and chickens, and a relentless war is waged against them. As they raise from 3 to 6 and occasionally 14 pups in a litter, and as they are wary animals which learn to recognize traps and poisoned meat, it is no easy task to reduce their numbers. Their fur, although coarse and grizzled, has a ready market. Their range extends from Alaska and the lower Mackenzie to Central America, and from the Pacific to the Texas-Missouri-eastern Ontario line. They resemble collie dogs and attain a length of 42 to 50 inches. *Canis latrans.*

◄ RED FOX

Foxy: "Wily, Cunning." Webster—According to the fables of Aesop, the fox lives by its wits, and lives well. According to Thoreau's famous piece on the fox circling over the snowy hills of New England, it has a precarious life indeed. The truth lies probably in the middle. While trappers are after the fox's pelt, and the farmer's rifle threatens near the chicken coop, and while dogs forever chase it — the scent seems to be maddening to them — the fox apparently enjoys matching wits with its pursuers. To confuse the dogs, it will crisscross its tracks, run in a circle, jump on a stone wall, run up brooks and streams, come up behind the yelping pack, and pass up perfectly safe dens because of the fun of the chase. Its call is a sharp bark or a high-pitched yowl, often heard on moonlight nights. Its reputation of being a ruthless killer of fowl and game birds is hardly justified; by far the largest part of its diet consists of mice and rabbits. Ranging over all of Canada and the cooler parts of the U.S. (except the Pacific coast region), its golden-reddish pelt is a popular catch, and that of its silver variation is highly prized; true strains of silver foxes are farmed successfully, the most famous producer is the Fromm Brothers Fur Farm in Hamburg, Wisconsin. The length of an average fox is 3 to 3½ feet, the weight, 5 to 10 pounds. *Vulpes fulva.*

COUGAR ►

Master of the Mountains — Silent death stalks the range; the victim hardly knows what happens; the attack is like a stroke of lightning. Step by step the big cat has moved its 160 pounds through the underbrush, without the slightest sound; suddenly it leaps on the victim and breaks its back. Death is instant. With a single stroke of its claw the cougar (or panther, puma, or mountain lion) rips open the carcass, tears out the intestines. After the warm feast, it covers the remains with litter for a second, cold meal. The prey is probably a mule deer or a flagtail, since elk have become scarce, or a smaller animal like a mountain beaver, or a cow or a colt. Colt indeed is its favorite meat, and in some Rocky Mountain regions which were infested with panthers, it used to be impossible to raise horses. At one time the mountain lion was truly the animal king of the New World, ranging and reigning throughout North and South America, in jungles, mountains, and deserts. Today it is restricted to the remote wilderness acres of the West; several species live from British Columbia and Alberta southward to New Mexico and Louisiana; Florida also has panthers. Mountain lions were sacred animals to certain Indian tribes, and have always been feared by hunters and settlers, but there is no authentic record of an unprovoked attack on man. Length: 6 to 9 feet, weight: 100 to 175 pounds. *Felis concolor hippolestes.*

Animals

BOBCAT ►

Fierce Cousin of the House Cat — "He can whip his weight in wildcats," — such an estimate of a man's prowess was the most flattering compliment any one could be paid in the jargon of the American frontier. Although a relatively small animal of 15 to 25 pounds weight and a length of approximately 3 feet, the bobcat (or wildcat) is a remorseless hunter, not only of muskrats and squirrels, mice and wood rats, grouse and game birds, but also of porcupine, sheep, and deer. Attacks of 20 pound bobcats on 200 pound does have been recorded. Although a good tree climber, it usually forages on the ground. It is too fierce to be tamed, and at night its shriek, sounding like the scream of an hysterical woman, is blood-curdling. As a nocturnal prowler, it ranges throughout the woodlands of the U.S. and the southernmost rim of Canada, including Nova Scotia, and is not driven away by neighboring settlements. Within its northern territory it competes with its somewhat larger cousin, the Canadian lynx, a handsome cat with tufted ears, cheek-whiskers and a black-tipped tail. The lynx takes up the range where the bobcat leaves off, spreading north to the Canadian timberline. The bobcat, by the way, is named for its abbreviated tail which looks bobbed in comparison with the long appendages of the mountain lion and the jaguar. In the spring 2 to 4 kittens are born in its cave. *Lynx rufus.*

◄ BLACK BEAR

A Famous Performer — Man has always been fascinated by the bear, because the bear looks like a man. Standing on its hind feet as it frequently does, it gives the impression of a hairy, stout-limbed, primitive human being. When the fur coat is removed from a bear's carcass the similarity is even more striking, and there are seasoned hunters in Maine who won't skin a bear, just for that reason. The beast also acts like a man in some ways. If it wants honey, it opens a hive; if it craves apples, it shakes a tree. It is vain and loves applause. If it finds that a little acting will produce some delicacy, it does not hesitate to act. Overindulgence turns it into a beggar or robber, which happened in our national parks. It is born either brunette, redhead, or blond; the cinnamon bear is but a color variation of the black species. Bears occur in all the woodlands of Canada and still live in 36 states of the Union. The 12 bear-less states are in the East and Midwest. Black bears are usually vegetarians, enjoying leaves, fruits, acorns, nuts and honey, also green corn if they can steal it. They lick up ants and other insects, and occasionally eat mice and squirrels. Pork and lamb are also favorite foods, and to get a side of bacon they will break into camps. They hibernate, and during the winter 1 to 2, rarely 3 tiny cubs are born, weighing less than a pound. *Euarctos americanus.*

GRIZZLY BEAR

Lord of the Woods — How can a traveler in the woods distinguish between a black bear and a grizzly? The lumberjacks recommend to irritate the beast and climb a tree. If the animal settles down for a wait at the trunk, it's a grizzly. If it climbs the tree with squirrel-like swiftness, it's a black bear. Besides, the grizzly has a sprinkling of silver-tipped hairs on its coat, and is usually larger. In fact, it is the biggest carnivore on earth, and fears nobody except another grizzly and man. When, on the old Spanish ranchos of California, a particularly fierce bull was bred, the caballeros trapped a grizzly and at the fiesta arranged for an arena fight between the bull and the bear. More than once a bull's neck was cracked with the very first blow of the grizzly's paw. It will carry a 200 pound deer under its arm, but will not attack man unless it is cornered. In that case it will maul and kill the hunter, but does not eat him. Its diet is similar to the black bear's, but some old grizzlies acquire a taste for moose and cattle, and there have been bounties of $1,000 on the head of certain vicious individual marauders. They inhabit the remote mountain wildernesses from Alaska to Utah, are very rare in the U.S., and a little more numerous in Canada. During hibernation 1 to 4 small cubs are born. *Ursus horribilis.*

WALRUS

The Valross—"Whale Horse"—of the Vikings — To keep cool, the walrus likes to sit on an ice floe. That might seem unnecessary as the two species of this animal, the Atlantic and the Pacific walrus, live in arctic oceans, usually in sub-zero temperatures. But they have a thick layer of fat under their hide which keeps them so insulated that in case of death their bodies will remain warm after floating in icy waters for 12 hours. The walrus also loves company, and will climb onto a floe which is already loaded with animals; top-heavy, the floe may turn over with a splash and dump all occupants (some of them had been dozing in the sun) into the icy sea. The excitement is accompanied by loud barks and bellows. Both the male and the female have ivory tusks which they use for fighting and for digging up mollusks; they dive to depths of 60 to 300 feet where they find big clams, starfish, shrimps, and sea snails. The females have one baby and nurse it for almost two years; often they let the young ride on their backs, an opportunity for killer whales to swim under the mother, bump the pup into the sea, and eat it. There used to be herds of tens of thousands, but the whalers almost exterminated them for their hides, ivory, and oil. Today the walrus communities hold their own and give economic security to many Eskimos. Atlantic species: *Odobenus rosmarus.*

ALASKAN FUR SEAL ►

Reunion on the Pribilofs — Fur seal families live separated by 3000 miles most of the year. The fathers enjoy themselves in Alaskan waters while the mothers, their pups and the young males spend the winter in the balmy seas of California. In spring the females and bachelors begin their northern voyage, and take a straight course to a narrow passage between the Aleutian Islands; from there they head to the rocky Pribilof Islands in the Bering Sea, the only land they ever touch. The bulls await them eagerly and herd as many females as they can collect into the world's largest mammal harems; the old "beachmasters" gather 40 to 60, and a super-strong bull may acquire 100 wives. The harems are strictly defined pieces of land, and when an intruder crosses the line, it has a fight on hand with blood streaming and pieces of flesh flying. The female then brings forth her single pup after which she is bred, and if she tries to escape or flirt with a neighbor, a heavy slap on the head will return her to the path of virtue. The master of the harem is in such a state of excitement that he hardly sleeps and never eats during the 3 months of family life. Early in August the fantastic show is over. The fur seals were almost exterminated by the whalers who killed them by the millions, but now they are under protection by international agreement and have recovered remarkably. *Callorhinus alascanus.*

◄ HARBOR SEAL

A Neighborly Fisherman — The only seals ever seen on our inhabited coasts are the playful, curious, and intelligent harbor seals, also called common, hair, or leopard seals. Several species occur from the arctic seas to southern New England, and from the Pribilofs to lower California. They are usually seen in small groups. They do not migrate and never stray far from shore as they apparently cannot sleep in the water, as several other seals do. While the Eskimos eat seal meat and make clothes and rawhide lines of their skins, and even use the membranes of the intestines for waterproof parkas, white man has few commercial uses for this seal. As the hair of its fur points backwards, skiers slip strips of sealskin over the bottom of their skis, as an aid in climbing snowy slopes. As to their family life, the harbor seals are promiscuous, do not form harems, and do not take on any responsibilities. Their single pups often still wear their soft, white, prenatal coat when they are born, exchanging them for the parent's spotted coats a few days later; the claws are already sharp and usable. They cry somewhat like a sheep while the adults utter a sharp bark. Their favorite fish are herring, cod, flounder, pollock, and others. The two great enemies of the harbor seals are the shark and the killer whale; against them the smaller seals have not even a chance of a fight and are swallowed whole. *Phoca vitulina.*

◄ MANATEE

Sea Cow and Siren — There were mermaids in Florida waters. Sailors had seen them. Out of the ocean they rose, holding up their infants and nursing them at their breasts. Behind this tale, widely believed in the days of the sea serpents, was probably the manatee mother which indeed nurses her baby in that fashion. Upright in the water, exposing her head and shoulders, she clasps her baby with her flippers and suckles it at her breasts which, as in a woman, are in the chest region. When the sailors of the mermaid era actually caught a manatee, they must have been terribly disappointed for they had on their hands not a seductive siren but a clumsy sea cow, with the bald head of a seal, no ears, tiny, expressionless eyes, and a swollen upper lip with whiskers. Yet, when science was called upon to classify and label the beast, it reverted to the romantic legend and named the family Sirenia. By size, the sea cows are monsters, having a length of 9 to 15 feet and a weight of perhaps a thousand pounds; but by temperament they are as placid as cows, eating huge quantities of grasses plucked from the bottoms of rivers. Although they are said to descend from the same ancestor as the elephant, they are so completely adapted to their element that they lost their hind legs. They range as far north as the Indian River, and are killed by cold currents. *Trichechus latirostris.*

SPERM WHALE ►

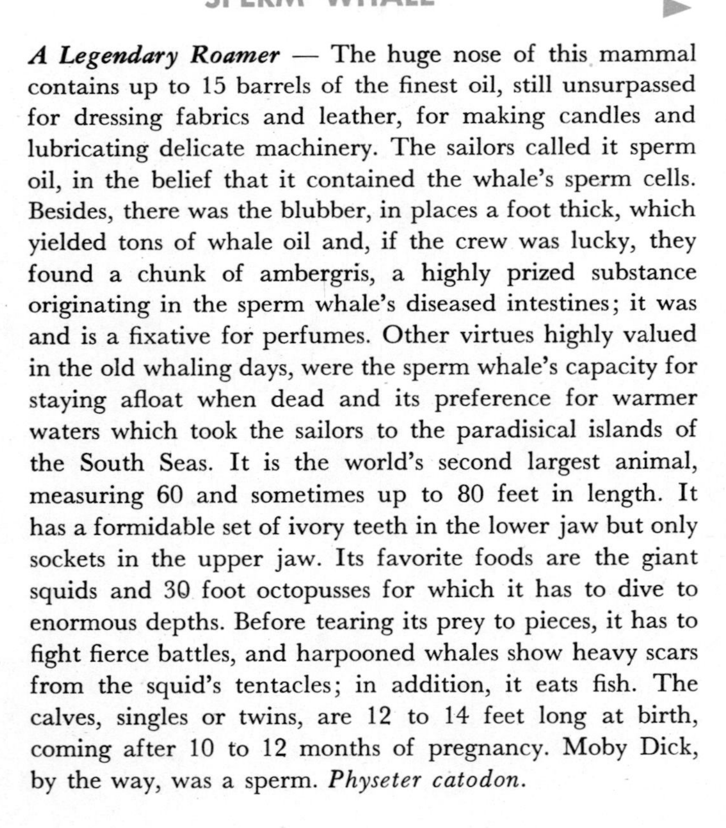

A Legendary Roamer — The huge nose of this mammal contains up to 15 barrels of the finest oil, still unsurpassed for dressing fabrics and leather, for making candles and lubricating delicate machinery. The sailors called it sperm oil, in the belief that it contained the whale's sperm cells. Besides, there was the blubber, in places a foot thick, which yielded tons of whale oil and, if the crew was lucky, they found a chunk of ambergris, a highly prized substance originating in the sperm whale's diseased intestines; it was and is a fixative for perfumes. Other virtues highly valued in the old whaling days, were the sperm whale's capacity for staying afloat when dead and its preference for warmer waters which took the sailors to the paradisical islands of the South Seas. It is the world's second largest animal, measuring 60 and sometimes up to 80 feet in length. It has a formidable set of ivory teeth in the lower jaw but only sockets in the upper jaw. Its favorite foods are the giant squids and 30 foot octopusses for which it has to dive to enormous depths. Before tearing its prey to pieces, it has to fight fierce battles, and harpooned whales show heavy scars from the squid's tentacles; in addition, it eats fish. The calves, singles or twins, are 12 to 14 feet long at birth, coming after 10 to 12 months of pregnancy. Moby Dick, by the way, was a sperm. *Physeter catodon.*

COMMON PORPOISE AND DOLPHIN ►

Roller Coaster — When the singer Arion traveled to Sicily he played his cithara so touchingly, according to Greek mythology, that an enraptured herd of dolphins followed the boat; the jealous sailors threw him overboard, but the dolphins carried him ashore to safety. Such pleasant thought associations still prevail. Every North Atlantic traveler has seen flocks of round-headed porpoises and beaked dolphins playfully swim around the ship, arching in and out of the water in a graceful roller coaster fashion, and almost always cavorting in company. Yet, for all their apparently joyful antics, they are among the most voracious killers alive. They are the smallest of the toothed whales, averaging 6 feet in length and perhaps 100 or 120 pounds in weight. With their big, snapping mouth they cause panic in a school of fish, and keep their own stock healthy by eating the weak and wounded members of their family. The giant porpoises, also called killer whales, reach a length of 20 feet; an Eskimo legend asserts that they are wolves which have transformed themselves into fishes; indeed they hunt like wolves, in packs, and spread terror in the arctic and temperate seas. They even gang up on the great whales, snapping their lips and tearing out their tongues. The various species of the group have single babies, about half the length of their mothers which suckle their young while swimming on the side. Common dolphin: *Delphinus delphis.*

◄ BLUE WHALE

A Retiring Giant — The largest mammal the world has ever known to exist must by necessity be a sea animal. No land creature could give birth to an eight-ton baby; but it is possible for the blue whale mother because the surrounding water acts as a supporting element. She is a foot or two longer than the male which attains a length up to 100 feet and a weight of 200 tons. The blue whale is a world-wide traveler, and it is encountered in Alaskan, Californian and North Atlantic waters feeding on tiny sea animals; this food is collected on its tongue while the water strains out of its mouth through the whalebone sheaths it possesses in lieu of teeth. A giant in size, it is a shy, timid, easily frightened creature. Before the use of modern harpoon equipment, landing this giant was impossible; his body sank to the depths after being killed. It is reticent in its love life. While humpback whales will lie side by side and stroke and pat each other lovingly with their long fins, the blue whales apparently prefer privacy and mate entirely under water. When nursing her baby, the mother raises her rear out of the water and two nipples are pushed out of the recesses of her body; the milk is forced into the baby's mouth and sometimes it spills and clouds a stretch of ocean water. *Balaenoptera musculus.*

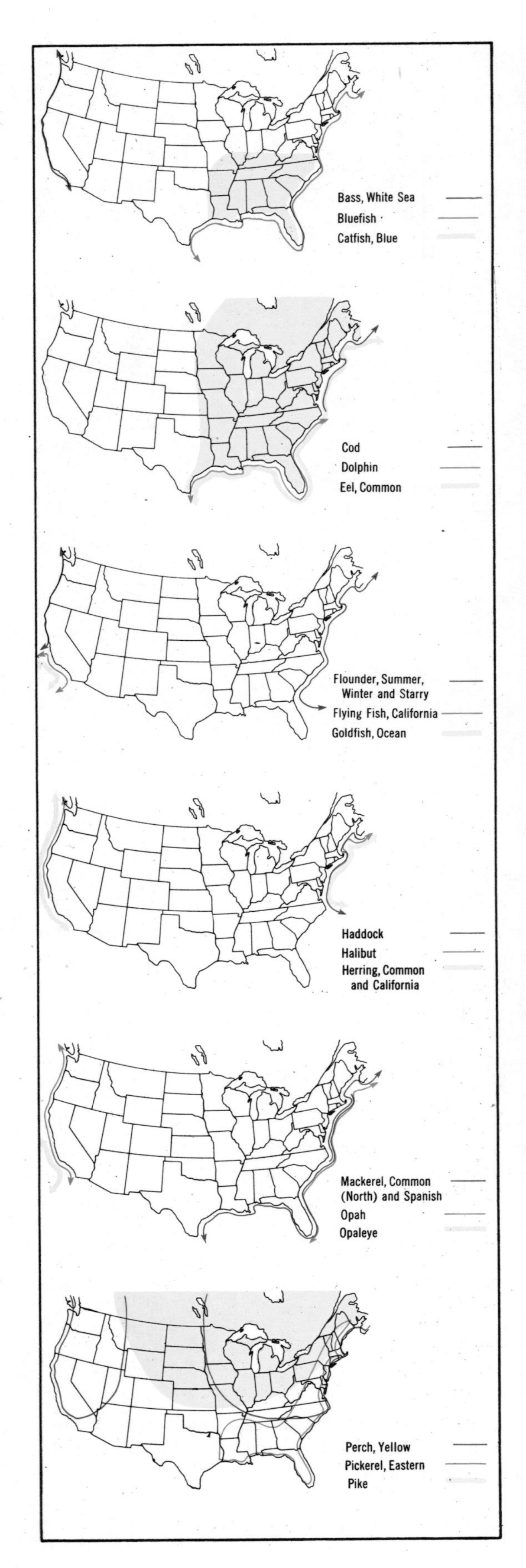

FISHES IN THE U.S. AND SOUTHERN CANADA

The following pages describe and illustrate those fishes which are most frequently encountered in the U.S. and southern Canada, or are of general interest for other reasons. The distribution of these fishes is outlined in alphabetical order on the range maps on this page. A key of the principal orders and families will be found on page 232.

The following notes refer to the maps. *Albacore* — occurs in all warm seas, rarely on Atlantic Coast. *Bass, Large-Mouth* — its original range is the Mississippi Valley, the Great Lakes region and the streams of the Gulf and south Atlantic Coasts; it has been introduced to the rest of the country. *Bass, Small-*

Fishes

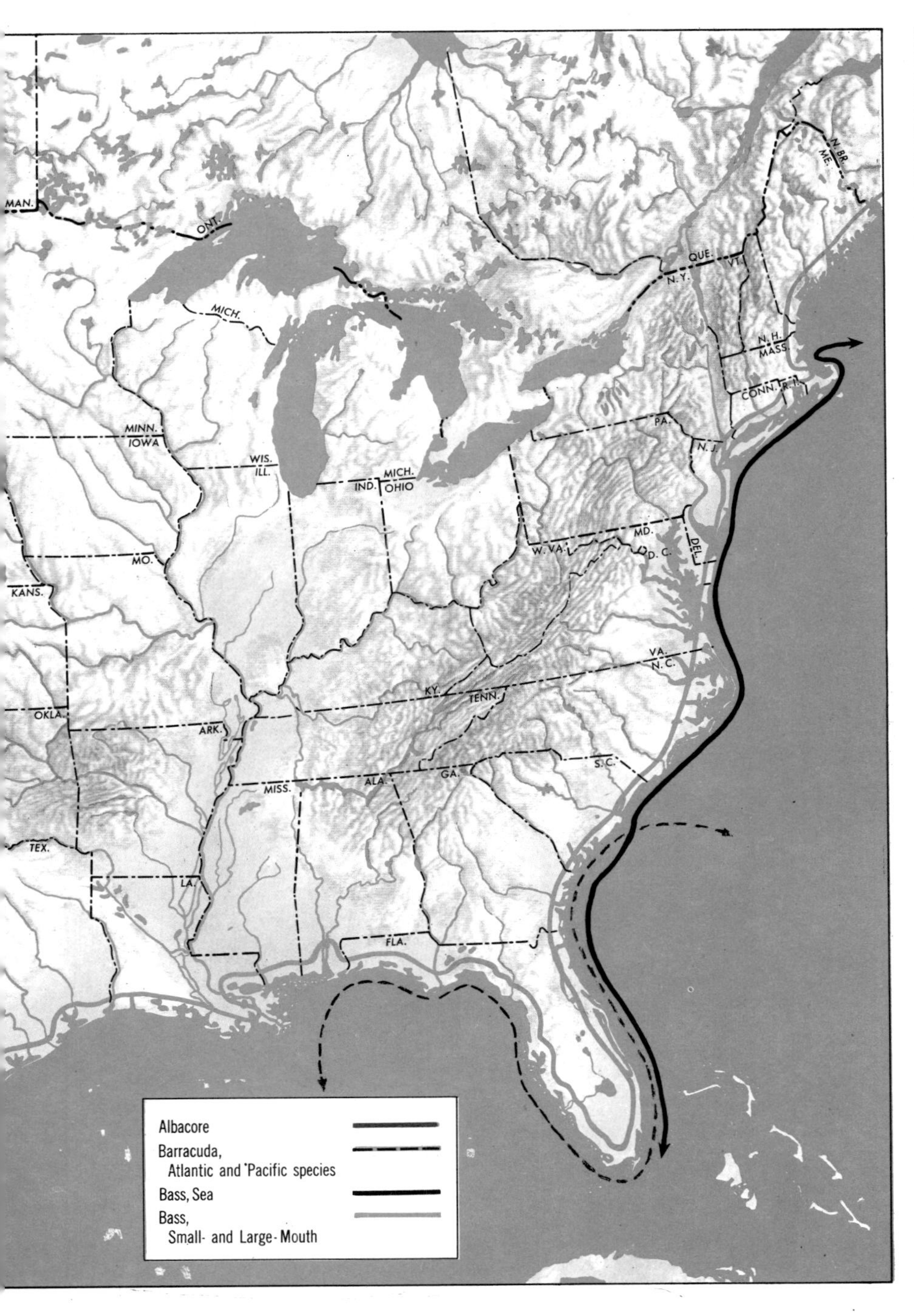

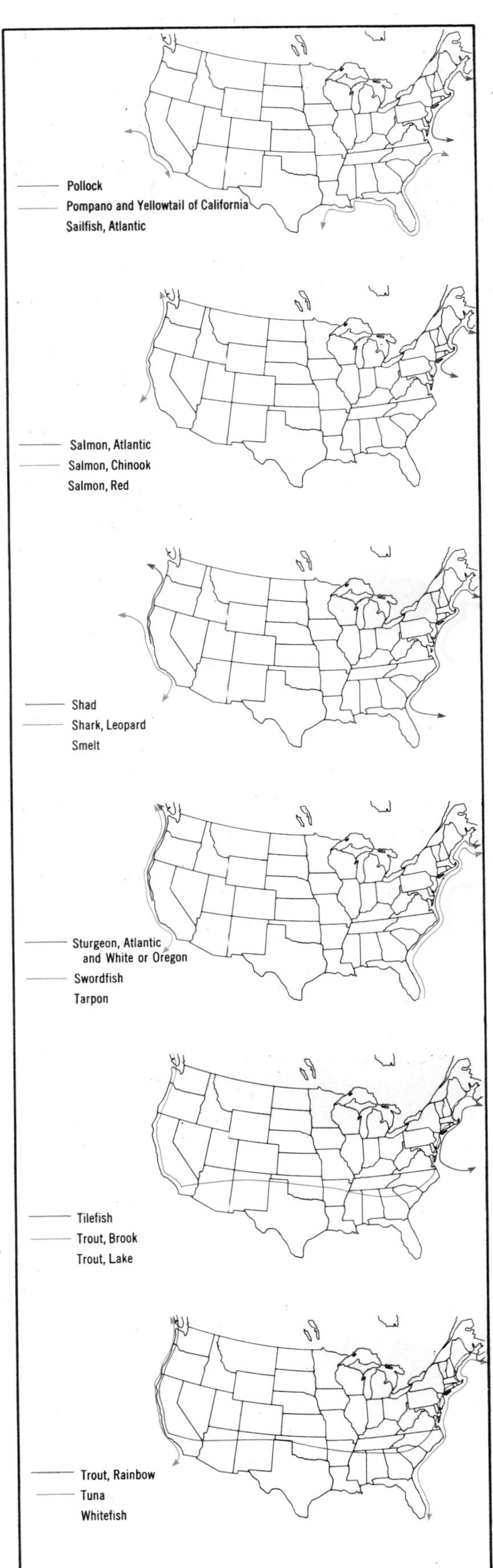

Mouth — its original range extended from Lake Champlain to Manitoba, Oklahoma, Tennessee, South Carolina; it has been introduced to the rest of the country. *Dolphin* — not encountered on west coast, but Kontiki crew reports its abundance in mid-Pacific waters. *Perch, Yellow* — its original range is the East; it has been introduced to the West. *Pompano* — this fish and the Yellow-tail are close relatives of the same family. *Shad* — its original range is the East; it has been introduced to the West. *Smelt* — originally a saltwater fish, it has become landlocked in Lakes Champlain and Memphremagog, and has been introduced to the Great Lakes. *Trout, Brook* — its original range is the East; it has been introduced to the West. *Trout, Rainbow* — its original range is the Pacific slope; it has been introduced to the rest of the country.

◄ STURGEON

Gourmet's Prize — Did Americans ever feed caviar to their pigs? Yes, they did, for about 200 years. Only after the middle of the 19th century did the fishermen realize that the roe of our sturgeon was the same expensive delicacy that had been imported from Russia, and that their previous practice of using it as bait for eel and perch or feeding it to the hogs was wasteful. In 1853 they began to prepare, salt and pack it as caviar. As to sturgeon meat, only poor folks had eaten it, but now it was considered tasty. Good-sized sturgeons that carried one-quarter of their weight in roe had previously sold for 25 to 30 cents. They had been of fairly frequent occurrence in their range between the St. Lawrence River and Mexico, particularly in the lower Delaware; with their sudden rise to fame and value they were vigorously overfished and have been rare ever since. As the sturgeon ascends the rivers to spawn, the pollution of our eastern streams contributed to its decline. With its bony head, its rows of bony shields, its shark-like tail and shovel-like snout it is easily recognized. The fish grows to a length of 10 feet, and giants of 18 feet have been reported. As the sturgeon has a small mouth and no teeth, it is a "mud-grubber," digging in the bottom sand, like a pig, for mollusks, worms, and small fish. *Acipenser sturio.*

TARPON ►

The Silver King — This is the greatest game fish of them all. Lovers of southern sea fishing are unanimous in giving the crown to the tarpon, and a struggle with the "silver king" is a supreme test of strength and skill. Occurring from Long Island to Brazil, it is sought most frequently on both Florida coasts and the Texas shore. It lies in ambush, along the bays and inlets, in the channels and between the banks, waiting for the tide to bring in the smaller fish on which it preys. It is taken by still-fishing or trolling. The popularity of the tarpon as a catch is the more remarkable as it is not especially large, varying from 2 to 6 feet in length and from 30 to 300 pounds in weight, with specimens over a hundred pounds not frequently encountered. Neither is its meat considered a delicacy. But its fight to free itself is fascinating and a classic in the war between man and fish. When it feels the point of the hook it throws its body into the air in a startling series of high and fast leaps, and often succeeds in liberating itself. But these violent jumps are exhausting, and if the hook is not thrown or the line not broken, the prize catch is boated. As its scales are large and iridescent, it makes a magnificent trophy on the clubhouse wall; the scales are also used in the souvenir industry. *Tarpon atlanticus.*

Fishes

HERRING

Staple for the Masses — The first seafish known to inland dwellers was the herring. Even in the Middle Ages it was salted in brine and sold all over Europe, and that powerful combine, the Hanseatic League, was largely built on the herring monopoly. When the herrings left their ancient grounds in the Baltic Sea, the migration was a major reason for the collapse of the league. On the American side of the North Atlantic the same fish was encountered in temperate and cold waters, and for generations was fished by the picturesque method called "torching." A birch-bark or oil torch was fastened to the bow of the boat which was rowed rapidly; great quantities of fish, attracted by the light, were easily dipped into the boat. The torch was also used to lure them into weirs. Now fishing has been modernized both in Europe and America, and billions of herrings are taken annually. Nevertheless, no reduction in numbers is noticeable. Strictly an ocean fish, it is not anadromous, and its reproductive season is very long, lasting throughout the spring, summer, and fall. Herrings feed on small crustaceans and tiny organisms, and are in turn the favorite food of cod and haddock, halibut, bluefish, and others. The principal fisheries are north of Cape Cod; the young are packed as sardines, the adults are sold fresh, or smoked, salted or pickled. A Pacific species occurs in western waters. Length: 10 to 15 inches. *Clupea harengus.*

SHAD

On a Staggered Visit — Nobody knows where the shad lives. But it arises out of the deep sea every year, gathers at the mouths of its several spawning rivers until the water temperature rises to about 60°, and then swims upstream to spawn. In December it invades the Florida rivers, in March it enters Chesapeake Bay, in April it appears in the Hudson, and in May in Canada's St. John. After the eggs have been laid, the adults return to their ocean depth. During their river excursion they do not seem to be interested in food, being intent on the business of propagation, and as they hardly ever eat, they cannot be fished with bait. But they are netted in great numbers and have become a famous American spring delicacy: "Planked Shad with Roe and Bacon." The young fry stay in their river cradle until the water temperature falls noticeably in the fall; then they leave, saltwater-bound, and do not return until the time of their own maturity, probably three or four years later. The shad has been transplanted to the Gulf and Pacific coasts; artificial propagation has been carried out for years, and protective laws have been enacted. In spite of these measures its numbers are on the decline, both because of overfishing and the pollution of river water. Formerly, specimens up to 14 pounds were caught. Now the average is probably under 4 pounds. It is the largest of the herrings in America. *Alosa sapidissima.*

ATLANTIC SALMON

International Aristocrat — ". . . the river salmon surpasses all the fishes of the sea." This is the oldest sentence in world literature in which the word salmon — "salmo" in Latin — appears; it was written 1900 years ago by Pliny, and shows that even the classical world prized highly the salmon which regularly ascended the northern rivers of the Roman Empire. The Anglo-Saxons loved it too and bestowed upon it a multiplicity of Saxon names some of which, strangely, are still in use along our Atlantic coast; "parr," for instance, is a young salmon in fresh water, and "smolt" is its name when entering tidewater with a new silvery coat. On the American side, Indians hunted salmon with torch and spear, and in Colonial days it was so abundant on the New England coast that apprentices in Connecticut stipulated in advance that they would not dine on salmon more than twice a week. Since then its numbers have decreased greatly, and the pollution of our rivers has driven it largely to Canadian waters; the natural range extends from Greenland to Cape Cod. The spawning occurs in the fall, but the eggs do not hatch until the following spring. The young remain in fresh waters for two years or longer, then migrate to their ocean home. They return to the river to spawn after 3 to 5 years in salt water. They do not die after spawning but repeat it 3 or 4 times. Some are landlocked. Length: 20 to 30 inches. *Salmo salar.*

SMELT

A Tasty Dish, and a Candle Burning — Captain John Smith of Jamestown was the first white person to report on the smelt. In 1622 he wrote that the Indians dipped baskets into the river like sieves, and raised them full of smelts. Today this small, shapely fish is still abundant and caught in great numbers during the winter; for its delicate flesh is good eating and contains a pleasant oil that aids digestion. For most species sea water is the proper habitat, preferably the North Atlantic and Alaskan waters, but some swim up the rivers to spawn. Quite a few have become landlocked in eastern lakes, as in Champlain and Memphremagog; they have also been introduced into the Great Lakes where they now thrive in enormous schools and are considered quite a nuisance as they begin to crowd out larger and more valuable fish. Shrimps and other crustaceans are their favorite diet. Structurally the smelt resembles salmon and trout. However, they differ in the formation of their stomachs and in their size; smelt attaining only 7½ inches. Although a favorite game fish, the smelt is not the fighter the salmon is. *Osmerus mordax.* A species of smelt which lives on the Pacific coast from Oregon northward is said to surpass even trout in its delicate flavor. Its strange feature is its extreme oiliness. If it is dried and stuffed with a wick it will burn like a candle; appropriately it is named candlefish. *Thaleichthys pacificus.*

BARRACUDA ►

Cold Eyes, Ferocious Temper — Big fishes bitten in two, or human limbs cut off neatly may be the work of either a shark or a barracuda. If the bite is crescent-shaped and jagged, it is a shark; if it is straight and clean, a barracuda. The teeth of the latter have cutting edges on both sides, the jaws are long and powerful, and the appearance of the open mouth is frightful. Cruising along, it looks for some floating cover under which it can hide, lying in ambush like an old sea-lane pirate. When an unsuspecting fish passes by, it hurls itself on its prey with a fierce dart and does not hesitate to attack fishes many times its own size. In the West Indies many natives fear it more than a shark. Its range extends from Cape Cod to Brazil, but it is most common in tropical and subtropical waters, for instance among the Florida Keys. A related species occurs along the Californian coast and appears as far south as Panama. Around Santa Catalina Island and also along the Florida coast, it is a popular game fish. Squid, live mullet, or other small fish are used as bait. When hooked, it will fight fiercely, but its violent action rarely lasts longer than a few minutes. While the California species reaches a length of 4 to 5 feet, the Atlantic barracuda averages 6 to 8 feet. Its value as a food fish is limited. *Sphyraena barracuda.*

◄ MACKEREL

Twenty Miles of Squirming Bodies — Large silvery patches begin to appear on the ocean near Cape Hatteras early in spring; they are schools of mackerel starting out on their northward journey which, in good mackerel years, becomes a veritable mass migration. Fish hordes of bonanza proportions have been measured to be 20 miles long and half a mile wide. As spring changes into summer, the voyage continues along the shores of New York, Maine, and Nova Scotia, apparently regulated by the fluctuating temperature of water. It ends at the Straits of Belle Isle in northern Newfoundland. Early in the year the mackerel is lean and its flesh of poor texture, but after spawning in rather deep water, between Long Island Sound and the Gulf of St. Lawrence, during May, June, and July, it becomes a fine, fat food fish. A streamlined, fast swimmer, it feeds largely on tiny crustaceans; its favorite is a red copepod called "red feed," and wherever this little creature is abundant, fishermen wait for mackerel to appear. In its struggle for life, the mackerel survives by sheer numbers, for its enemies are legion. Beside man, the gannets hunt them and often stuff themselves so hoggishly that they cannot rise from the waves and have to disgorge a few fish before their wings will lift them again. Whales, sharks, and porpoises like to feed on mackerel and follow their schools to feed. Length: 12-16 inches. *Scomber scombrus.*

◄ TUNA

The Wanderer — The tunas visit our Atlantic coast from early summer to October. Where they are the rest of the year is not known. Where they spawn is doubtful. No tuna eggs or small fry have ever been found in American waters, but from the Mediterranean Sea both eggs and young fish have been reported, and fry from the mid-Atlantic. Tunas appear from Norway to the Cape of Good Hope, seemingly of the same species but in varying sizes. In an attempt to shed some light on their global migrations, an effort has been made to examine the hooks sometimes found imbedded in their tissues when caught. In Sardinia, for instance, a tuna was caught which carried a hook made in Akron, Ohio. Even on our own coasts the tunas' wanderings are not recorded to any extent. They range from Newfoundland to Florida, and from Washington to lower California; in certain localities they abound for a while, then are not seen for years. They feed on all smaller schooling fish, particularly on their cousins, the mackerels and herrings; in turn they are pursued by killer whales which are reported to kill them instantly by hurling themselves on the tunas' nape and biting through their spinal cord. They are hunted by sportsmen and by high-powered tuna boats, and practically the entire catch is canned. They are taken with gill nets or are harpooned. Weight: 100 to 250 pounds. *Thunnus thynnus.*

SAILFISH ►

Glamorous Mariner — With its streamlined tail, its iridescent rays, and its pointed spear, this is the most spectacular trophy a fisherman can mount. Its value is enhanced by its size, approximately 6 feet in length and 120 pounds in weight, and by its relative rarity. Its glamor, gaminess and courage have probably contributed more than anything else to the development of the deep-sea fishing sport in Florida. Furthermore, it is an excellent food fish of fine texture and delicate flavor. That it has excited the imagination of fishermen is confirmed by its numerous names; it is known not only as sailfish but also as spikefish, voilier, aguja volador ("the flying needle"), boohoo and guebucu. It frequents our warmer Atlantic waters as far north as Savannah, but is more common about the Florida Keys. A near relative is the Spearfish, also called billfish or aguja blanca ("white needle") which attains an even greater size than the sailfish but possesses only one ray in the ventral fin. Spearfishes have been observed to pass Cuba in pairs in the summer and have been caught as far north as Cape Cod. They are also found in southern Europe. Arch enemies of the sharks, they become maddeningly furious at the sight of one; cases have been reported where spearfish attached to a fisherman's line changed their struggle to free themselves from the hook into an attack on an approaching shark. *Istiophorus americanus.*

SWORDFISH ►

Tiger of the Sea — Panic in a mackerel school: From the depth of the sea, a monster suddenly arises among the squirming fish and slashes about with its sword, striking left and right "with the force of fifteen double hammers and with the velocity of a swivel shot," killing dozens of mackerel all around and devouring them promptly. That, it is said, is the feeding habit of the swordfish, so named by Aristotle 23 centuries ago. It has an almost world-wide range and occurs both on the Atlantic and Pacific coasts. In American waters, they usually appear during the warm months from June on, and in a smooth sea they like to cavort near the surface and occasionally even leap out of the water. That is the fisherman's chance for a chase, and while the hunt proceeds with harpoon and whale lance, some of the thrills of the old whaling days are revived. The big game fish may even attack a yawl and ram its sword through the boat's side; many a small vessel has limped home to port with a leak in its bottom from a swordfish hunt. As a food fish this fierce fighter has gained favor during the past twenty years and today a swordfish steak is enjoyed as a choice dish. While catches of 800-pound specimens have been reported, the average weight is between 250 and 400 pounds. *Xiphias gladius.*

◄ POMPANO

The Cook's Delight — There are at least two dozen ways in which the chefs of our south Atlantic and Gulf towns prepare the pompano. A pompano steak covered with thinly-sliced, broiled almonds and smothered in browned butter is a culinary highlight. The common pompano inhabits American waters along the Gulf and South Atlantic coasts, is quite frequent in the Indian River region and occurs occasionally as far north as New Jersey. On the west side of the Gulf it seems to be uncommon. Several related species, like the round pompano and the great pompano, also occur in southern waters. It is highly valued not only by gourmets but also by commercial fishermen because it is present the year round, though more abundant in wintertime. It runs in schools, frequents inlets, swims in an out with the tides, and is quite easily caught. As a typical warm water fish, it abhors the cold, and an unusual cold wave refrigerating the water will not only drive it south but also actually kill great numbers. Small crustaceans, bivalve mollusks, and other minute organisms comprise its diet. In shallow waters and in the surf, pompanos root in the sandy or muddy bottoms for food, their fins sometimes protruding above the surface of the water. While they attain a length of 18 inches and a weight of 8 pounds, most specimens vary between 2 and 3 pounds. *Trachinotus carolinus.*

BLUEFISH

"An Animated Chopping Machine" — To destroy and cut to pieces as many fishes as possible seems to be the life aim of this exceedingly carnivorous beast. It does not kill to satisfy its hunger but just to kill, and it has been asserted that it sometimes disgorges the contents of its stuffed stomach to fill it anew. It has been estimated to devour twice its weight daily. Traveling in schools, the bluefish will charge into another school of somewhat smaller-sized fish like a pack of wolves, or like a chopping machine which reduces everything before it to fragments. Frequently their prey is too large to be swallowed whole, so they snap off the hind part and devour it while they leave the front part to rise or sink. In such a massacre the bluefish leave behind a mess of fish heads floating in bloody waters. In turn, the meat of the bluefish is excellent and considered second only to that of the pompano. Like the tunas, the bluefish are great roamers, reported in African, Indian, and Australian waters. On our Atlantic coast, they appear for about 120 days during the summer from Nova Scotia to Brazil; they are caught, in commercial quantities, between Massachusetts and Alabama. Their spawning habits are quite a mystery; they go through a larval stage, and while their larvae have been found at some distance at sea, their eggs have not been identified. Length: 15 to 24 inches. *Pomatomus saltatrix.*

DOLPHIN

A Miracle in Death — Ancient mariners' tales seldom fail to tell of the dolphin's brilliant hues of blue, vivid olive green, white and gold. In the narrative, a dolphin is caught and the sailors watch in awe the beautiful spectacle of its death: The fish begins to change hues, the tints fusing into each other rapidly with the iridescence of precious gems. Today the dolphin is quite rare, but occasionally one is caught in its range between the Carolinas and Texas, and the fishermen of this age stand in the same awe before the wonder of its color transformations in death. The dolphin is a strong and rapid swimmer, and seems to be equipped with superior eye sight. If it sees a likable prey or bait that is trolled, it will jump out of the water in a flashing leap, landing right on top of it. One of its favorite foods is flying fish which it trails anticipating the leaps and is at hand waiting for its prey exactly where it strikes the water. It is a gamey and sporty, but not very persevering, fighter. The high forehead is a characteristic of the adult male. With a length of approximately 6 feet, it reaches a weight of 75 to 100 pounds. Its meat is good eating. The name dolphin is a regrettable choice as a mammal of the porpoise family has been called dolphin since mythological times. *Coryphaena hippurus.*

SEA BASS

Well-Groomed and Tough-Mouthed — Any ship wreck on the bottom of the sea is a favorite hideout for sea bass; or you may search for it along breakwaters, jetties, piles, or on the open ocean where the bottom is rough and rocky. Fishing grounds that meet these specifications are found along Long Island and New Jersey where power boats carry metropolitan sportsmen to the sea bass banks by the thousands. 20 to 30 miles from the coast of North Carolina there is a large submarine area at a depth of 20 to 30 fathoms, the floor covered with rock cavities and coral formations. To fish sea bass over this ideal ground is, or at least used to be, a pleasure. Two handlines with 3 hooks each were operated simultaneously by fishermen who were kept busy drawing in the catch of the lines in turns; sometimes they worked without a let-up. Few were lost since the hook stays firm in the tough mouth of the captured fish. The sea bass, a handsome species whose skin has been compared to a tweed suit, ranges from Massachusetts to Florida; a second related species occurs from North Carolina southward but no distinction is made by fishermen. The sea bass are voracious feeders living on small fish and squids, crabs and shrimps, and when caught their stomachs are usually stuffed with food; to avoid decomposition and odors, they are dressed without delay. Length: 18 to 20 inches. *Centropristes striatus.*

TILEFISH

A Sea Mystery — In May, 1879, the schooner *Wm. V. Hutchings* trawled for cod south of Nantucket and caught 5,000 pounds of a fish none of the crew had ever seen before. It was as brilliantly colored as the coral reef fishes of the tropical seas, with bluish or olive-green tints on the upper, yellow or rosy hues on the lower sides. Small yellow spots extended to the back fin. At the home port, none of the Gloucestermen had heard of such a fish either, and when zoologists were called in, the catch proved to be new to science also. The flesh was boiled, fried, and smoked and tasted excellent. For three years there was wide interest in the discovery, when the tilefish, as it was called now, again appeared in the news. Steamers arriving from Europe reported that certain stretches of the Atlantic were literally covered with dead tilefish. The schooner *Navarino* had sailed through 150 miles of them. The number of carcasses was estimated at a billion. They were examined and found free of disease, infection or parasites. What had caused the catastrophe? After a careful investigation the scientists came up with a single answer: The fish had died of cold. Northern gales had cooled their habitat beyond their endurance. There were no tilefish for several years, then they reappeared gradually and are now a valuable food fish occurring from New England to Virginia. Length: 18 to 24 inches. *Lopholatilus chameleonticeps.*

COD

The Fish That Made History — 9,100,000 children from one mother in one year are a theoretical possibility for the cod. That is the number of eggs that the ovary of a 75-pound cod has been computed to hold; in a 21-pound cod the number is about 2,700,000. If every egg were hatched and every young reached maturity, the ocean would overflow with codfish. In reality, millions of eggs fail to be impregnated, myriads are eaten, and the newly hatched cod are reduced in numbers by a legion of enemies. Nevertheless, its extremely prolific reproduction is responsible for its survival in abundance in spite of grand-scale fisheries. It has flesh of a good flavor, few bones, and is adaptable to dry-salting, while oil-rich fish like salmon and mackerel have to be preserved in brine. It was probably a combination of these virtues that induced European fishermen to search for cod in American waters before Columbus; that encouraged England to establish its American colonies; and caused the Commonwealth of Massachusetts to place the cod on its seal and its state house. The cod is a cold water fish generally taken in depths of from 8 to 40 fathoms; it ranges from Cape Hatteras to the north and is important from Massachusetts to Newfoundland. As an omnivorous feeder, it makes a contribution to science: Rare or new species of fish, mollusks or crustaceans are occasionally found in its stomach. Length: 2 to 3 feet. *Gadus morrhua.*

POLLOCK

Open Sea Strategist — The pollock transforms excellent fish into fair-grade fish and is therefore unpopular. It devours first-rate food species while its own meat is considered mediocre by many. It is the arch enemy of the young cod, its cousin. Bands of adult pollocks have been observed to completely surround schools of half-grown cod. In a concerted effort the attackers squeeze their prey into a compact mass, then charge into it with systematic greed. As the pollocks work their way into their squirming food pile, sea gulls appear in the sky and join the witches' sabbath from above, diving into the center and sharing in the feast. The panicky young cod try desperately to break through the ring of killers but rarely succeed. Pollocks seem to specialize in feeding on young fish; they roam through our Atlantic waters, on the surface and at intermediate depths, and search for schools that may be devoured; they are also bottom feeders. They are quite abundant in northern waters and appear as far south as Cape Cod or even New York. Specimens measuring 4 feet and weighing 40 pounds have been caught, but a length of 2 to 3 feet is more common. As a game fish, the pollock takes the hook freely and in some localities fights with vigor and perseverance. It is as prolific as the cod; a 13-pound specimen produced more than 2½ million eggs. A favorite spawning ground is off Cape Ann. *Pollachius virens.*

Fishes

HADDOCK ►

An Old and New World Food Fish — While cod is salted in great quantities, haddock is rather frozen or eaten fresh; it is considered ideal for fish chowder and particularly tasty when boiled. It is also smoked; in that form it is called Finnan Haddie, after the towns of either Findon or Findhorn in Scotland. In Europe, it occurs all around the British Isles and from Iceland to France. On the American coast it ranges from the Straits of Belle Isle to Cape Hatteras and, as it is more gregarious than the cod and roams in huge, compact schools, it is caught in enormous quantities; it even exceeds the cod in the volume of the annual catch. The Massachusetts coast and the banks in the Gulf of St. Lawrence are favorite fishing grounds. The haddock, rarely seen on the surface, is a more or less omnivorous bottom-feeder, living on marine invertebrates and mollusks. One of its favorite hunting grounds is the clam-bank; for that reason the Germans call it Schellfisch. Specimens weighing 17 pounds have been encountered but the usual weight is 3 to 4 pounds and the average length 23 to 30 inches. The spawning takes places from April to June, and its egg-laying is as prodigious as that of the cod; therefore its stupendous numbers. Besides fecundity, it has another point in common with the cod: The eggs of both float on the surface. *Melanogrammus aeglefinus.*

◄ SUMMER FLOUNDER

A Marvel of Adaptation — Eye migration is the unique feature of the flounders. After birth they swim like other fishes, in an upright position, and their heads possess one eye on each side. But soon they take on the peculiar habit of the flatfishes — to rest on one side, to favor the sea bottom, and to cover themselves with sand. In such a state the eye on the lower side cannot serve any useful purpose and therefore it migrates to the upper side to assist the eye already there. Correspondingly, the flounder's bottom side remains pale while the topside, exposed to the light, becomes pigmented. Of the two related species which are distinguished commercially, the summer flounder rests on the right, the winter flounder on the left side. The former occurs from Cape Cod to South Carolina, being most numerous from New York southward, and the latter from northern Labrador to Cape Lookout. Both feed on small marine animals like mollusks and crustaceans, but the summer flounder has a somewhat larger mouth, eats more fish, and grows a little bigger, from 15 to 20 inches, as compared with the regular 15 to 17 inch size of the winter flounder. Occasionally a 2-foot flounder is caught. The summer flounder has a remarkable flair for camouflage; it will adjust its color to its background, taking on red, green or blue hues, and even mimicking the pattern. Both species spawn in the winter. *Paralichthys dentatus.*

◄ HALIBUT

A Giant Flounder — A flatfish 9 feet 2 inches long and weighing 625 pounds when dressed was captured 50 miles from Thatcher Island on the Massachusetts coast in 1917. This was probably the largest halibut ever caught. Specimens of 4 to 6 feet, weighing between 50 and 200 pounds are of average size. Males are smaller than females, and big, old fish do not furnish the most savoury flesh. From the chef's viewpoint, a fat, 80-pound female is ideal. The halibut inhabits both our Atlantic and Pacific waters and ranges from the icy-cold northern currents to New Jersey in the east, to northern California in the west. So enormous were early catches that a special train, "the halibut express" (faster than most passenger trains) ran from Vancouver to Boston, filled almost entirely with this one fish. Inshore fishing almost exterminated the halibut before government protection. It has now become a strictly deep-water fish. A voracious feeder, the halibut includes in its diet a multitude of fish from cods and haddocks to flounder and herrings, devours lobsters and clams, and even enjoys an occasional sea bird and refuse from ships. Like the winter flounder, it wears its two eyes and pigmented skin on the right side. When it transforms itself from an upright fish into a flatfish, in its early youth, the eye on the bottom side migrates with its socket. *Hippoglossus hippoglossus.*

CHINOOK SALMON ►

A River Trip of Life and Death — Reproduction of the species seems to be the goal in the life of the chinook and the other Pacific salmons. As soon as they have served that purpose and spawned, they die; they do so near their birthplace. In the Columbia River the ascent begins in March and lasts for three months. The travel, at first at a leisurely pace, gradually becomes a rapid race; the earliest ones go farthest, more than 1,000 miles from the sea to the Sawtooth Mountains in Idaho. The late-comers select tributaries nearer the coast. There is a similar movement on the Sacramento, the Yukon and the other large streams. Some salmon run from August to November, depending on the river. In fine gravel beds in clear, cool, mountain streams the chinooks deposit their eggs and fertilize them as soon as the water temperature falls to 54°. Having accomplished this chore for the first and last time, both the males and females die at an age of 4 or 5 years. Has, perhaps, the strenuous journey exhausted and mutilated the swimmers? It does not seem so for they arrive in fine condition. But pushing the gravel and rubbing against the pebbles of the spawning beds causes severe abrasions; they also fight with each other a good deal. In the ocean, the chinook is a valuable and abundant food fish, living on marine animals, especially on herring and anchovies. Length: 4 feet. *Oncorhynchus tschawytscha.*

RED SALMON ►

Source of An Industry — The Russians in Kamchatka call it krasnaya ryba, the Alaskans red salmon, the Canadians sockeye, and the fishermen of the Columbia River blueback. All consider it a magnificent food fish whose firm, red, well-flavored meat lends itself well to canning. It occurs from Alaska to San Francisco Bay but is not frequent south of the Columbia; in Alaska, however, it is the most abundant and valuable catch. The Fraser River in British Columbia was once its favorite spawning road and, at the height of the run, so many red salmons fought their way upstream that the river bed looked like a street paved with red fish-backs. A peculiarity which distinguishes the red salmon from the other species is its unerring instinct to ascend only those streams which end in lakes. They spawn in the tributary brooks and their young spend 2 or more years in the lake before returning to the ocean. Some adults remain landlocked as freshwater "red fish," as they are called. In these western lakes it has been possible to observe the courtship habits of the species: How they pair off; how the female builds a nest while the male drives off intruders; how the male touches his mate with his snout, moves his body against hers and for one or two seconds quivers sharply, an act often repeated. Their favorite food in fresh and salt water is plankton, especially its animal organisms. Length: 20 to 24 inches. *Oncorhynchus nerka.*

◄ CALIFORNIA FLYING FISH

Airplane Models — For centuries the would-be inventors of a flying machine turned to nature for guidance, but they watched the wrong model. They were always fascinated by the flapping wings of birds while they should have observed the flying fish: How its tail, vibrating vigorously in the water from side to side, acts as a motor propeller; how the flyer taxis over the water, the front part of its body raised over the surface at a slight angle; how it then takes off, making use of air currents and controlling its flight both on a horizontal and vertical plane. Their taxiing extends for perhaps 40 feet and the flight up to a hundred yards, as far as 200 yards in some species. These flights are perhaps a method of escape from their enemies, dolphins, sharks and tuna. While under water, both pairs of the fin-wings are folded and cling to the body; they spread when reaching the air and act as glider wings; they do not flap, and the fish do not truly fly but soar. When skipping the crests of rolling waves the tail touches the water, works again like a propeller for a moment and gives new impetus to the flight. Flying fish occur in the warm seas only, and the California species inhabits the southern coastal waters of the state. It is edible though rarely fished commercially. Length: 12 inches. *Cypsilurus californicus.*

◄ ALBACORE

Racer with the Long, Pectoral Fins — This relative of the tunas is streamlined to such an extent that its body provides grooves into which all its fins fit closely; there are even depressions for the jaws; it is expertly built for great swimming speeds. A roamer of the warm seas, it is rare in the Atlantic but quite abundant in Californian waters. Like the tuna, it prefers the open ocean and power fishing boats are now equipped to search for these food fish more than 1,000 miles from the home port. To attract a school of albacores, rag lures are used and, when located, pails of live bait are thrown over-board to keep the fish around the boat. As long as they stay, they can be hooked in great numbers by lines on hand poles, but they will vanish as suddenly as they appear. Their meat was once considered inferior, but it is in favor now and canned as tuna. It has a supposedly chicken-like flavor in salads. The albacore's own food consists of the smaller fishes of the open seas, like anchovies and sardines. From May to December, schools of albacores are encountered frequently, but their migrations during the rest of the year are unknown. Their spawning habits are also a mystery. An interesting sport of the Pacific coast fishermen is kite-fishing of tuna and albacore, i.e. bait and hook are administered with the help of a box kite. Length: 3 feet. *Germo alalunga.*

OPAH ►

A Glamorous Cosmopolitan — This fish is a work of art, a swimming display of striking colors, a living pattern of ultramarine and vermillion with silver spots. Its eye is described as very big and brilliant, with a golden ring around its pupil. Its appearance is startling, for it combines beauty and grace with size: the opah grows to a length of 2½ to 6 feet and a weight of 40 to 400 pounds; even 600-pound specimens have been reported. Its flesh has a red tint of varying shades and is described as firm, rich, oily, tender, flavorful and of choice taste. Furthermore, the opah is a cosmopolitan traveler and has been caught in the seas of California and Alaska, Cuba and Madeira, Newfoundland and Maine. No wonder, then, that it has excited the imagination of the world's fishermen and is known under a whole galaxy of additional fanciful names: mariposa and moonfish, San Pedro fish and Jerusalem haddock, cravo and soho, glance fish and gudlax. The French use a translation of moonfish: poisson lune. It lives singly and in schools, but as can be expected of such an exceptional creature, it is too rare and irregular in its appearance to have economic significance; on the Pacific coast where apparently most catches are made, it is not fished commercially either. It is the only species of its family; it has a small mouth without teeth, and is covered with minute cycloid scales. *Lampris regius.*

OPALEYE

Playing in the Greenish Pools — Incisors in the front of their jaws are the tools used by the opaleyes for cutting and eating green, brown, and olive algae. This species belongs to the family of rudderfishes which have no molars and are herbivorous; but as the seaweeds are covered with minute marine animals, they absorb a certain amount of flesh food. The opaleye can readily be seen darting back and forth in west coast rock pools. Its green tints grow lighter or darker as light conditions change, therefore, it is also called greenfish. It is easily recognized by the light blotches it displays on its back, one on each side of the dorsal fin; in the young these spots are whitish-yellowish, on the adults, white. Rather small and built as a compact, solid body, it is a swift and skillful swimmer and, as it has no other weapons, relies on speed and dashing activity to avoid its enemies and to escape when pursued. Anglers capture it by using hooks which are baited with worms or bits of fish or clams. But, while its meat is edible and of fair flavor, the fish is not especially in demand. The range of the opaleye is the California shore from Monterey or even San Francisco to Cape San Lucas and Guaymas; a relative is found near the east coast of Asia. Its length is from 10 to 12 inches, but occasionally specimens of 17 inches are measured. *Girella nigricans.*

WHITE SEA BASS

Pacific Fighter — This bass is not a true bass; it is the Pacific brother of the Atlantic weakfish or squeteague, and a member of the croaker family, the large carnivorous group which includes croaking, snoring and drumming species. Its range extends from the Gulf of California to Vancouver Island, and it even travels to Alaska, but as it prefers warmer waters, it is rare north of San Francisco. Sardines and anchovies, herring and smelts, crustaceans and squids are included in its diet, and it is caught in weights ranging from 20 to 90 pounds. Its firm white flesh is very tasty and popular, and it is not only a fine food fish but also a vigorous and sporty gamefish. There are reports of exciting 15 to 30-minute contests in which the fisherman had to exert all his skill and strength to haul in his catch. It is an important and frequent inhabitant in the waters surrounding Santa Catalina Island. Steelblue on its back, silvery on its sides, and white on its stomach, this fish is a handsome creature; occasionally some bronze and old-gold tints are noted. At the base of the pectoral fin the scaly pattern is interrupted by a dusky spot. The young have cross bars which disappear on the adults. Most of its relatives live in tropical seas, and more than 45 species are encountered off the coast of Central America. Length: 3 to 6 feet. *Cynoscion nobilis.*

◄ LEOPARD SHARK

Tough But Not Alarming — Even in Thoreau's day bathers on American beaches were gravely warned of the danger of sharks. Thoreau made fun of the bugaboo, and he was right: In our waters a swimmer is more apt to be struck by lightning than bitten by a shark. It is true that most sharks are voracious, have formidable jaws with various rows of triangular teeth, and bite large, clean chunks out of any fish. But the number of authenticated reports of attacks on man are very rare. Two of the largest species, the basking shark and the whale shark, with a length of 45 feet (the biggest living fish) are harmless even to other fish; for they feed on plankton; they catch it in a swallow of water, then strain it out of their mouths through gill-rakers that act as sieves. The leopard shark is a well known representative of the fish-eating group on western shores, ranging from San Francisco Bay to lower California. Its name is derived from the black cross bars on its back and its round, black spots. It never attacks man and is frequently caught by anglers. It is a nuisance when it crashes into a sardine seine, moves about and rubs the thousands of spines in its skin against the twine of the net. This abrasive contact ruins the net. Most sharks are viviporous, i.e. they give birth to living young. Length of the leopard shark: 3½ to 5 feet. *Triakis semifasciatum.*

OCEAN GOLDFISH ►

Dweller in the Reef Gardens — Sightseers in glass-bottom boats off Santa Catalina Island enjoy the scarlet-golden fishes which are called ocean goldfish or Garibaldi, the most brilliant dwellers of the submarine gardens. To make the moving pattern of colors in the rock pools and around the picturesque reefs even more striking, their young have intensely bright blue markings on their dusky-scarlet skins. For his pugnacity, agility (his only defense) and color the Garibaldi is named in honor of the Italian liberator and unifier whose volunteer troops were called the "red shirts." But the graceful family name Demoiselles seems more appropriate. Neither the Garibaldi nor its multi-colored relatives that float around the reefs and docks of Florida and other tropical regions, are of any commercial importance, but they lend glamor to the tropical seas. The Garibaldi is a small fish approximately 8 inches long, though 14-inch specimens have been encountered. It feeds on minute organisms in tidepools and among the rocks, ranging from Point Conception to Todos Santos Bay in Lower California. Atlantic species also have fanciful names. The yellow-tailed demoiselle contrasts a dark body with a brilliant yellow tail, and the abundant sergeant-major, about 6 inches long, proudly displays its yellow and black vertical bands, symbols of its military rank; playful and decorative, it fits perfectly into its sunny setting. *Hypsypops rubicundus.*

Fishes

BLUE CATFISH ►

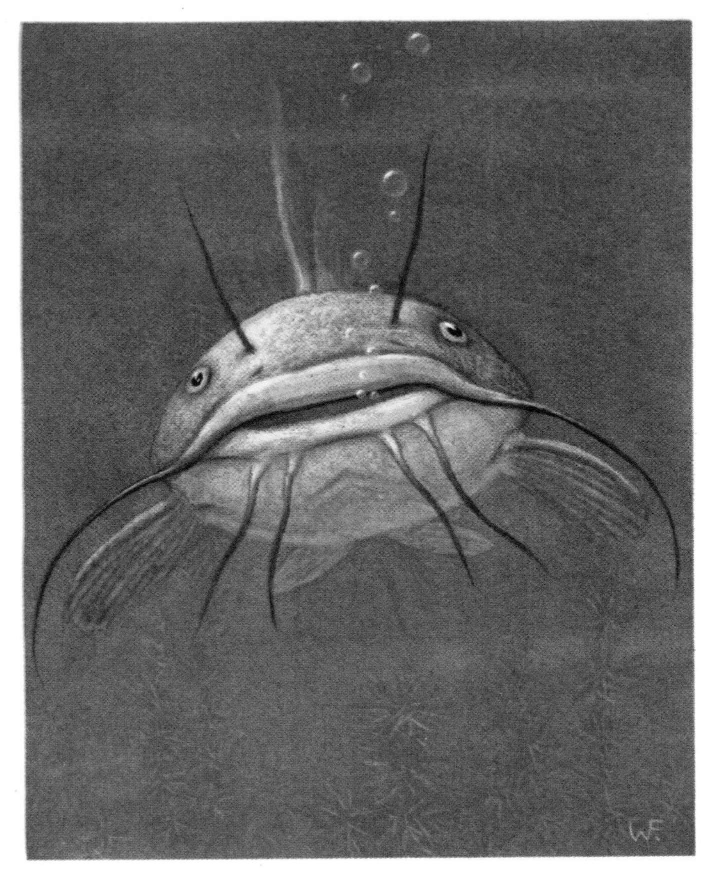

A Bewhiskered Southerner — "Oh, do not bring the catfish here! The Catfish is a name I fear." It had been proposed to introduce this American favorite to England's rivers, lakes and lochs, and the poem was the adverse reaction of *Punch*. Doubtlessly the English judgment was prejudiced by the ugly appearance of the catfish, its small eyes, scaleless skin, and long, dangling feelers. But on the credit side it should be mentioned that it lives in clear and swift streams, has a clean diet of fishes and crayfish, takes many kinds of bait, is easily caught, surrenders only after a fight, and furnishes a firm, flaky, nutritious and flavorsome meat. The average weight is a few pounds; occasionally 80-pound specimens are caught, and the giants attain a weight of 125 pounds. Its original home is the Mississippi Valley, but it has been successfully introduced to many other sections, both in the East and the West. In Louisiana, it is an integral part of the Bayou Country, and where, in spring, the Mississippi flood inundates forested areas, the catfish "takes to the woods." There, hooks and lines fastened to trees catch the "Mississippi cat," or, as the Creoles call it more elegantly, the "poisson bleu." Fishing is so heavy that the blue catfish could hardly survive in abundant quantities if it were not largely a night feeder, and if it did not protect its nest and care for its young as conscientiously as it does. Length: up to 5 feet. *Ictalurus furcatus.*

◄ COMMON EEL

Mysterious Traveler — Zeus was the progenitor of the eel, according to the ancient Greek poets who habitually attributed every case of doubtful paternity to the prolific god. For almost 2,000 years the mystery of the eel's reproduction remained; both in Europe and America it was known to inhabit rivers and lakes, then to swim to the sea and to vanish forever. In spring, myriads of small, transparent baby eels appeared at the mouths of the rivers and migrated upstream to live as far inland as the middle Mississippi Valley. The puzzle was solved not so many years ago: It was discovered that the reproduction cycle of the eel was the exact opposite of that of the Pacific Salmon. The latter is an anadromous ocean fish ascending the rivers to spawn and die. The former is a catadromous freshwater fish descending to the ocean to spawn and die. The eels' spawning beds were discovered south of the Bermudas, the grounds of the American eels lying westward of those of the European eels. From there the eastward voyage of the baby eels to Europe takes about 3 years, the westward trip to America only one year. The young ascend the gulf and Atlantic rivers of the U.S. and Canada, even to the remotest lakes. The eel is a scavenger in its diet, feeding on refuse, dead fish and animal matter. It is valued as food in certain sections of the U.S. and Canada. Length: up to 4 feet. *Anguilla bostoniensis.*

WHITEFISH

A Famous Midwesterner — The spawntaker grasps the female whitefish firmly, supports her head with his body; while holding her tail, he bends her into a crescent with one hand and with the other strokes her gently toward the vent: Easily, the eggs slide into the pan. Then the milt is procured from the male in the same way; eggs and milt are mixed, treated with water and forwarded to the hatchery. It is fortunate that the whitefish responds so freely to artificial propogation; it could hardly survive otherwise. Even so, its numbers are declining in the Great Lakes. Because of its superb flaky meat which is equally popular when smoked or prepared in any other way, it is considered one of the world's most important freshwater food fishes. Besides the Great Lakes, several other lakes in the U.S. and Canada are its habitat. It is rarely taken with the hook; the gill net is the principal method of making the catch. In midsummer it descends to cooler depths, and in the fall many whitefish approach the shore or enter streams to spawn; the movements vary in different lakes. The young seem to be slow in maturing and apparently do not spawn until they are five years old. The diet of the whitefish includes insect larvae, small mollusks and other minute animals. Old whitefish weigh up to 20 pounds, but specimens of 3 or 4 pounds are the norm. Length: 2 feet or more. *Coregonus clupeiformis.*

BROOK TROUT

Fish of a Thousand Tales — The female trout dashes into the gravel of the brook's pool against the current. As she turns on her side, a sweeping motion of her tail rubs her body against the sand, and after one or two days' labor the round or oval nest is ready; it is a hole 2 to 10 inches deep and 1 to 2 feet in diameter. All this time the male hovers around; he does not share in the work but is busy fighting off intruding rivals. After a round of courtship rites, the eggs are deposited. Then the female covers the eggs slightly with gravel and leaves them to rest throughout the winter. The mating usually occurs late in October, the hatching the following spring. The fish thus produced is the most talked-about and written-about game fish of our fresh waters. Its original home extends from Labrador to Saskatchewan in the West, and along the Alleghenies to Georgia in the South. But it has been introduced by fish culturists to almost any clear, cool, rapid, gravelly mountain brook in the U.S. and Canada. It is also raised for the market in artificial ponds and hatchery troughs with flowing spring water. Once trout of 10 pounds weight were taken; today the thousands of trout anglers consider a one-pound specimen a fine catch The appearance of the brook trout varies greatly; in some waters it is dark, in others it shows its famous spectacular pattern. Length: 8 to 24 inches. *Salvelinus fontinalis.*

Fishes

LAKE TROUT ►

On Midwestern Menus — Like a good housewife, the female lake trout begins to clean and tidy up her nesting site when spawning time approaches, in the fall. After having left the deep water, she selects a suitable spot around the reefs in a shallower part of the lake and, working mostly at night, she pushes and pulls away the debris of stones, the plants, and the slime, until the clean nesting site can be clearly distinguished from the untidy surroundings. The spawning takes place above the nest, the eggs settling into the crevices of the rock. This largest member of the trout family used to attain, on occasion, a weight of 100 pounds, but today specimens weighing from 5 to 10 pounds are the average. In the Great Lakes where it is called Mackinaw trout, its numbers are declining. It appears also in the bigger Maine lakes where it is known as togue, and in British Columbia, the Canadian arctic and subarctic, and Alaska where the Indian names are still in use: namaycush or masamacush. Though omnivorous, its diet includes largely smaller fishes; once 13 lake herrings were found in the stomach of a 20-pound lake trout. Commercially it is caught by grand-scale methods, and sportsmen like to catch it by ice-fishing in wintertime. The ice hole must be widest toward the water, and the line must be kept bobbing, ready for an instantaneous pull. Length: 2- 3½ feet. *Cristivomer namaycush.*

◄ RAINBOW TROUT

An All-American Favorite — When, with the advance of civilization, many streams became unsuitable for the brook trout, the rainbow trout came to the rescue of the sportsmen. Originally it is a native of the Pacific slope, inhabiting the streams in the western drainage of the Rockies and the Sierras, the Cascades and the Coastal ranges in the U.S., Canada and Alaska; but early experiments proved that it adapts itself readily to other parts of the country, and rainbow trout eggs were shipped from California, Oregon and Washington to many states and provinces in the East and in the Great Lakes region. There the rainbow trout was welcomed because it was less demanding than the brook trout as to cold water and rapid currents. Today it flourishes in rivers too warm for other trout, both in mountainous terrain and farther downstream. It is not as colorful as might be deduced from its name; but it has a broad band along its sides which is purplish-iridescent. There are several geographic races, and a good deal of hybridization has been carried out by fish culturists. Many eastern sportsmen do not rate the rainbow trout as highly as the brook trout, but western fishermen assert that in its native waters it is a superb game fish which will leap when hooked, a stunt rarely resorted to by the brook trout. A good average catch weighs 2 to 3 pounds, and its meat is delicious. Length: 1 to 3 feet. *Salmo gairdnerii.*

EASTERN PICKEREL

Lurking in the Lake Weeds — How can this voracious fish swallow a fellow fish half its own size? Opening its large mouth, it takes a hold of the tail end of its prey and slowly and by degrees works it down its throat. Where the hunting is good, it will grow into a two-foot specimen weighing 7 or 8 pounds. Its range extends from Maine to Florida and may be described as east and south of the Alleghenies. Except at spawning time, the eastern pickerel is a solitary dweller of rivers, ponds, and lakes; fishermen look for it among submerged water plants and weeds; in such an environment the spawning takes place, and the string of eggs settle on the under-water brush. It is a spring spawner, mating in April and May in the North and earlier in the South. Popular with sportsmen, it is a fair game fish and taken quite easily by various methods; fishes and frogs are effective live bait. As a human food, the eastern pickerel has a varying reputation; its flesh is dry but relatively firm and has a good flavor. A smaller species, the little pickerel, is fairly abundant west of the Alleghenies; it measures less than a foot. The eastern pickerel is also called the chain pickerel because of the markings on its sides which resemble the links of a chain. Length of the eastern pickerel: 22 inches. *Esox niger.*

PIKE

A Way-Laying Killer — "Choicely good" is Isaac Walton's verdict on freshly roasted pike. In fact, he declares, it is "too good for any but anglers and honest men." This favorable judgment reflects the high esteem in which the pike is held in Europe. America is not quite as enthusiastic. This notorious fish is so predatory and voracious that it will devour not only great quantities of fish — every other species in the pond is marked for death by the pike — but also suitable mammals and unsuspecting water birds. It is estimated a 10 pound pike eats 2 pounds of food each day, at least during the summer. Lurking in ambush among aquatic weeds, it darts out to catch its prey or the bait of an angler. Under these conditions, only two or three pikes can inhabit a small lake without starving; the pike should be propagated only where inedible and useless fish abound; in a pond stocked with choice species of game and food fish it would be disastrous. Large specimens attain a length of 4 feet and a weight of 40 pounds, but the average catch is much smaller. The pike ranges from the Hudson and Ohio rivers northward, is common in the Great Lakes and the surrounding bodies of water, and occurs also in Alaska. It is abundant in the fresh waters of northern Europe and Asia. In Siberia and Alaska, tales of pikes in monster sizes are current among the natives. Length: 30 - 50 inches. *Esox lucius.*

SMALL-MOUTH BASS ►

A Strong and Plucky Spirit — Can a sportsman who has hooked a black bass, but has not yet seen it, know whether he has caught one of the small-mouth or one of the large-mouth variety? The experts assert that he can. If the catch is gamey and plucky, courageous and unyielding to the last, it is the former; if giving up without much of a struggle, the latter. The meat, of course, is delicious in both species, and also in the third type of black bass, the spotted bass which was identified only 25 years ago, although it had been fished for two centuries. The original range of the small-mouth bass extends, in the South, from Oklahoma to the Tennessee River Valley and, in the North, to the Quebec-Minnesota line. The territory of the large-mouth bass does not reach quite as high in the northern direction, but includes the fresh waters down to Florida and the Gulf. But today both types have been introduced to most sections of America. For that purpose they are cultivated extensively, but they cannot be relieved of their eggs by hand, as is done in the case of the whitefish; the slower method of pond culture has to be used, i.e. ideal mating and hatching conditions have to be created. The small-mouth bass loves clear, big lakes and cool streams; a specimen of 3 or 4 pounds is a good average. Length: 12 to 24 inches. *Micropterus dolomieu.*

◄ YELLOW PERCH

"A Bold-Biting Fish" (Walton) — This is the fish for beginners. It will nibble any kind of bait, can be caught by a child, looks handsome in the basket with its black and yellow coat, and is perhaps the best-tasting pan fish. It is abundant in the East and North from Nova Scotia and Quebec to Minnesota; in the states bordering the Great Lakes; and on the Atlantic slope down to North Carolina. As an introduced fish, it flourishes in western waters. Its spawning habits are spectacular: In spring the female lays her eggs near the shore in a thin pencil-like mass which when it absorbs water, unfolds into a wide undulating ribbon which may sometimes exceed 7 feet in length; it contains thousands of minute eggs, measuring about 1/13 inch in diameter, and is draped over plants, roots and stones; two weeks later the young are hatched. This is a fast and effective method of propagation, and within a given body of water the yellow perch has the tendency to dominate the scene. This was proved in certain western lakes where the perch was introduced and soon crowded out the trout and salmon, infuriating the sportsmen. In some ponds it breeds in such numbers that food becomes scarce and the adults eat their own eggs; that restores or improves the balance. The usual weight of a catch is ½ to 2 pounds, the average length, 10 inches. *Perca flavescens.*

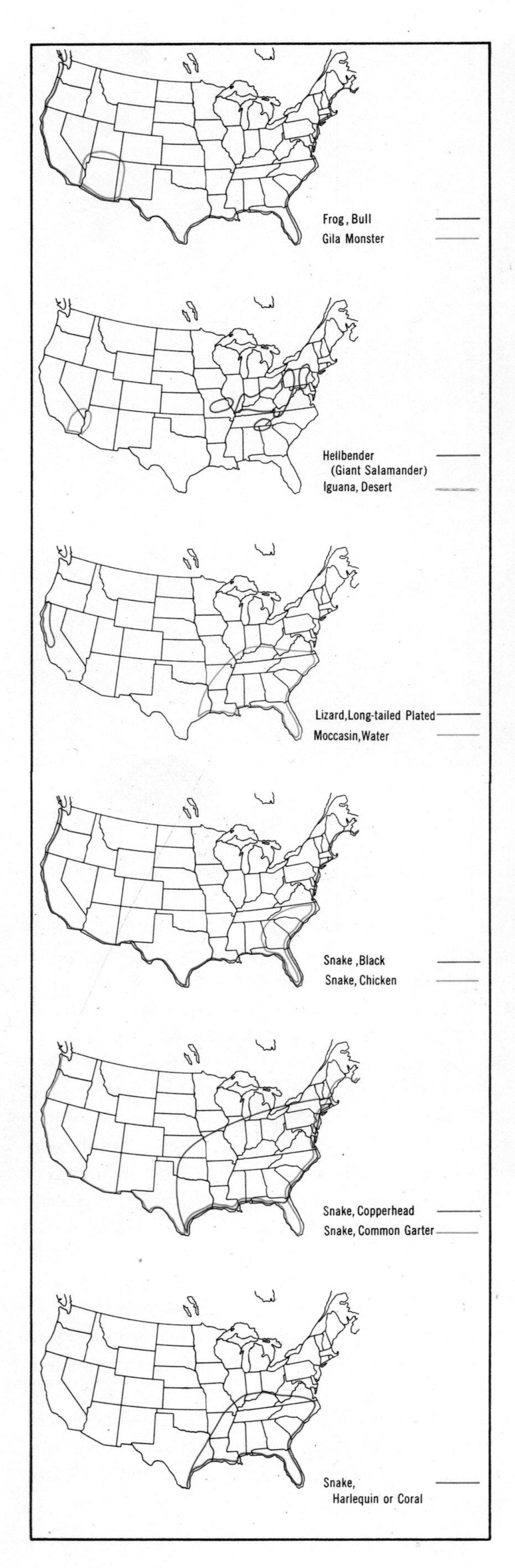

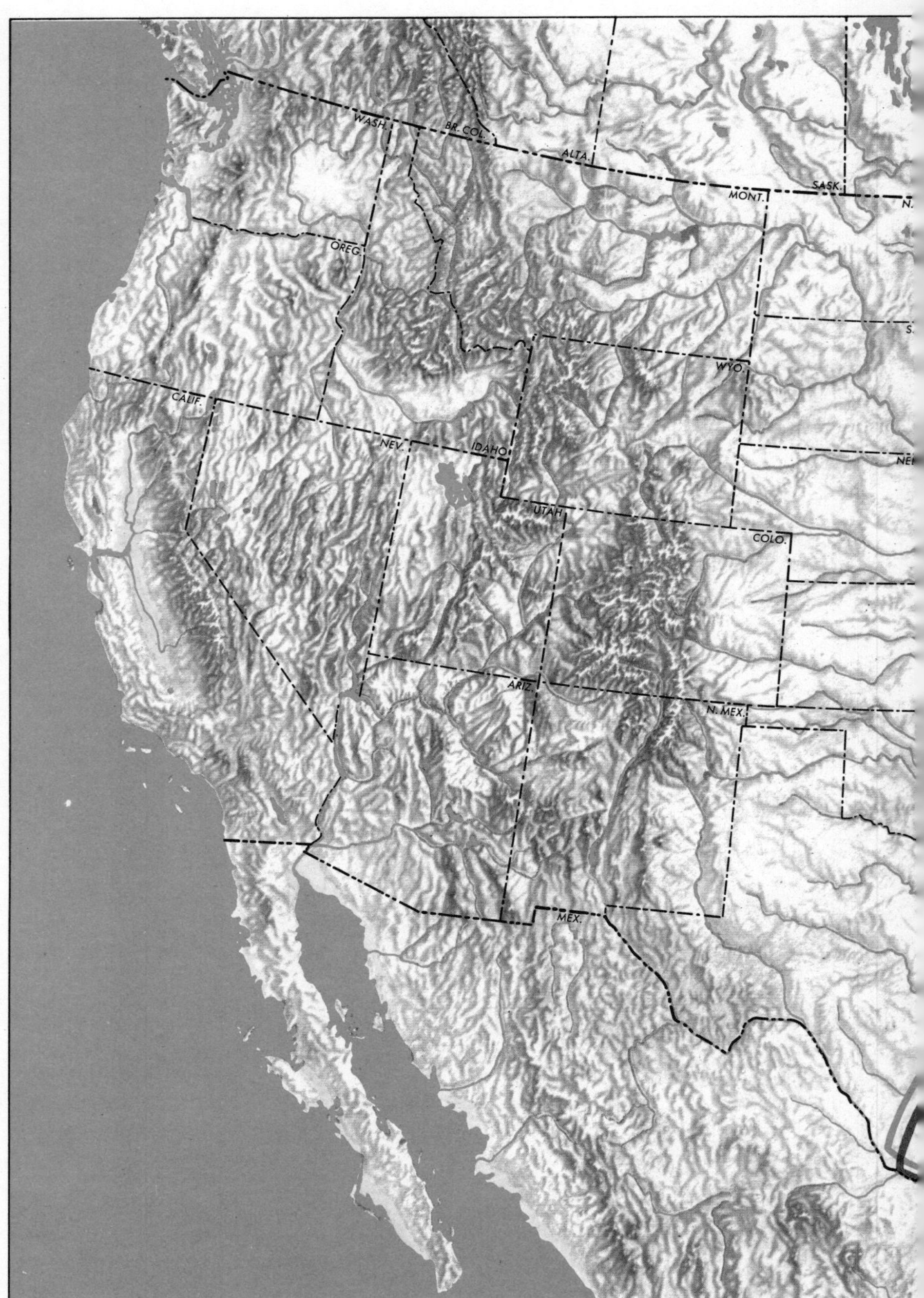

AMPHIBIANS AND REPTILES IN THE U.S. AND SOUTHERN CANADA

The day of the reptile, on this continent, dawned 200 million years ago. Dinosaurs and their kind roamed a lush, tropical land. The smallest were a few inches in length, the largest measured 80 feet. Possibly this huge bulk became their undoing; unwieldy, they fell prey to ferocious enemies. In quicksand they were trapped, and in floods they drowned. Washed into shallow waters, their carcasses were buried in mud flats, silt covered them, and the heaps of bones were impregnated with silica, becoming fossils. One place where they can be studied is the Dinosaur National Monument between Utah and Colorado.

Today Everglades National Park is a reptilian paradise, with snakes in the

Amphibians and Reptiles

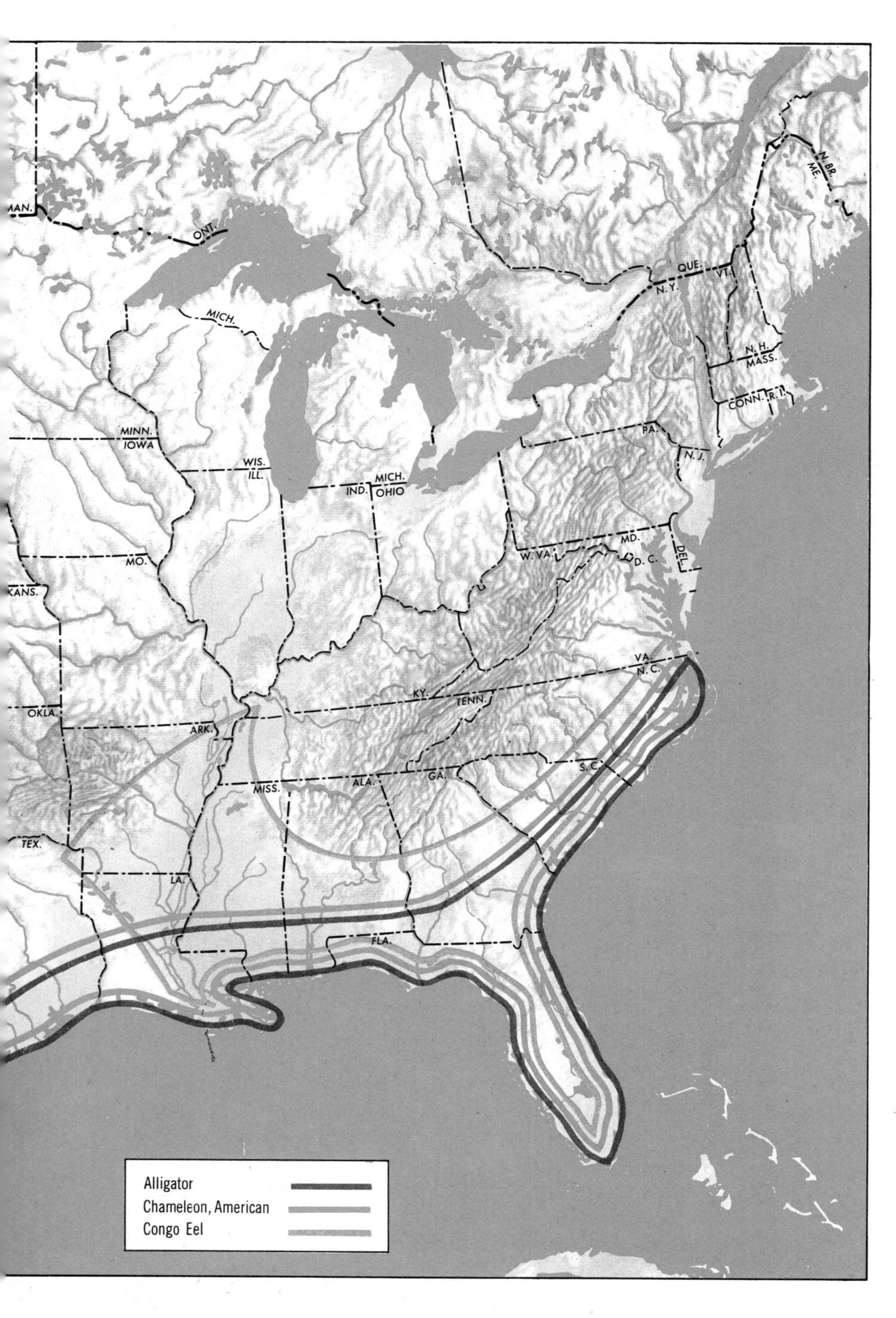

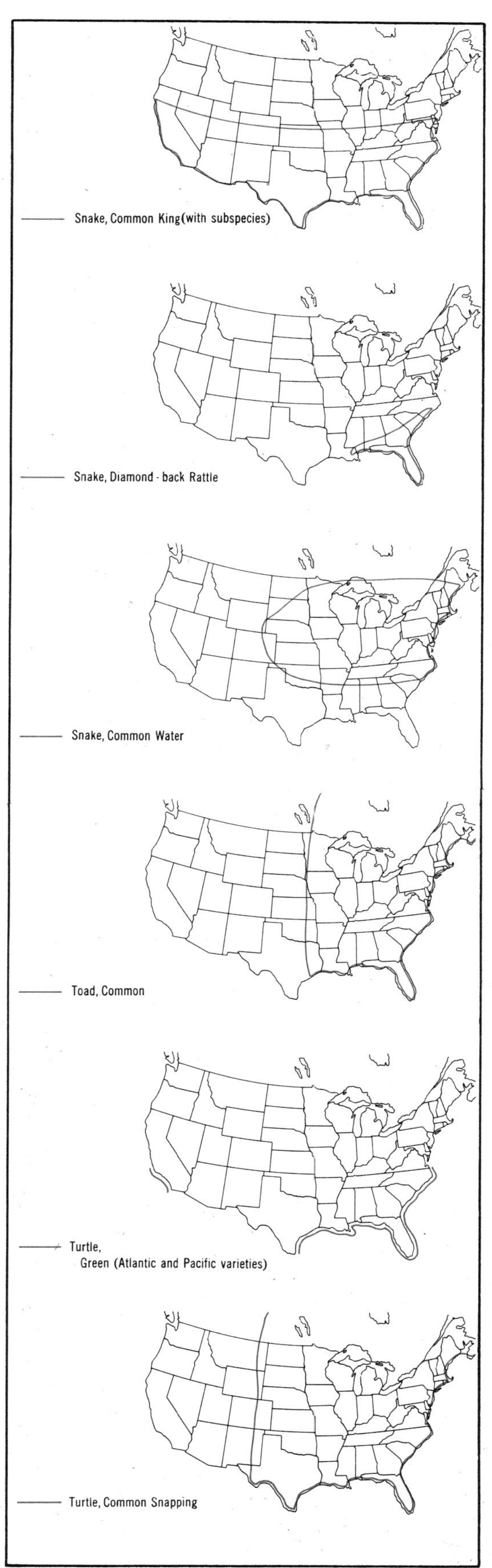

swamps and giant loggerheads on the beaches, alligators in freshwater pools and crocodiles in saltwater inlets or freshwater swamps.

The pages which follow describe and illustrate those amphibians and reptiles which are frequently encountered in the U.S. and southern Canada, or are of general interest for other reasons. The distribution of these animals is outlined, in alphabetical order, on the range maps on this page. An outline of the principal orders and families will be found on page 236.

The following notes refer to the maps. *Congo Eel* — the range includes both the 2 and 3-toed subspecies. *Frog, Bull* — originally it lived only east of the Rockies but was successfully introduced in the West. *Turtle, Green* — it occurs as far north as New Jersey and Massachusetts in the summer.

◄ HELLBENDER

A Stream-bottom Dweller — According to Webster a hellbender is, in American slang, "a reckless debauch." This unflattering comparison apparently refers to this salamander's voracious appetite. In many ways it is misleading though, for the hellbender is a rather shy character that hides by day under stones and other shelters at the bottom of streams. It is also a good father. During the mating season, in late summer, the male excavates a pan-shaped nest in the stream bottom under a rock. Here he welcomes female visitors and as the strings of eggs, that look like "rosaries," are laid, the male ejects a white, cloudy mass into the water which fertilizes them externally. One female will deposit 300 to 450 eggs, and several others may add theirs to the tangled pile at the bottom of the nest. The male does not relax his duties; he will lie among the eggs and watch the entrance of his nest. The hellbender is a large, soft-bodied creature with wrinkled folds on each side of the body, and has a compressed tail with a thin keel. The coloring varies considerably. They may have a yellowish to a very dark brown or rusty-red ground color and lighter or darker irregular spots dot the back. Adult males vary in size from 11½ to 22 inches, the larger females may attain a length of 27 inches. It is abundant in the Ohio, Tennessee, and lower Missouri River systems. *Cryptobranchus alleganiensis.*

CONGO EEL ►

Of Lakes, Bayous, and Cypress Swamps — This aquatic animal looks like an eel but is an amphibian with lungs. Diminutive limbs set it definitely apart from the true eels. Its southeastern range is probably responsible for the term Congo, a name used in the slave-holding states. There are two subspecies: The two-toed subspecies is deep brown on the head and greyish-brown on trunk and tail, slightly paler on sides and belly; it is usually found in swamps, muddy and sluggish ditches, pools and bayous from Virginia to southern Florida, also westward to Louisiana. The three-toed subspecies is lighter in color, especially on the belly; it prefers lakes and streams of running water, particularly those with lime-bearing rocks, but occurs also in bayous and wooded swamplands, from Alabama north to Missouri and west to eastern Texas. Hay was the first to describe the breeding habits of the 3-toed variety. In 1887 he came upon a large congo eel resting on a nest full of eggs, under a large log in a cypress swamp near Little Rock, Arkansas. The eggs were connected with each other by a thin cord, forming a pile of about 150. When opened, the egg produced a highly developed embryo which, when liberated, measured about 1¾ inches in length; it possessed well-developed legs and toes. Length of either subspecies: 2 to 3 feet. Two-toed, illustrated: *Amphiuma means means.*

Amphibians and Reptiles

COMMON TOAD ►

Farmer's Friend—This common inhabitant of the American East may not be pretty, with its many warts of various sizes; its roughly tubercular arms and hands, legs and feet; its dark spots and dirty olive-colored skin; and its protruding eyes. But it is a most useful collaborator of man; all night long it forages busily in garden and field, its tongue — a sort of loose flap — picking up its food: Cutworms are snapped up, chinch bugs, potato bugs — all the crawling pests are highly desirable delicacies to the toad. In our folklore the toad is always connected with witches' brews and magic spells; in reality it is an important helper in keeping the balance of nature in man's favor. Gardens and cultivated fields are its favorite haunts, but as it dislikes the rays of the sun, it spends the hours of sunshine in seclusion under a board or log, a stone or woodpile. At night it sallies forth to feast on insects. Its breeding call is a long-sustained, high-pitched trill. In the fall it retires into its hole, digging backward to make it deeper for hibernation, or may move to another locality. The breeding season, in spring, lasts from April through most of July; then the female lays her two strings of eggs, as many as 8,000; they hatch in 3 to 12 days, releasing small, almost black tadpoles. Its range extends from Hudson Bay southward throughout eastern North America. Length: 2¼ to 4¼ inches. *Bufo americanus.*

◄ BULL FROG

Basso Voice of the Summer Night — "—bottle-o'-rum, jug-o'-rum, more rum, more rum." That is supposedly the call of the bull frog on warm evenings in early summer when its resounding basso voice carries over the country side. When the croaking season opens, many males select certain perches from which their concert can be heard far and wide; they use the same place over and over again and look like so many rival kings, each with his private lily-pad or stump throne. Night hunting of bull frogs is a favorite sport of those who would eat or sell their succulent legs. This largest of all American frogs is aquatic and thrives in lakes and ponds throughout Canada and the U.S. east of the Rockies; it has also been introduced, beyond this original range, into the western states. In the North, the color of its skin may be described as greenish on the back and yellowish-white on the belly, while it is almost black above and mottled underneath in the Gulf States. Fine tubercles cover the skin. The breeding depends on the warm temperature of the air and the water, and begins in June or July in the North and much earlier in the South. The eggs are black and white and float in the form of a surface slime; the tadpoles are large, 4 to 6½ inches, including the tail. The adults average in size from 3½ to 8 inches. *Rana catesbeiana.*

◄ ALLIGATOR

Big Swamp Beast — The air is heavy with moisture; the shallow, warm waters of the remote, inaccessible swamp teem with small fish; the atmosphere is hot and steamy, and the sun, baking. Here the female builds her nest and raises her young; here the adults catch their prey: fish, smaller mammals or perhaps a water bird that swims unsuspectingly on the surface, is caught from below, and swallowed whole; here, at night, the old males bellow their reverberating calls and eject penetrating waves of a strong-smelling musk secretion into the steamy atmosphere. Unfortunately for the alligator, not many such retreats are left in its range from the Carolinas throughout the Gulf States. The old saying that a bullet will not penetrate a 'gator's hide is no longer true either, for modern rifles inflict mortal wounds in spite of the armor. So it is shot for sport and for its skin. Young alligators fall prey to big turtles and fish, and are caught and sold to curio dealers. The eggs are eaten in many southern localities, and consequently the nests are plundered. Still the big reptile survives, although the old 15-foot specimens are gone, and for this generation a length of 10 feet to 11 feet is considered large. It is hoped that this prehistoric relic that still carries the body plates and sharp ridges of its remote ancestors of millions of years ago, will survive as a part of our wildlife. *Alligator mississippiensis.*

AMERICAN CHAMELEON ►

A Temperamental Southerner — When two chameleons fight with each other, as they occasionally do, both shine in a brilliant green. That color indicates excitement or fright; they display a pale green when asleep. A rich, deep brown is another hue, especially during the hours of bright sunlight, and it is their habit to change color as promptly as the true chameleons of Africa. The transition takes about three minutes; the brown turns into a lovely golden yellow which changes to dull grey; white dots appear on the back; then a leaf-green color suffuses the body. Temperature, light, emotion, and sleep are responsible for the selection of the hue, not the color of the environment as is popularly assumed. In other ways, too, the chameleon is a most amusing little creature. The male carries a peculiar throat pouch called a dewlap; when making love or getting ready for combat he expands it at will while nodding his head emphatically. It stalks its prey like a cat; it slinks forward along the branch, quivers, then surges forward with open jaws and seizes the fly. Always, with its sharp teeth it chews its meal before swallowing it. Its gripping toe pads enable it to walk almost anywhere it wants to go, and its eyes roll independently of each other. Length: 7¼ inches. Range: From the south coast of North Carolina westward to the Rio Grande in Texas and southward throughout Florida. *Anolis carolinensis.*

Amphibians and Reptiles

DESERT IGUANA ►

A Lizard of the Sizzling Sands — On a hot, sandy desert plain, these agile reptiles dash back and forth between the scant cactus plants; extremely wary, they won't let an observer approach nearer than 30 to 40 feet. They thrive in the heat, and dislike cool temperatures. Largely herbivorous, they eat buds, alfalfa leaves, small flowers and fruits. This feeding habit is an interesting link to the huge prehistoric iguanas which were also vegetarians. When not in search of food, they live in small mammal burrows under desert shrubs. Practically nothing is known about their ways of breeding; in August they are sometimes seen in pairs and seem to occupy the same locality, which suggests that late summer is their mating season. In October they dig burrows under the surface of the soil — some just a few inches below, others to a depth of two feet — and retire to hibernate. The body of the desert iguana is stout; in proportion, the head seems small and the tapering tail (detachable when caught by an enemy), exceedingly long. Its scales are small, but on the center of the back a row of enlarged keeled scales runs from behind the head over a part of the tail; for that reason the desert iguana is also called northern crested lizard. Its range extends throughout the Colorado and Mojave Deserts and adjacent localities. Length: 16 inches. *Dipsosaurus dorsalis.*

LONG-TAILED PLATED (ALLIGATOR) LIZARD ◄

Confounding Its Enemies — Catch a lizard by its tail, and you will probably hold the wreathing appendage in your hand while the front part scampers away. The long-tailed plated lizard even goes one step farther; it seems to be able to shake off its tail by a sudden thrust, in a bloodless parting. Acting as a decoy, the cast-off tail wriggles violently, as though alive, to the confusion and delay of a pursuing enemy. In the meantime the lizard escapes, though shortened considerably, as the tail comprises about two-thirds of its body. An examination of the breaking point shows filaments of flesh protruding like the petals of a flower, while the detached tail has corresponding cavities. However, the two parts cannot be fitted together again; instead, a new but shorter tail will soon grow. All this is true of most lizards. When making the rounds, the two tips of its thick and well developed, forked tongue touch the ground lightly to pick up grubs, beetles and other insects. Occasionally a specimen is cannibalistic and eats smaller lizards of other species. After the meal, it wipes its lips vigorously with its tongue. The young of the species are born in a membranous sac, and are quite active from birth. The range of this lizard is limited to south central Washington, central Oregon, and central and coastal California. Its length averages 11¾ inches of which the tail comprises 7½ inches. *Gerrhonotus coeruleus.*

◄ GILA MONSTER

Gentle In Spite of Its Name — Ditmars describes an interesting though unusual struggle: With a sudden twist of the head and a sharp hiss the gila monster's wide-open jaws dig into the middle of a snake's body. The serpent coils and struggles furiously, but the jaws hold fast like those of a bulldog. In the meantime the lizard's poisonous saliva has begun to flow from the swollen glands, and the venom is conducted, through the lower fangs, into the wound. The snake will shortly breathe its last. This deadly weapon, however, is not used frequently; for it is not needed in foraging; while there is still considerable uncertainty as to the lizard's feeding habits, it seems to exist mostly on eggs. In captivity it becomes tame, but when placed outside in the sun, a peculiar change takes place; its flash movements come back, and the old agility reappears; back in the shade of the cage, calm returns; the same transformation is observed with many reptiles. The gila monster differs in two ways from all other American lizards: It is poisonous, and its body is not covered with scales but with bead-like tubercles. The trunk is stout as is the expandable blunt tail that may store fat for leaner days, similar to hibernating animals. The female buries her eggs — reportedly 5 to 13 in number — in moist sand exposed to direct sunlight. It occurs in desert regions in the Southwest, especially in Arizona. Length: 19 inches. *Heloderma suspectum.*

COMMON GARTER SNAKE ►

Hardy and Harmless — What is a snake den? Usually it is a slope of soft soil permeated with boulders, rocks, clefts and fissures that reach into a considerable depth. In the area surrounding such a hideout the garter snakes bask in the sun during the middle of the day and retire into the burrows and fissures when the sun's rays become paler toward evening. As early fall turns into late fall, the sunny hours grow shorter, and before the first frost arrives, the snakes stay deep in the den, beginning their hibernation. In spring, the garter snakes are among the first to reappear, and sometimes can be seen in March while there are still snowbanks in the forests and fields. Springtime is also the mating season, and as the snakes leave their winter quarters they generally copulate in the immediate vicinity of the den. When the weather becomes warm, they scatter into the woods; in August they bring forth their 20 to 50 living young. They are a hardy race and survive even within the limits of metropolitan cities. Frogs, toads and earthworms are their principal diet. There are a considerable number of species in this genus. The particular form illustrated here possesses three yellowish or greenish stripes on a darker background of green, olive, brown, or black. It occurs, with its relatives, throughout the continent from the Atlantic to the Pacific. Length: 30 inches. *Thamnophis sirtalis.*

COMMON WATER SNAKE ►

Bands and Blotches — Most people chase it or beat it to death when they find it hanging on a tree branch over a pond, calling it "a poisonous water moccasin." In fact, this reddish snake banded by dark brown stripes in front and by blotches on the posterior body, is non-poisonous, harmless and shy, and will glide into the water at the slightest disturbance. Although, if cornered and with no way to evade its pursuer, it will strike out violently in an alarming manner, it usually seeks escape rather than attack. In the Middle Atlantic States it is probably the best known water snake, quite abundant on the shores of several lakes and streams. As a method of catching it Ditmars suggests to tie a line with a small fish to a branch above the water, near a spot where snakes are known to sun themselves. One of them will probably devour the fish and most of the line and can be bagged easily. Ditmars also reports that the power of scent is well developed in the species; a pan containing a number of water snakes becomes the scene of wild confusion when a frog is rubbed across the bottom; the greedy reptiles will dart about, and in their vain search for the prey bite each other's bodies frantically. The species is vivaporous, and litters of 20 to 35 young have been counted. Its range is the entire eastern U.S. and southern Ontario. Length: 3½ feet. *Natrix sipedon.*

◄ BLACK SNAKE

A Snake-Lore Celebrity — A legend has been built around the black snake, but it is only a legend. This reptile is supposed to hypnotize birds and rodents before the deadly strike; yet it never does. It is said to be the arch enemy of the rattlesnakes; in fact, it does not pay any attention to them. It is reported to attack man and squeeze an arm or leg into unconsciousness; in reality it is not a constrictor, and slides away from human beings with the speed that has given it the name of black racer. It lives in open locations where birds have their nests in bushes and wild mice have theirs in rock walls. The black snake is fond of all, the mice, the nestlings, and the eggs. Frogs also are on its diet, and as to smaller snakes, it has cannibalistic tendencies. If cornered, it will fight courageously, and is said to strike at an observer who overtakes it on smooth ground where it cannot travel fast. During June or July the female lays up to 24 eggs which are hidden under rocks in soft, moist, warm soil; the young measure about 8 inches at birth, and have a color pattern of their own; only in their third summer do they take on the shiny black, with the white throat and chin, of their parents. The western forms have blue or bluish green dorsums. The range of the species extends all over the U.S. Length: 5 to 6 feet. *Coluber constrictor.*

◄ CHICKEN SNAKE

Hunting from Above — A rafter in a cabin, a limb of a live oak, the garret of a stable, or a beam in the chicken house are favorite hideouts of the chicken snake. What it is looking for are mice and rats, but occasionally it stages a raid downstairs and devours some young chickens. It may also make a meal of 6 or 7 eggs; they are swallowed whole but crushed farther down the throat. The chicken snake is a good climber and sometimes is seen 25 feet above the ground, on a tree branch. Certain swamps also are known as favorite hunting grounds for big specimens. It is quite fearless, and when cornered it raises its neck in a threatening S, ready for a long strike. When caught, it ejects a stinking secretion from glands on the tail, a weapon it has in common with many other serpents. The female lays approximately two dozen eggs during the early summer, and about nine weeks later the young are born, looking quite different from their parents. They have a vivid pattern of dark brown blotches on a grey background and only gradually take on the adult characteristics: a bright yellow, olive, or brown color with two dark brown or black back stripes and two side stripes. Their range extends from North Carolina to South Carolina, Georgia and peninsular Florida. Length: up to 6 feet. *Elaphe obsoleta quadrivittata.*

COMMON KING SNAKE ►

Perennial Champion — The strangest character trait of this reptile is its hostility to all other snakes. It engages serpents as large as itself, and always emerges the victor, thanks to its extraordinary strength. Contrary to legend, it does not go out of its way to search for copperheads and rattlers, but when it encounters a rattlesnake, a life and death duel is on. While the king snake coils around the enemy, the rattler will bite viciously and inject its venom into the body of its adversary. However, this otherwise deadly weapon has no effect on the king snake which soon overcomes its victim and eats it. This immunity from serpent poison has been tested and confirmed by laboratory tests. Other snakes are a favorite food of these cannibalistic reptiles, a diet supplemented by rodents and birds. The female lays up to two dozen eggs which hatch in approximately six weeks. With its subspecies the common king snake ranges throughout the U.S. south of the 40th parallel which crosses southern New Jersey. The typical form occurs from that state south to northern Florida and west to the Appalachians; it abounds along the southern coasts. Its length is about 3½ feet, north of North Carolina, while in the deep South, specimens of 6 feet are fairly frequent. The markings are reported to be white in the North, yellow in the South. *Lampropeltis getulus getulus.*

HARLEQUIN OR CORAL SNAKE ►

Masquerade of Danger — Neurotoxin does not in all cases cause such intense pain as the poison of the moccasin, rattler, or copperhead, but it works steadily, and death usually arrives within 24 hours. No antitoxin is prepared in the U.S. This is the venom of the harlequin or coral snake, so called because of its flamboyant coloration, and of the western or sonora coral snake. The dangerous twist arises from the fact that a number of harmless snakes — the scarlet and scarlet king snake in the Southeast, the western milk snake and the Arizona king snake in the Southwest — look very much like the poisonous corals. Often the harmless ones are killed, the others treated casually. Fortunately the coral snakes do not bite unless they are stepped upon or touched, and their fangs are too short to penetrate a leather shoe. Harmless and dangerous species can be quite easily distinguished: The former have a white or blotched belly, the latter have rings circling the body completely; they also have black rings bordered by yellow ones; the opposite pattern is true for the non-poisonous serpents. The length of the harlequin snake is approximately 28 inches, while the western species is shorter, about 15 inches. The range extends from North Carolina to Florida, Texas, and Mexico, also up the Mississippi Valley to southern Ohio. The western variety occurs in southern New Mexico and Arizona. *Micrurus fulvius.*

◄ WATER MOCCASIN

The "Cotton Mouth" of the South — When surprised, this snake draws back its head, opens its jaws wide, and the observer looks into an all-white mouth. From that sight the widely used term "cotton mouth" has originated. While greeting you with open jaws, the serpent beats its tail vigorously in a steady rhythm. Thriving in southern swamps, the water moccasin feeds on frogs, fish, birds, small mammals and snakes. In captivity, it has been observed to kill small animals by a single bite, the fangs remaining in the wound. But the sight of a large rat or rabbit excites the snake greatly; it strikes again and again, viciously and nervously. This moccasin looks as evil as he is. His thickset body, pudgy head and hostile eye portend no good for other snakes. Cases of hostility toward larger serpents have been reported. Ditmars relates how one morning he found a huge South American anaconda prostrate and dead on the floor of its cage, its 12 foot body bitten in a dozen places and contorted in the agony of the death struggle. The victor, a moccasin less than 4 feet long which had crawled in through the ventilator opening, quietly surveyed the scene. The cotton mouth brings forth living young, perhaps 8 or 12. It ranges from southern Virginia to eastern Texas including all of Florida, and up to the Mississippi Valley to the Ohio River. Length: 4 feet. *Agkistrodon piscivorus.*

◄ COPPERHEAD SNAKE

Serpent of Rocky Ledges — If you pin a copperhead to the ground with a forked stick, it will struggle furiously; while thrashing its body to the left and to the right it may even lash its tail into its own mouth and bite it. Nothing happens, though, as the copperhead is immune to snake poison. This is a serpent of high, dry and rocky places, and often chooses abandoned stone quarries as shelters for hibernation. It also likes the neighborhood of forests where it finds plenty of food: rodents and birds, frogs and snakes. In case of danger it tries to slide away; if that is not possible it defends itself courageously, coiling its body into a sequence of loops, vibrating its tail so that a rustling noise is made in dead grass or leaves, and striking rapidly. Females bear living young, a relatively small number of perhaps 6 to 9. They have bright yellow tails which, when wiggled by the little serpent, have great resemblance to yellow maggots. Therefore, it is supposed that the tail serves as a lure to attract small frogs which fall easy prey to the ever alert snake. The yellow fades during the second year. The range of the copperhead extends from Massachusetts to Illinois, and southward to Oklahoma, Texas and Florida. Because of this wide distribution, most venemous snake bites in the U.S. are inflicted by copperheads, but only a small number are fatal. Length: 2½ to 3 feet. *Agkistrodon contortrix.*

DIAMOND-BACK RATTLESNAKE ►

"—a bugbeare tale of horrible serpents—" (Morton, 1637) — There is a certain tense grandeur about America's most outstanding poisonous serpent. As a deep breath inflates the body, the rattle vibrates like an electric buzzer; its enormous fangs and big venom glands are ever ready, its 6 or even 8 feet of strong body are in perfect control. It does not get frightened, and it does not flee, nor even retreat. Calmly it watches, aims and strikes. It resents captivity; many specimens refuse to eat when deprived of their freedom, and starve to death. Character and courage are united here. The swampy lowlands of the Southeast are the habitat of this rattler, and cottontail rabbits seem to be its favorite food; its diet also includes other rodents, but apparently not birds. Ditmars describes how the diamond-back rattler devours a rabbit which has succumbed to the poison in less than a minute: The snake glides around its prey and tests it with its tongue; the head is examined most thoroughly, perhaps with a dozen touches of the tongue-tip. Finally the jaws are opened wide, the rabbit's nose is seized, and the swallowing begins. The female bears from 6 to 12 living young, in the coastal lowlands from North Carolina to the Mississippi River, including all of Florida. Length: 6 feet. *Crotalus adamanteus.*

GREEN TURTLE ►

Graceful and Clumsy — Turtle soup is the final destiny of the many live, green turtles that are offered for sale in our markets. The animals are all turned on their backs; for, unsupported by their life element, water, the soft plastron lets the weight of the body press on the internal organs, particularly on the lungs, and the turtles suffocate. The female does go ashore to lay her eggs, but in the process of digging a nest with her flippers, her weight rests mostly on the edge of the carapace. It has also been reported that in Hawaii green turtles like to sleep on remote, rocky ledges, in a normal position. The solution of the apparent contradiction may be this: While enough oxygen can be obtained by a calmly slumbering turtle, the amount is insufficient for one in panic and struggling for its life. The size of the specimens that are usually captured varies from 70 to 150 pounds, but a few weighing up to 500 pounds have been recorded. They feed on marine grasses and algae, and the delicate taste of their flesh is highly appreciated. Their fat has a greenish color, which accounts for the turtle's name. Their shells have a handsome pattern but are too thin to be of commercial value. This graceful swimmer occurs in American waters from the bays of North Carolina southward to the Gulf of Mexico, and the Pacific variety ranges along the coast of southern California. *Chelonia mydas.*

◄ COMMON SNAPPING TURTLE

Disaster Below — A duck on the pond suddenly vanishes as if by magic. The water is ruffled for a while, then duck feathers rise to the surface. What has happened? A snapping turtle, half-embedded in the mud at the bottom, has seized the legs of the unsuspecting water fowl, has dragged it down to drown it, has torn it to pieces and devoured it. A passing fish will experience the same fate. For this lazy kind of hunting, the snapping turtle is excellently armed. Its sinister, powerful head with small but keen eyes attacks like a snake, striking so rapidly that the eye can hardly follow the lurching head. Its sharp-edged, cutting mandibles terminate in strong hooks, so that a medium-sized turtle can easily snap off a human finger, a big one a human hand. Entirely carnivorous, snapping turtles always feed under water. They do not seem to be able to swallow their food otherwise. Some specimens get so stuffed with fat that their flesh hangs out on each side of the shell and they cannot move on land; they provide the best turtle steaks. The female leaves the pond or stream in early summer and digs a hole on dry land; there she lays her eggs and carefully covers them with sand. They are hard-shelled, white, and usually round. The range of the common snapping turtle extends all over the U.S. and southern Canada east of the Rockies. Its total length, with head and tail outstretched, is about 28 inches. *Chelydra serpentina.*

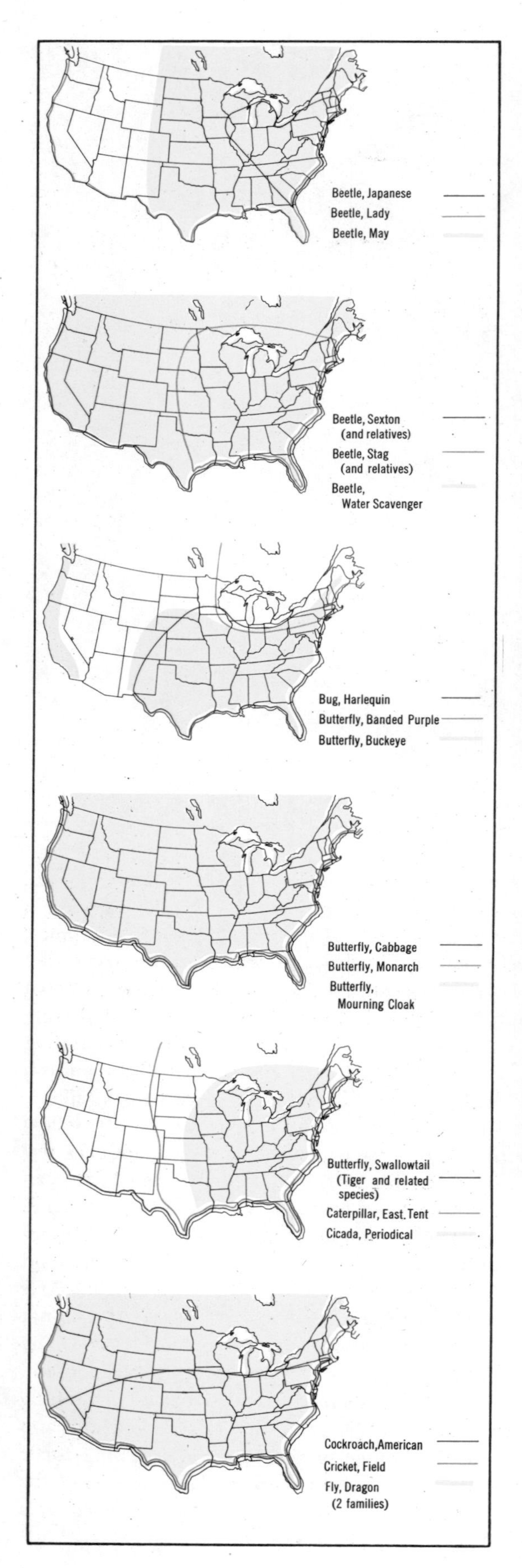

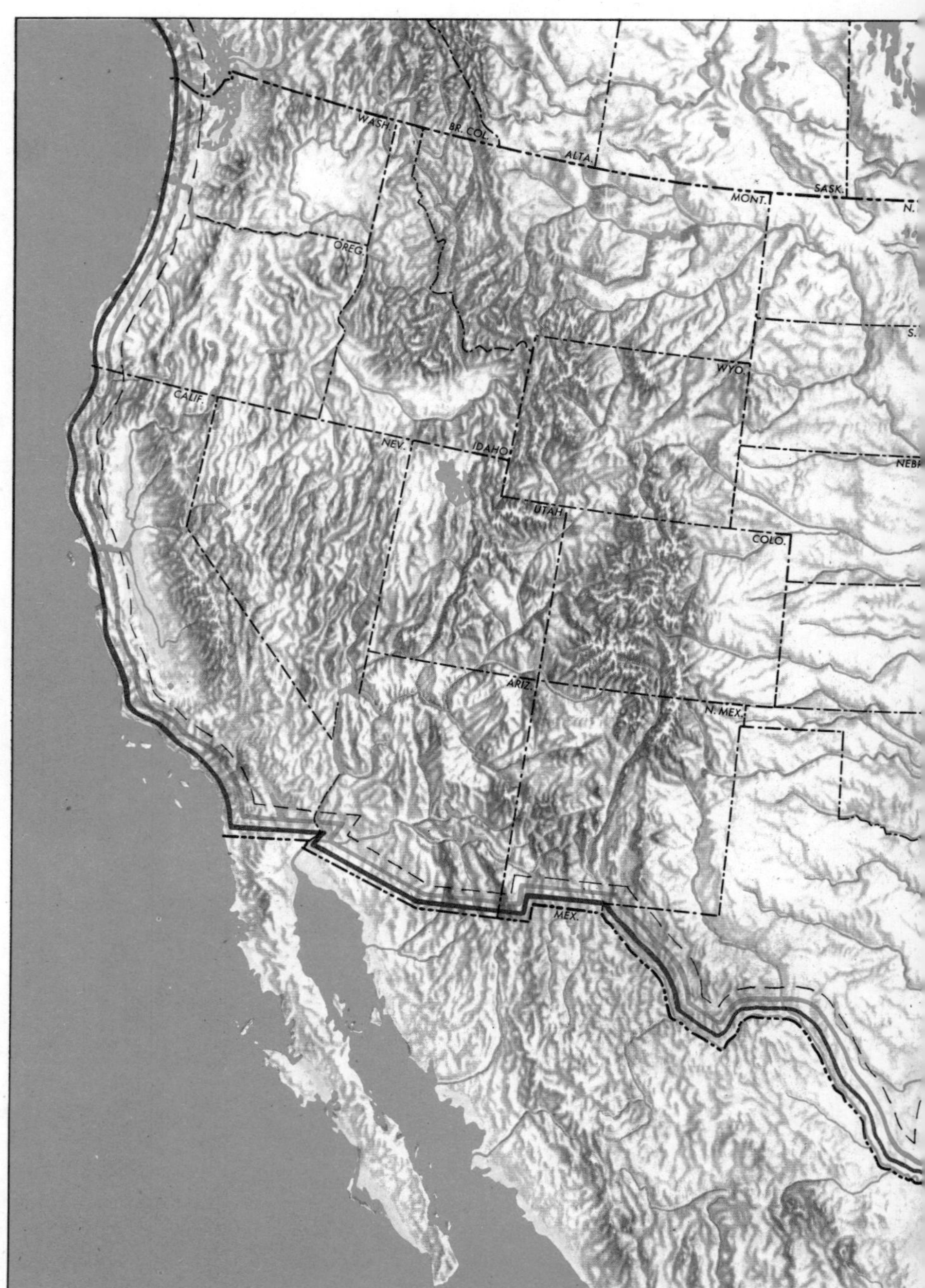

INSECTS IN THE U.S. AND SOUTHERN CANADA

Insects, the creatures with a kind of skeleton outside of their bodies, are by far the most numerous animals. Up to the present, more than 600,000 species have been identified; yet these represent only a part of all insects, and a tremendous task of classification still lies ahead of our entomologists. The layman will have to be content with a general knowledge of the important orders and families.

While insects destroy approximately 10% of our crops, they help maintain our fish and bird population and our rich plant life.

The following pages describe and illustrate those insects which are most frequently encountered in the U.S. and southern Canada, or are of general interest for other reasons. The distribution of these animals is outlined in alpha-

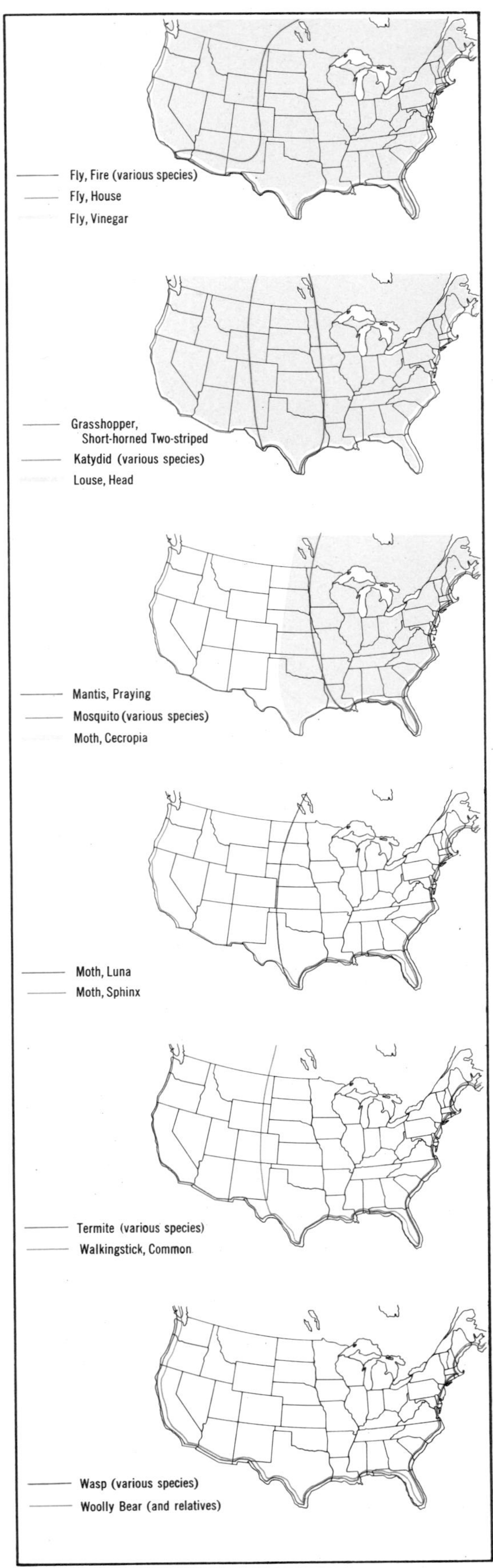

betical order on the range maps on this page; the maps, however, are only suggestive as our knowledge of the geographical distribution of insects is limited. A key to the principal orders and families will be found on page 238.

The following notes refer to the maps. *Bee, Honey* — does not occur in extreme North of Canada. *Beetle, May* — abundant in Northeast, fairly frequent in East, less frequent in West, apparently absent from Northwest. *Butterfly, Buckeye* — also found occasionally between two ranges and in northern regions. *Caterpillar, Eastern Tent* — common in East; the fall webworm occurs throughout the U.S. and southern Canada. *Cicada, Periodical* — the northern broods have a 17-year cycle, the southern a 13-year cycle. *Cockroach, American* — abundant in South; in North in heated buildings.

◄ DRAGONFLY

A Voracious Beauty — Could you imagine a creature so greedy that it would eat its own tail? The dragonfly is said to do just that, and will devour its abdomen for good measure if its tail is bent around to meet its mouth. It is a voracious eater and killer, consuming huge quantities of mosquitoes and other pests; it has been observed to swallow 40 houseflies in two hours. It is also a superb flyer. Although its four wings look as fragile as the finest gauze, they are able to whirr for hours, sometimes at a fantastic speed. It catches its prey and devours it while on the wing; it does its mating and most of its egg-laying in flight also. For this life in the air it is excellently equipped; its two eyes cover more than two-thirds of its head, and each eye consists of over 30,000 lenses directed up and down, forward and sidewise; for additional vision the head rotates through 180°. It rests with wings outstretched while its relative, the smaller damselfly, reposes with wings folded. Both lay their eggs in water or on water plants; from the egg an ugly nymph develops with a huge, mask-like underlip. After several stages of growth it leaves the water, the skin cracks, and the adult emerges. There are two families of dragonflies: the Aeschnidae are "the devil's darning needles"; of the more common Libellulidae the ten-spot dragonfly is illustrated here. *Libellula pulchella.*

AMERICAN COCKROACH ►

Hiding in the Moist and the Dark — The kitchen light turns on, and speedily these brown scavengers flit to their crannies. They feed on any garbage or victuals they can obtain, and destroy much larger quantities of stored food by tainting it with their fetid odor or dead bodies. They damage rugs and clothes and even books. This same insect, filthy in our eyes, probably spends more time cleaning itself than a kitten does. Its legs possess spines that are used as combs, stroking every part of the body over and over again to remove the dirt, and the leg combs are cleaned in the mouth. The antennae are also scrubbed there. Most species produce their eggs in capsules which protrude from the body of the female and are carried around for a few days until a suitable dank cavity is found or carved out; there the egg case is glued to the wall with a secretion, and often covered with a fragment of debris. The number of species of cockroaches is large, particularly in the Tropics. The American cockroach also prefers warmth and is much more frequent in the southern states; but it also occurs in buildings far to the north, particularly in heated houses. This roach was thought to be a native of America, but the researches of J. A. G. Rehn indicate that the insect originated in West Africa and was brought here by slave vessels and other ships. Length: 1½ inches. *Periplaneta americana.*

PRAYING MANTIS ►

A Hungry Hunter — The word "praying" in the insect's English name, and the term "religiosa" in its Latin label, seem amusing for an insect that is a cannibal. Its spiny forefeet, held in a prayerful attitude, are used to capture any passing insect; in captivity, that may be another praying mantis which will be promptly devoured. After mating, the female is apt to eat the male, and when the young arrive, they have similar cannibalistic tendencies at an early age. The structure of these insects is strange; they are, as Lutz remarks, the only ones that are able to look over their shoulders. Their green or brownish coloration is an excellent camouflage in the foliage or on the bark of a tree trunk. As they feed on nothing but insects, including a great many grasshoppers, and as they have a ravenous appetite, they are considered beneficial. Some species are native to North America, among them the Carolina mantis, but better-known are two introduced species, the Chinese and the European mantis. The latter first appeared in New York state around 1900 and has now spread over most of the eastern parts of the U.S. and Canada. It proved valuable in control of insect pests and has since been imported and colonized. The female lays a few hundred eggs in the form of a frothy, brownish substance that dries into a papery mass. The European species is the most common. Length: 3½ inches. *Mantis religiosa.*

◄ COMMON WALKINGSTICK

The Ultimate in Camouflage — "A twig with legs" is the best definition for this insect in our regions. In the Tropics it may be a branch with legs, showing even the flaky scales of the bark, or an almost perfect green leaf with legs. These creatures move slowly and in an ambitionless, stealthy way; they are harmless leaf eaters, preferring oak and walnut trees; but they do not cause great damage. Their mimicry is their only protection, and they like to assume a motionless "arboreal" position with antennae and legs in line with their bodies. Nevertheless, some 16 species of birds and a few lizards and rodents discover and eat them, and they are never safe from being devoured by their cousin, the praying mantis. The female drops her approximately 100 eggs to the ground like kernels of seeds, one at a time; when they hit the ground, the effect is that of a patter of rain drops. The eggs remain among the fallen leaves throughout the winter, and the young, which hatch in spring, resemble the adults. After 5 or 6 molts they attain their mature size of approximately 3 inches. If they lose a leg in the process of growing up, a new one, or at least part of one, will appear in a later molt. The most familiar species, the grey, green, or sometimes yellowish common walkingstick, ranges throughout the U.S. and Canada east of the Rocky Mountains. Length: 3¼ inches. *Diapheromera femorata.*

◄ SHORT-HORNED GRASSHOPPERS

The Fiddlers — Small, hard pegs project on the inside of the femur of the hind legs; they are rubbed over the thick veins on the first pair of wings, up and down, up and down, and with this complex instrument the grasshopper produces its well-known music. However, only the males are equipped with a "fiddle"; the females are silent. Both sexes possess big organs for hearing. This large, notorious family includes the non-migratory grasshoppers, most of which live and die in the field where they were born, and migratory species, which are commonly called locusts. All are destructive insects and, while normally some varieties are grass feeders and others foliage feeders, a migrating horde will devour and destroy anything green in its path. The Rocky Mountain locusts used to be a major plague of the old West and, to this day, many of our largest cooperative insect control projects are aimed at the grasshoppers, particularly in the western states. The female drills a hole into the soil (or into rotten wood in one species), with her abdomen, and lays a batch of 20 to 100 eggs. They are cemented together and, with the surrounding soil which adheres to them, form an egg pod. This act takes place in the fall, and normally the eggs do not hatch until the following spring. A familiar species in the central plains of the continent is the two-striped grasshopper. Length: 1¾ inches. *Melanoplus bivittatus.*

LONG-HORNED GRASSHOPPERS ►

The Plague — America's most famous story of the cricket plague refers to the year 1848 when swarms of long-horned grasshoppers descended upon the fields of the religious refugees in Utah and threatened them with starvation and destruction of their new foothold in the West. At the critical moment, droves of sea gulls arrived, devoured the pest, and saved the new settlement. The birds were honored with a monument, and the insects received a name: Mormon crickets. Their enormous bands are still a plague in the western states. In the eastern sections the green katydids are familiar members of the same group; they fill the summer nights with their persistent call which supposedly pronounces their name. They live and feed either in trees — oaks, maples and fruit trees are favorites — or in the grass, and as their wing covers look like leaves, they are not easily detected. Some species are partly insect eaters with cannibalistic tendencies. Their song is produced by rubbing together the projecting veins which grow at the base of the males' outer wings. Their ears are located on their front legs. Their antennae are almost as long as their bodies; in some species they are longer. With their saber-shaped ovipositors katydids lay their eggs on or inserted into leaf edges; Mormon crickets lay theirs in the soil. A common long-horned grasshopper is the angular-winged katydid. Length: 1⅛ inches. *Microcentrum laurifolium.*

COMMON FIELD CRICKET

Destructive Neighbor — Seedlings cut at the ground; cereal plants stripped of the grain; cavities eaten into peas and tomatoes, strawberries and other garden fruits — these are the misdeeds of the common field cricket which occurs throughout the U.S. and southern Canada; its labors become particularly damaging during the occasional increases in the cricket population, when it destroys fields, crawls into houses, and even eats textiles. Normally, crickets are vegetarians, but sometimes they feed on insects, including each other. Having an aversion to light, they are nocturnal, and by vibrating their forewings together, the males produce their high-pitched, shrill night music. Their ears are located on the forelegs. Females lay eggs in the ground using a sword-shaped ovipositor; the following spring the young emerge, looking like their parents; they acquire their wings in several stages. Tree crickets dwell in the foliage of small trees and bushes; in contrast to the brown and black field crickets, they are pale green; they inject their rows of eggs into plant stems or twigs. The mole crickets are subterranean diggers, and the wingless camel crickets make their homes in decaying logs and stumps, or beneath loose bark. Finally there are a few tiny species, less than ¼ inch long, which seem to obtain their food by cleaning certain ants and the sides of their tunnels, playing the role of chambermaids. Length: ⅞ inch. *Acheta assimilis.*

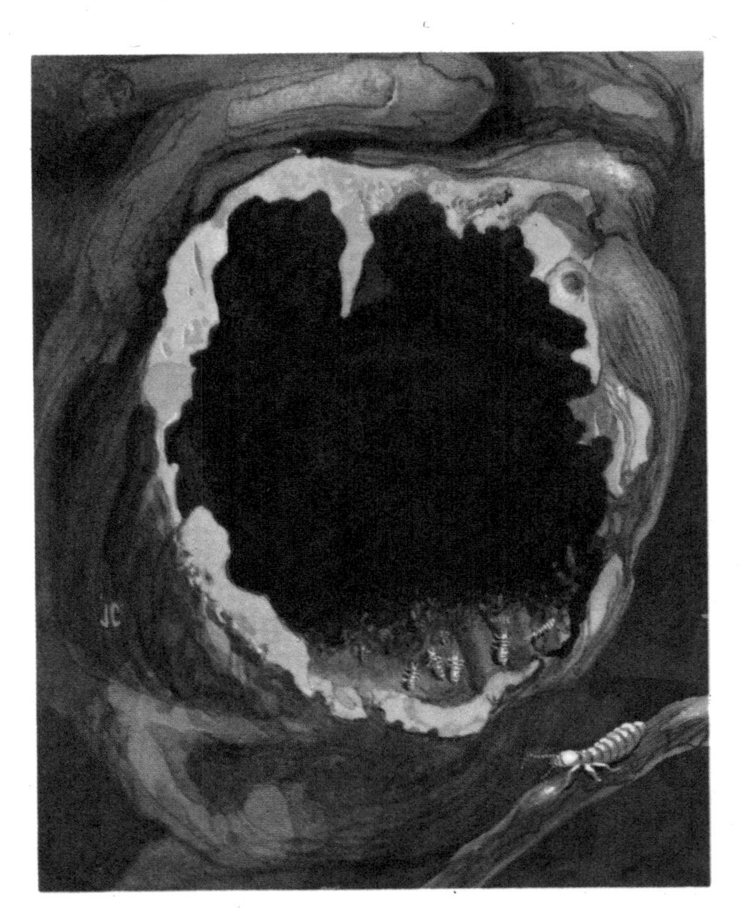

COMMON TERMITE

Insects with a Caste System — A highly developed, drab efficiency rules the society of termites. In spring, winged males and females emerge from the colonies of a certain district, almost at the same hour. In a mating flight, they pair off, then descend, and the couple is ready to start their nest; as their wings would detract from the big task ahead, they lose them. Now, being king and queen, they produce their own nation. All eggs are fertilized, and the queen becomes an enormous, large-scale egg producer, unable to move; in some species she lays about 4,000 eggs in 24 hours. Most of her offspring are workers, a pale, soft breed without eyes or sex, either of which would interfere with their labors of building the tunnels, feeding the queen, and caring for the progeny. The third caste are soldiers with enormous heads and powerful mandibles, the defenders of the colony. The fourth caste is the reproductive reserve, consisting of termites with eyes and wing buds. If the king or queen dies, they take over their functions. The nest is usually in the ground, connected, by tunnels, with dead wood in trees or buildings. In order to derive any nourishment from the wood they eat, termites carry, in their alimentary tracts, one-celled protozoa which are able to digest the wood cells and are in turn digested by the termites. The damage caused by various species throughout the continent amounts to millions. Common eastern species: *Reticulitermes flavipes.*

◄ WATER SCAVENGER BEETLE

The Pond Patrol — How do these air-breathing beetles, which live in the water most of the time, obtain their oxygen supply? They take their air along, under the fore wings and on the lower surface of the body. If the air becomes stale and a fresh supply is needed, they swim near the surface of the water, hold the side of the body at an angle and, through a notch between the head and the thorax, take in the oxygen. The antennae, which look like small clubs, have a definite function in the process: They break the film of the water's surface. These beetles, in swimming, use their hind legs like oars, striking the water alternately. As scavengers, they eat decaying animal and vegetable matter, but occasionally prey on other insects. The female carries her eggs under her abdomen in a silken case. The latter is attached to a water plant or a floating leaf, or simply set adrift. The long, spindle-shaped larvae feed on insects and other minute aquatic animals, and may even prey on small fishes. The pupa is developed ashore. Water scavengers range widely throughout southern Canada and the U.S., preferring small ponds and grassland pools. In China certain species are considered a desirable food, and one member of the family is used in biological insect pest control, in the sugar cane fields of Hawaii and the banana plantations of Jamaica, to fight certain boring larvae. Length: 1⅜ inches. *Hydrophylus triangularis.*

SEXTON BEETLE ►

The Undertaker — Nature is teeming with small animals, yet hardly ever do we encounter their dead bodies. This mystery can be explained largely by the nocturnal work of a beautiful black beetle with vermillion markings; it plays the part of a gravedigger. When a small beast dies, its odor attracts a male sexton beetle; soon a female companion arrives. As a foresighted undertaker the male selects a burying plot of loose ground, which may be right under the carcass or several feet away. In the latter case the digger performs a herculean task: Although the dead body may have many times the beetle's weight, the worker pushes it toward its grave, frequently lying on its back and shoving away with six, strong, black legs. The female helps by busily clearing the way and chewing through impeding rootlets. On the proper spot, the hole is dug below the corpse, which gradually sinks into its grave. Now the female lays her eggs in the burying ground under the carcass, but the couple's task is not yet fulfilled. While many insects are not at all concerned with their young, the sexton beetles patiently wait for the hatching while living on the carrion, and when the yellow grubs come to life, they tend them carefully and feed them partially predigested meat until they are ready to change to adults. These beetles, whose length is approximately ¾ of an inch, belong to the family Silphidae. *Necrophorus marginatus.*

STAG BEETLE ►

Knight in Armor — Stags and stag beetles have one feature in common: They both have antlers — at least the huge mandibles of the beetle look like antlers — and they use them to fight over their mates which, in either case, are weaker and smaller. There are photographs of such insect battles which show their life-and-death seriousness. On summer nights such encounters may be observed where there are electric lights, sometimes even on a sidewalk. Their hard forewings cover the abdomen and protect it like an armor. By rubbing their legs, or outer wings, they produce a certain noise. In spite of their formidable appearance and chivalresque duels, the stag beetles are harmless from the human viewpoint. Their feeding habits are not very well known, but honeydew, plant secretions and wood seem to be their principal nourishment. The whitish larvae are similar to those of the June beetle, and live in decaying wood, in rotten trunks or in dead limbs. The kind of timber they infest has no economic importance. The stag beetle, also called pinch bug in many sections of the country, belongs to the family Lucanidae which thrives mainly in the Tropics and includes the largest known beetles, some measuring more than 4 inches in length. Only a few species are found in the temperate zone of North America. They are a familiar sight in the eastern half of the U.S. Length: 1⅝ inches. *Pseudolucanus capreolus.*

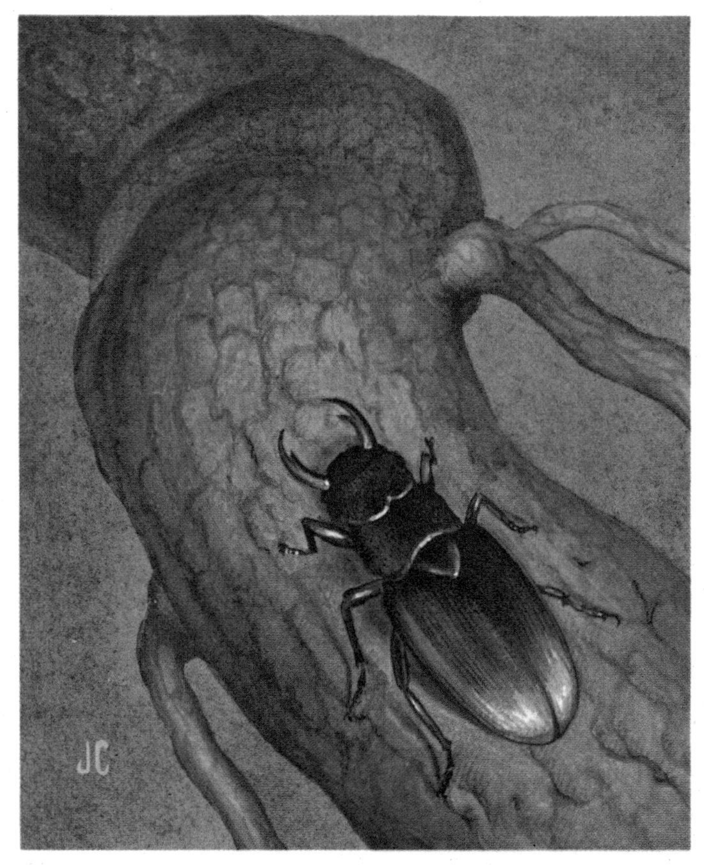

◄ JAPANESE BEETLE

The Invader — In Riverton, New Jersey, less than a dozen brown beetles with a metallic green sheen were discovered in 1916 and identified as a Japanese insect that had been accidentally introduced from the Orient. Soon there were thousands of them, and in a few years there were millions. Ever since they have been at work: Their larvae — white grubs — feed on the roots of grasses and other plants, injure lawns and are the curse of golf courses. The adults are even a worse plague, descending upon our rose bushes, feeding on flowers, devouring fruits, eating foliage, and damaging trees and shrubs. Besides, they are hardy, and the larvae dig deep underground when winter comes. Therefore a battle has been raging between our entomologists and the undesirable aliens for more than 30 years, and so far victory cannot be predicted with safety for either side. The Japanese beetles are still mainly restricted to the Northeastern and Middle Atlantic states, but word of sporadic infiltrations has come from such faraway states as Florida in the south and Iowa in the west. It seems they have broken through the quarantine. On the other hand the beetles have their troubles, too. Certain parasitic insects — their natural enemies — have been imported from Japan. The grubs contract a milky disease. Factors of this type may still check the pest, particularly as the biological controls are supplemented by numerous insecticides. Length: ½ inch. *Popillia japonica.*

◄ FIREFLY

A Lantern Bright and Cold — In our electric lamps only a fraction of the energy consumed is converted into light. The rest is wasted as heat. A much more efficient method is employed by the fireflies, which are not flies at all but soft-bodied beetles; their bodies glow with a greenish-white, heatless light. The glow area consists of a fatty tissue permeated with many air tubes and nerves; the nerves stimulate the tubes to produce oxygen for the fatty tissue; the latter contains several substances which combine with the oxygen and create light. Collected in a glass jar, these insects form a very usable though eerily shifting lantern. Scientific experiments have not yet fully succeeded in explaining the process. Light signals are the firefly's mating call, a unique phenomenon as hardly any other insect attracts a mate by vision. The glow worm is the wingless female of the common firefly, and in some cases also the larvae and even the eggs glow at night. The adults of many species do not eat, or take very little food while the larvae thrive on slugs, snails, and similar prey. Of the approximately 50 American species most are encountered east of the Rockies in the U.S. and Canada; in the Central States the "lightning bug," an insect of ⅜ to ½-inch in length, is well known. In the Tropics groups of thousands of large fireflies often flash in unison — a breathtaking spectacle. The illustrated species is *Photinus scintillans.*

MAY BEETLE ►

Under the Roots, Above the Trees — The ancient Egyptians adored their sacred scarab beetles because these insects seemed to emerge from the earth, generated spontaneously. The same could be imagined of the May beetle or June bug, a relative of the scarab, which also appears out of the ground, as a full-fledged adult, during the spring months indicated in its two names. The secret is, of course, simple: This beetle spends the 2 or 3 years of its youth underground. The white eggs are laid by the female in a soil-covered ball which is deposited among the roots of plants. After hatching, the white larvae — called grubs — live on these roots for a few years, pupate underground in the autumn, and the following May the beetles emerge. The grubs do a good deal of damage to grass roots and are particularly injurious to field crops in newly plowed sodland. On the other hand, the presence of the fat grubs is known to birds and certain animals which root for them; pigs, for instance, are fond of them. While the grubs often feed among the roots of coniferous trees, the adults take to deciduous trees and eat the foliage of oaks, elms and others. They are active at night, and electric lights attract them in swarms. They are encountered over a wide area, but are especially frequent in the northeastern parts of the U.S. and the neighboring provinces of Canada. Length: ⅞ inch. *Phyllophaga fusca.*

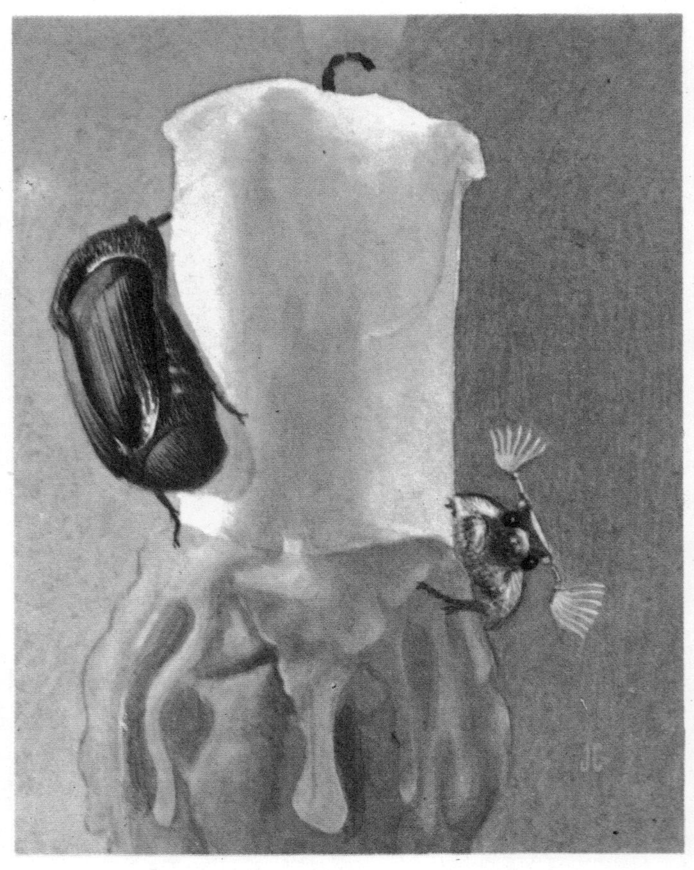

Insects

LADYBIRD ►

Fly Away Home! Your House is on Fire! Your Children do Roam — The hop vines are covered with aphids, and thousands of lady beetles and their larvae are feeding on them. At harvesting time it is the custom, in England, to burn the vines and as the flames spread, the beetles fly away and their larvae crawl to safety as fast as they can move. It was on such an occasion that the old nursery rhyme originated. The name of that insect — ladybird, lady beetle, or lady bug — has an even more ancient source: In the Middle Ages it was dedicated to the Virgin Mary. They enchant our children and help to keep our plants free from aphids and mealy bugs, scale insects and similar pests. Nowhere in America are the lady bugs more highly honored than in California where they once saved the citrus groves. The destructive, cottony, cushion scale from Australia was spreading through orange groves and threatening them with destruction when 500 lady beetles were imported from Australia; within a few years they and their offspring brought the plague under control. The female lays her spindle-shaped eggs, in clusters or singly, on plants which are infested with aphids and scale insects, and when the larvae are hatched they find an abundant food supply ready for them. Lady beetles occur throughout the U.S. and Canada. The illustrated variety is the convergent ladybird. Length: 1/4 inch. *Hippodamia convergens.*

◄ HEAD LOUSE

It Thrives in Filth and War — Today, few Americans are personally acquainted with this insect, or with its slightly different brother, the body louse. But before sanitation reached its present level, lice were an annoying plague, particularly in the old-time mining and lumber camps. They seem also unavoidable during war. These small insects have crab-like claws so they can cling to the hair of their host, and possess an elaborate piercing apparatus with which they stab into the flesh. The blood begins to flow and is sucked up; it is the louse's only food. The mouth parts, when not in use, are withdrawn into the head. The female glues her eggs, also called nits, to the hair of the host or, in the case of the body louse, to the seams of the clothes the host is wearing. The life cycle of the nymphs is completed on the human head and, as eggs are laid regardless of the season, 6 to 12 generations may grow up within one year. This parasite is the carrier of trench fever, European relapsing fever and typhus. Other species thrive on other mammals, but can exist only on one kind of host; horses, hogs, cattle, sheep and dogs are often infested with lice, also numerous wild animals from bats to lions. All of these parasites are "sucking lice," while another order, the "biting lice," live on birds and eat fragments of feathers, hair and skin. Length: 1/10 to 1/5 inch. *Pediculus humanus humanus.*

◄ HARLEQUIN STINKBUG

Barrel Maker, Cabbage Feeder — Squat little miniature barrels, beautifully decorated in various hues and provided with hinged tops, are glued to each other and cemented to a leaf. These grotesque kegs are the eggs of the harlequin stinkbug which itself is ornamented in striking colors. This insect, with slim legs and a smooth body, is a pretty but undesirable immigrant from the American tropics; from the Central American countries it spread northward to Mexico and was first seen in Texas in 1864. Since then it has invaded many parts of the U.S. and has been reported as high north as South Dakota and Massachusetts. It is a plant feeder and, especially in the southern states, devours enough cabbage, mustard and other cultivated vegetables to be considered a pest. It belongs to the family Pentatomidae, the so-called stinkbugs whose thorax glands emit a strong, disagreeable odor. That does not, however, afford them great protection as the birds do not mind the smell and eat them; in some localities English sparrows are said to have developed a fondness for harlequin bugs. The large triangular segment on the back is another identification mark, the whole body outline resembles a shield, and those members of the family whose large scutellum develops from the thorax and covers most of the underside, are called shield bugs. Various species occur throughout the U.S. and southern Canada. Length: 3/8 inch. *Murgantia histrionica.*

17-YEAR CICADA ►

Strange Cycle — Ancient fairy tales tell of enchanted people who appear from the depth of the earth for one day every hundred years. A similar story is that of the cicada which spends 17 years underground as a nymph, then emerges as an adult in bright daylight and lives there just long enough to mate and insert the eggs in the branches of trees or the stems of plants. The adult dies and the wingless young hatch, drop or crawl to the ground and burrow into the soil where they feed on root juices. There, in the earth, they spend from 13 to 17 years, according to the latitude; then they leave their shelter by night, climb upon a tree, and the adult emerges out of the splitting nymphal skin, its transparent forewings covering the body like a roof. The vibrating membranes on its thorax are ready to produce its whirring night music. As there are 17 broods, some adults appear every year in a different section; in the South the cycle is 13 years. For that reason the name "periodical cicada" is more appropriate. When large numbers emerge simultaneously, they do great damage to shade and orchard trees; for the branches into which they insert their eggs are weakened, and broken by the wind. At the same time their mass appearance offers a feast to gulls, terns, English sparrows and other birds. The periodical cicada occurs throughout the East to the Great Plains. Length: 1½ inches. *Magicicada septendecim.*

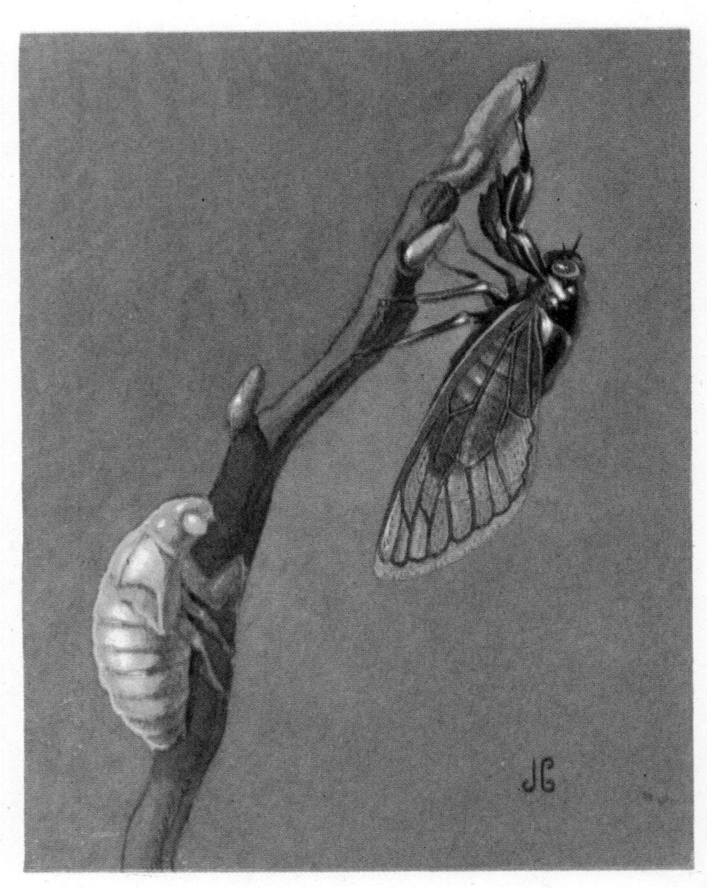

APHIDS ►

A Female World — The dairy cows kept by ants are aphids. The ants tend them and milk them, i.e. they stroke them gently which seems to increase the flow of a sweet secretion called honeydew. Ants love honeydew, and when their "cows" feed on a rootlet which is too crowded, they carry some of them to another pasture that is unoccupied. Bees and certain other insects are also very fond of honeydew. The aphids of the ants are mostly subterranean; even more species live on plants, feed on plant juices and, in doing so, spread a number of virus, fungus and bacterial diseases, for instance, the mosaic plant diseases. At one time a species of this group almost exterminated the world's grape cultures. The aphids or plant lice, as they are usually called, are entirely defenseless, yet they cover the earth. They are able to survive because of their vitality and incredible fecundity. In spring only wingless females are hatched from the eggs; throughout the summer they bear living young females without mating, sometimes 12 generations. When the host plant becomes overcrowded, some females emerge with wings, fly to another plant, and begin to give birth to living young there. In the fall normal males and females are born; their eggs carry the race through the winter, and in spring the new mass breeding begins. An example for this family is the melon aphid which is destructive to cucumbers and melons. Length: 1/4 inch. *Aphis gossypii.*

◄ SWALLOWTAILS

On Flickering Wings — There are swallowtails even north of the Arctic Circle in Alaska, and no section of the U.S. and Canada is without its species of these beautiful butterflies, the largest on our continent. With the exception of the South American owl and morpho butterflies, the swallowtails include the largest butterflies on earth. Most species have two tail extensions from which the name of the family is derived. Like butterflies in general, they are day flyers and like to alight on bright flowers, particularly on blossoms of thistles and milkweeds. There they suck in their nourishment with the help of a sucking tube which, when not used, is rolled into a tight coil. Rotting carcasses and decaying fruit also seem to have a special attraction for them. Their eggs are laid singly or in small groups on the host plant; their caterpillars have a smooth skin, and some species, like those of the tiger swallowtail which is illustrated here, bear large eye spots; whether these simulated eyes are supposed to have a protective function is not clear. However, another device is definitely of a protective nature: When disturbed, the caterpillars thrust out tube-like horns and give off a sickening odor. In the case of the parsnip caterpillar the smell resembles that of the host plant. The pupa is naked; it is suspended by the tail and a band of silk about its waist. The very common tiger swallowtail is illustrated. Wing spread: 3¾ inches. *Papilio glaucus.*

◄ MONARCH BUTTERFLY

The Wanderer — In the fall, enormous masses of these brightly colored butterflies gather in huge tribes and migrate to the extreme south of the U.S.; some swarms get as far as Central and South America. On their journey they roost, at night or on cloudy days, like flocks of birds, alighting on certain trees so that the branches are covered with reddish-brown wings; they are the famous butterfly trees of Florida and California. In their southern winter quarters the swarms stay together, and the following spring they fly back north, lay their pale green eggs on plants of the milkweed family, and die; 3 to 5 days later the larvae are born. Monarchs are wanderers in still another sense: Originally butterflies of the New World, they have spread to western Europe across the Atlantic, and to Hawaii and many South Sea islands across the Pacific. One of the fascinating aspects of this insect is the fact that it has an imitator. The viceroy, although belonging to a different subfamily, mimics the monarch not only in form and coloration but also in its ways of flying and its habits. Why? The monarch is distasteful to birds while the viceroy is edible; so the latter escapes death many a time by being mistaken for the other species. Of course, it is doubtful whether we can speak of imitation in nature; if not, the case of the monarch and the viceroy is one of coincidence. Wing spread: 4 inches. *Danaus plexippus.*

BUCKEYE ►

Of Southern Fields and Western Meadows — Old World chronicles report that in times of stress red raindrops fell from heaven. They were signs of the Lord's ire, and people came forth in awe and fear to repent and atone. As passions were aroused, even massacres occurred. The red raindrops still fall to the earth and explain the medieval miracle. It happens wherever certain butterflies gather — those of the Family Nymphalidae. After leaving the shell of the pupa, the nymphalid excretes a large drop of a liquid which, with some species, is usually red. If this occurs in the air, and if the nymphalids swarm in great numbers, there will be red rain. This largest of our butterfly families has a distinguishing feature: Both in the males and the females the reduced forelegs are unfit for walking: the insects are "brush-footed." In the South and West one of the best-known members of the group is the buckeye, spectacular with its beautiful eye spots. Southern meadows often swarm wih buckeyes, particularly where narrow-leaved plantains abound; for plantains and gerardia are the principal host plants for its dark green eggs, and its brown, bristly caterpillars whose spines branch out on all sides. Its chrysalis has a pale, wood-brown color and hangs head downward from the host plant, at less than a right angle. The buckeye shows a pugnacious disposition, dashes down on other butterflies. Wing spread: 2½ inches. *Junonia coenia.*

BANDED PURPLE BUTTERFLY ►

A Northern Beauty — Walking over a tote road in the northwoods of Wisconsin or Maine, the traveler is sure to be greeted by lovely butterflies with wings of a velvety, purplish black color and broad white bands. There may be a dozen or more around a moist spot; upon your approach they will rise and accompany you for a while, flying evenly, three to eight feet above the ground; they will dip or dodge suddenly to avoid a horsefly, then will rest again and sit on a low branch in a fashion quite typical for the banded purple: Nervously they open and close their wings. While abundant in the forests, they occur also in the suburbs of cities in its range. Their range extends from northern New England through Quebec and Ontario to the region surrounding the Great Lakes; Saginaw Bay in Michigan and the Pennsylvania woods are their southern limits. The female deposits her green eggs on deciduous trees, preferably willows, birches and poplars; here the larva, a naked, greenish-brown caterpillar, feeds on the leaves using a peculiar method: It begins at the tip and eats everything except the center rib; the latter, protruding like a thorn, is spared in order to serve as a resting place. For hibernation, the larva builds a winter shelter of a rolled leaf and ties it securely to a branch with silk. The chrysalis is white or silvery with brown markings. Wing spread: 2⅞ inches. *Basilarchia arthemis.*

◄ MOURNING CLOAK

Dark Silk Embroidered with Gold — This magnificent butterfly is another member of the world-wide Family Nymphalidae. The many names given to that group attest to their fame; they are called peacocks and emperors, anglewings and tortoise shells, fritillaries and leaf butterflies; the latter name refers to an Indian species which resembles a leaf when its wings are closed. The mourning cloak, one of the most common nymphalids in the U.S. and Canada, hibernates as an adult and is one of the first butterflies to emerge in early spring. Its eggs are dark, and as they are laid in rows on the twigs of trees, they look like miniature barrels. Poplars, elms and willows are preferred for the purpose. Its caterpillar, blackish brown with red spots, is covered with sharp spines; it is a gregarious creature; a number of them get together in a bush or small tree and fashion a net of silk over its branches; occassionally they strip the bush of its leaves; this is also the place where they shed their skins. The mourning cloak is not a specifically American butterfly but common in the whole northern hemisphere; in England, for instance, it is a beloved garden dweller known as "Camberwell beauty." In colder climates it produces one brood annually, but two in our South. Wing spread: 2½ inches. Other famous nymphalids are the red admiral and the painted lady which is said to be more widely distributed than any other. *Nymphalis antiopa.*

SPHINX MOTHS

Speed-Flyers — A large, green caterpillar raising its head belligerently in a snake-like attitude has a faint resemblance with a sphinx; it is the larva of a moth called sphinx moth for that reason, "Hummingbird moths" is another name for members of the family; for they hover in front of blossoms with wing motions so rapid that they are invisible. They extract nectar from the flowers and, as their sucking-tube mouth is exceptionally long — one species in the American tropics has a proboscis nearly a foot in length — they are able to get their nourishment from such blossoms as petunias, trumpet vines, and honeysuckle; in doing so they are effective pollinators. The adult moths are built for speedy flight, with long, narrow wings and tapering streamlined bodies, reported to be capable of a speed of 35 m.p.h. Their colors are not bright but exquisitely beautiful. The larvae bear a harmless horn on the last segment of the abdomen and are commonly called hornworms; the name of their food plant completes their designation. The species illustrated here is the tomato hornworm. Others feed on tobacco, grape and various garden crops. The pupa develops in a cell under ground. The tomato hornworm occurs throughout southern Canada and the U.S. It is attacked by a small braconid wasp which lays its eggs in the living caterpillar. Wing spread: 4 inches. *Protoparce quinquemaculata.*

CABBAGE BUTTERFLY

Tough, Common, Aggressive — It is estimated that almost one-fifth of the cabbage and cauliflower cultivated in the U.S. is destroyed every year by insects. By far the worst offender is a green, cylindrical caterpillar covered with fine fuzz, the larva of the white cabbage butterfly which, like the English sparrow, is an undesirable immigrant. Of European origin, it first appeared in the region of Quebec in 1860; in a few decades it had spread to the Rocky Mountains, and now has appropriated every cabbage patch in Canada and the U.S. In doing so it has crowded out some of the native butterflies, for its males show a great deal of pugnaciousness toward other species. They bear down on them, disturb them and drive them from their breeding sites. The female — with two black spots on the forewing, in contrast to the one spot of the male — deposits her conical eggs on cabbage leaves, and two or three broods mature annually. The last brood hibernates in the chrysalid stage, and the butterfly emerges the following spring. Sometimes a chrysalid is brought into a house attached to a fruit or vegetable basket, and on a cold, mid-winter day a newly hatched, white butterfly may erratically hover in a room and head for the window. The cabbage butterfly is a member of the Family Pieridae whose various species are named in accordance with their colors: "whites," "yellows," "sulphurs." Wing spread: 1¾ inches. *Pieris rapae.*

Insects

LUNA MOTH ►

Glamor Queen—This is, most probably, the first contender for America's loveliest moth. A white body and white legs are supported by delicate, light green wings that have a velvety look and end in tails resembling those of the swallowtail butterflies. The antennae are two tiny feathers. Each forewing has a purple margin on top, and each fore and hind wing has a transparent eye spot, a feature typical for several species of the Saturniidae to which the luna moth belongs. The female lays her eggs on the food plants of the larvae, preferably on the leaves of walnut and beech, hickory and persimmon, sweet gum and willow trees. The caterpillars, green with varicolored dots and bristles, feed on the foliage of their hosts but are not numerous enough to do great damage. The comparatively small, brownish cocoons are attached to the leaves and, when the winter winds blow, fall to the ground with them. Sometimes they are spun right on the ground. The adult males and females are similar in appearance; only the purple margin on the edges of the wings is variable. The range of the luna moth is the east of the continent, extending from southern Canada to Florida in the South and to the Rocky Mountains in the West. This species, a favorite with American collectors of moths and butterflies, has a body length of a little more than 3/4 of an inch and an expanse of wings from 3 to 3½ inches. *Tropaea luna.*

◄ CECROPIA MOTH

The Emperor — The emergence of the cecropia moth is a sight to behold: Out of a hard, grey-brown cocoon a big, wrinkled creature appears, stretches and sprawls until its wings unfold to a spread of five inches, displaying a beautiful color pattern. It is a grand entrance; but this superb insect is destined to die young: It is born with its mouth parts so reduced that it is not capable of eating. It lives just long enough to perform its task of reproduction; the male finds a mate apparently by its sense of smell, and experiments have shown that it may be attracted over distances of two or three miles. The female lays her eggs, singly or in clusters, on deciduous trees like maples, elms, wild cherry and apple trees. Sometimes her dead body is found under the shrub on which she has deposited her last eggs, a case of death while on duty. The caterpillars are bright green and, because of their large size and brightly colored tubercles, look quite formidable. When mature, they spin silk cocoons attached to twigs or rolled into leaves, and pass the winter in that stage. As the silk is not continuous it cannot be unraveled and is of no commercial value. However, the term giant silkworm is sometimes applied to the family of the cecropia moth, the Saturniidae, because some Asiatic species do produce silk; the famous shantung silk is extracted from their caterpillars. Wing spread: 5½ inches. *Samia cecropia.*

WOOLLY BEAR

A Would-Be Weather Prophet — Ever since colonial days American farm lore has stated that the woolly bear forecasts the weather of the coming winter. If the brown band around the caterpillar's center is broad, the winter will be mild, and vice versa. For several years the entomologists of the American Museum of Natural History have studied the case and kept statistics; so far the ancient observation has been confirmed; but it will take another 50 years to establish the facts. Covered completely with hair, the woolly bear looks like a "bottle brush"; when alarmed it rolls into a bristly coil or ball, and most birds avoid it; only the cuckoo does not seem to mind the bristles. The larva's favorite food consists of the leaves of plantains and similar plants. It hibernates in the larval stage under a piece of loose bark or under a fallen log; only when the sun shines warm again the following spring does it emerge from its winter quarters and begin to pupate. It spins some silk and uses it together with its own hair to weave a loose, brown cocoon. The adult which emerges from the pupa is the common isabella moth, an attractive insect of pinkish yellow color with an orange hue and three rows of small, black spots on the body. It belongs to the Family Arctiidae, the Tiger Moths. Its wing spread is about 1⅔ inches, the length of the woolly bear up to 2 inches. *Isia isabella.*

TENT CATERPILLARS

A Larval Community — The ugly nests or webs seen on shade and orchard trees in the spring should really not be there; for insect control is made very easy in this case. The owner can spray the tents with 5% DDT or just rip them out with all the caterpillars concentrated within. The colony is mothered by a brown moth with two white lines on its forewings; a creature so hairy that even its legs and eyes are covered with hair. The masses of eggs, topped with a foamy crust, are laid on a branch of the host plant and the larvae develop within the eggs to the point of hatching but remain dormant in that stage through the winter. In the warm days of spring the hatching takes place and the hairy, rather brightly colored caterpillars begin to build their family tent, a woven structure similar to that of the fall webworm. While the tent caterpillars build between the branches, the webworm covers the leaves. During the day all members of the tribe stay in the tent, but at night they crawl out to eat the young leaves and often defoliate big limbs or strip entire small trees. It is said that every caterpillar keeps a silken lifeline to the nest, to be sure of its retreat. When the larvae are mature, they leave the tent and search for hideouts where they spin their silken cocoons. Wing spread of the moth of the eastern tent caterpillar: 1¼ inches. *Malacosoma americana.*

MOSQUITOES ►

"Blood is a very Special Juice" — The mosquito has been called man's worst insect enemy; for some of its species have killed millions of people by infecting them with such dread diseases as yellow fever and malaria. As a pest, mosquitoes are difficult to control because their adaptability is as remarkable as their fecundity. Some occur in the Arctic Circle in huge numbers, others swarm in the Tropics. They spend the winter as eggs, or adults, or larvae frozen in ice, according to species. The female of the Genus Culex lays whole rafts of eggs on any big pond or tiny puddle. In a few days the larvae hatch — they are called wrigglers — and after four larval stages the new adults emerge. The whole process may take only 2 to 3 weeks. It seems that in most species the females have to fulfill one condition before their eggs can develop: They have to suck, at least once, the blood of a warm-blooded animal. They do so with their piercing and sucking mouth parts and on these occasions they may become carriers or transmitters of diseases. At best, their bite is mildly poisonous and annoying. The males are not able to sting or buzz. Of the many species, the anopheles mosquito is notorious as the carrier of malaria; the salt marsh or New Jersey mosquito is abundant but does does not transmit diseases; and the well known house mosquito is the one illustrated on this page. Length: ⅛ inch. *Culex pipiens.*

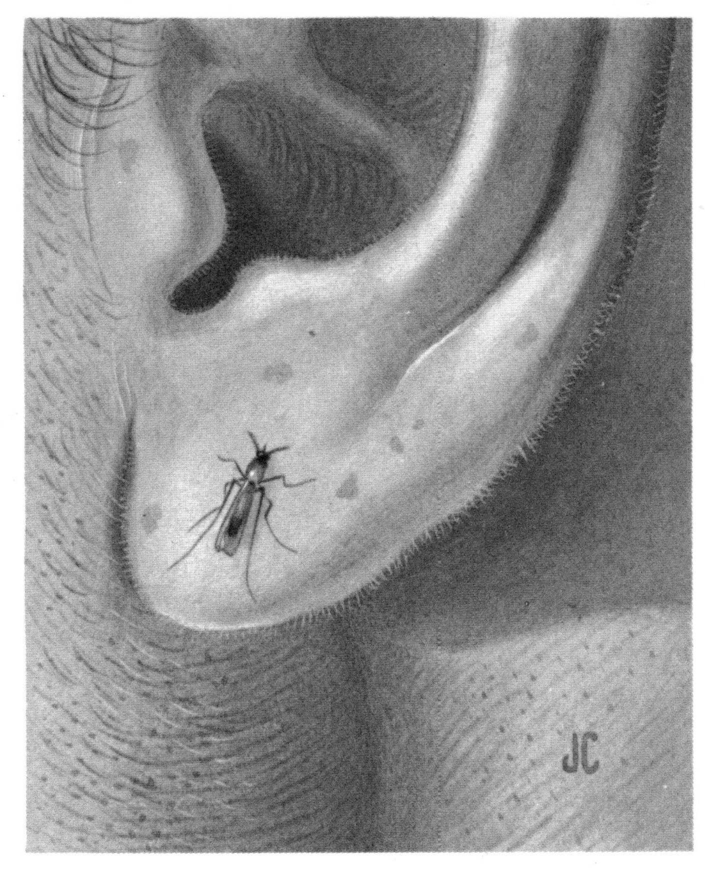

◄ HOUSE FLY

In Every House on Earth — If we try to define the average size of a living creature, including in our calculation the animal kingdom from the smallest protozoon to the largest whale, we arrive at the approximate size of the common house fly — according to Swain who made this interesting comparison. Other aspects of the house fly are also interesting, but almost all of them in a negative sense. This pest collects bacteria, particularly with the adhesive pads on its feet that enable it to climb walls and walk upside down on ceilings. A single fly may carry, according to recent estimates, up to 500 million bacteria; most of them are harmless, but others are not, and the house fly may transmit such diseases as typhoid fever, cholera, tuberculosis and amoebic dysentery — probably 30 to 40 diseases altogether. The female lays her white, spindle-shaped eggs in small clusters; the glossy-white maggot lives in dung or decaying plant and animal matter. The pupa looks like a brown seed, and a little over two weeks after the egg has been laid, the new adult emerges, ready to reproduce on its own. In the northeastern U.S. it hibernates as a maggot. While the house fly is a major pest in all inhabited regions of the earth, its numbers have been reduced in the U.S. and Canada by screening, spraying and more sanitary handling of food. Length: ¼ inch. *Musca domestica.*

◄ COMMON VINEGAR FLY

Its New Calling: Biology — If we know a good deal today about genetics and the laws and processes of inheritance, these common little flies have made a considerable contribution to that knowledge. In more than one way they are ideal objects for laboratory experiments: Their life cycle is completed in approximately ten days at summer temperatures, so that a steady flow of generations is available. They are particularly adapted to the study of genes as factors in inheritance, and have been exposed to experimental radiation to discover its influence on reproduction. In their natural habitat they are minute insects found in fruit stands, kitchens, and garbage pails, or wherever fruits or plants are decaying or fermenting. They carry the spores on their bodies and, as they eat and lay their eggs, contaminate the fruit and are the cause of the fermentation of grapes, without the injection of yeast. The white larvae live in the decaying vegetable pulp where the eggs had been deposited, and develop the puparium wherever they can find a fairly dry spot. Some related species, however, feed on fungi and flowing sap. The brown pupae have two short horns on one end which are respiratory tubes. The adults, tiny creatures with feathery antennae and red eyes, are a nuisance on warm summer days; they are also called fruit flies, for obvious reasons. Length: $\frac{1}{16}$ to $\frac{1}{8}$ of an inch. *Drosophila melanogaster.*

ANTS ►

The Most Abundant Animal on Earth — The story of the ants is fantastic: A single fertilized female starts a new colony; she needs a mate only once; for the rest of her life she will be fertile — 10 years, perhaps 15. She digs a nest in the ground, rears a brood, and feeds them until they are mature. After that, they in turn will take care of the queen and the colony; in time, the latter may contain some 500,000 inhabitants. All the work in this community is done by the infertile females, acting as laborers and soldiers. Some species keep plant lice, tend them, and obtain from them the much cherished honeydew. Sometimes tiny crickets and beetles live with the ants, clean their bodies and feed on the secretions they glean from them. A Texas variety lays out gardens where they raise a fungus on macerated leaf tissues; the fungus is their staple food. Slavery is a common practice with many species; raiders steal strange larvae or pupae and raise them to be servants of their masters. Among the honey ants in our Southwest certain individuals have to serve as living barrels for storing honey; they are bloated to the size of a large pea. A well-known species, particularly common in the East, but in various forms ranging throughout the temperate zones of the world, is the carpenter ant which excavates its galleries in dead timber, in stumps, old logs or buildings. Length: ½ inch. *Camponotus herculanius pennsylvanicus.*

HONEY BEE ►

The Only Domestic Insect — Bees existed in America when white man arrived, but not honey bees. However, they were brought here in early colonial days and have been thriving ever since. Great numbers escaped into the forests and reverted to their native habit of building hives in hollow trees. Honey-making is tedious work: A bee has to fly twice around the earth — in terms of mileage — to produce one pound of honey. The bee's contribution to pollination is more important: Most of our fruit trees and many other plants would not bring forth fruit without the bee's services. The bee community, containing up to 50,000 members, is a woman's world; the workers are infertile females, and the queen has to mate only once in her life of 3 to 5 years. Of the male drones, perhaps one in a thousand will mate a queen; otherwise they are useless, and after the mating season all are driven from the hive and starve to death. The queens develop from the same type egg as the workers. However their cells are peanut-shaped and attached to the face of the hive. During the 6 days of larval development, the queens are fed royal jelly, a rich secretion of the "nurse bees" while the workers receive this food for only 3 of the 6 days. In early summer the "swarming" takes place: The original queen leaves the hive with a retinue of workers to found a new colony. Length of worker: ½ inch. *Apis mellifera.*

◄ WASPS

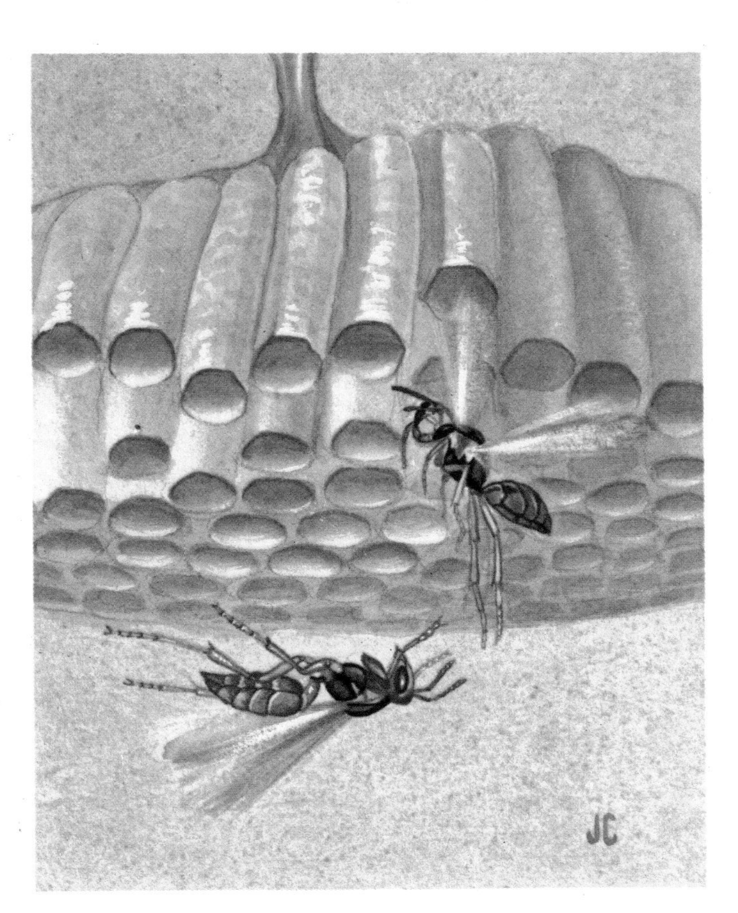

Extroverts and Introverts — Some wasps love crowds, others are solitary individualists. Among the former are the hornets and yellow jackets, social wasps which form busy communities of thousands, with queens, males and workers. They are the inventors of paper, producing it for their nests of chewed wood, plant fibers and saliva. Others, like the potter wasps and mud daubers, are solitary, i.e., each female builds a private nest for her young. In each cell she places several paralyzed spiders or other insects together with her egg and then seals the cell. This common mud dauber is often imposed upon by the blue mud dauber which throws out the contents of the former's cell, and refills it with her own egg and insect. Even worse is the cuckoo wasp which, when unobserved, lays her eggs in a mud dauber's nest and lets her larvae feed on the insects provided by the host. The tool and weapon of the steel-blue or black, yellow or reddish wasps is the sting of the females and workers, a thin, pointed drill hidden in the rear tip of the abdomen and used to paralyze their insect game or to attack an intruder. Wasps do not store food for the winter; all die in the fall except the queen which hibernates to carry on the race. The following spring she builds the initial shelter and feeds the larvae until the first workers are hatched. Paper wasps: ¾ to ⅞ inch. *Polistes fuscatus.*

CLIMATE AND VEGETATION IN THE U.S. AND CANADA

When white man landed in the eastern part of our continent he found a lustier climate than he had known at home. The summers were hotter, the winters colder. Great air masses from the west or south passed over huge land masses and heated or cooled to a much greater degree than the air masses over small-scale Europe. There was plenty of rainfall, as the map indicates. This humid, vigorous climate combined with a fertile soil to produce trees, and the land from the Atlantic to the Prairies was one huge forest. To a large extent it still is a forest, surrounding the cities and agricultural sections that have been carved out of the woods. Wherever farms are abandoned, as in New England and the southern mountains, the forest still reclaims the land and obliterates the work of man.

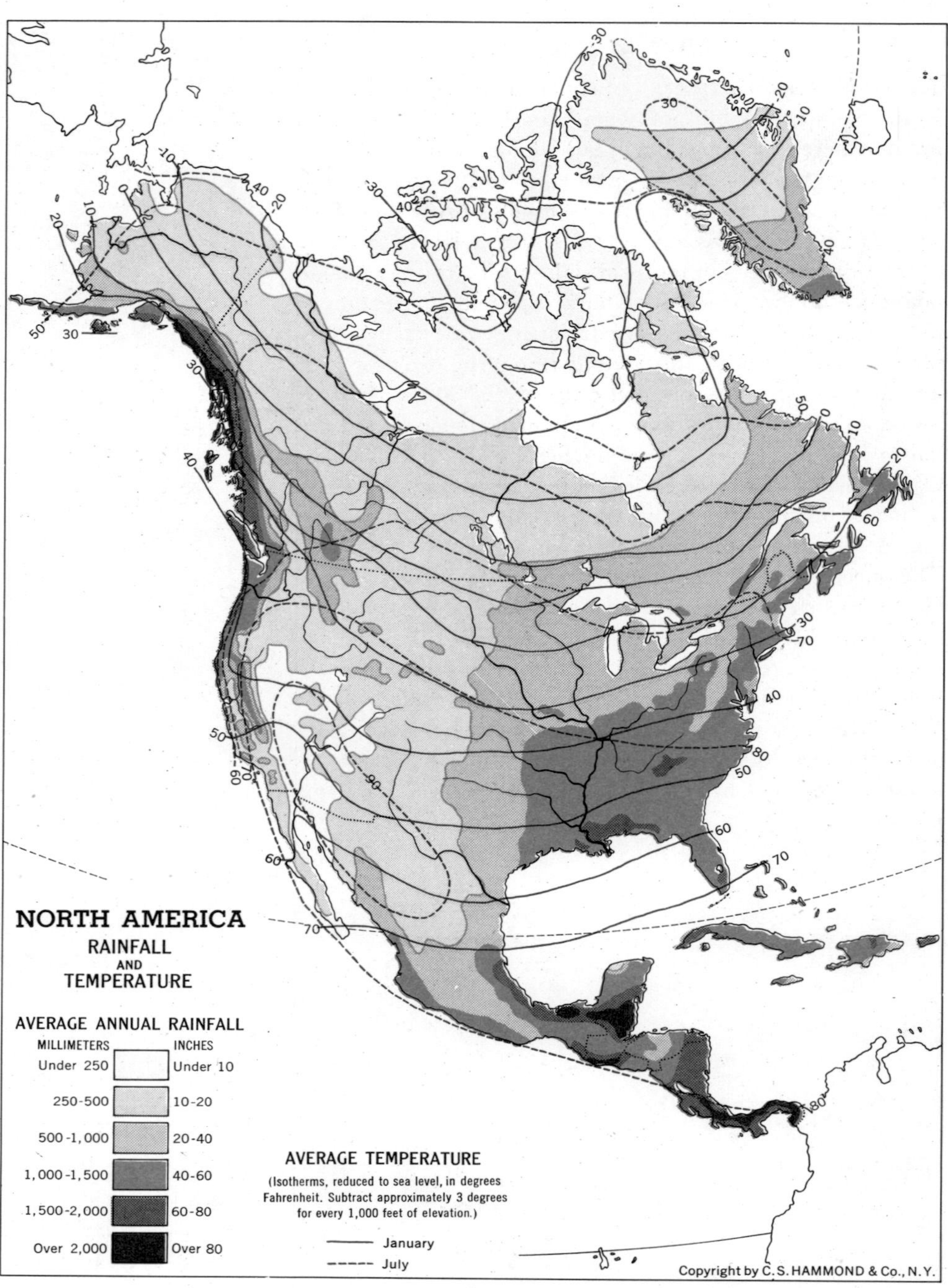

Where the eastern forest ceases, beyond the rainfall region of 40 to 60 inches and approximately at a line which marks an annual rainfall of 30 inches, the prairies begin. Here the landscape is quite uniform, but the temperature changes at the rate of approximately 2.5° for every 70 miles going north or south. The January mean for southern Texas is 50° to 55°, while the average midwinter temperature for North Dakota and northwestern Minnesota is 5°. The Texas "norther" is a gale of arctic air that may cause a drop of 50° in 2 hours. Prairie and Great Plains blizzards with fine, dry snow and bitter cold blasts are treacherous, causing death to man and beast. The original plant cover of most of these lands was the tall prairie grass that grew to heights of 3 to 10 feet. No trees existed, except along the water courses, but flowers like violets and phloxes, spiderworts and shooting stars bloomed among the grasses in profusion.

To the west of this huge flower garden, now a rich agricultural mosaic, the Great Plains form a belt of scarce rainfall (10 to 20 inches), at an elevation of 3,000 to 4,000 feet above sea level. The climate here is dry and irregular. There are dry spells of 120 days. The tropical maritime air of the Gulf tends to move up the Mississippi Valley and then eastward without touching the Great Plains. However, occasionally masses of very moist, tropical air do invade the plains; upon colliding with dry, polar air they cause such violent rainstorms that as much as a third of the annual rainfall may precipitate in a single day, or a fifth in an hour. Extremes of heat and cold are common; summer temperatures of 110° have been recorded throughout the region, just as below zero temperatures during the winter. The natural vegetation of the Great Plains is a group of short grama and buffalo grasses which are adapted to the climate; they rest but do not die during a drought, and after a rain falls they produce seeds in a surprisingly short time.

Climate and Vegetation

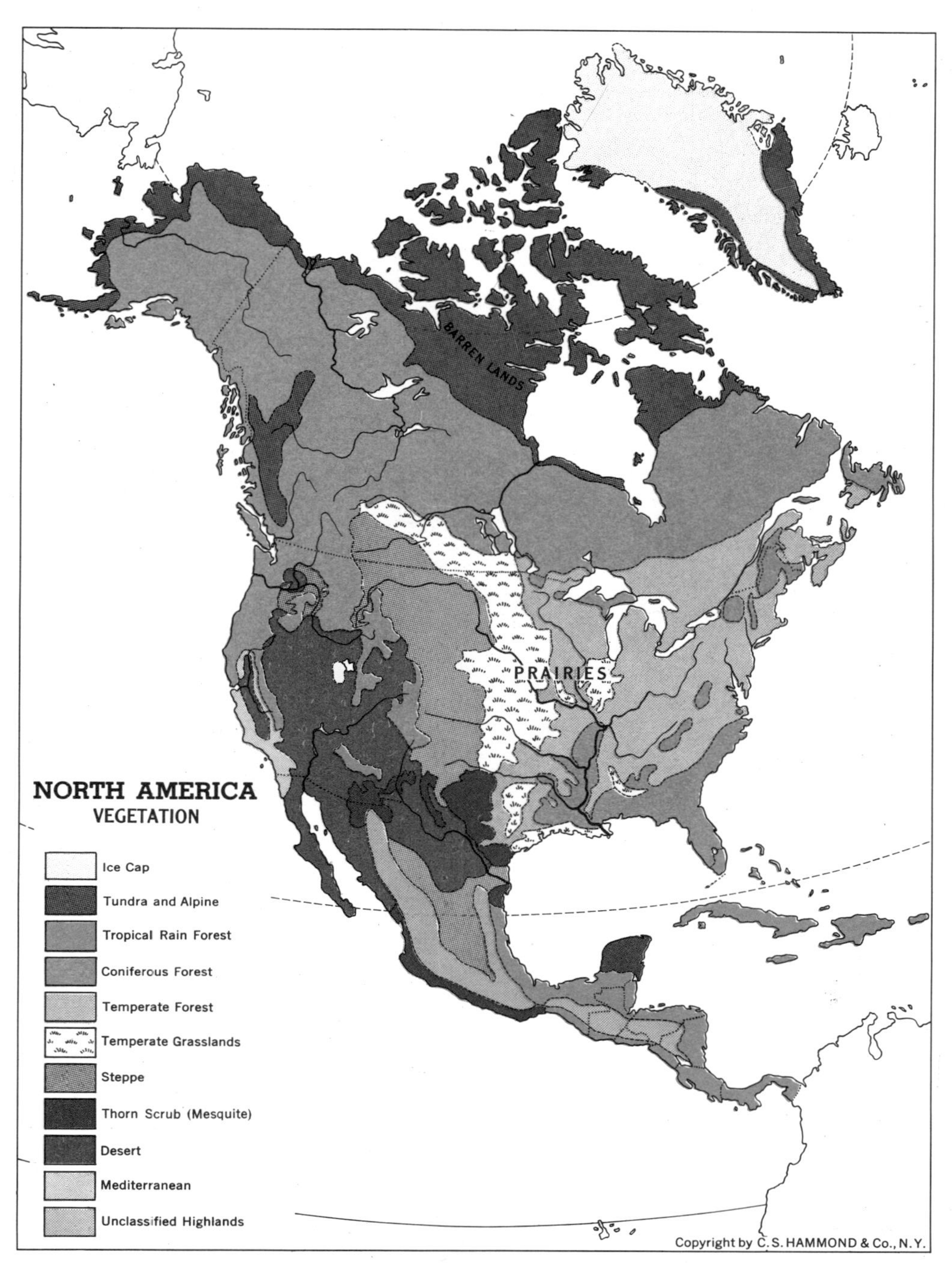

Between the plains and the western coastal belt lies a broad arid region of mountains, valleys and deserts, 600 miles wide and reaching far into the Canadian north and the Mexican south. This is the driest area on our continent; for the storms moving eastward from the Pacific first strike the barrier of the Sierra Nevada and the Cascade Mountains and precipitate most of their moisture as rain on their western slopes. The remnants of the storms proceed to the east, but each successive mountain range acts as another obstacle with the same effect. Consequently, "humid islands" exist on the western mountain slopes while great aridity reigns everywhere else. These humid islands, densely covered with trees and blanketed with snow in the winter, are usually inaccessible and uninhabitable.

The Pacific shore belt west of the Sierra Nevada and the Cascade Mountains has a so-called "summer-dry" climate, i.e. in many parts of the belt 40 to 60% of the total annual rainfall precipitates in December, January and February while the summer months are dry. Variations, however, are great; San Diego, for instance, receives only 9.7 inches annually, while Tatoosh Island south of Vancouver Island registers 83.5 inches. In some mountain regions a precipitation of 100 inches produces the heaviest forest in the U.S. and Canada. The winters along the coast are mild; air masses coming from the ocean have not been refrigerated by snow-covered land, and the mountains keep out continent cold waves. At the time of the discovery, the coastal belt was a pleasant, park-like landscape of grassland, forest and chaparral (shrub thickets).

As the vegetation map shows, the greater part of the continent is a varied forest land in which the following types are represented: In the U.S. the only *tropical forest* is the mangrove forest in southern Florida. The *coniferous forest* consists of (1) the southern pineries, (2) the spruce-fir forest of the north, and (3) the spruce-fir forest of the west which is supplemented by ponderosa pine forests and cedar-Douglas fir-redwood forests along the coast. The *temperate forest* includes (1) the great oak forests of the Middle-Atlantic and Midwestern states and (2) the northern and Appalachian hardwood forests of birch, beech and maple, often mixed with conifers. Southern Canada has the same types of forest as the northern U.S., with large stands of grey birch, paper birch, northern white cedar and quaking aspen. In northern Canada such conifers as tamarack, black spruce, white spruce and balsam fir prevail. In the far north of Canada and Alaska, bog-like *tundra* country prevails. This bleak vegetation of mosses, lichens and stunted flowering plants results from the permanently frozen subsoil which does not thaw sufficiently in the Arctic summer.

LAND FORMS AND NATURE IN THE U.S. AND CANADA

In its sweep and variety the North American continent is a grandiose setting for our nature heritage. It contains every known land form and shape: towering mountains and sandy beaches swept by arctic, temperate, and tropical waters; ancient masses of granite, and stretches of earth so new that water and terra firma have not yet separated; humid rain forests and sun-baked deserts; an inland sea and the world's longest river system; a gulf and a bay as large as seas.

Nature and urban civilization exist side by side. There are half a dozen ranges of wooded hills thirty miles or so from Times Square, lush crests and valleys where musk-rats build houses in ponds and deer jump through the clearings. So it is throughout the land. On the south side of the Great Lakes an industrial super-civilization has grown that handles more tools more expertly than any other region on earth; and on the north side of the lakes an immense wilderness lives on where the hammering of pileated woodpeckers resounds through the northwoods, bears lick wild honey, and the last timber wolves howl at night.

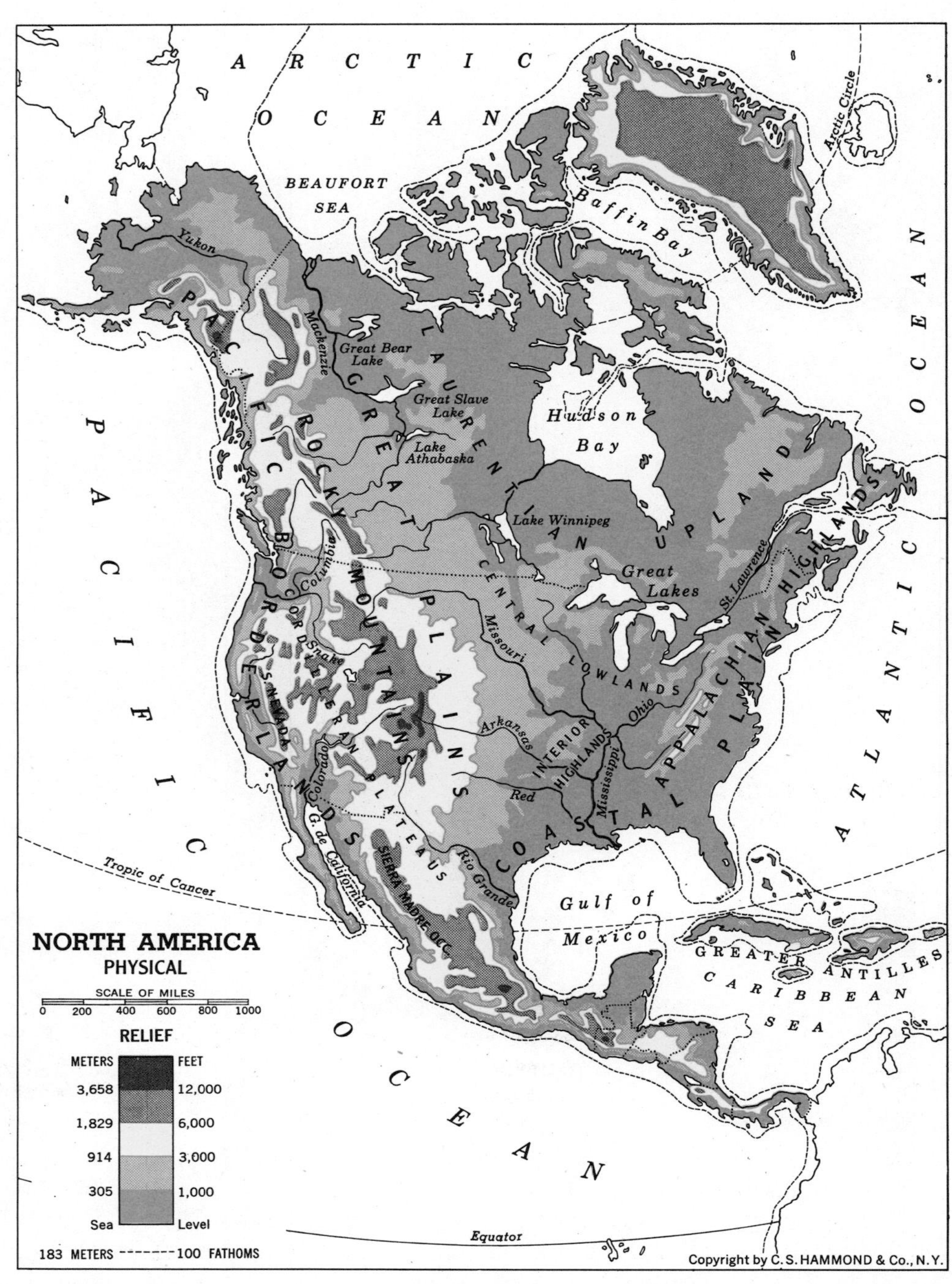

Modern geographers distinguish nine physiographic provinces which are, in the sequence used by W. W. Atwood, Sr., 1) The Coastal Plain along the Atlantic and the Gulf of Mexico. 2) The Appalachian Highlands, from the Newfoundland and New England ranges to the Cohutta Mountains of Georgia. 3) The Laurentian Upland, largely of Canada, but including the Adirondack Mountains of New York and portions of Wisconsin and Minnesota. 4) The Central Lowlands, our Midwest. 5) The interior highlands, i.e. the Ozark Plateau and the neighboring ranges. 6) The Great Plains. 7) The Rocky Mountains. 8) The Cordilleran Plateaus. 9) The borderlands of the Pacific.

These physiographic provinces show not only the variety of America's physical features but also their enormous scale: In the Rocky Mountains more than 40 peaks rise above 14,000 feet, and in the Central Lowlands, the natural waterway system of the Mississippi may carry a steamboat from Olean, New York, on the Allegheny River, to Great Falls, Montana, on the Missouri — an east-west voyage of some 4,000 miles. The coastal plain and the Appalachian Highlands on the Atlantic side, and the borderlands of the Pacific have a fascinating common bond: If the whole of our continent could be viewed from an airplane, we would see two broad forest belts circling a huge grassland and a semi-desert, and merging, in the Canadian north, into a single splendid wreath of trees. Many fascinating isolated phenomena occur within the nine provinces ranging from the active volcano of the Pacific borderlands, Mt. Lassen, to meteor carved Chubb Crater of the Laurentian Upland.

Classification Key

An Outline of Our Natural Environment by Orders and Families

WHILE THE COLOR SECTION describes and illustrates the most commonly encountered single species, this outline presents the structure and classification of orders and families, or groups and varieties in the case of rocks. It shows the place which each individual species occupies in the whole of our natural environment.

No classification can be definite as long as the natural sciences are in a constant flux of progress and discovery; new species are constantly being described, and new characteristics of known species are identified, which make reclassification necessary. Therefore, there cannot be a unanimous opinion among natural scientists as to all details; this survey uses the most generally accepted systems and lists. It includes only those orders, families and species that are of interest and importance to laymen nature lovers in search of a non-technical introduction.

Outline of the Principal Groups and Varieties of Rocks in the U.S. and Southern Canada

Atoms make elements; elements build up minerals; and minerals combine in various ways to form rocks. Rocks may also consist of mineral-like matter, like glass, or of organic matter, like coal. Rocks are natural, i.e. man-made concrete is not a rock.

Some important minerals of which our rocks are composed are described and illustrated in the color section: Agate and asbestos on page 32; beryl and copper on page 33; corundum and feldspar on page 34; flint and garnet on page 35; gold and graphite on page 36; hematite and mica on page 37; quartz and silver on page 38; sulphur and talc on page 39. The rocks are classified in three groups: igneous, sedimentary, and metamorphic rocks.

Igneous Rocks (i.e. rocks that at one time were hot and liquid or molten, and either erupted through volcanoes or hardened underground). *Important coarse-grained varieties:*

GRANITE, the rock of our mountains and monumental buildings is described and illustrated on page 40.

GIANT GRANITE or pegmatite is an industrially valuable rock. It is the source of feldspar which is used in glazing china; mica, an insulating material; uranite, an important source of radium; topaz and beryl for jewelry; fluorite for etching acid, etc. Occurrence: Maine, South Dakota, and a few other states.

GABBRO. This grey, green or black granular rock is quarried in the Adirondacks, Vermont, and the Lake Superior region. In New York and Minnesota masses of iron are found in gabbros, and in Ontario, nickel and copper ores.

DIABASE. The famous Palisades of the Hudson River opposite New York City are diabase, which is grey, black or deep green ("greenstone"). A tough rock, it occurs in the West and also in the Central East.

TRAP. This is a miner's term for gabbro, diabase, and other dark, heavy igneous rocks which break into step-like blocks and were called "Treppen," "steps," by German quarrymen. From Treppen the word trap is derived. It is not necessarily coarse-grained.

Igneous Rocks. *Important fine-grained varieties:*

FELSITE. These very dense types of rock have a dull appearance and are hard to break. They are found in almost any color except dark green. Occurrence: Maine, Pennsylvania, Wisconsin, many parts of the Rockies, western Coastal Ranges.

FELSITE PORPHYRIES. This group of light-colored porphyries includes the red, grey or pink andesites of which Mount Rainier is formed.

BASALT. The dark lava rock with a very old history is described and illustrated on page 40.

Igneous Rocks. *Important glassy varieties:*

OBSIDIAN. The glass-sharp tool of the Indians is described and illustrated on page 41.

FLOW BRECCIAS. These are angular fragments of lava enveloped in a later lava flow.

Igneous Rocks. *Important fragmental varieties:*

LOOSE FRAGMENTS OF LAVA. They consist of volcanic dust, volcanic ash, cinders, or volcanic bombs. The latter are blocks of solid lava that were broken in an eruption or melted into various forms, either spheric or massive, and sometimes even got twisted or hollow. Interesting bombs are found at Sunset Crater near Flagstaff, Arizona, and at the Craters of the Moon in Idaho.

AGGLOMERATE. VOLCANIC BRECCIA. Both are mixtures of broken rock material blown out of volcanoes or fissures. They contain ash, cinders, bombs, fragments of obsidian, limestone, sandstone, granite, and other materials. Occurrence: Frequent in many regions of the Rocky Mountains, Cascade and Coastal Ranges.

TUFF. This volcanic rock of fine grain and light weight consists of volcanic ash or cinders cemented by minerals.

Sedimentary Rocks (i.e. rocks that have been built up by water, ice, or wind, or have been deposited by plants and animals). *The Clastic Types* (clastic means "broken," i.e. these rocks consist of material broken or worn from older rocks). The important coarse-grained varieties; most of them are so common that no special locations are indicated.

TALUS. This is a typical pile of rocks, from tiny particles to large blocks, at the base of mountain sides.

BRECCIA is cemented talus, or any other mass of cemented rock fragments.

TILL is an unsorted miscellaneous mixture of rock fragments, deposited by melting glaciers. Its pieces may range in size from fine clay to boulders of many feet in diameter. If till is cemented, it becomes tillite.

GRAVEL is a mass of worn rock fragments, of pebbles, cobblestones, or even boulders.

CONGLOMERATE is a mixture of rounded pebbles cemented with silica or sand, clay, limestone, or iron oxide.

SAND is a loose mass of mineral grains which may be coarse or fine, rounded or angular. When rocks erode, they produce sand. Quartz is the most common mineral, but there are also sand grains of feldspar, lime and gypsum. Formations of dunes occur on the east and south shores of Lake Michigan, and the Great Sand Dunes of Colorado reach a height of 800 feet. The striking White Sands of New Mexico are dunes of pure white gypsum crystals or grains.

SANDSTONE i.e. sand grains held together by cement, is described and illustrated on page 41.

Sedimentary Rocks, *Clastic Types.* The important fine-grained varieties; most of them are so common that no localities are indicated.

MUD. A loose mixture of the fine grains of numerous minerals is called mud, a term that on land is usually applied to any wet soil (soil—fine mineral grains mixed with decaying vegetable or animal matter). In contrast to the more plastic clay, mud crumbles into lumps or dust when heated.

LOESS. This is a very fine-grained deposit similar to clay; it consists mostly of dust, i.e. tiny quartz grains blended with various minerals and also with clay. Many small tubes can be observed in loess; they have been caused by the decay of roots. Loess is usually of wind-blown origin.

ADOBE. This fine-grained rock which crumbles quite easily, ranges in color from whitish pink to chocolate brown. It is the raw material of the sun-dried adobe bricks; adobe is a popular construction material of the Southwest dating back to the building of the missions. It is very rich soil when irrigated.

CLAY consists of minute forms, crystals and others, of mineral matter held together by films of "water of crystallization." These particles are less than 1/250 millimeter in diameter. Important clay varieties are: *boulder clay* which is the fine-grained deposit in glacial till; *brick clay* is usually bluish-grey in color, but when fired becomes yellow, brown, or red and fuses. *Fire clay* is kaolin mixed with sand; the white or pale-buff bricks of this clay do not crumble even in great heat and are employed in lining blast furnaces, forges, fireplaces, etc. *Potter's Clay,* consisting of very fine grains of quartz and other minerals, is the raw material for inexpensive but highly usable earthenware. *Bauxite* consists of earthy layers or solidified balls, ¼ to 1 inch in diameter; if pure, it is white, but iron oxides usually color it brown or red. It is an aluminum ore and also the source of a number of chemicals and abrasives; deposits are found from Virginia to New Mexico. *Kaolin* is white when burned, and after careful grinding and mixing serves in the manufacture of high-grade porcelain; kaolin is also used in producing oilcloth, wallpaper, soap, paint, tooth powder, and other articles; important deposits are found in Georgia, North and South Carolina, Pennsylvania, and other states.

PIPESTONE OR CATLINITE is the compact rock of pale grey to deep red hues, which was used by the Sioux and other Plains Indians and also by white trappers and traders to make smoking pipes. It is soft when quarried and hardens when drying. The principal deposits are in Minnesota, Wisconsin, and South Dakota.

SHALE, the grey rock which often preserves the plant and animal life of ancient epochs, is described and illustrated on page 42.

Sedimentary Rocks from Solutions (i.e. rocks formed by the evaporation of mineralized water). Important varieties:

GYPSUM-OR-ROCK-SALT-BEARING SEDIMENTS. These sediments are composed largely of the minerals gypsum and rock salt which are described and illustrated on pages 42 and 43.

GEYSERITE is a brittle rock generally encountered at hot springs and geysers. On the whole it is limited to volcanic regions like Yellowstone National Park. Most geyserite is formed by simple algae which live in hot springs or on surfaces wetted by geyser spray.

Sedimentary Iron-Bearing Rocks.

HEMATITE, the red iron ore, is the mineral which occurs in great quantities in iron-bearing rocks. It is described and illustrated on page 37.

LIMONITE. One of the varieties of this mineral is the bog iron ore that, in pioneer days, was hauled out of swamps and shallow lakes in the East, and in revolutionary times furnished many a cannon ball. It is loose or firm, porous, of brown or brownish black color, deposited in shallow water with a layer of decaying plants on top and often a layer of clay below. Limonites occur from Vermont to Alabama.

Sedimentary Limestones and Related Rocks.

LIMESTONE, the world's most useful rock, is described and illustrated on page 43.

CHALK. This soft limestone consists of the tiny shells of microscopic one-celled animals called Foraminifera. It is a white, buff, grey or flesh-colored shallow-water deposit containing both marine fossils and the bones of land-dwelling reptiles. Its practical purposes are manifold: Occasionally it is used as a building stone; it is burned for lime; mixed with clay it serves the cement industry; as a chemical conditioner it is spread on acid soil; and it is an ingredient in such common products as glass polish, paint, and tooth powder.

OOLITE is the Greek word for "eggstone." This name refers to the small round grains of calcite of which the rock is formed. They look like fish eggs, measuring 2 millimeters in diameter and less. In the U.S. the best oolites are the Bedford limestones of Indiana which occur in solid beds of 20 to 70 feet in thickness, spreading over 70 square miles in south-central Indiana. Hundreds of thousands of tons of this rock are used every year in buildings throughout the continent.

PISOLITE is the Greek word for "peastone." It consists of round or oval grains which are as large as peas, all having a diameter of more than 2 millimeters. Aside from the size of the grains, "peastone" is essentially the same as "eggstone." A well-known deposit is encountered at Canada's Ptarmigan Pass near Lake Louise.

TUFA. This porous or spongy limestone is encountered in desert lakes and around springs, streams, and waterfalls. Its most spectacular examples are the terraces of Mammoth Hot Springs in Yellowstone Park. As long as the algae in the hot springs stay alive, the tufa deposits shine in yellow, orange, and red. When the flow of water stops and the algae die, the colors fade into white and the rock crumbles.

TRAVERTINE AND ONYX. Travertine is a hard and solid, banded type of tufa ranging in color from white to yellow to red. It is quarried in Montana and, as it takes a high polish, it is much used in decorating theaters and public buildings. Though porous with irregular cavities, it is very long lasting. Onyx, a mottled or banded variety of travertine, is even better known as a translucent ornamental stone. It occurs in Arizona, California, Kentucky and Utah, but mostly in the Mexican part of Lower California.

STALAGMITES AND STALACTITES are the limestone cave deposits that, through the action of trickling water, arise from the floor or hang down from the ceiling.

DOLOMITE. This rock, a mixture of the mineral dolomite or magnesium carbonate with calcite and impure elements, looks like limestone and is used in the same way. Particularly, it is burned to manufacture a heat-resisting substance for kilns and furnaces; it also plays a part in the production of insulating blocks and cement.

Sedimentary Rocks That Once Were Alive.

PEAT, a rock covering 50 million acres in the U.S. and Canada, is described and illustrated on page 44.

LIGNITE OR BROWN COAL. This yellowish, brown or black rock contains from 55-75% carbon, and its thin slabs, split along the bedding, burn with a yellow flame of pungent odor and heavy smoke. Enormous deposits occur under the surface of the Great Plains, from the Yukon Territory to Texas.

BITUMINOUS OR SOFT COAL, the great industrial fuel, is illustrated and described on page 44.

CHANNEL COAL is a lusterless rock of great density, burning readily and brightly, but is quite rare now.

ANTHRACITE, the hard coal of the American East, is described and illustrated on page 45.

Metamorphic Rocks (i.e. rocks that now are different from what they had been originally, the change having been effected by heat, mineral-bearing water, or pressure).

GNEISS, the granite-like banded rock, is described and illustrated on page 45. SCHIST is the name for a group of rocks which have finer texture than gneiss, with thin parallel layers of crystalline sheets; mica schist is the most common metamorphic rock; others are hornblende schist, quartz schist and talc schist. SOAPSTONE, the cooking plate of the Indians, and SLATE, of our roofs and blackboards, are described and illustrated on page 46, MARBLE, the rock of columns and statues, and JADE, of the famous green carvings, on page 47.

Outline of the Principal Classes and Families of Trees in the U.S. and Canada

The Class Gymnosperms, i.e. plants which do not develop true flowers and have exposed or "naked" seeds, includes 3 families common in America:

THE GINKGO FAMILY. Ginkgoaceae. This native of China, with fan-shaped leaves and light-grey bark, is very ancient: There are a great many ginkgo fossils but there is only one living species. It is used as an ornamental tree in the U.S. and Canada, with the exception of the North Central States. Height: 120 feet.

THE YEWS. Taxaceae. The strong, elastic wood of the yews was once highly valued, both by the ancient peoples of Europe and the American Indians, for it made excellent bows. While the low-growing evergreen American yew of eastern Canada and the U.S. remains a shrub of approximately 5 feet in height, the Pacific yew grows into a tree of 50 feet and ranges from California and Montana to Alaska.

THE PINES. Pinaceae. In our modern civilization this is probably the most valuable family of trees, providing us with a large part of our paper pulp and about four-fifths of our lumber. Almost all members of the group are evergreen, i.e. they have needle-shaped or scaly leaves which are dropped as new leaves are grown. They are wind-pollinated and produce the well-known conifer cones, although in some species the cones are berry-like. The seeds are full of vitality, survive under all sorts of adverse conditions, and grow into a trunk of strong and workable wood at a relatively rapid rate. The family includes many well-known genera and species. Some of its important eastern members are described and illustrated in the color section on trees:

white pine and red pine on page 50; red spruce on page 52; Norway spruce on page 53; eastern hemlock on page 54; and Atlantic white cedar on page 57. Other eastern species are the pitch pine (with a strong pitch flow when limbs are broken), the Scotch pine (Europe's most common pine tree which has been acclimatized in this country and Canada), the Austrian pine (introduced here as early as 1759 and thriving in many parts of the country), and the eastern red cedar (with tiny evergreen leaves, dark blue berries and shreddy bark).

Of the southern group, the bald cypress (page 56) and the Atlantic white cedar (page 57) are described and illustrated. Other predominantly southern species include the loblolly pine (with a deep-furrowed, cinnamon-red bark, growing in wet lowlands called "loblollies"), the pond pine (one of the so-called hard pines, with long, thin needles), the Virginia pine (the same as Jersey pine, and growing as far west as Indiana), the shortleaf and the longleaf pines (two of the commercially most important species), and the slash pine (preferring damp "slashes" and producing resin of high quality).

Of the northern group tamarack (page 53), white spruce (page 52), and balsam fir (page 54) are described and illustrated. The jack pine is a "pioneering tree," often on sandy and rocky soil. Black spruce (a slender, tall tree with short branches) has about the same range as white spruce. Northern white cedar, also called arborvitae, extends far into the Canadian north.

Of the Rocky Mountain species ponderosa pine is described and illustrated on page 51, the Douglas fir on page 55. Others are the limber pine (the white pine of the high ridges), the whitebark pine (also a high mountain dweller and often distorted in shape by high winds), the bristlecone pine (either a bushy tree or a contorted shrub), the Jeffrey pine (a symmetrical tree growing to a height of 180 feet), the lodgepole pine (the most abundant evergreen of the northern Rockies), the Engelmann spruce (one of the most admired American conifers), the alpine fir (a slender, symmetrical spire), the white fir (with a whitish cast on its pale green foliage), the noble fir (a magnificent specimen of 200 feet), the Utah juniper (a bushy tree with irregular branches and whitish berries), the alligator juniper (with checkered bark), and the short, chunky sierra juniper.

Of the species occurring in the far West the Norway spruce is described and illustrated on page 53, the Douglas fir and the giant sequoia on page 55, and the redwood on page 56. Important others are the sugar pine (the most majestic pine, with a recorded height of 245 feet and cones of 20 inches), the ponderosa pine, the Coulter pine (with bunches of long, bluish-green needles), the digger pine (with a twisted trunk and broad crown), the introduced Austrian pine, the mountain hemlock (of the high ranges of the Pacific slope), the white fir (resting its massive limbs on the ground), the silver fir (with a trunk like a spire and glossy needles), the California incense cedar (of the western Coast Ranges, at altitudes from 4,000 to 8,000 feet), and the Monterey cypress (the gnarled, picturesque tree occurring only on Monterey Bay).

The western white pine is an important timber tree in the Northwest. Other outstanding northwestern species are the western larch (which sheds its needles in the fall), the Sitka spruce (occupying a narrow coastal belt from Alaska to northern California), the western hemlock (the largest hemlock, growing to a height of 250 feet), and the western cedar (one of the largest trees of the coast, reaching a diameter of 8 feet and an age of 1,000 years).

Of the conifers of the Southwest, the pinyon pine is described and illustrated on page 51. An important mountain tree of the Southwest is the Arizona cypress, encountered at altitudes from 4,500 to 8,000 feet.

The Class Angiosperms — **"Flowering Plants"** — includes all other families of American trees:

THE PALMS. Palmaceae. Of approximately 1,500 species of this largely tropical family about 15 species are native in the southern and western states, and approximately 200 species are reported as introduced. Palms are monocots, i.e. they possess a single seed-leaf or cotyledon. Their leaves have parallel veins, and their stem contains a system of tubes. Well-known are the palmettos of the Gulf States, the wind-blown coco palms of Florida, the date palms of the California desert, and the royal palms, also of Florida, one of the world's most majestic trees. The coco palm, probably the most useful member of the family, is described and illustrated on page 57.

THE WALNUTS AND HICKORIES. Juglandaceae. These trees, as well as all following tree families, are dicots, i.e. the seed contains two seed-leaves or cotyledons. The leaves are net-veined. The Walnut Family furnishes excellent hardwood and tasty nuts; the butternut and the black walnut are described and illustrated on page 58, the pecan and shagbark hickory trees on page 59. Other important species are the black hickory of Texas; the shellbark hickory of the Midwest; the mockernut of the East; the nutmeg and water hickories of the South; and the bitternut hickory of the East, with thin-walled, round, bitter fruits. Height 50-150 feet (walnuts); 30 to 160 feet (hickories).

THE WILLOWS. Salicaceae. This family comprises the willows, poplars, aspens, and cottonwoods. Because of their soft wood these trees were held in little esteem and, except for the manufacture of charcoal, excelsior and crates, were considered quite useless. But now many species are accepted as raw material for wood pulp and, because of their quick growth, have been successfully employed in erosion control. The quaking aspen and the eastern cottonwood are described and illustrated on page 60, and the black willow on page 61. Other species include the black cottonwood, the largest American poplar, of the western river bottoms; the bigtooth aspen of the Northeast; the swamp cottonwood of the Atlantic seacoast and the Mississippi Valley; the white poplar, a native of Europe; the balsam poplar of the North; the Lombardy poplar introduced from Italy; the coastal plain willow of the South; the peachleaf willow of the Midwest, the Great Plains and Canada; the shining willow of the northeastern U.S. and Canada; the ornamental golden willow; the celebrated weeping willow, a native of China; the pussy willow of the Northeast, with furry, white catkins; and the shrubby Bebb willow which occurs in most sections of the U.S. and in Canada. Height: 70 to 200 feet (poplars); 25 to 80 feet (willows); 70 feet (black willow).

THE BIRCH FAMILY. Betulaceae. Birches occur as far south as the Gulf States where the river birch is native. But they are at their best in the North, on both sides of the American-Canadian border. The paper birch, with the smooth, creamy-white bark, is described and illustrated on page 61. The sweet birch with dark brown bark occurs from the southern mountains to the Northeast, as does the yellow birch and the grey birch, the smallest member of the family. Also to this group belong the alders, and the filberts or hazelnuts. Height: 40 to 120 feet. Among other members of the Birch Family are the American hornbeam, a bushy tree of the East, and the hophornbeam, whose fruit resembles that of the hop vine, and whose wood has a horny texture. Height: 30 feet.

THE BEECHES, CHESTNUTS, OAKS. Fagaceae. While the official name of this group is "the Beech Family," it contains three genera of America's most magnificent forest trees. As their representatives the following species are described and illustrated: the American beech and the American chestnut on page 62, the northern red oak and the black oak on page 63, the live oak and white oak on page 64. The American beech is the only native North American species of beech, although the European beech has been introduced here. The only companions of the American chestnut are the chinquapins, small chestnuts of the Southeast. But the roster of American oaks is long; of the approximately 300 species that have been described, about 65 occur in the U.S. and Canada; all are recognized by their fruit, the acorn. Besides the illustrated members, several others are important: the stout post oak prefers the South; the overcup oak is a tree of wet grounds, as is the swamp white oak and the swamp chestnut oak; the range of the bur oak extends throughout much of the East to the edge of the Great Plains. On the west coast and the Pacific slope we encounter the tan oak, the canyon live oak, the California and Oregon white oak.

THE ELMS. Ulmaceae. A row of tall elms forming gothic arches over a farmhouse or a country road is a truly American sight. Hardly any other tree has been so closely identified with the "old" American landscape as the American elm, described and illustrated on page 65. Of the other species the slippery elm ranges over a similar territory, usually divided, a few feet above the ground, into a few large limbs. The rock elm is, on the whole, a northern tree while the winged elm prefers the South; the Siberian, Chinese and English elms have been successfully introduced. Height: 50 to 135 feet. The hackberry tree, with purple, cherry-like fruits, (100 feet), and the southern sugarberry tree (80 feet), also belong to this family.

THE MULBERRY FAMILY. Moraceae. While the red mulberry is a native of America (east and south), the white mulberry was introduced here from China for the feeding of silk worms. The paper mulberry is a native of Asia, and the common fig, of the Mediterranean region. Height: 30 to 70 feet.

THE MAGNOLIAS. Magnoliaceae. The romantic beauty of the South is closely linked with two trees, the live oaks, with their huge branches and their deep shade, and the magnolias with their shiny leaves and their frosty-white blossoms. The southern magnolia and its cousin, the equally magnificent tulip tree, are described and illustrated on pages 65 and 66. The sweetbay, the bigleaf magnolia and the Fraser magnolia are predominantly southern varieties; the cucumber tree is also a species of the Magnolia Family. Height: 40 to 100 feet.

THE CUSTARD APPLE FAMILY. Annonaceae. The best-known member of this family is the pawpaw, a shrub or small tree of the East and South with banana-like fruits. Height: 40 feet.

THE LAURELS. Lauraceae. Besides the aromatic sassafras tree, which is described and illustrated on page 66, this family includes the red bay of the South (height 70 to 80 feet), so-called because its wood is bright red, and the California laurel of the coastal mountains which attains a height of 175 feet. The mountain laurel belongs to the Heath Family.

THE WITCH-HAZEL FAMILY. Hamamelidaceae. A well-known representative of this group is the straight, symmetrical sweetgum which grows to a height of 120 feet. Its fruits appear in a ball-like mass. It occurs most frequently in the South, but also as far west as Texas. Witch-hazel is the shrub or small tree, about 25 feet tall, which gives this family its name; it is famous for its use in medicine and cosmetics.

THE PLANE TREES. Platanaceae. A native species of this family, the American sycamore, is described and illustrated on page 67. It is the largest tree, in diameter, of the eastern and central U.S., and reaches a height of 120 feet. The London plane, a relative of the sycamore, has been introduced here.

THE ROSE FAMILY. Rosaceae. This large family is a combination of small plants, shrubs and trees. Besides the roses, it includes the blackberry, raspberry, and strawberry. Among its trees, the mountains ashes are to be mentioned, and the wild fruit trees. The common pear and the quince are immigrants from Europe and Asia. The prairie crab apple, growing in dense thickets 25 to 30 feet high, occurs in the East, but especially in the Prairie States, and the southern crab apple thrives in a warmer climate. Others are the wild apple tree of European origin, which grows to a height of 40 feet, the wild black cherry of the East, the common chokecherry which occurs in the U.S. and Canada from the Atlantic to the Rockies; the pin cherry of the northern states and Canada; the chickasaw plum of the South; the Canada plum, encountered between the Atlantic and the Rockies; the apricot and the peach, both introduced from China via Europe. The extremely numerous hawthorns also belong to this family; more than 800 species have been recorded in this country alone; their identification is often difficult.

THE PEA FAMILY. Leguminosae. Besides the various species of peas, beans, lentils, peanuts, soybeans, alfalfas and clovers, this family also includes several trees: the honey locust (140 feet) is described and illustrated on page 67. The water locust (60 feet) occurs from Texas to Florida; the ornamental redbud (40 feet) is encountered from Connecticut to Texas. The Kentucky coffee tree (100 feet), the yellowwood (160 feet) the black locust (100 feet) and the clammy locust (40 feet) are at their best in the mountainous regions of the South.

THE RUE FAMILY. Rutaceae. The native species of this family are the common prickly ash of the North, a shrub or tree 25 feet high; the Hercules club of the South, reaching a height of 40 feet; and the common hop tree, 25 feet tall, whose fruits have been reported sometimes to replace hops in brewing. But this family also includes a group of introduced trees that have become tremendously important in the daily life of America: the various types of oranges, citrons, lemons, grapefruits, tangerines and kumquats.

THE MAHOGANY FAMILY. Meliaceae. The chinaberry is a representative which is widely known in America although its original home is Asia. Particularly the ornamental variety called umbrella chinaberry is a very common shade tree throughout the South and Texas. Height: 50 feet.

THE CASHEW FAMILY. Anacardiaceae. This family of shrubs and trees includes the common sumachs: staghorn sumach with its brownish-red fruits, bunched in panicles 6-9 inches long; the shining sumach; and the poison sumach which is highly toxic and grows in swamps. Height: 25 to 40 feet. Poison ivy also belongs to this family, just as the highly popular cashew and pistachio nuts.

THE HOLLY FAMILY. Aquifoliaceae. The American holly of Christmas fame is described and illustrated on page 68.

THE BITTERSWEET FAMILY. Celastraceae. Every fall thousands of American homes from the east and south to the prairies are decorated with bittersweet bouquets, consisting of the deeply lobed, bright, salmon-colored fruit. The common bittersweet is a climbing woody vine, the wahoo a shrub or small tree 6 to 12 feet high.

THE MAPLES. Aceraceae. Deeply rooted in the history of the American Indians and the pioneers, the maples still are closely linked with the American scene, especially in early spring at "sugaring time," and in their resplendent foliage of the fall. The sugar maple is described and illustrated on page 68. There are many other varieties: the striped maple of the Appalachian Mountains and the North; the small mountain maple of Canada, our northern states and the Appalachians; the southern Florida maple; the eastern silver maple, raising its crown 120 feet high; the common red maple; the bigleaf maple of the Pacific coast; the box elder whose various varieties spread throughout the U.S. and Canada from the Atlantic to the Great Plains; and the introduced Norway maple which is well acclimatized both in the East and the West. Height: 30 to 120 feet.

THE HORSE-CHESTNUTS AND BUCKEYES. Hippocastanaceae. The members of this family have hand-like compound leaves consisting of five or seven leaflets. The stately horse chestnut with its shiny brown mahogany seeds is a native of southern Asia; it is described and illustrated on page 69. The Midwestern Ohio buckeye has given Ohio the name of the Buckeye State; its leaves and seeds are poisonous to cattle. The yellow buckeye and the red buckeye have a more southerly range. Height: 35 to 100 feet.

THE SOAPBERRY FAMILY. Sapindaceae. This southwestern shrub-like tree produces yellow "soapberries" which hang on the branches all winter. Height: 45 feet.

THE BUCKTHORNS. Rhamnaceae. The Carolina buckthorn with dark yellow-green leaves occurs in the South. The cascara buckthorn is a western species. Height: 40 feet.

THE LINDENS. Tiliaceae. The tall American basswood or linden tree with its widely spreading branches and blossoms of basswood honey fame is described and illustrated on page 69. The white basswood occurs both in the Southeast and throughout the West. Also, the small-leaved European linden has been introduced here. Height: 90 to 125 feet.

THE CACTUS FAMILY. Cactaceae. This is an almost entirely American plant family with more than 1,000 species, many of them not yet named. Usually they grow without leaves, in the shape of thorny globes, cylinders, columns, or stems with flattened, joint-like divisions. The stem carries out the leaves' task of conserving the small quantities of water encountered in arid surroundings. While we normally associate the cactus with deserts and the Southwest, some species grow in the North, for instance in New England. Many cactus varieties have beautiful, delicate flowers and some grow edible fruits. Height: From small plants, not exceeding half an inch in diameter, to trees of 50 feet. The saguaro cactus is described and illustrated on page 70.

THE LOOSESTRIFE FAMILY. Lythraceae. The common crape myrtle, a native of China, is a small tree or shrub widely planted in the South Atlantic and Gulf States because of its profusion of large pink flowers. Height: 25 feet.

THE MYRTLE FAMILY. Myrtaceae. All members of this family have oil glands in their leaves. The group includes two interesting trees: the tall eucalyptus tree which in its various species has been successfully introduced from Australia to California; it grows fast and furnishes both eucalyptus oil and excellent timber; and the small guava tree of southern Florida and California whose pear-shaped fruits make the delicious, spicy guava jam or preserve.

THE GINSENG FAMILY. Araliaceae. The shrublike, thorny devil's walkingstick occurs in the East and South. Its berries and the bark of its roots were used for medical purposes. Height: 30 feet.

THE DOGWOODS. Cornaceae. The very attractive flowering dogwood is described and illustrated on page 70. The alternate leaf dogwood with cream-colored blossoms occurs from Canada to the middle South, while the roughleaf dogwood extends to the Gulf States and central Florida. The Pacific dogwood with small, greenish-yellow flowers, associated with 4 to 6 large, showy, white or pinkish bracts, is a western species; it is similar to the flowering dogwood of the East and attains a height of 30 to 50 feet. Also, the southern black tupelo and the water tupelo belong to this family.

THE HEATH FAMILY. Ericaceae. This is largely a family of shrubs with leathery leaves, including the laurels, rhododendrons, azaleas, cranberries, blueberries, huckleberries and wintergreen. However, some of these shrubs occasionally attain the status of trees, i.e. the mountain laurel (40 feet), the rosebay rhododendron (40 feet), and the southern sparkleberry (30 feet); the sourwood (60 feet) and the Pacific madrone (125 feet) are always trees.

THE SAPODILLA FAMILY. Sapotaceae. The gum bumelia is a shrub or tree with black berries which occurs both in the South and Southwest. Height: 60 feet.

THE EBONY FAMILY. Ebenaceae. The outstanding American species of this family, the common persimmon, is described and illustrated on page 71.

THE SNOWBALL FAMILY. Styracaceae. The Carolina silverbell is so-called because of its white, bell-shaped flowers. Height: 40 feet.

THE OLIVE FAMILY. Oleaceae. No olive trees are native to America, but the important ash belongs to this family. The white ash is described and illustrated on page 71; other species are the pumpkin ash of the East and South, the smaller Texas ash; the red ash which occurs over most of the eastern half of the U.S. and Canada and thrives on the Appalachian Mountains; the green ash of approximately the same range; the black ash of the northern states and Canada; the blue ash of the Midwest; the Carolina ash of the South Atlantic and Gulf States, and the Oregon ash of the west coast. Height: 60 to 120 feet. The fringetree (30 feet) with fringe-like, drooping, white flowers and the privet are also members of this family; among the bushes of the olive family are the lilacs and jasmines.

THE BIGNONIA FAMILY. Bignoniaceae. The northern and the southern catalpa trees belong to this family. They are popular shade trees, and their wood is valued for fence posts, because of its resistance to decay. Height: 60 feet.

THE MADDER FAMILY. Rubiaceae. The common buttonbush with its red-brown fruit balls is encountered throughout the U.S., with the exception of the Northwest. Height: 50 feet. The gardenias and the tropical and subtropical coffee tree belong to the Madder Family, also the cinchona tree, from whose bark quinine is extracted.

OUTLINE OF THE MAJOR FAMILIES OF WILDFLOWERS IN THE U.S. AND SOUTHERN CANADA

All wildflower families belong to the class Angiosperms—"Flowering Plants".

THE CAT-TAILS. Typhaceae. Indians and early settlers alike prized highly these perennials of the marshes (4 to 8 feet tall) which were a double blessing: their starchy rootstocks furnished food, and their narrow leaves, shaped like swords, were ideal for making rush chair seats or plaiting mats. Even today these plants are useful: Their masses of chocolate-brown flowers form a dense spike, an almost perfect cylinder, the down of which is used as insulation material. The range of the broad-leaved cat-tail includes the temperate U.S. and Canada.

The Water Plantain Family. Alismaceae. This is another group of shallow water perennials. Their most outstanding members are the arrowheads, so called because of their arrow-shaped leaves. The beautiful broad-leaved arrowhead is described and illustrated on page 74.

The Arum Family. Araceae. The best-known representatives of this large, mostly tropical family are the skunk cabbage of our swamps, with the heart-shaped, cabbage-like leaves and the odor suggestive of skunk or garlic, and the jack-in-the-pulpit, the familiar spring flower of rich, moist woods. Both plants occur in the Canadian and American East.

The Spiderworts. Commelinaceae. The few American species of this large family include the ephemeral blue day flowers which bloom only for one sunny morning or one cloudy day, and the blue to rose spiderworts to which a common house plant belongs: the wandering Jew or inch plant. All thrive in moist soil.

The Pineapple Family. Bromeliaceae. A famous American species of this family is the Spanish moss or tillandsia whose grey-green festoons adorn many southern trees. However, Spanish moss is not a parasite, it just chooses the branches as its habitat; it lives on the dust and humidity in the air. It is not a moss either but a flowering plant.

The Pickerel Weeds. Pontederiaceae. These herbs live in or on shallow fresh water bodies. The widely distributed pickerel weed is described and illustrated on page 74. Another famous species is the spectacular purple-blue water hyacinth which blossoms in ponds and streams from Georgia to Florida and Texas.

The Lilies. Liliaceae. Among the members of this large family of more than 2,000 species are such beautiful garden varieties as the tulip, the hyacinth, the lily-of-the-valley, and the garden lilies, and such delicious vegetables as the onion, leek and asparagus. The wild members of the lily family are perennials which develop from bulbs or fleshy rootstocks and grow parallel-veined leaves. As their representatives, the Solomon's seal and the adder's-tongue are described and illustrated on page 75, and the ruby lily on page 76. Other interesting species are the western desert lily with fragrant, white flowers like an Easter lily; the wild onion (east of the Rockies), and the wild garlic (East and South); the deep-red prairie lily, the emblem of the province of Saskatchewan; the lovely yuccas, shrubby plants from which tall stems of large, white, bell-shaped flowers arise; and the waxy-white, large-flowered trillium.

The Amaryllis Family. Amaryllidaceae. Such celebrated spring flowers as the snowdrop, the daffodil and the poet's narcissus belong to this family of perennial herbs.

The Iris Family. Iridaceae. Decorative garden plants like the crocus, the gladiolus and the various varieties of iris are among these perennial herbs which grow from rootstocks, or corms.

The Orchids. Orchidaceae. With over 17,000 members this is probably the word's largest flower family; but only about 140 species occur in America, from Newfoundland and Manitoba southward to Florida. The most spectacular orchids grow in the Tropics, some of them airplants attached to the branches of tall forest trees. The seed pods of two of the climbing orchids furnish our natural vanilla. The orchids of the temperate U.S. and Canada are less conspicuous but well-known; they include the yellow, white and purple fringed orchis, the various pink and purple pogonias, the pink arethusa, the white-yellowish ladies' tresses, and the pink lady's slipper which is the state flower of Minnesota and is described and illustrated on page 76.

The Buckwheat Family. Polygonaceae. The name buckwheat is a translation of the German Buchweizen, meaning beech wheat; for the three-sided fruits look like beechnuts. The family includes, besides buckwheat and rhubarb, the numerous erigonums of the West, one of which, the so-called butter balls, is described and illustrated on page 77. Another member is the sheep sorrel whose greenish or reddish flowers are a common summer sight everywhere except in the far North. The familiar and often noxious knotweeds are described and illustrated on page 77.

The Goosefoot Family. Chenopodiaceae. These annual or perennial herbs with small, inconspicuous flowers include among their members the two garden vegetables, beets and spinach.

The Amaranth Family. Amaranthaceae. The spectacular, many-colored cockscombs of our gardens and the tumble-weed, famed in song, are members of this family which largely consists of obnoxious weeds.

The Pokeweeds. Phytolaccaceae. The most common representative of this group is the pokeweed or pokeberry, a stout, branched, country-wide perennial 4 to 12 feet tall. The flower is white, the berries are dark purple and inflict nausea, and the root is poisonous. Root and berry extracts are used in medicines.

Four-O'Clock Family. Nyctaginaceae. Some members of this largely western family open their blossoms during the afternoon, like the bright pink western four o'clock. The popular sand-verbena and the showy bougainvillea which flourishes in Florida belong to this group.

THE PINK FAMILY. Caryophyllaceae. Although enough species of this family bear pink blossoms to justify the name, it is the pinked margin of the flower petals that is the name's source, "pinked" meaning scalloped or toothed as in dressmaking. Several fine garden flowers are members of the family, i.e. the various carnations, sweet william and baby's breath. But many more wild species are included, among them the brilliant red Indian pink of the Northwest and the common or scarlet fire pink of the East and South. The Indian pink is described and illustrated on page 78.

THE PURSLANE FAMILY. Portulacaceae. Purslane is a weed of such vitality that its seeds will germinate and grow after a lapse of many years. It thrives throughout America except in the far North. The saying "mean as pussley" reflects the disrepute in which purslane, commonly called pussley, is held. Other more popular members of the family are the white or pink spring beauty and the familiar portulaca of our gardens.

THE WATER-LILIES. Nymphaeaceae. The celebrated lotus of Egypt and the fragrant white water-lily are the best-known members of this small aquatic family whose plants have thick horizontal submerged rootstocks. The American lotus, also called great yellow water-lily, and the yellow pond-lily occur east of the Rockies. The water-lily is described and illustrated on page 78.

THE CROWFOOT FAMILY. Ranunculaceae. The annual and perennial species of the Crowfoot Family include many well-known groups of wild and garden flowers. The marsh marigold or American cowslip, an attractive golden-yellow blossom, has been over-picked (for its leaves make a fine spring salad). The black snakeroot, also called rattlesnake weed, has a white, fetid blossom sought by carrion flies. Also the lovely and colorful columbines belong to this family, both the wild and the garden varieties; their name is based on the Latin columba, "dove", and fancifully imagines the blossom to look like a group of doves sitting around a fountain; about 23 species occur in North America. The wild columbine is described and illustrated on page 79. The bright and graceful blue larkspurs are common western wildflowers although, of course, they grace our gardens anywhere in the temperate U.S. and Canada. Other garden species are the peony, clematis and the Christmas rose. The perennial monkshoods, blue or white nodding flowers of meadows and woods, have thick roots from which a narcotic poison is extracted. Of the delicate white or purplish anemones approximately 20 species occur in the U.S. and Canada as far north as the subarctic. The name of this genus means "shaken by the wind", a proper characterization for these delicate flowers. The pale blue, violet, pinkish or white hepaticas have supposedly medicinal properties; their three-lobed leaves resemble the liver and were thought to be curative in diseases of the liver; they were also called liverworts. Of the very common buttercups or crowfoots the tall buttercup is described and illustrated on page 79. The meadow-rues grow to a height of 10 feet, have beautiful foliage and terminate in panicles of white or purplish flowers.

THE BARBERRY FAMILY. Berberidaceae. Besides the familiar barberry bushes of our hedges, the white-flowered may apple or wild mandrake is a member of this family; it forms dense thickets in our woodlands.

THE POPPIES. Papaveraceae. This celebrated family consists of plants with milky or colored sap which is acrid or bitter; in some instances it is narcotic, as in the case of the opium poppy which, however, is a native of Asia. The best-known representatives of this group are the California poppy and the thistle poppy which are described and illustrated on page 80. The European poppy is cultivated here, and since World War I is also called Flanders poppy.

THE FUMITORY FAMILY. Fumariaceae. This small family of delicate plants with finely dissected leaves includes the creamy-white dutchman's breeches and the beloved white and red bleeding heart.

THE MUSTARD FAMILY. Cruciferae. Some very annoying and some extremely useful plants live side by side as members of this extensive family. It includes several noxious weeds like the various wild mustards and shepherd's purse, but also many lovely flowers like sweet rocket, sweet alyssum and wallflower. It contributes most heavily to our common vegetables; among its members are mustard, water cress, radish, turnip, horseradish, broccoli, brussels sprouts, cauliflower, cabbage and kale.

THE PITCHER PLANT FAMILY. Sarraceniaceae. "Meat-eating" seems a strange adjective for a plant, yet it appears that the 9 or 10 species of this entirely American family receive at least part of their nourishment from insects that fall into their pitcher or trumpet-like leaves and decay in the pool of water inside. 8 species of these swamp plants are natives of the southeastern and eastern U.S. and Canada.

THE SUNDEW FAMILY. Droseraceae. The members of this bog-loving family are insect-catchers. Their leaves bear reddish bristles which shine with a clear, viscid substance. They lure and catch insects and gradually digest the body juices of their prey. The Venus's flytrap of the savannas of North and South Carolina is a famous species.

THE SAXIFRAGE FAMILY. Saxifragaceae. Saxifrage, "rock breaker", is a rather grandiose name for a family of mostly small herbs; it refers to those species which frequently grow in crannies of rocks. Besides the various wild saxifrages and alum roots which are distributed throughout the U.S. and Canada, the family includes the mock orange, hydrangea, currant and gooseberry.

THE ROSES. Rosaceae. This family is described in the section on trees, page 214.

THE PEA FAMILY. Leguminosae. This third largest plant family has been described under trees on page 214, as far as its tree members are concerned. The vegetables belonging to the group have also been mentioned. Among its herbaceous plants are numerous well-known species, most of them bearing winged, butterfly-like blossoms. Of the beautiful lupines which thrive in abundance in our western states, the blue lupine is described and illustrated on page 81. The blue bonnet of Texas fame, the official flower of the Lone Star State, is also a lupine. The clovers, of which about 75 species are found in the U.S. and Canada, are an excellent forage crop and a soil-building fertilizer. As a representative, the red clover is described and illustrated on page 81. Among the milk vetches the loco-weeds are to be mentioned; on western pastures they prove injurious to sheep, cattle and horses and turn them "loco", i.e. crazy. The true vetches are trailing herbs, about 25 species occurring in the U.S. and Canada. The common vetch is described and illustrated on page 82.

THE FLAX FAMILY. Linaceae. Flax has been raised since prehistoric times, as the raw material of linen and for the oil extracted from its seed. Several species are native in the U.S. and Canada, and the important common flax, cultivated in the Dakotas, Minnesota and Canada, thrives as an escaped herb along highways, railroads, country lanes and waste places almost anywhere in North America.

THE WOOD SORRELS. Oxalidaceae. These annual or perennial herbs contain oxalic acid which gives them a typical sour taste. The white, violet and yellow wood sorrels occur widely east of the Rockies. The yellow species is described and illustrated on page 82.

THE GERANIUMS. Geraniaceae. Approximately 75 species of herbs belonging to this family, among them the cultivated geraniums, are distributed over most of the U.S. and Canada. The wild geranium, a magenta-pink or purple flower, is described and illustrated on page 83.

THE MILKWORTS. Polygalaceae. The milkworts, widely distributed weeds of which some 50 species grow in North America, superficially resemble the pea family as to their flowers; however, in contrast to the simple milkwort leaves the plants of the pea family usually have compound leaves. Some species bear interesting subterranean flowers. The field milkwort, with globular or oblong clusters of magenta or white flowers, is common in fields and along roadsides.

THE SPURGE FAMILY. Euphorbiaceae. The members of this family produce a milky sap which, in several species, is the raw material of rubber; one is the useful castor oil plant. Some members have brightly colored leaves, like the poinsettia, the Christmas flower. Other ornamental garden plants are the crown-of-thorns and the snow-on-the-mountain.

THE JEWELWEEDS. Balsaminaceae. The balsam or touch-me-not is a well-known member of this family. It bears both jewel-like, pale yellow, hanging blossoms and ripe green fruits which pop open when touched. It occurs east of the Rockies.

THE MALLOWS. Malvaceae. This family of herbs and shrubs includes a plant of great commercial importance: cotton. The root of the marshmallow is used both by the pharmaceutical and the candy industries. Also such popular garden plants as hollyhocks, mallows, and hibiscus belong to this group. The rose mallow is described and illustrated on page 83.

THE ST. JOHN'S-WORT FAMILY. Hypericaceae. This small family has a long Old-World history: Its members bloom around St. John's Day, and in ancient tales were used for black magic. St. Andrew's cross is a lemon-yellow eastern flower.

THE VIOLETS. Violaceae. As a representative of this celebrated family the prairie violet is described and illustrated on page 84.

THE CACTUS FAMILY. Cactaceae. This desert-loving family is described in the section on trees on page 215.

THE MEADOW BEAUTIES. Melastomaceae. These showy, delicate, four-petaled flowers, ranging in color from white to purple, are natives of the eastern and southern states.

THE EVENING PRIMROSE FAMILY. Onagraceae. Of this abundant family the common evening primrose and the fireweed are described and illustrated on pages 84 and 85.

THE GINSENG FAMILY. Araliaceae. Fragrant foliage, roots and berries are characteristics of many species of this medicinally important family. It includes bristly sarsaparilla and two species of ginseng plants whose roots are valued as medicines in the Far East. See also section on trees, page 215.

THE PARSLEY FAMILY. Umbelliferae. Some members of this interesting family are valuable food plants, like celery, carrot and parsley; others are poisonous pests. As a representative, Queen Anne's lace is described and illustrated on page 85.

DOGWOOD FAMILY. Cornaceae. This family is described in the section on trees on page 215. A well-known herbaceous member is the bunchberry whose showy white bracts and "bunches" on bright-red berries are a common sight in American and Canadian woodlands.

THE HEATH FAMILY. Ericaceae. This family is discussed in the section on trees on page 215. Among its ground-loving members is the highly-prized trailing arbutus which is described and illustrated on page 86.

THE LOGANIA FAMILY. Loganiaceae. The outstanding

species of this family is the yellow jessamine or jasmine whose fragrant, funnel-like flowers are beloved in our southern states; the plant, the state flower of South Carolina, is an evergreen vine growing to a length of 20 feet. From the seeds of one species the poison strychnine is extracted.

THE GENTIANS. Gentianaceae. One of the most common members of this widely distributed family of colorful flowers, the bottle gentian, is described and illustrated on page 86.

THE DOGBANE FAMILY. Apocynaceae. While many species of this family contain strong poisons, others grow nutritious fruits, or are popular because of their fragrance, like the star and the crape jasmines. Perhaps the most famous member is the maile of Hawaii, the scented blossom of the charming wreaths of welcome called "leis". The shrub oleander also belongs to this group. The most common species in the U.S. and Canada is the spreading dogbane, also called bitterroot or milk ipecac. Its flowers, somewhat similar to those of the lily-of-the-valley, are pink on the outside and white-striped on the inside.

THE MILKWEEDS. *Asclepiadaceae*. As a representative of this family which contains many plants with medicinal properties, the common milkweed is described and illustrated on page 87.

THE MORNING GLORIES. Convolvulaceae. The common morning glory, a trailing vine with spectacular flowers of various hues, is described and illustrated on page 87.

THE PHLOX FAMILY. Polemoniaceae. While some species of phlox occur in the eastern half of the U.S. and Canada, the brightly colored gilias thrive mainly in the western deserts and mountains. The scarlet gilia is described and illustrated on page 88.

THE WATERLEAF FAMILY. Hydrophyllaceae. These perennial or biennial herbs are mostly natives of our West. They include such picturesquely named flowers as baby blue-eyes, California bluebells and the yellow whispering bells. Their leaves were formerly believed to contain water cavities, hence the name waterleaf.

THE BORAGE FAMILY. Boraginaceae. The annual, biennial or perennial members of this large family are quite versatile: Some are used for medicinal purposes; from the roots of others a dye is extracted; several are popular because of their lovely blossoms, like the Indian heliotrope and the forget-me-not. The Virginia cowslip or bluebell is described and illustrated on page 88.

THE VERVAINS. Verbenaceae. The best-known genus of this family is that of the verbenas whose approximately 100 species are all natives of the Americas, some 20 occuring in the U.S. Their blossoms are white, violet, purple, lilac, or reddish. The garden hybrids of the verbenas are common in the U.S. and Canada.

THE MINTS. Labiatae. Such names as sweet lavender, peppermint, spearmint, sage, thyme, rosemary, sweet marjoram and sweet basil conjure the illusion of fragrant perfume, pleasant candy and spicy cooking. All these plants have the characteristics of the mint family: the normally squared stems and the fragrant leaf glands which contain the various volatile, aromatic oils. Their flowers are generally small and two-lipped, and offer nectar for bees. The scented American pennyroyal and the catnip, used as a nerve tonic, also belong to this family.

THE NIGHTSHADE OR POTATO FAMILY. Solanaceae. Economically, this is one of the most important plant families on earth, for it includes such herbs, vines and shrubs as the potato, tomato, red pepper, and tobacco, also decorative plants such as the Chinese lantern and the petunia. Their fruits are true berries (sometimes capsules), often poisonous and narcotic; in other cases they are edible. Usually the leaves have an unpleasant odor.

THE FIGWORTS. Scrophulariaceae. Such well-known flowers as the Indian paintbrush and turtle head, monkey flower and mullein, snapdragon and foxglove are members of this family. The lovely penstemons, ranging in color from blue, lavender and purple to red, yellow and white, are typical Rocky Mountain plants, although there are also species in the East and South. The mullein and the false foxglove are described and illustrated on page 89, and the Indian paintbrush on page 90.

THE PLANTAINS. Plantaginaceae. The common plantain is one of the most familiar weeds in the U.S. and Canada, except in the far North. Its slender stalk topped by a spike of greenish flowers, 3 to 12 inches long, is a common sight at roadsides and waste places.

THE MADDER FAMILY. Rubiaceae. This group is also mentioned in the section on trees on page 215. Smaller members of the family are wild madder and wild licorice (both east of the Rockies in the U.S. and Canada), the widely distributed bedstraws, and the handsome partridge berry which is described and illustrated on page 90.

THE HONEYSUCKLES. Caprifoliaceae. These fragrant, beautiful plants are mostly natives of the northern hemisphere. They include such popular wild and garden varieties as the scented honeysuckle vine, bush honeysuckle, snowberry, elderberry and viburnum. They occur throughout the country.

THE VALERIAN FAMILY. Valerianaceae. Of the herbs and shrubs of this small family the common valerian, also called garden heliotrope, is grown as a decorative flower in gardens (where its scent is said to attract cats), or raised commercially for its medicinally valuable root sap.

THE TEASEL FAMILY. Dipsacaceae. Several ornamental members of this Old-World family have acclimatized themselves very well in American gardens, especially the scabiosas. Fuller's teasel used to be cultivated for its elastic bracts which were employed in the woolen industry to raise the nap on woolen material.

THE BELLFLOWERS. Campanulaceae. The graceful bell-shaped blossoms of this family are usually blue. The blue bell of Scotland is described and illustrated on page 91.

THE LOBELIA FAMILY. Lobeliaceae. The plants of this group resemble those of the Bellflower Family, except that their blossoms are irregular. The lovely, brilliantly red cardinal flower is described and illustrated on page 91.

THE COMPOSITE FAMILY. Compositae. More than 13,000 species, distributed all over the earth, form this famous family which represents the highest point in plant development, in the opinion of botanists. In the U.S. and Canada its members are largely perennial herbs; generally, they have numerous small flowers or florets (as many as 200 in a dandelion) in a compact flower head sitting on the receptacle, i.e. the broadened end of the flower stem. Most of them have a single pistil and 5 stamens; their anthers form a tube around the pistil. Their one-seeded fruits are disseminated by various methods: Some grow barbs and attach themselves to animal pelts, bird feathers, or the clothes of human beings; others have delicate, bristly hairs and are blown overland by the winds. The following representatives of this family are described and illustrated in the color section on wildflowers: tall ironweed and Joe-Pye-weed on page 92, New England aster and plume goldenrod on page 93, black-eyed susan and common sunflower on page 94, yarrow and daisy on page 95, common thistle and dandelion on page 96, chicory and orange hawkweed on page 97.

THE GRASS FAMILY. Poaceae. Finally this family should be mentioned here although it does not include any wildflowers; its blossoms have no petals and therefore are inconspicuous. It is the world's most important plant family, embracing not only the myriads of different grasses that cover our lawns and pastures, but also bamboo, corn, oats, rice, sorghum, sugar cane, and wheat.

Outline of the Principal Orders and Families of Birds in the U.S. and Southern Canada

The Order Gaviiformes — Loons — consists of one family:

THE LOONS. Gaviidae. The weird, laughing calls of these large water birds are symbols of our lonely, northern lakes. Six species inhabit the continent, mostly the northern parts, although the Pacific loon occurs as far south as Lower California. The common loon is described and illustrated on page 100.

The Order Colymbiformes — Grebes — consists of one family:

THE GREBES. Colymbidae. Sometimes a nest with eggs can be observed on an island of vegetation floating on a lake. It probably belongs to one of the grebes which occasionally select such a strange location as the birthplace of their young. The water birds resemble ducks but have a less striking plumage. Six species in Canada and the U.S. Length: 7 to 26 inches.

The Order Procellariiformes — Tube-nosed Swimmers — consists of 3 families:

THE ALBATROSSES. Diomedeidae. A wingspread up to 12 feet and a 9 inch width of wing seems an unbalanced combination of measurements, yet it enables the albatross to soar on the winds of the southern oceans for weeks. Coming from their breeding grounds on lonely islands, 4 species are occasionally reported on the waters of North American coasts. They are among the world's largest flying birds. Length: 32 to 36 inches.

THE SHEARWATERS, FULMARS, AND PETRELS. Procellariidae. In sailing ship days birds of this family were burned as torches, for their oily bodies are often storehouses of fat. They are typical inhabitants of the shore and, unlike the gulls, do not fly inland. Usually they are mistaken for gulls, but are lighter and more elegant in flight. 21 species are encountered on American and Canadian coasts during the summer; they breed on the islands of the southern oceans. Length: 6 to 20 inches.

THE STORMY PETRELS. Hydrobatidae. This graceful water bird seems to walk over the waves, as Saint Peter is reported to have done; therefore it is called Petrel, a diminutive form of Peter. Another name for one species of these common black and white sea birds is Mother Carey's chickens. Length: 5½ inches.

The Order Pelecaniformes — Totipalmate Swimmers — consists of 6 families:

THE TROPIC BIRDS. Phaethontidae. Phaeton (from whom this family name is derived) was the high-soaring son of the sun god Apollo. These high-soaring, long-tailed, whitish birds occur in 3 species and belong to the North American ocean fauna, although they do not reach our shores proper. Length: 30 inches.

THE PELICANS. Pelecanidae. Pelicans are fascinating birds: With huge bodies measuring from 4 to 6 feet, they are grotesquely awkward on land, but are fully at home on the water. A gregarious family, they breed in huge rookeries, building their clumsy nests on the ground. The 3 American species inhabit both the southern Atlantic and the Pacific coasts; the white pelican occurs as far inland as Yellowstone Park. The eastern brown pelican is described and illustrated on page 100.

THE BOOBIES AND GANNETS. Sulidae. Heavy and goose-like, these fishermen are strictly ocean birds; however, they remain near the coast, gorging themselves on mackerel and other fish. 7 species live on the Atlantic and Pacific shores of the U.S. and Canada. Length: 27 to 35 inches.

THE CORMORANTS. Phalacrocoracidae. These cousins of the pelicans do not plunge into the waves but pursue their game fishes under water. When sitting they clasp their flexible, rubber-like feet tightly around their perch. 10 species of these dark-colored, big birds, which grow to a length of 30 inches, are known in Canada and the U.S., living both on the coasts and on some inland freshwater lakes.

THE DARTERS. Anhingidae. Snake bird, water turkey and anhinga are other names for these swamp birds. One species occurs in the deep South of the U.S. Length: 34 inches.

THE MAN-O-WAR BIRDS. Fregatidae. Off the Florida coast one species of this graceful, mainly black ocean bird is encountered. Length: 40 inches.

The Order Ciconiiformes — Herons and allies — consists of 4 families:

THE HERONS AND BITTERNS. Ardeidae. Thoreau once found a live turtle with its intestines ripped out through the rear hole in its shell; he discovered a bittern to be the surgeon of this gruesome operation and concluded that the innards of turtles were the bitterns' favorite dish. Both groups of these long-billed and long-necked swamp birds are solitary in their hunting and fishing habits; during nesting time, however, many species become gregarious and congregate in big settlements. About 24 species are widely distributed in the U.S. and Canada. The great white heron and Ward's heron are the largest, reaching a length of 50 to 52 inches. The great blue heron and the American egret are described and illustrated on page 101.

THE STORKS AND WOOD IBISES. Ciconiidae. According to legend and fact the stork is an Old World bird, and several attempts to introduce it into America have failed. Only one species of the stork family, the white and black wood ibis, is native to this country and nests in huge colonies in Florida. Length: 40 inches.

THE IBISES AND SPOONBILLS. Threskiornithidae. "Father of the Sickle" was the Egyptian name for the ibis, because of its long sickle-like bill. On the American continent 3 species and 1 subspecies occur in the southern states. One species of the spoonbills, the roseate spoonbill which swings its beak back and forth just under the surface of the water to catch its prey, is reported in the Gulf States. Length: 24 to 40 inches (ibises); 32 inches (spoonbill).

THE FLAMINGOES. Phoenicopteridae. Throughout the world these birds are celebrated for their vermillion and black plumage, their exceedingly long necks and legs, and their red bills with black, flattened and decurved tips. One species occurs sparingly on the southernmost tip of Florida. Length: 60 inches.

The Order Anseriformes — Swans and allies — consists of one family:

THE SWANS, GEESE, AND DUCKS. Anatidae. The members of this family used to live here by the millions, but their numbers have dwindled because of over-hunting, draining of marshes and clearing of lands. Now only restrictive laws and bird refuges keep them from extinction. Even swans were numerous in pioneer days, and trumpeter swans, great white birds with voices as loud as a clarion, sailed over American skies in huge V-shaped flocks. They are now in danger of extinction, a few wild specimens surviving in British Columbia and the Yellowstone Park region. 50 species representing 75 kinds of the Anatidae Family are encountered in the U.S. and Canada. Length: 55 to 65 inches (swans); 25½ to 45 inches (geese); 14 to 22 inches (ducks). The Canada goose and the common mallard are described and illustrated on page 102; the black duck on page 103.

Other well-known members of the family Anatidae which can be observed in our wildlife refuges are the whistling swan, a large white bird (55 inches) with black bill and feet and a high, shrill call; the blue goose which summers near Hudson Bay and winters on the Gulf of Mexico; the cackling goose which is similar to the Canada goose but smaller; the various species of the arctic snow goose; the white-fronted goose which is also arctic; the American brant, the smallest of our wild geese, and the black brant with a black neck and breast; the baldpate, a brown-black-white duck; the canvas-back, a duck with a handsome chestnut-brown head; the gadwall, a finely mottled brown freshwater duck whose meat is prized by gourmets; the mottled duck which resembles the black duck but has mottled under-parts; the New Mexico duck which resembles the mallard; the pintail, a neat and trim duck with elongated, black tail feathers, the "greyhound among water fowl;" the ruddy duck, a toy-like, little duck with reddish-brown upper parts; the ring-necked duck with a narrow chestnut-brown collar around the black neck; the various species of scaups, ducks which "scaup" rather than "quack;" the brown-green shoveller duck; the blue-winged teal, a duck with large white crescents on its cheeks; and the beautiful wood duck with its plumage of bright, iridescent colors.

The Order Falconiformes — Birds of Prey — consists of 3 families:

THE VULTURES. Cathartidae. The Greek word kathartes, from which this family name is derived, means cleanser. It adequately describes the function of these carrion eaters. 3 species occur in the U.S., south of the Connecticut line. They include the very rare California condor whose wingspread of about 10 feet is exceeded only by that of the wandering albatross. Length: 24 inches (black vulture); 30 inches (turkey vulture); 50 inches (condor). The turkey vulture is described and illustrated on page 103.

THE KITES, HAWKS, AND EAGLES. Accipitridae. We are thoroughly informed about the food eaten by this family to which the kites, hawks, eagles, goshawks and ospreys belong. After they have struck their prey with their stout and powerful feet, have torn it to pieces with their strongly hooked beaks, and swallowed it in large chunks, they eject the indigestible parts, like bones and fur, through the mouth in the form of compact pellets. An examination of the pellets discloses the birds' diet. Other characteristics are their unsurpassed vision, their harsh and piercing voices, their curved and sharp talons, their broad wings. For centuries they have been roughly persecuted, and only today they are recognized as truly useful helpers to the sportsman and farmer. 35 species and subspecies occur throughout the U.S. and Canada. Length: 15 to 22½ inches (kites); 10 to 23½ inches (hawks); 32½ to 43½ inches (eagles); the red-tailed hawk and the osprey are described and illustrated on page 104, the bald eagle on page 105.

THE FALCONS. Falconidae. Fearless, fierce and swift, they are the hunters in the ancient sport of falconry. They proceed through the air with rapid wing strokes, in contrast to the hawks which like to soar. 20 species are distributed all over the continent from the Arctic to the Tropics. Length: 15 to 17½ inches.

The Order Galliformes — Gallinaceous Birds — consists of 5 families:

THE CURASSOWS AND GUANS. Cracidae. Crested heads and scratching feet distinguish these large, hen-like birds. One species, the chachalaca, is an inhabitant of the lower Rio Grande region of Texas. Length 21¾ inches.

THE GROUSES AND PTARMIGANS. Tetraonidae. These terrestrial dwellers of the woods build their nests on the ground and, when startled, dart into the air with great speed. Their short bills have a rounded upper edge, and the hind toe on their stout legs is raised above the ground. Their young are born with heavy down of protective coloration. Ptarmigans are the arctic version of the grouse; one species, the northern white-tailed ptarmigan, has a wide range: It extends from British Columbia and Alberta southward along the Rocky Mountains to New Mexico. A pure-white mountain species, quite common in Glacier National Park, is practically invisible in the snow. 46 species of the Tetraonidae live in the cooler parts of the continent. Length: 17 to 21½ inches (grouses); 13 to 15 inches (ptarmigans). The ruffed grouse is described and illustrated on page 105.

THE PARTRIDGES AND QUAILS. Perdicidae. The European partridge is probably the most prominent member of this family. It has been successfully introduced into New York, Pennsylvania, some prairie states, Minnesota and southern Canada. The other 18 American and Canadian members include 5 species of bob-whites. Length: 12½ inches (partridges); 9½ to 11 inches (quails); 8½ to 10 inches (bob-whites). The eastern bob-white is described and illustrated on page 106.

THE PHEASANTS. Phasianidae. The spectacular ring-necked pheasant, an introduced species, is described and illustrated on page 106.

THE TURKEYS. Meleagrididae. Flocks of these spendid birds, some of them attaining a weight of 40 pounds, were common all over the East in pioneer days. They were particularly frequent in Massachusetts and occurred as far north as Ontario. Today their range is restricted from Pennsylvania southward to Florida and Texas, and westward to Oklahoma. Their characteristics are similar to those of the domestic turkey. Length: 49 inches.

The Order Gruiformes — Cranes and allies — consists of 3 families:

THE CRANES. Gruidae. While herons in flight pull their necks into the shape of an S, cranes extend their heads straight forward. Otherwise they resemble the herons with their long legs, necks, and bills. 2 species with 4 members occur in the U.S. and Canada; 3 of them are brownish-grey while the magnificent whooping crane is pure white; its bare head and throat are brownish-red and have a thin growth of black hair. Formerly a common American bird, it has become extremely rare; small colonies spend the summer in Saskatchewan and Mackenzie, and the winter in Texas. Length: 44 to 50 inches.

THE LIMPKINS. Aramidae. In the Okefinokee Swamp in Georgia, the Everglades in Florida and other marshy regions of the southeastern states, one species of the brownish limpkins is encountered. Length: 28 inches.

THE RAILS, GALLINULES, AND COOTS. Rallidae. "Mud hen" is another name for these inconspicuously colored swamp birds with small heads and cackling, hen-like voices. They live among the reeds and marshes. 18 species occur in the U.S. and Canada. Length: 5½ to 17½ inches (rails); 13 to 13½ inches (gallinules); 15 inches (coots).

An Outline of Our Natural Environment

The Order Charadriiformes—Shore Birds and allies—consists of 10 families:

THE JACANAS. Jacanidae. The spectacle of a bird walking over the water by stepping with its enormous feet from floating leaf to floating leaf can be observed in the lower Rio Grande valley in Texas. It is the habit of one species of the rail-like Jaçana Family. Length: 8½ inches.

THE OYSTER-CATCHERS. Haematopodidae. Bright-red bills are the trade marks of these sandpiper-like, mainly black and white birds. 4 species are encountered along the Gulf coast and the Atlantic coast as far north as Virginia, with occasional stragglers in New England and New Brunswick. Length: 16 to 19 inches.

THE PLOVERS, TURNSTONES, AND SURF-BIRDS. Charadriidae. The eggs of these little birds are conical so that the wind will roll them in a circle but not away. Many species are speckled. 21 species occur in the U.S. and Canada. Length: 6 to 17½ inches (plovers); 9 to 9½ inches (turnstones); 10 inches (surf bird).

THE WOODCOCKS, SNIPES, AND SANDPIPERS. Scolopacidae. As inconspicuous as these grey and brown birds are, so elaborate and amusing are their courtship habits. Solitary during the nesting season, the sandpipers gather in large flocks on wintry beaches. 55 species and subspecies of the Scolopacidae are recorded in the northern portions of the continent. Length: 11 inches (woodcocks); 8½ to 11¼ inches (snipes); 6 to 9 inches (sandpipers). The spotted sandpiper is described and illustrated on page 107.

THE AVOCETS AND STILTS. Recurvirostridae. These are graceful shorebirds wading in shallow water. Two species have been recorded in the U.S. and Canada, both with a touch of cinnamon in their plumage. Length: 18 inches (avocet); 15 inches (stilt).

THE PHALAROPES. Phalaropodidae. The female is boss in this peculiar family of "swimming sandpipers." She is larger and more brightly colored (bluish-grey, white and reddish-brown) than the henpecked, rather passive male; she performs the courting and selects the nesting site while her husband takes on the female chore of incubating the eggs. All 3 species reside in North America; 2 of them spend the winter at sea. Length: 7¾ to 8¾ inches.

THE JAEGERS AND SKUAS. Stercorariidae. "Jaeger" is the German word for "hunter;" actually the word "robber" would be a more appropriate name, for these fierce pirates outfly the fastest sea birds, attack them, and rob them of their prey. On their nesting grounds on the tundras of the north they feed largely on eggs stolen from other birds. 5 species of these dark brown, hawk-like gangsters are encountered in the U.S. and Canada, mostly in the northern regions. Length: 17 to 22 inches.

THE GULLS AND TERNS. Laridae. This world-wide family of approximately 100 species is well represented in America. Both the gulls and the terns have webbed feet and are predominantly white, grey, brown and black, although there are color exceptions like the roseate tern. On the whole, terns are slender and long-winged "sea swallows," gulls are heavy-bodied. Terns have pointed, gulls have hooked bills. Terns dive for living prey, gulls suck down soft organic matter from the surface; they also feed on scraps thrown overboard and are the most valuable scavengers of our harbors and bays. While the seashore is the principal habitat of the Laridae, they are also found on a number of inland lakes. 46 species and subspecies occur in the U.S. and Canada. Length: 11 to 29 inches (gulls); 9 to 21 inches (terns). The herring gull is described and illustrated on page 107, the common tern on page 108.

THE SKIMMERS. Rynchopidae. Skimming over quiet water with its bill open and scooping up small aquatic animals, the black skimmer is encountered in the eastern states and occasionally in Nova Scotia. It is the only representative of its family in the U.S. Length: 18 inches.

THE AUKS, MURRES, AND PUFFINS. Alcidae. The lives of these brown, black and white ocean birds are spent mostly on the open seas, but they visit bays and harbors at times. More than 20 species live largely in Alaska and the arctic regions but occur also as far south as Massachusetts in the east and lower California in the west. Length: 16½ inches (auk); 16 to 16½ inches (murres); 13 to 15 inches (puffins). The family Alcidae has some interesting members. The now legendary great auk was a big, flightless bird which could be killed easily with clubs, and was slaughtered mercilessly for its flesh, oil, and feathers. No living great auk has been seen since 1844. The California murres breed in large rookeries on the Farallone Islands off the California coast; in the 1850's egg production soared: Some four million, murre eggs were brought to the San Francisco markets and sold for less than hens' eggs. Puffins look like little parrots and are actually called "sea parrots."

The Order Columbiformes — Pigeon-like Birds — consists of one family:

THE PIGEONS AND DOVES. Columbidae. 600 species or more belong to this sleek-looking family. 21 members reside on this continent, mostly in western Canada and the western and southern states of the U.S. Length: 13½ to 16¼ inches (pigeons); 6¾ to 13 inches (doves). An extinct member of this family is the famous passenger pigeon, a beautiful bluish bird with a neck of metallic iridescence. In earlier days vast flocks of them swept over the eastern parts of the U.S. and Canada, actually darkening the sky. They bred in enormous colonies, one tree sometimes supporting more than 50 nests. They were netted and trapped, clubbed and stoned, shot and choked by smoke, to be eaten and also to be used as fertilizer. The last wild passenger pigeon was shot in 1906, the last captive one died in 1914. The mourning dove is described and illustrated on page 108.

The Order Psittaciformes — Parrots and allies — consists of one family:

THE PARROTS AND PAROQUETS. Psittacidae. The thick-billed parrot occurs very rarely in southern Arizona. Length: 16½ inches. The paroquets, formerly common birds in the South, seem to be extinct now.

The Order Cuculiformes — Cuckoo-like Birds — consists of one family:

THE CUCKOOS, ROAD-RUNNERS, AND ANIS. Cuculidae. The American cuckoo is a better citizen than its European counterpart, for while its Old-World cousin is a parasite which always lays its eggs in other birds' nests and lets its young be raised by their foster parents, the American cuckoo takes its family duties seriously and builds its own nest. Only very rarely a yellow-billed cuckoo is reported to deposit an egg in a black-billed cuckoo's nest, and vice versa. The anis like to associate themselves with cattle, and the road-runner is the racer of the cactus-covered range. 10 species and subspecies of the Cuculidae are encountered in the U.S. and Canada. Length: 11¾ to 13½ inches (cuckoos); 22 inches (road-runner); 13¾ inches (anis). The road-runner is described and illustrated on page 109.

The Order Strigiformes—Owls—consists of two families:

THE BARN OWLS. Tytonidae. The one species of this family is described and illustrated on page 109.

THE TYPICAL OWLS. Strigidae. The more than 500 members of this family spread over the whole globe. Their characteristics are well known: The birds' heads can be turned around nearly 180° toward either side, so that the owls look almost straight backward between their shoulders. Their keen eyes in a circular face see particularly well in twilight and in moonlight, but not in total darkness. Their ears are so sensitive that they hear the softest noises. Like the hawks, they eject pellets of bone and fur through their mouths, after a meal. 55 species occur in the U.S. and Canada, from the tiny elf owl (5⅞ inches) to the great grey owl (28 inches). The eastern screech owl is described and illustrated on page 110.

The Order Caprimulgiformes — Goatsuckers and allies — consists of one family:

THE GOATSUCKERS. Caprimulgidae. The chuck-will's-widow, the whip-poor-will and the nighthawk belong to this family. All three are well prepared for insect hunting: their deep, wide mouths are, at the base, fringed with long, stiff bristles which serve as a net. They do not build nests but lay their eggs on the ground in any slight depression. The name goatsucker refers to an ancient Italian superstition which asserts that the birds suck the teats of goats. 17 forms occur in the U.S. and Canada. Length: 8½ to 10 inches. The whip-poor-will is described and illustrated on page 110.

The Order Micropodiformes — Swifts and Hummingbirds — consists of two families:

THE SWIFTS. Micropodidae. The salivary glands of these swallow-like birds excrete a sticky substance that is used like a cement in building the nest. As the name implies, they are extremely fast flyers. 5 species and subspecies are encountered in the U.S. and Canada. Length: 5 2/5 inches. The chimney swift is described and illustrated on page 111.

THE HUMMINGBIRDS. Trochilidae. Only a blur can be seen and a humming be heard when hummingbirds move their wings; they are among the world's best flyers. Their plumage has a scintillating iridescence, therefore the name "feathered gems." They form a large, all-American family of some 750 species and subspecies, ranging in size from the giant hummer of the Andes Mountains (8½ inches) to the fairy hummingbird of Cuba (2¼ inches), the world's smallest bird. 19 species and subspecies occur in the U.S. and Canada. Length: 3 to 5 inches. The ruby-throated hummingbird is described and illustrated on page 111.

The Order Trogoniformes — Trogons — consists of one family:

THE TROGONS. Trogonidae. The magnificent quezal, the holy bird of the Aztecs, is the best-known member of the family. In the U.S. the strikingly colored coppery-tailed trogon is found in southern Texas and Arizona. Length: 11½ inches.

The Order Coraciiformes — Kingfishers and allies — consists of one family:

THE KINGFISHERS. Alcedinidae. The word "top-heavy" seems to describe most adequately the peculiar shape of this bird with a big head and tiny feet. 4 members are recorded throughout the continent. Length: 8 to 16¼ inches. The belted kingfisher is described and illustrated on page 112.

The Order Piciformes — Woodpeckers and allies — consists of one family:

THE WOODPECKERS. Picidae. About 700 species are known, and most of them have the same distinct characteristics. They make their nests in tree cavities either natural or hewn out; in the Southwest they will excavate holes in giant cactus plants; but they will not work on living hardwood. 64 species and subspecies occur in the U.S. and Canada. Length: 6⅝ to 11 inches, with the pileated woodpecker reaching a length of 17⅝ inches, and the magnificent ivory-billed woodpecker 20 inches; the latter has retreated to the cypress forests of the deep South and is threatened with extinction. The northern flicker is described and illustrated on page 112, the northern downy woodpecker, on page 113.

The Order Passeriformes — Perching Birds — consists of 27 families:

THE COTINGAS. Cotingidae. These "chatterers" of the western hemisphere are birds of brilliant plumage. Only one species, Xantus's becard, is reported in the U.S., in the Huhchuca Mountains of Arizona. Length: 6¾ inches.

THE FLYCATCHERS. Tryannidae. A flycatcher will sit motionless on an exposed perch with a broad view, then suddenly dart out and snap up a passing insect. In catching its prey, it is helped by several large bristles that project at the base of its wide mouth and bill and act as a screen. Usually the hunter returns to its old perch. Grey, olive green, brown and white are the chief colors of this family which is not classed among the true song birds although the singing of some species, like the eastern phoebe or the wood peewee, is musical and pleasant. Of the approximately 750 members recorded in the Americas, 42 are encountered in the U.S. and Canada. Length: 4½ to 13½ inches. The eastern phoebe is described and illustrated on page 113.

THE LARKS. Alaudidae. Whether the expression "happy as a lark" has a basis in reality, is difficult to determine. It is true that larks like to cavort in flocks, and they love to sing, even while on the wing. Dull-colored, brownish birds but with light underparts, their heads bear "horns," i.e. tufts of feathers. Of the 17 species found in the U.S. and Canada, 16 are native, and one is a celebrated importation, the skylark of England, favorite of English poets. Length: 6¾ to 7¾ inches.

THE SWALLOWS. Hirundinidae. Twelve feathers make a swallow's tail which is either notched or deeply forked. Swiftly sailing on the breeze and swooping down on all sorts of insects, these streamlined, graceful birds with long, crescent-shaped wings spend their days mostly in the air. Blue, purple, brown and white are the predominant colors of this family whose range is global. 18 members are recorded in the U.S. and Canada. Length: 5½ to 7½ inches. The tree swallow and the barn swallow are described and illustrated on page 114.

THE JAYS, MAGPIES, AND CROWS. Corvidae. Black is the predominant color of this family, although there are notable exceptions like the handsome blue jay. All members have in common large feet, heavy bills, and raucous voices. 41 species and subspecies inhabit the U.S. and Canada; among them are, besides the common crows, jays, and magpies, the large black ravens; the English rook which is a straggler in Greenland, and the nutcracker of the western mountains. The latter likes to play a startling game: It drops from a cliff, opening its wings after a deep fall. Length: 11⅜ to 13⅛ inches (jays); 17 to 17½ inches (magpies); 16 to 19½ inches (crows); 24¼ inches (raven); 18 inches (rook); 12½ inches (nutcracker). The northern blue jay and the American magpie are described and illustrated on page 115, the eastern crow on page 116.

THE TITMICE, CHICKADEES, VERDINS, AND BUSH-TITS. Paridae. Forever bustling with activity, inquisitive about their surroundings, nervously twittering yet apparently in the best of spirits, these small gregarious birds are largely forest dwellers. Like acrobats they move among the leaves and twigs. The chickadees are the best-known members of the family of which 39 species and subspecies occur in the U.S. and Canada. Length: 4¾ to 6 inches (titmice); 4¾ to 5⅜ inches (chickadees); 4⅜ inches (verdins); 4¼ to 4⅜ inches (bush-tits); the latter weave long, grey, gourd-shaped, swaying nests hanging from the tips of branches. The black-capped chickadee is described and illustrated on page 116.

THE NUTHATCHES. Sittidae. Along the tree trunks and branches they crawl busily back and forth, moving horizontally, vertically, or diagonally; their heads point upward or downward or sideways, as they turn about like mice on a barn beam. Thus the bluish-grey nuthatches inspect their dwelling place, using their well-developed toes and claws for climbing, and their straight and sharp bills for examining the crevices of the bark. Woodlands and orchards are their habitat. 13 species and subspecies are encountered in the U.S. and Canada. Length: 4⅜ to 6 inches. The white-breasted nuthatch is described and illustrated on page 117.

THE CREEPERS. Certhiidae. Quietly going and coming, these inhabitants of the deep woods or lonely mountainsides conceal their nests to the point of invisibility. The birds themselves are inconspicuous, with their dull-colored plumage in grey, brown, black and white. Their long, pointed tails have stiffly spined feathers which serve as props in climbing trees. The best known species is the tree creeper which occurs in 5 subspecies in the U.S. and Canada. Length: 5⅝ inches.

THE WREN-TITS. Chamaeidae. California is the home of these small, greyish-brown birds which racially stand between the wrens and the titmice. There are 5 subspecies. Length: 6½ inches.

THE DIPPERS. Cinclidae. A bird that dashes through the wet curtain of a waterfall; that cavorts in the icy spray of a mountain brook, fully at home amid whirlpools and rapids, boulders and caves; that walks on the bottom of a shallow pool, completely under water; and that has been observed to force its way even under a sheet of ice, — such a creature is a remarkable specimen in the American scene. But there are more accomplishments to report: It is a song bird whose loud and varied musical harmonies resound through the mountain woods as liquid, bubbling and clear as "white water" itself. And finally it is a master builder. Its nest is a work of art, a beautiful globe of green mosses, six or seven inches in diameter; usually it is located in a crevice between boulders, by the roots of a tree, or even behind the veil of a cascade, but always so that the drifting spray will continually moisten the mosses of the nest and keep them green, fresh, and lovely. The name of this phenomenal diver — singer — builder is dipper or water ouzel, a brownish-greyish bird with a short bill, short wings, and a short tail, but large and sure feet. It is the only North American representative of the dipper family and inhabits the Rocky Mountains and the western Coastal Ranges in the U.S. and Canada. Length: 7¾ inches.

THE WRENS. Troglodytidae. If you find a bulky little nest on a lamp post or in a shoe, it's a house wren's. Wrens also may select a nook or corner in a shack or barn; they may choose an upturned tree and build their nest in the jumble of broken roots and soil, or they may find a suitable cavity on a rock or branch. The cactus wrens weave flasks that lie on the side, the marsh wrens construct globes of grasses; they may even build several globes, and only after their completion decide where to lay the eggs. The little brownish birds themselves are inconspicuous with their round wings, short tails and slender bills which are often curving at the tip. 46 species and subspecies are recorded in the U.S. and Canada. Length: 4 to 7½ inches. The house wren is described and illustrated on page 117.

THE CATBIRDS, MOCKINGBIRDS, AND THRASHERS. Mimidae. We have no nightingales in America, but our Mimidae, an all-American family of natural songsters, compensate us for the loss. While the mockingbirds are known for their imitative powers, they also may sing their own exuberant multiple melodies far into the night, like nightingales, or even throughout the night at full moon. Grey, white, and black are their colors. The catbirds, also of grey and blackish plumage, are perhaps not quite as proficient and varied as singers; their name is derived from the fact that they like to build their nests in "catbriar" tangles, placing them among the thorns at almost inaccessible spots. The thrashers, usually of brownish coloration, are also fine musical performers; they like to perch on solitary trees when chanting their sweet, well-phrased songs. 18 species and subspecies are reported in the U.S. and Canada. Length: 10½ inches (mockingbirds); 8⅞ inches (catbird); 8½ to 12¼ inches (thrashers). The mockingbird is described and illustrated on page 118.

THE THRUSHES, ROBINS, BLUEBIRDS, AND SOLITAIRES. Turdidae. This famous family of superlative singers is world-wide in its distribution; its outstanding European member is the nightingale, and in America robins, bluebirds, and reddish-brown hermit thrushes are renowned. The solitaire is, in accordance with its name, a dweller of the lonely mountain ranges where its songs ring clearly between dwarf trees and bare rocks. 34 species and subspecies inhabit the U.S. and Canada. Length: 7⅛ to 10 inches (thrushes); 10 inches (robins); 7 to 7¼ inches (bluebirds); 8⅝ inches (solitaires). The robin is described and illustrated on page 118, the wood thrush and bluebird on page 119.

THE WARBLERS, GNATCATCHERS, AND KINGLETS. Sylviidae. Of these pleasant but not, save in one instance, the ruby-crowned kinglet, overly distinguished singers 15 species and subspecies are recorded in the U.S. and Canada. The family consists of two species of rather dull-plumaged Old-World warblers (not to be confused with our much brighter-colored native wood warblers), of the tiny greyish-olive green kinglets which are so called because they wear small crowns of gold or orange on their heads; and the greyish, longtailed gnatcatchers which look like miniature mockingbirds. All Sylviidae build neat, cup-shaped nests. Length: 5 inches (warblers); 4 to 4⅜ inches (kinglets); 5 inches (gnatcatchers).

THE WAXWINGS. Bombycillidae. Only two species inhabit Canada, the northern states of the U.S., and the Allegheny Mountains. In winter, they spread toward the West Indies. Length: 7¼ inches. The cedar waxwing is described and illustrated on page 120.

THE SHRIKES. Laniidae. Here is a spectacle with a surprising turn: You hear a sweet strain from a lovely white-black-grey bird and then see this songster dart after a little chickadee or warbler in an acrobatic flight, dash it to the ground, kill it by several blows, and impale it on a big thorn. You have seen a shrike in action. Additional evidence of its menacing habits may be a frog stuck on a sharp splinter, or a mouse on display on the barb of a fence. Finally, you may see the hunter tear its prey apart with its hooked bill that looks like that of a miniature hawk, and swallow the chunks. Butcher bird is another, well-deserved name for the shrike. It is a true songbird, and, on the whole, considered a useful destroyer of pests. 8 species and subspecies occur in the U.S. and Canada. Length: 8¾ to 10⅜ inches.

THE STARLINGS. Sturnidae. The one American species of this family is described and illustrated on page 120.

THE VIREOS. Vireonidae. "Greenlet" was the former name of this family of small grey-yellow-olive-green birds which inhabit the leafy parts of the tree tops; there they build their perfectly formed nests that look like deep cups. They are not distinguished singers. The red-eyed vireo is common even in the trees of city streets, forever warbling its song of three syllables. 25 species and subspecies are found in the U.S. and Canada. Length: 4½ to 6¼ inches; the yellow-throated vireo attains a length of 10 inches.

THE WOOD WARBLERS. Compsothlypidae. The wood warblers do not warble. Their name is a misnomer. They utter short sibilant strains, not unlike the sounds of insects. They have a brilliant plumage, and some of them are beauties, like the blue-winged and the golden-winged warblers, the black and white warbler with jet-black and pure-white streamlines, and the magnolia warbler with a charming black-grey-yellow pattern. Being insect eaters, these all-American birds travel thousands of miles each year and seem to be always busy and hurrying. 82 species and subspecies are recorded in the U.S. and Canada. Besides the wood warblers proper, the family includes the yellow-throats of the vine tangles, marshes, and other inaccessible places; the water-thrushes of the tree-lined brooks; the ovenbird which builds a nest like an old-fashioned round oven, with a side opening; the redstarts with brilliant orange-red patches on a black and white body (the Cubans call them "candelitas," little torches); and the chats with yellow breasts which are the clowns and ventriloquists of the bushy pastures and groves; fine imitators, they are able to "throw" their voices like vaudeville artists. Length: 4¼ to 6 inches (wood warblers); 7½ inches (chats); 5⅜ inches (yellow-throats); 6⅛ inches (ovenbird); 5½ to 6¼ inches (water thrushes); 5¼ to 5⅜ inches (red starts).

THE WEAVER FINCHES. Ploceidae. The principal representative of this group, the English sparrow, is described and illustrated on page 121.

THE BLACKBIRDS, ORIOLES, MEADOWLARKS, COWBIRDS, AND BOBOLINKS. Icteridae. Black is a prominent color in the plumage of these all-American birds with stout, sharp bills and roundish or squarish tails of 12 feathers. 42 species and subspecies are reported in the U.S. and Canada, among them the tame, "black" blackbirds of the western cities; the red-winged blackbirds congregating in huge flocks in the East; and the yellow-headed blackbirds of the West. There are the beloved orioles with their purse-shaped nests; the meadowlarks with their flute-like song, which breed in hay fields and walk (not hop) about, consuming large quantities of cutworms, crickets, caterpillars, and other farm pests; the effusively singing bobolinks of northern pastures which in winter become the pillagers of southern rice fields; the cowbirds which are our only parasites: they build no nests but lay their eggs in the nests of warblers, sparrows, and similar species, forcing the foster parents to raise an adopted youngster much larger than their own young; and the purplish-black grackles. Length: 8¼ to 9½ inches (blackbirds); 7¼ inches (bobolink); 7⅝ to 7⅞ inches (cowbirds); 12¾ inches (grackles); 10¾ inches (meadowlarks); 7¼ to 8⅞ inches (orioles). The bobolink is described and illustrated on page 121, the Baltimore oriole and the meadowlark on page 122, and the red-winged blackbird on page 123.

THE TANAGERS. Thraupidae. Five species of these stout perching birds occur in the U.S. and Canada. The most prominent member of the family, the scarlet tanager, is described and illustrated on page 123.

THE GROSBEAKS, CROSSBILLS, FINCHES, SPARROWS, AND BUNTINGS. Fringillidae. This world-wide bird family is a world-wide blessing, for in every quarter of the globe they help the farmer in a twofold fashion: They eat immeasureable quantities of seeds of pestiferous weeds (their bills are stout and conical, just right for the splitting of hard seed shells), and they catch billions of crop-damaging insects. Besides, they are lovely songsters, 1,200 species and subspecies strong, the largest bird family on earth. In the U.S. and Canada alone 240 members have been recorded, all of them a joy to encounter in our gardens and parks, in the woods and the countryside. Among the finches, the red house-finch and the goldfinch are famous; the cardinal is a most decorative visitor to our gardens; the grosbeaks are delightful birds with rosy or blue hues; the native sparrows are dull-colored, earthy birds, but lovely and cheerful singers; among the buntings the snow bunting delights in the icy blasts of a snow storm, the deep-blue indigo bunting is a tireless musician; the siskins resemble goldfinches and love to associate with them; of the towhees the red-eyed towhee with the black head is a bird of dry lands; the juncos with the subdued plumage are common winter birds; the redpolls have a bright crimson crown and like to play with the goldfinches and siskins; and the chattering red crossbills have beaks with crossed tips, suited for opening pine cones. Sometimes they also swing by their beaks from a twig. Length: 5½ to 6⅝ inches (finches); 7 to 9⅛ inches (grosbeaks); 5¼ to 6⅞ inches (buntings); 4¾ to 7¼ inches (sparrows); 5 inches (siskins); 6⅝ to 8⅞ inches (towhees); 5 to 6 inches (redpolls); 6 to 6¼ inches (crossbills). The cardinal and the rose-breasted grosbeak are described and illustrated on page 124, the goldfinch and the song sparrow on page 125.

Outline of the Principal Orders and Families of Wild Animals in the U.S. and Canada

The Order Insectivora — Insect Eaters — consists of two families:

THE SHREWS. Soricidae. The world's smallest mammal is a member of this tiny, fierce and forever hungry family: It is the pygmy shrew measuring a little over three inches from nose to tail. The shrews have silky fur of inconspicuous color and narrow heads with long, tapering noses. Because of their fighting disposition they have become symbols of scolding women. Their six genera and innumerable species range all over the continent. The short-tailed shrew is described and illustrated on page 128. Length: 3 to 6½ inches.

THE MOLES. Talpidae. Moles are natural tunnel diggers. Their paddle-shaped front paws are powerful, and on their bodies all parts that might interfere with the tunnel passage, like external ears have disappeared. Their fur pushes forward as easily as backward. The eyes are degenerate or sealed. Five genera occur throughout the U.S. and Canada, except in the arid sections. Length: 4½ to 9 inches.

The Order Chiroptera — Bats — includes:

THE COMMON BATS. Vespertilionidae. These mammals of the night search for their insect food during the hours of darkness. They fly with complete assurance, apparently guided by a radar-like sixth sense. Their ten genera range all over the U.S. and Canda. The little brown bat is described and illustrated on page 128. Length: 3 to 5 inches, expanse of wings: 6 to 12 inches.

The Order Xenarthra — Strange-jointed Mammals — consists of one family.

THE ARMADILLOS. Dasypodidae. The nine-banded armadillo, a relic of prehistoric eras, is illustrated and described on page 129.

The Order Rodentia — Gnawers or Rodents — consists of 8 families:

THE SQUIRRELS AND MARMOTS. Sciuridae. Chisel-like, gnawing teeth are the tool and weapon of this order and family. The teeth grind each other but never wear out as they grow like human fingernails. The breaking of a chisel tooth is usually fatal since, in that case, two teeth no longer meet each other, grow wild, and lock the gnawer's jaw. The squirrel and marmot group occurs in innumerable forms and species all over the continent. It includes such interesting members as the flying squirrel (9-14 inches) which glides from tree to tree over distances of 50 or even 100 feet like a soaring hawk; however, it cannot truly fly. The chipmunks, the prairie dogs and the woodchucks belong to the same family. The hoary marmot (15-30 inches) is also a member. Living on the lonely heights of the Rockies and the High Sierras, this shy, grizzled-grey vegetarian has a loud, piercing call of warning which can be heard far and wide: the marmot's whistle. Representing this group, the grey squirrel (17-23 inches) is described and illustrated on page 129, the eastern chipmunk (9-11 inches) and the prairie dog (12-15 inches) on page 130, and the woodchuck (18-25 inches) on page 131.

THE BEAVERS. Castoridae. This famous dam builder is illustrated and described on page 131. It is the only species of its family. Length: 3-4 feet.

THE MOUNTAIN BEAVERS. Aplodontiidae. These primitive brown animals are not true beavers. They are shy, and little is known about their habits. Their range is the Pacific coast from British Columbia to central California. Length: 12 to 17 inches.

THE PORCUPINES. Erethizontidae. Of these grotesque mammals there are two species, the Canada porcupine of the eastern and the yellow-haired porcupine of the Midwestern and western states. The porcupine is described and illustrated on page 132. Length: 3 feet.

THE POCKET GOPHERS. Geomyidae. Although among our most abundant mammals, they are hardly ever seen as they spend their lives underground. They have a number of unusual and curious characteristics: Their cheeks have outside pockets used as handy food baskets; their gnawing teeth stick out of their mouths, with their lips meeting behind, which gives them a fierce appearance; their eyes are tiny but weep profusely, to wash away the dirt; and their tail has a tactile tip with a sort of nerve conductor. Gophers move backward almost as easily as forward. There are three genera in the U.S. and Canada, the eastern, the western, and the chestnut pocket gopher, with numerous local species and varieties. Length: 7 to 14 inches.

THE POCKET MICE. Heteromyidae. Desert land where there is no water to drink, is the habitat of most of these tiny mammals. As they manufacture water in their bodies, like so many other animals of the desert, they do not die of thirst. Like the gophers they have cheek pockets for food storage; but unlike the gophers, they are jumpers rather than diggers. Their hind legs are long, their tails often tufted. Four genera occur in the U.S. and Canada: The pocket mouse, the kangaroo rat, the dwarf pocket rat, the spiny pocket mouse. Length: 4½ to 14 inches.

THE JUMPING MICE. Zapodidae. An extraordinarily long tail, very long hind legs, a white belly and a brownish back are typical for these small mice of which numerous species and subspecies live from the Arctic Circle throughout most of Canada and the U.S. as far south as the North Carolina-California line. They are wonderful jumpers, but rarely seen in daytime. In the fall, before they retire to hibernate, they get very fat. Their winter sleep is deep, they become cold to the touch and almost stop breathing. Their food consists of insects, seeds and grasses. Length: 7½ to 9 inches.

THE NATIVE RATS AND MICE. Cricetidae. This large family of rodents includes the common field mouse, one of the worst farm pests; the pine mouse, a glossy, bright reddish-yellow relative of the field mouse; the red-backed mouse, a bright chestnut-colored forest dweller; the muskrat, one of the most important fur bearers; the brown lemming, a mouse of the arctic regions of Canada and Alaska; the collared lemming which is brown in summer, white in winter; the red tree mouse of the evergreen forests of northern California and Oregon; the handsome white-footed mouse which occurs from the Arctic to the Mexican tropics; the grasshopper mouse that thrives on a meat diet of grasshoppers, scorpions, lizards, other mice caught in traps, various insects and seeds; the pack rat, a country dweller which does not have the filthy habits of the house rat; the cotton rat that inflicts great damage upon the cotton crops of Texas; and the rice rat of the extreme South of the U.S. The house mouse and the house rat do not belong to this family but to the Old World family Muridae; they are immigrants from Europe but have overrun this continent to an alarming degree. The common field mouse (4½-8½ inches) is illustrated and described on page 132; the muskrat (17-23 inches) and the house mouse (6-8 inches) on page 133; the house rat (15-18 inches) on page 134.

The Order Lagomorpha — Hares and Rabbits — consists of two families:

THE HARES AND RABBITS. Leporidae. While the true rodents have two upper gnawing teeth, the hares have four; they chew with a sidewise, grinding motion. Members of this family are the snowshoe hare which changes its brown summer coat into a white winter coat; the white Arctic hare, one of the few permanent residents of the far North; the swift black-tailed jack rabbit of the plains which can outrun any dog except a greyhound; the big, white-tailed jack rabbit of the prairies which is killed for its meat in large numbers and sent to western and southern markets; and the downy, soft-eyed cottontail rabbit. The black-tailed jack rabbit (20 to 26 inches) is described and illustrated on page 134, the cottontail rabbit (11-20 inches) on page 135.

THE PIKAS. Ochotonidae. Around cliffs and caverns, at altitudes from 5,000 to 13,000 feet, these stockily built mountain animals, which look like guinea pigs, lead a life untouched by man. Since they do not hibernate, they have to store food for the winter and gather grasses, leaves, and plants at harvest time, stack them in haycocks near their homes, and dry and cure them. Therefore they are also called "haymakers." They live on the western mountains from Alaska to Mexico, forming several species whose fur coloration varies slightly between cinnamon, brown, and grey. Length: 7 to 8 inches.

The Order Marsupialia — Marsupials — consists of one family:

THE OPOSSUMS. Didelphidae. Australia, the land of the kangaroos, abounds with primitive marsupials. But in the U.S. and Canada the only marsupial is the opossum, illustrated and described on page 135. Length: 2½-3 feet.

The Order Ungulata — Hoofed Animals — consists of several families:

THE CATTLE FAMILY. Bovidae. Our barnyard cows are closely related to America's wild cattle; all have the same cloven hoofs, the same complicated stomach divided into four parts, they all are cud-chewers, and their true horns are unbranched; the solid bony part is permanent; they grow one pair only. The family's four genera are the bison (8-12½ feet) whose herds once darkened the continent; the musk ox (7-8½ feet), a warmly clothed arctic animal that is brown on the back and white on the belly; it lives on moss, lichens, grass and bark, in herds of 10 to 100, around Hudson Bay; the mountain sheep (4½ to 6 feet) with their splendid horns; and the Rocky Mountain goat (5 to 6 feet) which is a wonderful climber. The American bison and the mountain sheep (bighorn) are described and illustrated on page 136, the Rocky Mountain goat on page 137.

THE PRONGHORN ANTELOPES. Antilocapridae. This swift runner and jumper, one of America's most beautiful animals, is illustrated and described on page 137. Length: 4 to 4½ feet.

THE PECCARIES. Tagassuidae. This southern animal with the tusk-like teeth and pig-like snout, the omnivorous appetite and the strong-smelling glands is described and illustrated on page 138. Length 3 to 3½ feet.

THE PIGS. Suidae. This is not an American family, and no native animals belong to it; but the introduced wild boar is an interesting addition to our wildlife. When a group of English sportsmen established a hunting club on the North Carolina-Tennessee border, they stocked their large, wooded tract not only with elk, bear and buffalo, but also imported wild boars from Europe. The club failed, and about a hundred boars escaped into the neighboring wilderness. Today these impressive animals, standing 3 feet high at the shoulder and weighing up to 400 pounds, range through the back hills of North Carolina and Tennessee but have also been introduced to New Hampshire and California.

THE DEER FAMILY. Cervidae. Once a year the members of this family shed their handsome antlers — a remarkable feat in view of their size and sweep. While the antlers grow during the summer they are covered with a velvety skin, becoming mature by the mating season when fights occur between bucks (zoologists consider the antlers a secondary sexual characteristic). Many species of deer shed them after the breeding season. The important members of this family are the mule deer with the large ears; the high-jumping white-tailed deer with the white flag; the elk, called wapiti by the Indians; the moose of our northwoods; and the caribou (5 to 7½ feet), our native reindeer which, however, has never been tamed like the reindeer of Lapland; both males and females grow antlers; their sharp and round hoofs, shaped like cups, are designed for running over frozen surfaces in winter, and on swampy soil in summer; their coats are grey-brown above, whitish below. The mule deer (4½-5½ feet) is described and illustrated on page 138, the white-tailed deer (5-6 feet) and the elk (up to 10 feet) on page 139, and the moose (9½-10 feet) on page 140.

THE HORSE FAMILY. Equidae. No member of this odd-toed or single-hoofed family is a native of America. But the introduced mustang has become an interesting part of the American West; it is described and illustrated on page 140.

The Order Carnivora—Flesh Eaters—consists of 6 families:

THE WEASELS. Mustelidae. The flesh eaters vary greatly in size, the weasels belonging to the smallest. The weasel family includes many fur and game animals which possess musk glands and exude a musky odor when excited, among them the following well-known genera and species: The true weasel (6-20 inches), a natural killer; the black-footed ferret, a rare weasel of buff, yellow and brownish hues which lives on the Great Plains and is the arch enemy of the prairie dog; the mink (20-30 inches), a restless hunter; the common skunk (24-30 inches); the spotted skunk (14-22 inches) of the South and West; the hog-nosed skunk (25-33 inches) of southern Texas, Arizona and New Mexico; it sports a white back and tail; the pine marten (22-30 inches), a large weasel spending much of its time in the treetops; the brown-furred fisher (36-42 inches) which is equally at home on the ground and in the trees but never fishes; its range extends from Hudson Bay to the Tennessee-California line; the wolverine (36-44 inches), a fierce glutton; the badger (25-30 inches), prospector of the western plains; the water-loving otter (3½-4½ feet); and the rare sea otter of California (4-5 feet). The following representatives of this family are described and illustrated: the weasel and mink on page 141; the common skunk and pine marten on page 142; the wolverine and badger on page 143; and the otter on page 144.

THE RACCOONS. Procyonidae. This black-masked cousin of the bear is illustrated and described on page 144. A second species, the desert raccoon, is pale in color, adapted to its surroundings; a Mexican member of the family, the coatimundi, rarely finds it way into the U.S.

THE RING-TAILED CATS. Bassariscidae. These animals with white and dark bands on their bushy tails are not cats, in spite of their catlike feet. They are cousins of the raccoon, and at night like to prowl through the streets of the small western towns. Their range extends through Arizona, New Mexico and Texas; occasional specimens occur in Nevada, Colorado and Oregon. They are also known as coon cats or civet cats. Length: 25-30 inches.

THE DOGS. Canidae. The wild relatives of our domestic dogs are a family of medium-sized flesh eaters. Among its prominent members are the timber wolf (4 to 7 feet), a clever outlaw; the white wolf which is not always white but varies to nearly black; it stuffs itself on arctic mice in season, and hunts the caribou, the arctic hare, and the musk ox at other times; the coyote (3½ to 4 feet), with its human-sounding call; the red fox (3 to 3½ feet) which supposedly lives by its wits; the kit fox (2 to 3 feet), the slender hunter of the Great Plains and the mesquite and cactus country, with a color range from buff yellow to reddish grey; the grey fox (3½ feet) which climbs trees when pursued, or when berrying or sightseeing; it occurs south of the New Hampshire-Oregon line; the Arctic fox (2½ feet), a smaller animal which wears a brown coat in summer and a white one in winter; and its variation, the valuable blue fox, which has been developed on the Pribilofs and other Alaskan islands. The timber wolf and coyote are described and illustrated on page 145, the red fox on page 146.

THE CATS. Felidae. All wild American cats belong to the same family as our domestic cats. They have in common the ability to sheathe their sharp claws. Originally they ranged over most of the continent from the Arctic to Mexico, but now are restricted to certain inaccessible sections. Their roster includes such beasts as the cougar, panther (the black panther is a color variation of this family), or mountain lion (6 to 8½ feet); the jaguar (6 to 7 feet), a powerful jungle hunter which formerly lived throughout the lower Mississippi Valley but now rarely crosses from Mexico into the U.S.; occasionally a specimen is reported in the jungles of Florida; the ocelot (3½ to 4 feet), a small tiger cat with an intricate pattern of dark spots on a yellow background, a visitor from Mexico in the lower Rio Grande valley; in that same locality the jaguarundi (3 to 4 feet) occurs, a smoky-grey cat of the chaparral and the jungle underbrush; the Canadian lynx (2½ to 3 feet), brown in summer, grey in winter; and the bobcat (2½ to 3½ feet), a southerly cousin of the lynx. The cougar is described and illustrated on page 146, the bobcat on page 147.

THE BEARS. Ursidae. Most animals walk on their toes, but these largest of the flesh eaters walk on the soles of their feet. The family consists of the black bear (4½ to 6½ feet) and its color variation, the cinnamon bear, which live in the densely forested parts of Canada and the U.S.; the ferocious grizzly bear (6 to 9 feet) of the western mountains; the Alaskan brown bear, a variety of the grizzly, the world's largest bear (the species on Kodiak Island weighs up to ¾ of a ton); and the polar bear (7 to 9½ feet) whose white, thick hair covers even the soles of its feet; it is a slow but strong swimmer, above or under water, and catches its food, mainly seals, by strategy. The black bear is described and illustrated on page 147, the grizzly bear on page 148.

The Order Pinnipedia — Fin-footed Mammals — consists of 3 families:

THE WALRUS FAMILY. Odobenidae. Although descendants of early land animals, the fin-footed mammals now spend most of their lives at sea. Their feet have become webbed paddles, their legs flippers, and their bodies have developed streamlines. There are only two species in the Walrus Family, the Atlantic and the Pacific. The Atlantic walrus is described and illustrated on page 148. Length: 10 to 12 feet.

THE EARED SEALS. Otariidae. This family of seals with furry bodies and external ears includes 4 genera: the Alaskan fur seal(6 feet), the fabulous traveler; the Guadalupe fur seal of Lower California, a nearly extinct species; the California sea lion (10 to 13 feet), the skillful performer of zoo and circus, which may reach a length of 8 feet and weigh 500 pounds; it looks black in the water, reddish brown when dry; and Stellar's sea lion, with a range from San Francisco to Bering Strait; the latter is an even larger animal, the bull weighing up to 1,800 pounds. The Alaskan fur seal is described and illustrated on page 149.

THE EARLESS SEALS. Phocidae. The members of this family cannot use their hind flippers for moving ashore and are almost helpless on land. Their small, hidden ears close under water. Included in the group are the harbor seal of our rocky coasts and sandy bays; and the harp seal, so-called because of a harp-shaped brown band on the grey fur of the males; the latter spends the winter near the Grand Banks of Newfoundland, the summer on the west coast of Greenland towards Baffin Bay. The ribbon seal is a rare, small seal of the Aleutian Islands with striking, yellow ribbon markings on a brown coat. The male hooded seal, a bluish-grey animal with brown blotches and white underparts, wears a hood on its head, i.e. a bag of muscular tissue which may be inflated. This cousin of the harp seal uses, to a certain extent, the same routes of migration. The northern elephant seal (15 feet) is the largest member of the family, with a thick, pendulous nose that looks like an elephant's trunk; nearly extinct, the last of the sea elephants live on Guadalupe Island, off the coast of Lower California, under the protection of the Mexican government. The harbor seal is described and illustrated on page 149.

The Order Sirenia — Sirens — consists of one family:

THE MANATEES. Trichechidae. The one American species of this family, the manatee or sea cow of Florida, is illustrated and described on page 150. It used to be seen in Florida and gulf waters in herds of 10 to 15, but is very rare now. A near relative flourishes in the Amazon River. Length: 7 to 15 feet.

The Order Cetacea — Whales — is the group of mammals that look like fish; it comprises the suborder Mysticeti, Whalebone Whales, and the suborder Odontoceti, Toothed Whales. As the name indicates, the latter have teeth, from a full set to a single tusk in one species. They possess but one nasal opening and they spout through this single hole. Their group includes the following families:

THE SPERM WHALES. Physeteridae. The commercially important giant sperm whale is illustrated and described on page 150. Length: 65 feet.

THE PYGMY SPERM WHALES. Kogiidae. This rare species is closely related to the giant sperm whale; it occurs infrequently on both American coasts. Length: 9 to 13 feet.

THE DOLPHINS AND PORPOISES. Delphinidae. This family is composed of the smaller whales. While the two names are often used interchangeably, the term dolphin should be applied to those species whose snouts terminate in beaks, while the porpoises are beakless. Both are well-known, playful and voracious inhabitants of American waters. A certain confusion results from the fact that there is also a true fish called dolphin (see page 160). One of the giant porpoises, reaching a length of 20 feet, is called killer whale; it is a handsome black and white creature and a fast swimmer, overtaking dolphins and porpoises and swallowing them alive; like wolves on land, killer whales hunt in packs. The white whale, the only completely white sea mammal, is a small arctic whale of 12 to 15 feet which migrates as far south as the St. Lawrence River and Quebec during the summer. The blackfish, which attains a length of 24 feet, is a rather stupid animal with a sheep-like herd instinct; when fishermen encounter a school and succeed in driving one ashore, the rest follow and dozens or even hundreds will be beached and killed; this exciting sport is the topic of numerous Cape Cod stories. The one-toothed narwhal is the "sea unicorn" of the Arctic. The common dolphin is described and illustrated on page 151.

THE BEAKED WHALES. Ziphiidae. These whales, rare

on the coasts of North America, range in length from 15 to 30 feet. Their long jaws are bottle-shaped or beaked, which accounts for the name of the family.

The Whalebone Whales have no teeth but narrow plates of baleen (whalebone) hanging from the roofs of their mouths. These hairy-looking formations, fringed in the front and on the bottom, form screens between the jaws, where the abundant small animal life of the ocean is trapped while the water strains out again. The prey is swallowed alive and unchewed. The Whalebone Whales have two nostrils through which they spout. Their group includes the following families:

The Right Whales. Balaenidae. In early whaling days these were the only whales hunted, because they were the "right" ones: Their wealth in oil and whalebone made them most desirable; being slow, they were caught quite easily; and being lighter than water, they floated after death and could be handled leisurely. The most outstanding member of this family is the bowhead, a 60 foot giant; of that, 20 feet comprise the head; most of its head is mouth, and most of the mouth is lower jaw and underlip. The North Atlantic and the Pacific right whales belong to a similar genus.

The Grey Whales. Rhachianectidae. The members of this family used to bring forth their young in the shallow lagoons of California. The outgoing tide left just enough water for the young ones to swim, but the mothers were stranded and often fell prey to whalers. Consequently they are almost extinct now.

The Finbacks or Rorquals. Balaenopteridae. In contrast to the right or grey whales, the finbacks have dorsal fins. Another characteristic is the large number of grooves on their throats and chests. The family includes the humpback which forms a huge, round hump with its back when diving; it is black above, marbled or white below; although reaching a length of 75 feet, it is an exceedingly graceful and playful swimmer. The common rorqual, measuring about 65 feet, prefers more temperate water, and is often observed by steamship travelers as it throws its tall spouts into the air. The blue whale, which grows to a length of 95 feet, is the biggest creature on earth, both of our time and any by-gone epoch. It is described and illustrated on page 151.

Outline of the Principal Orders and Families of Fishes in American and Canadian Waters

The illustrations and descriptions of fishes on pages 154 to 173 are presented in a geographical sequence, the Atlantic species being followed by the Pacific and freshwater species. Such a pattern is not feasible here as the orders and families are based on anatomical characteristics and are grouped regardless of geographical distribution.

Before the fishes proper are discussed, the *Order Petromyzonoidea* — the Lampreys — should be mentioned here; for these animals have become an alarming pest in American waters, particularly in the Great Lakes. Without limbs, they look like eels; however, they are not fishes at all but aquatic vertebrates. They have no jaws; their mouth is a large circular sucking apparatus with many conical teeth. The larger species attach themselves to fish, rasp off the flesh, and suck the blood. In this way they inflict serious damage upon our fish population; so far no effective means of curbing them seems to have been discovered, in spite of intensive research. The lampreys occur both in salt and fresh water. Length: 20 inches.

While the large majority of fishes are "bony fishes," the sharks and rays stand out as a special group because their skeleton is cartilaginous; they are divided into several orders and families of which the *Requiem or Cat Sharks,* Galeidae, are important. They include the tiger shark, the blue shark, and the leopard shark of the Pacific coast which is described and illustrated on page 168. Other families are the Whale Sharks, the Mako Sharks, the Thresher Sharks, the Basking Sharks, and the Hammer-head Sharks.

The following orders and families refer to the "bony fishes."

The Order Chondrostei — Sturgeons — comprises one family:

The Sturgeons. Acipenseridae. These famous producers of caviar inhabit the northern oceans and also fresh waters. Most of them are migratory. Among the various American species the lake sturgeon (40 inches) is the largest fish of the Great Lakes, and the white sturgeon (40 inches and more) of the Pacific coast lands is the largest freshwater fish in North America; it used to be abundant in the Columbia River. The common sturgeon of the Atlantic is described and illustrated on page 154.

The Order Isospondyli — Herring-like Fishes — includes some widely known families:

The Herrings. Clupeidae. The members of this family are not game fishes but most important food fishes. The common herring and the shad are described and illustrated on page 155. The alewife (11 inches) is a close relative of the herring, but unlike the herring runs up the streams to spawn. A small western member of the family that is commercially important is the California sardine, called pilchard on the coasts of Washington and British Columbia. This silvery fish of approximately 10 inches is caught in enormous purse seines, one haul yielding as many as 35 and occasionally up to 100 tons. Almost the entire catch is turned into oil and fish meal, a valuable chicken feed and fertilizer.

The Anchovies. Engraulidae. An extremely long lower jaw is a characteristic of these fishes; they like to swim in large schools along sandy coasts and feed on minute animals and plants. Various species occur both on the Atlantic and Pacific coasts, and are an important food for salmons and seals. Length: 5 inches. The canned anchovies, popular as hors d'oeuvres, are imported from Europe.

THE SALMON AND TROUT FAMILY. Salmonidae. This is not a particularly large group but its members stand out as far as size, beauty, quality and flavor of the flesh, and gaminess are concerned. They are confined to the northern hemisphere and include both saltwater and freshwater species; some live in the sea and enter fresh water streams for spawning. The best-known representatives are described and illustrated in the color section on fishes: Atlantic salmon on page 156, Chinook salmon on page 164, red salmon on page 165, brook trout on page 170, lake trout on page 171, and rainbow trout on page 171. Of the Pacific salmons which live in a wide geographical arch stretching from northern Japan and arctic Siberia to arctic Canada, Alaska and central California, three species should be mentioned: the chum or dog salmon (18 inches) which does not take readily artificial lure and is therefore not appreciated by sportsmen; the pink or humpback salmon (18 inches) so called because of the hump on the back of the male at spawning time — not a game fish either, it is caught in purse seines and canned in Alaska in huge quantities; and the silver or coho salmon (24 inches) whose delicious pink to deep salmon red flesh is canned, frozen and smoked; of its roe, salmon caviar is prepared. The land-locked Atlantic salmon of Maine which has also been introduced to other sections of New England and to New York, is as highly prized as the trout.

Among the various species of the trout group are the western cutthroat trout (12 inches) whose name is derived from the pair of red color bars along the inner edge of the lower jaw bones; they look like cuts on the trout's throat. The Dolly Varden trout (24 inches) has a color arrangement in common with its relative, the eastern brook trout; both show light spots on a dark background while all other trouts have black spots on a light ground color; they also have a few scarlet spots on their sides; the Dolly Varden is quite abundant in western mountain streams but does not leap and is not ranked high as a game fish. The beautiful golden trout (8 inches), originally of the Mt. Whitney area, is now much more widely distributed. The Yellowstone or Montana black-spotted trout (12 inches) is the only game fish in Yellowstone Lake, a gorgeously colored trout that will take almost any kind of bait.

THE TARPONS. Megalopidae. The "silver king" of our Atlantic shores is described and illustrated on page 154.

THE SMELTS. Osmeridae. This small, delicate food fish is described and illustrated on page 156.

THE WHITEFISHES. Goregonidae. This famous freshwater fish is described and illustrated on page 170.

The Order Apodes — Eels — comprises several families; the most important one is the following:

THE EELS. Anguillidae. There is only one genus and one species in this family, in American waters, the common eel; it is described and illustrated on page 169.

The Order Eventognathi — Carp-like Fishes — comprises several families:

THE SUCKERS. Catostomidae. The "vacuum-cleaner" mouth of these bottom-feeders is responsible for the name "suckers." As food fishes they do not rank high; the flesh is well flavored, but it contains numerous bundles of small, annoying fagot bones. They are not game fish either. On the Pacific coast the Sacramento Sucker (15 inches) is a silvery fish with yellowish sides, common in the streams of British Columbia and the U.S. It feeds on small organisms and plants on the stones of stream bottoms.

THE CARPS AND MINNOWS. Cyprinidae. The carps proper are not native American fishes, but as they are a very popular food in Europe and Asia, they have been introduced here by fish culturists and are thriving now in many parts of the country. They attain a length of 3 feet but usually are smaller. Minnows are the best live bait an angler can obtain. Since they are by far the largest group of North American freshwater fishes, with many more species than any other family, and since the individuals are also exceedingly abundant, they are easily trapped and caught. Most of them are small fish; some reach a foot in length, like the common chub which is hooked everywhere but eaten only in emergencies; it is excessively bony like all minnows. The largest of the family, the well-known squawfish of the West averages a length of about 18 inches. The adult squawfish lives largely on other fish including young salmon and trout, and because of its voracious habits is also called Sacramento pike.

The Order Nematognathi—Catfishes—comprises a famous family:

THE CATFISHES. Ameiuridae. This large family of naked fishes prefers the warm fresh waters; they are abundant in North America. Among the species in the U.S. the channel or spotted catfish (20 inches) is common in the Mississippi Valley and the Great Lakes, the horned pout or bullhead in the eastern and middle states. The widely distributed blue catfish is described and illustrated on page 169.

The Order Haplomi—Pike-like Fishes—is represented by:

THE PIKES. Esocidae. The members of this family are so greedy and voracious, they have been called "mere machines for the assimilation of other organisms"; but from the human viewpoint they are good food and game fishes. The eastern pickerel and the pike are described and illustrated on page 172. The largest species of the group, the muskellunge, is an inhabitant of the Great Lakes, the St. Lawrence River, and the adjoining American and Canadian fresh waters. With an average length of 3 feet, a weight of 40 pounds, and a fighting disposition, the "musky" requires expert handling to be boated. Its strong and narrow body is built for swift swimming, and it is given to sudden bursts of speed.

The Order Synentognathi — Synentognathous Fishes — includes an interesting family:

THE FLYING FISHES. Exocoetidae. The California flying fish, a spectacular representative of this family, is described and illustrated on page 165.

The Order Anacanthini is represented by a most valuable family:

THE CODFISHES. Gadidae. The world-famous cods of the northern seas include such valuable food fishes as the cod, the pollock, and the haddock. They are described and illustrated on pages 162 and 163. The squirrel hake (15 to 20 inches) also belongs to the Cod Family, and although its meat is soft, it is quite popular; the range extends from the Gulf of St. Lawrence to North Carolina.

The Order Selenichthys includes the spectacular family of THE MARIPOSAS. Lampridae. The only known species is the big, gorgeously colored opah or moonfish, described and illustrated on page 166.

The Order Heterosomata contains a family known everywhere:

THE FLOUNDERS AND HALIBUTS. Hippoglossidae. The summer and winter flounder and the halibut are described and illustrated on pages 163 and 164. On the Pacific coast the starry flounder belongs to this family.

The Order Acanthopteri — Spiny-rayed Fishes — is an outstanding order of fishes with a list of important families:

THE MULLETS. Mugilidae. A very abundant species, the common or striped mullet occurs both in the Pacific and Atlantic Oceans. It is reported as far north as Cape Cod, but only from Chesapeake Bay southward is it a year-round resident. During the fall run, enormous schools collect in southern bays and shoals, all members being of nearly the same size or age. They feed on microscopic organisms on the surface but also like to search the ground sediment. They are a fine food fish caught in tremendous numbers in nets and haul seines, and are eaten fresh, or frozen, or salted; they are also a popular bait for various hand-line fisheries. Their backs are dark bluish with yellowish tints; their sides, silvery with a dark stripe along each row of scales. Length: 8 to 15 inches.

THE BARRACUDAS. Sphyraenidae. The barracuda of our southeastern waters is described and illustrated on page 157.

THE SAILFISHES. Istiophoridae. The highly prized sailfish is described and illustrated on page 158.

THE SWORDFISHES. Xiphiidae. The single species of this family is described and illustrated on page 159.

THE MACKERELS. Scombridae. Most of the numerous species of this family are valuable food fishes with firm and oily, though sometimes coarse flesh. The following well-known members are described and illustrated in the color section: mackerel on page 157, tuna on page 158, and albacore on page 166. A close relative of the common mackerel, though of smaller and thicker proportions, is the Spanish mackerel, one of the most popular food fishes along our Atlantic and Gulf coasts; it occurs from Cape Ann to Brazil. Its body has a metallic beauty and attains a weight of 10 pounds. An even larger species is the kingfish (not to be confused with the kingfish of the Whiting Family) which may attain a weight of 20 pounds or more, although 5 pounds is the average; its range extends from Cape Cod to Brazil. The meat of the bonito (18 to 24 inches) is often sold as Spanish mackerel, although it is inferior in flavor and texture. The streamlined body of the bonito is that of a large mackerel, with bluish stripes on its back as a distinguishing mark. On our Atlantic coast it ranges from southern Canada to Cape Sable in Florida and along the Gulf coast, but usually it remains in large schools on the open seas and approaches the shores only erratically. A voracious, predatory species, it feeds on other schooling fish, particularly on alewives and its own cousin, the mackerel. Strangely, almost nothing is known about its life history; not even its eggs have been identified. The Pacific mackerel is smaller, approaching the common species of the Atlantic in length (15 inches) and weight (2 pounds); it occurs from Alaska to California and is caught and consumed in great quantities. The Pacific species, also called greenback or zebra mackerel because of the greenish-yellow and black markings on its back, is omnivorous and devours anything it can swallow.

THE POMPANOS. Carangidae. The pompano, delight of all gourmets, is described and illustrated on page 159. A Pacific member of the group, the yellowtail, sometimes called the amberjack, is a beautiful and spectacular fish with yellow fins and a broad yellow stripe dividing its dark upper from its whitish lower body. Along the California coast it is recognized as one of the finest game fishes. Length: 30 inches.

THE BUTTERFISH. Stromateidae. The delicious but rather rare harvestfish and the more common butterfish are the only members of this family occurring on the Atlantic coast. The latter is caught from Nova Scotia to

North Carolina, preferably in bays, sounds, and inlets, but only during the summer months; it is not known where it spends the winter. This is the dollarfish of Maine, the sheepshead of Cape Cod, the pumpkinseed of Connecticut, the starfish of Norfolk; other names are shiner and skipjack. Both the small harvestfish (6 inches) and the larger, silvery butterfish (7 to 9 inches) like to swim about various jellyfishes.

THE BLUEFISHES. Pomatomidae. The only species of this family is described and illustrated on page 160.

THE DOLPHINS. Coryphaenidae. There are two species in this family, but only one is recorded in American waters: the common dolphin which is described and illustrated on page 160.

THE BASSES. Centrarchidae. A characteristic of most species of this freshwater family is their habit of building nests for their eggs and of defending them with great courage. Two species, the black crappie or calico bass and the white crappie, have about the same length (8 inches), the same weight (1 pound), range through the same American and Canadian territory east of the Rockies, have innumerable local names, and vary in the darker markings of the black crappie. The principal difference between the celebrated small-mouth bass which is described and illustrated on page 173, and the large-mouth variety lies in the upper jaws which extend to the rear margin of the eye in the former, and considerably beyond the eye in the latter. The popular rock bass is one of the most common game fishes from Vermont and New York westward to Manitoba and southward to Louisiana and Texas; it is a delicious, meaty panfish.

THE PERCHES. Percidae. This popular family comprises several of the best known American fishes, like the handsome, delicately flavored and abundant yellow perch which is described and illustrated on page 173, and the wall-eyed pike which is also called yellow pike-perch. It ranges from Lake Champlain and southern Canada to Minnesota, particularly throughout the Great Lakes region, south to Georgia and Alabama. An inhabitant of clear water, it has a firm, flaky, white meat. This fish of about 20 inches is quite variable in color, as such local names as yellow pike, grey pike, and blue pike indicate. Minnows, shad and other fishes are its diet. The sauger or sand pike (20 inches) is a similar species and has the same distribution.

THE SEA BASSES. Serranidae. This is one of the largest families of fishes; all members are carnivorous and restricted to warm and temperate seas; several species live in fresh water. A prominent species, the handsome sea bass, is described and illustrated on page 161. The white perch also belongs to the Sea Bass Family, a fish of the tidal regions from Nova Scotia to South Carolina; like the striped bass it is a most adaptable fish, common in brackish water but also living either in salt or fresh water. It has even become landlocked in some lakes. A good eating fish, it will average a pound in weight. Length of white perch: 8 to 10 inches.

THE RUDDERFISHES. Kyphosidae. A well known member of this family inhabits our Pacific shores, the greenfish or opaleye. It is described and illustrated on page 167.

THE GREENLINGS. Girellidae. This carnivorous family of the North Pacific includes the cultus cod or ling (30 inches), the chinook word cultus meaning "worthless"; since its flesh is good eating, the term is a misnomer. An outstanding characteristic of this "chameleon of the sea" is its capacity for varying its colors; the fish seems to adapt its hues to its environment.

THE DEMOISELLES. Pomacentridae. The spectacular ocean goldfish or Garibaldi of the west coast is described and illustrated on page 168.

THE TILEFISHES. Branchiostegidae. There is only one species in this family, the tilefish, which is described and illustrated on page 161.

THE CROAKERS. Sciaenidae. Most species of this family produce a peculiar noise which is hard to define: They croak or snore, apparently using the air bladder. One of their principal representatives is the weakfish or squeteague, of our Atlantic and Gulf coasts. It is highly esteemed as a food fish in the South, but less so in the North. A fine game fish, it has to be handled with care as its mouth is very tender. Also the king whiting or kingfish (12 to 18 inches) belongs to this group; it ranges from Maine to Florida, but by far the greatest catches are made from North Carolina southward. In fact, three closely related species live along our Atlantic Coast; but commercially they are not separated. With its yellow and black markings, the king whiting is a handsome fish; as it is sensitive to sudden waves of cold and heat, it is called the weather prophet of fishdom. The white sea bass is not a bass but a species of the croakers; indeed it is the Pacific version of the Atlantic weakfish to which it is very closely related. It is described and illustrated on page 167. A freshwater member of the Sciaenidae is the drum of the Great Lakes region and the Mississippi Valley, a large fish attaining a length of 3 feet; it is a source of mother-of-pearl. The saltwater counterpart of the freshwater drum is the sea drum, ranging from New England to the Rio Grande.

The Order Cataphracti includes a family of wide distribution:

THE ROCKFISHES. Scorpaenidae. This large family inhabits all seas, particularly the temperate parts of the Pacific. Many species are viviparous, i.e. they bring forth living young. On the Atlantic Coast the rose-fish, also called snapper, red perch, redfish, bream or John Dory, ranges from the Arctic to central New Jersey and is of ever increasing commercial importance. The biggest specimens reach a length of 2 feet, but the average is much less. It can easily be identified by its orange-red color and spiny head. On the west coast the red rockfish (12 inches) is even handsomer, displaying a spectacular color pattern of orange, red and purple.

Outline of the Principal Orders and Families of Amphibians and Reptiles in the U.S. and Southern Canada

The most easily recognized difference between amphibians and reptiles is their external appearance. Amphibians are commonly covered with a skin (which often has irritating or poisonous secretions), while nearly all reptiles are covered with scales or bony plates. Amphibians pass through a complete metamorphosis; during their aquatic or larval stage they are equipped with gills which they lose upon maturing; they then breathe through lungs or, as in the case of certain salamanders, through the skin or a mucous membrane of the mouth. The reptiles do not pass through a metamorphosis and are always air-breathing. In many characteristics the amphibians stand between the reptiles and the fishes. In the following outline the salamanders, frogs, and toads are amphibians, the other orders and families are reptiles.

The Order Caudata — Salamanders and Newts — is represented in the U.S. and Canada by several families:

THE MUDPUPPIES. Proteidae. Mudpuppies are permanent aquatic larvae ranging in size from 6 to 17 inches; they have a brownish color; several varieties are dotted with dark spots or blotches. The 7 species and subspecies occur in many regions of the East from southern Canada to the Gulf States.

THE CONGO EELS. Amphiumidae. As a representative of this group the congo eel of the southeastern U.S. is described and illustrated on page 176.

THE HELLBENDERS. Cryptobranchidae. As a representative of this family the hellbender is described and illustrated on page 176.

THE NEWTS. Salamandridae. The members of this family which produces both aquatic and terrestrial stages, are small, ranging in size from 2½ to 8½ inches. Brown is the predominating color; some species are spotted. Newts occur in the East from southern Canada to the Gulf States, and also in the far West.

THE BLUNT-MOUTHED SALAMANDERS. Ambystomidae. This family, on the whole terrestrial except in the breeding season, contains 19 species and subspecies of various sizes. It includes some spectacularly colored species like the ringed salamander of Arkansas and Missouri (yellow bars and spots on a brown background); the California tiger salamander (lemon-yellow spots on a lustrous black background); the spotted salamander which occurs in numerous localities from southern Canada to the Gulf States (bluish black with yellow or orange spots on either side); the marbled salamander of the Southeast (black with white markings); the eastern tiger salamander whose range, for the various subspecies, extends from the eastern seaboard to the Rocky Mountains (deep brown or black with pale brownish blotches); and the spectacular yellow-barred tiger salamander of various localities in the west-central states (deep brown or black with yellow markings).

THE LUNGLESS SALAMANDERS. Plethodontidae. This family comprises the majority of the American salamanders, with 79 species and subspecies. Some of them have small, limited ranges. Among the better known varieties of broader ranges are the northern and the southern dusky salamanders, the eastern red-backed salamander, the slimy salamander, the yellow-blotched salamander, the eastern four-toed salamander, the mountain purple salamander, the northern two-lined salamander, and the long-tailed salamander. In this family several interesting examples of environmental adaptation are reported. In the darkness of the caves of Missouri and Arkansas a salamander is found which is blind in its adult stage, and in the caves of Texas a permanent larva is found which is blind and has also lost nearly all its skin pigment; but its slim legs are elongated.

THE SIRENS. Sirenidae. This family comprises 3 species of aquatic salamanders with eel-like, elongated bodies. They range in size from a little over 8 inches to 3 feet. Their habitat is predominantly the South, although one species occurs in the Mississippi Valley northward to Lake Michigan.

The Order Salientia — Frogs and Toads — includes the following families which occur in the U.S. and Canada.

THE BELL TOADS. Ascaphidae. This small two-inch toad occurs in the American Northwest and British Columbia. Its color is grey or brown to almost black, with numerous black spots. It is solitary and awkward on land.

THE SPADEFOOTS. Pelobatidae. The 7 species of this family have hind feet provided with spades; with them they dig the burrows in which they live. They breed in rain pools and temporary overflow areas. Their color ranges from green to greyish, yellowish and brown. The spadefoots occur all over the U.S., but most species live in the West (including British Columbia) and the Southwest.

THE TOADS. Bufonidae. As a representative of this family of 20 species and subspecies the American toad is described and illustrated on page 177.

An Outline of Our Natural Environment

THE TREE FROGS *(Including Cricket Frogs and Chorus Frogs)*. Hylidae. The 28 species and subspecies of this family commonly have sucking disks on their digits, useful on trees. Some have exceptionally loud voices, and some can change their colors. A familiar species is the common tree toad which varies in hues from pale brown to ashy grey or green; it has a granular skin and attains a length of 2 2/5 inches. It ranges from the Maine - southern Canada - Minnesota line to the Gulf States. Other species occur in various parts of the country.

THE ROBBER FROGS. Leptodactylidae. A dog-like bark is typical for the 6 species of this family which occurs only in the southernmost parts of the U.S. Some have fanciful color patterns.

THE TRUE FROGS. Ranidae. This family includes 26 species and subspecies. The best-known member is the bull frog, the largest American frog. It is described and illustrated on page 177.

THE NARROW-MOUTHED TOADS. Microhylidae. The 4 small members of this family are lovers of moist places; they are largely nocturnal and subterranean; 2 occur in the East, 2 are confined to Texas.

The Order Loricata—Crocodilians—consists of one family:

THE CROCODILE FAMILY. Crocodylidae. Two species occur in North America, the rare American crocodile and the more frequent alligator. The latter is described and illustrated on page 178.

The Order Squamata — The various lizards form the sub-order Sauria; it includes numerous North American families; the more important ones are:

THE GECKOS. Gekkonidae. In contrast to other lizards the geckos have such minute scales that their skin appears to be soft like that of a toad. The tropical geckos reach the size of a foot or more, but the 7 North American species are diminutive creatures which live in the southernmost regions of the U.S. The banded gecko, 3 inches long and of a rich yellow color either crossed by bands of chestnut brown, or spotted with brown blotches, occurs in the Southwest and Lower California.

THE AMERICAN CHAMELEONS, IGUANAS, ETC. Iguanidae. This family includes a number of interesting genera. The strange and amusing American chameleon is described and illustrated on page 178, and the desert iguana of the Southwest on page 179. Other representatives of the Iguanidae are the large chuckawalla, the collared lizard with a double black collar, the leopard lizard (yellowish with dark blotches), the zebra-tailed lizard with whitish and dark bands on the tail, and the striking sand lizard which seems to wear a pattern of light embroidery on a dark background. The collared swift is a representative of the swifts, small lizards with rough scales. Also the horned lizards, commonly called horned toads, belong to this family. They are distinguished from all other lizards by their toad-like bodies and cone-shaped horns.

THE PLATED LIZARDS. Anguidae. These reptiles have slender bodies and very long and brittle tails, often twice as long as the head and body. They show square scales on top, arranged in ring-like rows. The long-tailed plated lizard is described and illustrated on page 179. One lizard member of this family has an appearance all its own: the glass snake, so-called because of its serpentine body which shows no traces of limbs, and its smooth, glassy surface. However, it is clearly distinguished from a snake by its well-developed eyelids and its ear cavities.

THE BEADED LIZARDS. Helodermatidae. The only species encountered in the U.S. is the famous gila monster, described and illustrated on page 180.

THE SKINKS OR SMOOTH-SCALED LIZARDS. Scincidae. These small lizards with glossy scales are represented in North America by 16 species; one member is particularly interesting because of its complete color change. When young, it is called the fine-lined skink; it is coal black, striped with vivid yellow lines; its tail shows a brilliant blue. When adult, the reptile takes on a brownish color while its head becomes bright red. It is then called red-headed lizard or "scorpion." It reaches a length of 9½ inches and ranges from Massachusetts to Florida and Texas, extending also through the Mississippi Valley to southern Canada.

The snakes belong to the same order as the lizards, but form the special sub-order Ophidia.

THE TYPICAL NON-POISONOUS SNAKES. Colubridae. The striped or garter snakes are important members of this family: These reptiles usually show 3 yellow stripes on a darker background shade. The common garter snake is described and illustrated on page 180. The Water Snakes are another genus of the Colubridae; as a representative of these dim-colored, ugly-looking reptiles, the common water snake is described and illustrated on page 181. The Garter Snakes and Water Snakes are supplemented by a number of satellite genera, the so-called Small Swamp Snakes and Brown Snakes. The Racers are large, slender, non-constricting serpents of great agility and activity; one of the best-known species is the blacksnake or black racer, illustrated on page 181. The Flat-nosed Snakes, Leaf-nosed Snakes and the Bull Snakes are largely inhabitants of the Southwest. The Pine Snakes of the Southeast belong to the bull snake group. The Rat Snakes, powerful constricting serpents, are valuable destroyers of farm pests; the chicken snake is described and illustrated on page 182. The King Snakes are so-called because they seem to dominate the other snakes, both harmless and poisonous; they attack them, kill them and eat them; a description and illustration of the common king snake is found on page 182. The Ring-necked Snakes include the well-known grass snake which attains a length of 15½ inches and occurs east of the Rockies; it is common in New England and New York. The Rainbow Snakes show brilliant patterns of coloration, and their scales have an opalescent luster; they grow to a length of 6 feet; but in spite of their showy appearance they are burrowers and are rarely seen above ground. The thick-bodied, pugnacious Hog-nosed Snakes are equipped with an upturned, flat, hog-like snout; typical is their way of lowering their heads and necks and hissing loudly; they are the notorious "adders" and "vipers" but their antics are not to be taken too seriously as they bite quite seldom. There are eastern, southern and western species. Finally, the Rear-fanged Snakes belong to this family; they are scantily represented in the southern regions in the U.S. Mildly venomous, they use their poison to benumb their prey.

THE HIGHLY POISONOUS SNAKES WITH SHORT AND ERECT FANGS. Elapidae. The Old World Cobras and the American Coral Snakes are the best-known members of this family. The harlequin or coral snake is described and illustrated on page 183.

THE HIGHLY POISONOUS SNAKES WITH LONG, FOLDING FANGS IN THE UPPER JAWS. Crotalidae. Of these venomous snakes, as dangerous as they are famous, the water moccasin is described and illustrated on page 183, the copperhead and the diamond-back rattlesnake on page 184.

The Order Testudinata — Turtles and Tortoises — comprises 6 families.

THE LEATHER TURTLES. Dermochelidae. The leather-back turtle is the largest of all turtles, attaining a weight of 1,000 pounds and a length of 6 feet. Its dark brown, leathery shell is sometimes spotted with yellow. The huge front flippers, the rear flippers and the head have no coarse armor plates, in contrast to the heavy armor of the other marine turtles. With its powerful, seal-like flippers it swims gracefully and comes ashore only to deposit its eggs. It is found in the American waters of the Atlantic, sometimes as far north as Nova Scotia, also on the Pacific coast as far north as Vancouver.

THE SEA TURTLES. Cheloniidae. The best-known species of this family, the loggerhead turtle, (300 pounds) and the green turtle (up to 500 pounds) have about the same range as the leather-back. One species occurs also along the coast of Lower California. The green turtle is described and illustrated on page 185.

THE SNAPPING TURTLES. Chelydridae. These are the largest freshwater turtles in the U.S. and Canada. The common snapping turtle is described and illustrated on page 185.

THE MUSK AND MUD TURTLES. Kinosternidae. These small reptiles — few grow to a length of 5 inches — emit a heavy odor of musk when disturbed. If caught, they snap viciously and bite fiercely. They will nibble at the hook and cause a commotion in the water, to the annoyance of freshwater fishermen. The common musk turtle grows a dull brown shell approximately 3¾ inches long; two bright yellow stripes on each side of the head are its characteristic markings. Its range extends from southern Canada to Florida, and westward to Texas and Oklahoma.

THE FRESHWATER TURTLES. Testudinidae. This family includes the terrapins, i.e. the semi-aquatic North American turtles of which the larger species are edible. The most familiar is the southern diamond-back whose olive-colored shell is marked with a diamond pattern. Its average length is 8 inches, and its market value increases greatly with every additional half inch. One habit in which it differs from other terrapins is its occurrence in brackish and salt water, especially salt marshes. The coastal area from Cape Hatteras to Florida is its range; several subspecies extend to New England in the North and the Gulf States in the South. The northern diamond-back occurs in Delaware and Chesapeake bays. Among the smaller terrapins are the so-called painted varieties, i.e. the painted turtle which ranges from New Brunswick to the Gulf. Its marginal plates have red blotches. Its average length is 4⅝ inches. The Box Turtles also belong to this family; they have high, globular shells and are quite terrestrial.

THE SOFT-SHELLED TURTLES. Trionychidae. "Flapjack turtles" is the name given to these aquatic reptiles whose shell is flat, forming an oval or almost a sphere. The southern soft-shelled turtle is edible and for sale in many markets.

Outline of the Principal Orders and Families of Insects in the U.S. and Southern Canada

The Order Thysanura — Bristletails — includes several families of wingless, elongated, usually white insects that are also called silverfish or fire brats. They may be seen running over the cellar floor or found out of doors under the bark of trees or feeding on dry leaves in damp places. Length: ⅝ inch.

The Order Odonata — Dragonflies and Damselflies — comprises four families, *the Aeschnids* (Aeschnidae), the largest species; *the Skimmers* (Libellulidae) to which most common dragonflies belong; *the True Agrionids* (Agrionidae) with broad wings and metallic colors; *and the*

Damselflies (Coenagrionidae). The ten-spot dragonfly of the Libellulidae is described and illustrated on page 188. The smaller damselfly has also four wings, but they operate without coordination and cause a kind of bouncing flight. Male and female damselflies frequently fly together in tandem fashion, the male grasping the thorax of his mate while the female deposits her eggs on water plants. This practice is also occasionally observed with dragonflies. Length of odonata: 1½ to 2¾ inches; expanse of wings: 1¾ to 4⅛ inches.

The Order Ephemeroptera — Mayflies — is a short-lived race. Adult mayflies exist only for a few hours, or at the most, in some instances, a few days. They arise from the aquatic nymph at sunset, a moult takes place, and the mating dance begins; it is over by sunrise when the eggs are laid and the insects die. Length: ⅝ to ⅞ inch.

The Order Plecoptera — Stoneflies — is closely connected with the maintenance of our freshwater fish population. Millions of stoneflies are devoured by fishes. Billions of eggs are hatched, as each female deposits 5 to 6 thousand; but only a small percentage of stonefly nymphs ever reach maturity; the remainder form an abundant food supply for fishes in brooks, ponds, and rivers. The adult brown stonefly has long, threadlike antennae and two pairs of wings but is not a skillful flyer. Other regional names are salmon fly, trout fly, shad fly, etc. Length: ½ to ¾ inch; giant stonefly: 1½ to 2⅜ inches.

The Order Orthoptera — Cockroaches, Crickets, etc. — includes several interesting families:

THE COCKROACHES. Blattidae. These furtive pests of human habitations are described and illustrated on page 188.

THE PRAYING MANTIS. Mantidae. This unusual insect, a predaceous eater of other insects, is described and illustrated on page 189.

THE WALKINGSTICKS. Phasmidae. The wingless, herbivorous walkingstick is described and illustrated on page 189.

THE SHORT-HORNED GRASSHOPPERS. Locustidae. These insects have been responsible for tremendous crop losses in the history of man. The two-striped grasshopper is described and illustrated on page 190.

THE GROUSE LOCUSTS. Tettigidae. These diminutive grasshoppers — the name "grouse" remains unexplained — are found in almost any pasture in the U.S. and Canada. They are greyish to blackish, sometimes with a large white spot on the back. Length: ⅜ to ⅝ inch.

THE LONG-HORNED GRASSHOPPERS. Tettigoniidae. An important member of this family is the bright green katytid whose description and illustration are found on page 190.

THE CRICKETS. Gryllidae. As a representative of this omnivorous family the common field cricket is described and illustrated on page 191.

The Order Isoptera — Termites — is encountered throughout the U.S. and southern Canada. This destructive wood-eater is described and illustrated on page 191.

The Order Dermaptera — Earwigs — consists of small insects whose name has probably been corrupted from ear-wings, as the hind wings of those species which fly, suggest the outline of a human ear. Two of its families are very common, the black or brownish *European Earwig Family,* Forficulidae, which, by means of potted plants, has spread to every temperate and tropical region on earth, and the black, flattened *Small Earwig Family,* Labiidae, whose members often fly at lights. Length: ⅜ to ⅝ inch (European); ⅛ to ¼ inch (Small).

The Order Coleoptera — Beetles — includes approximately 40% of all known species of insects. Characteristic is the hard shell on their back; this shell is really the first pair of wings; it covers and protects the more delicate second pair which is neatly folded beneath. In size, the beetles range from the Trichopterygids which are so small that quite a number of them can find room on the head of a pin, to the hercules beetle which measures 6 inches in length. Of the large number of families the following are important in the U.S. and Canada:

THE WHIRLIGIGS. Gyrinidae. These black beetles with a metallic luster commonly swim in large colonies on the calm surface of a pond. They are probably the best equipped insects for an air and water life because they have well developed wings and are also excellent swimmers, both on the surface of the water and underneath. Some species exude a peculiar odor which faintly resembles the fragrance of apples, hence the name "apple bug." Length: ⅜ to ½ inch.

THE WATER SCAVENGERS. Hydrophilidae. Abundant are the water beetles. Their largest representative, the water scavenger beetle, is described and illustrated on page 192.

THE DIVING BEETLES. Dytiscidae. If you see a dull reddish beetle with black markings hanging head down from the surface of the water, with two large breathing pores protruding from the water, it is probably one of the predacious, carnivorous Diving Beetles. This is their method of supplying themselves with air. Both the adults and their very long, slender larvae, with big heads and long mandibles, prey upon minute vertebrates and invertibrates. Length: 1 inch.

THE WEEVILS. Curculionidae. A snout-like projection of the head is typical for the weevils or "snout beetles;" these slow and secretive grey and brown insects are considered a pest as they are injurious to cotton, corn and other agricultural plants, and also to stored grain.

THE ROVE BEETLES. Staphylinidae. This large family is abundant in decaying organic matter. When annoyed, the long, slender beetles run about with the tip of their abdomen turned up, as if they are ready to sting. Although they have no sting, this bluff doubtlessly affords them a measure of protection. The largest species attain a length of 1/2 inch, but most are smaller than 1/8 inch. Many have a dark metallic luster.

THE SCARABS. Scarabaeidae. A large family of medium-sized beetles, ranging in color from metallic green to bronze or purple, they include the dung-eating beetles (among them the sacred scarab of Egypt), the leaf-eating May beetle or June bug, the long-legged, yellowish-brown rose-chafer and the Japanese beetle, an introduced pest. The May beetle and the Japanese beetle are described and illustrated on pages 194 and 193.

THE STAG BEETLES. Lucanidae. The formidable looking stag beetle is described and illustrated on page 193.

THE TIGER BEETLES. Cicindelidae. All species of this small to medium-sized family are considered beneficial because they feed on other, often injurious insects. Abundant in wooded areas, they are active by night and hide beneath the surface litter by day. A few species are brightly colored, but dark brown and black hues are prevailing. Several exude a bad-smelling secretion, sometimes in the form of a volatile gas expelled in explosive puffs which can be heard and seen; they are called bombardier beetles.

THE BLISTER BEETLES. Meloidae. These small beetles, grey or black, sometimes with markings, are frequently found on potatoes and flowers, particularly on goldenrods. They have chemical properties: They secrete cantharadine which raises blisters on the human skin, and from the dried bodies of certain species a medicinal substance is extracted and used as an aphrodisiac and for other purposes. Some species secrete an oily fluid on leg and body joints when alarmed, and are called oil beetles. They have a complicated life history; in one stage they are parasites of bees.

THE FIREFLIES. Lampyridae. This light-producing beetle is described and illustrated on page 194.

THE SOLDER BEETLES. Cantharidae. With their soft bodies these insects resemble the fireflies. In the late summer and fall they are common on flowers, particularly on goldenrods, and while some species live on insects, others feed on pollen and nectar. They are yellow marked with black.

THE SEXTON OR CARRION BEETLES. Silphidae. These busy undertakers are described and illustrated on page 192.

THE LONGHORNS. Cerambycidae. Long antennae, often longer than their bodies, are typical. They like garden flowers and are capable of producing a buzzing sound. Most females deposit their eggs in dead or decaying trees, but some species prefer the living tissue and occasionally infest the plant so badly that it dies. The front segments of their larvae are greatly enlarged and look like big round heads; therefore they are called round-headed borers.

THE METALLIC WOODBORERS. Buprestidae. These hard, compact beetles have a metallic luster which makes them look like brass pieces. Their antennae are fashioned like saws, each part forming a tooth. They are active by day, particularly in the warm days of August and September. The first segment of the thin larva is greatly expanded, hence the name hammerhead borer; they excavate flat tunnels in trees, and include also a few leaf-miners and gall-makers. Length: 3/8 to 5/8 inches.

THE LEAF BEETLES. Chrysomelidae. A destructive and common representative is the yellow or orange potato beetle whose shell is marked with longitudinal black lines. The female deposits her eggs on the underside of the potato leaves, and from the eggs the potato bugs emerge, i.e. the red, plump larvae. Originally feeding on the wild members of the potato family, like the night-shade, they have quickly adapted themselves to the cultivated variety.

THE LADY BEETLES. Coccinellidae. The one beetle that is popular with human beings, is described and illustrated on page 195.

THE CLICK BEETLES. Elateridae. These small brown or black beetles have a unique method of righting themselves when they are turned on their backs. They spring into the air, and 2 or 3 flips are usually sufficient to land them right side up. One common North American species has two large black eye spots. The long reddish-brown larva looks like a piece of rusty wire and is called wire worm.

The Order Mallophaga — Biting Lice — and the **Order Anoplura** — Sucking Lice — are described and illustrated (picture of head louse) on page 195.

The Order Hemiptera — True Bugs — includes those insects whose outstanding characteristics are long, sucking mouth parts and a gradual development. The word Hemiptera means half-winged and describes the front pair of wings which are thick at the base and thin at the apex, appearing to be divided in half. Most true bugs feed on living plant tissues, but some capture other insects and feed on their body fluids. Among the more important families are the following:

LACE BUGS. Tingidae. When seen under a microscope, the front parts and the first pair of wings of these small insects seem to be made of the most delicate lace; they are usually white.

The Shield Bugs. Scutelleridae. They look like miniature turtles and commonly have a light brown color.

The Stink Bugs. Pentatomidae. Among them the harlequin bug is best known; it is described and illustrated on page 196.

The Water Striders. Gerridae. These insects skate over the quiet surface of pools and ponds. Their long legs are covered with minute hairs which do not become wet and maintain them on the surface.

The Damsel Bugs. Nabidae. These grey, brownish, reddish or black bugs are, on the whole, predaceous; they feed on the body fluids of other insects.

The Plant Bugs. Miridae. This family comprises several thousand species, most of which suck the juices of plants; small to medium-sized, they are usually oval in shape and fragile, and vary from dull brown to brilliant colors.

The Chinch Bugs. Lygaeidae. These insects are, to a large extent, agricultural pests; the true chinch bug, a small black and white insect with red legs, is particularly injurious to grain and corn.

The Squash Bugs. Coreidae. As the name implies, an important species of this family, a large, brown-speckled bug, feeds upon the plants of the squash family; many species have scent glands and exude a penetrating, nauseating odor.

The Ambush Bugs. Phymatidae. These hunters hide in flowers, particularly goldenrods, to catch bees, flies, and other insects on whose body juices they feed; one frequent species is green and yellow in color, with a broad black band across the abdomen.

The Assassin Bugs. Reduviidae. These bugs feed largely on other insects, but some species will also suck the blood of rodents and small mammals and even attack man; they are also carriers of diseases, such as the black sickness of India; some are brightly colored, but the majority are dark brown or black, and covered with many large and small hairs; dust and dirt will cling to the hairs and serve as camouflage. Strangely, they are also called "kissing bugs," because of a much publicized incident in which a young lady was bitten by one of these insects.

The Bed Bugs. Cimicidae. The presence of these wingless parasites in a home is considered an embarrassing indication of lack of cleanliness. Bed bugs are small, usually measuring less than a quarter of an inch; they have the shape of a strawberry and are reddish brown. Hiding by day, they are active at night. Only one American species attacks human beings, but others are parasitic on birds and mammals.

The Flat Bugs. Aradidae. In wooded areas the notion prevails that bed bugs may be introduced into houses by old lumber. Such a misconception results from the fact that the flat bugs living beneath the loose bark of logs look very much like bed bugs. But there are two important differences: They have wings, and they are not bloodsuckers; for the most part they feed on fungi or, rarely, living plants.

The Giant Waterbugs. Belostomatidae. Small heads, large eyes, and front legs held before the body in readiness to seize their prey of young fish, tadpoles, and insects are characteristics of these brown bugs; they wait in ambush, partly buried in mud or hiding between water plants in ponds and pools. For obtaining oxygen, they have a breathing tube which protrudes from the apex of the abdomen and is held above the surface of the water. Length: 2 to 2¼ inches.

The Water Scorpions. Nepidae. A long breathing tube at the hind end of the body is typical for these thin, predacious aquatic bugs. Their coloration is mostly brown, their length, 1⅜ to 1⅝ inches.

The Water Boatmen. Corixidae. With their elongated middle and hind pairs of legs these brownish bugs row through the water; as the legs are fringed with hairs, they have the effect of oars. Probably from this arrangement the name "boatmen" is derived. Their air supply is preserved in a hollow space in the abdomen beneath the wings.

The Backswimmers. Notonectidae. As the name implies, these bugs swim upside down. Their back is pale, often pearl-like in lustre, a protective adaptation to the sky-reflected surface of the water, while their underside is light brown. They have a sharp pointed beak which they use as a hypodermic needle for injecting a poison into their struggling prey of fish, tadpoles, crustaceans and insects. After paralyzing the creature, they use their beak for sucking out the body fluids of their prey. Length: ⅜ to ½ inch.

The Order Homoptera — Membranous-winged Bugs — ranges in size from a species so small they are hardly visible to the naked eye, to others that measure 3 inches in length. They include a number of well-known families:

The Cicadas. Cicadidae. These musical bugs are described and illustrated on page 196.

The Lanternflies. Fulgoridae. This is largely a tropical and sub-tropical family, but several species are frequent in our own pastures. They look like moths. Certain species produce a waxy secretion that may form long filaments, others secrete a powdery wax on wings and body which enhances their mothlike appearance. Length: ⅜ inch.

The Treehoppers. Membracidae. These small insects have grotesquely distorted front parts. The green to brownish buffalo treehopper has a broad, hoodlike covering; another species grows a "thorn" on its head, as a mimicry. Many members of the family produce the clear, sweet secretion called honeydew which is collected by ants.

THE LEAFHOPPERS. Cicadellidae. In spite of their name these slender insects are more abundant in the grass than among the leaves of bushes and trees. They feed on plant juices and do much damage to our crops, particularly to cotton. Their body is usually brown.

THE FROGHOPPERS. Cercopidae. Small clumps of white froth on grasses, bushes, and low trees are a common sight during the summer months; they are usually called "frog spit," "snake spit," or "cuckoo spit." An examination of the bubbles will reveal the builder of this strange home: a small, dusky grey or brown bug with dark spots. Length: ¼ to ⅜ inch.

THE SCALE INSECTS AND MEALY BUGS. Coccidae. The winged males of this family do not possess a mouth and consequently are short-lived. In fact, they are so unimportant that in several species the females lay their eggs or produce living young without sexual union. The wingless female builds around her body a waxy or powdery covering in the shape of an oyster shell or a cushion. The mealy bugs cover themselves with a powdery secretion that resembles corn meal. The yellowish young are active for a while but the dark adults usually spend their life in one spot, sucking the juices of the host plant and doing considerable damage; they are frequent on potted plants. Length: 1/16 inch.

THE WHITEFLIES. Aleyrodidae. These tiny destructive insects are frequent in greenhouses and multiply rapidly. Their nymphs look like scale insects. Length: 1/16 inch.

THE APHIDS. Aphididae. These "milk cows of the ants" are described and illustrated on page 197.

The Order Neuroptera — Net-winged Insects — has a common characteristic, the net or nerve-veined type of wing; it has, however, no monopoly on this feature. The water-loving small brown or black Alderflies belong to this group, as well as the Dobsonflies whose big larva is prized for trout and bass fishing. Other families are the arboreal Snake Flies and the Green Lacewings which are also called Golden Eyes because their eyes have a metallic golden color, or Stink Flies, because they exude a nauseating odor when disturbed. One family is of special interest:

THE ANT LIONS. Myrmeleontidae. The yellow-brown adult lion resembles a damselfly but has longer and broader wings. Nevertheless it is a poor flier. Its larva is the celebrated doodle-bug, a plump insect with sickle-like mandibles; it digs a small cylindrical pit in the sand or dry soil, entrenches itself at the bottom, and waits for a passing ant that may tumble down.

The Order Trichoptera — Caddisflies — have larvae that are architects; for most of the caddisworms, as the larvae are called, build themselves houses or cases of sticks (so that a stream of water always runs through them) or of stones, if the species lives on a rocky stream. The adults are not often seen on the wing. As many species do not eat during their adult stage, they are short-lived; the males die soon after mating, the females after egg-laying. Most caddisflies are dull brown or black.

The Order Lepidoptera—Butterflies and Moths—includes the insects whose wings are covered with overlapping scales, in numerous cases in the most brilliant colors. The following are the more important families of butterflies:

THE SWALLOWTAILS. Papilionidae. The tiger swallowtail is described and illustrated on page 197.

THE SKIPPERS. Hesperiidae. These active butterflies are a common sight as they skip from bush to bush. The more frequent species are light or dark brown with yellow, orange, or white patches. Their caterpillars present a bizarre appearance with their reddish-brown, large heads and thin, yellow necks and bodies; during the heat of the day many of them crawl on leaves, fold them over their bodies, and fasten them with silk threads. At night they venture out and search for food.

THE MILKWEED BUTTERFLIES. Danaidae. As a representative of this family the well-known monarch is described and illustrated on page 198.

THE MEADOWBROWNS. Satyridae. This popular family is often identified by eye spots on their wings. The buckeye is described and illustrated on page 198.

THE FRITILLARIES. Nymphalidae. Of this dominant family two species are described and illustrated in the color sections: The banded purple and the mourning cloak on page 199.

THE BLUES AND COPPERS. Lycaenidae. The blues are small but bright. The reddish-brown coppers are their relatives. The caterpillars of this family are flat and slug-like and some exude a fluid secretion of which the ants are fond.

WHITES AND SULPHURS. Pieridae. The very common white cabbage butterfly is described and illustrated on page 200.

The moths vary greatly in size; the smallest species have a wingspread of less than 1/16 of an inch, the giant atlas moth has an expanse of 9 to 10½ inches. Among the better-known families are:

THE CLEARWINGS. Aegeriidae. These small moths have probably survived because they strongly resemble wasps. They are incapable of stinging, but their enemies stay away from them. Their wings are usually clear, their abdomen has black, yellow or red rings.

THE SPHINX MOTHS. Sphingidae. Of these moths the two best-known species are the tomato sphinx moth which is described and illustrated on page 200, and the tobacco sphinx moth.

THE GIANT SILKWORMS. Saturniidae. As representatives of this family of large and beautiful moths the luna moth and the cecropia moth are described and illustrated on page 201.

THE SMOKY MOTHS. Amatidae. This small and feebly flying species that is common in the U.S. and Canada has smoky brown wings; the hind wings, however, become clear toward the center. They wear a yellow collar, have a metallic blue abdomen, and are active by day.

THE TIGER MOTHS. Arctiidae. A well-known caterpillar produced by this family, the woolly bear, is described and illustrated on page 202.

THE GEOMETERS. Geometridae. Geometers, or measuring worms, are "land measurers" or surveyors. The caterpillars of these moths move over the ground as if they are measuring it. Having legs only on each end but none in the middle, they draw the hind end to the front, and proceed in a looping motion. When still, they look like twigs. The adult moths are frail insects with long and slender legs; they have dark brown markings on a tan background and are poor fliers. Expanse of wings: 1¼ inches.

THE TENT CATERPILLARS. Lasiocampidae. These builders of web-like tents are described and illustrated on page 202.

THE BELL MOTHS. Tortricidae. The English name is derived from the shape of the front wings of these moths; they are narrow at the base end and broad at the top, jointly forming a bell. Among their destructive species are the apple worm and the small caterpillar inside the Mexican jumping bean, the cause of the jumping. The spruce budworm is misnamed because it prefers balsam to spruce, and is not a worm. Feeding both on the needles and on the buds, this small caterpillar has destroyed thousands of acres of balsam in various parts of the U.S. and Canada. The fruit tree leafroller is a serious pest in American orchards.

THE TUSSOCK MOTHS. Lymantriidae. The term "tussock" concerns the cluster of hair which sticks up on the backs of most caterpillars of this family, like the hairs of a nail brush.

THE MILLER MOTHS. Noctuidae. More than 3,000 species of this night-flying family have been described for the U.S. and Canada alone. Most of them are drab-colored, usually with an inconspicuous pattern on a brown background; they are easily attracted by sugar bait and electric lights. Many of their caterpillars are "semi-loopers" living on host plants, but some naked brown species are subterranean: They are the vicious cutworms which attack small seedlings and cut their stems off near the ground. Also such pests as the greasy cutworm, the mealy stalkborer, and the corn earworm belong to this family.

THE CLOTHES MOTHS AND LEAF MINERS. Tineidae. The larvae of two species of this family ravenously devour textiles. One spins a case for its body, the other casts a loose web over the material it is eating. The adults of the case-makers are yellowish brown with brown marks on the front wings, the others are more lightly colored and not spotted. Wing spread: ½ to ⅝ inch. Some Leaf miners also are members of this family. Their larvae produce the well-known tunnels in leaves, burrowing along between the upper and the lower sheets.

The Order Mecoptera — Scorpionflies — includes a few families whose male members possess a scorpion-like sting at the apex of the abdomen; unlike the organ of the true scorpion, however, it is not a stinging device. Another interesting characteristic of many species is the structure of the wings: They are membranous and conspicuously marked with brown spots. The scorpion flies are encountered, sometimes quite abundantly, in wooded districts.

The Order Diptera — Flies — contains those insects which possess only one pair of wings; the second pair is vestigial; they are the swiftest fliers among the insects, and speeds of 50 to 60 miles per hour are accepted as possible for certain species. Of their larvae, called maggots, many are headless and legless. Their breeding habits are varied; most of them deposit their eggs on or near the food supply; some lay living young, the eggs being hatched within the body of the female; others lay pupae, the eggs being hatched and the larvae developed to the stage of the pupa within the female insect. On the whole flies are considered pests and carriers of diseases, but a great many are active plant pollinators, and they furnish a most important food supply for fishes and birds. In the final analysis the benefits derived from flies outweigh the damage. The order includes many well-known families:

THE BLACK FLIES. Simuliidae. During the early summer, after the ice has left the lakes, the visitor in our northwoods will find the black flies most annoying. Their swarms seem endless, and their appetite for blood ravenous; as they are tiny, not even fine netting will keep them away. Usually the act of biting and feeding does not hurt, but an irritation and sometimes a painful swelling follow. Their eggs are placed on the banks of rapid streams.

THE CRANEFLIES. Tipulidae. Daddy longlegs is a more common name for the members of this family. In size they range from very large specimens to others not larger than a mosquito which they resemble in various ways; but because of their poorly developed mouth parts crane flies are harmless. Some northern species are wingless and can be seen crawling over the snow in wintertime. The name daddy longlegs, by the way, is also used for the Phalangida (an order of the spiders and their allies).

THE MOSQUITOES. Culicidae. This fascinating insect is described and illustrated on page 203.

THE MIDGES OR GNATS. Chironomidae. These tiny relatives of the mosquito may be annoying, but they are harmless. A swarm of them will settle on a walker in the woods and get into his hair, eyes, ears, and mouth, but most of them are unable to bite. In a swarm they produce a high-pitched, buzzing noise.

THE SOLDIER FLIES. Stratiomyidae. These bluish-black flies have yellow or green markings and look as the name implies, like soldiers in uniform. They are attracted by flowers, particularly yellow ones. Their worm-like larvae live in decaying organic matter.

THE DEER FLIES. Tabanidae. On warm summer days the medium to large-sized members of this family land on a man's neck or arm and bite viciously. Of animals, deer and horses are especially subject to their attack, hence the names deer fly or horse fly. As they like to alight on ears, they are also called ear flies. Commonly their very large eyes are metallic green in color, and the name green-headed monster is sometimes heard. Finally the term gadfly is used. Only the females are biting bloodsuckers; the males are harmless vegetarians and live on the nectar of flowers. Their long and flat eggs are black and are laid in a cluster.

THE ROBBER FLIES. Asilidae. These large insects, also called assassin flies, capture their prey on the wing; in flight their hairy legs form a basket to trap insects.

THE BEE FLIES. Bombyliidae. These small bee-like flies with stout, hairy bodies are attracted by brightly colored flowers. They are excellent fliers, darting through the air at great speed or hovering at the same spot in the fashion of a helicopter. Their wings are usually transparent, but some species show brown cross bands. Their larvae are parasites on other insects; they eat the eggs of grasshoppers and beetles, or, when hatched within the nests of bees and wasps, feed upon their young hosts. THE FLOWER FLIES (Syrphidae) resemble bees and wasps still more closely; they even hum and buzz, but, of course, do not sting.

THE BLOW FLIES. Calliphoridae. The well known bluebottles and greenbottles belong to this family. They are identified by their metallic blue or green coloration.

THE HOUSE FLIES. Muscidae. This unpopular insect is described and illustrated on page 203.

THE VINEGAR FLIES. Drosophilidae. This scientifically important fly is described and illustrated on page 204.

The Order Siphonaptera — Fleas — comprises a group of curious insects: They are laterally flattened so that they may proceed swiftly between the hairs of their host. The most common species live on cats and dogs; the so-called human flea attacks man, dogs, hogs, skunks, rats, and poultry; others specialize in one particular bird or mammal host. At least 11 species are reported to transmit bubonic plague, others are carriers of murine typhus fever, and most likely additional diseases are also spread by fleas. When the host of a flea dies of a contagious disease, the flea leaves the corpse and seeks a new host.

The Order Hymenoptera — Bees, Wasps, Ants — includes a number of insects which seem quite different in structure and habits yet have several important characteristics in common. They possess, for instance, two pairs of membranous wings arranged in an unusual manner; the hind pair is considerably shorter than the front pair, and normally both pairs are joined by tiny hooks so that the four wings act as two units — an improvement in efficiency. These wings are membranous and show a few large veins and cross veins, but they have not the network of small veins found on the dragonflies. Finally, the members of this large order are equipped for sucking and biting. Among the families which use the sting as a weapon, only the females and the workers (which are under-developed females) are able to do so, as the stinging apparatus is really an ovipositor; in many species it is actually used for depositing eggs. Every member of this order goes through a complete life history from egg to larva, pupa, and adult. There are a number of important families:

THE SAWFLIES. Tenthredinidae. These wasp-like insects are small to medium-sized. Their name derives from a saw-like ovipositor with which the female saws a number of slits in the leaves or stems of the host plant where she deposits the eggs.

THE HORNTAILS. Siricidae. The name of these large, brown and yellow insects is derived from the stout, horn-like ovipositor of the female which is inserted into a tree for the laying of an egg. Sometimes it is so deeply embedded in the wood that the female has difficulties pulling it out.

THE ANTS. Formicidae. This family is described and illustrated on page 204.

THE ICHNEUMONS. Ichneumonidae. Many of these parasitic wasps insert their eggs in the bodies of larvae or caterpillars. Their own minute larvae hatched from the eggs begin to eat their host's fatty tissues, and the host may live for a while while numerous tiny larvae feed on its inside. Only when the vital organs are affected and destroyed, the host gives up its life. The ichneumons are considered most useful in pest control, and foreign species have been frequently introduced to aid in the scientific procedure called "biological control."

THE BUMBLE BEES, Bombidae, and THE HONEY BEES, Apidae. The bees are described and illustrated on page 205.

THE PAPER WASPS, Vespidae; THE POTTER WASPS, Eumenidae; and THE MUD DAUBERS, Sphecidae. The wasps are described and illustrated on page 205.

Tables of Wildlife Refuges

NORTH EASTERN SECTOR *Map Pages 18 and 19*

State	Name	Acreage	What to Observe
Maine	Moosehorn	21,972	Woodcock, grouse.
	Widow's Island Migratory Bird Refuge	12	Waterfowl, shorebirds.
Vt.	Missisquoi	1,656	Canada goose, black duck, woodcock.
	Morgan	952	Waterfowl, upland game, fur animals.
Mass.	Monomoy	3,000	Waterfowl, shorebirds.
	Parker River	12,367	Black duck, woodcock, grouse, muskrat.
New York	Fort Tyler	14	Migratory birds.
	Montezuma	5,819	Mallard, black duck, quail, terns, shorebirds.
	Shinnecock	8	Waterfowl.
N. J.	Brigantine	2,222	Snow goose, black duck, quail, terns, shorebirds.
	Killcohook	1,362	Mallard, black duck, pintail, teal, muskrat.
Del.	Bombay Hook	13,811	Snow goose, black duck, quail, mourning dove, muskrat, shorebirds.
	Cape Henlopen	212	Shorebirds.
Maryland	Blackwater	10,584	Canada goose, mallard, black duck, quail, muskrat.
	Patuxent	2,623	Research refuge.
	Susquehanna	18,413	Canvasback, ruddy duck, ring-necked duck, whistling swan.
Virginia	Back Bay	4,589	Whistling swan, snow goose, Canada goose, ring-necked duck, canvasback, pintail, shorebirds, muskrat.
	Chincoteague	8,809	Snow goose, waterfowl, shorebirds.
	Fisherman's Island	225	Herons, shorebirds, terns.

There are no federal wildlife refuges in New Hampshire, Rhode Island, Connecticut, Pennsylvania and West Virginia. However, these states own state-operated facilities for the preservation and scientific management of wildlife. New Hampshire, for instance, has 9 game preserves totaling 16,100 acres, and Pennsylvania operates 61 wildlife refuges totaling 38,743 acres. Rhode Island, too, owns several preserves. In the other states the same function is fulfilled, to a certain extent, by state parks and forests.

SOUTH EASTERN SECTOR *Map Pages 20 and 21*

State	Name	Acreage	What to Observe
North Carolina	Mattamuskeet	50,228	Canada goose, whistling swan, pintail, black duck, mallard.
	Pea Island	5,880	Greater snow goose, American brant, Canada goose, shorebirds, terns, otter, diamond-backed terrapin.
	Swanquarter	15,501	Whistling swan, scaup, buffle-head.

SOUTH EASTERN SECTOR *(Continued)*

State	Name	Acreage	What to Observe
Tennessee	Lake Isom	1,744	Mallard, blue-winged teal, wood duck, mourning dove, herons.
	Reelfoot	9,273	Ring-necked duck, gadwall, wood duck, canvasback, mallard, quail, mourning dove, herons, muskrat, raccoon, mink.
	Tennessee	49,510	Waterfowl.
Arkansas	Big Lake	9,602	Geese, mallard, pintail, wood duck, gadwall, baldpate, quail, muskrat, mink, raccoon.
	White River	110,354	Mallard, pintail, black duck, Canada goose, teal, woodcock, herons, rails, black bear, raccoon, mink.
South Carolina	Cape Romain	34,015	Black duck, teal, scaup, wild turkey, brown pelican, shorebirds, terns, deer, sea turtle.
	Carolina Sandhills	40,829	Wood duck, quail, wild turkey.
	Santee	78,370	Waterfowl, mourning dove, herons, raccoon, otter.
	Savannah	7,149	Mallard, black duck, pintail, wood duck, ruddy duck, white ibis, wild turkey, mourning dove, herons, raccoon, otter.
Georgia	Blackbeard Island	4,854	Sea turtle, scaup, ruddy duck, pintail, blue-winged teal, shorebirds, herons, deer.
	Okefenokee	328,551	Limpkin, white ibis, Florida crane, wood duck, kite, herons, alligator, black bear, otter.
	Piedmont	29,211	Quail, mourning dove, beaver.
	Savannah	5,460	See Savannah, South Carolina.
	Tybee	100	Shorebirds.
	Wolf Island	538	Brown pelican, shorebirds.
Alabama	Petit Bois	134	Brown pelican, herons, gulls, shorebirds.
	Wheeler	38,448	Geese, mallard, pintail, black duck, quail, mourning dove, mink, muskrat, raccoon.
Miss.	Noxubee	38,120	Mallard, wood duck, turkey, deer, quail, mourning dove.
	Petit Bois	596	Brown pelican, herons, gulls, shorebirds.
Florida	Anclote	197	American egret, snowy egret, man-o-war bird, cormorants, gulls, terns.
	Cedar Keys	379	Brown pelican, white ibis, herons.
	Chassahowitzka	5,343	Pintail, baldpate, canvasback, scaup.
	Chinsegut	2,033	Herons, waterfowl, upland game.
	Everglades	55,647	Herons, ibises, roseate spoonbill, limpkin, Everglade kite, manatee.
	Great White Heron	1,000	Great white heron, brown pelican, white-crowned pigeon, key deer, shorebirds.

SOUTH EASTERN SECTOR *(Continued)*

State	Name	Acreage	What to Observe
Florida	Island Bay	11,100	White ibis, brown pelican, herons.
Florida	Key West	2,033	Great white heron, brown pelican, white-crowned pigeon, gulls.
Florida	Sanibel	2,394	Waterfowl, herons, terns, shorebirds.
Florida	St. Marks	64,095	Canada goose, pintail, scaup, ring-necked duck, white ibis, limpkin, turkey, herons, shorebirds, deer.
Florida	Besides, there are refuges for pelicans, white ibis and other shorebirds on 7 small islands, covering 2 to 40 acres each.		
Louisiana	Breton	7,158	Baldpate, pintail, redhead, scaup, brown pelican, man-o-war bird, shorebirds, gulls, terns.
Louisiana	Delta	48,788	Blue goose, pintail, mottled duck, gadwall, baldpate, blue-winged teal, mourning dove, raccoon, mink, otter, alligator, muskrat.
Louisiana	East Timbalier Island Reservation	337	Brown pelican, gulls, terns.
Louisiana	Lacassine	31,125	Blue goose, snow goose, mallard, mottled duck, fulvous tree duck, herons, rails, muskrat, otter.
Louisiana	Sabine	142,749	Roseate spoonbill, snow goose, mallard, mottled duck, glossy ibis, herons, muskrat, raccoon, mink.
Louisiana	Shell Keys	77	Brown pelican, royal tern.
Louisiana	Tern Islands	1,000	Brown pelican, gulls, terns.

NORTH CENTRAL SECTOR *Map Pages 22 and 23*

State	Name	Acreage	What to Observe
Ohio	West Sister Island	82	Great blue heron, black-crowned night heron.
Ky.	Kentucky Woodlands	63,323	Wild turkey, deer, waterfowl.
Michigan	Huron	147	Double-crested cormorant, herring gull, terns.
Michigan	Seney	91,097	Canada goose, black duck, mallard, spruce grouse, ruffed grouse, sandhill crane, prairie chicken, muskrat.
Illinois	Chautauqua	4,474	Mallard, pintail, wood duck, scaup, muskrat, raccoon.
Illinois	Upper Mississippi River Refuge	5,256	Canada goose, mallard, pintail, scaup, baldpate, blue-winged teal, wood duck, muskrat, raccoon.
Wisconsin	Gravel Island	27	Great blue heron, herring gull, Caspian tern.
Wisconsin	Green Bay	2	Herring gull, Caspian tern.
Wisconsin	Horicon	15,078	Canada goose, mallard, black duck, pintail, wood duck, redhead, ring-necked duck, mink, muskrat, raccoon.

NORTH CENTRAL SECTOR *(Continued)*

State	Name	Acreage	What to Observe
Wisconsin	Long Tail Point	103	Waterfowl.
Wisconsin	Necedah	39,361	Canada goose, mallard, black duck, baldpate, wood duck, ruffed grouse, sharp-tailed grouse, prairie chicken, beaver, deer, muskrat, mink, raccoon.
Wisconsin	Trempealeau	707	Mallard, baldpate, blue-winged teal, scaup, mourning dove, American egret.
Wisconsin	Upper Mississippi River Refuge	67,312	Canada goose, mallard, pintail, scaup, baldpate, blue-winged teal, wood duck, muskrat, raccoon.
Missouri	Mingo	3,243	Waterfowl.
Missouri	Squaw Creek	6,836	Blue goose, mallard, pintail, shoveller, white pelican, muskrat.
Missouri	Swan Lake	10,672	Geese, mallard, pintail, prairie chicken, mourning dove, rails, raccoon, muskrat.
Iowa	Union Slough	1,850	Waterfowl, upland game birds.
Iowa	Upper Mississippi River Refuge	24,639	Canada goose, mallard, pintail, scaup, baldpate, blue-winged teal, wood duck, muskrat, raccoon.
Minnesota	Mille Lacs	1	Waterfowl, gulls, terns, purple martin.
Minnesota	Mud Lake	69,719	Canada goose, mallard, blue-winged teal, baldpate, ring-necked duck, scaup, ruffed grouse, sharp-tailed grouse.
Minnesota	Rice Lake	15,356	Scaup, mallard, ring-necked duck, ruffed grouse, muskrat, beaver.
Minnesota	Tamarac	29,908	Scaup, ring-necked duck, blue-winged teal, redhead, ruddy duck, ruffed grouse, prairie chicken, muskrat, beaver.
Minnesota	Upper Mississippi River Refuge	25,265	Canada goose, mallard, pintail, scaup, baldpate, blue-winged teal, wood duck, muskrat, raccoon.
Nebraska	Box Butte	2,210	Waterfowl.
Nebraska	Crescent Lake	46,547	Canada goose, mallard, pintail, shoveller, canvasback, ruddy duck, sandhill crane, long-billed curlew, antelope.
Nebraska	Fort Niobrara	18,719	Buffalo, Texas longhorned cattle, elk, prairie chicken, sharp-tailed grouse, mallard, beaver.
Nebraska	North Platte	5,107	Sandhill crane, mallard, pintail, quail, pheasant.
Nebraska	Valentine	69,719	Mallard, blue-winged teal, shoveller, pintail, redhead, canvasback, sharp-tailed grouse, pheasant, shorebirds, muskrat.

Tables of Wildlife Refuges

NORTH CENTRAL SECTOR *(Continued)*

State	Name	Acreage	What to Observe
South Dakota	Bear Butte	436	Waterfowl.
South Dakota	Belle Fourche	13,680	Herons, waterfowl, shorebirds, gulls.
South Dakota	Eagle Creek	1,201	Waterfowl.
South Dakota	Lacreek	9,915	Canada goose, mallard, blue-winged teal, pintail, shoveller, sandhill crane, pheasant, sharp-tailed grouse, shorebirds, muskrat.
South Dakota	Lake Andes	7,435	Canada goose, white-fronted goose, mallard, pintail, shoveller, shorebirds.
South Dakota	Sand Lake	21,212	Canada goose, snow goose, blue goose, mallard, pintail, blue-winged teal, shoveller, pheasant, prairie chicken, Franklin's gull, Hungarian partridge, white pelican, cormorant, muskrat.
South Dakota	Twin Lakes	277	Waterfowl.
South Dakota	Waubay	4,659	Mallard, pintail, blue-winged teal, goldeneye, ruddy duck, pheasant, Franklin's gull, shorebirds, muskrat, deer.
North Dakota	Ardoch	2,738	Whistling swan, geese, scaup, mallard, pintail, white pelican, Hungarian partridge, gulls, muskrat.
North Dakota	Arrowwood	16,079	Whistling swan, geese, mallard, pintail, scaup, prairie chicken, sharp-tailed grouse, pheasant.
North Dakota	Buffalo Lake	2,061	Mallard, pintail, sharp-tailed grouse, prairie chicken, pheasant.
North Dakota	Chase Lake	3,233	White pelican, redhead, upland game birds, shorebirds, gulls.
North Dakota	Cottonwood Lake	973	Waterfowl.
North Dakota	Dakota Lake	2,633	Waterfowl.
North Dakota	Des Lacs	19,495	Mallard, pintail, redhead, sharp-tailed grouse, prairie chicken, pheasant.
North Dakota	Johnson Lake	2,008	Geese, mallard, pintail, scaup, sharp-tailed grouse, prairie chicken.
North Dakota	Lac Aux Mortes	5,882	Geese, mallard, pintail, sharp-tailed grouse, prairie chicken, Hungarian partridge, muskrat.
North Dakota	Lake George	3,128	Waterfowl, grouse.
North Dakota	Lake Ilo	3,212	Mallard, pintail, sharp-tailed grouse, Hungarian partridge, pheasant.
North Dakota	Lake Zahl	3,603	Waterfowl, upland game birds, shorebirds, muskrat.
North Dakota	Long Lake	19,340	Geese, mallard, pintail, Franklin's gull, pheasant, Hungarian partridge, sharp-tailed grouse, shorebirds.
North Dakota	Lostwood	26,308	Mallard, pintail, shoveller, sharp-tailed grouse, sandhill crane, shorebirds, muskrat.

NORTH CENTRAL SECTOR *(Continued)*

State	Name	Acreage	What to Observe
North Dakota	Lower Souris	58,565	Geese, mallard, pintail, blue-winged teal, redhead, prairie chicken, sharp-tailed grouse, white pelican, mourning dove, muskrat, beaver.
North Dakota	Silver Lake	3,348	Geese, mallard, pintail, scaup.
North Dakota	Slade	3,000	Mallard, pintail, redhead, canvas-back, sharp-tailed grouse, prairie chicken, deer.
North Dakota	Stewart Lake	2,330	Waterfowl, sharp-tailed grouse.
North Dakota	Tewaukan	3,074	Waterfowl, pheasant, muskrat.
North Dakota	Upper Souris	32,168	Geese, mallard, pintail, gadwall, baldpate, blue-winged teal, pheasant, sharp-tailed grouse, prairie chicken, sandhill crane, shorebirds, muskrat, beaver.
North Dakota	Willow Lake	2,848	Waterfowl, ruffed grouse, sharp-tailed grouse.
North Dakota	The State of North Dakota is host to 77 national wildlife refuges; the above table lists only the more important ones with areas of 2,000 acres or more. The smaller refuges have a similar bird and animal population.		

There are no federal wildlife refuges in Indiana and Kansas. However, both states own state-operated facilities for the preservation and scientific management of wildlife. Indiana operates 7 game preserves totaling 18,883 acres, and in Kansas there are three large wildlife refuges totaling 25,223 acres; Ottawa County State Park includes a bird sanctuary and a hatchery for quail and pheasant.

SOUTH CENTRAL SECTOR *Map Pages 24 and 25*

State	Name	Acreage	What to Observe
Oklahoma	Salt Plains	31,350	Geese, mallard, pintail, Mississippi kite, white pelican, quail, mourning dove, Franklin's gull, herons.
Oklahoma	Tishomingo	13,449	Waterfowl.
Oklahoma	Wichita Mts. Wildlife Refuge	61,287	Buffalo, elk, antelope, Texas long-horned cattle, deer, wild turkey, quail, mallard, Mississippi kite.
Texas	Aransas	47,261	Roseate spoonbill, whooping crane, sandhill crane, reddish egret, herons, geese, mottled duck, pintail, wild turkey, Attwater's prairie chicken, shorebirds, deer, peccary.
Texas	Hagerman	11,300	Waterfowl.
Texas	Laguna Atascosa	11,275	Waterfowl, doves.
Texas	Mesillo	17	Waterfowl, doves.
Texas	Muleshoe	5,809	Canada goose, mallard, baldpate, sandhill crane, scaled quail, mourning dove, shorebirds.
Texas	Santa Ana	1,980	Tree ducks, doves, chachalacas, red-billed pigeons.

SOUTH CENTRAL SECTOR (Continued)

	Name	Acreage	What to Observe
New Mexico	Bitter Lake	23,803	Baldpate, mallard, pintail, little brown crane, scaled quail, nutria.
	Bosque del Apache	56,238	Canada goose, gadwall, mallard, New Mexico duck, shoveller, Gambel's quail, scaled quail, mourning dove, beaver, muskrat.
	Carlsbad	16,234	Mallard, shoveller, scaup, scaled quail, white pelican, sandhill crane, shorebirds.
	Rio Grande	73,228	Canada goose, mallard, New Mexico duck, gadwall, pintail, scaled quail, Gambel's quail, shorebirds.
	San Andres	57,215	Bighorn sheep, mule deer, white-winged dove, Mearn's quail, scaled quail.

NORTH WESTERN SECTOR Map Pages 26 and 27

	Name	Acreage	What to Observe
Wyoming	Bamforth	1,166	Waterfowl, shorebirds, antelope.
	Evanston	360	Waterfowl.
	Hutton Lake	1,969	Waterfowl, shorebirds, antelope.
	National Elk Refuge	24,271	Elk, blue grouse, sage hen, Franklin's grouse, Canada goose, mallard.
	Pathfinder	43,341	Waterfowl, shorebirds, antelope.
Montana	Benton Lake	12,235	Snow goose, mallard, pintail, shorebirds.
	Black Coulee	1,480	Mallard, pintail, shoveller, sage hen.
	Bowdoin	14,402	Canada goose, mallard, pintail, canvasback, redhead, white pelican, sage hen, antelope, shorebirds, pheasant.
	Creedman Coulee	2,648	Mallard, pintail, prairie chicken, sage hen, shorebirds, muskrat.
	Fort Keogh	56,954	Upland game, waterfowl.
	Fort Peck Game Range	946,944	Mallard, sharp-tailed grouse, sage hen, pheasant, antelope, deer.
	Hailstone	2,665	Mallard, pintail, sage hen, Hungarian partridge.
	Halfbreed Lake	3,097	Mallard, pintail, sage hen, Hungarian partridge.
	Hewitt Lake	1,360	Mallard, pintail, sage hen, Hungarian partridge.
	Lake Mason	6,607	Mallard, pintail, shoveller, sharp-tailed grouse, sage hen, muskrat.
	Lake Thibadeau	3,721	Mallard, pintail, sharp-tailed grouse, sage hen.
	Lamesteer	800	Waterfowl, sharp-tailed grouse.
	Medicine Lake	31,458	Geese, mallard, pintail, sandhill crane, sharp-tailed grouse, shorebirds, gulls, terns, muskrat, badger.
	National Bison Range	18,451	Buffalo, deer, bighorn sheep, blue grouse, Franklin's grouse, mallard.

NORTH WESTERN SECTOR (Continued)

	Name	Acreage	What to Observe
Montana	Nine-Pipe	2,088	Whistling swan, Canada goose, mallard, baldpate, pheasant, shorebirds, muskrat.
	Pablo	2,868	Canada goose, mallard, baldpate, pheasant, shorebirds, muskrat.
	Pishkun	8,195	Mallard, baldpate, sharp-tailed grouse, Hungarian partridge, shorebirds.
	Red Rock Lakes Migratory Waterfowl Refuge	32,174	Trumpeter swan, whistling swan, redhead, canvasback, pintail, scaup, sage hen, Columbian sharp-tailed grouse, Shiras mouse, muskrat.
	Willow Creek	3,199	Whistling swan, Canada goose, mallard, pintail, canvasback, goldeneye, sharp-tailed grouse, shorebirds.
Idaho	Camas	10,535	Canada goose, whistling swan, mallard, pintail, sage hen, Columbian sharp-tailed grouse, pheasant, long-billed curlew.
	Deer Flat	10,252	Canada goose, mallard, pintail, white pelican, pheasant, shorebirds, gulls, terns.
	Minidoka	25,332	Canada goose, mallard, gadwall, pintail, redhead, scaup, sage hen, shorebirds.
	Snake River	355	Canada goose, mallard, gadwall, pintail, scaup, goldeneye, buffle-head.
Washington	Columbia	9,212	Waterfowl.
	Lenore Lake	6,159	Mallard, buffle-head, ruddy duck, California quail, shorebirds.
	Little Pend Oreille	40,809	Franklin's grouse, blue grouse, ruffed grouse, mallard, pintail, goldeneye, deer, black bear.
	Skagit	5,074	Waterfowl, shorebirds.
	Turnbull	11,173	Mallard, green-winged teal, ruffed grouse, valley quail, shorebirds.
	Willapa	3,519	Black brant, Canada goose, pintail, scaup, blue grouse, shorebirds, black bear, black-tailed deer, raccoon, muskrat.
	In addition there are 9 refuges of small acreage for such birds as cormorants, petrels, murres, auklets, puffins, harlequin ducks and band-tailed pigeons.		
Oregon	Cape Meares	139	Shorebirds, band-tailed pigeon, black-tailed deer.
	Charles Sheldon Antelope Range	627	Antelope, mule deer, sage hen, waterfowl.
	Cold Springs	2,677	Waterfowl, shorebirds.
	Hart Mountain National Antelope Refuge	226,891	Antelope, mule deer, sage hen, valley quail.
	Lower Klamath	61,139	White-fronted goose, cackling goose, pintail, mallard, gadwall, redhead, ruddy duck, California quail, shorebirds.

Tables of Wildlife Refuges

NORTH WESTERN SECTOR (Continued)

	Name	Acreage	What to Observe
OREGON	Malheur	174,366	Whistling swan, snow goose, white-fronted goose, pintail, sage hen, valley quail, sandhill crane, white pelican, shorebirds, antelope, mule deer.
	McKay Creek	1,813	Waterfowl, sandhill crane.
	Oregon Islands	21	Cormorants, gulls, murres, puffins.
	Thief Valley	1,495	Waterfowl.
	Three Arch Rocks	17	Cormorants, gulls, murres, puffins, sea lion.
	Upper Klamath	8,140	Pintail, shoveller, redhead, shorebirds.

SOUTH WESTERN SECTOR

Map Pages 28 and 29

	Name	Acreage	What to Observe
COLO.	Kit Carson	664	Whooping crane, waterfowl.
UTAH	Bear River Migratory Bird Refuge	64,899	Whistling swan, Canada goose, pintail, green-winged teal, shoveller, white pelican, shorebirds, muskrat.
	Locomotive Springs	1,031	Waterfowl.
	Strawberry Valley	14,080	Mallard, gadwall, pintail, sage hen.
ARIZONA	Boulder Canyon	312,047	Bighorn sheep, Gambel's quail, redhead, scaup, pintail, mallard, white pelican.
	Cabeza Prieta Game Range	860,040	Bighorn sheep, Mexican antelope, peccary, Gambel's quail, white-winged dove.
	Havasu Lake	21,426	Bighorn sheep, white-winged dove, geese, pintail, Gambel's quail, herons, muskrat.
	Imperial	28,711	Bighorn sheep, Gambel's quail, geese, pintail, green-winged teal, white pelican, roseate spoonbill, herons, rails, muskrat, beaver.
	Kofa Game Range	660,040	Bighorn sheep, white-winged dove, Gambel's quail.
	Salt River	21,120	Waterfowl, upland game birds.
NEVADA	Anaho Island	248	White pelican, cormorant, gulls.
	Boulder Canyon	346,571	Bighorn sheep, Gambel's quail, redhead, scaup, pintail, mallard, white pelican.
	Charles Sheldon Antelope Range	584,373	Antelope, mule deer, sage hen, waterfowl.
	Desert Game Range	2,022,000	Bighorn sheep, mule deer, elk, Gambel's quail, mourning dove.
	Fallon	17,902	Waterfowl, California quail, pheasant.
	Railroad Valley	133,397	Mallard, gadwall, cinnamon teal, sage hen, shorebirds.

SOUTH WESTERN SECTOR (Continued)

	Name	Acreage	What to Observe
NEVADA	Ruby Lake	35,578	Canada goose, whistling swan, gadwall, pintail, mallard, redhead, canvasback, sage hen, sandhill crane, blue grouse, shorebirds.
	Sheldon National Antelope	34,050	Antelope, mule deer, sage hen, waterfowl.
	Winnemucca	10,006	Waterfowl, white pelican, gulls.
CALIFORNIA	Clear Lake	25,300	Cackling goose, snow goose, white pelican, shorebirds.
	Colusa	2,385	Waterfowl.
	Farallon	91	Murres, auklets, guillemots, puffins, shorebirds.
	Havasu Lake	14,472	Bighorn sheep, white-winged dove, geese, pintail, Gambel's quail, herons, muskrat.
	Imperial	18,130	Bighorn sheep, Gambel's quail, geese, pintail, green-winged teal, white pelican, roseate spoonbill, herons, rails, muskrat, beaver.
	Lower Klamath	20,928	White-fronted goose, cackling goose, pintail, mallard, gadwall, redhead, ruddy duck, California quail, shorebirds.
	Sacramento	10,776	Snow goose, cackling goose, whistling swan, Ross's goose, pintail, baldpate, mallard, pheasant, shorebirds.
	Salton Sea	32,407	Snow goose, fulvous tree duck, pintail, baldpate, green-winged teal, shoveller, ruddy duck, shorebirds.
	Sutter	1,272	Waterfowl.
	Tule Lake	37,337	White-fronted goose, cackling goose, snow goose, whistling swan, Ross's goose, pintail, mallard, redhead, canvasback, ruddy duck, muskrat, shorebirds.

CANADA

Map Pages 18-19, 22-23, 26-27

CANADA

Canada maintains 80 bird sanctuaries located in all provinces except Manitoba. They comprise a total area of 1,800 square miles; the largest refuge is Akimiski Island in the Northwest Territories, with an area of 1,300 square miles; the smallest is Rideau Island in Alberta, with an area of one acre. However, no maps showing the location of the sanctuaries are available for distribution. Also many of Canada's national and provincial parks are wildlife refuges, particularly the following:

NEW BRUNSWICK: Fundy N.P. (mink, otter, weasel, great blue heron, falcon); Plaster Rock-Renous Game Refuge. NOVA SCOTIA: Cape Breton Highlands N.P. (black bear, snowshoe rabbit, bald eagle, golden eagle). QUEBEC: La Vérendrye Provincial Park (formerly a fishing preserve). MANITOBA: Riding Mountain N.P. (mule deer, white-tailed deer, elk, moose, bear, buffalo). SASKATCHEWAN: Prince Albert N.P. (caribou, buffalo, double-crested cormorant, white pelican). ALBERTA: Elk Island N.P. (buffalo, big game); Wood Buffalo N.P. (wood buffalo, big game); Banff and Jasper N.P. (mountain sheep, mountain goat, mule deer, black bear, grizzly bear, coyote, mountain lion, marten, marmot).

Alluvial — soil carried away by flowing water from one place and deposited in another is alluvial.

Amphibole — a silicate of calcium and magnesium; frequently one or more other metals are added.

Anadromous — certain ocean fishes such as the shad and the salmon ascend rivers in order to spawn in fresh water; they are called anadromous fishes.

Andesite — an eruptive rock so called because it occurs frequently in the Andes; it is also common in the western mountains of North America; its color is normally dark grey.

Aphrodisiac — a sexual stimulant, usually a drug or certain types of food.

Arborescent — looking like a tree; the word refers also to the woody growth of the stalk.

Bivalve — provided with two valves, particularly in reference to a shell with two parts that open and close.

Bluegill — a sunfish encountered in the waters of the Mississippi Valley; it is a fine food fish of approximately one pound weight.

Braconid — also braconic, the adjective of Braconidae, the family name of the ichneumon flies; some species lay their eggs on living larvae.

Bract — a leaf which grows directly under a flower or a cluster of flowers.

Bream — any one of the various species of fresh-water sunfishes.

Cairn — a pile of stones in the shape of a cone or mound, set up as a landmark or memorial.

Calcareous — adjective of calcite or calcium carbonate; anything which contains calcium.

Calcified — anything which is permeated with calcareous material.

Carapace — the shell of a turtle, or the bony armour protecting the back of an animal.

Carat — in determining the approximate proportion of gold, a twenty-fourth part; in weighing diamonds and other precious stones, 200 milligrams (international metric carat).

Carnivorous — living on the flesh of other animals.

Cartilaginous or cartilagineous—like the elastic tissue called cartilage, i.e. gristly, firm, and tough.

Catadromous — certain freshwater fishes such as the common eel descend rivers to the ocean to spawn in salt water; they are called catadromous; the opposite is anadromous.

Chaparral — a thicket of thorny shrubs or small trees, often so dense as to be impenetrable.

Chrysalid or chrysalis — the pupa of butterflies and other insects which remain in a dormant condition during their pupal stage.

Conchoidal — shaped like one-half of a bivalve shell.

Coniferous — cone-bearing, referring to such evergreen trees as pines, spruces, and cypresses.

Copse — a grove or thicket of small trees used as a supply of fuel.

Corm — a fleshy stem resembling a bulb, bearing thin scale leaves and buds.

Corolla — botanically, the petals of a flower as a unit; the petals may be separate or more or less grown together.

Cycloid — circular, or laid out in circles; "cycloid scale" is an expression which refers to a thin fish scale with concentric lines of growth; it has no serration on the margin and is not enameled.

Deciduous — trees whose leaves are shed at certain seasons are deciduous; evergreen or coniferous trees are the opposite.

Ductile — metals or other materials which can be thinned and extended by pressure without reverting to their previous form are ductile.

Eocene — geologically, this term refers to the earliest main subdivision of the Tertiary period.

Family — biologically, it is a group of related plants or animals; in our system of classification it stands higher than a genus and lower than an order.

Fault — a rock crack or fissure with a dislocation of the strata, caused by movements of the crust of the earth; this dislocation has occurred in such a way that one wall of the fracture has slipped past the other wall.

Femur — the thigh bone.

Fetid — emitting an offensive smell.

Gall — when certain parasitic fungi, bacteria, or insects attack a plant, a swelling of the tissues occurs which is called a gall.

Genus — biologically, a group of related plants or animals; in our system of classification it stands below a family and above a species.

Gill net — a flat net which catches fishes by their gills; it is suspended vertically in the water and allows the heads of fishes to pass through the mesh; but when the fish try to free themselves they are caught in the gills.

Herbivorous — feeding on plants.

Igneous — geologically, igneous rocks were at one time hot and liquid or molten, and either erupted through volcanoes or hardened underground.

Lamellar — consisting of lamellae, i.e. thin plates or layers.

Lanceolate — botanically, lance-shaped; broadest at or below the middle; narrow at the apex.

Launce — a fish of the family Ammodytidae.

Lenticle — a lenticular formation; lenticular means "in the shape of a double convex lens."

Lochleven trout — a variety of trout introduced to the U.S. from Loch Leven and other lakes in Scotland and northern England.

Glossary

Macerate — to soften fibrous material by placing it in a liquid.

Magenta — a purplish shade of red.

Magma — geologically, a liquid mass within the earth; it erupts as lava and, if solidified, forms igneous rocks.

Malleable — metals or other materials which may be shaped by hammer blows or roller action are malleable.

Mandible — zoologically, this term refers to the upper or lower jaw of an animal; it is applied particularly to birds and reptiles which have beaks.

Metamorphic — geologically, metamorphic rocks now are different from what they had been originally, the change having been effected by heat, mineral-bearing water, or pressure.

Milt — the reproductive secretion of the male fish, or the reproductive gland containing the secretion.

Mucilaginous — adjective of mucilage; moist, viscid, sticky.

Nodule — a lump which has a rounded, irregular shape.

Order — biologically, a group of related plants or animals; in our system of classification it stands below a class and above a family.

Ossified — bone-like, or converted into bone, or hardened by minerals.

Ovipositor — most female insects have an ovipositor, a special, drill-like organ for laying their eggs in plants, in the ground, etc., wherever conditions will favor the development of the larvae.

Pan fish — any small fish that can be fried whole.

Pistillate — applied particularly to flowers which have pistils but not stamens.

Piute trout — a western species of trout named after the Piute Indians who live between the Rocky Mountains and the Sierras.

Plankton — a collective name for the minute plants and animals floating or swimming in water; the animals of the plankton range from protozoans to jellyfishes, but do not include fishes proper.

Plastron — zoologically, that part of the shell of turtles or other animals which protects their undersides.

Pleistocene — geologically, this period follows the Tertiary period.

Pliny the Elder — Roman naturalist, A.D. 23 to 79.

Predaceous — preying on other animals; predatory.

Prehensile — certain animals are able to use their tails to grasp bars or branches, by wrapping them around the seized object; such tails are called prehensile.

Proboscis — a tube-like prolongation of the head of an animal, as for instance with certain insects.

Protozoa — a phylum of primitive minute animals, usually composed of a single cell.

Purse Seine — a large purse net; this fishing net has a mouth which closes like a purse.

Pyrite — any of a number of sulphides; pyrites are the source of huge quantities of sulphur.

Raceme — a simple cluster of flowers on an elongated flowering stem; each flower is attached to a separate stalk.

Rookery — a breeding colony of rooks (a common European bird of the crow family) or other gregarious birds.

Scape — botanically, a leafless or nearly leafless flower stalk arising from the ground and bearing a flower or a cluster of flowers.

Scutellum — in reference to an insect, the scutellum is the third of the four parts which form the upper piece of a thoracic segment.

Seine — this large net hangs vertically in the water, kept in position by floats on the upper and sinkers on the bottom ends; the fish are caught when both ends are brought together.

Semi-looper — describing half loops, usually referring to the crawling method of certain caterpillars which possess legs only in the front and in the rear and describe loops or semi-loops when moving.

Sibilant — a hissing sound; or spoken, sung, or uttered with a hissing sound.

Species — biologically, a group of related plants or animals; in our system of classification it stands below a genus or subgenus and above a subspecies or variety; members of a species of animals are related closely enough to interbreed and pass on their characteristics to their offspring.

Stalactite — a rock deposit hanging from the ceiling of a cave, formed by trickling water which leaves a part of its mineral contents on the protruding rock.

Stalagmite — a rock deposit formed on the floor of a cave by drops of mineralized water.

Sun squall — a general term applied to any large jelly fish.

Tuber — a short, thick, fleshy branch which grows underground and possesses many buds or "eyes."

Tundra — an arctic plain beyond the tree line; its subsoil is permanently frozen; mosses and lichens grow in its black, mucky soil.

Ventral — this term refers to the belly or abdomen.

Vestigial — this term expresses that just a vestige or trace of an object or growth is noticeable.

Viscid — sticky, adhesive.

Viscosity — a viscous, i.e. adhesive or sticky condition.

Viscous — sticky, adhesive.

Viviparous — almost all mammals, many reptiles and a few fishes are viviparous, i.e. they give birth to living young.

Voracious — greedy in reference to food; ravenous.

Index

*NOTE—The letter F stands for Family, the letter O for Order—Asterisks * refer to color illustrations—Latin names are printed in italics*

Hammond's

Guide to Nature Hobbies

By

E. L. JORDAN, PH.D.

Rutgers University

Drawings

By

HERBERT PIERCE

C. S. Hammond and Company

MAPLEWOOD, N. J. NEW YORK, N. Y.

Foreword

HOBBIES IN MODERN LIVING. The concept of a "hobby" has undergone a complete change during the past twenty years. It used to be considered a child's play or a grown-up person's somewhat eccentric pastime; Webster still defines it as "a subject or plan to which one is constantly reverting; a favorite and ever recurring subject of discourse, thought or effort; a topic, theme, or the like (considered as) unduly occupying one's attention or interests." The most significant phrase in this definition consists of the words "unduly occupying one's attention;" it is also interesting to note that here a hobby is largely talk ("subject of discourse, topic, theme, plan"); in its most exalted form it becomes an "effort," but never reaches the level of achievement and accomplishment.

Webster correctly summarizes what a hobby meant to our parents. But his dictionary will have to add an entirely new definition for the present generation. For due to a number of causes, particularly the greater amount of leisure time which is at everybody's disposal today, the lowly hobby has emerged a major factor in modern living. Psychologists recommend it as a means of keeping on an even keel in a chaotic world, and doctors prescribe it for mental hygiene. Young people take to it naturally, and retired folks depend on it to fill the long and quiet days. Millions of people carry on their hobbies just because they like them.

The number and variety of hobbies is great, and there is no limit to the imagination and ingenuity of their followers. Within this vast complex one group is increasing in popularity year after year, the nature hobbies, and to their potential and actual devotees this guide is dedicated, in the hope that it will be both interesting in theory and helpful in practice.

Acknowledgements

A NUMBER OF FRIENDS assisted me in this venture, and I am particularly grateful to Mr. Charles Vogel of the Radio Corporation of America who was consulted repeatedly on the question of field equipment for nature photography and whose constructive criticism, upon reading the wildlife photography section, was greatly appreciated. I am thankful also for the cooperation of Miss Ruth Sage of the Nature Section of the Photographic Society of America; and to the Eastman Kodak Company (especially Mr. R. W. Brown of the Editorial Service Department) for placing at my disposal the excellent wildlife photographs reproduced on pages 47 to 59.

Several government agencies, notably the Fish and Wildlife Service of the U.S. Department of the Interior, collaborated by furnishing valuable material, as for instance the illustrations on pages 29, 31 and 32. All other illustrations are the original drawings of Herbert Pierce, of the Cartographic Division of C. S. Hammond & Co.

E. L. J.

Contents

COLLECTING ROCKS AND MINERALS

Why Rocks Are Interesting — Getting acquainted with rocks will help us to understand the planet on which we live. For our earth is a gigantic ball of rock. But rocks do not only form the firm foundation on which all plants and animals have settled, but are essential to life itself. What we call soil is decayed or weathered rock, and with the help of the dissolving agent of water the plants growing there absorb the minerals they need. Animals, including human beings, eat plants and thus assimilate the mineral substances without which we could not exist. Even mammals which eat nothing but meat, like the lions, receive their necessary mineral quota regularly; for they devour other animals which are plant eaters, like antelopes or zebras. When we realize that human and animal life depends on plant life, plant life on soil, and soil on the rocks from which it has been worn, broken or dissolved, we recognize one of the important chains controlling life around us.

In the history of mankind rocks have played an outstanding part. When primitive man stopped using a natural boulder to hit his prey or break a bone, and began to chip off pieces and give his weapon or tool a more efficient form — a process which led to the invention of the ax, the knife, the saw — civilization was born. Also the value of precious stones was recognized by primitive prehistoric peoples. In the middle ages the alchemists hunted for the magic touchstone, a cure-all which was to perform veritable miracles. In our own day rocks are one of the principal bases of our industrial civilization, and are transformed, more widely than ever before, into an endless variety of products ranging from skyscrapers and super-highways to knife sharpeners and tooth powder. To explore the rocky materials that on one side tell us of the earliest youth of our planet and on the other side surround us daily, in nature and as industrial products, seems an interesting venture indeed.

Illustration Number 1

Geologist's Hammers

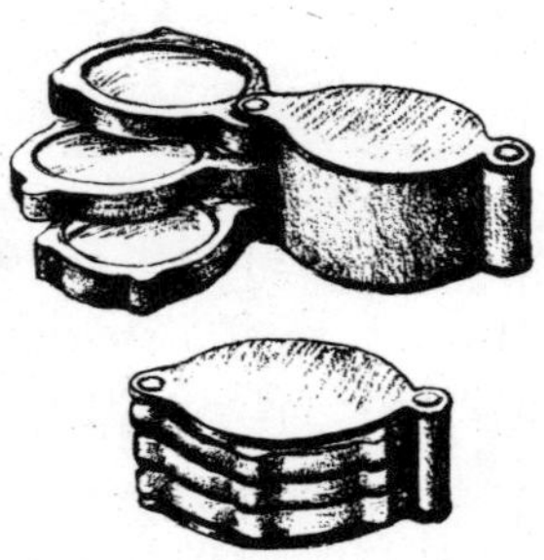

Pocket Magnifier

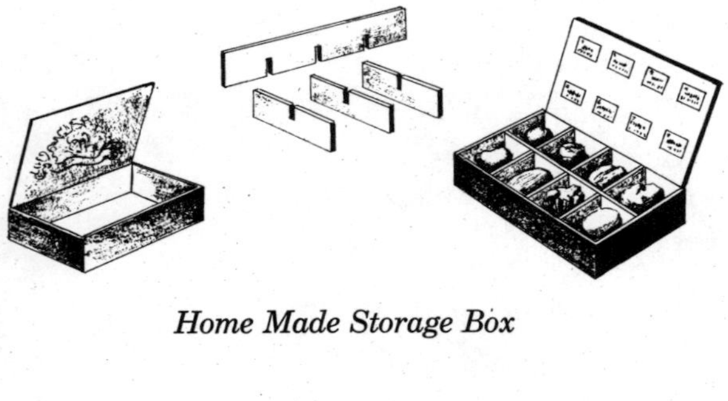

Home Made Storage Box

Viewpoints for a Rock Collection — 1) General — This will almost always be the start of a rock collection: On a hike, an excursion or a vacation trip a few stones are found which because of their color, texture or form attract the attention of the prospective collector. Other specimens are acquired for comparison or supplementation, and the collection is on the way. As it grows, the owner might decide on specialization. Among the many possibilities the following are mentioned here:

2) Geographical: Your Home Region — To tell the geological story of your home district through a rock collection is a fascinating project, particularly if you live in one of America's mountainous regions where a great variety of minerals and rocks are available.

3) Geographical: Your Travels — Rock specimens brought home from your journeys are among the most meaningful souvenirs. Particularly in connection with photographs, such specimens will illustrate vividly America's most scenic sections: the white gypsum sand dunes, the rocky sea coasts, the Great Lakes cliffs, the painted desert, the western canyons, the innumerable ranges of varied geological ages. Besides the nature interest proper, there may be aspects of history, ethnology or folklore connected with your rocks that lend an extra touch of attraction. White quartz crystals from New Hampshire explain the name of the White Mountains in whose peaks quartz of light color occurs frequently. The Indians called these ranges "Mountains with Snowy Foreheads" ("Waumbeck Methna"). The first white man to climb Mount Washington — Darly Field, an Irish settler from Portsmouth — returned from his feat in 1642 with joyous news. His pockets were stuffed with diamonds he had found. The diamonds turned out to be quartz crystals, still plentiful in the region. In getting specimens of marble from the famous quarries of Vermont you may not only find out about the tremendous inner stresses to which

metamorphic rocks are subjected — occasionally a huge marble block will split spontaneously and explosively, or a big block freed on all sides except the bottom will, for the same reason, suddenly snap loose, with the sharp bang of a gun — but you will also discover that handling rocks and cutting stones is a most ancient art. The Vermonter helping you to your marble slabs will probably be a descendant of stone cutters from the quarries of Saragossa, Spain, or Carrara, Italy, or Edinburgh, Scotland, a direct scion of the artists who shaped columns or carved statues of marble for the Roman emperors 2000 years ago. In Minnesota, Wisconsin or South Dakota you may pick up specimens of catlinite or pipestone, in almost any color ranging from light grey to deep red, and remember that from that rock the Sioux and other Plains Indians used to make their smoking pipes, and trade them to other tribes over wide distances, long before white man arrived. That soft rock stands at the very beginning of the present world-wide habit of smoking. Examples of this sort, illustrating the possibilities of combining imaginatively travel and rock collecting, could be multiplied when proceeding to the mountainous regions of the west.

4) Rocks and Soils — A collector interested in agriculture and soils may gather an interesting group of specimens which show how the various types of rocks break down into the various types of soil.

5) Technical — The structural-technical qualities of rocks may serve as guideposts for the collector. Small initial collections to be used as basis and starting point may be secured from a scientific supply house like Ward's Natural Science Establishment, Beechwood Station, Rochester, N. Y. A *cleavage collection* illustrates the important forms of cleavage observed in rocks; a *fracture collection* demonstrates such fractures as even, uneven, conchoidal, sub-conchoidal, splintery, and hackly; a *luster collection* shows various types and degrees of luster ranging from metallic to vitreous, resinous, greasy, pearly, silky, shining, glistening, glimmering, and dull; a *crystal collection* consisting of both single and twin forms is an attractive introduction to the field of crystallography.

6) Nature History — A particularly interesting though more difficult type of collection specializes in rock slabs or layers (for instance of flagstone or shale) which show the action of nature and wildlife throughout the ages; ripple marks reflect the tides and currents, waves and winds that once swept over that spot, and trails, tracks and burrows tell the story of living creatures that once jumped, ran, crawled or dug in that locality, ranging from tiny worms to huge dinosaurs. In this connection fossil collections may be mentioned as an interesting link between geology and zoology. One leading supply house offers a beginner's collection which includes such fossils as a protozoan (single-celled animal), a sponge, two corals, a sea bud, a sea urchin, two types of sea moss, two lamp shells, one clam, one sea snail, one shell devil, one shark's tooth, and part of a mammal bone.

7) Anthropological — Collections of rocks slightly worked by primitive peoples seem especially appropriate in those regions of America where ancient Indian cultures flourished. They would contain arrowheads of flint, knives of obsidian, cooking plates of soapstone, pipes of catlinite, bowls fashioned of various types of soft rocks, and similar implements of stone.

8) Artistic — This is not the viewpoint of the natural scientist, but it is a very valid one for a collector with an artistic bend of mind. The banded beauty of agate, for instance, or the delicate colors, designs, and textures of various marbles may make a most attractive series. Some rocks like jade have been used for centuries as raw material for artistic carvings, and jade collections are often extremely valuable possessions. But even if the beauty of the stones is the starting point of the collection, a scientifically correct identification and description of the specimens is advisable.

These are mere examples of endless possibilities of specialization that exist, or of combinations that serve a specific purpose. Boy scouts, for instance, may use collection type 2 or 4 to win a merit badge. There is, of course, no definite need to specialize; one consideration, however, seems to favor it: You can make an actual scientific contribution to the field in which you specialize. Amateurs are often timid about the scientific aspects of their hobby, but the knowledge gained in a specialized field and the collections gathered in the process have in more than one case extended the frontiers of human knowledge.

Illustration Number 2

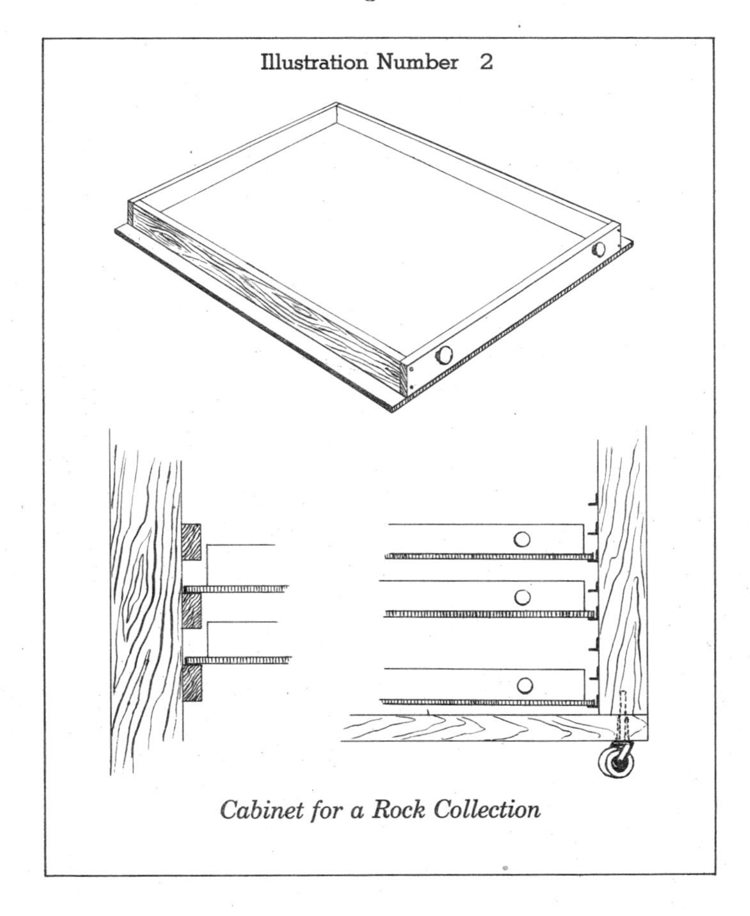

Cabinet for a Rock Collection

Where to Obtain Rocks — The most satisfactory method is to search personally for specimens of minerals and rocks. Mines and quarries, dumps and old ore piles, road cuts and ancient glacier beds are the best hunting grounds, although abandoned underground mines should never be entered alone by an inexperienced person. Outcroppings of rocks in fields and woods and even excavations for new buildings may furnish specimens.

The Smithsonian Institution recommends examining steep cliffs as they usually consist of firm rocks which are not deeply weathered. In volcanic areas rocks with cavities often contain minerals. The banks of rivers and the beaches are of special interest to rock collectors because their pebbles, gravels and sand give a good indication and preview of the types of rocks that prevail toward the headwaters of the drainage area to which the shore and beach belong. Besides, the heavy river sands of mountainous districts often contain deposits of gold, platinum, tin, and precious stones.

In some localities it is difficult to obtain fresh, firm material; in such cases remove the external or weathered layer of the rocks with a hammer. Wherever water is available it is recommended to wash and clean the specimens collected on that spot. Thus their true color, luster and texture will come out clearly and make it possible for the collector to select the best specimens for packing, leaving behind the poor ones.

In the southernmost parts of the United States, for instance along the shores and in the shallow waters of the Florida Keys, numerous corals of great beauty may be found. They are desirable specimens for rock collections. Living corals are preferable to dead and worn corals that have been tossed about by waves. The specimens have to be dried in the sun, a process in which the flesh disintegrates and gives off an offensive smell. For transportation each piece must be individually wrapped to avoid breakage.

As you will not only wish to expand your collection in quantity but also improve it in quality, you will look out both for new specimens and for better samples of varieties which you already possess, so that you can discard your inferior specimens.

When traveling in the mining districts of the west, you may be able to buy pieces of locally prominent minerals and rocks from mine workers who sometimes provide this service for visitors, or even from gift and souvenir shops. As your collection extends, and you may wish to add specimens that are not available in your locality, you can secure them by trading and exchanging. In that respect a magazine like "Rocks and Minerals" which is published bimonthly by the Rocks and Minerals Association in Peekskill, New York, will be helpful. Samples may also be obtained from various natural science supply houses. Among the latter Ward's is outstanding in the field of geology.

Illustration Number 3

Tray for a Rock Collection

For Rock Exhibits

How to Identify Rocks — Whether you plan a general or a specialized rock collection, you will organize it according to scientific principles. You will build up one group consisting of minerals, many of which have an important function as ingredients and raw materials of rocks, and another group made up of rocks proper; the latter will be subdivided into a series of igneous rocks (which at one time were liquid or molten, and erupted as lava or solidified under ground, like basalt and granite), a series of sedimentary rocks (which were built up by wind, water, ice, plants or animals, like sandstone and limestone), and a series of metamorphic rocks (whose original status has been changed to their present status by heat, pressure, or mineral-bearing water, like marble and slate). For an introduction to this field, and as a helpful tool in identifying minerals and rocks, the following group of reference and field books is recommended; those particularly useful for the beginner are starred.

*Jordan, E. L., Hammond's Nature Atlas of America, the section on Rocks and Minerals, New York, 1952

*Hawkins, The Book of Minerals, J. Wiley & Sons, New York, 1945

*Spencer, L. J., The World's Minerals, Frederick A. Stokes Co., New York, 1916

George, R. D., Minerals and Rocks, D. Appleton-Century Co., New York, 1943

Pirsson, L. V., and Knopf, A., Rocks and Rock Minerals, 3rd Edition, J. Wiley & Sons, New York, 1947

Loomis, F. B., Field Book of Common Rocks and Minerals, G. P. Putnam's Sons, New York, 1948

*Fenton, C. L. and M. A., Rocks and Their Stories, Doubleday & Co., New York, 1951

*Fenton, C. L. and M. A., The Rock Book, Doubleday & Co., New York, 1951

Merrill, G. P., A Treatise on Rocks, Rock Weathering and Soils, Smithsonian Institution Series, New York, 1913

Even with well illustrated books as guides it will often not be easy to identify certain rock specimens. One major difficulty is the fact that color is no reliable distinguishing mark, and depending on admixtures granite, sandstone, marble, and numerous other rocks may vary considerably in hues and tints. The beginner who is in doubt about some of his specimens will readily receive information and advice from more advanced fellow collectors, scientists, and museums.

Two tools of identification which are popular with experienced collectors are a *set of hardness points* on small brass rods, for mineral identification, marked 5-10 as in Moh's Scale: apatite, quartz, pyrope, topaz, sapphire, diamond; and *streak plates,* inexpensive pieces of unglazed porcelain employed in identifying ore minerals; when scratched with the specimen, the white plate will identify the mineral by the color of the streak.

Field Equipment for Rock Collectors — To Pry Loose and Break Pieces of Rock — Any well-made hammer will serve the purpose. Special hammers for geologists and prospectors are offered by scientific supply houses; some of them are made of a single piece of non-rusting metal so that hammer head and hammer handle cannot separate. One type of hammer is provided with a sharply pointed pick, another with a broad edge. The latter proves useful when working with rocks which, like slate, split in layers. Occasionally a two-foot iron bar will be handy to pry off or break a boulder, but this is a rather heavy and bulky tool; it will hardly be necessary under normal conditions. Also a prospector's pick, a little over a foot in length, is available; it is equally usable in chipping hard rock as it is for securing fossils from shale. To test rocks and minerals for hardness and to check the grain a pocket knife and a cold chisel (possibly two, a small one and another approximately an inch wide) will be useful. To measure boulders or outcroppings from which specimens are taken, a tape measure or steel rule will be taken along, and for checking the external appearance of the rocks a magnifying glass, possibly with 2 or 3 lenses, will be employed. Such pocket magnifiers are available in various types, the more expensive ones magnifying up to 20 times. The Coddington Magnifier, costing approximately six dollars, contains a solid cylinder of optical glass with an internal diaphragm for the finest possible definition in magnifications of either 7, 10, 14 or 20 x. The novice will probably choose a simpler type. A looseleaf notebook is, of course, an indispensible piece of field equipment.

To Transport the Specimens — Newspapers or brown wrapping paper, and for samples of various types of soils and ashes small paper or cloth bags will serve as the primary packing material. To carry rock specimens and soil samples a knapsack made of canvas is recommended; dealers in sports equipment offer suitable types. A pack board inserted between the knapsack and the collector's back distributes the heavy load more evenly.

Illustration Number 4

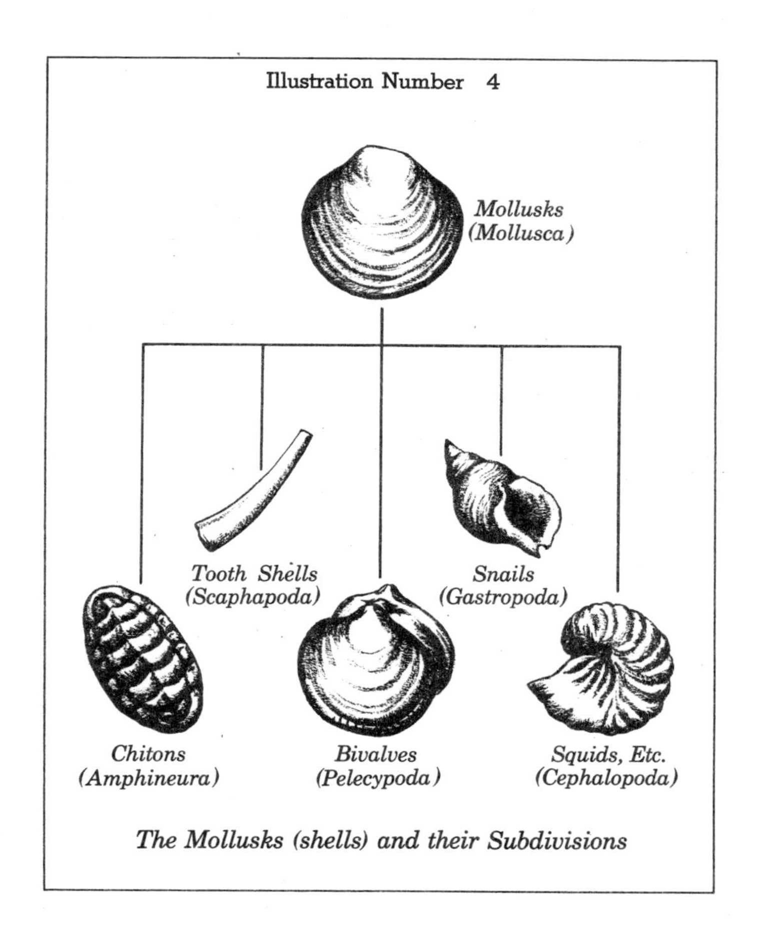

The Mollusks (shells) and their Subdivisions

Home Equipment for Rock Collectors — For the sake of appearance a fairly uniform size should be maintained for all specimens of the collection, except, of course, for those pieces which show prehistoric animal tracks or wind marks on a larger surface. To obtain approximately equal sizes various methods will be used as the hardness of rocks and minerals varies greatly. Gypsum and adobe, for instance, may be cut neatly by a sharp knife into any desired shape; however, a part of the surface should be left in its rough condition to show its natural state. Somewhat harder rocks will respond to a trimming treatment by a chisel, while the hardest varieties will have to be handled with regular household tools, a heavy hammer, pliers and nippers.

Polishing stones which in some cases brings out beautiful and interesting characteristics not visible on broken surfaces, is an art that requires a certain amount of special equipment. A relatively simple home method is recommended by Carroll L. and Mildred A. Fenton, the well-known geologists and nature writers:

The preliminary work of trimming the rock to a fairly even surface should be done with hammers, chisels, and other appropriate tools.

Take some carborundum No. 120 and put it, together with a small amount of water, on a piece of plate glass. Rub

Illustration Number 5

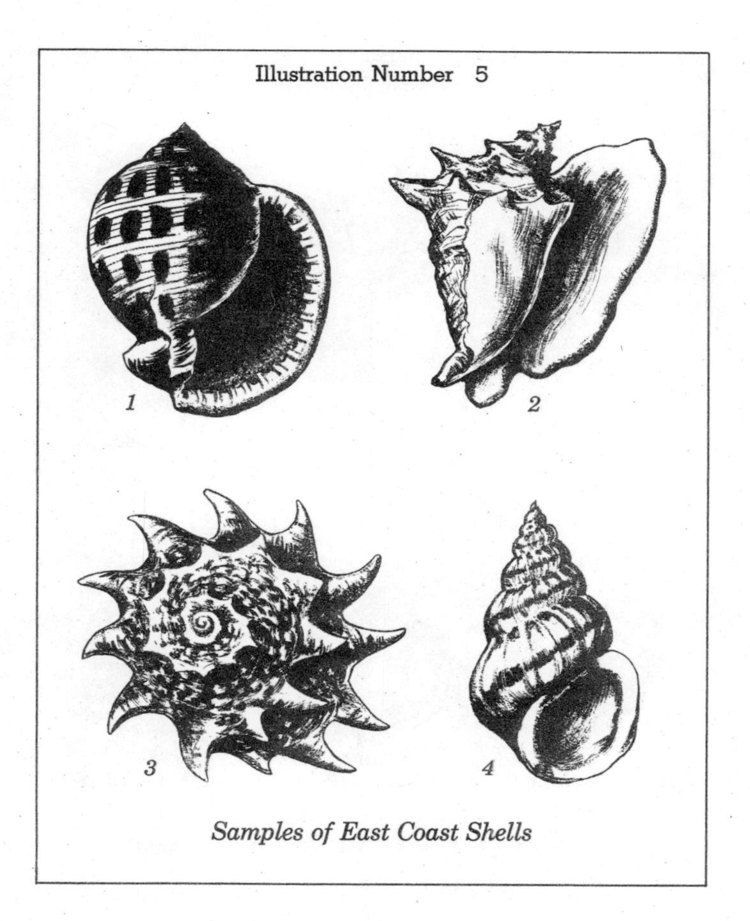

Samples of East Coast Shells

the surface of your rock specimen on the plate glass. Replenish carborundum and water when necessary. A flat though scratchy surface will emerge on the rock specimen after sufficient grinding.

Clean your plate glass or provide a new piece. Take some carborundum F F and put it, together with a little water, on the plate glass. Rub out the scratches on the surface of the rock specimen.

Take a new piece of plate glass used especially for this purpose. Put on it carborundum No. 600, together with a few drops of water. Continue rubbing until the surface of the rock specimen is satisfactorily smooth.

Take a small box partly filled with sand; place in it the rock specimen so that its newly ground surface is in a horizontal position. Apply a thin coating of Duco Cement or a similar product, using a spatula or knife. The cement should dry where no dust will settle on it. The final result will be a smoothly polished surface presenting the desired details in grain, color, pattern, and texture.

But even semi-professional equipment is not difficult to handle and is not overly expensive either. An All-Purpose Gem Maker unit is offered by the scientific supply houses for little more than thirty dollars; it can be mounted on a table 1½ by 2 feet and transforms stones into gems by sawing, grinding, shaping and polishing. The necessary tools, grinding and polishing compounds, brushes, etc. are included, together with exact instructions and even an assortment of gem stones ready to be cut, ground, and finished.

Equipment for Storing — Provisional Storage — Old cigar boxes or shirt boxes, subdivided by cardboard or wooden partitions (see illustration No. 1) will prove serviceable.

Permanent Storage — A cabinet with drawers, the latter interchangeable, is recommended. The drawers should consist of a plywood bottom and a border of pine or any other soft wood available. The size of the tray will depend on the collector's preferences and on the space and material on hand. A tray 1½ feet wide and 2 feet long might be suggested. The height of the simple external frame structure will also depend on individual circumstances, particularly the size of the collection to be stored. The drawers will run on woodstrips nailed to the inner side of the frame, or on angle irons screwed to the frame. It is suggested not to fit the trays too tightly into the cabinet but allow a little marginal space. This leeway will make the drawers truly interchangeable.

A more elaborate but also more satisfactory construction is suggested by the Fentons and described on illustration No. 2. Here the number of runners is about twice as large as the number of drawers, and the wooden borders of the trays recede on both sides to leave space for the horizontal parts of the angle irons or the wooden runners immediately above. In such an arrangement the drawers may be kept two or three runners apart if certain larger specimens require more space.

The sides and the top of the cabinet may be left open, or be covered with plywood or similar material to shut out the dust.

The professional method of storing rocks is to place them in cardboard trays on the drawers; such trays may be bought from supply houses or may be made of cardboard and tape, as shown on illustration No. 3. The size of these trays should be figured carefully so that they fill the exact drawer space available. Since some rock specimens will be larger and others smaller than the regular size, some cardboard trays may be made in twice the normal size, and others in half the regular size.

In certain cases it might be advisable to fasten the rock specimens to the plywood bottom of the drawer with thin wire, with a label below the specimen (see illustration No. 3). This method is used where the specimens are occasionally on exhibition, as in schools or boy scout troop headquarters.

Numbering, Labeling, Cataloguing — Every specimen of the rock collection should have a number, the first piece being No. 1. The number may be written with India ink on a small piece of white tape, and the tape attached to the rock; or it may be written on a piece of heavy paper, and the paper glued to the specimen with household cement; or a circle of white enamel may be painted on an appropriate, carefully cleaned spot on the rock. After the white enamel has dried, the number may be painted on the circle with black enamel, applied with a very fine brush. The latter method is the most professional and permanent one, but also requires the most skill.

Every specimen should also have a label indicating the number of the rock in the collection, the name, the type (whether igneous, sedimentary or metamorphic), and the locality where found, for instance:

Soapstone
No. 79 Metamorphic
Dorchester, Vermont

Typed labels are, of course, neatest, but as to size, arrangement and their place on or in the cardboard tray the collector will proceed according to his own preferences.

Finally there should be a catalogue which contains additional data for those specimens for which more information is available. The most convenient form is that of a card index or loose-leaf book where cards or leaves can be removed and substituted easily if inferior specimens are discarded and better ones added in their place. Each card or leaf bears the number of one specimen, and the information may describe the details of the environment from which the rock was taken, the name of the finder, the date on which it was found, etc. A photograph of the whole formation may be added, or a reference to a photographic negative stored elsewhere. With increasing knowledge of the field, various interesting geological observations may be added.

Meteorites — Meteorites are fascinating; for they are the only known objects which have not originated on this earth. Consequently they are of definite scientific significance, and rock collectors who on their field trips happen to find meteorites, are requested to note them, to preserve them and to make them available to the scientific institutions which possess large collections of meteorites and study and examine them systematically. For rock collectors who are willing to cooperate the Smithsonian Institution issues the following instructions:

"Meteorites — are so rare that they are found usually by accident rather than by search. They may hit the earth anywhere, and no place is too remote for one.

Meteorites are of two kinds — stone and iron. The latter are more easily recognized because of their weight and metallic character. Nothing similar to them in appearance exists in nature. It is unusual to find large masses of metallic iron scattered in remote places, and consequently any metallic object answering the following descriptions should be investigated.

The surface of iron meteorites is usually rusty brown and is dotted with holes or depressions which resemble thumb marks in putty. The sound produced by striking an iron meteorite with a hammer or rock is different from that produced by striking a large stone. Hammering on the surface only dents or batters the metal, and chips do not easily break off . . . To remove a sample the collector usually has to resort to cutting with a hacksaw.

Stony meteorites are more difficult to recognize. They are made up of heavy silicate minerals, and the presence of iron inclusions adds greatly to their weight. Therefore a stony meteorite is likely to be heavier proportionally than the other minerals or rocks in its vicinity. If a great number of similar pieces are found scattered over wide areas, they are probably *not* meteorites.

Collect the entire specimen wherever possible and submit it for study. If it is too large to handle easily remove a piece about the size of a silver dollar and forward this directly to the U.S. National Museum (Smithsonian Institution, Washington, D.C.) for identification. Be sure to include the location of your find and your name and address on the accompanying label.

If your find is a meteor, the American Meteor Society will pay you a dollar per pound, plus a bonus of $5.00.

COLLECTING SHELLS

Why Shells Are Interesting — Adornment, decoration, art, —words of this kind summarize the role which shells have played in the history of civilization, ever since its dawn. In the caves of stone-age peoples, archaeologists have found pierced shells that had been used as jewelry, perhaps the first jewels to adorn human necks, arms, and ankles.

Fifteen hundred years before Christ, possibly earlier, rich purple dyes were extracted from shells, or rather shell-bearing mollusks; on the Tyrian coast of the Mediterranean which was famous for this art, cavities can still be seen, chiseled into the rock, where the shells were crushed in preparation of the dye. So costly was the process that for centuries purple

Illustration Number 6

Samples of East Coast Shells

remained the royal color reserved for kings. In the days of Emperor Augustus wealthy Romans paid two hundred dollars for a pound of wool colored with the purple dye of the shells.

The Orient detected pearls in shell-bearing mollusks, particularly in certain oysters and clams, — nobody is certain how many centuries ago. The pearls appeared in various colors, but those that were satiny white received highest honors. The perfectly round, separate specimens were preferred over those attached to the shell. Later on the experts discovered the mollusk's secret of pearl making: They inserted a fragment of a foreign substance into the body of the mollusk, and the oyster covered it with layer after layer of finest mother-of-pearl. Thus the cultured pearl industry of the Far East was born.

In the declining decades of the Renaissance, throughout the 17th century, the form of the shell became so dominant as a decorative motif in architecture and the arts in general, that a whole period was named after it: the Baroque. This word is derived from the Italian adjective "barocco", which originally meant "irregularly round like a sea shell."

In our own native American history, many Indian tribes used shells not only as jewelry — particularly in the graves of the ancient Mound Builders shell ornaments have been found — but also as a medium of exchange. The shells so employed, the "wampum", were dyed in purple or other colors.

In Victorian days our grandfathers collected spectacular shells not so much by gathering them at the seashore but rather by acquiring them in spirited bidding at sea shell auctions which were held regularly in all large cities. Sometimes hundreds of dollars were paid for rare and beautiful specimens which then gathered dust on a corner shelf or nick-nack table in a Victorian living room.

Illustration Number 7

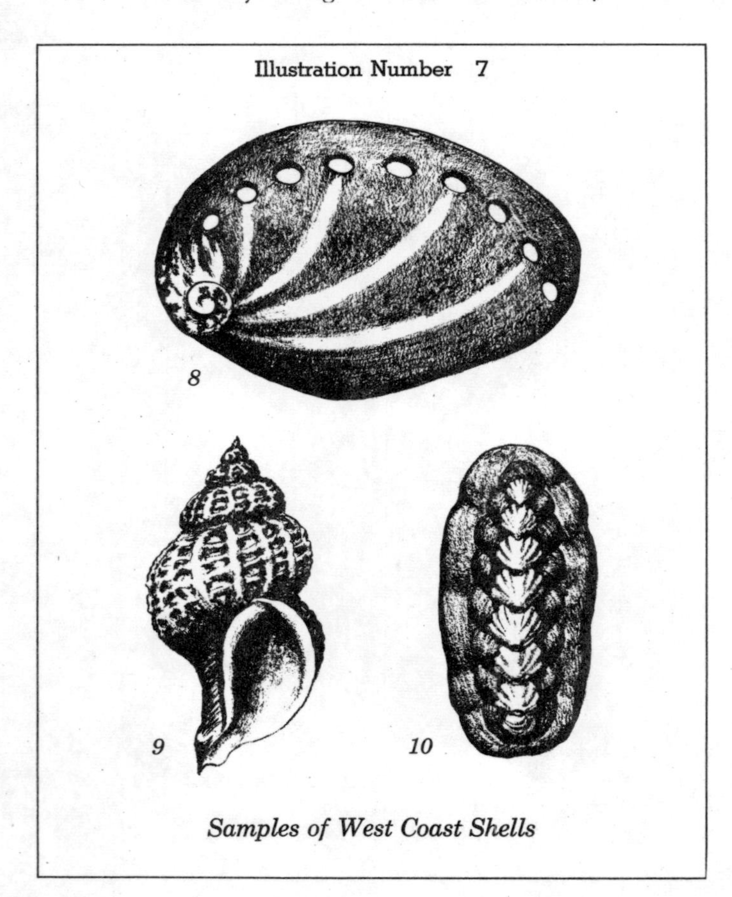

Samples of West Coast Shells

After the First World War interest in shell collecting declined, but at present a definite upswing in this hobby is noticeable. A number of good field books have appeared recently which in turn encourage shell-collecting under a more scientific angle than had been done previously.

Viewpoints for a Shell Collection — 1) GENERAL — Like a rock collection, a shell collection is likely to grow out of a few specimens which attracted the attention of the potential collector because of their beauty or striking form. In order to identify, compare, and supplement the initial pieces, others are acquired, and the collection is under way. With a growing knowledge of shells, the new "conchologist" may wish to specialize, and while he is the sole judge as to the organization of his collection, he will probably proceed along one of the following lines.

2) BY CLASSES—The animals which produce and inhabit shells are the mollusks, a name derived from a Greek-Latin stem meaning "soft", and said to have been originated by Aristotle 2300 years ago. The mollusks ("Mollusca") form a phylum, one of the great subdivisions of the animal kingdom, just as for instance all animals with a backbone ("Chordata") comprise a phylum. The phylum Mollusca contains approximately 75,000 species, and as it represents one of the most ancient forms of life on earth it is also found in thousands of fossil species, in the oldest fossil-bearing rock formations. Approximately three fourths of all shells are univalves, twenty per cent are bivalves, and the remaining five per cent belong to various other classifications. The phylum is divided into five classes, each of which offers an interesting field of specialization (see illustration No. 4). They are:

The Chitons or Amphineura (the Greek term for "having nerves on both sides") are sluggish and primitive animals which favor shallow water and can be collected close to the shore. A typical chiton is pictured in illustration No. 4 (1); it has an armor of eight shells shaped like saddles; these plates overlap and form a row on the back. With its flat "foot" the chiton adheres to the rock by suction or "creeps" to another location. Conchologists believe that the most ancient ancestral form of all present-day mollusks closely resembled the chiton.

The Tooth-Shells or Scaphapoda (the Greek term for "bowl-footed") are also called Tusk-Shells because their tapering shell cones look like miniature elephant tusks. The "foot" and a few tentacles protrude from the larger end. The mollusks of this small group prefer clean sand as a habitat.

The Clams or Pelecypoda (the Greek word for "hatchet-footed") include, besides the clams proper, such well-known bivalves as oysters and mussels. Typical representatives of this class are shown in illustrations No. 6 (7) and 8 (1).

Collecting Shells

The Snails or Gastropoda (the Greek word for "stomach-footed") comprise the mollusks that crawl on their stomach in the manner of the snails, slugs, and limpets. While the slugs produce only fragments of shells or no shells at all, the snails' houses are known to everybody.

The Squids and allies or Cephalopoda (the Greek term for "head-footed") are a group of mollusks with parrot-like beaks including the octopus, the cuttlefish, the beautiful paper argonaut and the spectacular pearly nautilus of the South Seas. The Cephalopoda appear also in a great many fossil forms which are called Ammonites.

A good many collectors specialize in a single genus of shells.

3) Geographical — The collector's residence may determine the extent of his hobby, and collections of East Coast sea shells, West Coast sea shells, land shells, and fresh water shells are a logical specialization. Sea shells are the biggest and handsomest specimens, and therefore are more attractive to collectors than the others which are interesting scientifically but somewhat neglected by amateur conchologists. While sea shells present themselves in clear ocean water in all their glory, land shells of snails and their relatives are usually dusty and dirty and therefore inconspicuous. Fresh water shells, while yielding fine mother of pearl for the pearl button industry, are usually of dull external colors, frequently in greenish shades, and are therefore not so eagerly sought.

4) Artistic — This is not the scientist's viewpoint, but as some of nature's most magnificent creations are sea shells, excelling in line and form, texture and color, and displaying what we would call an exquisite taste in art, the viewpoint is more than valid. If the collector is interested in shellcraft, perfection of the specimens gathered will be the determining factor. But also the "artistic" collector will derive a certain satisfaction from identifying properly the species he acquires.

How to Identify Shells — Latin Names — Almost every person can tell the names of the principal birds, trees, insects, and other creations of nature, but nobody except a shell collector can tell the names of the shells. The reason is one of language difficulties rather than of scientific hurdles. For most species of shell-bearing mollusks have Latin names only. In the relatively few cases where English names exist, they are local and cannot be used universally. To connect a Latin double name with a small shell may seem cumbersome to a beginner, but it is easy enough to get accustomed to it. Many Latin names show their close, ancestral relationship with common English words and are easily recognized in their meaning; longispina, for instance, obviously means "with long spines", and a five-syllable word like oregonensis simply turns out to mean "of Oregon". A few Latin names have actually a humorous touch, like the scientific name of the chiton shell in illustration No. 7 (10): "Katharina tunicata" is "Katy in a tunic". The Katy in this case was Lady Katharine Douglas who sent the first specimen of the species to the British Museum.

Even if the Latin name has no direct meaning to the novice-collector, the connection between name and shell is soon established. A few examples will illustrate this tie, in several drawings of outstanding East Coast and West Coast specimens.

Illustration Number 8

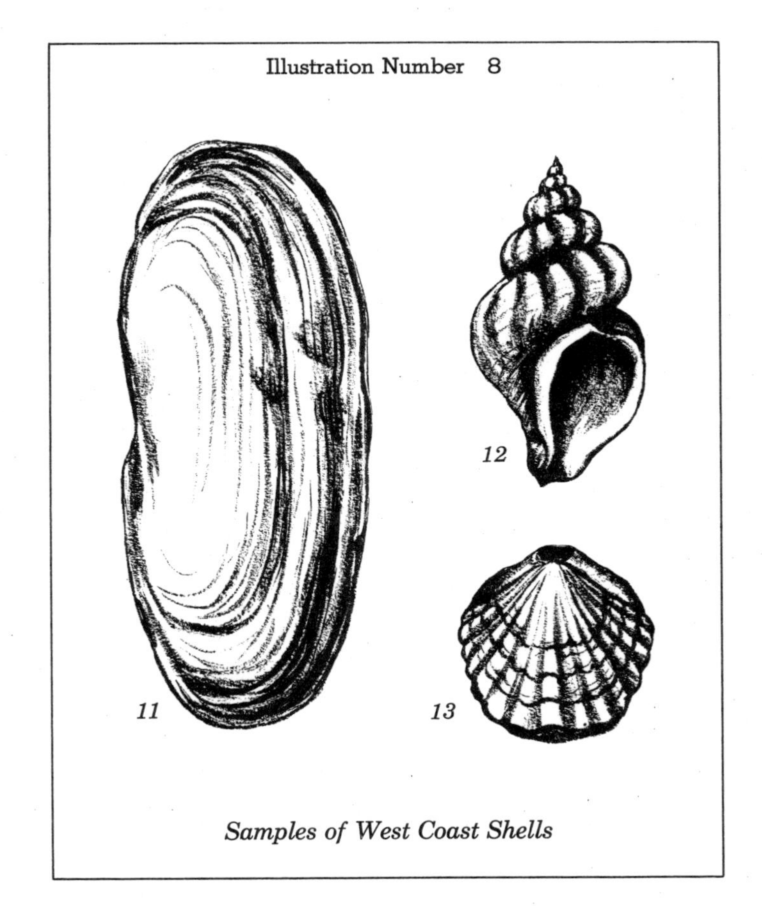

Samples of West Coast Shells

Ill. 5 (1): Phalium granulatum. North Carolina to West Indies; 2 inches; white or light yellow with brownish spots; this form is frequently offered for sale in southern souvenir and shell stores, sometimes under the name of Scotch Bonnet or Scotch Helmet.

Ill. 5 (2): Strombus gigas. Northern Florida to West Indies; 8 to 12 inches; weighs up to 5 pounds; exterior yellowish, interior pink, the latter an excellent base for carving fine cameos; these shells are made into scrapers and other tools; in Victorian days they were also used as borders of flower beds. The mantle fold contains sometimes semi-precious pearls. Local names are great conch or queen conch.

Ill. 5 (3): Astraea longispina. Southern Florida; 2 inches in diameter; silvery or greenish white, iridescent; a strong and magnificent species, in great demand with collectors and makers of shell jewelry.

Ill. 5 (4): Epitomium lineatum. Massachusetts to Florida; 1½ inches; pinkish white, often with one or two brownish bands. More frequently found in the stomachs of fishes than on beaches. Local name: banded or lined wentletrap.

Ill. 6 (5): Pecten nodosus. Cape Hatteras to Gulf Coast; 3½ to 6 inches; purple to orange to red; interior pink. One of the world's most beautiful shells, it is not frequently found on the beach. Dredged at 10 or more fathoms, and often brought up by sponge fishermen. Local name: lion's paw.

Ill. 6 (6): Epitomium groenlandicum. Northern waters,

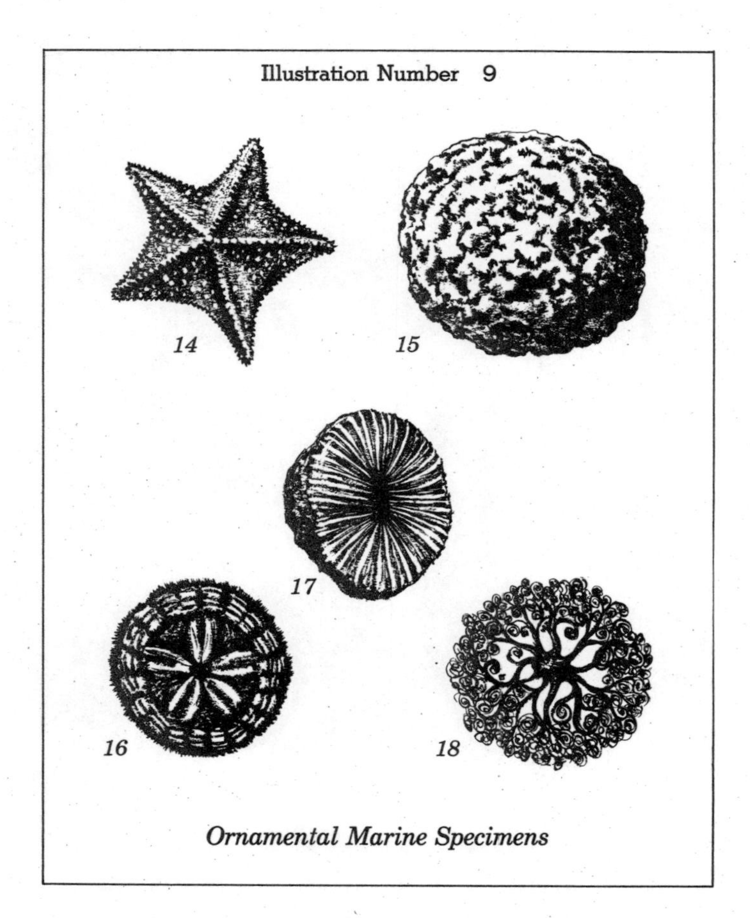

Ornamental Marine Specimens

particularly Maine coast; 1½ inches; white or brownish white. This splendid shell is often found in the stomachs of fishes caught near the Grand Banks. Local name: ladder shell.

Ill. 6 (7): Venus mercenaria. Gulf of St. Lawrence to Florida; up to 6 inches; whitish-grey, with a concentric pattern of numerous grooves. Next to the oyster, this is the most important commercial clam in the eastern states, known as hard-shelled clam, round clam, or little neck; when half-grown to a length of about 2 inches, it is known as cherry-stone clam. On the New England coast the Indian term quahog is in use; the early Indians were very fond of this variety, and ancient heaps of quahog shells are reminders of prehistoric clam feasts. This is also the shell used as "wampum".

Ill. 7 (8): Haliotis chacherodii. Oregon to Lower California; up to 6 inches; greenish-black outside, splendidly iridescent inside. Clings to cracks and boulders on the rocky coast. Popular name: black abalone.

Ill. 7 (9): Argobuccinum oregonensis. Alaska to Monterey; 4 inches; it has a hairy brown epidermis and a clear-white inside. This beautiful "Oregon Triton" is a typical cold-water shell.

Ill. 7 (10): Katharina tunicata. Oregon to Catalina; 2 to 3 inches; the back with the eight plates is black, the "foot" reddish. Local name of this chiton: Black Katy.

Ill. 8 (11): Siliqua patula. From Oregon northward; 5 inches; yellowish brown, with some violet touches. Known as "flat razor clam," it is one of the first West Coast shells to have been described systematically. Captain George Dixon gave a fine scientific picture of it in his book "A Voyage Around the World," published in London in 1789, and called it "exceeding good food."

Ill. 8 (12): Beringius kennicottii. Alaska; 5 inches; epidermis yellowish-brown, shell white with touches of purple and pink. This large cold-water shell is well-known on Kodiak Island where its mollusk spawns in shallow water.

Ill. 8 (13): Terebratalia occidentalis. From Monterey to the south; 1¼ inches; local name: western lampshell. The species of this family derive their popular name from their resemblance to classical Roman oil lamps. Innumerable fossil forms are found in the rocks.

Field Guides and Books — Once the novice collector has accustomed himself to Latin names, and has become familiar with the large subdivisions of the field, he will have no difficulties identifying his shells with the help of a field guide. The following books are recommended (all are useful both for beginners and for advanced shell collectors):

Morris, P. A., A Field Guide to the Shells of Our Atlantic Coast, Houghton Mifflin Co., Boston, 1947

Morris, P. A., A Field Guide to the Shells of our Pacific Coast, Boston, 1952

Keep, Josiah, West Coast Shells, Stanford University, California, 1935

Webb, Walter F., United States Mollusca, W. F. Webb, St. Petersburg 6, Florida

Webb, Walter F., Handbook for Shell Collectors, 9th edition, W. F. Webb, St. Petersburg 6, Florida

Webb, Walter F., Foreign Land Shells, W. F. Webb, St. Petersburg 6, Florida

Hausman, Leon A., Beginner's Guide to Seashore Life, G. P. Putnam's Sons, New York, 1949

Hausman, Leon A., Beginner's Guide to Freshwater Life, G. P. Putnam's Sons, New York, 1950

Rogers, H. E., The Shell Book, Garden City Publishing Co., Garden City, N. Y., 1914

In cases of doubt do not hesitate to get in touch with a museum of natural history to have your question answered and your problem explained. Unusual variations of shells may be of definite scientific interest.

Collecting Shells: When and Where — Sea Shells — Low tide in the early morning is recommended as the most auspicious time for shell collecting, especially after a storm. Sandy beaches with swift currents which provide a constant new supply of the microscopic organisms on which the mollusks feed, and rocky beaches with a great many small inlets and tidal pools will yield a good harvest. As tourists and travelers know, some beaches seem to be especially abundant in beautiful shells of great variety, as, for instance, many stretches of the Gulf Coast. Some geographical hints like those given by Walter F. Webb, the veteran shell collector and dealer, will be useful:

The beach of Cape Sable, Florida, is a favorite spot for

Collecting Shells

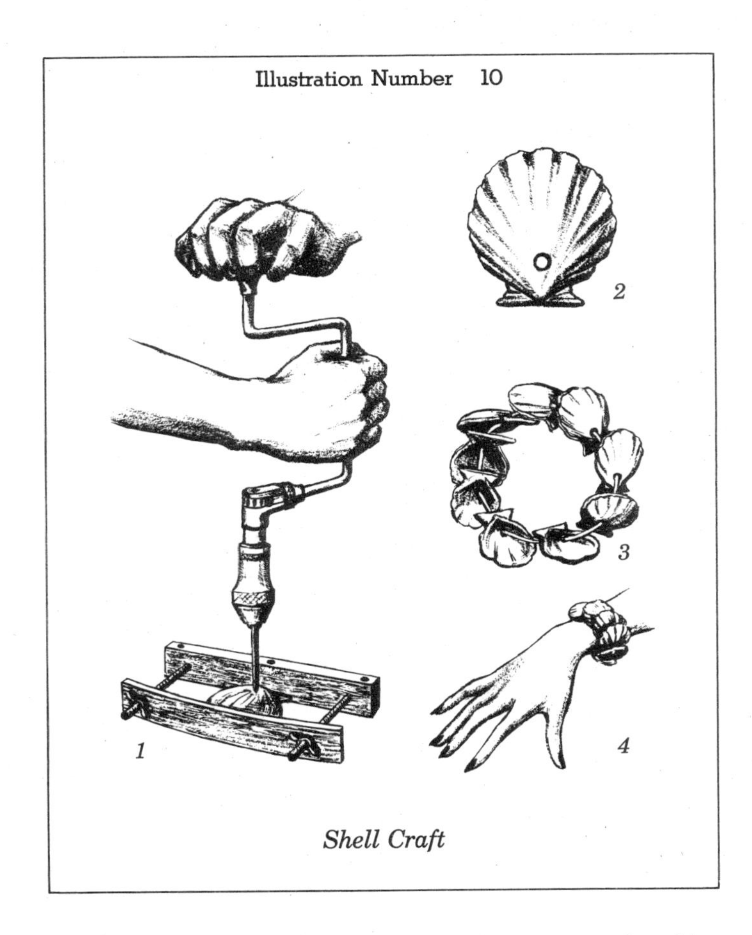

Shell Craft

collectors of fine shells. Its sands are magnificently white and curve abruptly into deep water; strong currents are sweeping along, unhampered by mangroves, and the tides have a range of up to 5 feet. After a storm, thousands of exquisite specimens cover the beach.

The banks of the numerous drainage canals that have been dug in the Everglades and other parts of southern Florida contain a great many marine shells, the same species that exist on the beaches.

In the state of Washington, Puget Sound has an excellent reputation as a shell-collecting ground. It seems that climate and geography combine to make that region unusually rich in sea life and mollusks. On Tomales Bay extensive mud flats appear when the tide goes out; they are ideal gathering areas. On San Juan Island the University of Washington has established a Biological Station to take advantage of the abundance of specimens for research.

On the Californian coast large beds of Mytilus californianus, the California mussel, are found. These shells are remarkable both for their size — they grow as big as eight inches — and for their beautiful purple color which is set off by occasional streaks of brown. If polished on a lapidary's wheel, they become exquisite show pieces. This is another West Coast shell reported by Captain Dixon in 1789. He observed specimens 9½ inches long and saw Indians file them to a point and use them as harpoons in fishing.

A great variety of interesting shells, especially of abalones, may be gathered at Pacific Grove and on Monterey Bay. On the vast mud flats along the coast from Puget Sound to Mexico the huge shell of the so-called rubberneck clam Schizothaerus nuttalii which grows to a length of 10 inches, may be spotted by the jets of water thrown up for a foot or higher.

Outside of the United States and Canada the Gulf of Dulce on the Pacific Coast of Costa Rica and Panama and the Santa Elena Bay of Ecuador are recommended as a collector's heaven, extremely rich in marine life.

Interesting semi-fossilized shell specimens may be secured from the "kitchen middens" encountered along the Atlantic coast from Canada to Florida. The "middens" are huge heaps of oyster and clam shells discarded by prehistoric Indians after their seafood feasts.

When gathering specimens on a rocky shore, watch for such birds as hawks and gulls picking up shells, lifting them to a considerable height, and dropping them above the cliffs. The shells break and the birds swoop down to eat the mollusks.

LAND SHELLS — The northern forms of land shells are usually produced by ground-dwelling mollusks and are found under the cover of leaves, logs, boulders, etc. In the south many species have arboreal habits and can be picked from the lower parts of tree trunks, during the rainy season. Land shells will be more abundant in limestone regions, and if several living specimens are kept in a container for study or research purposes, a piece of limestone should be provided for them as their shells — like the shells of all mollusks —

Avoid Poison Sumach
(Also called Poison Oak or Poison Ash)

are composed principally of carbonate of lime. Otherwise the mollusks' quest for lime may induce them to eat each other.

FRESH WATER SHELLS — Almost any brook, river, pond or lake produces some shells, but the quantity varies greatly. Water of a moderate temperature is better suited than cold water; consequently more shells will be found in southeastern rivers and lakes than in the water bodies of the north or those of the western mountains. But a most important prerequisite for an abundance of shells is the presence of limestone in the drainage system. In limestone regions shallow streams, shoals, creeks and ponds with algae and other vegetation will furnish a large amount and variety of shells.

The mother-of-pearl of fresh water mussels is splendidly iridescent, their tints ranging from white to reddish, violet and purple. A properly lighted collection on glass shelves will be an attractive exhibit.

SUPPLY HOUSES — While the personal collecting of shells is the most enjoyable part of the hobby, supplementary species may be bought from shell stores — there are quite a number in Florida and California — and supply houses. A well-known shell dealer, Walter F. Webb of 2515 Second Avenue North, St. Petersburg, Florida, has a catalog and price list of thousands of species.

Field Equipment — Old clothes, a pair of rubber boots, a shovel for securing those species that live in the sand, a strong pocket knife for prying loose shells that cling to rocks, a container for the gathered specimens, a notebook and pencil — these objects comprise the simple field equipment of the shell collector. Deep digging will unearth a great many specimens that are rarely found on the surface of the beach. If large and small living shells are gathered, it is recommended to keep the small ones in a separate jar; otherwise they might be devoured by their bigger fellow-mollusks. A magnifying glass may be useful at times. In the notebook the day's discoveries should be listed, with exact locations; note the number of miles from the nearest town or village.

A dredge or scraper made of wood and iron may be used just below the low water line of the ocean, or in rivers, ponds and lakes. A dredge with a D-shaped frame, steel runners and heavy brussels netting, suitable for both salt and fresh water, can be bought from natural science supply companies like the General Biological Supply House of Chicago. This, however, is a rather professional piece of equipment.

A towing net pulled on a rope by a boat will often catch fine specimens, both during daylight and at night when certain varieties rise to the surface of the water. This is particularly effective in warmer ocean waters. Such a towing net consists of a wooden hoop, 12 to 14 inches in diameter; a bag of strong material (for instance bunting), two feet long, its mouth sewn around the hoop; and three cords a foot and a half long, fastened to the hoop at equal intervals, while the other ends are tied to the tow line.

For collecting small freshwater shells of bivalve mollusks a sieve may be used. There are several hundred species of shells under half an inch in length, and in very small creeks, ditches, and ponds an inexpensive hand sieve will be effective in scooping up the bottom soil, washing and rinsing it in the water, and picking out the desired shell specimens. If conditions warrant it, the sieve may be tied to a pole, to increase the radius of exploration.

Home Equipment — CLEANING — A good part of the shells gathered will be empty; in others the mollusk will still be present. To remove it, place the shell in hot water for a few minutes; then bend a hairpin into a hook and pull the soft parts out. If any fragments remain inside, immerse the shell in alcohol for several days and dry it in a shady spot. No offensive odor will remain.

Many shells have an outer cover which is called periostracum, epidermis, or simply skin. In most cases you will want to retain it as it is the natural state of the shell. Where an especially decorative appearance is desired, for instance for the use in shellcraft, the epidermis can be removed by a solution of caustic soda in which the shell is placed for about 24 hours; the usual proportion of the solution's ingredients is a pound of caustic soda to a gallon of water. Don't let the solution touch your fingers as it will burn your skin; use tweezers.

To clean and brighten up shells without epidermis, a commercial cleaner like Clorox is recommended by some collectors. Land shells usually need only to be washed with water and a brush. Fresh water shells are sometimes dis-

Illustration Number 12

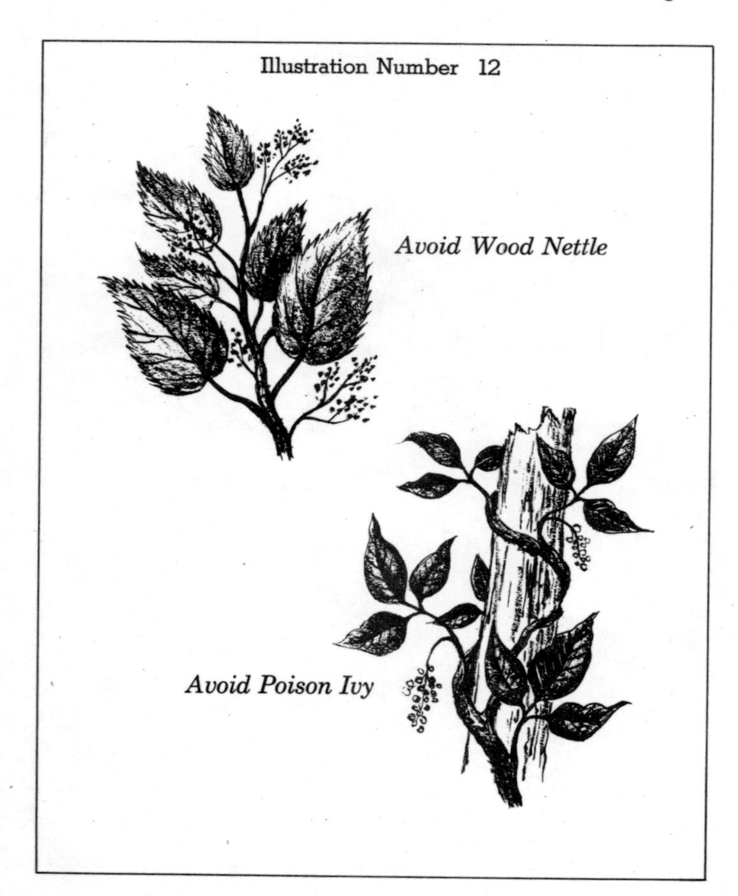

colored by green mould or algae which cling to them. Such growths can be removed by soaking the shells in oxalic acid for about an hour, and then rinsing them in water and scrubbing them with a brush.

In the case of very small live shells it will be difficult to pull the mollusk with a hook. The simplest procedure is to immerse them in alcohol for several days, then spread them to dry in the shade.

STORING — Shell collections are kept in cabinets similar to those described previously for rock collections. Shelves of plywood with a raised wooden border are used as drawers which run on angle irons or strips of wood, in a simple frame or an elaborate cabinet. The dimensions of the drawers and the height of the cabinet will depend on the collector's preferences and the size of the collection.

As in the case of rocks, the shells should be placed in individual cardboard trays. If the sizes 1½ x 2, 2 x 3, 3 x 4, and 4 x 6 inches are selected, the shelf space will be covered completely as each larger size corresponds to two trays of the smaller size. Three-quarters of an inch is the generally preferred depth for the trays. Some collectors use glass vials to store small species of which they have a good many specimens.

CATALOGUING AND LABELING — As in the case of rock and plant collections, each specimen of your shell collection should have a number, beginning with 1 and proceeding without repetition. The number should be marked 1) on the specimen, with indelible ink, in small figures; 2) on the label attached to the tray; and 3) on the index card of the catalog. The label should record, besides the number, the Latin name, the date when found, the place where found, and the person by whom it was found:

Shell Collection of Henry F. Black
Conus spurius
No. 372 DATE: 8-19-53
FOUND: 2 miles south of Clearwater, Fla.
BY: Mary H. Black

The catalog may be a card index or a loose-leaf notebook. Under the number of the label and the shell it will give details on the specimen (whether picked up as a living or empty shell), on the marine community in which it was found, on the condition of the beach, the tide, etc. The more familiar the collector becomes with his hobby, the more pertinent and interesting his observations and notes will be.

The "Marine Touch" — Some shell collectors like to add the skeletons of a few ornamental sea urchins, sea stars, corals, or sponges to their collection or exhibit, for the sake of a decorative and interesting "marine touch." Several specimens suited for such a purpose are pictured in illustration No. 9. They are:

The giant sea star (14), a spectacular massive star, approximately 4 inches thick and 12 inches wide, fairly common in the shallow waters of the Bahamas and occasionally found on the southern Florida coast.

The sand dollar (16), a sea urchin, covered with small black spines, moving about quite freely; it is commonly gathered from Canada to Florida, and similar forms exist on our Pacific coast; 4 inches.

Illustration Number 13

An Airtight Terrarium

The basket sea star (18), from the deeper waters from Canada to Florida. When preserved for a marine collection, it is usually compressed to a diameter of about 10 inches; floating in the ocean it spreads its hundreds of arms over a wide surface, sometimes with a radius of 7 feet.

The rosette coral (17), which is often brought up by sponge divers from depths of 10 to 20 fathoms. It grows on reefs in the Gulf of Mexico. Approximately 3 inches.

The so-called velvet sponge (15) of the Gulf of Mexico, usually living at a depth of from 10 to 20 fathoms, is commercially important.

It is well worth-while to visit Tarpon Springs, on the west coast of Florida, the center of the sponge fisheries of the Gulf of Mexico. The unusual trade is in the hands of a colony of Greek sponge divers who were transplanted to this spot from the Aegean Islands of the Mediterranean; they carry on an age-old Greek craft that is mentioned by Aristotle and Homer and can be traced back for thousands of years.

From the seaside resorts of Florida and California glass-bottomed boats make excursions to the so-called marine gardens where shells, sea stars, sea feathers, corals and brightly colored tropical fishes may be observed beneath the boat, in their natural habitat.

Shellcraft — Persons with skill and artistic taste can make

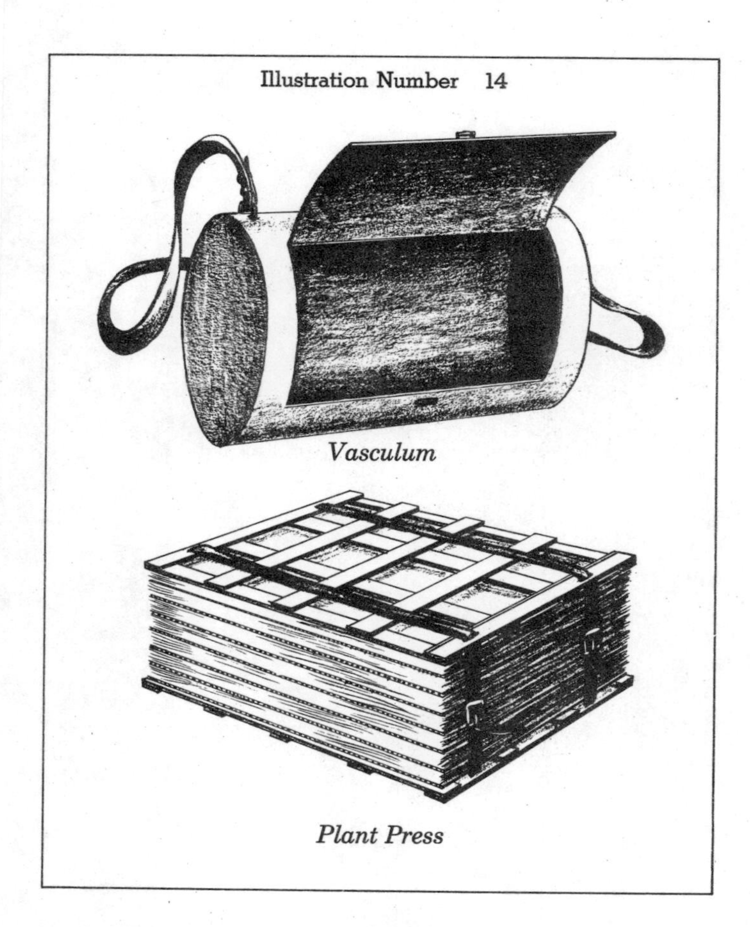
Illustration Number 14

Vasculum

Plant Press

lovely shell jewelry at home, from bracelets and necklaces to belts and earrings. For most pieces a considerable number of perfect shells of uniform size, shape, color and texture are needed.

The only tool for this project is a small brace and bit; a small electric drill is even handier. A ⅛-inch drill, a 1/10-inch drill, or a fine nail filed to a round point may be used for boring. Some practice will be necessary to acquire the light touch that will drill the hole without cracking the shell.

Illustration No. 10 shows how to make a shell bracelet (a—drilling the hole; b—shell showing the proper place for the hole; c—shells strung on an elastic, under side; d—same, upper side). Other shell jewelry may be made in a similar fashion.

PLANT HOBBIES

Viewpoints for a Plant Collection — When we speak of collecting plants we usually have in mind the gathering and pressing of plant specimens for inclusion in a herbarium. While that is indeed the most usual form, it is also perfectly possible to collect living plants. In either case the collector will have to restrict himself to a certain field or region, as a general collection would be quite pointless because of the enormous size and variety of the plant kingdom.

While the interest and imagination of the collector are the principal and indeed only important guideposts, the following suggestions may be helpful in selecting a special field.

1) Geographical: Your Home Region — Wildflowers will probably be your "first love" for a plant collection. But soon you will branch out to include other members of the various plant families, regardless of the showy appearance of their flowers. If you collect your plants in a definitely circumscribed district — your farm, village, township, a 3-mile or 5-mile circle around your home, etc. — the result will have definite significance as a botanical survey, perhaps the first one made in that locality. It may correct the generally accepted and known range of certain species, and thus make a contribution to botanical science in the field of plant distribution.

2) Geographical: Your Travels — If you own a camp in the mountains or spend a vacation on the coast you may, of course, proceed in the same way. But even if you just gather along the road specimens that strike you as beautiful or interesting, press and preserve them properly so that they keep most of their original color, and mount them together with your own annotations, such a collection will be a meaningful and worth-while botanical souvenir and record of your trip.

3) By Family or Genus — A particularly scientific approach is the one that restricts the collection to a certain genus or family. It may be a relatively small group like the Water Lilies, or a very large one like the Composite Family; in each case you will, if you pursue this hobby long enough, become an expert who might very well make a scientific contribution. Through clubs and associations you will get in touch with collectors of the same plant group in Minnesota or New Jersey, Oregon or Iowa, and exchange both specimens and data. You will become aware of variations in color and form that occur within the same species, conditioned by differences of soil, altitude, rainfall and temperature. If such observations are made over a wide-enough range and long-enough period of time, they may be of definite scientific value. Whether you will become interested in technical publications, including doctor's dissertations, which deal with your special plant family, will depend entirely on the amount of time and effort you are willing to devote to your hobby.

4) Tree Leaves — The leaves of deciduous trees — the branches of pines, spruces and other conifers, of course, can not be collected in a herbarium — are so characteristic and beautiful in form and seasonal color, that they are the favorite object of a novice plant collector. As in the case in all plant collecting, it is essential to select and include only samples that are complete, healthy, and as typical for the tree as you can possibly find them. Therefore spring is an especially favorable gathering season as the leaves are not yet attacked by fungus diseases and parasites. On your herbarium page the two specimen leaves of the tree, one showing the upper, the other the lower side, will be the central display, but certain additions will make the sheet more interesting. In some cases the tree's beautiful flower

may be added; that, however, will not always be possible as many species of trees produce blossoms so small, green, and inconspicuous that they are hardly noticeable. On the other hand, a sample of the seeds may be added, for instance a specimen of the maple's winged seeds which may fly over considerable distances before they fall to the ground. The viewpoint for a collection of tree leaves may again be local — geographical, or by families or genera.

5) FERNS—These most graceful plants are an interesting group by themselves and make most attractive herbarium specimens. They are not flowering plants but reproduce by spores which may be found either on special stalks or on the backside of the leaves. On the herbarium sheet the spores should always be shown; in the latter case one of the pressed leaves should be turned. What we see of the ferns above ground are the leaves called fronds; the stem proper grows horizontally on or slightly below the surface. A piece of the rough stem should be included on the herbarium display of the ferns as it is essential for the identification of the species.

A living collection of ferns can easily be organized in your garden. You may either prepare a bed of ferns or plant them in clusters around existing groups of bushes. However, before transferring various types of ferns from the forest to your garden, the soil has to be prepared correspondingly. It should have a good deal of humus, and it might be worthwhile to work rotting leaves or other decayed vegetable matter into the ground. Also be sure that the specimens of your "fernery" enjoy approximately the same amounts of sunlight, shade, and moisture they received in the forest.

Ferns, by the way, are not only interesting as plants of our own environment, but also because of the important role they played in the history of life on earth, and in the development of our huge coal deposits. For at one time, between three and four hundred million years ago, plants of the phylum ferns were the outstanding examples of vegetable life on our planet. They grew in enormous, rich forests in wet and swampy soil, and although they reached the size of trees, they crashed and tumbled easily in floods and storms. Layer after layer of fern fronds piled up in the marshy lowlands, and when later eras covered the plant mass with sand and clay, the pressure transformed the ferns into peat, then into lignite, later into soft coal and finally into anthracite. So it happens that fossil prints of ferns are not infrequently discovered in deposits of coal and sometimes also in sandstone. Such specimens are found in our coal-producing states, like Pennsylvania, West Virginia or Illinois, and collectors are always eager to add to their collections of contemporary ferns the latters' early ancestors in the form of fossil specimens.

6) ALGAE—These plants that live in the ocean (and, to a lesser extent, also in fresh water) are so varied in shape and color that they make attractive specimens for a special herbarium. To a certain extent the collecting of algae is geographically limited as the thousands of miles of sandy beaches along our coast do not yield a considerable and varied harvest of algae. On the other hand, all rocky coasts are ideal haunts for algae collectors: stretches of the Massachusetts and Maine coasts, and parts of the Washington, Oregon, and California shores; also the coral deposits of Florida are a worth-while hunting ground. The method of preparing and preserving algae differs somewhat from that applied to land plants; it will be described in the chapter on Collecting, Pressing and Mounting. For research purposes algae are usually not dried and preserved in a herbarium but kept in vials filled with formaldehyde and alcohol or another preservative solution. Collectors specializing in algae and other lower plant groups like mosses, lichens, and fungi should get in touch with the Farlow Reference Library and Herbarium, Harvard University, Cambridge, Mass., which is devoted to this field exclusively.

7) THE ECOLOGICAL APPROACH — In a collection of this type the assembled plants are not the members of the same family or genus, as in a collection described under 3). They are probably not related at all, but they form a natural community conditioned by their environment. Ecology, which might be called the science of living nature communities arising in various surroundings, finds an abundant field in America because of the fantastic variety of our physical geography. Ecological plant collections may depict desert plant life in the Southwest, alpine plant life in the Rockies or Sierras, swamp plant life in the Everglades, or a hundred others, all gathered within our own borders.

8) LIVING PLANT COLLECTIONS — Although every garden

Illustration Number 15

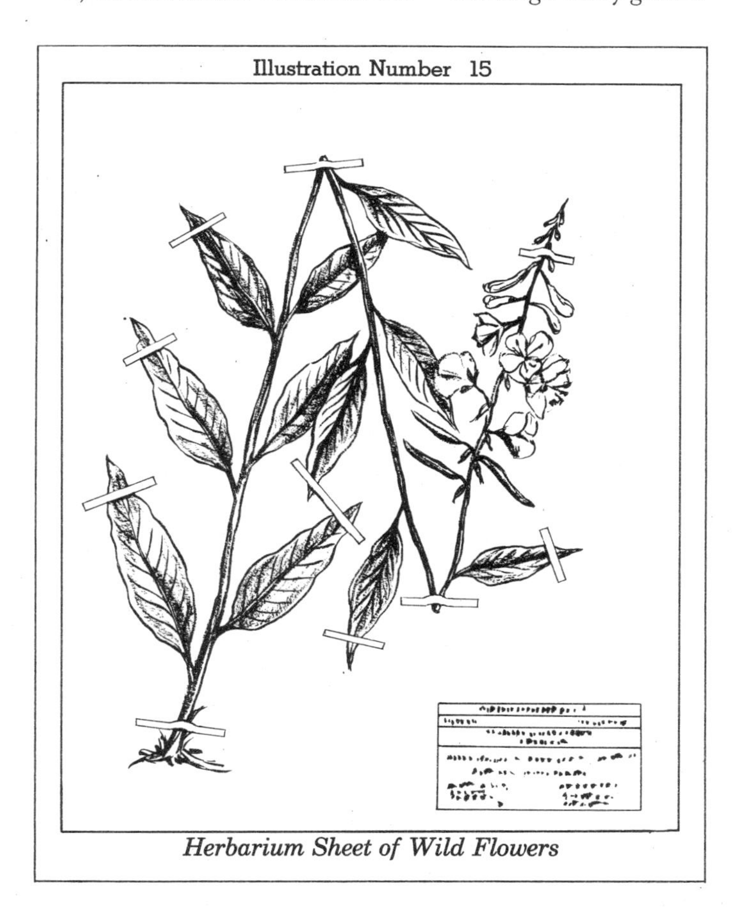

Herbarium Sheet of Wild Flowers

is a plant collection, and although the viewpoint and purpose of a flower garden, a vegetable garden or an orchard is very obvious and definite, we would hardly apply the term collection to a bed of spring flowers or a cabbage patch. However, an herb garden like that of the Cloisters in New York, the branch of the Metropolitan Museum of Art, could well be called a plant collection as it faithfully reproduces the herbs that were cultivated in a medieval convent for a double purpose, the flavoring of food and the use as medicines. For collectors with money, time and imagination the possibilities in this field are endless; a garden displaying all the plants mentioned in the works of Shakespeare used to be (and possibly still is) maintained in a park in New York City, and any favored literary work from Alice in Wonderland to the New Testament may serve as the starting point for such a plant collection. All Botanical Gardens belong to this group.

9) A Living Collection of Miniature Plants — A conventional glass-walled terrarium may, of course, be used for the study of a special group of plants. But as it normally houses not only plants but also frogs, turtles, salamanders, and other amphibians and reptiles, it will be discussed later on in a special chapter. However, the so-called air-tight terrarium (see illustration No. 13) is strictly a plant collection. It consists of a one or two-gallon glass jar in which originally pickles had been packed, or a similar container with a wide mouth. It is placed sideways on a simple wooden stand and provided with a bottom of two layers, the lower one consisting of sand and charcoal, and the upper one of good soil. This operation may be carried out with the help of a tablespoon. Now a carefully selected group of plants gathered in the forest will be set firmly into the soil; all should be of miniature proportions, like various mosses and lichens, tiny ferns and such small plants as the Twin Berry. Members of the fast-growing and domineering grass family are not recommended for inclusion in the group, but perhaps some tree seeds may be planted, like a beechnut, a chestnut and an acorn. If conditions are right they will sprout and start out on their slow growth into potential big shade trees. After the internal arrangements have been completed, the whole is sprinkled with water and the metal cap is screwed on tightly. It must not be taken off again, and although it may seem strange that the plants should take root and thrive without any further supply of water and air, they do so by producing a sufficient amount of moisture and oxygen of their own. They will not last indefinitely in their air-tight greenhouse, but will live perhaps for a year. Much depends on just the right exposure and sunlight; too much or too little will shorten the life of the plant group.

Illustration Number 16

Herbarium Sheet of Tree Leaves

This type of bottle terrarium is employed in shipping rare plants all over the world, between botanical gardens and other scientific institutions.

Identification of Plants — The more common plants in garden and farm are familiar to most of us. However, as you become more deeply interested in plant collecting or leaf collecting it will be necessary to consult field guides and reference books. Some of the best-known publications are the following (books useful to the beginner are starred):

Wildflowers:

Moldenke, H. N., American Wildflowers, D. Van Nostrand & Co., New York, 1949

*Hausman, E. H., The Illustrated Encyclopedia of American Wildflowers, Garden City Publishing Co., New York, 1947

*Wherry, E. T., Wildflower Guide, Doubleday & Co., New York, 1948 (eastern U. S. and Canada)

*Zim, H. S., and Martin, A. C., Flowers, a Guide to Familiar American Wildflowers, Simon & Schuster, New York, 1950

Armstrong, M., Western Wildflowers, G. P. Putnam's Sons, New York, 1927

Ferns:

Durand, Herbert, Field Book of Common Ferns, G. P. Putnam's Sons, New York, 1928

Wherry, E. T., Guide to Eastern Ferns, The Science Press, Lancaster, Pa., 1942

Algae:

Arnold, Augusta, The Sea Beach at Ebb-tide, Appleton-Century Co., New York, 1901

Smith, Gilbert M., The Fresh Water Algae of the U. S., McGraw Hill Book Co., New York, 1933

Trees:

Sargent, C. S., Silva of North America, Houghton Mifflin Co., Boston, 1891-1902

Sargent, C. S., Manual of the Trees of North America, 2nd Edition, Houghton Mifflin Co., Boston, 1933

U. S. Dept. of Agriculture, Trees: The Yearbook of Agriculture, Government Printing Office, Washington, D. C., 1949

Britton, N., North American Trees, Charles Scribner's Sons, New York, 1908

Keeler, H. L., Our Native Trees, Charles Scribner's Sons, New York, 1931

*Collingswood and Brush, W. D., Knowing Your Trees, Washington, D. C. (The American Forestry Ass'n.), 1949

*Peattie, D. C., A Natural History of Trees of Eastern and Central America, Houghton Mifflin Co., New York, 1950

*Jaques, H. E., How to Know the Trees, Wm. C. Brown Co., Dubuque, Iowa, 1946

GENERAL:

*Jordan, E. L., Hammond's Nature Atlas of America, the sections on Wildflowers and Trees, C. S. Hammond & Co., New York, 1952

Robinson, B. L., and Fernald, M. L., Gray's Manual of Botany, 7th Edition, American Book Co., New York, 1908

*Zim, H. S., Plants, Harcourt, Brace & Co., New York, 1947

Hitchcock, A. S., Field Book for the Local Botanist, J. Wiley & Sons, New York, 1931

Smithsonian Institution, A Field Collector's Manual in Natural History, Washington, D. C., 1944

Johnston, I. M., The Preparation of Botanical Specimens for the Herbarium; Arnold Arboretum, Cambosco Scientific Co., Boston, Mass., 1939

Collecting, Pressing, and Mounting — A pocket knife or pruning shears for cutting plants with a woody stalk; a small trowel for digging out herbacious plants for which you wish to save and press part of the root; and a notebook are the only field equipment needed for the non-professional plant collector. A magnifying glass may be added. The securing of the plants themselves is easy, but good care should be taken of exact annotations. If you are certain of the common and scientific names of the plant, write them down; otherwise leave this space open until you have an opportunity to identify the plant at home. However, the following data are indispensible: Number in your collection (start with 1 and proceed as you add specimens), date, place (describe the geographical relationship to the nearest road so that it can be reached again), environment (swamp, desert, mountain top, forest, etc.) and soil (sand, clay, loam, humus, etc.). If you know the elevation and are familiar with other plants in whose association your specimen is found, note also these data. If you collect leaves of trees, describe the trees, their shape, approximate height, color and texture of bark, etc.

As to the next step, one of two methods may be followed. The specimens may be gathered in a metal container, to be

Illustration Number 17

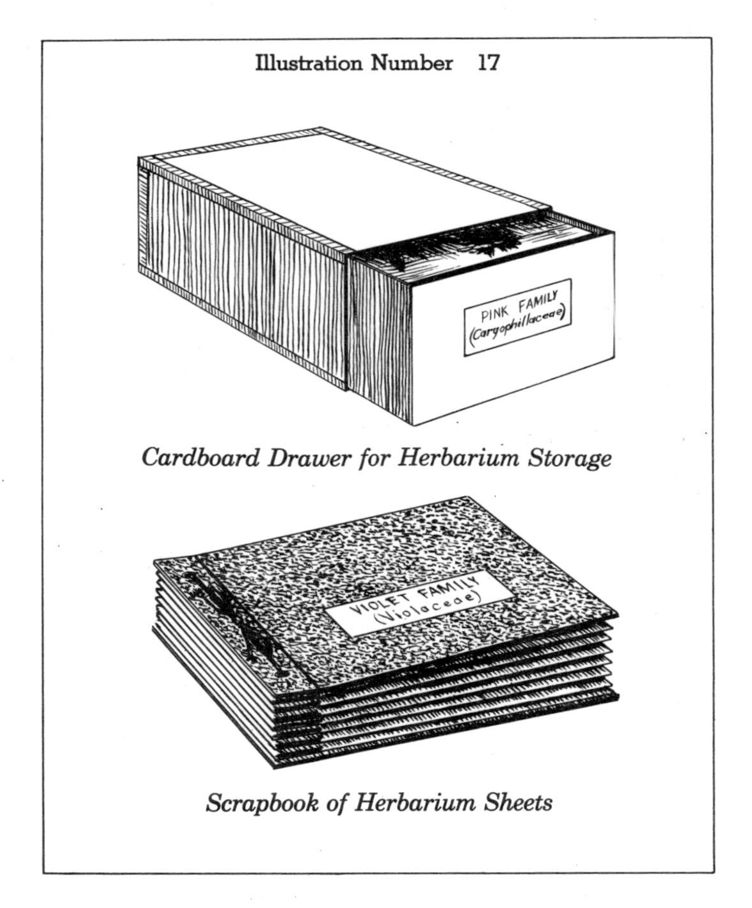

Cardboard Drawer for Herbarium Storage

Scrapbook of Herbarium Sheets

prepared and pressed later on at home. Any long and round or oval tin can will serve the purpose, although the so-called vasculum which can be bought at scientific supply houses, is probably the most practical container; it has a wide opening on the side and is provided with a strap for carrying it over the shoulder (see illustration No. 14). If the specimens are sprinkled with water or the vasculum contains a piece of wet moss, the collected plants will remain fresh for many hours. Once this was the only method ever followed, and the vasculum became the—sometimes humorous—trademark of the 19th century botanist.

The other method provides for the pressing of the plants in the field and is followed by most professionals. It requires the carrying of bulkier equipment but preserves best the color of the flowers and the leaves, and as there is little spoilage, it is also less expensive in the long run. The press to be used in the field (see illustration No. 14) consists of the following materials:

1) A pile of old newspapers; tabloid-size papers (11 x 16 inches) are just right while regular-size papers should be folded in half.

2) About 20 pieces of cardboard cut from old grocery boxes to the same size; the cardboard should be corrugated because it will act not only as a support but also as a ventilator. To fulfill better the latter purpose the rills or flues should run not lengthwise but parallel to the 11 inch side, and only strong corrugated cardboard should be used which will not collapse under the influence of pressure or

Illustration Number 18

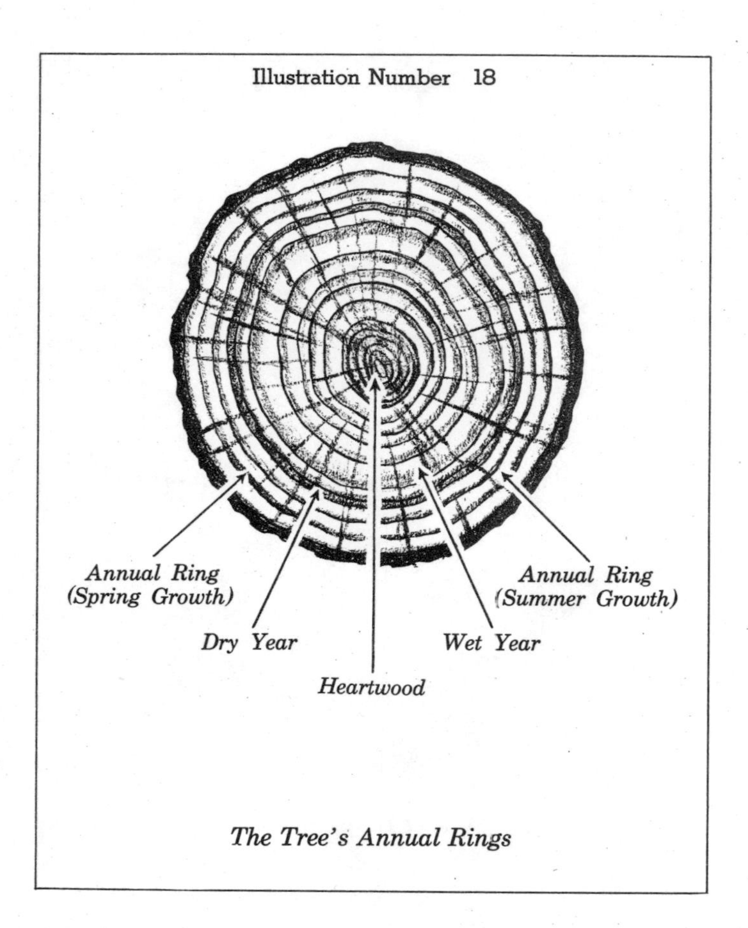

The Tree's Annual Rings

moisture. Some prefer ventilators of loose woven wickerwork.

3) Two simple wooden outside frames 12 x 17 inches; slightly flexible lattice work is best. While slats of tough wood (ash, for instance) are ideal, any type of wood will answer the purpose.

4) A stout cord, or more neatly, two straps with buckles. Slits should be provided on the wooden frame near the top and the bottom of either end.

These materials are combined in the following sequence:

The wooden frame at the bottom;
two cardboards;
four layers of newspaper;
the first plant specimen to be pressed;
four layers of newspapers;
the second plant to be pressed—and so on.

Between the fifth and sixth plants insert again two cardboards; continue in the same fashion until the day's collection is completed; place two cardboards and the other wooden frame on top; tie cord or straps around press.

The plants, always carefully selected, perfect, typical specimens, should be placed between the newspapers in such a way that they show the botanical essentials and offer an attractive display (see illustrations No. 15 and 16). Large plants may have to be folded in a V or N shape, or the middle part of the stalk may be cut out and only the top and bottom may be pressed. The collection number, the same as in the notebook, should be written on the newspaper on which the plant rests.

For aquatic plants some blotters should be ready; as soon as the plant is removed from the water, it should be blotted gently and placed in the press right away. For certain aquatic plants some botanists recommend the same method which is applied to algae, i.e. the specimens are floated in a pan of water, and the specimen-paper is slipped under it and raised out of the water with the plant on top of it.

The next step is the definite pressing and drying of the collected specimens. For that purpose the press and the process described above may be used again, but with new newspapers as layers below and above the plants. Heavy sheets of blotters of tabloid size are ideal for the purpose but quite a bit more expensive. From now on the one point to be watched constantly is that the contacting paper remains dry; at first it will have to be changed every two days, then every three days, and later every week, until the pressed plant is completely dry. The press should be placed in a warm and dry spot.

Care should be taken not to draw out the process of drying over too long a period; it may discolor or even blacken the specimens; mold may appear. On the other hand, rapid drying will help greatly to retain the original natural color. Experience will teach the collector the most favorable condition in which the specimen should be removed from the press. If a plant is taken out before it is completely dry, the leaves may curl and wrinkle and develop mildew. If the specimen is left in the press too long, it will become brittle and may break. For the right stage — dry and stiff but not brittle — the collector will soon acquire a special touch.

The dry specimens, all numbered, may be stored in boxes until they are mounted; then they are laid out either on herbarium sheets — the official size is 11½ x 16½ inches — or on the pages of a large loose-leaf scrapbook which can be expanded. The herbarium sheets are usually kept in folders, or drawers, by family or genus. The plants may be fastened to the paper by strips of gummed paper, gummed tape or cellophane; the latter is transparent and disturbs least the attractiveness of the display, but sometimes cracks and is not as permanent as paper or tape.

In the case of algae the procedure is somewhat different. They will have to be collected at low tide, preferably in shallow tidal pools where they can be gathered by hand, by pulling or scraping them from the rocks. They will be kept in a pail filled with salt water. For the next step the heavy mounting paper should be ready — not a temporary newspaper or blotting paper but the mounting paper itself — and a large pan filled with sea water. Let the algae specimen float on the surface in its normal, beautiful shape, push the mounting paper gently under the algae, raise it and drain the water. The specimen will be displayed most attractively. If necessary, an eye-dropper filled with water and thin wire may be used to straighten out some of the delicate branches. The drying process is the same as the one described before, but it is necessary to place a sheet of wax paper or light cloth over the specimen to avoid the algae's sticking to the upper sheet. Most algae are provided with a glue-like coating and will adhere to the mounting paper; only occasionally strips of paper or cellophane will be necessary.

I. M. Johnston, of the Arnold Arboretum of Harvard University, summarizes the operation of pressing and drying plants as follows: "The collecting and preparation of botanical specimens can be an art. Excellent specimens are not the product of laborious effort. They are the result of thought and care during simple operations, and they are the result of practice."

Labeling and Cataloguing — How much information on each specimen should be given on the label and how much in the catalog, under the same number, is for the individual collector to decide. Usually the information on the label is restricted to the data that are uniformly available for each specimen in the collection; and whenever there are additional descriptions and annotations, particularly of characteristics which the dried specimens will not show, they are reserved for the catalog. The latter may be a card index or a loose-leaf book. A typical label in the herbarium may contain these details:

Herbarium of Henry P. Smith
No. 961 Date: May 27, 1953
Lobelia Cardinalis
Cardinal Flower
From: Maine, Penobscot County, Mount Chase Township, Foot of Sawtelle Falls
Habitat: Along bank of brook, in large flower bed.
Soil: Sandy humus Altitude: 800 ft.
Color: Deep red Odor: None

The Artistic Touch — Pressed flowers have always been used for artistic and decorative purposes, mounted as pictures in the form of bouquets, wreaths and in similar designs. Today pressed flowers are more appropriate for decorative uses than ever because the modern methods of pressing, as described previously, preserve the color of the blossoms and of the leaves much better than methods formerly applied. One striking new use for pressed flowers or ferns is their mounting on plastic lamp shades. Between two layers of whitish, semi-transparent plastic material spectacular blossoms in clear colors are mounted, or a wreath of attractively shaped leaves running around the shade, or artistic designs of graceful grasses and ferns. Lampshades of this type are beautiful, and their pressed plants keep their color and form for many years.

A Wood Collection — TIMBER IN AMERICA: Trees and forests have always been close to the heart of America. When this continent was first settled, the whole East was one huge, continuous ocean of trees, and to this day no country in the temperate zone can match the U.S. in the variety, size, and beauty of her trees. Practically speaking, wood has played a most important role in the life and growth of America; no people has used wood so extensively in the building industry, and for 250 years European immigrants have been—and still are—surprised at our hundreds of thousands of wooden frame houses. The significance of wood and of trees in our national life is in fact increasing, and the importance of trees for the preservation of our natural resources, including the soil and the climate, is clearly recognized not only by the government but also by many leading lumber, pulp, and paper interests which own great tracts of our forests. Reforestation is practiced extensively, and the utilization of wood has undergone many refinements which stretch the available supply and make more efficient use of it, for instance in the form of plywood and laminated wood.

To the amateur-nature lover the comparative study of woods is fascinating. Great differences in weight, color, and texture are obvious, and a microscope or even magnifying glass will reveal the variations in structure. Each type serves best a special purpose; the color section on trees and the survey of orders and families of trees in the Nature Atlas of America describe this aspect: The wood of swamp trees like cypresses is excellent for outdoor use, as it is little affected by wind and weather; certain light woods are ideal for crating; pine, durable and easily worked, is a prime building material; among the pulp woods some produce fine magazine and book papers, others cheap newsprint; and among the hardwoods many types are reserved for highly specialized tasks and parts, from baseball bats to piano keys, from venetian blinds to clothespins, from ax handles to weaver's shuttles.

Illustration Number 19

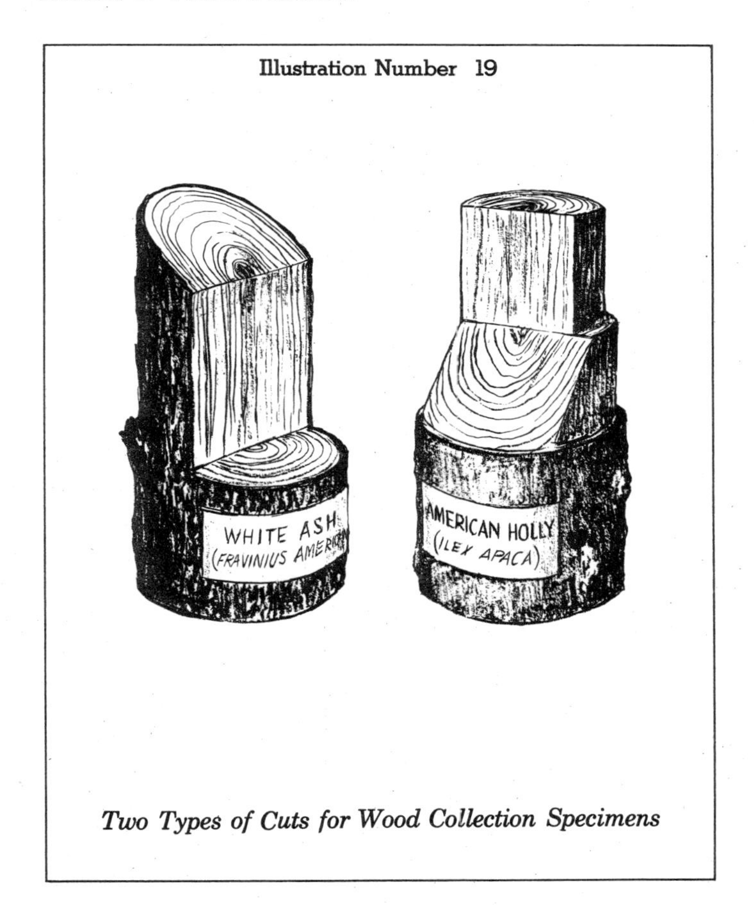

Two Types of Cuts for Wood Collection Specimens

Tree Trunks and History: A freshly cut tree trunk tells its age in its annual rings, but it often reveals also a good deal of local history, like a fire during a certain year. A nail or a screw deeply embedded in the wood and grown over by later rings may indicate that some 20 years ago some object was nailed to the young tree (perhaps a fence), but ripped off again 5 years later. Evidence of this sort is sometimes important in court cases.

The great trees of the West embrace in their tree rings a fantastic panorama of history; on the stump of a giant sequoia the tree rings of the years in which Christ was born and America discovered may be pointed out. As narrow rings indicate dry and broad rings moist years, we know from trees whose age is certain, when major droughts occurred, and by comparing the pattern thus established with the ring patterns of ancient pieces of wood found in Indian ruins, a good deal of prehistoric chronology has been reconstructed. Certain Indian cliff dwellings in the Southwest, for instance, had been deserted at an early time; the inhabitants seemed to have left voluntarily, without any evidence of struggle or violence, and their motives for doing so were quite puzzling to the archeologists. Now we know, thanks to the tree rings, the major cause of the exodus: a severe drought reigned throughout the last quarter of the 13th century in what are now our Southwestern States.

A Wood Display: In establishing a wood collection, branches of old trees or stems of young trees should be cut neatly with a saw, specimens that are 3 to 4 inches in diameter, and a second cut should turn them into straight pieces of approximately seven inches in length. When dry, the specimens should be cut in such a fashion that they show the bark on the lower part, and the rings, the grain and the rays on the upper part. Two ways of cutting are suggested in illustration No. 19, but the wood collector may figure out any system he may prefer for showing the horizontal, vertical, diagonal and possibly tangential surfaces. The exposed parts of the wood may be sandpapered, polished and varnished with colorless varnish, and the result is very neat and pleasing. For the purpose of comparison the surfaces of one half of the specimen may be left in their natural state, the other half may be finished.

Here again various viewpoints are possible under which a wood collection may be set up. A person interested in cabinet making, in furniture manufacture and interior decorating may gather wood specimens illustrating that phase of usage; a paper company may display in its showroom a collection of all the types of wood that are converted into pulp and ultimately into paper; such a collection may be extended, historically, to other plants that at one time or another have furnished the raw material for paper, going back to the papyrus of Egypt. Or the viewpoint might be botanical and refer to all woods of the pine or oak families.

On the labels of a wood collection it will be quite proper to indicate, besides the scientific name and the botanical English name, the term applied to the wood by the lumber-

Illustration Number 21

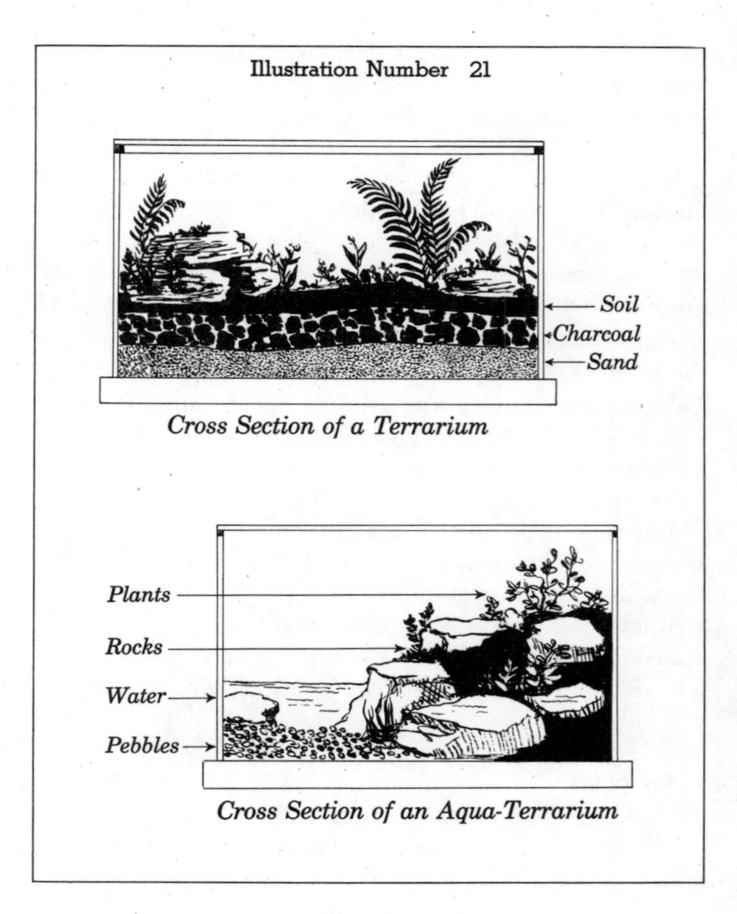

Cross Section of a Terrarium

Cross Section of an Aqua-Terrarium

Illustration Number 20

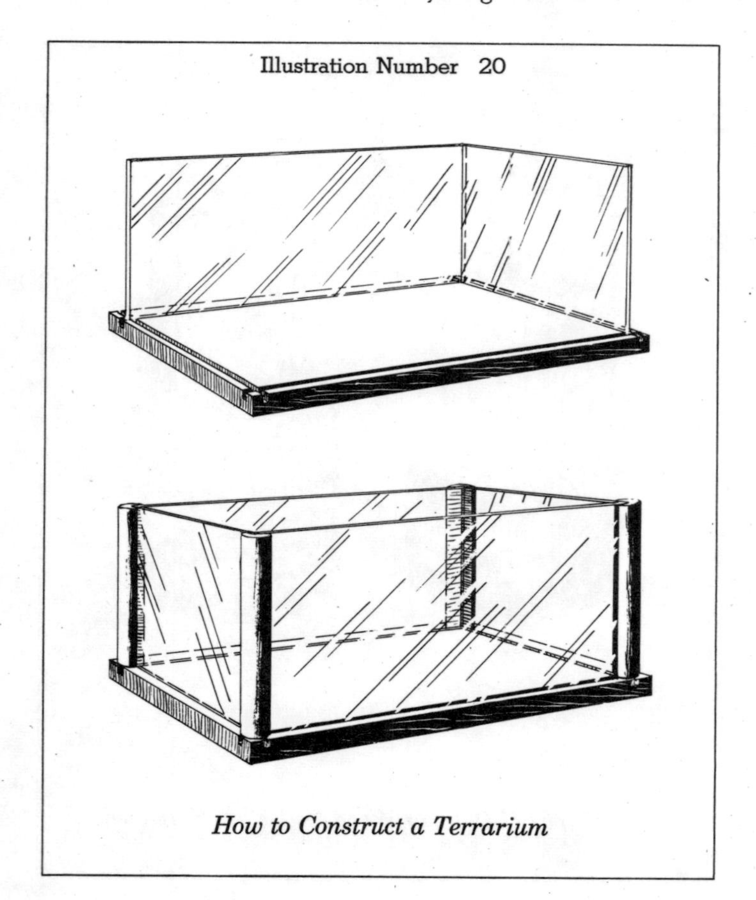

How to Construct a Terrarium

men; for the lumbermen's name is sometimes a different one, as mentioned on various occasions in the section on trees of the Nature Atlas of America. The lumbermen are sometimes extremely specific, using different names for the various cuts of the same tree (as in the case of certain hickories), or they are extremely general, including under a single name any number of species, some of them inferior to the wood which furnishes the label for the whole group.

THE TERRARIUM HOBBY

Why a Terrarium is Interesting — There are vastly more terrarium fanciers in Europe than in America. Yet, when looking at their often beautiful exhibits, in England or in continental Europe, one is surprised to discover how many of their striking and interesting salamanders, lizards, turtles, and other amphibians and reptiles are Americans by origin. Considering the fact that we have at our disposal, in our own nature environment, a great number of potential inhabitants for a terrarium, and that most of us know very little about the fascinating living habits of these animals, the terrarium hobby offers broad new horizons for observation and knowledge.

Constructing a Terrarium — To construct, at home, a terrarium is a much simpler task than building an aquarium, because the former does not have to be waterproof. The size will depend on individual circumstances, the room available and the number and type of animals to be kept, but it should not be smaller than 10x20 inches at the foundation, with a height of 10 or 12 inches. The needed materials are a wooden base, four window glass panes, four pieces of ¾ round molding, and some standard household cement. The self-explanatory illustration No. 20 shows how these materials are joined. The terrarium should be covered with wire netting or, more neatly, a pane of glass. The latter should be raised slightly with rubber or cork pads at the four corners, to permit the free entrance of air.

If an especially sturdy construction is desired, or if a so-called "aqua-terrarium" is contemplated, for amphibians or reptiles which live both on land and in water, the instructions in the following chapter, on the aquarium hobby, should be followed.

Managing a Terrarium — The Moist-Temperate Terrarium — As the first step it will be necessary to decide what natural environment the terrarium is to recreate. The moist-temperate type is most easily organized, for obvious reasons. On a bottom layer of sand, a layer of charcoal or pebbles will provide the necessary drainage; on top of that, the soil for the plants is spread (see illustration No. 21). Some rocky ornamentation is always attractive, and stones can be cemented together to form ledges and caves, natural bridges and cliffs; the porous varieties of rock or even clinkers have the advantage that small plants find enough cracks and openings there to grow their roots in the crevices and spread decoratively over the rock structure. Such ornaments also act as moisture holders.

Illustration Number 22

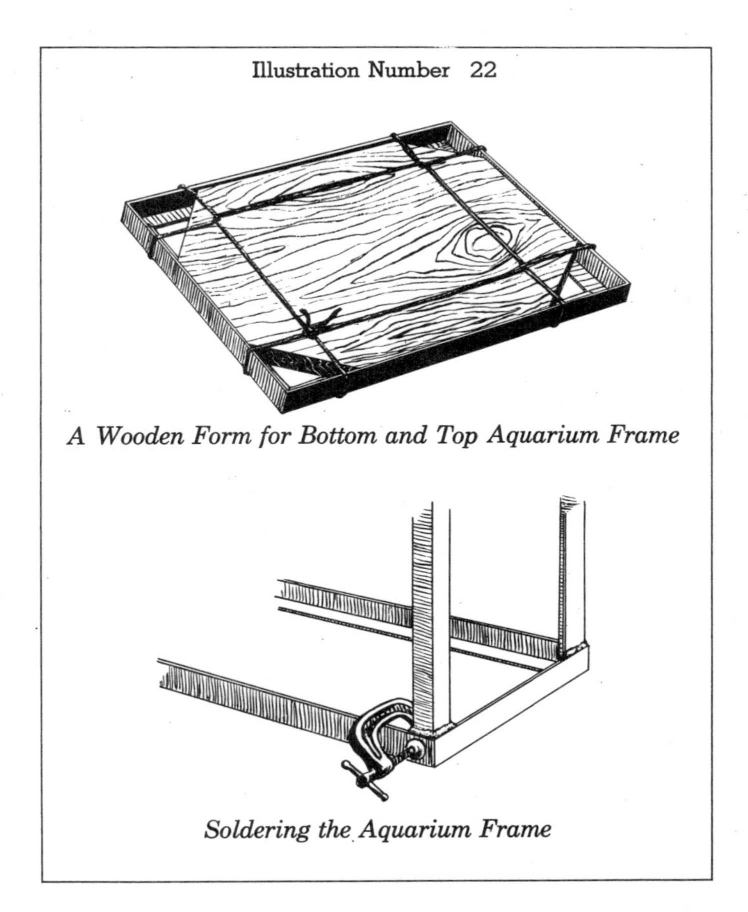

A Wooden Form for Bottom and Top Aquarium Frame

Soldering the Aquarium Frame

Embedded in the soil there should be a pool of water, perhaps an earthenware bowl, to provide not only drinking water but also a moist resting place.

As the next step the plants should be inserted; for that purpose the lower stratum of the soil may be fertilized, but only slightly. As to the plants that may be used to advantage, the choice is almost unlimited for a terrarium of moist-temperate climate; the owner may use his own judgment. As the atmospheric conditions of a sparsely ventilated terrarium resemble those of a greenhouse, the same type of plants that thrive in the latter environment may be utilized. It is, of course, also possible to employ separate pots for plants or groups of plants, an arrangement which makes any desired changes in the interior of the terrarium easy. In grouping the plants, the habits and preferences of the future occupants should be considered; the snakes, for instance, like a dry spot to take their sun baths, while salamanders look for a dark, shady, moist place to hide under leaves or rocks. Suitable inhabitants for such a terrarium are frogs and turtles, newts and salamanders, and certain kinds of small snakes, like garter and green snakes.

The Dry-Temperate Terrarium — The arrangement of the soil and of the rocks is similar in this case, but only a small dish with drinking water needs to be provided. The experts advise to fasten a mirror on the bottom of the bowl, or to make a pool by providing a small round mirror with an edge of concrete; otherwise some of the shy inhabitants of the terrarium will not recognize the water. Here the range

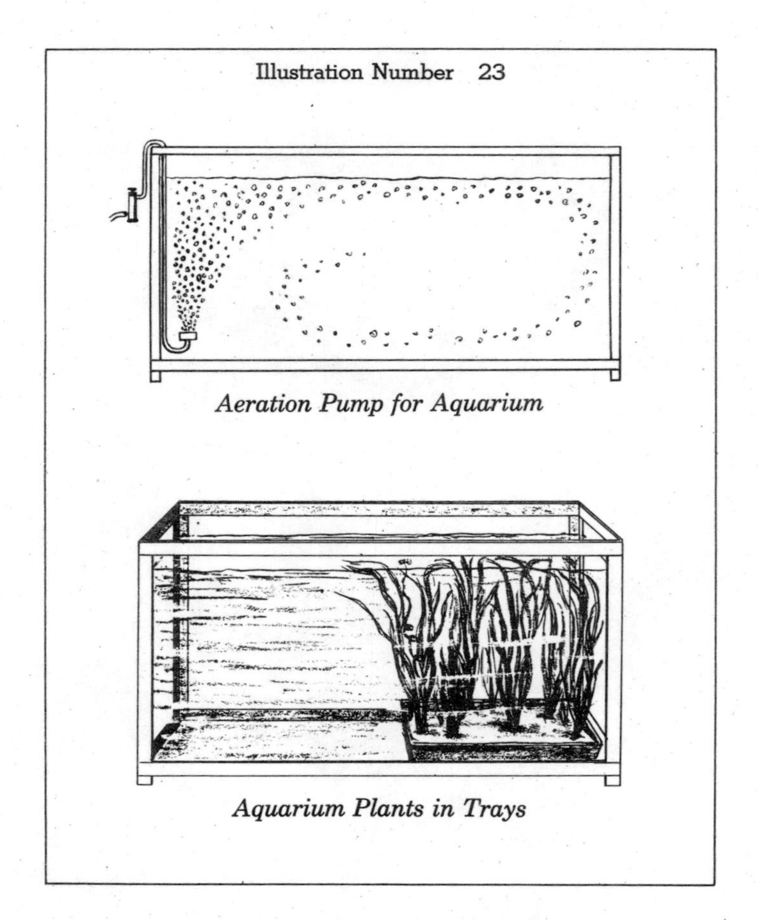
Illustration Number 23

Aeration Pump for Aquarium

Aquarium Plants in Trays

of plantings is limited, but the various cactus plants — some weird, some handsome — the aloes and agaves, the yuccas, and dry-soil ferns can make a most attractive setting.

Among the occupants of a dry-temperate terrarium the chameleon is a most amusing pet, changing colors according to its moods and emotions, watching the world warily with its independently moving eyes, and stalking its insect prey like a wildcat. It may also be kept in a moist-temperate terrarium. Other prospective occupants are lizards and tortoises, tree toads and horned toads, snakes and beetles, butterflies and moths. For the tree frog a small wooden ladder should be provided. Supposedly, it forecasts the weather by either staying on the ground (rain) or on top of the ladder (sunshine); there may be a grain of truth in this old folk belief as the frog, no doubt, acts under the influence of atmospheric pressure.

Other Types — In the U.S. and Canada the moist-tropical and dry-tropical kinds of terrarium have to be heated artificially by coils arranged under the bottom. Both are better suited for scientific observation and research than for the purpose of a hobby.

The aqua-terrarium may consist of one dry half and one half of water, or of a full surface of water with one or two islands covered with bog plants (see illustration No. 21). It is particularly appropriate for the observation of those insects which start their lives in the water and develop through several aquatic stages to become terrestrial insects. It is also an ideal environment for most amphibians.

Catching and Feeding Amphibians and Reptiles — How to Secure Them — Some of the previously mentioned animals may be secured in our own nature environment. Frogs and toads may be caught with a heavy insect net, or in case of the aquatic species with a kitchen sieve on a pole. A handy tool for catching snakes is a stick with a three or four inch angle iron screwed to the lower end to form an L with a very long upright and very short horizontal line. Such a snake stick is useful for turning up boulders and poking under logs; when a snake is located, the angle iron will pin it to the ground. The small, harmless snakes that are suitable for a terrarium, may then be secured by hand.

Salamanders are more numerous than is generally supposed; they are rarely seen because they avoid bright daylight, but if you know where to look for them, under rocks, leaves, and fallen trunks in moist locations near brooks, you can catch them quite easily. Don't hesitate to use your hands; the animals won't bite. They have to be kept moist.

Lizards are caught by various nets, traps and snares; avoid holding them by the tail; it might separate from the body in a quick and bloodless operation, and you will hold the tail while the rest of the lizard escapes. Lizards are lightning-quick in the warm sun but sluggish and more manageable on a cool morning.

Land turtles are easily captured by hand. For the aquatic species a net with a long pole is an indispensable tool.

Feeding the "Boarders" — The following table gives a short survey of the meals that might be served to the inhabitants of a terrarium:

Small Amphibians and Reptiles	*Menus*
Snakes and lizards	Insects and worms; small live animals and fish; toads.
Carnivorous turtles, newts, salamanders, also baby alligators	Small pieces of meat, fish, and oyster; worms; scrambled eggs.
Box turtles	Earthworms and slugs, table scraps.
Chameleons, frogs, and toads	Flies; meal worms, meal bugs.

The owner of a terrarium will do well to operate a fly trap during the summer. To empty the catch of the trap into the terrarium and to watch the ensuing chase, is a most amusing spectacle. During the winter, when no flies are available in the northern parts of the continent, meal worms and meal bugs may take their place; they are easily raised in bran or other flour.

Books on the Terrarium Hobby — Apparently no books have been published specifically on this subject. But there is an informative chapter on the terrarium in W. T. Innes' "The Complete Aquarium Book," Halcyon House, New York, 1936. A terrarium for plants is described in Ted Pettit's "The Book of Nature Hobbies," Didier, New York, 1947. Many books are available which describe and identify the animals suitable for a terrarium.

The Aquarium Hobby

The books of the following list are recommended both for the beginner and for the advanced student:

Bishop, S. C., Handbook of Salamanders, Comstock Publishing Co., Ithaca, N. Y., 1943

Wright, A. A. and A. H., Handbook of Frogs and Toads, Comstock Publishing Co., Ithaca, N. Y., 1942

Ditmars, R. L., The Reptiles of North America, Doubleday & Co., New York, 1942

Smith, H. M., Handbook of Lizards, Comstock Publishing Co., Ithaca, N. Y., 1946

Ditmars, R. L., A Field Book of North American Snakes, Doubleday & Co., New York, 1939

Curran, C. H. and Kauffeld, C., Snakes and Their Ways, Harper & Brothers, New York, 1937

Pope, C. H., Turtles of the U.S. and Canada, Alfred A. Knopf, New York, 1939

Jordan, E. L., Hammond's Nature Atlas of America, the Section on Amphibians and Reptiles, C. S. Hammond & Co., New York, 1952

THE AQUARIUM HOBBY

Why an Aquarium Is Interesting — Keeping an aquarium is one of America's fastest growing hobbies. The reasons are not hard to discern. Fishes are animals of beauty and grace, and since the introduction and ascent to popularity of the so-called exotics, a touch of far-away tropical waters and unknown foreign seas has been brought to our homes. It is also fascinating to observe the life cycle of fishes, — their feeding and fighting, mating and breeding. To the uninitiated, fishes seem far removed from the sphere of the human mind; to them they are either game for sportsmen or food. Only aquarium fanciers learn to know them and discover that each of them has what in human terms might be called a personality.

How to Construct an Aquarium — SIZE — While aquaria of various types and sizes may be bought from the supply houses, many fanciers prefer to construct their own aquarium at home. However, only those should undertake such a task who have some experience in metal work.

The size will depend on the owner's requirements, but the following points should be kept in mind:

The water surface should be as large as possible, in proportion to the volume of water, to insure an ample supply of oxygen. Consequently low side walls are ideal, but they should be high enough to accommodate the water plants.

An aquarium that is too wide, loses much of its transparency; in such a case it is difficult to get a side view of the fishes, especially if the water is slightly cloudy. Therefore, a moderate width is advocated. There are no restrictions on the length, aside from unwieldiness. On the whole, a relatively large aquarium is advocated; its maintainance requires hardly more time and effort than a small one.

MATERIALS — While there are many ways of building a good aquarium, in accordance with each owner's experiences and preferences, the advice of the experts is summarized in the following instructions. Particularly the ideas of William T. Innes, one of America's leading authorities in the field, are emphasized here.

The materials needed will be 1) angle brass (90° molding) for the frame, i.e. for the bottom, the top, and the four uprights; the builder should use his own judgment as to the suitable dimensions of the molding; also angle iron or angle aluminum may be used, but they are more difficult to handle; 2) four panes of window glass (double thickness) or plate glass, as side walls, and a piece of thick plate glass as a base; the latter can be secured cheaply from an automobile junk dealer, from a discarded windshield; 3) aquarium cement; the cement base sold under the trade name of Gilsonite, or a similar type, is recommended.

STEPS OF CONSTRUCTION — 1) Cut the angle brass to the needed lengths for the four uprights, and for the bottom frame and the top frame; 2) cut the ends of the pieces for the bottom frame at 45 degree angles so that they will fit together at 90 degree angles; solder them together slightly; 3) make a form of an old wooden box top, cut to the exact size of the aquarium bottom but with the corners sawed off (see illustration No. 22) to leave space for working on the edges of the frame; 4) fit the brass frame around the wooden form and secure it with a cord; 5) solder the four corners permanently; 6) solder an angle flange on each corner, to strengthen the frame; 7) take out the wooden form; solder the four uprights to the frame (see illustration No. 22); 8) build the top frame exactly like the bottom

Illustration Number 24

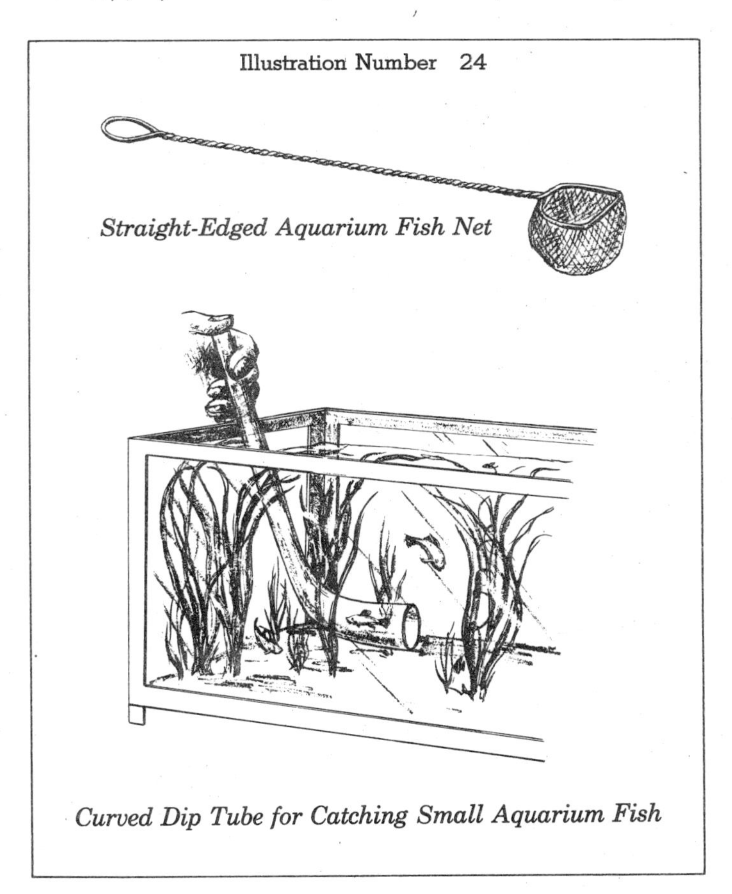

Straight-Edged Aquarium Fish Net

Curved Dip Tube for Catching Small Aquarium Fish

frame and solder it to the uprights; 9) clean the contact parts of glass with alcohol or ammonia; apply a thin layer of aquarium cement to the glass, and a thick layer to the inside of the frame; 10) insert glass base first; it should be cut to cover the inside of the bottom frame completely, so that the glass walls will stand on top of it; 11) press glass walls against frame; force a few thin sticks of the proper length between opposite glass walls to hold them firmly against the frame until the cement is dry; 12) let the aquarium dry for about two weeks; then keep water in it for one week; then empty the water and fill the aquarium again. Now it is ready for the plants. Cover it with wire netting or with a glass pane; the latter should be raised a little by four cork or rubber pads on each corner, although the fishes won't suffocate if the pane lies right on the frame.

Principles of Aquarium Management — How Many Fishes Should be Kept? — The old rule of one gallon of water per fish really misses the point, although ordinarily it is quite workable. The well-being of the fish is influenced not only by the amount of water but primarily by the contact surface with the air which furnishes the needed oxygen. On the whole it might be said that at a temperature of 74°F the minimum requirement for a fish 3½ inches long is 20 square inches of surface, with larger or smaller specimens requiring correspondingly more or less. Twice the air surface is advocated for growing young fish.

The situation is improved by water plants which give off oxygen for the benefit of the fishes; they do so, however, only under the influence of sunlight. The function of oxygenation is even more important in aquarium plants than their decorative properties.

Illustration Number 25

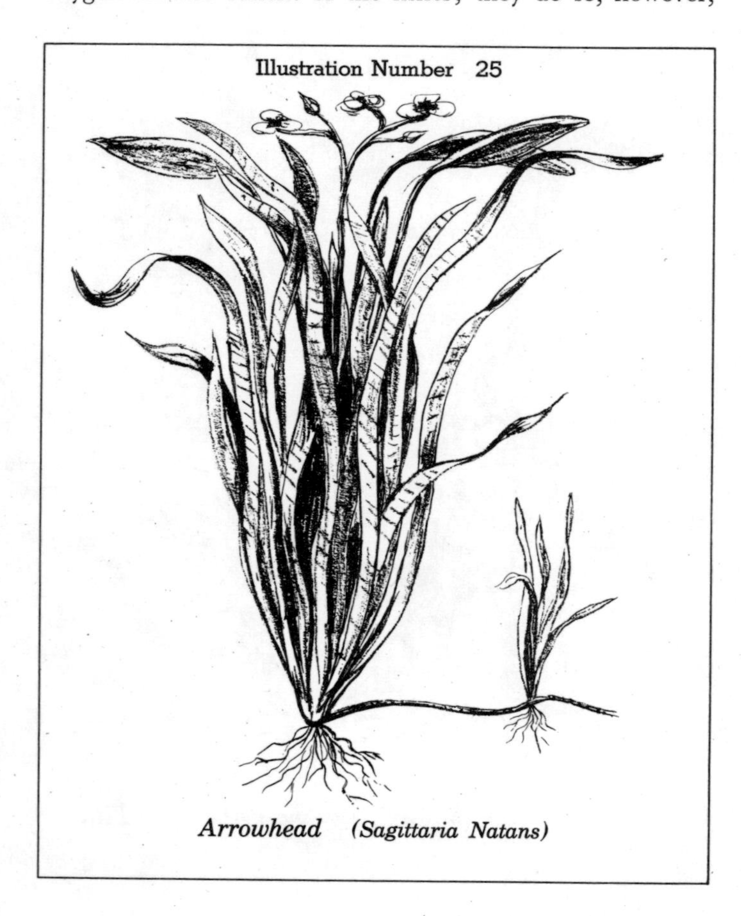

Arrowhead (Sagittaria Natans)

A modern attachment which helps to solve the oxygen problem is a small electric aeration pump which, from an opening at the bottom of the tank, lets small air bubbles rise through the water and causes a slow and healthy circulation (see illustration No. 23). Such pumps are quite regularly in use in large aquaria, but less frequently in the smaller types. They are recommended for all saltwater aquaria.

What Kind of Water Should Be Used? — Some writers recommend pond or rain water which recreates natural conditions. It is, however, not necessary to use either; in most places tap water will be satisfactory. Mild chlorination can be removed by aeration; wherever the chlorine content is strong, boiling will eliminate the chlorine. Such boiled water may be used, but it must be aerated; in simple terms, it must be poured into the aquarium through a sprinkling can, from a certain height. Such aeration is recommended for every type of aquarium water, no matter what its source.

Many beginners feel that the water should be changed often. That, however, is not the case, at least not as far as the total contents of the water is concerned. A gradual renewal of the water is now recommended by several leading authorities in the field, approximately 10 per cent of the volume weekly during the winter and more during the summer. The water should stand for a while and be brought to the right temperature before it is poured in. If, for some reason, as much as 50 per cent of the water has to be changed, it should "ripen" for about two days. Sudden temperature changes are harmful.

The correct temperature of the water depends on the type of fishes that inhabit it. In a general way it might be said that for native species a temperature somewhat below 70°F is appropriate, and for exotic species a slightly greater warmth. Saltwater aquaria are, as a rule, cooler than the freshwater types.

Indirect light, with perhaps two hours of direct sunshine, is best-suited for the home aquarium. If the water becomes green, the aquarium has probably too much light. When the amount of light is reduced, the green color will, in most cases, disappear.

In a newly built aquarium the water is often cloudy, either because the sand used on the bottom was not well cleaned or because the newly set plants are not yet functioning properly. Therefore it is recommended to let a new aquarium stand for a week, after setting the plants; then the fishes may be introduced gradually.

Aquarium Equipment — The following utensils will be useful in managing an aquarium:

Nets — A larger and a smaller fish net with a long wire handle (see illustration No. 24) will be needed whenever certain specimens have to be caught.

Dip Tube, Straight — This is a glass tube with a diameter

of approximately ¼ of an inch, and somewhat longer than the height of the aquarium. It is used for cleaning purposes, especially for removing particles of surplus food from the bottom or from plants. Press your thumb on the top opening of the tube, insert the tube into the water over the particle, lift your thumb until the tube has sucked up some water with the particle, close the tube opening with your thumb, and lift the dip tube out of the water.

Dip Tube, Curved — This tube is curved like a pipe, and much wider at the lower end. It is employed in catching small fish, as shown on illustration No. 24. The operation is the same as described above.

Siphon — This is a rubber or plastic hose used to remove water from the aquarium; it should be approximately twice as long as the aquarium is deep. Fill the hose with water and close both ends with your fingers. Hold one end in the water of the aquarium, and the other outside, as low as it will go. Remove your fingers from the openings simultaneously, and the water will begin to flow out.

Planting Stick — One or two long sticks with a notch in one end are helpful in setting and arranging the plants.

Cleaner for Inside Glass — A razor blade in a holder with a handle (the kind which can be purchased at any hardware store) is the best tool for cleaning the inside of the glass walls, especially for scraping off unwanted algae.

Aquarium Plants — Ornamentation and Oxygenation — The purpose of plants in an aquarium is twofold, as has been mentioned before: Ornamental beauty and oxygenation, although the latter plays a negligible part in the case of saltwater plants.

The Method of Planting — The most usual procedure is this: Spread half an inch of thoroughly washed sand on the bottom. Do not use earth as it clouds the water. If you care to have a rock ornamentation (see also the chapter on the terrarium hobby), set it in its proper place. After filling in water to a level of about 4 or 5 inches, insert the plants, spreading the roots on the bottom. Add another layer of sand, this time of the coarse type, one to two inches thick. Fill the aquarium, and straighten out the leaves and stems. Some experts recommend covering the sand and the plants with a piece of paper while filling, to keep the water clear. As was suggested previously, a sprinkling can should be employed.

In a freshwater aquarium the plants may be set in pots or trays (see illustration No. 23) so that they can be easily removed or rearranged. Each pot or tray should be filled with a layer of pebbles, a layer of (preferably alluvial) soil, and a thin layer of sand. The latter has the purpose of keeping the soil in the pot and preventing it from clouding the water.

Freshwater Aquarium Plants — The five favorites which are easily obtained and generally used are described in the following:

Arrowhead — Sagittaria. This plant is so-called because of its arrow-shaped aerial leaves, reminiscent of Sagittarius, the archer in the zodiac. Other leaves are lance-

Illustration Number 26

Eelgrass (Valisneria Spiralis)

shaped. The white blossoms with yellow centers rise above the surface like lovely small cups. The species Sagittaria natans (see illustration No. 25) has been a popular standby of aquarium fanciers for generations. It is adaptable to varying conditions, grows slowly but continually, and is supposed to be an especially good provider of oxygen. Sagittaria gigantea attains a height of 15 to 18 inches; it is a big, sturdy plant with firm roots. In contrast, Sagittaria subulata is a small species which grows to a height of from 3 to 7 inches. Its narrow leaves are quite dark green.

Eel Grass — Valisneria spiralis. This graceful plant, shown in illustration No. 26, is especially suited for larger aquaria as it reaches a height of 18 and more inches. Its ribbon-like leaves are translucent and light green, its small white blossoms float on thin, spiral stems. It reproduces largely from runners. The common wild eelgrass is not as satisfactory as the cultivated variety.

Water Milfoil — Myriophyllum verticillatum. Besides its delicate, graceful appearance, this plant has two advantages: Its fine leaves are excellent spawn holders, catching the spawn of those fishes which drop their eggs, and they are a popular construction material for those species that use vegetable fibers in building their nests. The plant is pictured in illustration No. 27.

Fanwort — Cabomba caroliniana (see illustration No. 27). Although there is the same touch of oriental beauty on this plant that distinguishes the fancy breeds of goldfishes, both may not be kept in the same aquarium. For the

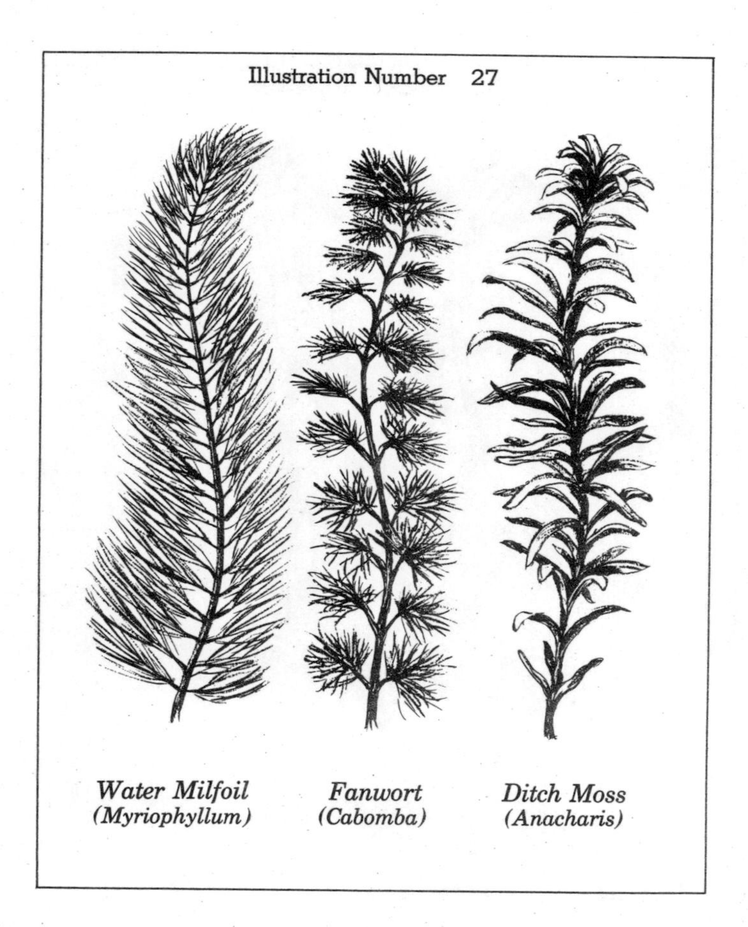

Water Milfoil *(Myriophyllum)* *Fanwort* *(Cabomba)* *Ditch Moss* *(Anacharis)*

goldfishes eat it. However, it is a popular plant for aquaria with other species of fish.

Ditch Moss — Anacharis. A cultivated variety derived from the wild Elodea canadensis is sold widely, although many experts recommend it rather for outdoor fish pools. It grows very rapidly, and in a home aquarium tends to lose vigor and take on an unhealthy, pale, and stringy appearance. It is shown in illustration No. 27.

Other well-known freshwater aquarium plants are the water hyacinth, hornwort, willow moss, hair grass, sword plant, moneywort, ludwigia, water lettuce, water fern, duck weed, and water poppy.

Saltwater Aquarium Plants — The great majority of aquaria are of the freshwater type as saltwater aquaria are normally maintained only close to the coasts, at least for the sake of a hobby. However, ocean saltwater will be shipped anywhere in 10-gallon containers by the biological supply houses.

The range of suitable saltwater plants is very limited. One plant that thrives in marine aquaria and can be easily secured is the Ulva, the so-called sea lettuce. You may also experiment with other algae which may be obtained from tide pools on our rocky coasts. The splendid sea anemones—Actiniae—have the appearance of beautiful, dahlia-like flowers but they are animals of a low type. Usually they attach themselves to a rock, and they should be transferred to the saltwater aquarium and placed there in that form, i.e. together with the rock.

A natural and attractive ornament for a marine aquarium is a reef formation of coral. However, as coral in its natural habitat is filled with all manner of minute marine life, it has to be boiled and thoroughly cleaned before it is inserted in the aquarium. Otherwise the decomposition fouls the water.

Keeping Native Freshwater Fishes — The popularity of exotic species has somewhat obscured the fact that we have among our own native fishes many decorative and interesting varieties which are eminently suitable for an aquarium. The fun of searching for them in our own brooks and rivers, ponds and lakes, of watching them in their habitat and of catching them for further study in our aquarium, is a pleasure unknown to the fancier of exotic species.

While any of the various methods of fishing will secure the desired specimens, as long as they are not killed in the process, the approved procedure for collectors is the use of the hand net and the seine. The former should be of 18 or 20 inches in diameter, and should be employed in brooks and streams. Experienced fishermen warn that the upward scoop will not bring results; instead, push the net downward and pull it toward your feet, scraping the bottom. All this should be carried out in a quick movement.

The seine should be of the type employed for minnows, with poles on both ends and sinkers and floats attached. Two persons are needed to handle the seine; they ought to proceed slowly, preferably toward a little cove or bay on the shore, and see to it that the lower side of the seine is in front of the upper side.

As quality counts and not quantity, only those few specimens should be carried home in a pail or can that are actually suitable and desirable for the aquarium. If the container is crowded, the health of the fishes will be harmed and their life span shortened. Always wet your hands when handling live fish.

The following species are recommended by such authorities as William T. Innes, and others, for their decorative appearance and pleasant ways:

The rainbow darter, also called soldier fish—Poecilichthys coerueleus. Color pattern: vertical bars with red, orange, blue, and green. It swims in a quaint, jerky fashion. Cool water is its element.

The killifish, also called bullhead minnow — Fundulus heteroclitus. Color pattern: dark vertical bars on sides, iridescent. Very hardy.

The silverfin — Notropis analostanus. Color pattern: pale blue, scales on sides black-edged; ends of fins silky-whitish during summer. A beautiful and playful aquarium fish; two of them will often play a graceful game of tag.

The mud trout — Umbra pygmaea. Color pattern: brown with dark lateral lines and a few dots. An alert, curious and friendly fish that will leap out of the water for a bit of raw meat or a piece of a worm on a toothpick.

The roach, also called shiner — Abramis crysoleucas. Color pattern: bright silver. Good-natured and hardy.

The redfin — Notropis cornutus. Color pattern: the pectoral fin and the upper parts of the other fins are bright red, during the breeding season. Unfortunately this blazing beauty fades at the beginning of winter.

The chaetodon, also called black-banded sunfish — Mesogonistius chaetodon. Color pattern: silvery with vertical black bands. The fins are almost transparent, which creates the impression of a body propelled by some invisible power. A hardy, well-mannered fish. Other sunfishes suitable for the aquarium are the blue-spotted, the orange-spotted, and the blue-gill. One trait of the latter three that may be disturbing in a home aquarium, is their pugnacity.

The red-bellied dace — Chrosomus erythrogaster. Color pattern: A pale golden band on each side, framed by two black lines; during the breeding season the mouth, the belly and the lower part of the dorsal fin are flaming red. Beautiful, agile, friendly and hardy.

The black-nosed dace — Rhinichthys atronasus. Color pattern: White belly, with a black band along the center of the sides. This 2-to-3-inch-long fish is an extremely rapid swimmer.

The rosy-sided dace — Clinostomus vandoisulus. Color pattern: silvery greenish, with a dark, almost black line running along the sides of the body; below the line, the males have a color patch which is bright red during the summer and paler during the winter.

The mullet, also called chubsucker — Erimyzon sucetta. Color pattern: white belly, yellow sides, green back.

Other attractive aquarium fishes from native waters are the hardy carps, particularly the colored varieties; the stickleback which builds a charming little basket-like nest around the stems of water plants, using a silky thread produced by special glands; the green tench and the golden tench; and the sole or freshwater flounder.

In a freshwater aquarium snails are usually employed as scavengers; they help to keep the water clean by feeding on small dead fishes and other animal matter in a stage of decomposition; but only those snail varieties will serve the purpose which do not eat the plants. The snails have another useful function: If they insist on staying at the edge of the water, it has probably become fouled, and the owner is warned to investigate and correct the condition.

The following species are preferred: The Japanese snail, Viviparus malleatus, which brings into life completely developed young, tiny but able to take care of themselves; the very common pond snail; the coral snail, and others. Some exotic fishes and also several natives (like a few species of sunfishes) will eat the snails; obviously, the latter are not employable in all cases.

One or two freshwater mussels will keep the water in the aquarium from turning green.

Keeping Exotic Fishes — The term "tropicals" which prevailed for several decades, has now been replaced by the word "exotics." The latter term is more accurate as the beautiful foreign species which are so popular now, have been acclimatized both from tropical and temperate seas.

The splendid forerunner of this trend was the goldfish, the product of countless generations of patient breeders in China, Japan, and Korea, who gradually transformed lowly carps into red-golden beauties. However, the career of the goldfish is definitely in the eclipse; it is yielding to the greater variety and individuality of the exotic importations, with their magnificent color patterns and forms. Therefore, the goldfish is mentioned here only in passing.

The common goldfish is handsome and easily tamed; fortunately it is hardy and survives much abuse in the form of fancy goldfish bowls with an insufficient oxygen supply, overfeeding, and other harmful conditions. The shubunkin is a mottled goldfish with transparent scales.

The fancy breeding of goldfishes has branched out in two directions: In one group of strains the fins have been developed into fantails, fringetails, and majestically flowing veils of truly oriental splendor. The other trend is toward "telescopic" species, i.e. some varieties with far-protruding big eyes have been developed. Many nature-lovers fail to see the "weird beauty" that is claimed for these creatures of Chinese origin. The "celestial telescope" type, for instance, has the protruding eyeballs turned upward so that the pupils, on a horizontal plane, stare heavenward. To increase the absurd effect, the dorsal fin is missing, and the tail spreads out in a fan with four long points. The height of eccentricity is the goldfish called lionhead or buffalohead whose frontal extremity is well described by its name although some people rather liken it to a big raspberry. In all these cases patient breeders have transformed certain arbitrary quirks of nature which occasionally occur, into strains

Illustration Number 28

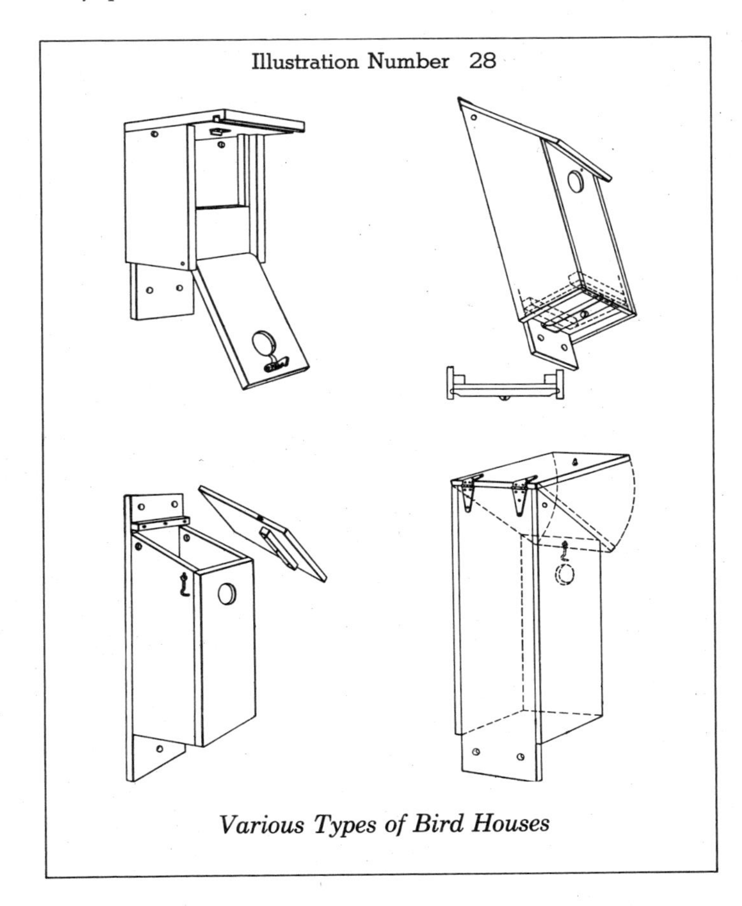

Various Types of Bird Houses

which reproduce their absurd characteristics not always but frequently.

The number of exotics whose popularity is growing rapidly is legion. Therefore only the most outstanding species are mentioned here. Most of them have been introduced in North America within the last 20 years.

The guppy — Lebistes reticulatus. There are millions of guppies in the world, glistening in all colors of the rainbow, and yet not two males are alike. The 2 or 3 big black dots that appear on their colorful coats, on the tail or the fins or the sides, make fascinating patterns of unending variety. Besides being handsome, the guppies are also playful and active, amusingly intense in feeding, courting and mating; they are great lovers, chasing a female even after fertilization; the latter bring forth tiny living young. They are easy to keep and survive in a wide range of temperatures (60° to 100°).

The angel fish — Pterophyllum eimekei. Like a swimming silver dollar with streamlined top and bottom fins, black vertical stripes, red eyes and drooping whiskers, the angel fish makes a most decorative inhabitant of an aquarium. However, this 5 to 6 inch long South American is no gentle beauty. It will bully the smaller fishes and occasionally eat them.

The veiltail betta — Betta splendens. Magnificent, spectacular, extraordinary — these are the adjectives showered upon the famous fighting fish from Siam; its fins are gracefully flowing veils, its colors blazing. This 2½-inch long species is now bred in red and blue, lavender and green, although the ventral fins are bright red in almost every variety. Only one male may be kept in a general aquarium; two will come to grips readily, attacking each other with such quick viciousness that the human eye is hardly able to follow the combatants' movements. The fins will be torn to shreds, and occasionally blood may flow. In Siam, bets are won on the fish which is eager to continue while its adversary gives up the struggle. However, the bettas do not attack other species. Jack Long describes the amusing courting habits of his red betta: It begs for the female's favor by gracefully swimming around her in a sort of water ballet. But suddenly the sweetness comes to an end; the master in the male asserts himself: He beats her up. After that, both embrace happily.

Illustration Number 29

Rustic Bird Houses

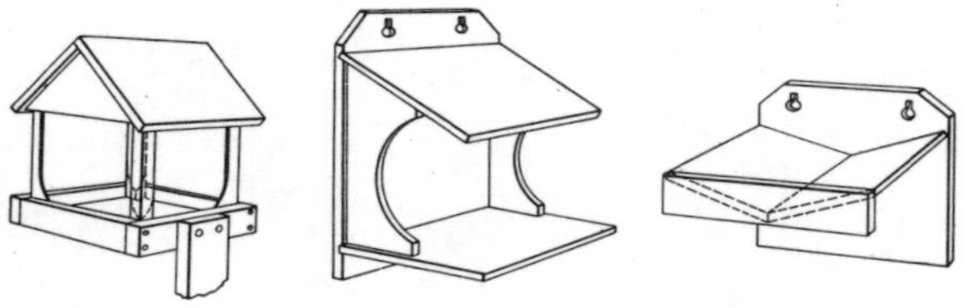

Nest Brackets and Shelves

The neon tetra — Hyphessobrycon innesi. This is a fascinating small fish (1¼ inches) from the upper Amazon. A blue-green band that extends along its body, has such brightness that it appears luminous, and a streak of scarlet flashes on its lower sides. As its fins are transparent, the body seems to be propelled by an unknown force. The species is difficult to breed in captivity.

The zebra fish — Brachydanio rerio. The effect of the horizontal iridescent blue stripes that cover the body and tail of this active small fish (1¾ inches) is heightened by the fact that it swims in schools. Lovely blue ribbons seem to float through the water.

The leopard coydoras — Coydoras julii. This popular Brazilian which grows to a length of 2½ inches has unusual markings — resembling those of a lizard rather than those of a leopard — and a black spot on the dorsal fin.

The silvery-reddish Copeina arnoldi (3 inches) has a perfectly fantastic procedure of mating and breeding; the male and the female interlock fins and together leap out of the water toward a pane of sanded glass leaning against the wall of the aquarium; they glue to the glass a jellied mass of about ten eggs, approximately 2 inches above the water line. This acrobatic act is repeated perhaps 10 times. From then on the male passes under the spot at frequent intervals and splashes it with his tail to keep the spawn wet; 72 hours later the eggs hatch and the young drop into the water.

Other interesting exotics desirable for an aquarium are the flame fish or tetra from Rio, the glow-light tetra, the tet from Buenos Aires, the head-and-tail-light fish, the red nose, the riddle-eye, the bloodfin, the rosy barb, the clown barb, the cherry barb, the black ruby, the white cloud, the bitterling, the Argentine pearl fish, the blue gularis, the lyretail, the flagfish, the Egyptian mouthbreeder, the big Jack Dempsey (7 inches), the almost transparent glassfish, and many others.

Keeping Saltwater Fishes — The special features of a marine aquarium have been mentioned before: It has few plants but a coral reef formation serving both as ornament and refuge. It needs artificial oxygenation by means of an aerating pump, and prefers subdued light. One important additional point should be mentioned here: Replace evaporated sea water with pure fresh water. The reason for this rule is simple: The salts do not evaporate and produce a higher concentration in the remaining water. The temperature should be in the low sixties for species of the temperate zone, and in the low seventies for tropical marine fishes. For an unexplained reason the inhabitants of a marine aquarium thrive more vigorously if the natural ocean water is somewhat diluted to a strength of about 1.020.

Those aquarists who wish to stock their saltwater aquarium with native marine life, will find the tide pools and coves, pockets and bays, breakwaters and piers of our rocky coasts in the East and West an ideal hunting ground. Your hands and your net are the most effective tools. Again quality is far more important than quantity, both in transporting your harvest home and in organizing your aquarium which, particularly in the case of the marine type, should be understocked rather than overstocked.

Among our natives, the prize exhibit in any saltwater aquarium is the sea horse, probably the most un-fishlike looking true fish in existence. Its upright position and its slow, deliberate locomotion are amusing, and its breeding procedure is extraordinary: In numerous face-to-face approaches and retreats the female transfers her eggs to the male in whose belly pouch they are hatched. The pouch splits open, the father rubs it lightly against a stone, and the young emerge.

Among the suitable exotic saltwater fishes such species as the small puffer fish, the colorful sergeant major, and the spade fish are suggested. One species that prospers in an aquarium is the black-and-white damsel fish, Dascyllus araunus (2 inches), whose color pattern of vertical broad black and white bands is of striking simplicity. However, not more than one male can be kept in a home aquarium, because of the vicious fighting habits of this visitor from the South Pacific. Finally the 2-inch-long clownfish, Amphiprion percula, is recommended. It is quite rare because so far no one has succeeded in breeding it in captivity, but it is of perfectly startling appearance. Three broad, irregular vertical bands are brilliantly yellow, set off with black edges. The other 4 bands are a clear white. The fish looks like a 2-inch toy composed of 7 chunks of alternating color; but the chunks do not seem to fit together too well.

Fish Foods — General Hints — The food consumption of fishes, like that of all cold-blooded animals, varies considerably with the temperature. Therefore one daily feeding is recommended for aquaria with a water temperature of less than 70° F, and two or more feedings for higher temperatures.

Outstanding aquarists recommend that the amount of prepared food fed at one meal should be the quantity that is consumed in 5 minutes. After 5 to 10 minutes all surplus food should be removed because it will foul the water.

As dried foods swell when moistened, it is better to feed them slowly.

Prepared Foods for Freshwater Fishes — The various brands of prepared fish foods that can be purchased at pet shops consist of a ground and dried mixture of such

Illustration Number 30

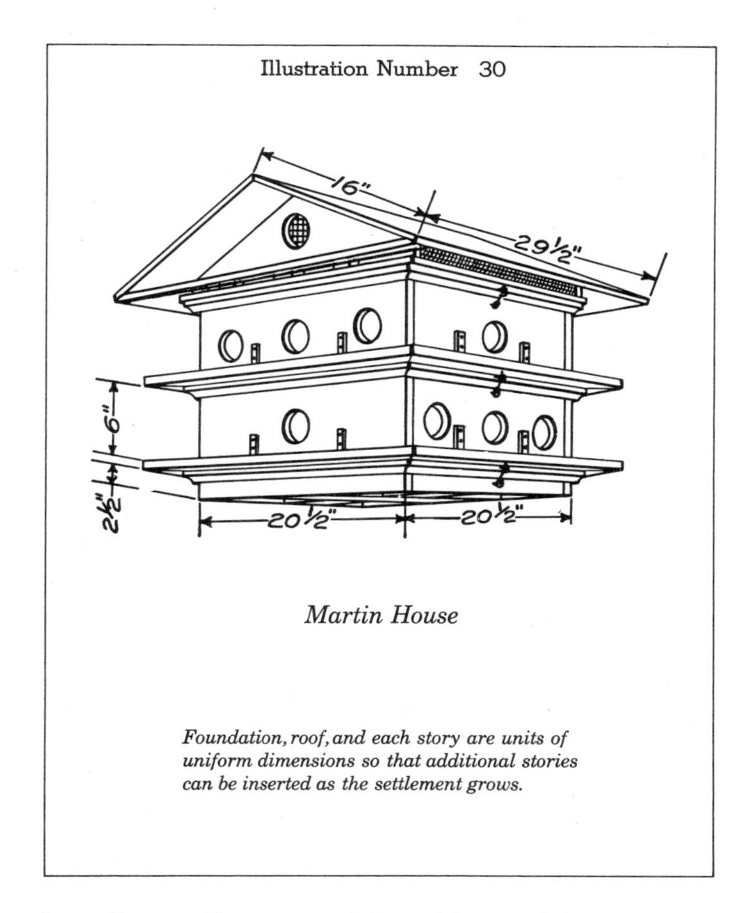

Martin House

Foundation, roof, and each story are units of uniform dimensions so that additional stories can be inserted as the settlement grows.

ingredients as flour, meat, fish, and insects. Many aquarists vary the brand occasionally as the fish seem to thrive on a change of diet.

Other popular foods are canned herring roe mixed half and half with corn meal; ground puppy biscuits, preferably with the addition of powdered shrimp; pablum or similar baby foods; canned dog food; scrambled eggs; chopped lettuce or chopped boiled spinach which apparently act as a substitute for certain soft algae not obtainable in the aquarium.

Live Foods for Freshwater Fishes — Live foods are not indispensable but desirable. Obviously earthworms, the ideal live bait, are also the choice live food for the aquarium; they are the kind of nourishment that puts the fishes into a breeding condition. The 1-to-3-inch worms are tender, the bigger ones quite tough. They may be cut into suitable pieces with a pair of scissors. Many aquarium owners collect a winter supply in the fall, keeping the worms alive in damp earth, with corn meal or mashed potatoes. White worms, the one-inch relatives of the earth worms, are also a popular fish food. Meal worms are an ever ready stand-by as they are easily raised on bran in a tin box; there they multiply, passing through a complete life cycle including the beetle stage.

Among the crustaceans the daphnia, popularly called ditch fleas, are an excellent supplement to prepared foods. They appear in grey, green, and red colors, the latter being preferred by most aquarists. Although they live in fresh-

Illustration Number 31

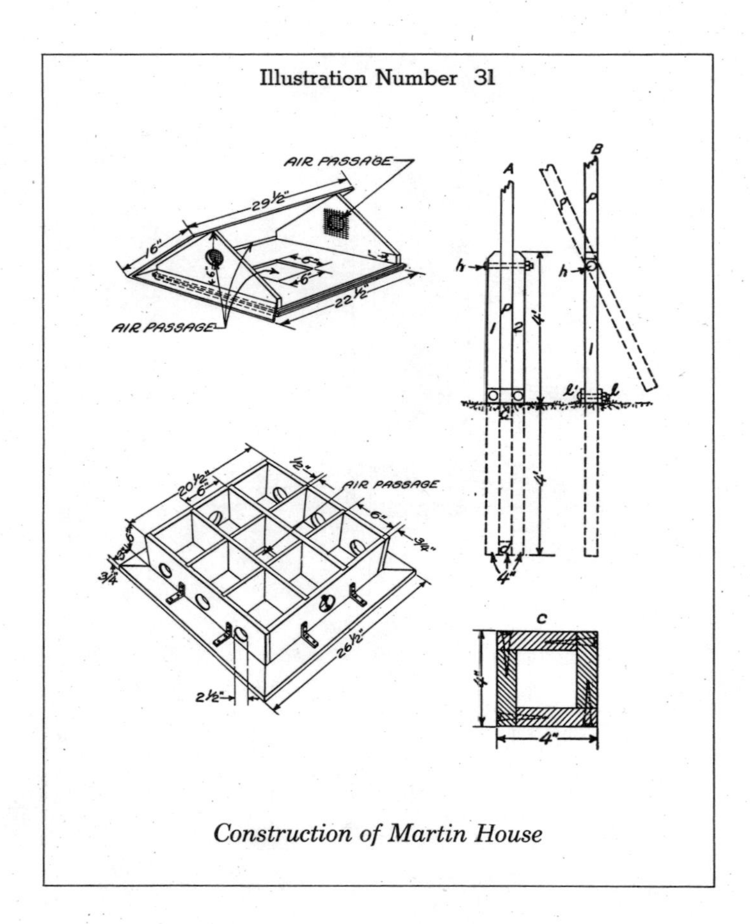

Construction of Martin House

water ponds and ditches almost anywhere, the beginner will do well to accompany an experienced collector to learn the most effective technique of gathering them. Field equipment are a net on a long pole and a pail of water for transportation. Breeders of exotic fishes raise daphnia in large quantities, but for most amateurs it is too cumbersome a task.

Cyclops, another tiny crustacean; mosquito and similar insect larvae; freshwater shrimps, other minute water animals, and an occasional house fly are desirable live foods.

FOODS FOR SALTWATER FISHES — Almost all marine fishes are carnivorous and thrive on chopped raw fish, shrimp, shellfish, and crabmeat. Live small fishes are a welcome meal.

Books on the Aquarium Hobby and on Fishes.

Innes, W. T., The Complete Aquarium Book, Halcyon House, New York, 1936

Innes, W. T., Exotic Aquarium Fishes, Innes Publishing Co., Philadelphia, Pa., 1952

Boulenger, E. G., The Aquarium Book, D. Appleton-Century Co., New York, 1926

McClintock, Theodore, The Underwater Zoo, The Vanguard Press, New York, 1938

Boardman, E. T., Field Guide to Lower Aquarium Animals, Cranbrook Institute of Science, Bloomfield Hills, Michigan, 1939

Jordan, E. L., Hammond's Nature Atlas of America, the Section on Fishes, C. S. Hammond & Co., New York, 1952

Jordan, D. S. and Everman, B. W., American Food and Game Fishes, Doubleday & Co., New York, 1923

La Gorce, J. O.; Schultz, L. P.; and Nichols, J. T., The Book of Fishes, National Geographic Society, Washington, D.C., 1939

Breder, C. M., Field Book of Marine Fishes, G. P. Putnam's Sons, New York, 1929

Schultz, L. P., The Ways of Fishes, D. Van Nostrand Co., New York, 1948

Roule, L., Fishes: Their Journeys and Migrations, W. W. Norton & Co., New York, 1933

BIRD HOBBIES

Why Birds Are Interesting — From time immemorial birds have fascinated man's imagination. The birds' plumage is often striking, and in the manifold activities of bird life — in flying and singing, courting and mating, nesting and rearing the young — they have a grace and a charm that are captivating. Their beauty is of a shy and fleeting kind, an enjoyment to be experienced for moments only, and therefore prized more highly. In the appearance and behaviour of birds we see reflected, rightly or wrongly, all human moods and emotions, from gloom and ill temper to light-hearted merriment. Particularly songbirds in spring seem to radiate a magnificent love of life and joy of love. Of course, we cannot ascribe human traits and reactions to animals, but the nature lore that turns birds into symbols, is deeply rooted in our folk life; the owl has always been worldly wise and the lark supremely happy.

Some of nature's great mysteries are connected with birds. Flying has appeared to man a most desirable achievement ever since Ikarus is said to have attempted the feat. Naturally man watched the birds, but as long as he imitated their flight he failed, and only when he developed an entirely different set of aero-principles, did he succeed. According to the mechanics of airplane engineering the birds should not be able to carry on any distance flying at all; yet they fly far and wide and the mystery has deepened.

Most men love to travel and look with awe at the world's greatest travelers, the birds. How and why tiny birds fly from continent to continent, between nesting grounds and winter quarters, some of them covering up to 18,000 miles in the round trip, is one of creation's unsolved secrets. Often the selection of routes is equally mystifying; the storks of northern Europe spend the winter in Africa; those that are bred east of the Elbe river (which meanders from the heart of Czechoslovakia to the North Sea) fly south over the Balkans and Asia Minor, those bred west of the Elbe River travel via southern France and Spain. There are no exceptions.

How migratory birds find their distant goal, often sailing over long stretches of ocean where no landmarks can be distinguished and no food is obtainable, and how most of them manage to arrive at their destination not only not exhausted but in prime condition, is not easily explained.

Bird Hobbies

As to the Why of the migrations such factors as the food supply and the change of the seasons certainly play a part, but as considerable groups of birds do not migrate, a fully convincing explanation still has to be found. So far there seems to be no answer to the question; nevertheless, science has discovered solutions to many seemingly unanswerable problems, and it is certain to make progress in unraveling this one.

One strange aspect of bird migration is the so-called homing instinct. It is best known in the homing pigeon, but exists also in innumerable other birds. Starlings taken to a distant place by a wide, semi-circular detour, fly home, when released, in a straight line. Song birds return from Central and South America to the same county and township, sometimes to the same backyard and maple tree.

Therefore it is not surprising that thousands of people go beyond the casual observation of birds and take up a bird hobby. Bird hobbies will be described here, for the sake of organization, as "attracting birds" and as "watching birds," the first term referring to the various measures a home owner may take to attract songbirds to his windows and his garden, in most cases just for his general human enjoyment, and the second term implying a more systematic field study of birds and their ways. Frequently both aspects overlap; the building of a feeding station may lead to intensive "bird watching," and some interesting bird observations in the woods may cause the observer to build bird houses or to plant bird-attracting shrubbery in his backyard.

How to Attract the Birds: Landscape with Bath — A beautiful garden is a great attraction to birds whose notions about a desirable environment coincide with ours, though for other reasons. The right proportion of trees, shrubs, vines and open spaces will allow the plants to asborb plenty of sunlight and produce ample fruits and seeds; it will also increase the insect population which is another incentive to the birds. The greater the variety of the setting, the greater will be the variety of the bird species. Lawns, as everybody knows, are the happy hunting grounds of robins which, however, need also good-sized trees with strong branches as building sites for their nests. Fully grown trees whose crowns buzz with thousands of insects of various kinds, offer desirable shelter to warblers, orioles, and vireos. Big trees which are somewhat neglected attract chickadees and titmice, woodpeckers and nuthatches. Groups of shrubs that are often pruned when young will have many crotches, — ideal supports for the nests of cardinals and thrashers, catbirds and mockingbirds, particularly if the shrubs are allowed to grow into a thicket.

In hot weather a bird bath — used also as a drinking well — is a prime attraction, and even in the cool months when hardly any human being would think of taking an outdoor shower, some birds like to splash and cavort in their "pool." In times of drought a garden bird bath may actually be a life saver for dozens of birds.

A watering place for birds may take on various forms:

1) A small bowl or the saucer of a flower pot will serve the purpose, although the water will have to be renewed frequently.

2) The regular bird bath of concrete, with a rough bottom gradually rising toward the edge, is the most frequent form; it can be bought, in various decorative versions, at a modest price, or it can be made at home. A flat bowl of concrete placed on the ground will be welcomed, although the birds will be better protected from sudden attacks by cats and other enemies if the bowl is elevated. Even the top of a garbage can or a similar metal receptacle will be useful; in that case, however, the bottom should be covered with gravel to afford a safe foothold for the bathers.

3) A bird pool will be an attractive addition to a larger garden, and will be even more popular with the birds. The size will depend on the space available, but 3 x 8 or 4 x 10 feet will be convenient. To keep the pool free from mosquitoes, a few small fishes may be placed in the water; in that case it will be necessary to provide a number of water plants for oxygenation.

4) A trickling fountain set up in a bird bath or in a pool will be more expensive but will be the birds' delight (see illustration No. 34). Even a revolving sprinkler on the lawn will attract robins and other birds, for a twofold reason: The food supply of earthworms and cutworms becomes more easily available, and the water spray creates the mud which swallows, robins and some other species utilize for the building or reinforcing of their nests.

In wintertime water is needed as much as during the

Illustration Number 32

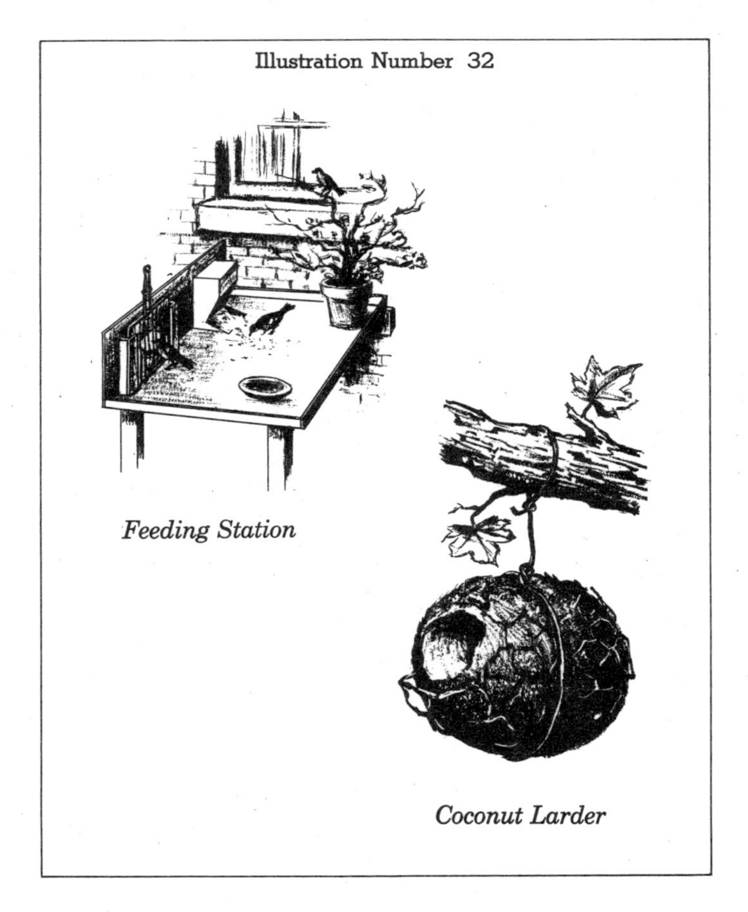

Feeding Station

Coconut Larder

summer. The usefulness of a bird bath can be prolonged far into the cold season by renewing the water daily and by adding a little glycerin which delays freezing of the water.

How to Attract the Birds: Bird Houses—Modern advances in gardening have not always helped the birds; a garden whose trees are groomed to perfection by a staff of tree-surgeons, leaves one large group of birds stranded without nesting sites: those which utilize tree holes and cavities. This situation can be remedied, to a large degree, by furnishing bird houses which are accepted by approximately 50 species. For this reason plenty of bird boxes are indeed needed throughout the country. The number of pairs of birds in the suburban areas of the large cities in the U. S. and Canada is approximately ten per acre; this is considerably higher than the average for the country as a whole, and has been accomplished largely because bird houses are made available there. A fair number and variety of birds are not only a welcome and pleasant ornament to any garden but also help to keep insect pests under control.

Bird houses may be bought or built at home in many different forms and versions. The types pictured in illustrations 28 and 29 are recommended by the U. S. Fish and Wildlife Service. All should be solidly built to keep their tenants cool in warm weather and protected from rain at all times.

The principal points to remember are these:

1) Building Materials — Wood is the accepted standard material; pine, yellow poplar, cypress, or any other kind that is easily worked, serves the purpose. Bird houses of pottery are usable but not easily made at home.

Illustration Number 33

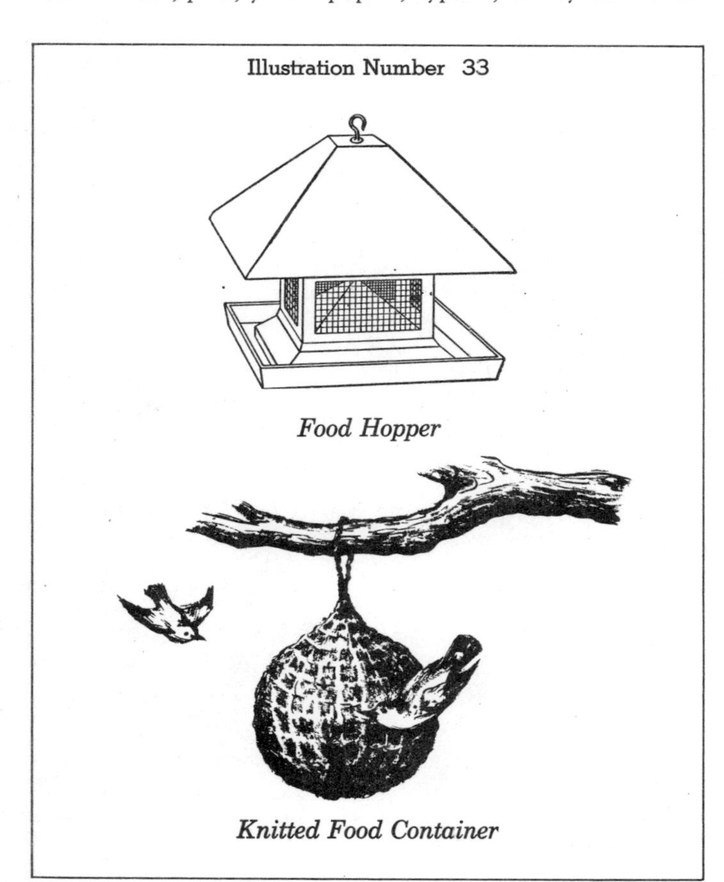

Food Hopper

Knitted Food Container

Bird boxes with a straight rather than a pitched or slanted roof, may have a tar-paper covering on the roof.

2) External Appearance — Bird boxes may be painted as a protection against the weather. Inconspicuous shades like brown, grey or a subdued green are best. A fancier way which will give a touch of rustic beauty to the bird box is to cover the exterior with slabs of wood with the bark on, which can be obtained cheaply or entirely free at any sawmill, from the waste pile. Such rustic boxes (see illustration No. 29) are actually preferred by some species of birds.

3) Ventilation — On warm days the heat in the small box with only one opening may become uncomfortable. Therefore two small holes should be drilled into the sides of the bird house near the top. They will not cause a draft but will help to circulate the air.

4) Observation — The upper left bird house in illustration No. 28 may be built as a kind of observation post if for the part inserted in back of the hinged front a piece of glass is used. If the owner is carrying out, for a whole season, a systematic observation of bird life histories (see the chapter on "Contributing to Man's Knowledge of Birds"), such an arrangement will be very helpful, and the nest and family life of the birds will not be disturbed.

5) Special Houses — Robins, barn swallows, phoebes and song sparrows will not normally accept the type of bird houses described so far. For them nest brackets or nest shelves will have to be provided, as shown in illustration No. 29.

Purple martins are said to be the only birds that like to live in apartment houses, although the author has seen, in northern Maine, martin houses that were occupied by swallows. The external appearance of a martin house is shown in illustration No. 30. While illustration No. 31 is self-explanatory, these measurements are recommended for the martin-house pole: The supports A and B (1 and 2) are 4 inches square and 8 feet long; they are buried 4 feet in the ground, aligned by the 4-inch blocks c and d. The pole itself is built of ⅞ inch hardwood; its cross section is shown in C. The hinge h consists of a piece of pipe or a heavy bolt. Two hardwood blocks or iron plates bolted together (l and l') hold the base of the pole in position.

The house may have two, three, or more stories; each story has eight outside rooms with separate entrances. The central squares form an air shaft.

The martin house is usually painted white to reflect the sunlight.

6) Sanitation — All bird houses should be constructed in such a way as to be easily cleaned. Every spring and preferably after each nesting (as soon as the fledglings have left the nest) the houses should be cleaned of old rubbish, sterile eggs, and dead nestlings. The tendency of certain insect pests, for instance the gypsy moths, to lay their eggs in bird boxes is an additional reason for a thorough periodical housecleaning. If the birds living in a certain box seem

Species	*Floor Space*	*Depth of Cavity*	*Entrance Above Floor*	*Diameter of Entr.*	*Height Above Ground*	*Notes*
Bluebird	5x5″	8″	6″	1½″	5-10′	Orchards are favorites. Open spaces with sunlight preferred.
Robin	6x8″	8″	open sides	—	6-15′	In partly shaded spots on trees or under overhanging eaves of shed or porch roof.
Chickadee	4x4″	8-10″	6-8″	1⅛″	6-15′	Prefer rustic bird houses but will accept others also. Old orchards and edges of woodlands are favorite locations. Feeding stations with suet and nuts will be an inducement to accept a house.
Titmouse	4x4″	8-10″	6-8″	1¼″	6-15′	
Nuthatch	4x4″	8-10″	6-8″	1¼″	12-20′	
House Wren	4x4″	6-8″	1-6″	1-1¼″	6-10′	
Bewick's Wren	4x4″	6-8″	1-6″	1-1¼″	6-10′	Partly sunny spots in yards and orchards are favored. Instead of round holes they like oblong slots to carry in "bulky" nesting material.
Carolina Wren	4x4″	6-8″	1-6″	1½″	6-10′	
Violet-green Swallow	5x5″	6″	1-5″	1½″	10-15′	A dead tree is a good spot for several swallow houses. Bodies of water, even a small pool, are a great attraction.
Tree Swallow	5x5″	6″	1-5″	1½″	10-15′	
Barn Swallow	6x6″	6″	open sides	—	8-12′	Will accept a nest bracket or shelf, like robin.
House Finch	6x6″	6″	4″	2″	8-12′	Box may be attached to trees, posts, or buildings.
Starling	6x6″	16-18″	14-16″	2″	10-25′	Box close to human habitations preferred.
Phoebe	6x6″	6″	open sides	—	8-12′	Likes shelf near water, loves nest under bridge.
Crested Flycatcher	6x6″	8-10″	6-8″	2″	8-20′	Rustic bird house in orchard, open woodland.
Flicker	7x7″	16-18″	14-16″	2½″	6-20′	Flickers are most likely to accept a house. For all flickers and woodpeckers, cover the bottom of the box with small chips to a depth of 1-2 inches, for the shaping of the nest; otherwise the birds will mutilate the box.
Red-headed Woodpecker	6x6″	12-15″	9-12″	2″	12-20′	
Downy Woodpecker	4x4″	8-10″	6-8″	1¼″	6-20′	
Hairy Woodpecker	6x6″	12-15″	9-12″	1½″	12-20′	
Screech Owl	8x8″	12-15″	9-12″	3″	10-30′	Owls take bird houses readily, the first two preferring orchards and groves, the last one quiet spots high on barns. Screech owls are sometimes destructive to other birds.
Saw-whet Owl	6x6″	10-12″	8-10″	2½″	12-20′	
Barn Owl	10x18″	15-18″	4″	6″	12-18′	
Wood Duck	10x18″	10-24″	12-16″	4″	10-20′	Boxes on lowland trees ¼ to ½ mile from water are favorite nesting sites.

to be badly infested with parasites it is suggested to treat the inside and the nest with liberal doses of derris or pyrethrum powder.

7) Easy Access — Because the cleaning of the boxes is so important, bird houses should be set up where they can be reached without difficulty, with the help of a regular household ladder.

8) Details of Construction and Location — The table above gives the desirable measurements and other notes for the more important species that use bird houses.

How to Attract the Birds: Feeding Stations — Nothing has fostered the acquaintance and friendship between birds and man as much as the winter feeding of those species that stay at home during the cold season. This hobby is increasing in popularity throughout the country, and it saves thousands of bird lives every year. But it has to be carried on as long as the winter lasts; a sudden stoppage of the food supply may be fatal to those birds that have become accustomed to your hospitality and rely on it. There is no compelling reason either to stop the feeding when spring arrives, although the natural food supply will be plentiful by then. Some birds will continue visiting your station during the nesting and egg-laying season, and will be grateful for some broken shells of hen's eggs and for some chopped suet which they may even feed to their young.

Starlings and blue jays are also eager customers at all feeding stations, and readily eat almost all of the foods mentioned in the table. Nobody cares to attract them as their rough and noisy manners often crowd out cardinals and other shy birds which will not feed when they are annoyed. But it is difficult to keep out the "bullies," or even to keep them at a distance. One advice which is sometimes given suggests that coarser foods and crumbs that appeal to starlings, English sparrows, and blue jays be scattered farther away while the daintier foods are offered closer to the house to more welcome guests. This method seems to be quite effective, at least in reference to starlings and English sparrows.

Illustration Number 34

Bird Fountain

Permanent Food House

For the birds that benefit most from winter feeding stations, the U. S. Fish and Wildlife Service recommends the following "menus":

Bird Species	*Favorite Foods*
Titmice, chickadees, nuthatches	Suet, cracked nuts, shelled and broken peanuts, sunflower seeds, bread crumbs.
Mockingbirds, catbirds, thrashers, hermit thrushes, robins	Cut apples, cut oranges, currants, raisins, bread crumbs.
Blackbirds, cardinals, towhees	Sunflower seeds, corn, shelled and broken peanuts, scratch feed.
Finches, juncos, native sparrows	Scratch feed, millet, wheat, screenings, small seed mixtures, bread crumbs.
Woodpeckers	Suet, cracked nuts, corn.

Besides the favorite foods listed above, the number of foodstuffs that may be fed and are fed to birds is legion; they include any kind of fat, pork rinds, bones with fragments of meat, cooked meat, cheese, chopped hard-boiled eggs, buckwheat, crackers, coconut meat, popcorn, corn bread, corn meal, broken dog biscuits, doughnuts, pastry, fresh and dried fruits, hominy, whole oats, rolled oats, peppers, pumpkin seeds, squash seeds. Whatever is handiest and most readily available may be used; there is no need for a great variety of offerings.

Moist foods like bananas, cooked rice, potatoes and boiled corn meal freeze easily in wintertime, as do table scraps which also sour quickly in summertime; therefore they should be used only sparingly and where they are consumed immediately.

Insect-eating birds love earthworms, mealworms, and ant eggs, but to provide such delicacies is more than can be expected from the regular bird lover; the birds will be quite content to find suet or suet mixtures at the station.

In some parts of the country bird cakes are prepared from such ingredients as ground grains (corn meal, oat meal, etc.), bread crumbs, chopped nuts, and currants. The cereals are partly cooked, mixed with eggs, and baked; or they may be combined with melted suet; occasionally some thick sweetening (honey or molasses) is added. The cakes are "served" in various ways, as described later.

Feeding stations may be bought in pet shops, but they are just as easily made at home. The number of possible variations is almost unlimited, and the personal preferences of the owner will decide the type to be used. A few common and less common forms, as recommended by the U.S. Fish and Wildlife Service, are described here:

1) A Simple Food Tray or Shelf — It must have a raised border around the edge to prevent the scattering of seeds and other foods by wind and rain. One sidewall should be raised against the prevailing winds. It may or may not have a roof. It should be set up at a fairly protected place that is not too much exposed to storms, driving rains, and heavy snow. It may be fastened to a tree, or set on top of a pole, or attached to a window that has plenty of sunlight. Sometimes a pulley arrangement of wire is used between a window and a tree; the station is filled at the window and pulled out to the tree; after the birds have become accustomed to feeding there, the tray may be gradually placed nearer and nearer to the window, for closer observation.

Illustration No. 32 shows a simple food shelf by a window. The hopper used there may be bought or built at home of wood and wire mesh; while it protects the food, it is not necessary. A double grill made for broiling hamburgers at picnics, holds the suet in the right position. Other ingenious devices may prove just as effective.

In windy areas, windproof stations are sometimes erected. A food tray with three side walls and a roof is set on a pivot so that it will revolve. One or two weather vanes are attached to the station in such a way that they always turn the open side away from the wind.

2) A Food Hopper — A protected feeding station with a detachable roof, as shown in illustration No. 33, may be either bought or made of wood and wire screening.

3) A Stationary Food House — This is a more or less permanent garden structure, as pictured in illustration No. 34. Its roof and four glass walls completely protect the food from wind and weather yet allow observation of the feeding. It is provided with two trays; the one containing the food is within the walls; the other one, perhaps a foot below, has the function of attracting the birds; it serves as a sort of entrance hall, and after a while the birds learn to fly from there to the upper tray where they find the food.

4) A Coconut Larder — This is an effective device, popular with many birds. Carve or drill a hole in a coconut, drain the coconut milk, and fill the cavity with bird cake, chopped suet and nuts, peanut butter, or similar food. The birds will eat with relish both the stuffing and the natural inside lining of coconut meat. If you want to reserve this treat for small birds, cut only a small hole. The coconut larder is suspended from a tree branch with wire, as shown in illustration No. 32.

5) Specialties — To serve bird cake, metal cans with small openings or baskets of wire netting are useful during the summer and in mild winters. In severe cold the tongues of the birds may be hurt if they touch the frosted metal and adhere to it; therefore knitted baskets of twine or yarn are preferable in cold climate. When filled with food, these baskets have the shape of a ball (see illustration No. 33). Bird cake made with suet or other fat may also be served "au naturel," i.e. poured into natural or drilled holes and cavities in tree trunks or limbs where birds will find it readily.

If you hammer two or three small nails part way into the feeding shelf so that they stand upright and serve as holders of pieces of apple which are forced down over them, mockingbirds will appreciate such an arrangement; occasionally also catbirds or cedar waxwings will be attracted by the "apples on a stick."

A ripe sunflower head suspended from the limb of a tree will be the scene of an amusing acrobatic performance. When nuthatches, chickadees and titmice discover it, they will cling to the flower and pick the seeds, their little feet up and their heads down.

To cater to hummingbirds, a few small bottles, vials or drinking fountains with syrup should be supplied. A solution of regular white sugar seems to be the favorite, but strained honey and other syrups are also welcome. To help the hummingbirds find the new food supply, the syrup in the vial may be colored red by adding a little vegetable coloring, or a bright red or orange flower, genuine or of paper, may be affixed to the bottles. After the hummingbirds have discovered the syrup and visit it regularly, there is no further need for special "come-ons."

How to Attract the Birds: Planting Their Food — A more permanent way of attracting and maintaining a bird population is to plant those trees, shrubs, herbs and flowers whose seeds or fruits are favorite foods of well-loved birds. It is also a relatively simple method as the birds will readily discover your offerings and do their own harvesting. Insect eaters are, of course, not included here, but for the other groups the following plantings are recommended, in accordance with the researches and findings of the U.S. Fish and Wildlife Service:

1) Seed Eaters — Goldfinches, Siskins, Juncos, Native Sparrows, and Others — Their favorites are the seeds of garden flowers and field plants like asters, centaureas, California poppies, cosmos, marigolds, sunflowers, tarweeds, forget-me-nots, princesplumes, portulacas, zinnias, sorghum, Japanese millet (also called barnyard grass), Hungarian grass.

Goldfinches, siskins and redpolls are fond of alders and birches, during the winter, because their cones supply palatable seeds. In spring, the goldfinches and purple finches like to stay in the neighborhod of elms which bear the first tree seeds of the year. With the grosbeaks the box-elders and ashes are popular; their winged fruits are opened and yield the seed. Pines, larches, and other coniferous trees are the favorites of many seed-eaters, for instance of the crossbills whose bills are especially constructed for securing the seeds from the pine cones. Woodpeckers and jays, nuthatches and grackles, crows and game birds are attracted by oaks and beeches, i.e. by acorns and beechnuts; woodpeckers and jays depend on them, to a great extent, for their livelihood.

2) Seed-Eating Game Birds — The raising of food patches in the open country is recommended, particularly of alfalfa, beggarweed, buckwheat, clover, corn, cowpeas, flax, hemp, millet, oats, peanuts, rice, rye, sorghum, soybeans, sunflowers, vetches, wheat, winter peas.

3) Fruit Eaters — For this group of birds the food supply is abundant during the summer and fall, but winter and early spring are often critical seasons. Therefore plantings destined for the fruit-eating birds should concentrate on shrubs and trees whose fruits will stay on the branches throughout the cold season. Such long-lasting fruits are produced by the bayberry, bush honeysuckle, dogwood,

Illustration Number 35

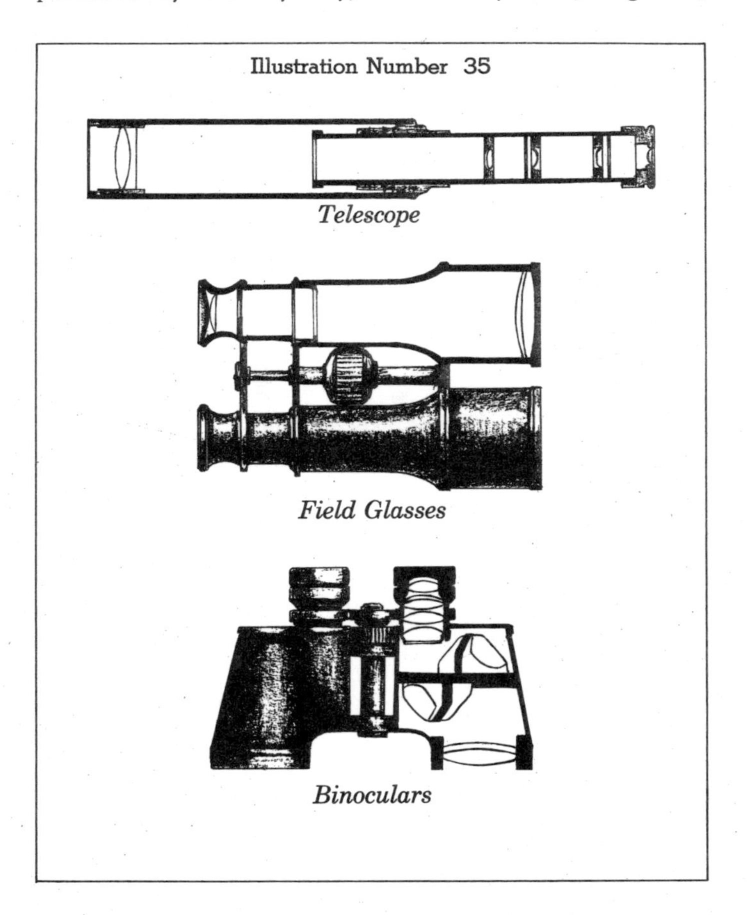

Telescope

Field Glasses

Binoculars

flowering apple, hackberry, holly, juniper, mountain ash, persimmon, snowberry, sour gum, thorn apple, Virginia creeper.

From a survey based on careful observations and statistics, the following fruits emerge as the favorites of fruit-eating birds:

More than 100 species of birds like to eat	Raspberries, blackberries, elderberries.
50 to 99 species like to eat	Berries of dogwood, sumach, and red cedar; juniper berries, bayberries, mulberries, pokeberries, strawberries, blueberries; grapes.
35 to 49 species like to eat	Fruits of the greenbrier, crab apple, flowering apple, thorn apple, holly, Virginia creeper, sour gum; hackberries, juneberries, crowberries, bearberries, huckleberries, snowberries, cranberries, and others.

4) HUMMINGBIRDS — The bright blossoms of garden flowers readily attract hummingbirds; red, orange and purple seem to be the favorite shades. Some commonly cultivated species are special attractions: daylilies, lilies cannas, morning glories, petunias, honeysuckles, fuchsias, jasmines, royal poincianas, coralbells; jewelweeds and trumpet vines are great favorites.

5) DUCKS AND OTHER WATER FOWL — These birds are attracted by the following plants which will increase the food supply: bulrushes, coontail waterlilies, duck potatoes, duck weeds, musk grasses, pond weeds, water cress, wild celery, wild millet, wild rice. For marshy flats and wet margins wild millet and smartweeds are recommended, for ponds and lakes duckweeds and longleaf pondweed.

Illustration Number 36

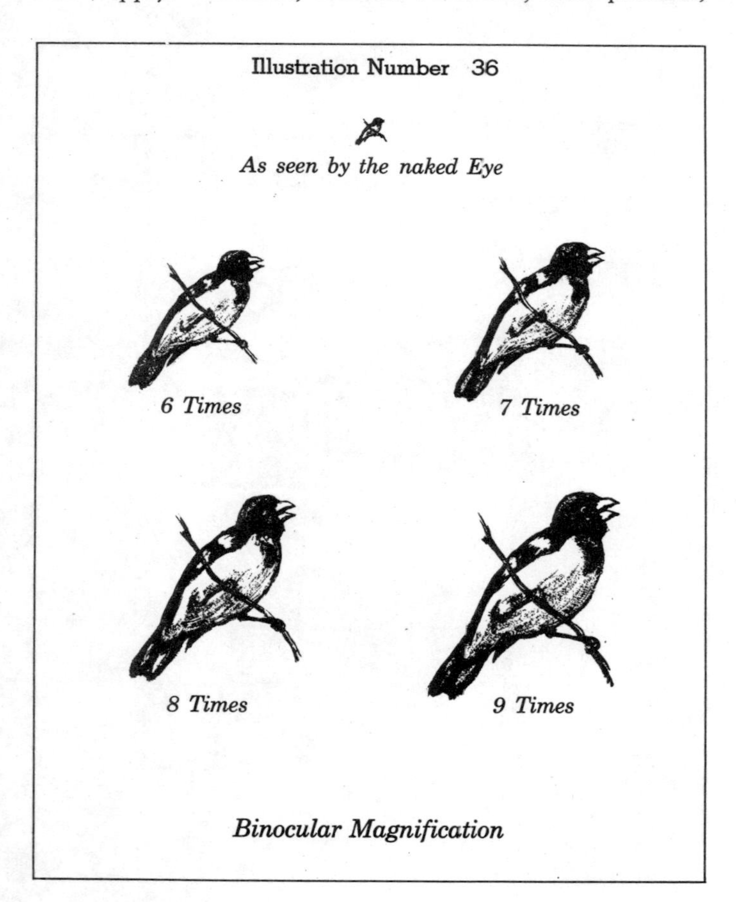

Binocular Magnification

Bird Watching: Field Equipment — While some excellent bird watching can be carried on in the observer's own backyard, especially if he employs one of the methods previously recommended for attracting birds, the common usage of the term implies a hike to the woods and open fields to watch bird life in its untamed environment. Normally it is also assumed that the bird watcher will take notes of what he sees and hears, especially of the birds which he identifies.

There was a time when many "practical" people considered bird watching a slightly ridiculous hobby favored by teen-age boys, school teachers, and elderly spinsters. Fortunately that stage has passed, and among the country's most enthusiastic bird watchers — some of them laymen who have made definite contributions to science — are prominent lawyers and engineers, bankers and business executives, and men and women from every walk of life.

The field equipment for this hobby is limited. It consists of a notebook and pencil — items of negligible cost — but includes one piece that is fairly expensive: field glasses or binoculars. Technically, the first term refers to the straight glasses without prisms which rarely magnify more than 5 times, while the second name concerns the prismatic type (see illustrations No. 35 and 36). Conversationally, both terms are often applied to either system. The initial outlay for a pair of good binoculars may be considerable, but they will last a lifetime.

Many beginners use opera glasses which happen to be in their possession; as such glasses magnify two or three times, they are welcome at the start. Sooner or later, however, the bird lover will feel that stronger binoculars are indispensable. Whether he will acquire glasses that magnify 4, 6, 8, or 10 times, will depend on his personal preferences. The buyer will have to keep in mind that the greater the magnifying power, the smaller will be the field of vision. In open woodlands where various trees and bushes limit the view, a good-sized field may be important; on the beach or the ocean distance may count, i.e. magnifying power. If different brands offering the same magnification vary in price, the cheaper ones have probably a smaller field of view.

Brightness is another factor to be weighed, as it aids in the recognition and identification of birds; it depends on the size of the objective lens which is farthest away from your eyes. It is not recommended to buy glasses with an objective lens diameter of less than 30 millimeters. The objective lens, by the way, has nothing to do with the size of the field.

Also the weight of the glasses is worth considering; a pair of 8 x binoculars (this is the accepted form of indicating the magnifying power) is heavier than a pair of 5 x binoculars; some people object to the frequent lifting of heavy glasses while others, with a stronger constitution, do not mind at all. A very steady hand is necessary for 10 x or 12 x binoculars because each jerking or trembling motion of your fingers is magnified 10 or 12 times just as the bird on the lens.

The final choice will be a compromise between highest possible quality and available means, with personal preferences deciding the details of magnification, field of vision, brightness, and weight. In an informal poll conducted among bird students by George Dock Jr., 7 x binoculars with a 35-millimeter objective lens emerged as the first choice.

In two points all experts in this hobby agree: The binoculars should have a central focusing screw as the adjustment of two individual screws is too slow and cumbersome in the field; and the glasses should be worn around the shoulder on a short strap as a long strap swings in too wide a radius; the latter might result in damage to the glasses, especially when the wearer suddenly bends down.

There seem to be fashions in binoculars, as in everything else. Sometimes German Zeiss glasses are considered the last word, at other times French Le Maire products; lately American binoculars seem to be in special favor, for instance those of Bausch and Lomb. In any case it is worth-while to consider also the second-hand market.

Bird Watching: When and How — At four o'clock in the morning the swelling chorus begins; the wood peewee is usually the first singer although not a very conspicuous one; soon the robins join in, and the cardinals and Baltimore orioles add their clear and loud whistles to the morning symphony. The bushes along the old wagon road are stirring with bird life, and so are the crowns of the trees. This is the bird watcher's hour, and although it may not be easy to obey the alarm clock at five A.M. and to leave a comfortable bed, the reward will be worth it. For not only the bird world is alive at that time, but wildlife is stirring everywhere; particularly in the mountains it will delight you: Two deer may be grazing at the edge of the forest; a skunk mother may be crossing your path with two youngsters toddling behind in Indian file; a shaggy bear may be tearing through a raspberry thicket; or a wildcat — they are more frequent than is commonly supposed — may be following you curiously.

The second period of the day when bird watchers may stalk their prey, is the dusk and nightfall. Then another feathered group will be in its glory, from the whip-poor-will and the insect-hunting night hawk to the tribe of the owls. Among the night singers the mockingbird, the ovenbird, and the woodcock will excel.

Your own experience will teach you how to extract an optimum of pleasure and profit from your "bird hikes" and "bird sittings." But the advice of the experts should not be neglected, and in the following I would like to present some of the hints given by my colleague Dr. L. A. Hausman, one of America's outstanding naturalists:

1) Don't set out on a morning watch with an empty stomach. Eat a good breakfast; drink hot coffee or chocolate.

2) Don't walk toward the east; the rising morning sun will make it almost impossible to recognize the colors and patterns of birds. Walk with the sun on your back.

Illustration Number 37

Various Types of Bird Nests

3) Select a calm morning; on windy days many birds seek shelter in the dense foliage of bushes; whether the morning is warm or cool does not make a great deal of difference. Ravines and narrow valleys may be suitable even in windy weather.

4) Dress simply and soberly. If you adapt your clothes to the subdued colors of nature the birds will accept you as a part of the environment; bright, conspicuous colors will cause alarm.

5) Needless to say, move quietly and slowly. Sudden starts and jerky motions will frighten the birds away. Don't talk, whistle, sing, whisper. Keep your dog at home.

6) Take a notebook and pencil along. Keep a bird list. Jot down your notes on what you see and hear. If you have the thrill of discovering a bird you have never observed before, and you do not know its name, describe it so that you can identify it later with the help of a field guide.

The Audubon Society issues an "Audubon Daily Field Card of Birds" in three versions, one for bird watchers in North America East of the Mississippi River, another for the Central United States, and a third for the Pacific States. Each card records such data as the observer, the locality, the date, time, weather, and wind, and contains 8 columns of names of the more common bird species of the region concerned. The bird watcher has just to enter the number of birds of each species he encounters. These cards, printed as four-page folders, are definite time savers in the field

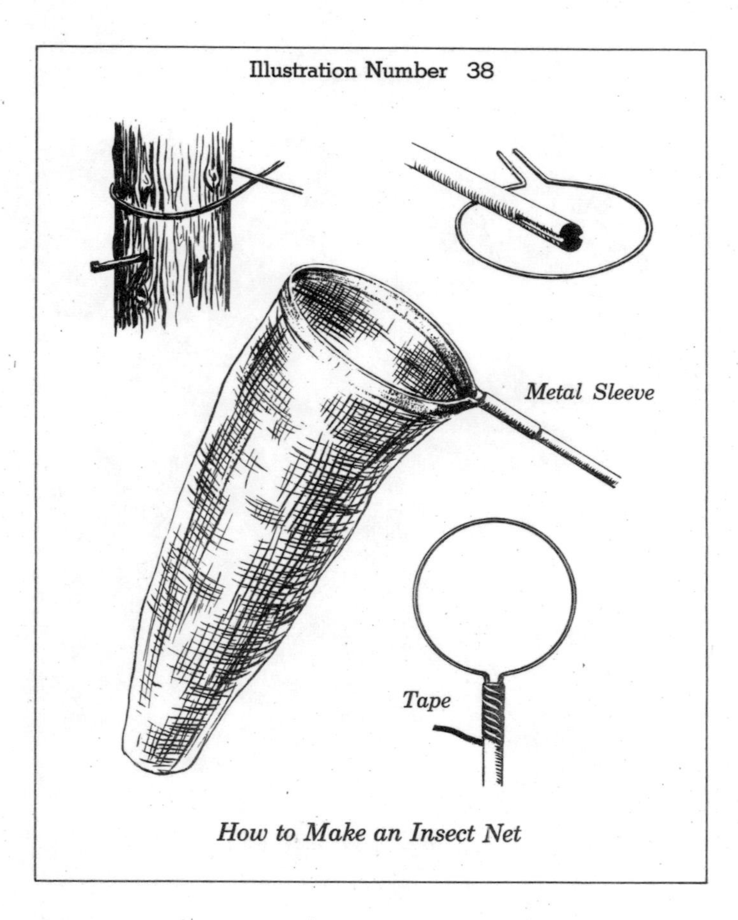

How to Make an Insect Net

but are not intended as a substitute for your individual notes.

Identifying Birds — To a beginner it may seem an almost insurmountable task to identify "the birds," i.e. to learn their names. Yet with persistence and enthusiasm every one can master the art. There is, of course, no set formula in so highly individualistic a venture, but most experts advise the following steps:

1) Observe and identify the most common birds at a close range.

2) Make good use of modern field guides and bird books which offer not only fine illustrations, many of them in color, but also show the appearance of a bird at a great distance and in flight. Various patterns of flying or running, peculiar to certain birds, are described, and habits and habitats are explained. All these details will be helpful in the field.

3) Associate the name of a bird with that of the family to which it belongs. In that way the characteristics of the family will become clearer, and you will find it easy to identify other species of the same group. Everybody has definite thought associations with such bird families as the Herons, the Ducks and Geese, the Owls, the Gulls and Terns, the Nuthatches, and so forth. Expanding from that basis, a mental picture of the bird world as a group of families rather than individuals will help to bring order into the chaos.

4) Finally the bird student will be able to identify many birds at fair distances, learning by experience the pitfalls caused by special conditions of weather, light, and motion. He will be aware of the fact that under certain circumstances not even the experts can make their definitions with complete assurance.

5) Learning the bird songs is important as some birds are more frequently heard than seen. It is not as difficult as it may appear, especially if one is introduced to the calls and melodies by an experienced bird student. Some naturalists connect definite syllables and words with the various calls and songs, others record them in a sort of shorthand consisting of consonants, vowels, and rising and falling lines. The reporters have to keep in mind that some species have more than one song, and individual birds often enjoy their own little variations.

Most helpful are the excellent recordings of 132 song birds, made from nature by the ornithological laboratory of Cornell University and sold by the Cornell University Press in Ithaca, N. Y.; the six records present Birds of the Northwoods, of Northern Gardens and Shade Trees, of Southern Woods and Gardens, of the Fields and Prairies, of Western North America, and North American Game Birds; also, Some Familiar Birds of Gardens and Shade Trees, Some Familiar Birds of the Roadside, Some Birds of Lakes and Marshes, More Birds of the Marshes, and Some North American Warblers; also, Florida Bird Songs. The latter record contains the song of the Ivory-billed Woodpecker which by now may be extinct.

The number of books on birds is legion. Only a few are mentioned here (all are suited for beginners and more experienced students):

Field Guides

Peterson, Roger T., A Field Guide to the Birds, Houghton Mifflin Co., Boston, 1947

Peterson, Roger T., A Field Guide to Western Birds, Houghton Mifflin Co., Boston, 1947

Hausman, L. A., Beginner's Bird Guide, G. P. Putnam's Sons, New York, 1948

Hausman, L. A., Field Book of Eastern Birds, G. P. Putnam's Sons, New York, 1946

General

The Bird Section of Jordan, E. L., Hammond's Nature Atlas of America, C. S. Hammond & Co., New York, 1952

Hausman, L. A., The Illustrated Encyclopedia of American Birds, Halcyon House, New York, 1944

Grosvernor, G., et al., The Book of Birds, Vol. I and II, National Geographic Society, Washington, D.C., 1939.

Pearson, T. G., ed., Birds of America, Garden City Publishing Co., Garden City, N. Y., 1948

Hickey, Joseph, A Guide to Bird Watching, Oxford University Press, New York, 1946

Specialties

Allen, A. A., Stalking Birds with Color Camera, National Geographic Society, Washington, D.C., 1952.

Saunders, A. A., A Guide to Bird Songs, Doubleday & Co., New York, 1935

Hausman, L. A., Bird Hiking, Rutgers University Press, New Brunswick, N. J., 1948

Audubon Magazine, published by the National Audubon Society, 1000 Fifth Ave., New York City.

Audubon Field Notes — bi-monthly reports especially designed for bird watchers, bringing observations on distribution and migration of birds, including the annual Christmas Bird Count. Published by the Audubon Society.

Outdoors Illustrated — five annual issues on outdoor activities and hobbies, with many how-to-do reports for youth leaders and nature lovers in general. Published by the Audubon Society.

Collecting Eggs, Prints of Tracks, and Nests — The gathering and systematic collecting of eggs of the various species of birds was in vogue some fifty years ago, but it is doubtful whether any laymen-nature lovers indulge in such a hobby today.

The identification and "collecting" of bird tracks by means of impressions in wax, plaster casts, exact measuring and redrawing on sheets of cardboard is a specialty of definite value to nature study but it is a restricted, difficult field; for tracks will vary for the same bird depending on a hard or soft walking surface, and on the age of the specimen.

Collections of bird nests (see illustration No. 37) are instructive for school and boy scout exhibits, particularly if for each nest a picture of the bird responsible is shown: An oriole for a nest that looks like a pendant flask, a hummingbird for a compact little cup saddled on a limb, etc. For collecting nests, winter is obviously the best season as the bare trees and bushes expose the existing nest structures.

Contributing to Man's Knowledge of Birds — For more experienced bird watchers the point will come at which they wish to do more than just watch and identify the birds. They wish to make a real contribution to the science of birds, and may be a little discouraged at the thought that the scientists and experts seem to have already explored and discovered everything that can possibly be discovered. Fifty years ago the reply of the ornithologists may indeed have been pessimistic; at that time science was hardly interested in anything but the anatomy and physiology of the birds, the proper fields of trained experts. Today, however, the answer is about the opposite. For science today is also greatly interested in the "sociology" of birds, in their life histories, their communities, migrations, etc., and only a great amount of data and statistics taken by many different bird lovers at various points can bring clarity into the picture. A cooperative effort of bird clubs on a national scale will be necessary to coordinate the material, but the individual bird watchers have to provide the basic information.

Life Histories of Birds — If you are interested in projects of this type, you will find a detailed outline of the data that should be gathered, in Joseph J. Hickey's "A Guide to Bird Watching," on page 193. It is a kind of questionnaire, and by observing the daily life of a certain species nesting in your backyard or at some spot in the field where it can be watched regularly, throughout the season, you can collect significant notes and statistics. It will not be possible to answer all questions, but condensed notes even on a small phase will be valuable. To give you a general idea of the material to be collected, some areas and phases may be mentioned here:

The arrival dates of males and of females; the period of time over which the birds appear in spring; the relationship between the development of vegetation, especially the blooming of flowers and trees, and the arrival dates.

The number of songs of the male of the species; the frequency of song at various times of the day and the season; the use of singing perches.

The territory of the male and his family, and whether it is defended; the average size of the territory; the relationship between the male and his mate, particularly the question of dominance; evidence of the selection of the largest or best-looking males by the females.

The question whether the male or the female chooses the nesting site, and whether both build the nest; the reaction of the female when the eggs are taken or the nest is destroyed; evidence that the species is able to recognize its own eggs and, in the case of ground-nesting birds, will roll back an egg that is placed outside the nest.

The development of the young; the number of days for which they are blind; their gaping at moving objects including cardboard outlines of their parents; their begging from

Illustration Number 39

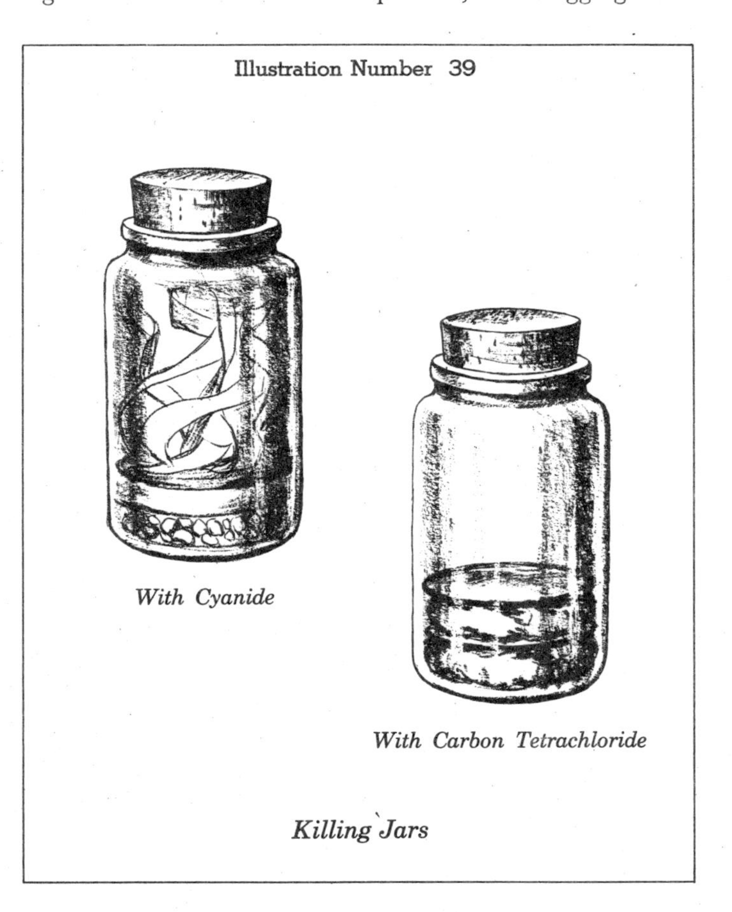

With Cyanide

With Carbon Tetrachloride

Killing Jars

birds of other species after leaving the nest; their first tentative song.

The ratio of male to female birds and the behavior of unmated birds during the breeding season; the question whether they make attempts at sexual relationships with mated birds.

These are only a few samples of the bird problems to be observed and studied systematically; they show the type of material that may be investigated, by laymen-bird watchers, for the enrichment of science.

BIRD COUNTS — A census of the bird population is of interest both to the scientists and the laymen-nature lovers. The practical implications of bird counts may not be apparent at first, but they are significant for effective wildlife management. Everybody, for instance, deplores the fact that the imported starlings have crowded out countless numbers of lovely native songbirds; to what extent that has really happened nobody can say, at least not in the eastern states; for no bird census existed at the time of the arrival and expansion of the starling population, early in the 19th century. However, in several western areas which are only now being invaded by the starlings, such data do exist, and the effect of the penetration can be gauged accurately.

The annual Christmas Bird Census, inaugurated in 1900 by Dr. F. M. Chapman, receives considerable newspaper publicity every year, and has become quite well known; in the first one 27 bird watchers participated, while today several thousand take part. The results are published in the March issue of the "Audubon Field Notes." County lists of bird populations are compiled in a few districts of America.

For the individual bird watcher a local study area offers probably the most satisfactory way of bird counting, especially if it is continued for a number of years over the same terrain; 25 to 50 acres are the recommended sizes; the stretch should be larger on pastures and open fields, and smaller in the forest. Such a census will take two to four visits; it will be more time-consuming in woodlands.

As bird counting includes a great deal of estimating, beginners will make a good many errors. They tend, for instance, to overestimate the number of large birds (a flock of 500 wild ducks will look like "thousands") and to underestimate the number of little birds, (8000 small shore birds huddled together on a beach will seem like half that figure). Large flocks of sitting birds may be effectively counted by determining the number of birds per square yard, and by estimating the size of the area.

Counting birds in process of migration has proved a significant means of checking the migratory routes and habits of many species. Flight lines of migrating hawks, for instance, have been established between Mount Tom in Massachusetts and Hawk Mountain in Pennsylvania. The latter had been a famous outpost for shooting hawks until it was converted into a sanctuary; the hunters departed and the watchers took over. On Mt. Tom as many as 765 flying hawks have been in view at the same time, in the migrating season during the second half of September.

BIRD BANDING — This is the scientific method to which we largely owe our knowledge of the world-wide, intercontinental travels of birds. Its first beginnings date back to the early years of this century; it came of age in 1919 when the U.S. Fish and Wildlife Service took charge of furnishing all bands and keeping all records; today the U.S. and Canada have a common set of numbers.

There are several thousand bird banders in this country and Canada, most of them laymen to whom bird study is a hobby. Whoever wishes to take up the banding of birds, will have to secure two permits, one from the Chief of the U.S. Fish and Wildlife Service (or the Department of Resources and Development in Canada), the other from the conservation department of the state where the banding is to take place. The former is the more important one and will be granted if the applicant is able to identify birds; the government may require a letter of recommendation from a reputable ornithologist, to that effect. It is also recommended to describe the project so that the Wildlife Service will recognize it as serious and valuable to science. It will also be very helpful to add a report about the bird studies you have carried out in your area.

Together with the permit the government will send you the requested number of aluminum bands, free of charge. Now you will obtain your birds which will either be nestlings still unable to fly and therefore easily secured, or adult birds which will have to be trapped. You will probably limit your project to one species, and as the advice of experienced bird

Illustration Number 40

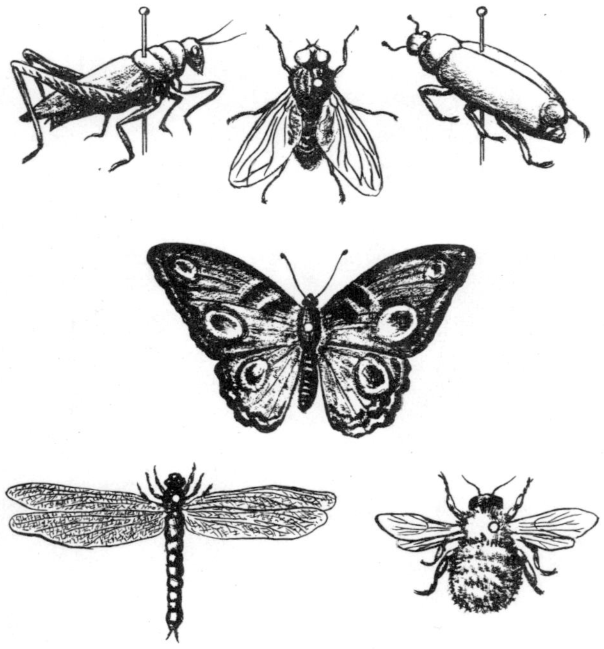

How to Pin the Insects

students and, if possible, of trained ornithologists is more essential in a venture of this kind than with other bird hobbies, it is suggested that you discuss your banding problem in your local bird club.

With all preliminaries decided upon, the banding itself is simple; you just fasten a small aluminum ring to the leg of the bird and release your prisoner. The band will have an inscription like "Notify U.S. Fish & Wildlife Service, Washington, D.C.", together with a number. When the bird is caught or shot and the ring dispatched to Washington, the government will send the finder an acknowledgment with a thank-you note, and to you a report of the interesting news, indicating the date on which your bird was caught, and the place where it was found — which may be Utah or Maryland, Quebec or Guatemala, the Yukon territory or the Pampas of Argentina.

COLLECTING BUTTERFLIES AND OTHER INSECTS

Why Insects Are Interesting — At the first glance a definition of the term insect seems as unnecessary as a definition of the words fish or bird. Yet, when we speak, for instance, of "spiders and other insects" we betray, technically at least, our ignorance. For spiders are not insects proper. To define an insect we have to list the following characteristics:

1) It is an invertebrate, i.e. an animal which has no vertebral column or backbone.
2) Its body is divided into three distinct parts, the head, thorax, and abdomen; this, however, is true only of the adult insect; caterpillars, pupae, etc. which are insects in a stage of development, do not have these body divisions.
3) Normally it has one or two pairs of wings.
4) Normally it has six legs in three pairs.

Many of us have a certain aversion to insects and like to label them pests. When we get better acquainted with them —and nothing will foster that acquaintance more thoroughly than a collection of insects, — we discover that not more than five to ten per cent of all insects are harmful, and that as a group they play an indispensible part in the balance of nature on earth. The damage done by some insects which are destroyers of plant tissues or carriers of diseases is great, but the benefits we derive from others, which act as pollinators of plants and are one of the principal foods maintaining our bird and fish population, are incomparably more important.

There are more insects on this planet than any other kind of living creatures; so far some 625,000 species have been described and named; but while practically all mammals and birds living on earth are officially known to us, there may be from three to four hundred thousand species of insects that still have to be defined and classified. To the scientifically-minded this fact will be a definite challenge; there are still a great many contributions to be made to the science of entomology.

Illustration Number 41

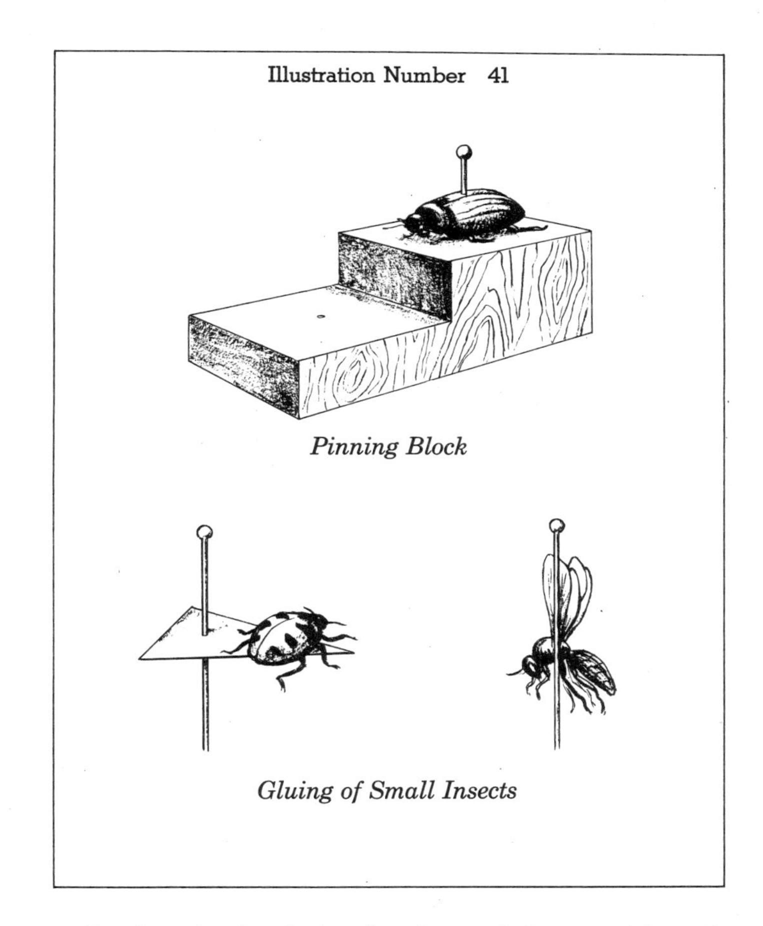

Pinning Block

Gluing of Small Insects

On the other hand, the abundance of the material available may have a somewhat deterring effect on the beginner. That should not be so, as he can proceed from the well-known to the less-known. He may start with the eye-catching insect families, as most insect collectors do, and begin to collect butterflies and moths. Their number is limited, relatively speaking; they are easily identified; and they make beautiful display specimens. Special interests or personal preferences may suggest a bee and wasp collection, or an ant collection. For a more diversified collection the geographical-local viewpoint will prove satisfactory: You collect the species of insects that occur in your flower garden, your orchard, your farm, your neighborhood.

Where to Find Insects — Everybody who has a little experience in nature hiking knows that the concentration of insects is greater in some spots than in others. Under logs and stones, under heaps of debris and rotting vegetable matter, in decaying wood (in stumps, logs, and beneath the bark), under the loose bark of living trees, and on all the various parts of plants insects tend to congregate. Beating bushes and smaller trees will produce fine results, particularly if a light cloth is spread under the plants to catch the harvest. However, such less conventional spots as the tissues of mushrooms, toadstools and other fungi, the droppings of animals, and the ground under the carcasses of animals will also yield a good crop of insects.

If water insects are to be captured and collected, the same objects and places are to be investigated on the shore

Illustration Number 42

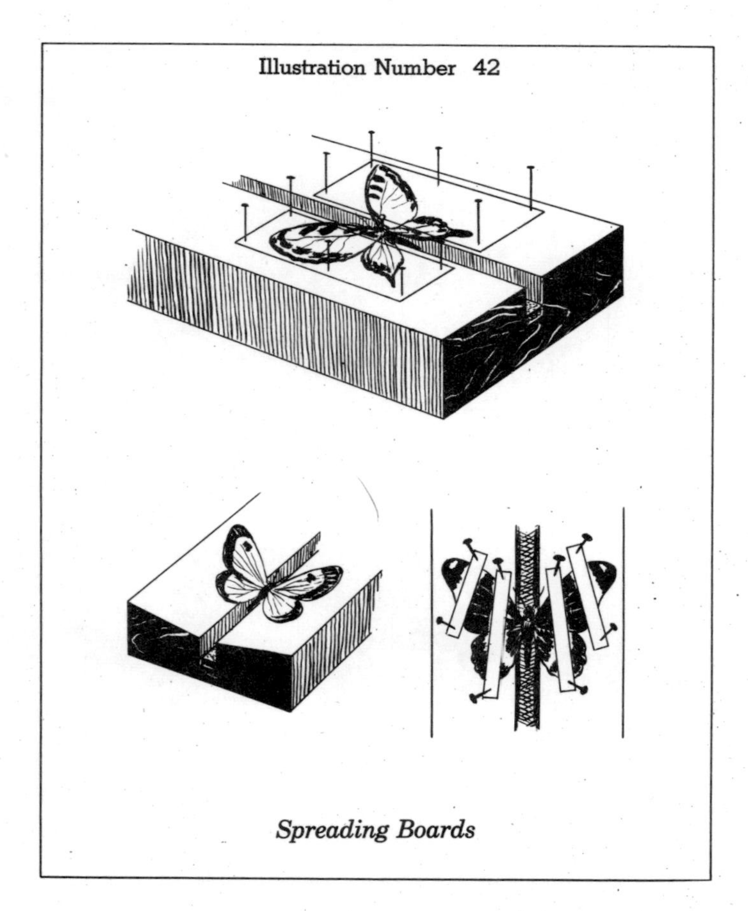

Spreading Boards

or in the water of a pond, a lake, a brook or a river. The bottom mud and the aquatic vegetation are good hunting grounds.

Experienced collectors advise to restrict each collecting excursion to one environment, i.e. to open fields, or woods, or swampland, etc., as the best means of getting familiar with the groups of insects that may be caught in certain types of surroundings.

Insects may also be caught by trapping; the following suggestions will be helpful.

For trapping moths: With a small brush apply a sugar solution to a tree trunk; various formulas are used for this purpose, but fermenting mixtures of molasses with rotting apples or with beer are considered most effective. The smell of the bait draws from the tree's neighborhood moths of different species, in the course of the night, and with the help of a flashlight the specimens may be picked from the bark. Urquhart recommends this method particularly for the trapping of the lovely red underwing moths.

An especially bright sign or light at a restaurant, motel or service station in a countryside of woodlands and pastures will also yield, at night, a collection of moths, together with many other insects which have been attracted by the light.

For trapping beetles: Bury an old tin can without top in the soil so that the upper edge just reaches the surface of the ground. Sprinkle some molasses on the bottom of the can. During the night the molasses will attract various species of beetles and other insects which crawl toward the source of the sweet smell, fall into the can, and are trapped. You may protect the can from rain by placing a small log or a stone on top of it, but slightly raised so that the access to the rim is free.

For trapping scavenger beetles: Take a metal sheet and cover it with soil. Place a small dead animal like a mouse, a baby rabbit or a bird on the sheet, and soon you will find under it scavenger beetles, some of which are very worthwhile specimens for an insect collection because of their beautiful color patterns.

How to Identify Insects — The most common insects are known quite generally. But as the number of species is enormous, it takes time to acquire a fair knowledge in this field. As an aid in studying and identifying insects the following books are recommended (those useful to the beginner are starred):

*Jordan, E. L., Hammond's Nature Atlas of America, the section on Insects, C. S. Hammond & Co., New York, 1952

Metcalf, C. L., and Flint, W. P., Fundamentals of Insect Life, McGraw-Hill Book Co., New York, 1932

*Swain, R. B., The Insect Guide, Doubleday & Co., New York, 1948

*Urquhart, F. A., Introducing the Insect, Henry Holt & Co., New York, 1949

Jaques, H. E., How to Know the Insects, Wm. C. Brown Co., Dubuque, Iowa, 1947

*Zim, H. S., and Cottam, C., Insects, a Guide to Familiar Insects, Simon & Schuster, New York, 1951

Howard, L. O., The Insect Book, Doubleday & Co., New York, 1937

Lutz, F. E., Field Book of Insects, G. P. Putnam's Sons, New York, 1930

*Klots, A. B., A Field Guide to Butterflies, Houghton Mifflin Co., New York, 1951

Macy, R. W., and Shepard, H. H., Butterflies, University of Minnesota Press, Minneapolis, 1941

Field Equipment for Collecting Insects — The few pieces of equipment needed for the collection of insects may either be bought from scientific supply houses or made at home at very little cost.

1) The Insect Net — Ready-made insect nets may be bought at prices ranging from about two dollars up. For the home-made type an old broomstick, a piece of strong wire (perhaps a coat hanger), a cord (or some tape) and the netting are the needed raw materials. The procedure is simple: Bend the wire into a loop, around a tree or telephone pole of approximately 14 inches in diameter; at the meeting point bend the ends of the wire at a right angle, away from the tree, and cut them to a length of about four inches, with a hacksaw. Carve two grooves into the end of the broomstick into which the wire ends will fit (see illustration No. 38); place the ends into the grooves and tie a cord or wrap some tape around the broomstick. If you want to make the loop detachable, fashion a metal sleeve which can be pushed over the grooves and back again.

Collecting Butterflies and Other Insects

For the net proper mosquito netting is frequently used, but experienced collectors are not too well impressed with the field performance of that material, particularly when it gets wet. It expands in places and develops holes through which insects may escape. A sturdier material which will not fray is marquisette, the netting of which most of our house curtains are manufactured, and the transformation into an insect net will give an outmoded living room curtain a useful old age.

For a 14-inch loop the net should be at least 30 inches long. A greater length is better as it affords more room for the captured insects after a turn of the hand closes the loop by overlapping. The net should have a broad bottom, not a point, for easier emptying. On top it should be sewed sturdily around the wire loop so that it will withstand rough treatment.

A kitchen sieve may be used to scoop water insects out of a brook or pond. For a greater operating radius it may be tied to a pole.

2) Killing Bottles — Killing jars and bottles may be purchased at scientific supply houses, at about 40 cents for a four-ounce size to 60 cents for a 32-ounce size. However, they can easily be made at home, using old olive or mayonnaise glass jars. Cork stoppers are preferable to metal lids. There are two systems in use, as shown in illustration No. 39, one employing carbon tetrachloride, the other cyanide.

In the former case soak a piece of cotton with carbon tetrachloride which may be obtained at a hardware store. Cover it with a circular piece of cardboard that fits quite tightly into the jar. Add another dry piece of cotton and another cardboard circle on top to keep the insects from touching the tetrachloride which may damage them.

If you prefer the other system, cover the bottom of the jar with about half a dozen small lumps of potassium cyanide or a layer of half an inch of sodium cyanide. Mix a thick liquid of water and plaster of Paris and pour it over the cyanide so as to cover it completely. Let it dry and harden. Cut a circular piece of cardboard to fit the bottle and place it on the plaster of Paris.

Cyanide is a poison and should be labeled as such. Take care in handling it and use a pair of forceps and other tools rather than your fingers.

Many collectors put some strips of paper into the jars; if several insects are dropped into the jar, the strips will keep the specimens from damaging each other.

The amateur-collector should take along on his field trips at least two killing bottles, one large and one small one. Some prefer three, reserving the biggest for moths and butterflies, the second for fragile types of insects like the Mayflies, and the third for beetles and other insects with hard bodies.

Professional collectors even go one step farther and provide two killing bottles for each type, i.e. they carry six bottles altogether. They place the specimen in the first killing jar and leave it there until it stops moving, which is in about three minutes. Then they transfer the insect, which does not flutter any longer but may not yet be entirely dead, to the second killing jar in which they leave it until they are back home; the second jar serves as a storage container. This method facilitates the handling of the butterflies, beetles, etc. in the field.

The process of transferring the insects from the net to the killing jar will have to be worked out individually, by experience. After several insects have been caught and sealed off by the turning of the handle of the net, some collectors insert the hand into the net, get hold of one insect, take it out and drop it into the killing bottle. Others prefer to insert an opened killing jar into the net with one hand and cautiously push the insect into the jar with the other hand, holding the insect in a fold of netting from the outside. As soon as the specimen is in the jar, they put the hand over the mouth of the jar, remove it from the net, and close it with the top. It is suggested to pinch the bodies of butterflies and moths with two fingers to stop their ruinous beating of wings.

3) A Collecting Bag — A bag of canvas or a haversack is needed to carry along the field equipment. Inside the bag, some straps should be so arranged as to hold the killing jars. Such secondary tools as a pocket knife, a pair of forceps, a small paint brush for picking up tiny insects, and a magnifying glass will be useful at times.

Home Equipment for Collecting Insects — Temporary Storage — If upon the return from the field trip some time elapses before the gathered specimens can be mounted, they

Illustration Number 43

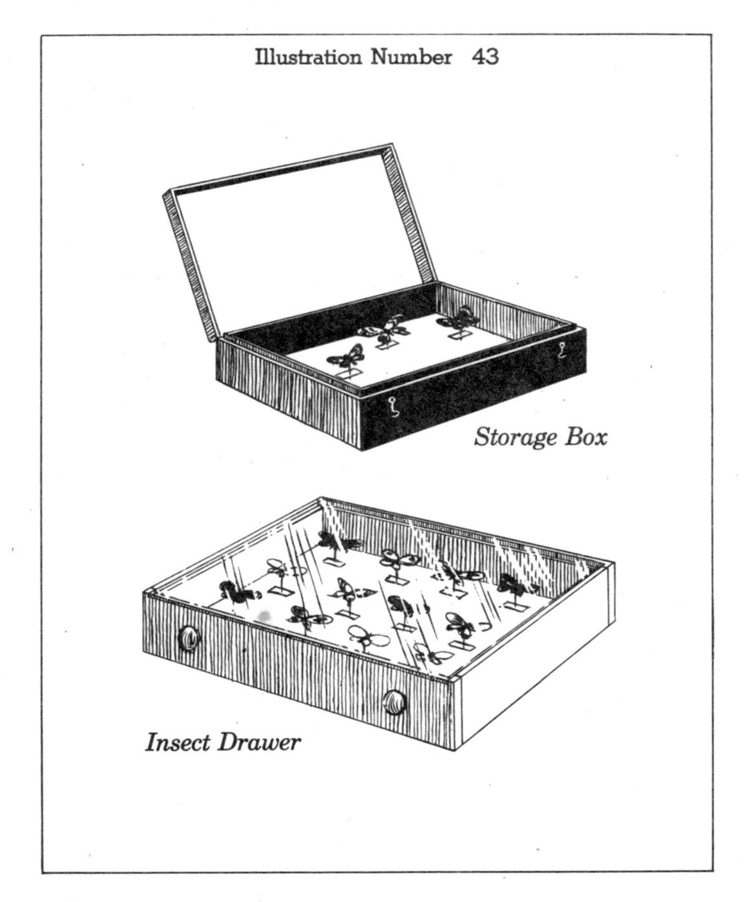

Storage Box

Insect Drawer

are kept in envelopes of paper or cellophane, particularly the moths and butterflies. Many collectors use an oblong piece of paper and fold it into a triangle over the body of the specimen.

MOUNTING — The so-called pinning is the established method of mounting insects so that they may be handled and studied without being touched. Special insect pins are used to impale the specimens, strong, non-rusting steel pins with very sharp points which may be purchased from the scientific supply houses. Ordinary household pins are not recommended, but fine needles may be used.

The question on which spot each type of insect should be pinned has been solved by a standard procedure which is in use very generally. Pictures on illustration No. 40 show how butterflies and moths are impaled in the center of the thorax but that most other specimens are pinned to the right of the middle; in that way the left half remains undamaged for identification and study.

Also impaled on the needle is the label which usually indicates the English and the scientific names of the insect, the place where found, the date when found, and the name of the finder.

In order to achieve uniformity in mounting — the specimen should be about one-third below the top of the needle, and the label on the level of the bottom of the box — a pinning block may be used. This is a small wooden block (see illustration No. 41) into which two holes are drilled, a deeper one for pushing the specimen, and another one less deep for placing the label into its exact position. In this way all specimens and all labels of the collection will be at uniform levels, which adds to an attractive appearance.

Illustration Number 44

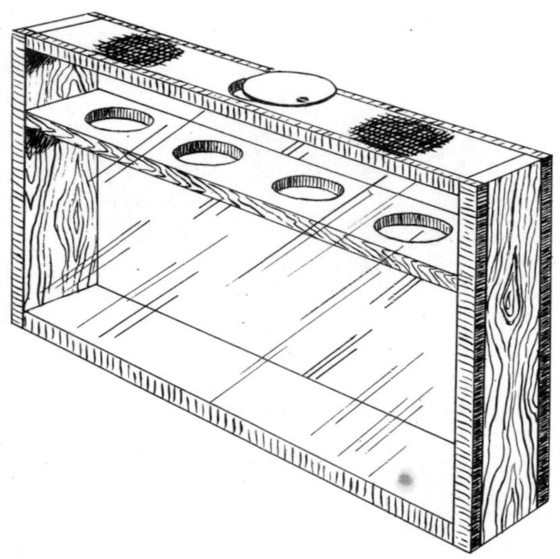

Ant House

A considerable number of species like mosquitoes and gnats are too tiny to be pinned. They are either glued to the pin, with a small drop of household cement, or glued to a cardboard triangle which in turn is impaled on the pin (see illustration No. 41).

Sometimes specimens get dry and brittle before they can be mounted. In such a case they have to be "relaxed," i.e. they are softened so that they won't be damaged when handled. Normally it is sufficient to place them in a tight box together with some wet blotting paper; in about 24 hours they should be in a sufficiently pliable condition. However, occasionally mold may form on the bodies of the specimens if this simple process is employed, and the professional collectors have a more elaborate method: To avoid the development of mold they use a weak solution of carbolic acid (one teaspoonful to a quart of water); a wad of cotton is soaked with it and placed in a box; a wire screen, supported by four wooden blocks, is mounted over the cotton; a piece of paper rests on the screen; the insect specimens are placed on the paper. Within 24 hours they will be ready for mounting.

TREATMENT OF MOTHS AND BUTTERFLIES — As the wings are the most beautiful and interesting parts of this group of insects — and of a few other species like the dragonflies—care has to be taken to mount and present the wings in their proper position. For that purpose a so-called spreading board is employed. Two popular types are shown in illustration No. 42, one which spreads the wings on a horizontal plain, the other at a slight angle. Such boards can be bought from biological supply houses or made at home from a few blocks of wood; most of the commercially sold boards are 14 inches long and vary in width from 2¾ to 8 inches; to the bottom of the groove into which the body of the butterfly is inserted, a strip of cork, beaverboard or corrugated cardboard is fastened. Into it the mounting pin of the insect is stuck while its wings are being "spread."

If the butterfly, in dying, has folded its wings under its body, which is a frequent occurrence, you can open the wings by taking hold of the body with a pair of tweezers and squeezing it gently at the base of the wings.

As the next step you place the butterfly on the spreading board and flatten its wings. This is done by a few strips of paper which are laid over the two left wings and the two right wings (see illustration No. 42). These paper strips are pinned to the wood of the block with ordinary pins which, however, do not perforate the wings of the butterfly. Now the wings have to be properly arranged so as to show their color and markings to the best advantage. An insect pin may be employed for this task, and by loosening one or the other regular pin holding a paper strip, a good display position can be achieved without damaging the wings. Only in especially stubborn cases should insect pins be used to pin the wings directly to the board.

Collecting Butterflies and Other Insects

After the wings have been laid out satisfactorily, a larger piece of paper may be placed over each side of the butterfly (see illustration) so as to cover the wings completely. These pieces of paper are secured by ordinary pins inserted into the wood around the edges of the wings. Instead of the paper, strips of glass of the same size may be employed. The specimen should remain on the spreading board for one to one and a half weeks. Then it will be ready for the collection.

General Storage — Until you own enough specimens to organize them systematically in various boxes according to orders and families, you will need one or several general storage boxes. Various kinds of wooden boxes may be used for the purpose; a bottom layer of cork or corrugated cardboard serves to hold the pins of the mounted specimens. It is advisable, however, to use only a box whose lid overlaps the sidewalls (see illustration No. 43); as to cigar boxes, only the most expensive brands will fulfill this condition. The complete tightness of the box is necessary because of the various species of tiny insects which live on the carcasses of other insects and which will find their way through the slightest cracks and openings. They can ruin an insect collection with surprising speed. While a sturdy, tight box will insure permanence, white surfaces inside (painted or papered, possibly with glazed white paper), will help to make the mounted insect specimens stand out clearly and attractively.

Permanent Storage — For a definite collection, glass-topped drawers kept in a frame or a cabinet are standard equipment. Such pest-proof drawers may be bought from the scientific supply houses at various prices; the more expensive ones are provided with brass hardware, are lacquered and expertly finished, and furnish the fitting background for a collection of spectacular butterflies and moths. But home-made drawers can also be built to look very attractive and serve their purpose effectively. They may be fitted into a simple or more elaborate cabinet-frame of boards, the drawers sliding on angle irons or wooden runners (see illustration of drawers in chapter on Collecting Rocks).

As in the general storage box, a "pinning bottom" of semi-soft material will hold the specimen pins. The wooden drawers should be tight, and the simplest way of attaching the glass panes is to fit them into the margin of the outer boards which are recessed on top, as shown in illustration No. 43.

Both in the storage boxes and in the glass-covered drawers it will sometimes be advisable to use pest repellants. For that purpose napthalene flakes are normally used.

Supplementing Your Collection — To obtain specimens that are not available in your neighborhood, you may trade with collectors in other parts of the country or purchase specimens from scientific supply houses like Ward's Natural Science Establishment in Rochester, N. Y. Among the insects sold commercially, exotic specimens of unusual size or beauty are most in demand. For an Atlas moth — the world's largest — with nine inches wingspread the price is about seven dollars, although specimens with smaller wingspreads can be bought for less than half that price. The Atlas moths are imported from the islands of southeastern Asia. For the Brazilian Morpho butterfly (Morpho aega), famous for its iridescent blue, a current price of $1.50 is quoted. Goliath beetles from Central Africa, giant grasshoppers from Peru, ten-inch "walking sticks" from New Guinea — the number and variety of specimens available is legion. If you state your special fields of interest, the supply houses will be glad to furnish specimen lists with prices.

Illustration Number 45

Collecting Living Insects — The Insect Cage — Some insects make amusing pets although, of course, they are quite short-lived in comparison with other pets. Any large glass jar covered with cheese cloth or mosquito netting may serve as an insect cage; the bottom should be covered with top soil, and a small bowl of water should be provided. Whether you place a few plants into the soil will depend on the kind of insects you plan to keep; if they are meat eaters, like the praying mantis, plants will make the cage attractive; if your pets are leaf eaters, plants would not last long. Among the various insects that may be kept in such a terrarium, crickets are especially interesting. A few of them may be collected in almost any pasture with tall grass, particularly under rocks, logs, or other debris. In the cage they may be fed green leaves, and occasionally a small drop of corn meal in water will be welcome. Their daily routine

Illustration Number 46

of feeding and living, including a little music now and then, is amusing to observe.

A praying mantis may become a pet even without a cage. The best time to catch an adult specimen, with an insect net, is August, and if it is fed regularly and has the run of the house, it will stay and join the household. Small insects are its preferred food, and if you offer it a fly or mosquito with your fingers, the praying mantis will seize the morsel with its front legs and then bite off the creature's head, the wings, and finally munch the body.

If no insects are available, as from the late fall on, small pieces of raw meat offered on a tooth pick will be accepted eagerly. The mantis will eat only a little at any time, but several times a day. A dish of water should be available at a definite place where the mantis can find it easily. An especially amusing gesture of this pet is its habit of "washing its face" after a meal is devoured.

Outside, the praying mantisses die, like so many other insects, when the cold season begins. Inside a building they may live until the second half of December.

THE ANT HOUSE — A home-made ant house is a fascinating device to observe the living habits of an ant colony. The following plan for an ant house is adapted from a design suggested by Ted Pettit, the author of various books on nature activities.

Make a wooden frame, as shown on illustration No. 44, about twelve inches long, six inches high, and two inches wide. Drill three holes with a diameter of one inch in the top board. Cover two holes with fine wire mesh, for the purpose of ventilation. The third hole is the gate through which the ants are fed; it has to be provided with a "door," i.e. it is covered with a circle of tin or any other soft metal which is fastened to the board with a tack; revolving around the tack, it opens or closes the hole.

Take a board that fits into the frame and drill four one-inch holes, as shown in the sketch. Nail this board into the frame, two inches below the top.

Fasten a piece of window glass 12 x 6 inches to one side of the frame by means of one-inch adhesive tape. Fill the lower part of the frame with good dirt, preferably topsoil, so that it is full up to the board with the four holes. Attach another pane of glass 12 x 6 inches to the other side in the same fashion.

From an ant hill in an orchard, field or forest dig up some ants together with a shovelful of dirt and put them in a paper bag. Most of them will be workers; if you can find an unusually large one, take it by all means; for it is probably a queen. If you can see some pupae which look like eggs, take them along. At home open the bag and with a pair of tweezers seize one ant after another by a leg and drop them into the ant house until there are twenty to thirty inside.

The best food to be dropped through the opening on top is a solution of sugar and water. Any sweets, from lump sugar to cake crumbs, will be welcome.

There are, of course, any number of similar ways in which an ant house may be built, in accordance with the collector's own ideas, plans and designs. Helpful suggestions on various constructions will also be found in William Hillcourt's "Field Book of Nature Activities" (New York, 1950). The matter of size will have to be decided individually. In every case, however, the watching of the new ant community and its daily life will be a unique experience.

COLLECTING CATERPILLARS AND COCOONS — To observe the metamorphosis of insects, particularly the transformation of a weird-looking caterpillar into an inconspicuous pupa or cocoon, and then into a beautiful butterfly or moth, has always intrigued and delighted human imagination. To watch the process at home, a caterpillar may be kept in any box covered with mosquito netting; it has to be fed with the leaves of its host plant, i.e. normally the plant on which it was found. A branch should be added, as the support to which the cocoon will adhere.

After the caterpillar has changed into a cocoon, no further feeding will be necessary. The pupa-cocoon may be hung on a spot where it can be observed, either outdoors or indoors. In combination windows the space between the screen and the glass pane is a good spot.

Many insect collectors begin the project at the point of the pupa. As many insects hibernate in the cocoon stage, it is not difficult to find various cocoons or pupae in the woods, particularly along brooks on trees which, like oaks, hold on to their old, dead leaves. In nature's mimicry, cocoons attached to the branches often look like such dead old leaves. It is also possible to buy cocoons from the scientific supply houses, for instance Ward's. A cocoon price list will be sent upon request.

If left outside, the cocoon will develop into a moth or butterfly as it would in nature. Inside, in the warmth of the house, the process will be speeded up and the adult insect will emerge more quickly. If it is to be used as a specimen in a butterfly collection, the premature birth does not matter as the newcomer will be killed shortly after its emergence.

Nobody has described the miracle of the metamorphosis as well as America's greatest nature writer, our own Henry David Thoreau. In his journal he describes, under the date of June 2, 1855, the change from pupa to adult of one of the so-called emperor moths, in his home in Concord, Massachusetts:

"From that cocoon of the Attacus cecropia which I found — I think it was on the 24th of May — on a red maple shrub, three or four feet from the ground, on the edge of the meadow by the new Bedford road just this side of Beck Stow's, came out this forenoon a splendid moth. I had pinned the cocoon to the sash at the upper part of my window and quite forgotten it.

About the middle of the forenoon Sophia came in and exclaimed that there was a moth on my window. At first I supposed that she meant a cloth-eating moth, but it turned out that my Attacus cecropia had come out and dropped down to the window-sill, where it hung on the side of a slipper (which was inserted into another) to let its wings down and develop themselves.

At first the wings were not only not unfolded laterally, but not longitudinally, the thinner ends of the forward ones for perhaps three-quarters of an inch being very feeble and occupying very little space. It was surprising to see the creature unfold and expand before our eyes, the wings gradually elongating, as (if) it were by their own gravity; and from time to time the insect assisted this operation by a slight shake. It was wonderful how it waxed and grew, revealing every fifteen minutes, which I called Sophia to see, but never losing its hold on the shoe. It looked like a young emperor just donning the most splendid ermine robes that ever (an) emperor wore, the wings every moment acquiring greater expansion and their at first wrinkled edge becoming more tense.

At first its wings appeared double, one within the other. At last it advanced so far as to spread its wings completely but feebly when we approached. This occupied several hours. It continued to hang to the shoe, with its wings ordinarily closed erect behind its back, the rest of the day; and at dusk, when apparently it was waving its wings preparatory to its evening flight, I gave it ether and so saved it in a perfect state."

NATURE AND WILDLIFE PHOTOGRAPHY

Hunters and Photographers — Hundreds of thousands of Americans like to hike out into the fields and woods to "shoot" — not with a gun but with a camera. They make no sentimental comparisons between the hunters' killing of the deer and their own picture-taking which records the beauty and grace of the deer. They have no hard feelings toward hunting which is a fine, ancient sport and very necessary in modern wildlife management. The wildlife population has to be kept at an optimum balance just as the trees of the forest have to be thinned out.

Wildlife photographers have chosen their hobby not because they are against hunting and fishing but for other, constructive reasons. They are nature lovers and individualists who cannot be bothered with buying licenses and studying the game laws of every state in the Union and every province of Canada. They know nothing of restricted seasons but go out into the woods whenever they please. Hunters "jacking" with a flashlight will be thrown into jail; photographers "jacking" with a flashlight will not be molested. And while nothing is left of the hunters' and fishermen's exploits after the trout and venison have been eaten, the photographer's wildlife prints and slides will last as long as he lives.

There is another challenge: It is more difficult to photograph a water lily than to pick it; it requires more skill and thought to take a picture of a wild duck than to take its life. Besides, the same bird can be portrayed more than once; in fact, its whole life history can be recorded photographically, from the egg to the adult. The same is true of other living creatures, and wildlife photographers have

Illustration Number 47

often made valuable contributions to the study of nature's "sociology."

Viewpoints for Nature Photography — SCENIC PHOTOS — Our first nature pictures are frequently of the scenic type; we shoot a craggy mountain peak that impresses us or a peaceful green valley that enchants us. These are nature photographs in the best sense of the word, and as the physical geography of North America is fantastically varied, we are able to present to our camera practically every landform that exists on earth. In order to get a picture of a typical desert we do not have to travel to the Sahara; the great sand dunes of Colorado are just as genuine. The fjords of Norway are famous, but those of Alaska are wilder, and even some of the rocky inlets of the Maine coast are a good facsimile. High mountains? Purely as a phenomenon of nature, the Rockies and the Sierras are more beautiful than the Alps. The typical tropics? Try the palm-studded white beaches of Florida. The Mediterranean landscape? Southern California will give you an excellent idea of its nature.

There is, however, a serious flaw to be considered. Although these gems of nature are all to be seen and photographed within our own borders, few Americans or Canadians can travel extensively enough to make use of their photogenic country for their photographic hobby. And unless they are very skillful and experienced, they will discover that panoramic views are difficult to take, and that the prints and color slides sold commercially are often superior to the products of their own labor. Usually it is at this point that they turn from the sweeping views to smaller objects of more specific interest, like blossoms or animals.

Illustration Number 48

JUST NATURE—Among the thousands who practice nature photography as a hobby, the majority are not scientifically minded. They do not care whether they make a contribution to ornithology or entomology, conchology or ichthyology. They take nature pictures because the topics that offer themselves are handsome or graceful, interesting or curious, unusual or startling. If they specialize, they hardly do so in the selection of subjects but on the quality level, eliminating the obvious and the commonplace. Composition, balance, proper distribution of lights and shadows, background; framing of the main object with branches, leaves, cliffs, or in other ways; emphasis on contrasts; moods of the season or of the day — these are all factors of prime importance to the nature photographers in the general group.

NATURE — A RESTRICTED AREA — Some wildlife photographers limit their activities to a restricted area, perhaps the acres adjoining their orchard. This method of specialization was mentioned also in connection with the rock collector, the amateur-botanist, the bird-watcher, and others. But in the case at hand the purpose of the geographical restriction is not to make a complete survey or to take a census, but to get thoroughly acquainted with the terrain and its wildlife. For the casual observer does not notice even a fraction of the goings and comings in nature, of the teeming microcosm of life. On the other hand, a patient and recurrent inspection of the same territory, at various times of the day and of the year, will reveal an unsuspected wealth both of nature information and of material for nature photography.

Taking a walk through the well-familiar haunts in December, for instance, the observer will be surprised to see how many cup-shaped little nests of vireos cling to the bare branches of the thickets along the road. He knew nothing of their existence and will make a mental note for certain vireo pictures next spring. Or he may be well aware of the bird, insect, and amphibian life in his preserve but be sure that few mammals live in his domain. Then, on a January morning after a light snowfall, he walks over his terrain and sees that it is actually criss-crossed by animal tracks. There may even be proof of the visits of a fox or a muskrat, and plans for some flashlight pictures of these guests may be laid.

A large-scale map of the territory may be one result of such a specialization, a map indicating every boulder and stone wall, bush and thicket, creek and water hole, with annotations that some day may be useful in local wildlife photography.

BY SEASONS — A specialization "by seasons" does not mean that there are nature photographers who take pictures only in spring, or in the fall. But they arrange their albums of prints or their slide collections in such a fashion. "Spring in Texas" when the bluebonnets are in their glory and the prairie is in bloom, or "Spring in the South" when the azalea gardens from Chesapeake Bay to Louisiana are glowing patches of color, or "Fall in New England" when oaks and maples turn their foliage into masses of red, orange, and yellow, are most attractive topics which can be enlarged and improved from year to year.

By Groups — From Rocks to Insects — Although nobody has ever collected any statistics on this subject, it is certain that most of the nature photographers who specialize at all, do so in the field of birds, with the flower enthusiasts forming the second-largest group. Others have worked out especially interesting techniques for animal photography which may involve trapping or automatic release devices. Amateur geologists, dendrologists and entomologists may specialize in taking pictures of rocks, of trees and of insects, supplementary to their rock, wood, and insect-collecting hobbies.

Life Histories: From Bud to Seed, from Egg to Butterfly — This viewpoint has more serious, scientific aspects. To take pictures of the same tree showing successively the buds, the blossoms, the fruits, the seeds; to present the development of life from the egg to the caterpillar to the pupa to the butterfly; or to follow bird family life from the arrival of the adults to the mating, the building of the nest, the brooding of the eggs, and the care of the fledglings, are topics that transcend the merely picturesque. Particularly the last-mentioned sequence skirts the field of animal "sociology" (see also the chapter on Bird Hobbies).

Specialties: Rare Flowers, Odd Trees, Clouds — The photographing of highly individualistic specialties has an intriguing angle: In most cases the specialist is extremely well informed about his hobby. The photographer who has built up a collection of color slides on the wild orchids of temperate North America is probably able to talk most interestingly about this plant family; the nature lover who for a number of years has photographed odd trees, will know the species that become twisted and gnarled; he will have discovered the relationship between climatic and geographic conditions on one hand (the timber line on mountains, the arctic tree line, etc.) and unusual tree growth on the other. In pursuing his hobby he will probably have learned a good deal of amusing local tree and timber lore. The cloud specialist who is building up a collection of prints or slides on cloud formations, will not only be well informed about the various types of clouds — the feathery white cirrus clouds, the towering masses of cumulus clouds, the even layer of stratus clouds and their innumerable subdivisions and combinations — but also about the effect of the camera equipment — lens, filter, type of film, etc. — on the outcome of cloud, sunrise, sunset, and simliar pictures. Probably he has also made some spectacular photographs of lightning which are quite easily taken at night, with the camera turned toward the storm cloud and the shutter left open to record the flash. Sheet lightning will not produce an image, but forked lightning will do so.

Technical — Photography is not only an amateur's hobby but also a branch of the sciences of physics and chemistry, and many scientifically-minded nature lovers are attracted by the technical aspects of nature photography.

Illustration Number 49

There is, for instance, the use of motion pictures as a medium of recording the processes of nature, the problem of close-up photography with the help of various portrait lenses and other attachments, and the technique of microphotography, i.e. the photographing of prepared specimen slides under a microscope on top of which a ground-glass-back camera is mounted, on a wooden stand. An outside source of light is reflected in the swinging mirror of the microscope. This taking of enormously magnified pictures is an intriguing specialty in which quite a few amateurs have become proficient.

Photographers with an interest in chemistry will develop their films and make their own prints at home in an improvised dark room.

Field Equipment — Selection of Cameras — The great difficulty in advising on the selection of a camera is the rapid technical progress made by the optical industry. New and improved camera models appear on the market frequently, and it will be wise for the prospective nature photographer to discuss this matter with friends who have some recent experience in the use of cameras, and with a reputable camera dealer. Prices range from a few dollars to five or six hundred; obviously it will be wise to begin with simple equipment and to switch to a more effective and more expensive camera as the photographer acquires a reassuring familiarity with all the optical and pictorial details involved. The more costly camera is generally more complicated and requires greater skill in handling; therefore

Illustration Number 59

beginners would often not get the full benefit out of such a precision instrument while they would enjoy it greatly and use it to full advantage at a more advanced stage of their hobby.

Because wear and tear in a camera is negligible, real bargains are often available in the second hand camera market. However, used cameras should be purchased only from reputable dealers who will guarantee the instrument for a reasonable period. Cameras that show evidence of damage, repairs, and alterations should be strictly avoided.

THE STILL CAMERA — Fine nature pictures can be taken with "brownies" and simple folding cameras of the traditional type (see illustration No. 59). They are all-round cameras serving every purpose, and with special equipment such as portrait lenses, filters and photo-flash bulbs may be adapted to many specialized functions. However, the more ambitious nature and wildlife photographer will wish to own a camera that is especially constructed to accomplish the tasks he has in mind.

In the literature available on this subject numerous cameras are described which today are outmoded. Therefore we shall limit our discussion to a few basic types which at this time are considered the answer to the wildlife photographer's requirements. They are on the market at sensible prices well within the range of most prospects, although a prosperous camera fancier may spend hundreds of dollars if he wishes to do so.

THE MINIATURE OR 35 MILLIMETER CAMERA — This type of camera (see illustration No. 59) has become popular over the entire world. Its lightness and compactness make it easily portable, and it has lens and shutter combinations that will handle a wide range of photographic problems. Cameras of this size are available to fit every purse; the more expensive, precision-built models are equipped with additional refinements such as a greater number of shutter speeds, a coupled range finder for exact focusing, and interchangeable lenses. In addition, various types of accessories including wide angle, high speed or telephoto lenses, reflex view finders and many other items may be purchased to adapt these cameras to particular kinds of work. The 35 millimeter perforated black and white or color film is available in rolls of 20 or 36 exposures.

While this camera will produce prints or slides, it is particularly well adapted to the making of color slides which are, at present, a most widely accepted form of photographic reproduction. To see their nature pictures in brilliant hues and greatly enlarged, thrown on a screen by a projector, is considered by many the most satisfactory climax of their hobby. To show to a group of friends not only travel views but also series of slides of flowers, birds, animals, insects, and wildlife in general has almost become a national pastime, and a most pleasant, constructive and stimulating one at that. A good choice of projectors for the home or the lecture hall is available in every price bracket.

THE REFLEX CAMERA — This is the camera (see illustration No. 59) of the professional nature photographer or of the amateur who has arrived at the advanced stages of his hobby. It may be purchased with double-extension bellows which have a telephoto effect. It derives its name from its reflex device; by means of a diagonal mirror the full-sized reflected image of the picture to be taken is viewed on a ground glass panel mounted on top of the camera case. A hood, released by pressing a button, provides a dark channel at the end of which the reflected image stands out brightly. While a popular negative size is 4 by 5 inches, reflex cameras are available from the 35 millimeter type to models with a 5 by 7 inch negative.

The outstanding advantage of this camera is its precise preview of the picture to be taken. Looking at the groundglass panel, you can adjust rapidly and exactly right up to the time of exposure 1) the most desirable size of the object to be photographed; 2) the sharpness of focus; and 3) the general composition of the picture including the interplay of lights and shadows, interesting contrasts and angles, and similar factors. When you release the shutter you have produced a correctly focused, carefully adjusted, and well composed photograph.

Most reflex cameras accommodate interchangeable lenses and also permit a wide choice of negative material in black and white and in color. While the transparencies of the 35 millimeter cameras are usually too small for publication in magazines and books, those of the larger reflex cameras are highly suitable for that purpose.

Many of the best wildlife shots in existence have been

taken by reflex cameras; the focused preview of each picture eliminates numerous defects and errors beforehand and gives its owner a certain sense of mastery. On a summery meadow where butterflies leisurely float between the blossoms, you may actually "stalk your prey" with a reflex camera, and watching the ground-glass panel through the hood you may take a number of completely natural butterfly shots — a refreshing change from the numerous "posed" butterfly pictures (see also the chapter on Shooting Insects). If an old abandoned orchard has an unusually large songbird population, you may, during the nesting season, even "stalk" the birds in the same fashion.

On the other hand, reflex cameras are expensive, heavy, and unwieldy, and the debate as to the relative merits of the reflex type and the miniature type continues. Some experienced nature photographers contend that they supplement each other excellently, and therefore both should be owned.

THE TWIN-LENS REFLEX CAMERA — This is a popular and efficient camera (see illustration No. 59) with two lenses equal in focal length and field of vision; one lens is set, in the camera, above the other. The upper lens which is used for viewing, catches the picture and throws it on a diagonal mirror which in turn reflects it onto a panel of ground glass on top of the camera. As in the case of the reflex camera, a hood provides a dark channel, and you see the image of the picture you are about to take. The lower lens is the so-called "taking lens." While a fine all-round camera, the twin-lens reflex is, on the whole, better suited for landscape and portrait work than for close-up nature photography.

THE VIEW CAMERA — This is the old stand-by: a folding camera with a ground glass panel on the back. The panel shows the inverted picture; after focusing, the panel is removed and a plate or a pack of cut film or roll film is inserted and the exposure is made. It is the professional choice for photographing still objects and, with some practice, of moving objects, although for the latter purpose the reflex camera offers advantages.

The view camera is usually equipped with interchangeable lenses and with a double-extension bellows which permits extreme close-up work; it is equally well suited for black and white or color work. It is available in various sizes, from 2½ by 3¼ inch models to large professional instruments.

PHOTO-FLASH EQUIPMENT — The present trend favors the shooting of nature and wildlife pictures at a close range with photo-flash equipment, even during the day and while the sun is shining. Not only will the quality of your wildlife pictures be uniform if you do so, but as a small lens opening may be used, the photos will have depth and warmth. Interestingly, the birds and other wild creatures do not seem to mind the flash.

The flash is so intense that the surrounding sunlight plays only a small part in exposing the film; therefore the film should be chosen correspondingly. Instructions as to shutter speed, lens opening, and distance of lamp to object are enclosed with the film. New, strong batteries are essential for perfect synchronization. Today many cameras have a built-in synchronizer which synchronizes the flash and the opening of the shutter — a feature most desirable for nature work.

CLOSE-UP LENSES — Regular cameras usually focus down to a range of approximately four feet. For close-up wildlife pictures you will have to employ supplementary lenses which are not expensive and can be attached easily. Kodak, for instance, offers the so-called Portra Lenses 1+ (for taking pictures at 20 to 30 inches), 2+ (for distances of 13 to 20 inches), and 3+ (for distances of 10 to 13 inches). Other manufacturers sell similar equipment. A table of lens data for pictures of birds and other small creatures may be found on page 9 of the pamphlet "How to Take Bird Pictures," and a table for pictures of flowers and similar nature objects may be found in the pamphlet "Flower Pictures in Color"; both are issued by the Eastman-Kodak Co. of Rochester, New York, and may be obtained free of charge.

Both pamphlets also give advice on another problem, the so-called problem of parallax: In close-range photography the picture shown in the view-finder no longer corresponds to the actual picture to be taken. As much as the upper quarter of the view-finder image may not appear on the photograph at all, and to compensate for this you will have to give your camera a little upward tilt. For an exact solution of this difficulty the aforementioned circulars should be consulted.

As was emphasized before, the parallax occurs only in

Illustration Number 51

connection with close-range pictures. For regular photography your view-finder will work very satisfactorily.

Tripod and Light Meter — The human hand is not steady enough for an exposure of more than one-fiftieth of a second, but a tripod is; as wildlife is photographed at various angles, a tilting top is recommended for the tripod.

In nature photography light conditions are often unusual; therefore the use of an exposure meter is suggested.

Release of Shutter — Since birds and other animals do not cherish the presence of man, some way of tripping the camera's shutter from a distance must be devised. The simplest way of doing so is to use a string which pulls the shutter release. A fishing line will be most effective because of its smoothness; other useful hints are: Run the line so that friction from obstructions is avoided; run it on a reel; keep the line taut for immediate reaction; don't pull so hard that the tripod topples over or the shutter is damaged.

Electrical tripping gadgets which function instantaneously upon the pressing of a button may be obtained at camera supply stores.

Motion Picture Cameras — Close-ups which are of prime importance in nature and wildlife photography, are often obtained with still cameras by taking a small, sharp picture and having it enlarged. That technique is not possible with motion picture cameras.

Most 8 or 16 millimeter home movie cameras are equipped with a fixed lens of standard focal length which is satisfactory for all regular pictures taken by the camera; if a larger

Illustration Number 52

image of the object to be photographed is desired, the camera has to be moved closer to the object. For extreme close-ups Portra Lenses or their equivalent may be employed. You have to keep in mind, however, that a movie camera cannot normally be camouflaged, like a still camera, near the photographic object, and operated by long-distance release; the camera and the cameraman are inseparable.

Other motion picture cameras may have an interchangeable lens system; the standard lens may be removed and other lenses may be attached; or they may be equipped with a so-called turret device which holds two or three lenses in a turret in front of the camera. Any of the lenses on the turret may be turned into position as required, using the optimum combination for each specific situation. With this equipment fairly large images are obtained even if the camera operates at distances of 30 or 40 feet.

To those interested in this type of nature photography the pamphlet "The Selection and Use of Cine-Kodak Lenses" is recommended; it contains detailed instructions and tables about the proper use of wide-angle lenses, extension tubes, and the filming of small objects.

For bird-movie enthusiasts the study of the previously mentioned pamphlet "How to Take Bird Pictures," pages 12 to 15, is suggested; besides the essential general information it contains practical hints about taking pictures of birds in flight, the use of the automobile as a blind, and similar advice.

"Shooting" Rocks — Photographs of rock formations, rock structure and rock texture are excellent supplements to a rock collection, and therefore of special interest to amateur geologists. A scenic photograph kept in an index-catalog of a rock collection with reference to a definite specimen may show the broad landscape from which the rock specimen was taken (see illustration No. 45), or it may present a smaller segment that shows the actual surface of the boulder or cliff (see illustration No. 46). In connection with illustration No. 45 the question may be asked whether the presence of human figures is desirable on a nature photograph of this type. The answer is yes; for they indicate the scale that should be applied to the scene.

The essential aspects of rock photographs are, by and large, the following:

1) Typical Rock Exposures — These are exposures of sandstone, granite, limestone, marble, trap rock, slate, or other important rocks which are quarried for building or industrial purposes. Quarries where such pictures may be taken are numerous but by necessity limited to the mountainous regions of the continent.

2) Structural Features — These photographs show rock strata which in the process of mountain building, millions of years ago, have been squeezed, folded, and twisted; the so-called "faults" belong to this group, i.e. breaks occurring in a "growing" mountain where under tremendous pressure one side of the break has slipped beyond the other, for as little as an inch or as much as several feet.

3) Glacial Drift and Erosion — Pictures of grooves

(so-called striae) that were scratched into the bedrock by sharp rocks frozen into the bottom of a moving glacier, record an interesting ice-age phenomenon; they indicate the direction in which the receding ice cover moved. The southern terminus of the glacial sheet is indicated today by the glacial till, a mass of sand, clay and boulders, the latter sometimes with one or two facets ground on their sides.

Also the process of erosion may be photographed in various ways at numerous points, the most magnificent example being the Grand Canyon of the Colorado.

4) SPECTACULAR STONES AND MINERALS — Many specimens have such striking colors and patterns that they are natural objects for color photography, as for instance quartz crystals whose shades range from white to dark amethyst; green, yellow, pink, white or bluish beryl; tourmalines in various hues of pink, black, or green; red garnets embedded in a light grey rock; the beautiful surface of banded agate.

"Shooting" Trees — The individuality of trees will become apparent only when single trees or small groves are photographed. The best time of the day for taking such pictures is the late afternoon. As every nature lover knows, a small group of trees will seemingly glow on their western exposure, in the rays of the sinking sun, and throw deep, long, and often dramatic shadows toward the east. Trees on the shore of a lake, their life-size image reflected in the still water, are magnificent photo-objects (see illustration No. 47).

Tree photography is largely a seasonal enterprise:

1) SPRING — Trees in bloom, from fruit trees and dogwoods to horse chestnuts and magnolias, to tulip trees and hawthorns, are among the most splendid and photogenic creations of nature. They have an air of perfection, at this time of the year when insect pests and fungus diseases have not yet launched their annual attack.

2) FALL — Autumnal hillsides of bright-yellow aspens and birches, scarlet and orange maples, red and brown oaks, saffron-tinted hickories and deep-green pines and spruces are a challenge to the color film. Black and white photography is frankly useless here, although a few artists have occasionally managed to capture the mood without colors.

Wild fruits, berries, and nuts, in their natural setting or arranged at home, make attractive and often artistic still-life prints or slides. The cones of evergreens are also picturesque objects growing in a great variety of size and form. Some are tiny knobs like those of the tamarack, while the cones of the white pine and the ponderosa pine may attain a length of six inches. On the other hand, the huge redwoods on the West Coast have cones only one inch long. Balsam cones stand upright like little candles, pine cones hang down like bells.

3) WINTER — This is the season to picture the typical shapes of trees. Free of the concealing cover of leaves, the elm reveals its fountain shape — a row of them will form a series of magnificent Gothic arches — the poplar its cylindrical form, the maple its oval skeleton. Set against the clear winter sky, the branches often make a striking and beautiful design (see illustration No. 48).

Illustration Number 53

Bark photographs are botanically important, and the field books on trees offer them as outstanding marks of identification. Bark is most accurately photographed in wintertime, as the lights and shadows caused by the leaves during the summer, may change the surface pattern on the picture.

Among the most popular tree pictures are those taken after a sleet storm when the freezing rain has coated branches and twigs with translucent ice so that they look as if made of shiny crystal. Another wintery tree topic irresistible to nature lovers is a group of evergreens heavily loaded with snow; fluffy, dry, cold-weather snow is not ideal for this purpose; but an early March storm will bring the heavy, wet kind of snow that clings to the tree limbs and drapes them in a most decorative fashion.

4) SEMI-TROPICAL TREES — In the southernmost parts of the United States the several dozen varieties of palm trees are most photogenic. Also the semi-tropical tree crowns covered with bright, spectacular blossoms are a specialty of the warm weather belt. The usually very clear atmosphere of the Deep South, the South West and the southern West Coast makes all colors appear doubly bright and creates ideal conditions for color photography.

"Shooting" Flowers — THE RIGHT FOCUS — If you are about to photograph a Maine meadow studded with blooming daisies and orange hawkweed, or an Arizona desert patch with blossoming cactus plants, or a rose garden in Oregon, no special instructions or equipment are necessary. But if you wish to take a close-up picture of a large blossom

Illustration Number 54

or a single small plant you will have to attach a close-up lens to your camera. A 2+ Portra Lens, for instance, will get a clear picture at 20 inches, a 3+ lens at 13 inches, a combination of a 2+ and a 3+ lens at 8 inches.

At such a narrow range, correct focusing is all-important. If, for instance, you use a 3+ lens — the camera focus should be at infinity — you must actually measure a distance of 13 inches with a ruler. One handy shortcut is a string tied to the Portra Lens, with a knot exactly 13 inches from the rim of the lens. Hold the string in a straight line so that the knot touches the front of the nearest flower (see illustration No. 60).

For pictures of flowers and other small objects at a close range, a so-called focal frame is often used. It may be obtained through a photo supply store or it may be made at home. For the camera it provides automatically the right focus, the proper distance, and the exact size and shape of the image that will appear on the photograph.

The focal frame is a simple but effective instrument. The camera, equipped with a 3+ lens, is secured on a wooden board as on a tripod. From the board two strong wires extend ahead for 13 inches, and then form a frame comprising the exact view "seen" by the camera. Any flower, plant, butterfly, etc. placed within the frame will be correctly focused and will be within the scope of the picture (see illustration No. 61). If you wish to make a focal frame at home, instructions can be found in the previously mentioned pamphlet "Flower Pictures in Color."

THE PROPER EXPOSURE — If the photograph is to be taken in sunlight, use the regular exposures recommended for your camera. If the flower is in the shade, the photo-flash process is the proper technique. However, numerous nature photographers today use their photo-flash equipment also in direct sunlight, with fine results, for a good reason: A wildflower in the field is almost constantly in a swaying motion, which makes a time exposure difficult but does not interfere with the photo-flash process.

If a time exposure is contemplated, the early morning is the most appropriate period of the day, because of occasional lulls in the wind. The dew should be shaken off, because a part of the blossom, weighted down by a dew drop, may recoil during the exposure. On the other hand, a photo-flash picture taken in the morning may well record some clear dew drops on the flower as an artistic touch. The "dew drops," by the way, can also be provided by an atomizer.

THE UNIFORM BACKGROUND — Wherever the wildflower stands, its background is apt to be indistinct, confused, and unfavorable for a sharply centered photograph. In that case a piece of cardboard may be set up as a background, preferably in a plain pastel shade. Some nature photographers prefer two cards, a lighter one for dark blossoms and a darker cardboard for light blossoms. Still others denounce the use of a cardboard as a sacriligeous interference with nature. In such a dilemma it is suggested that you exercise your own judgment.

ORCHID AND DANDELION — While fairly rare and beautiful flowers like the trailing arbutus, the cardinal flower, the fringed gentian, the pink lady's slipper and other wild orchids are eagerly sought as photographic objects; and while unusual growths like the insect-eating pitcher plant or the magnificent waxy blossoms perching on the weird limbs of big cactuses in the South West are topics greatly in demand, we should keep in mind that several of the most common flowers make highly artistic nature pictures, like the daisy, the chicory, or the dandelion; the latter's globe of seeds is indeed a masterpiece.

THE FAIRY RING — Finally the striking photographs that have been made of mushrooms and toadstools should be mentioned here. They concern both single specimens and whole colonies, particularly the mysterious "fairy rings"; the latter are settlements of certain mushrooms in ring form, the diameter of the ring growing from year to year, from an original few inches to a final stretch of several feet. Folklore ascribes the phenomenon to the fairies; science explains it in this way: The mushroom settlement grows in all directions in a circular fashion. As the organic food supply is exhausted, the old mushrooms in the center die off while the new generations appear on the outside rim. A "fairy ring" is an interesting and unusual addition to any collection of nature pictures.

Illustrations No. 49 and 50 show a regular-view flower picture and a close-up flower picture.

"Shooting" Birds—WHERE TO PHOTOGRAPH BIRDS—There

are two occasions on which you may induce birds to pose for pictures: Either when they visit you, or when you visit them. In the first case your reception room will be the feeding station in wintertime, and the bird bath in summertime. In the second case you will take your camera to the pastures, forests, and brooks.

Referring to winter feeding stations, a few hints about tried and tested procedures will be welcome:

1) Although the winter visitors at your feeding station may be fairly regular, you cannot count on their prompt appearance when you need them. In order to shorten your wait, it is suggested to select a day on which the ground is covered with snow and the general food supply greatly reduced. If there are other feeding stations in the neighborhood, cover them up for that day. Under such circumstances your seeds and suet will be a prime attraction.

2) Create a photogenic setting by decorating the tray with a few branches of evergreen.

3) If you wish to have a fairly large image of the bird, use a Portra or equivalent close-up lens. Place the seeds or whatever food you may offer in the center of the tray and focus the camera on the food; use the focusing methods described previously for flower close-ups.

4) If your feeding station is attached to a window, you may take the picture from the inside, through the window glass, without any loss of sharpness. Otherwise you will have to mount the camera outside, on a tripod, branch, fence, or similar support. Camouflage it with a few evergreen branches. Employ a long-distance release, as explained previously. As soon as a desirable bird appears, release the shutter.

5) On sunny days a regular daylight exposure will be satisfactory, but more often photo-flash exposure will be a more reliable solution. The birds do not object to the flash; some will fly away but return; others will go right on eating.

6) All previous instructions, with the exception of those referring to winter conditions, apply also to pictures taken at a bird bath.

NESTS — If you go out to the fields and woods in search of birds, you will naturally look for nests. A few nests with attractive bird families may, of course, be in your own backyard. Again, several points of advice may be summarized here:

1) To locate nests in spring, a pair of binoculars is most useful. If two companions pool their efforts, the searching time will be cut considerably. In order to locate nests of ground-nesting species, the two collaborators may drag a thin string lightly over the meadow, so as to flush the birds without damaging the nests.

2) A nest under construction is a charming object if you can get with it a picture of the builder.

3) A nest with eggs guarded by the mother (see illustration No. 51) is one of the most sought-after prizes of the wildlife photographer.

4) A batch of nestlings is easily photographed as they are more or less stationary. Before you take the picture make a twittering or chirping sound, perhaps by kissing the back of your hand; the little rubber-necks will shoot up, their mouths wide open. At that moment release the shutter.

To turn back a few branches that half-conceal the nest, will do no harm. But under no circumstances is it permissible to remove the nest with the young from its original place to improve lighting conditions. The parents will abandon such a nest, and the most perfect print or slide will not give satisfaction to the photographer if he knows that his models paid for the picture with their lives.

5) Fledglings nine to ten days old, able to stand on their feet and about to leave the nest, may be carefully taken out of the nest and lined up on a branch in a row. The result will be a charming picture. If you can set up your camera, focus it, keep the little ones in line until the father or mother arrives to feed them, and then release the shutter, you will have a picture to be proud of; to keep everything under control is not easy, but quite a few nature photographers have succeeded in obtaining perfectly enchanting family scenes.

Here is a warning again: If you try this venture with fledglings that are too young, they may pay for it with their lives.

6) If you just photograph a nest with eggs or with nestlings, you can approach it personally, holding your camera or mounting the camera on a tripod and releasing the shutter on the spot. In all other cases you will have to set up the camera near the nest, camouflage it, focus it, wait for the

Illustration Number 55

return of the adult bird, and trip the shutter by long-distance release.

7) The use of photo-flash equipment is recommended, just as much for the sake of the picture as for the sake of the eggs and the nestlings which should not be exposed to the sun for any length of time.

8) After you have photographed one or a few scenes of bird life at one session, do not return to the same nest a second time, to avoid too great a disturbance.

9) Birds in flight are more properly in the realm of motion pictures. But very fine still pictures of flying birds may be achieved either with a reflex camera whose ground glass image makes instantaneous focusing possible, or with any other camera equipped with a range finder. Looking through the latter, you follow the flying bird until its two images merge into one. That instant you release the shutter (see illustration No. 52).

BLINDS — Many professional and quite a few amateur photographers like to build blinds for bird and animal photography. The advantage of a blind over a camouflaged camera with a long-distance release is the photographer's chance of taking immediate action in adapting the camera to the circumstances of the moment which are never quite predictable. Blinds are practical because birds do not pay attention to immovable objects, or at least they get easily accustomed to them. Blinds are even more useful for movie cameras which cannot be concealed by themselves and run by a long-distance release. The usual forms are these:

Illustration Number 56

1) The simplest blind is set up with large, leafy branches, small logs, pieces of bark, or anything that is handy at the site. The blind should harmonize with the natural environment of the spot.

2) A few poles are mounted in the fashion of an Indian tepee and covered with pieces of burlap or similar coarse cloth. The outside may be decorated with evergreens or other branches, or the burlap itself may be dyed in the green-brown-grey camouflage patterns of the army. Two inconspicuous holes will provide openings for the camera lens and the eyes of the photographer. There should be no moving parts that flap in the wind.

3) An umbrella blind is essentially of the same type, only that it is based on the following skeleton: A pointed pole is pushed firmly into the ground; an opened umbrella is tied to the upper end of the pole; the burlap cloth is draped over the umbrella.

4) If a whole series of pictures is to be taken from the same spot, it may be worth-while to use an old large packing box or wooden framework covered with the artificial grass carpeting that is used by undertakers at funerals and on the stage. Several professional naturalists report that this system is especially effective.

5) Sometimes trees are excellent spots to set up a blind; in each individual case the photographer will have to decide which of the previously mentioned materials he should use. Especially cherry trees and mulberry trees will attract a great variety of "customers" at the time of the ripening fruit.

If the family life of high-nesting birds like hawks and eagles is to be photographed, a rope ladder will be useful. Percy A. Morris, the outstanding nature photographer, recommends the use of one-half inch rope, with strong rungs of oak tied to it every two feet and secured with nails; it will be 40 or 50 feet long and thrown over the lowest big branch with the help of a piece of light twine, weighted at the end with a stone. The other end of the rope ladder is pulled down over the limb, and fastened to a nearby tree. Such a ladder is cumbersome to carry around, but seems to be the only method available where the tree trunks are too thick to be "shinnied." The climbing irons of telephone repair men work well on smooth telephone poles of soft wood, but are not reliable on bark.

Again a word of warning must be added: Throw the ladder only over a sound limb as near to the trunk as possible, and never over a half-dead branch. And never use the ladder when you are alone, but only when a companion is ready to stand by in an emergency.

BIRD MOVIES — In a way, motion pictures are the natural medium for bird photography; for graceful and almost constant motion is an integral part of all bird life. For that same reason it is technically easier to record bird activities with a movie camera than with a still camera.

Large birds, particularly if they are tame like ducks, starlings, robins, or pelicans, may be filmed with regular equipment, in the same fashion in which other outdoor movies are taken. If smaller birds of a shy disposition are to be filmed, lenses of long focal length will have to be attached. In that way an area as large as 2x2½ feet may be pictured from 40 feet away, and interestingly intimate movies can be obtained. Magazine-loading cameras or those with a long run for each winding are preferable because valuable time and the chance to conclude or take a fascinating bird scene may be lost by the necessity of rewinding.

As everybody knows, too many amateur motion pictures show jumpy and jerky movements, due to the difficulty of holding the camera steady. Therefore a tripod should be used whenever possible, and if that is not feasible, as for instance in filming birds in flight, it is recommended to mount the camera on an old gun stock which can be held securely against the shoulder blade. An army surplus gun stock of a wooden drill rifle is very satisfactory.

Some movie fans like to combine their bird and wildlife shots into a consecutive story; this is a highly subjective undertaking for which no general formula can be prescribed. However, it will probably include some sights of your trip, your car, and the scenic environment in which the wildlife movies were taken.

Technical details on special lenses for movie cameras will be found in the previously mentioned circulars "How to Take Bird Pictures" and "The Selection and Use of Cine-Kodak Lenses."

Mounted Birds — In magazine illustrations, advertisements, and elsewhere you have probably seen some lovely colored bird pictures that appear as life-like as if they had

Illustration Number 58

Illustration Number 57

come directly from pasture or forest. In fact, a good many of them are indoor photographs of mounted and stuffed specimens borrowed from a museum or a private collection. There is no objection to such a technique as long as the photographs are not presented as typical wildlife pictures taken in the great outdoors.

Hints on Birds — In the following, various useful bits of information coming from active wildlife photographers, are summarized; they include experiences by Roger T. Peterson, the author of the famous field guides; Percy A. Morris of the Peabody Museum of Yale; the author of this guide, and others.

Chickadees are among the boldest birds in wintertime and easily photographed at feeding stations. In contrast, they are extremely wary and frightened during the nesting season, will not suffer any disturbance, and easily abandon their eggs.

Vireos construct the neatest little nest cups, interweaving the usual nesting material of fibers and grasses with silky threads of spider webs, bits of wood and little pieces of newspaper. The nests can be found in the forks of small branches, rarely higher than 5 or 6 feet.

Crested Flycatchers almost always work discarded snake skins into their nests and let one end of such a skin hang down flapping in the air.

Warblers sometimes build two-or-three-story nests. They seem to be particularly exposed to the attention of cowbirds which lay their eggs into warblers' nests. But the warblers

Illustration Number 59

Folding Camera

Twin Reflex Camera

Reflex Camera

35 Millimeter Camera

Types of Cameras

are not fooled. They construct a new bottom to insulate the cowbird's egg, raise the walls of the nest, and proceed with their regular family life. Sometimes they have to accomplish this extra work three times during the summer.

Hummingbirds have so rapid a wing action that not even a high-speed camera can "freeze" the movement of the wings. The best that can be achieved is a blur (see illustration No. 53).

Flickers are amusing photographic objects. If you spy a flicker hole, the entrance of an occupied cavity, not higher than 10 feet on an old orchard tree, set up your camera and focus it on the hole. Rap at the tree and watch the flicker stick out its head and neck to welcome you curiously. Release the shutter.

Also barn swallows may be photographed peeking out of their nests, little mud houses plastered under the barn roof. Great numbers of barn swallows perching on telephone wires and chattering gaily as if they were holding a convention, offer an amusing photoscene.

The oven birds, a species of large warblers, build nests in thickets on the ground. Their nests have complete roofs and small door-openings on the side, in the fashion of old-time Dutch ovens.

A male ruffed grouse in the act of drumming makes a prize photograph. Each male performs his drumming on the same "drumming perch" or log, and if you happen to locate such a perch it is quite possible to set up a blind nearby, and with great patience snap a picture of the grouse in the act of "drumming." Early spring is the most auspicious season.

The nest of a bob-white or quail is a rare photographic find; 12 to 15 white eggs are neatly laid out there, in the tall grass, and the mother, relying on her mimicry, will not easily fly away.

Owls will be fooled by a small rubber mouse pulled gently over the ground with a string. Set up your camera near the nest of a barred owl and introduce the mouse at dusk. The owl will swoop down and offer its image to the photo-flash camera.

The grebe often uses a self-made floating island of reeds and mud as a nest for its 10 to 12 eggs — a most unusual arrangement.

Wild ducks are attracted by domestic mallards and can be photographed quite easily, especially in wintertime when ice covers a good part of their haunts. Also waving with a handkerchief and similar motions will often cause them to approach you to the point of camera range.

Sandpipers and other shore birds travel largely on the narrow rim of the shore that lies between high tide and low tide. Set up your camera in the blind or just camouflage it — in that case you will also have to camouflage your body, by covering it partly with sand, and your head with dry seaweeds or a branch — focus on a spot marked by two stones, and wait for the procession of birds to pass by. The parade will be speeded up if a companion drives the birds to you by slowly, quietly walking along the beach.

Interesting and often rare bird pictures may be taken at many of the nearly 300 national wildlife refuges in all parts of the country. Along the Atlantic, Mississippi and Pacific flyways innumerable migratory birds find food and shelter on the way, and the enormous southern refuges protect the breeding grounds of millions of American birds. A table listing the national wildlife preserves together with the birds that may be found and photographed there, is included in Hammond's Nature Atlas of America, by E. L. Jordan, on pages 245 to 249.

"Shooting" Animals — The term "animals" is used here in the sense of "mammals."

SMALL FUR BEARERS — Experienced wildlife photographers feel that the most satisfactory way of shooting mice, shrews, chipmunks, and other small fur bearers is to trap them first and then to take their pictures indoors. Two simple but effective designs that will trap but not kill the animals, are shown in illustration No. 62. They follow the suggestions made by Percy A. Morris. The upper one consists of a wooden box with a wire top and the trap proper which can be carved of three splinters of wood. The lower device may also be made at home with a regular mouse trap, an old tin can with one end open, and a piece of wire netting; these parts are combined as shown in the self-explanatory sketch. When set, the traps should be camouflaged with leaves and branches and baited with bacon. But also cheese, bread crust, or other table scraps will serve the purpose.